W9-BHG-975

A Birder's Guide
To
Florida

by Bill Pranty

ABA/Lane Birdfinding Guide Series

Copyright © 2005 by American Birding Association, Inc.

All rights reserved. No part of this publication may be reproduced, stored in a retrieval system, transmitted in any form or by any means, electronic, photocopying, or otherwise, without prior written permission of the publisher.

Library of Congress Control Number: 2005926760

ISBN Number: 1-878788-24-8

Fifth Edition

1 2 3 4 5 6 7 8

Printed in the United States of America

Publisher

American Birding Association, Inc.

Production Editor

Virginia Maynard

Maps

Virginia Maynard and Cindy Lippincott, using CorelDRAW, version 8

Cover Photograph

White-crowned Pigeon with nestlings
Reed Bowman

Back Cover Photographs

Scaly-headed Parrot
John H. Boyd III

Black Rail
Lee F. Snyder

Other Photographs

Lyn S. Atherton, Andrew Boyle, Drew Fulton, Bruce Hallett, Helen W. Lovell, Larry Manfredi, Arthur Morris/ www.birdsasart. com, Kurt Radamaker, and Darcy Stumbaugh.

Distributed by

American Birding Association Sales
115 Fairview Rd, Asheville, NC 28803
toll-free (800) 634-7736 (in USA and Canada)
or (828) 274-5575 (international)
fax (800) 590-2473 (in USA and Canada) or (719) 578-9705 (international)
email: abasales@abasales.com
website: www.americanbirding.org/abasales

*With deep regret that they are not here
to see it, I dedicate this book to
the memory of my parents,
the late Dom and Peggy Pranty.
Dad missed seeing the book by one month.*

TABLE OF CONTENTS

ACKNOWLEDGMENTS

As with all of its predecessors, the rewriting of the fifth edition of this guide required the knowledge and talents of dozens of individuals, to whom I am most grateful. Some individuals edited entire sections of text, while others simply verified one or two bits of information. Thanks to the following:

Brian Ahern (Tampa area), Bruce Anderson (Lake Woodruff, Orlando area), Lyn Atherton (Fort De Soto Park), Gian Basili (Crescent Beach–Matanzas Inlet), Wes Biggs (Ponce Inlet–Sebastian), Sandra Bogan (Port St. Lucie), Chris Borg (Keys), Jeff Bouton (Punta Gorda), John H. Boyd III (Miami–Everglades National Park), John Bridges (Avon Park Air Force Range), Jane Brooks (Fort Pierce–Port St. Lucie), Roger Clark (Amelia Island–Jacksonville), Ruth Clark (Kissimmee–St. Cloud), Buck and Linda Cooper (Lakeland area, Kissimmee Prairie Preserve, Lake Kissimmee State Park), Jim Cox (Tall Timbers Research Station), Fritz Davis (Tallahassee, Wakulla Springs), Robin Diaz (Key Biscayne area), Terry "Darth" Doyle (Naples–Big Cypress Swamp, Southern Lake Okeechobee, Lower Keys), Jack Dozier (Panacea area), Bob and Lucy Duncan (Pensacola–Gulf Breeze, Blackwater River State Forest), Charlie "Chewy" Ewell (Fort Myers, Southern Lake Okeechobee), Judy Fisher (Largo–Seminole), Phil Frank (Lower Keys refuges), Wally George (Pompano Beach–Fort Lauderdale), Dave Goodwin (Ruskin, Tarpon Springs–St. Petersburg areas), Jack Hailman (Palm Beach area), Al and Bev Hansen (Crystal River area, Weeki Wachee–Brooksville), Mark Hedden (Lower Keys), Dale Henderson (Cedar Key and Goethe State Forest), Bill and Shirley Hills (Turkey Creek Sanctuary), John Hintermister (Live Oak and Lake City), Jackie Kern (St. Augustine), Gloria Hunter (Palm Beach to Boca Raton), Fran James (Apalachicola National Forest), Dean and Sally Jue (Marianna–Blountstown and Tallahassee areas), Jerry Krummrich (Keaton Beach–Steinhatchee), Ed Kwater (Clearwater), Thom Lewis (Apalachicola area), Marian Lichtler (Avon Park Air Force Range), Doug Linden (Three Lakes Wildlife Management Area), Casey Lott (Middle Keys), Donna Marchant (Middle and Lower Keys), Peter May (Emeralda Marsh and Lake Woodruff), Peter Merritt (Hobe Sound), Vince Morris (Withlacoochee State Forest), Linda Most (Palm Beach–Boca Raton), Brennan Mulrooney (Upper and Middle Keys), Kathy O'Reilly-Doyle (Lower Keys), Cheri Pierce (Orlando area), Peggy Powell (Amelia Island–Jacksonville), John Puschock (Ocala National Forest), Diane Reed (St. Augustine), Bryant Roberts (Everglades Agricultural Area), Rex Rowan (Gainesville),

Mark Sees (Orlando Wetlands Park), David Simpson (St. Sebastian River Preserve), Ron Smith (St. Petersburg, Bradenton, and Sarasota areas), Betty Smyth (Crystal River), Ken Spilios (Withlacoochee State Forest), Doug Suitor (Naples), Hilary Swain (Archbold Biological Station), Ken and Linda Tracey (Hudson–Holiday), Billi Wagner (Sebastian–Vero Beach), and Don Ware (Fort Walton Beach). Holly Lovell and James Tucker helped me check some sites.

I am grateful to the American Birding Association for publishing the fourth and fifth editions of this guide. For this edition, I thank Matt Pelikan, who did much of the text editing, Virginia Maynard for final editing and layout of the text, and for revision of Cindy Lippincott's original maps as well as creation of the new maps, Bob Berman and Cindy Lippincott for producing the bar graphs, and Allan Burns, Ted Floyd, and Bryan Patrick for other assistance. I thank Bruce Neville for his critical review of the fourth edition, published in *Florida Field Naturalist*. David Allan, Thomas Driscoll, Bob Falconer, Lauren Gilson, Nikolas Haass, Paul Lehman, Gordon Payne, Bob Pittell, P. William Smith, Gary Stitzinger, John van der Woude, George West, and Dan Willliams corrected errors in the fourth edition or suggested improvements. John Epler compiled the damselfly list and revised the dragonfly list. Buck and Linda Cooper updated the butterfly list. Gloria Hunter graciously provided copies of correspondence she exchanged with Jim Lane in 1980. Thanks to Jon Greenlaw for information on FOSRC matters. The photographs on the front and back covers and inside the guide are wonderful additions; my thanks to Lyn S. Atherton, Reed Bowman, John H. Boyd III, J. Andrew Boyle, Drew Fulton, Bruce Hallett, Helen W. (Holly) Lovell, Larry Manfredi, Arthur Morris, Kurt Radamaker, Lee F. Snyder, and Darcy Stumbaugh.

For support through the years, I especially thank my parents, the late Dom and Peggy Pranty, plus Bruce Anderson, Gian and Allison Basili, Wes Biggs, Reed Bowman, Dave Goodwin, Stephanie Johnson, Ed Kwater, Geoff LeBaron, Holly Lovell, Dave Powell, Cindy and Kurt Radamaker, Helen Violi, Glen Woolfenden, and numerous other friends and colleagues. I enjoyed discussing issues about birdfinding guides with Giff Beaton, the author of *Birding Georgia*. Wes Biggs, Dave Goodwin, Erik Haney, and Dave Powell assisted with updates to the bar graphs. I thank Cheri Pillsbury for correspondence on access for disabled birders (which regrettably could not be added to site descriptions, due to time constraints; we will hope to change that in the next edition). I especially thank Gian Basili for his fine Preface. Finally, to anyone who has assisted me in the past three years and whose name I have unintentionally omitted, please accept my apology. And of course, all errors of omission or commission are solely my responsibility.

Bill Pranty
Avon Park, Florida
15 September 2005

PREFACE

The first edition of *A Birder's Guide to Florida* was written in the 1970s by the late James A. Lane (1926–1987) and was published in 1981. Lane pioneered the use of site-specific birdfinding guides, and eventually produced a total of seven books, which became widely known as the "Lane Guides". His Florida guide was reprinted with minor revisions in 1984 and 1989, after which the American Birding Association assumed responsibility for maintaining the series and for adding new titles.

In 1996, ABA published the fourth edition of *A Birder's Guide to Florida*, which was completely revamped compared to the earlier editions. It was written by Bill Pranty, a local birder and ornithologist. The fourth edition of the Florida guide, which quickly became known as the "Pranty Guide," sold more than 15,000 copies between 1996 and 2004, establishing it as the best-selling birdfinding guide ever produced.

It is hard to find someone more dedicated to Florida birds than Bill Pranty. He arrived in Florida as a young boy in 1978 from Pittsburgh, Pennsylvania, and was fortunate to be exposed to birding by members of the West Pasco Audubon Society. Too young to drive, Pranty was chaperoned on numerous field trips throughout the state, and these experiences helped to create the foundation for his passion toward Florida birds and natural systems. Everyone who knows Pranty knows that since those formative years in his early teens, he has been immersed completely in the study of Florida birds. This is why he was the perfect choice to write the fourth and now fifth editions of *A Birder's Guide to Florida*.

Bill is perhaps best known for his birdfinding guides. However, his other contributions to Florida ornithology are significant and often unheralded, and they are worthy of mention, as they provide the knowledge base and relationships necessary for assembling such a comprehensive guide as this fifth edition. Every time I speak with Pranty, he is working on some bird-related project, most of which are done in his "spare time". True, much of his knowledge for this series has come on-the-job in positions such as state coordinator for both the Florida Breeding Bird Atlas (1991–1992) and Important Bird Areas Program (1999–2002), and studying Florida Scrub-Jays with the exceptional team from Archbold Biological Station. But Bill's understanding of Florida birds and birding is further broadened by extracurricular efforts, which include compiling seasonal bird observations for *North American Birds* and *Florida Field Naturalist*, his research and writing on various native and exotic species, and his herculean Christmas Bird Count schedule each year, as well as editing all of Florida's 60-plus counts.

Like the fourth edition, Pranty has packed this new and improved fifth edition with a wealth of information on Florida ornithology. It includes numerous meticulously compiled and informative sections such as a primer on Florida ecosystems, a calendar of bird activity, an updated list of Florida birds, a new section on West Indian vagrants, and chapters devoted to birds of particular interest (Florida specialties) and exotics. But make no mistake about it; the most powerful component of this guide is in directing you to the right place at the right time of year to experience Florida birds in their natural habitats. From the famous National Wildlife Refuges to the unknown yet productive secret spots of local birders, Pranty and his collaborators have provided the reader with a treasure map to Florida birds and birding. I commend Bill Pranty, his collaborators, and the American Birding Association for continuing to update this series in the ever-changing state in which we live, and for helping me and numerous others to experience the inspiring world of Florida ornithology.

Gian Basili
St. Augustine, Florida
September 2005

Gian Basili is a Senior Project Manager
working on ecological restoration projects
for the St. Johns River Water Management District

Osprey with chicks.

Arthur Morris/www.birdsasart.com

INTRODUCTION

Florida is a birding paradise. From the tall coastal dunes and great river swamps of the Panhandle and the unique terrain of the Red Hills, through the flatwoods, scrubs, dry prairies, and wetlands of the Peninsula, to the West Indian hardwood hammocks and coral reefs of the Keys, the state offers superb birding opportunities at all seasons. Through January 2005, the official Florida bird list, with 481 native species and 12 established exotics, is the largest of any state east of the Mississippi River and the fifth largest overall. Florida is the first landfall for tens of millions of migrants moving north from wintering grounds in the Caribbean and tropical America, and the last departure point for migrants during fall. When temperatures to the north drop below freezing, Florida's wetlands support wading birds and wintering waterfowl; its beaches attract shorebirds and larids; prairies and other grasslands host wintering sparrows; and woodlands contain mixed flocks of landbirds. The regular breeding avifauna of the state is rather depauperate—only about 150 native species—but the North American breeding ranges of 11 of these are mostly or entirely limited to Florida. Developed areas in the southern half of the Peninsula, especially the metropolitan areas of Fort Lauderdale and Miami, host large and increasing populations of exotic birds. Countable ABA-area populations for six of these exotics—Muscovy Duck, Budgerigar, Black-hooded Parakeet (pending ABA acceptance), White-winged Parakeet, Red-whiskered Bulbul, and Spot-breasted Oriole—are limited to Florida.

While not the largest state in the East, Florida is the longest. The distance from Pensacola to Key West is more than 800 miles. Florida contains the least topographic relief of any state; its tallest point, Britton Hill, in the western Panhandle, is only 345 feet above sea level. (The highest point in the peninsula is Iron Mountain, near Lake Wales, at 298 feet.) But what Florida lacks in topography, it more than makes up in biological diversity. The state contains 81 formally recognized natural communities, including some of the most diverse grasslands and forests in North America; 7,800 lakes and ponds of at least one acre in size; 1,700 rivers, sloughs, and creeks; 3,600 native plants; more than 700 native vertebrates; 750 miles of beaches, and—excluding those in the Keys—450 miles of saltmarsh or mangrove forest shoreline.

Florida Before Human Arrival

The existence of what is known today as Florida can be traced back about 600 million years, to when the state was a submerged part of Africa, itself a part of the supercontinent of Gondwanaland. It was not until about 25 million years ago that falling sea levels and uplifting land allowed Florida to become exposed. During its lengthy inundation, the region accumulated a thick layer of limestone deposits from the fossilized remains of coral reefs. Eventually, a vast, dry, arid ecosystem of woodland savannas and plains covered Florida. This habitat extended west to the Pacific Ocean and south through much of South America, and animals from these regions colonized Florida. Mammals that inhabited the state during this period included mastodons, bison, horses, camels, llamas, jaguars, sabertooth cats, giant ground sloths, capybaras, porcupines, peccaries, vampire bats, and giant tortoises. Prehistoric birds of Florida included California Condor, Yellow-headed Caracara, Northern Jaçana, Ringed Kingfisher, and Black-billed Magpie, as well as several now-extinct species: a loon, an anhinga, a cormorant, an ibis, a stork, *Titanus walleri* (a 10-foot-tall flightless predatory species), Merriam's Teratorn (a vulture with a 12-foot wingspan), a hawk-eagle, a woodcock, and one or more pygmy-owls. Emslie (1998) offers a look at the fascinating avifauna that has occurred in Florida over the past 2.5 million years.

One of the most extensive ecosystems in Florida up to about 11,000 years ago was scrub, a desert-like habitat that grows on well-drained, sandy soils. During the Ice Age, sea levels were as much as 300 feet lower than they are at present, and the Florida peninsula was at times twice its present width. As sea levels rose due to glacial melting, much of Florida flooded. Scrub communities became restricted to the only well-drained soils that remained: the tops of coastal and inland ridge systems that represent earlier shorelines. The plants and animals that survived on these ridge systems, now isolated by many hundreds or thousands of miles from their western and southern relatives, would eventually evolve into distinct species. Chief among these is the Florida Scrub-Jay, one of the most range-restricted bird species in North America.

By about 11,000 years ago, a habitat mosaic of pine flatwoods, oak hammocks and scrub, dry prairies, and myriad wetlands had come to dominate the peninsula. The lower-lying Everglades region was not formed until about 5,000 years ago, and vegetation on the Keys is more recent. Even today, wind and tidal currents continue to move around sand and shell, creating new land. As one of the last states to be "conquered" by humans (due in part to its abundance of wetlands, and therefore mosquitoes), Florida remained a "prolific reservoir of biological diversity" (Fitzpatrick *in* Loftin et al. 1991) until recently. But the face of Florida began to change forever in the mid-1800s, and vast alterations continue to be wrought upon the state. Today, only vestiges of the original Florida remain. Although even these remnants have been altered, in some cases probably permanently, they represent the last refuges for Florida's native flora and fauna.

HUMAN HISTORY

Unlike Florida's long 25-million-year floral and faunal history, human settlement of the state dates back to only about 12,000 years ago, when Paleo-Indians migrated south from what today is Georgia. They were nomadic people, hunting mastodons, bison, horses, deer, and smaller animals. As the Florida peninsula shrank as a result of sea-level rise, Florida's first human inhabitants began to form permanent settlements, and many began to cultivate crops. Eventually, six major Indian tribes with a total population of about 25,000 inhabitants lived in Florida. By the late 1700s, these Indians had been extirpated from the state. Most had succumbed to diseases brought by European explorers or had been captured and put into slavery; the few survivors fled to the West Indies, where they were later exterminated.

Florida was the first mainland area in the present U.S. to be discovered and occupied by European explorers. In 1513, Juan Ponce de Leon of Spain landed near present-day St. Augustine, searching for the Fountain of Youth. Ponce de Leon's "discovery" of Florida fueled later explorations by the Spanish, French, and British. By the late 1600s, Spain had established many colonies in Florida, including forts at Pensacola, near St. Marks, and at St. Augustine, and had built more than 30 missions to convert the Indians to Christianity. The late 1600s and early 1700s marked a period of warfare among Spain, England, and France, as these countries battled for control of North America. In the mid-1700s, Lower Creek Indians moved southward and eastward into Florida. Eventually, they would split into two distinct tribes: the Miccosukees and the Seminoles. The Seminole tribe was the larger of the two and became involved in extensive warfare with armies of the European countries, and later with U.S. forces.

In 1763, with the end of the French and Indian War, the Treaty of Paris gave England control of Florida. In October of that year, Florida was divided into two provinces, East Florida and West Florida. St. Augustine became the capital of East Florida, Pensacola the capital of West Florida, which extended west to the Mississippi River. The economies of both territories were small and relied heavily on agriculture, including the production of cotton, tobacco, and sugar. Possession of Florida was returned to Spain by the 1783 Treaty of Paris, but Spain was unable to govern the land. The sale of the Louisiana Territory, including a portion of West Florida, to the United States in 1803 signaled the beginning of the end of Spanish rule in North America. In 1818, General Andrew Jackson invaded Florida to recapture fugitive slaves, to pacify the Indians who controlled the cattle trade, and to trade cattle. This invasion was called the First Seminole War. On 22 February 1822, Florida was ceded from Spain to the United States. The population of the territory was about 4,300.

The Second Seminole War began in 1835, lasted seven years, and cost the government $20 million and the lives of 1,466 of its soldiers. More than 3,800 of the surviving Indians were removed from the state and sent to reservations in the West. The 300 Indians who resisted fled into the Everglades, where they battled U.S. forces until the end of the Third Seminole War, in 1858. A few survivors evaded capture and remained in the Everglades. Florida became a state in 1845, with a population of about 65,500. It seceded from the Union and joined the Confederacy in 1861. The state supplied men, cattle, and salt to the Confederate Army. Although there were many skirmishes in the state during the Civil War, only one major battle was fought here, at Olustee. After the war ended in 1865, Florida was placed under military rule for three years. For the next few decades, Florida's primary industry was the production of cattle, an industry that remains important to this day. Early Spanish excursions into Florida left about 400 to 500 cattle descended from the same breed as Texas Longhorns. These Florida Longhorns became acclimated to the natural range-grasses of the state. By the latter half of the 19th century, "cow towns" such as Kissimmee and Arcadia had sprung up to move cattle from inland foraging grounds to coastal cities for export.

In 1884, Henry Plant began building a railroad south along the Gulf coast. Two years later, Henry Flagler began a similar line down the Atlantic coast, and the Great Florida Land Boom was on. The timber industry followed the railroads and wrought havoc on the state's forests beginning in the 1880s. Within a few decades, massive logging had clear-cut virtually every pine and cypress in Florida, and the era of widespread environmental destruction—which, sadly, continues to this day—had begun. By 1896, Flagler's railroad had reached Miami, and in 1904 he began building a line to Key West. After eight years and 43 bridges, Flagler's "Overseas Railroad" finally reached Key West. Success was short-lived, however: a hurricane in 1935 destroyed several bridges, and the line was abandoned. The railroad bed was converted to a roadway named the Overseas Highway, which opened in 1938. This road, now U.S. Route 1, remains the sole route through the Florida Keys.

In 1905, the Everglades Drainage District was created to drain 7,500 square miles of the Everglades for agriculture and cattle ranching. Eventually, most of the southern peninsula would be criss-crossed by canals draining the Everglades. These canals continue to disrupt the entire Everglades ecosystem, sending into the Atlantic Ocean millions of gallons of fresh water each day. Excessive drainage threatens the drinking-water supply of the 5.1 million residents of the region. Beginning in the late 1940s, extensive areas of second-growth forests throughout the peninsula were cleared for cattle grazing, while scrub and other well-drained uplands fell prey to the ever-growing citrus industry. Finally, the widespread availability of air conditioning in the 1950s assured the success of Florida's primary cash crops: single-family homes, beachfront condominiums, and high-rise hotels.

Florida's population increased from 1.9 million residents in 1940 to 2.7 million in 1950, then 4.9 million in 1960, and 6.7 million in 1970. The population reached 9.7 million in 1980, 12.9 million in 1990, and 15.9 million in 2000. Currently, 700–900 people move into the state *every day*. To accommodate these

Black Skimmer, adult.

Arthur Morris/www.birdsasart.com

millions of new residents, an appalling amount of habitat has been destroyed in Florida, which has caused many of the state's native inhabitants to decline. In 1994, 803 species or subspecies of native plants and animals in Florida were considered endangered, threatened, vulnerable, or of conservation concern (Wood 1994). Five of Florida's native birds (Passenger Pigeon, Carolina Parakeet, Ivory-billed Woodpecker, Bachman's Warbler, and Dusky Seaside Sparrow) now are extinct (or at least probably extirpated).

Thankfully, government agencies, nongovernmental organizations, and citizens have realized that the only way to prevent the continued destruction of Florida's vital environmental and ecological sites is public purchase. Since 1964, Florida's state and local governments have spent more than $3.7 billion to preserve over 4.6 million acres of land. Federal conservation areas total an additional 4 million acres. By the end of 2001, there were over 1,200 conservation areas in Florida (Jue et al. 2001), which collectively preserve—theoretically in perpetuity—about one-quarter of the state's land area. On average, 200,000 additional acres of land were preserved each year. But regrettably, land values began to sky-rocket beginning in 2003, jeopardizing future public land-acquisition efforts. It is to the credit of the government and citizens of Florida that such steps are being taken, but there is really no alternative; our natural heritage is at stake. Our actions within the next 30 years will determine whether we succeed or fail in preserving the remainder of Florida's privately owned lands, water, and wildlife.

A BRIEF HISTORY OF FLORIDA FIELD ORNITHOLOGY

The first recorded observations of birds in North America were made in Florida by Alvar Nuñez Cabeça de Vaca, a Spanish explorer, in 1528. Near present-day Tallahassee, de Vaca reported seeing, "Geese in great numbers. Ducks, mallards, royal-ducks, fly-catchers, night-herons and partridges...falcons, gerfalcons, sparrow-hawks, merlins, and numerous other fowl" (Johnston 2002). Formal surveys of Florida's flora and fauna began 250 years later, with a series of explorations by John and William Bartram in the 1770s. Sixty years later, John James Audubon explored northeastern Florida and the Florida Keys for six months in 1831 and 1832. About 30 Florida birds were included in his monumental work, The Birds of America, published in sections between 1826 and 1838.

Ornithological interest in Florida began in earnest after statehood in 1845. The state was visited by many well-known ornithologists, numerous obscure ones, and countless "sportsmen", all of whom brought along shotguns and blasted essentially every bird within range. A more serious problem for Florida birds arose in the mid-19th century, when it became fashionable for women in America and Europe to adorn their hats and dresses with feathers (and often entire birds). The range of species killed to supply this "millinery trade" was quite wide and included Snowy Egrets, Herring Gulls, Pileated Woodpeckers, and Wilson's Warblers. Wading birds, especially Great and Snowy Egrets, were desired especially by milliners for the fine plumes (aigrettes), produced for the birds' courtship displays.

Florida was at the forefront of the American conservation movement because of the vast numbers of wading birds threatened by relentless hunting. To protect wading birds, wardens were hired to patrol the rookeries. In 1902, Guy Bradley was hired for $35 per month to patrol rookeries from present-day Naples through Flamingo to Key West—a huge area. On 8 July 1905, Bradley was murdered by poachers at Flamingo. Two other wardens (Columbus MacLeod in Florida and L.P. Reeves in South Carolina) were killed in 1908. These murders, coupled with stricter laws and a change in the public's attitudes about the killing of wild birds, led to the end of the millinery trade in 1913. In 1903, President Theodore Roosevelt set aside Pelican Island, north of present-day Vero Beach, as a rookery for colonial waterbirds. Pelican Island became the country's first National Wildlife Refuge, one of 53 established by Roosevelt. (A century later, there are now more than 530 refuges in the country.)

Despite all the ornithological attention that Florida received in the late 19th and early 20th centuries, the first state bird book was not published until 1925. In that year, Harold H. Bailey published The Birds of Florida, with accounts for 370 species, all natives. The book contains little specific information on bird distribution and occurrence, but the paintings by George Miksch

Sutton are wonderful. In 1932, *Florida Bird Life* was published. Written by Arthur H. Howell and illustrated by Francis Lee Jaques, it was instantly a classic, and it continues to be cited in scholarly works more than 70 years after its appearance. The book includes accounts for 361 species, including two exotics. In 1954, *Florida Bird Life* was updated by Alexander Sprunt, Jr., with additional plates by John Henry Dick. An addendum published later (Sprunt 1963) boosted the bird list to 411 species, including five exotics.

The Florida Ornithological Society was formed in 1972 and immediately established itself as the primary ornithological and birding organization in Florida. The Society publishes an excellent peer-reviewed quarterly journal, *Florida Field Naturalist*, which emphasizes field-oriented articles about birds, including seasonal summaries of significant observations. Occasionally, longer manuscripts are produced as Special Publications, and two of these are of interest to birders. *The Carolina Parakeet in Florida* by Daniel McKinley (1985, Special Publication No. 2) details the complete history of human involvement in the extinction of Florida's only native parrot. It is as sobering as it is informative. To quote McKinley: "It would be unfair to call the 1890s the decade when bird-lovers of the world lined up for a chance to shoot the last Carolina Parakeet...however, it would be easy to do so." *Florida Bird Species: An Annotated List*, written by the late William B. Robertson, Jr. and by Glen E. Woolfenden, was published in 1992 (Special Publication No. 6). An extremely accurate and concise summary of the state's avifauna since European discovery, *Florida Bird Species* became an immediate classic and provided the first comprehensive treatment of Florida's avifauna since *Florida Bird Life* was published 60 years earlier. The book contains accounts for 681 species: 461 "verified" species (including four recently extinct and 11 established exotics), 75 "unverified stragglers", and 145 unestablished exotics. Costing less than $20, this book is an essential reference for all Florida birders, and it is also recommended to visitors to the state. (A revision is in preparation.)

In 1994, the long-awaited tome, *The Birdlife of Florida* by the late Henry M. Stevenson and by Bruce H. Anderson, was published. Almost 20 years in the making, the book offers up-to-date, comprehensive information on all aspects of birds in Florida. It contains accounts for about 666 species, with 481 "accredited" species (including four recently extinct and 22 established exotics) and about 185 non-accredited species (unverified native species and unestablished exotics combined). In addition to a reported 9,000 bibliographic references, the 907-page book includes 450 range maps that show *seasonal* distribution for nearly all species *in each of Florida's 67 counties*. Because it sells for $120, *The Birdlife of Florida* is found in the personal libraries of only the most serious students of Florida ornithology.

THE FLORIDA BIRD LIST

The official names of birds and the order in which they appear are determined by the Check-list Committee of the American Ornithologists' Union (AOU). The ABA Checklist Committee follows the AOU in all matters of nomenclature (species names) and taxonomy (the evolutionary order in which birds are placed). The nomenclature used in this guide matches that of the 7th edition of the AOU's *Check-list of North American Birds* (1998), and supplements through the 45th supplement published in July 2004 of the *Auk*, the journal of the AOU. The Florida Ornithological Society Records Committee (FOSRC) is the keeper of the official Florida bird list. Through January 2005, this list numbered 493 verifiable species (those documented by photographic or specimen evidence), 481 natives and 12 established exotics (Bowman 2000, 2004; Jon Greenlaw, personal communication). The Florida bird list has grown by an average of two species annually over the past 25 years (Table 1, next page). Literally dozens of other species have been "hypothetically" reported to occur in Florida, but without verifiable evidence. The breakdown of verifiable species is shown below.

Verified native species:	481	Reguar visitors:	17
Permanent (breeding) residents:	122	Irregular visitors:	128
Summer (breeding) residents:	28	Extinct or exirpated:	5
Migrants:	52	Established exotic species	12
Winter residents:	129	Official Florida list:	493

Note that the largest category of regularly-occurring native species is that of winter residents. Florida may be unique among the states in this regard. Also verifiably documented in Florida are 103 exotic birds (Pranty 2004); see page 335 for a list of these species.

It is always entertaining to predict which species may be found next in a given area. Such guesses are based on patterns of vagrancy elsewhere in a region—in Florida's case, the Southeast. However, unprecedented and completely unexpected surprises sometimes appear. Several of the birds in Table 1 (among them Short-tailed Shearwater, Zone-tailed Hawk, Gray-hooded Gull, Eurasian Kestrel, White-tipped Dove, and Mangrove Swallow) were not on birders' "radar screens" to occur in Florida—or perhaps anywhere else in the Southeast. With that caution in mind, here is my "Top 20" list of naturally-occurring vagrants expected to be eventually documented in Florida: Garganey, Yellow-billed Loon, Northern Fulmar, Neotropic Cormorant, Little Egret, Red-necked Stint or Little Stint, Black-tailed Gull, Mew Gull, Inca Dove, Green Violet-ear, Magnificent Hummingbird, Hammond's Flycatcher, Bicknell's Thrush, Virginia's Warbler, Hermit Warbler, Painted Redstart, Smith's Longspur, Great-tailed Grackle, Lesser Goldfinch, and Common Redpoll.

Table 1. The 55 birds added to the official Florida list between 1980 and 2004, arranged in reverse chronological order

With three exceptions, this list includes only native species; asterisks (*) mark established exotics added to the official list by the Florida Ornithological Society Records Committee (FOSRC) or by Robertson and Woolfenden (1992). Not included in this table is Caribbean Elaenia, observed in 1984. Although accepted by the ABA Checklist Committee, the record was not accepted by the FOSRC (or the AOU Check-list Committee) and therefore is not included in the official Florida bird list.

Year	Species	Year	Species
2004	Black-hooded Parakeet*[1], Broad-billed Hummingbird	1991	Piratic Flycatcher
2003	Eurasian Kestrel	1990	European Turtle-Dove[1], Yellow-faced Grassquit, Green-tailed Towhee, Golden-crowned Sparrow
2002	Slaty-backed Gull, Mangrove Swallow, Mountain Bluebird, Hooded Oriole	1989	Thick-billed Vireo
2001	—	1988	Anna's Hummingbird, Calliope Hummingbird, Cassin's Kingbird
2000	Red-necked Grebe, Short-tailed Shearwater, Rough-legged Hawk, Zone-tailed Hawk, Heermann's Gull, Broad-tailed Hummingbird	1987	Ross's Goose, Buff-bellied Hummingbird
1999	Elegant Tern, Snowy Owl	1986	Black-bellied Whistling-Duck, Long-billed Murrelet, Atlantic Puffin
1998	South Polar Skua, Gray-hooded Gull, California Gull, MacGillivray's Warbler, American Tree Sparrow	1985	Shiny Cowbird
1997	Northern Lapwing, Allen's Hummingbird	1984	—
1996	Tropical Kingbird	1983	Yellow-nosed Albatross, Ferruginous Hawk
1995	White-tipped Dove, Western Wood-Pewee, Cuban Pewee, Sulphur-bellied Flycatcher	1982	La Sagra's Flycatcher, Rock Wren
1994	—	1981	Black-tailed Godwit, White-collared Swift, Golden-fronted Woodpecker
1993	Vaux's Swift	1980	Lesser Nighthawk
1992	Muscovy Duck*, Thick-billed Murre, Monk Parakeet*		

[1] These species have been accepted by the FOSRC, but have not yet been accepted by the ABA Checklist Committee.

WEST INDIAN VAGRANTS

The West Indies are a chain of islands that separate the Atlantic Ocean from the Caribbean Sea. They are composed of three primary island groups: the Bahamas, the Greater Antilles (including Cuba, Hispaniola, Jamaica, and Puerto Rico), and the Lesser Antilles (including numerous independent islands such as Antigua, Barbados, the Grenadines, and Martinique). West Indian species that stray to Florida are one of the primary attractions of birding in the extreme southern part of the state. More than 20 species largely or exclusively restricted to the West Indies have wandered to Florida (Table 2). Some of these species, such as La Sagra's Flycatcher, Bahama Mockingbird,

Table 2. Source countries of all non-pelagic West Indian species that have strayed to Florida

Scarlet Ibis, Red-legged Honeycreeper, and Cuban Grassquit are included here even though the provenance of the Florida records is unknown—they may represent vagrants from Tobago, or from Cuba or Mexico, respectively, or they may be escaped cage birds.

Species	West Indian Range	Species	West Indian Range
Least Grebe	Throughout	Cuban Martin	Cuba
Scarlet Ibis	Tobago (or escapees)	Bahama Swallow	Bahamas
White-cheeked Pintail	Throughout (or escapees)	Cave Swallow	Cuba
Masked Duck	Cuba	Thick-billed Vireo	Bahamas, Cuba
Scaly-naped Pigeon	Cuba	Bahama Mockingbird	Bahamas, Cuba
Zenaida Dove	Throughout	Bananaquit	Bahamas and other islands
Key West Quail-Dove	Throughout	Red-legged Honeycreeper	Cuba (or Mexico or escapees)
Ruddy Quail-Dove	Cuba	Western Spindalis (black-backed race)	northern Bahamas
Short-eared Owl	Cuba and Hispaniola	Western Spindalis (green-backed races)	Bahamas and Cuba
Antillean Palm-Swift	Cuba, Jamaica, and Hispaniola	Cuban Grassquit	Cuba (or escapees)
Bahama Woodstar	Bahamas	Yellow-faced Grassquit	Cuba, Hispaniola, and other islands
Cuban Pewee	Bahamas and Cuba	Black-faced Grassquit	Bahamas and other islands
La Sagra's Flycatcher	Bahamas and Cuba	Tawny-shouldered Blackbird	Cuba and Haiti

and Western Spindalis, occur annually or nearly so. Others, such as Scaly-naped Pigeon and Tawny-shouldered Blackbird, have occurred only once. Although the West Indies comprise numerous countries, possessions, and other holdings, vagrants to Florida probably originate mostly or entirely from the Bahamas and Cuba. West Indian strays to Florida arguably originate about equally from these two points of origin, even though considerably more species are endemic to Cuba than to the Bahamas. Species may be more sedentary on the large, diverse island of Cuba than they are on the 700 or so much smaller and less diverse Bahamian keys. Most species in the Bahamas probably "island-hop" on a frequent basis, which may explain why the Bahamas have so few endemic bird species relative to other West Indian countries.

Few species remaining in the West Indies appear likely to stray to Florida. Red-legged Honeycreeper and Cuban Grassquit already have been documented here, but there are questions about provenance of these birds (i.e., both of these species are imported for the cage-bird trade, and the Florida observations may represent escapees rather than natural vagrants). Several other species—West Indian Whistling-Duck, Cuban Emerald, Red-legged Thrush, Cuban Bullfinch, and Greater Antillean Bullfinch—have been reported in the state, but verifiable evidence is lacking—and questions of provenance would undoubtedly complicate most of these reports, as well. Tricolored Munia, which seems to be well established in Cuba as an exotic, may be straying to southern Florida, but again, the issue of provenance arises. In addition to West Indian Whistling-Duck, which Robertson and Woolfenden (1992) called a "plausible, even a likely, natural vagrant", there are perhaps only two remaining West Indian endemics that may be expected to occur in Florida naturally. One is Caribbean Martin (*Progne dominicensis*) of the southern West Indies, which occurs as a vagrant in the Bahamas. Males are similar to male Purple Martins but have gleaming white underparts. Females are similar to female Purple Martins. Reports of Caribbean Martin in Florida exist, but none has been accepted by the FOSRC. The other species that may stray to Florida is Pearly-eyed Thrasher (*Margarops fuscatus*), native to the southern Bahamas, Puerto Rico, and islands farther south and east. Pearly-eyed Thrashers seem to be moving northward, and one or more individuals may eventually reach the southeastern mainland or the Upper Keys. Both species are illustrated in A Guide to the Birds of the West Indies (Raffaele et al. 1998).

EXOTIC BIRDS IN FLORIDA

An exotic species is one that occurs in an area to which it is not native, through either deliberate or inadvertent introduction by humans. A few exotic birds are familiar to all ABA-area birders: Rock Pigeon, European Starling, and House Sparrow, for example, plus a few game birds released for hunting purposes (e.g., Ring-necked Pheasant). But most exotics are poorly known and have been ignored by both ornithologists and birders. Fortunately, the tendency to ignore exotics is beginning to change, as many birders now realize that *ignoring exotics does not make them go away; it only prevents accurate determination of their status and often, even their correct identification.* Birders concentrate on exotics that are, or someday might be, "countable" on

Table 3. New exotics reported in Florida from 1993 through 2004, arranged in reverse chronological order, and based on Pranty (2004).

Taxonomy and nomenclature follow AOU (1998) and supplements through 2003, or Clements (2000). Several of these species may represent natural vagrants rather than escapees.

Year	No.	Species
2004	5	Green-rumped Parrotlet (*Forpus passerinus*), Southern Ground-Hornbill (*Bucorvus leadbeateri*), Black-chested Jay (*Cyanocorax affinis*), Gouldian Finch (*Chloebia gouldiae*), Red-and-yellow Barbet (*Trachyphonus erythrocephalus*)
2003	5	Gray Partridge, Scaly-headed Parrot (*Pionus maximiliani*), White-necked Raven (*Corvus albicollis*), Superb Starling (*Lamprotornis superbus*), Red-legged Honeycreeper
2002	2	Trumpeter Swan, Rosy-crested Pochard (*Netta rufina*), Lady Amherst's Pheasant (*Chrysolophus amherstiae*) × Golden Pheasant (*C. pictus*)
2001	6	Pink-backed Pelican (*Pelecanus rufescens*), Red-breasted Parakeet (*Psittacula alexandri*), Red-throated Parakeet (*Aratinga rubritorquis*), Red-and-green Macaw (*Ara chloroptera*), House Crow (*Corvus splendens*), Bronze Mannikin (*Lonchura cucullata*)
2000	5	Philippine Duck (*Anas luzonica*), Sacred Ibis (*Threskiornis aethiopicus*), Malabar Parakeet (*Psittacula columboides*), Sun/Jandaya Parakeet (*Aratinga solstitialis* or *A. jandaya*), Knysna Turaco (*Tauraco corythaix*)
1999	5	Golden Pheasant, Black Crowned-Crane (*Balearica pavonina*), Dusky Lory (*Pseudeos fuscata*), African Gray Hornbill (*Tockus nasutus*), Tricolored Munia (*Lonchura malacca*)
1998	4	Great White Pelican (*Pelecanus onocrotalus*), Abdim's Stork (*Ciconia abdimi*), Black Bulbul (*Hypsipetes madagascariensis*), Village Weaver (*Ploceus cucullatus*)
1997	0	
1996	1	Purple Swamphen (*Porphyrio porphyrio*)
1995	2	Bar-headed Goose (*Anser indica*), Ringed Kingfisher
1994	7	Common Shelduck (*Tadorna tadorna*), Woolly-necked Stork (*Ciconia episcopus*), Schalow's Turaco (*Tauraco schalowi*), Wreathed Hornbill (*Aceros undulatus*), Silvery-cheeked Hornbill (*Ceratogymna brevis*), Common Raven, Orange Bishop (*Euplectes franciscanus*)
1993	4	Coscoroba Swan (*Coscoroba coscoroba*), White Stork (*Ciconia ciconia*), Eurasian Spoonbill (*Platalea leucorodia*), Black-headed Parrot (*Pionus melanocephala*)

personal lists, but those few species represent just a fraction of the exotic avifauna currently winging its way around Florida. As Robertson and Woolfenden (1992) pointed out, "It seems that the exotic avifaunal element is in Florida to stay, and we need to know much more about it." Smith and Smith (1993) agreed, and added, "If birders really care about birds and the environment, then they should care about the identity and impact of exotics, too."

Through 2003, the number of exotic bird species reported in Florida was 209 (plus one hybrid), although several of these are potential natural vagrants (Pranty 2004). Three or four exotics new to the state are discovered in most years (Table 3). Of these 209 species, 68 have been reported to breed in the wild in the state, but only 12 are considered "established" by the FOSRC: Muscovy Duck, Rock Pigeon, Eurasian Collared-Dove, Budgerigar, Monk Parakeet, Black-hooded Parakeet, White-winged Parakeet, Red-whiskered Bulbul, European Starling, Spot-breasted Oriole, House Finch, and House Sparrow. To increase awareness of the multitude of exotic birds found in Florida, this book includes information on several species that are considered not established by the FOSRC.

In most states, the presence of a parakeet, myna, or finch seen in the wild means simply that a pet owner or aviculturist (bird breeder) inadvertently left open a cage door. Most escaped cage birds last only a few days or weeks before succumbing to cold temperatures, predators, or starvation. In a few southern states, however, numerous species of escaped cage birds have bred successfully, and some of these have attained sizable populations. Three states in particular have many "naturalized" exotics reproducing in the wild: California, Florida, and Hawaii. These three states share several important features: mild year-round climates, extensive urban and suburban areas landscaped with tropical or subtropical vegetation (usually exotic), and major ports of entry for imported wildlife. The variety of exotics is surprisingly large, but many are parakeets, parrots, macaws, and the like, collectively called psittacids (pronounced sit-TASS-idz).

A complete list of all exotic birds documented in Florida begins on page 335. Fortunately, most exotic birds seem to have little to no impact on native species or ecosystems, because they are limited to developed areas from which most native species have been eliminated. If they remain limited to developed areas, as seems likely, then exotic birds probably will continue to avoid eradication efforts by government agencies, which already are fighting losing, under-funded battles against invasive exotic plants, from which native ecosystems face severe and well-documented threats.

BIRD COLLECTIONS IN FLORIDA

Specimen collections form the foundation for bird study around the world. There are four major bird collections in Florida, with the largest at Gainesville. These collections exist for a number of scientific purposes and may be examined by prior arrangement with the curators: **Archbold Biological Station** (123 Main Drive, Venus, FL 33960; 863-465-2571), **Florida Museum of Natural History** (University of Florida, Gainesville, FL 32611; 352-392-1721), **Tall Timbers Research Station** (13093 Henry Beadel Drive, Tallahassee, FL 32312; 850-893-4153), and **University of Central Florida** (Department of Biological Sciences, University of Central Florida, Orlando, FL 32816-3268; 407-823-2917).

CALENDAR OF BIRD ACTIVITY

This calendar briefly summarizes predictable bird occurrences in Florida during each month of the year. It should be understood that this is only a general guide: some birds are unpredictable in their occurrence, substantial regional differences exist in the distribution of many birds, and weather conditions can greatly affect bird abundance and distribution. For more precise information, consult the bar graphs on page 342.

January: The beginning of the new year marks the middle of the breeding season for Bald Eagles, Barn Owls, and Great Horned Owls. Some other species (e.g., most wading birds and other colonial breeders, Crested Caracaras, and several doves) may nest in Florida in nearly any month of the year. Masked Boobies are nesting at Dry Tortugas National Park, Sandhill Cranes begin egg-laying in January, and American Woodcocks are performing courtship flights in the Panhandle and northern half of the Peninsula. January marks the beginning of "spring" migration for Purple Martins—the first male scouts arrive from Central and South American wintering grounds around the middle of the month. Breeders and migrants aside, January is a mid-winter month and a good time to look for waterfowl, loons, grebes, shorebirds, and larids (gulls, terns, and Black Skimmers) along Florida's extensive coastlines. Wintering landbirds such as Yellow-bellied Sapsucker, Blue-headed Vireo, both kinglets (only Ruby-crowned in the southern half of the Peninsula), Hermit Thrush, and several wood-warblers are widespread in oak hammocks, while Wilson's Snipe, Sedge Wren, Palm Warbler, and several species of sparrows are commonly found in grassy or shrubby fields. The occurrence in Florida of irruptive wintering species such as Red-breasted Nuthatch, American Robin, Cedar Waxwing, Purple Finch, and Pine Siskin is highly variable. Even during "invasion" years, the nuthatch, finch, and siskin remain rare and are generally restricted to north of the central Peninsula, while robins and waxwings occur statewide. The first five days of January conclude the Christmas Bird Count season; see the December account for more information.

February: The final winter month is a relatively quiet one. Waterfowl generally depart in February, but most other winter residents remain through the month. Individuals of a few Neotropical migrant species such as Swallow-tailed Kite and Northern Parula return to Florida, usually around mid-month. Short-tailed Hawks begin to move north from their southern

Willet in breeding plumage.   Arthur Morris/www.birdsasart.com

Florida wintering grounds to breeding areas farther north in the peninsula. Many permanent residents begin singing, especially in years with mild winter temperatures. American Woodcocks begin nesting activities, primarily in northern Florida.

March: Most winter residents are still present at the beginning of the month, but many have returned to northern breeding grounds by the end of March. Permanent residents begin nesting, and more spring and summer residents arrive by late month (e.g., Chuck-will's-widow, Great Crested Flycatcher, Eastern Kingbird, Red-eyed Vireo, and Orchard Oriole). Wood-warbler migration is dominated by understory species such as waterthrushes and Kentucky and Hooded Warblers. West Indian strays may show up along the southeast coast or in the Keys. Mid-March gives Floridians an opportunity to hear Chuck-will's-widows and Whip-poor-wills singing side by side before the latter depart to breed father north.

April: The vast majority of winter residents that did not depart in March will do so this month. The first individuals of Florida's migratory spring and summer resident specialties (e.g., Antillean Nighthawk, Gray Kingbird, Black-whiskered Vireo) return by mid-April. The height of spring landbird migration occurs this month, often between the 10th and the 20th. Shorebird migration is also at its peak, and birders head to coastal areas such as Fort Pickens, Fort De Soto Park, Bill Baggs Cape Florida State Park, and Dry Tortugas National Park to witness the migration of shorebirds and landbirds. During fallouts, 20 or more species of wood-warblers may be seen, along with

Summer and Scarlet Tanagers, Rose-breasted and Blue Grosbeaks, Indigo and Painted Buntings, Orchard and Baltimore Orioles, and many other species. April is also the month when most birders visit Dry Tortugas National Park via boat trips from Key West. Additional West Indian vagrants may continue to show up along the southern Atlantic coast and in the Keys. Breeding residents are nesting, and a few early breeders (e.g., Florida Scrub-Jay and Pine Warbler) fledge young by the end of the month.

May: Most species are nesting, and singing is at its peak. Purple Martins have completed their breeding cycle in Central and South Florida, and colonies may be deserted by late May. (It is not known whether Florida's martins fly north to breed again, or whether they return south for the "winter".) Bald Eagles also have completed nesting, and many migrate northward out of Florida for the summer. Shorebird migration continues through the month, but landbird migration largely ends by mid-May. A few migrants (e.g., White-rumped Sandpiper and Connecticut Warbler) are more common in May than in April. Most Breeding Bird Survey (BBS) routes are run from mid-May to early June. These surveys are 24.5-mile-long transects along public roadways that consist of 50 stops, one every half-mile. BBS route-runners spend three minutes at each stop and record all birds seen or heard during that time within a quarter-mile radius. BBS data have been recorded since 1966 and are a critical tool for monitoring the abundance and distribution of breeding birds throughout North America. For more information on Florida BBS routes, contact the BBS coordinator, Florida Fish and Wildlife Conservation Commission, 4005 South Main Street, Gainesville, Florida 32611; 352-955-2230.

June: Intense sun, heat, and oppressive humidity characterize this month, and these conditions continue through at least August. Most breeding species have fledged young (many have laid second or third clutches), and the breeding season is winding down. Individuals of some species (e.g., White-rumped Sandpiper, Barn Swallow, and American Redstart) are still moving north in the first part of June, while some non-breeding shorebirds and gulls appear to remain in Florida through the summer. "Fall" migration begins in mid-June with the appearance of a few Purple Martins and Louisiana Waterthrushes away from breeding areas. June marks the beginning of hurricane season in Florida. Tropical storms and hurricanes often push pelagic species, especially Magnificent Frigatebirds and Bridled and Sooty Terns, to shore and even inland.

July: Blue Jays, Florida Grasshopper Sparrows, and a few other species are still nesting, but the breeding season generally is over by the beginning of July. Fledglings of most species are present and conspicuous. Fall migration of landbirds is obvious by the middle of the month, with the appearance of the first wood-warblers: Yellow, Yellow-throated, Prairie, Prothonotary, Black-and-white, and Hooded Warblers, and American Redstarts. Some Ruby-throated Hummingbirds seen in late July may also be migrants. Fall migration of shorebirds is well under way by the end of the month, with thousands of yellowlegs and peeps massing at favored areas. Roseate Spoonbills, mostly juveniles, appear inland after dispersing from coastal breeding sites, and the first Belted Kingfishers return to winter in the southern half of the Peninsula. Swallow-tailed Kites mass at large communal roots before island-hopping through the Keys and Cuba on their way to wintering grounds in South America.

August: Shorebird migration reaches a peak, and many birders head to shallowly-flooded vegetable fields such as those in the Everglades Agricultural Area. Fall migration begins for Kentucky Warblers, Louisiana and Northern Waterthrushes , Lark Sparrows, and others, and peaks for Yellow Warblers. Southbound flocks of Eastern Kingbirds are conspicuous by the end of the month, and movement of Ospreys in the Keys is obvious. Southbound Barn Swallows appear in early August and become common within a few weeks. Early-returning ducks such as Blue-winged Teal appear by mid-month. Most Swallow-tailed Kites have departed Florida by the end of August. Migration of Black Terns and some other larids begins in earnest, and pelagic species increase offshore. The last singing Chuck-will's-widows are heard this month.

September: Temperatures begin to cool a few degrees, although the humidity remains high. The height of wood-warbler migration occurs in September, and birders enter mosquito-filled oak hammocks and riparian habitats in search of Florida's 36 regularly-occurring species. Other landbirds also are moving through in numbers: flocks of hundreds of Common Nighthawks are frequent by mid-month, and diurnal flocks of Eastern Kingbirds continue southbound through the first half of September. Shorebird migration reaches a second fall peak. Raptor migration continues, with Mississippi Kites and Broad-winged Hawks moving through the western Panhandle, and the first Merlins and Peregrine Falcons appearing throughout. Hawkwatch stations at Guana River State Park south of St. Augustine and Curry Hammock State Park in the Middle Keys begin daily observations in September. Some breeding species, such as Mourning Dove, Northern Mockingbird, and Northern Cardinal, resume singing after a two- or three-month hiatus.

October: Raptor migration peaks in the first half of the month, and birders head to the Atlantic coast and Keys to witness large numbers of accipiters and falcons. Dozens of Peregrine Falcons may be seen daily at selected sites during the first half of October. Migration of thrushes and some wood-warblers such as Bay-breasted Warbler also peaks in the first half of the month. Western-breeding species that winter in Florida arrive, especially along the Gulf coast: look for White-winged Dove, Vermilion Flycatcher, Western Kingbird, and Scissor-tailed Flycatcher. Other winter residents, such as Wilson's Snipe, Eastern Phoebe, and Palm Warbler, are conspicuous by the end of the month. Migration of pelagic species offshore increases (especially in the Atlantic), and large numbers of Pomarine and Parasitic Jaegers may sometimes be seen from shore.

November: Fall migration of birds *through* the state generally ends early in the month, although a few migrants may be found later. But southward movement of birds *into* Florida continues for waterfowl, Yellow-rumped Warblers, and irruptive species such as American Robin and Cedar Waxwing. Flocks of dozens to a hundred or more Turkey Vultures move into the state. Numerous jaegers moving off the Atlantic coast are joined later in the month by Northern Gannets and Black Scoters. In the latter half of the month, high-flying migratory flocks of Greater Sandhill Cranes can be seen (or, more typically, heard) as they head south over the Peninsula. Toward the end of November, waterfowl, loons, and grebes are widespread along both coasts, and some are found inland on larger lakes. Most winter residents are present in numbers by the end of the month. Nesting season begins for Bald Eagles and Great Horned Owls.

December: The final month of the year marks the beginning of winter. Southbound flocks of Greater Sandhill Cranes continue into the first part of December. Nearly all winter residents are present by the beginning of the month, although a few species (e.g., Bonaparte's Gull and Cedar Waxwing) may not appear until late in the month, or even later. Pelagic birds are still moving offshore early in December. Landbirds form mixed-species wintering flocks that may contain 20 or more species. These flocks forage through habitats during the day, and are most easily observed by judicious use of an Eastern Screech-Owl tape. The birds mob the tape (screech-owls are predators of small birds, among other prey) but generally lose interest after five to ten minutes, presumably because they cannot locate the "owl". Certainly the biggest birding events in December are Christmas Bird Counts (CBCs), day-long surveys of 15-mile diameter circles. The CBC season begins on 14 December and continues through 5 January. More than 60 CBCs are conducted annually in Florida, with circles concentrated along the coasts in the southern half of the Peninsula. For more information, go to the CBC website <www.audubon.org/bird/cbc>. The entire 100-year CBC database may also be accessed from this site. The Florida Ornithological Society website, which lists CBC dates and contact information, is found at <www.fosbirds.org>.

FLORIDA HABITATS AND TYPICAL BIRDS

Florida supports more than 300 species of trees, representing almost half of all species native to the United States. Historically, the state was nearly 90 percent forested, but human development has reduced this amount considerably and has severely fragmented many wooded habitats. Although the highest point in Florida is only 345 feet above sea level, elevational differences (sometimes measured in feet or even *inches*) are important in determining the composition of plant communities. Florida's abundant rainfall, high humidity, varied drainage patterns, extensive coastline, and subtropical climate also affect the distribution of plant life, which in turn affects the distribution of birds and other animals. For more information, consult the superb reference book, *Ecosystems of Florida*, edited by Ron Myers and John Ewel (1990), from which much habitat information found here was taken.

Many of Florida's 481 native bird species occur statewide, or nearly so. For instance, nearly all wooded areas in the state contain Eastern Screech-Owls, Downy Woodpeckers, White-eyed Vireos, and Carolina Wrens. Because repetitive reference to these and several others would be tedious and would take up space better devoted to other, more specialized species, most of these common species are listed together here, grouped by habitat. You should be able to find most of the birds listed below, provided that you visit the proper habitat during the proper season (and, for some species, the proper region of Florida). In this section, "northern Florida" refers to the Panhandle and the northern peninsula (south roughly to Gainesville), "central peninsula" refers to the area between Gainesville and Lake Okeechobee, and "southern Florida" refers to the peninsula south of Lake Okeechobee and the Keys.

PINEWOODS were formerly the most widespread terrestrial plant community in Florida, covering about half the state's uplands. In central Florida, these forests are called "flatwoods" because of the terrain, which stretches for miles with little or no elevational relief. Frequent low-intensity, growing-season lightning fires maintained pine flatwoods as open forests with an understory dominated by Saw Palmetto and Wiregrass. Three dominant species of pines make up Florida's pinewoods: Longleaf Pine, Slash Pine, and Pond Pine. Longleaf Pine was the most widely distributed pine in North and Central Florida up to the late 1800s or early 1900s but was logged extensively and failed to regenerate in many areas, apparently because feral hogs consumed most of the seeds. Many writers of the late 1800s and early 1900s commented on the extent of Florida's open Longleaf Pine flatwoods. Below is a typical example, written by Arthur Cleveland Bent (1947):

> The northern tourist, seeking a winter sojourn in Florida, rides in the south-bound train for hour after hour with nothing to see from the car window but apparently endless miles of uninteresting flat pine barrens, until he wearies of the monotony. He does not appreciate the intriguing vastness of these almost boundless flatwoods, nor does he admire the stately beauty of the Longleaf Pines....One may wander for many miles through these park-like woods, along the winding, grass-grown cart roads, but he never seems to get anywhere, as the trees seem to lead him on indefinitely....

Today, development and agriculture have obliterated most of Florida's pinewoods, while others have been converted to pine plantations. As a result, Slash Pine now is the most widely distributed pine in the state. Habitat fragmentation and resultant fire suppression have turned most of the surviving flatwoods remnants into dense forests with thick understories of oaks and other woody invaders. Eventually, the shaded understory prevents young pines from flourishing, and the pines give way to an oak forest. Because some other habitats are strongly protected from development, Florida's pinewoods, under little or no environmental protection, are being destroyed at an alarming rate. As a result, one of Florida's most abundant plant communities has now become perhaps its most threatened.

Permanent residents: Northern Bobwhite, Black Vulture, Turkey Vulture, Red-shouldered Hawk, Red-tailed Hawk, Mourning Dove, Common Ground-Dove, Eastern Screech-Owl, Great Horned Owl, Red-headed Woodpecker (local), Red-bellied Woodpecker, Downy Woodpecker, Hairy Woodpecker (local), Red-cockaded Woodpecker (extremely local), Northern Flicker, Pileated Woodpecker, White-eyed Vireo, Blue Jay, American Crow, Fish Crow, Carolina Chickadee (except southern Florida), Tufted Titmouse (local in southern Florida), Brown-headed Nuthatch (local in southern Florida), Carolina Wren, Blue-gray Gnatcatcher, Eastern Bluebird (local in southern Florida), Northern Mockingbird, Brown Thrasher, Yellow-throated Warbler (does not breed in southern Florida), Pine Warbler, Common Yellowthroat, Eastern Towhee, Bachman's Sparrow (local in southern Florida; difficult to find throughout when not singing), Northern Cardinal, Common Grackle, and Brown-headed Cowbird (uncommon during summer in central and southern Florida).

Summer residents: Mississippi Kite (northern Florida only), Broad-winged Hawk (northern Florida only), Yellow-billed Cuckoo, Common Nighthawk, Chuck-will's-widow, Great Crested Flycatcher, Eastern Kingbird, Purple Martin (around human habitation), Northern Parula, and Summer Tanager (rare in southern Florida).

Winter residents: Sharp-shinned Hawk, American Kestrel (local permanent resident), American Woodcock, Yellow-bellied Sapsucker, Eastern Phoebe, Blue-headed Vireo, House Wren, Ruby-crowned Kinglet, American Robin, Gray Catbird (local breeder in northern Florida), Cedar Waxwing, Orange-crowned Warbler, Yellow-rumped Warbler, Palm Warbler, Black-and-white Warbler, and American Goldfinch (irruptive in southern Florida).

OAK FORESTS of different varieties comprise another widespread habitat in Florida, especially on interior peninsular ridge systems that have gently rolling reliefs. In these areas, Longleaf or Slash Pines have mixed with Turkey Oaks and other species to form a habitat known as sandhills. In the Panhandle, these areas are called clayhills because of the clay soils. After the pines were logged and fires were suppressed, oaks dominated. Other types of mixed forests also occur widely in the state. Along the coast especially, but inland as well, oak forests and oak hammocks are popular birding sites during migration. (Migrant landbirds strongly prefer oak habitats to pines, presumably because oaks offer more food and cover.) Widespread in Florida, and one of its most characteristic species, is the Live Oak, which grows very large but rarely tall, with limbs that spread out and hug the ground.

A few of these trees are more than 1,000 years old. The tree is named because it is nearly or entirely evergreen, a rare quality among oaks, shedding and replacing its leaves in a short period during spring. Huge solitary Live Oaks growing in fields and pastures are still familiar sights in Florida's less developed areas. On old dune systems, the vegetation is often dominated by endemic oaks classified as xeric oak scrub; see the next section on scrub.

Permanent residents: Wild Turkey, Northern Bobwhite, Black Vulture, Turkey Vulture, Red-shouldered Hawk, Red-tailed Hawk, Mourning Dove, Common Ground-Dove, Eastern Screech-Owl, Barred Owl, Red-headed Woodpecker (local), Red-bellied Woodpecker, Downy Woodpecker, Hairy Woodpecker (local; sandhills), Red-cockaded Woodpecker (extremely local; sandhills), Northern Flicker, Pileated Woodpecker, White-eyed Vireo, Blue Jay, American Crow (mainly inland), Fish Crow, Carolina Chickadee (except southern Florida), Tufted Titmouse (local in southern Florida), Carolina Wren, Blue-gray Gnatcatcher, Brown Thrasher, Pine Warbler (sandhills), Eastern Towhee, Northern Cardinal, and Common Grackle.

Summer residents: Swallow-tailed Kite, Mississippi Kite (northern Florida only), Broad-winged Hawk (northern Florida only), Yellow-billed Cuckoo, Common Nighthawk, Chuck-will's-widow, Great Crested Flycatcher, Red-eyed Vireo (local in southern Florida), Purple Martin (around human habitation), Northern Parula, and Summer Tanager (rare in southern Florida).

Winter residents: Sharp-shinned Hawk, American Kestrel (local permanent resident), American Woodcock (breeds in northern Florida), Yellow-bellied Sapsucker, Eastern Phoebe, Blue-headed Vireo, House Wren, Ruby-crowned Kinglet, Hermit Thrush, American Robin, Gray Catbird (local breeder in northern Florida), Cedar Waxwing, Orange-crowned Warbler, Yellow-rumped Warbler, Yellow-throated Warbler, Palm Warbler, Black-and-white Warbler, and American Goldfinch (irruptive in southern Florida).

S CRUB is a plant community dominated by stunted oaks and woody shrubs that grow in well-drained sandy soils along both coasts and on ancient coastal dunes that now constitute interior ridges of the Peninsula. The largest of the central ridges, the Lake Wales Ridge, was formed two to three million years ago when sea levels were much higher than they are today, and the rest of the Peninsula was submerged. Because of their long geographic isolation from the rest of the continent, many scrub plants and animals have evolved into distinct species: in fact, the Lake Wales Ridge contains more endemic plant species than any other region of Florida, and it is one of the most endemic-rich areas in the country. About half of Florida's scrub plants are endemic.

Because scrub soil is pure sand dozens of feet deep, rainwater filters quickly through the ground, creating a nutrient-poor, well-drained environment not unlike a desert. As a result, scrub vegetation is frequently sparse and stunted, dominated by evergreen oaks, palmettos, shrubs, cactuses, and flowering plants. Fairly frequent (roughly every five to 15 years), intense fires maintained the scrub as a low, open habitat. In a long (40-year) absence of fire, many scrubs succeed into forests of Sand Pine, a scrub endemic tree. Under these conditions, many of the scrub's other specialized species decrease in abundance or die out entirely. Ocala National Forest, where fire is excluded specifically for the production of pulpwood, is an example of a Sand Pine forest. Other Sand Pine forests occur in a narrow band along some of the Panhandle coast and elsewhere in the Peninsula. Examples of oak scrub remain as a narrow strip along much of the Atlantic Coast (now fragmented heavily by human development), including Canaveral National Seashore, Merritt Island National Wildlife Refuge, and Jonathan Dickinson State Park, in Oscar Scherer State Park near Sarasota, and along the Lake Wales Ridge from Lake Wales to Venus. The Lake Wales Ridge National Wildlife Refuge is the nation's first refuge established specifically to preserve endangered and threatened plants. Because most interior scrubs have been destroyed by the citrus industry, and those along the coast have been lost mostly to residential and commercial development, scrub is one of Florida's most imperiled natural communities.

> **Birds typical of oak scrub** include Northern Bobwhite, Common Nighthawk (spring and summer), White-eyed Vireo, Florida Scrub-Jay (endemic), Gray Catbird (migration and winter), Northern Mockingbird, and Eastern Towhee. **Sand Pine forests** contain an almost completely different suite of species, such as Cooper's Hawk, Eastern Screech-Owl, Hairy Woodpecker (local), Great Crested Flycatcher (spring and summer), Blue Jay, Pine Warbler, and Summer Tanager (spring and summer). Many other species found in pinewoods and oak forests will also occur, depending partially on the extent of pine overstory.

H AMMOCKS are island-like stands of palms, Red Cedars, or deciduous trees surrounded by pine flatwoods, marshes, or prairies. Cabbage Palm hammocks are a conspicuous part of coastal marshes and of the extensive prairie region west and north of Lake Okeechobee. The tropical hardwood hammocks dotting the Everglades are unique in the United States to Florida because the vegetation is largely of West Indian origin. Tropical hammocks contain species such as Mahogany, Gumbo Limbo, Jamaican Dogwood, Royal Palm, and various figs.

> **Breeding birds** vary with the type of hammock and the location within Florida but can include Red-shouldered Hawk, Wild Turkey (local in southern Florida and absent from the Keys), White-crowned

Pigeon (southern Florida), Yellow-billed Cuckoo (spring and summer), Barred Owl (absent from the Keys), Great Crested Flycatcher (mostly spring and summer), and White-eyed Vireo. Upland hammocks will have most species found in oak forests, while wetter hammocks will contain many birds found in swamps. Hammocks also support large numbers of *migrant and wintering passerines*.

SWAMPS are poorly drained and frequently flooded areas grown mostly to hardwoods and other non-coniferous trees. Many different species of trees are found in swamps, depending on water levels, geographic location within Florida, and other factors, but the Bald Cypress is probably Florida's best-known swamp tree. Others include Grand Magnolia, Tupelo, Swamp Bay, Sweet Gum, Red Maple, and various oaks and willows. Swamps vary in size from small depressions to vast areas such as the extensive river swamps of the Panhandle or Big Cypress Swamp in South Florida.

Permanent residents: Wood Duck, Wild Turkey, Anhinga, Great Blue Heron, Great Egret, Snowy Egret, Little Blue Heron, Tricolored Heron, Green Heron, Black-crowned Night-Heron, White Ibis, Wood Stork, Osprey, Bald Eagle, Red-shouldered Hawk, Limpkin (Peninsula mostly), Eastern Screech-Owl, Barred Owl, Red-bellied Woodpecker, Downy Woodpecker, Pileated Woodpecker, White-eyed Vireo, American Crow, Fish Crow, Carolina Chickadee (except in southern Florida), Tufted Titmouse (local in southern Florida), Carolina Wren, Blue-gray Gnatcatcher, Northern Cardinal, Red-winged Blackbird, and Common Grackle.

Summer residents: Swallow-tailed Kite, Mississippi Kite (northern Florida only), Broad-winged Hawk (northern Florida only), Yellow-billed Cuckoo, Acadian Flycatcher (northern Florida only), Great Crested Flycatcher (year-round in southern Florida), Red-eyed Vireo (local in southern Florida), Northern Parula, and Prothonotary Warbler (rare in southern Florida).

Winter residents: Sharp-shinned Hawk, American Woodcock, Belted Kingfisher, Red-headed Woodpecker (irruptive), Yellow-bellied Sapsucker, Blue-headed Vireo, Ruby-crowned Kinglet, Hermit Thrush, Gray Catbird, Cedar Waxwing, Orange-crowned Warbler (uncommon), Yellow-rumped Warbler, Yellow-throated Warbler, Black-and-white Warbler, Ovenbird (mostly southern Florida), Chipping Sparrow, Rusty Blackbird (mostly northern Florida), and American Goldfinch (irruptive in southern Florida).

MANGROVES comprise three species and genera of salt-tolerant trees that form extensive forests in coastal areas. Red Mangroves are identified easily by their complex network of curved "prop roots" that rise above the water. The other two species in Florida are Black Mangrove and White Mangrove. (Buttonwood often is mentioned as Florida's fourth mangrove species but is not a true mangrove.) Tropical trees, mangroves cannot tolerate cold temperatures and generally are limited to the central and southern Peninsula and the Keys. Black Mangroves are the most cold-tolerant and therefore range farther north than the other two species. Mangrove forests reach their greatest extent along the extreme southern Peninsula and in the Keys.

Many large birds nest in mangroves in Florida, including Magnificent Frigatebird, Brown Pelican, Double-crested Cormorant, all wading birds, and even Osprey and Bald Eagle, but six landbirds are especially associated with mangrove forests: White-crowned Pigeon, Mangrove Cuckoo, Gray Kingbird, Black-whiskered Vireo, Florida Prairie Warbler, and Cuban Yellow Warbler.

TIDAL MARSHES AND ESTUARIES represent two of the most extensive coastal habitats found in Florida. Tidal marshes occur where wave action is insufficient to create beaches and dunes. In Florida, tidal marshes reach their greatest extent along the Gulf coast from Apalachicola to Tarpon Springs. Other saltmarshes form behind barrier islands and at the mouths of rivers. Many species of sedges and grasses are found in Florida's saltmarshes, but needle-rush (*Juncus*) and cordgrass (*Spartina*) are two principal plants. Because these wetlands are now protected from development, extensive areas of saltmarshes remain in Florida. Sea-level rise, however, may pose a significant threat to tidal marshes in the not too distant future. Estuaries are shallow areas where fresh water and salt water mix, creating salinities dependent upon rainfall, tides, and other factors. Bays and lagoons are two examples of estuarine habitats.

Permanent residents: Mottled Duck (mostly absent from northern Florida), Brown Pelican, Double-crested Cormorant, Great Blue Heron, Great White Heron (southern Florida), Great Egret, Snowy Egret, Little Blue Heron, Tricolored Heron, Reddish Egret (rare in the western Panhandle), Green Heron, Black-crowned Night-Heron (local), Yellow-crowned Night-Heron, White Ibis, Wood Stork, Bald Eagle, Osprey, Clapper Rail, Killdeer, American Oystercatcher, Willet, Laughing Gull, Royal Tern, Black Skimmer, Marsh Wren, Seaside Sparrow (mainly northern and central Gulf coast), Red-winged Blackbird, and Boat-tailed Grackle (rare in the western Panhandle).

Summer residents: Magnificent Frigatebird (mostly the Peninsula; resident in the Keys), Least Tern, and Gray Kingbird.

Migrants: Semipalmated Sandpiper, Common Tern, and Black Tern.

Winter residents: American Wigeon, Blue-winged Teal, Northern Shoveler, Green-winged Teal, Canvasback (except southern Florida), Redhead (except southern Florida), Lesser Scaup, Bufflehead (except southern Florida), Hooded Merganser, Red-breasted Merganser, Ruddy Duck (local), Common Loon, Pied-billed Grebe, Horned

Grebe, Northern Harrier, Virginia Rail, Sora, Black-bellied Plover, Semipalmated Plover, Greater Yellowlegs, Lesser Yellowlegs, Spotted Sandpiper, Whimbrel (local), Marbled Godwit (local), Ruddy Turnstone, Western Sandpiper, Least Sandpiper, Dunlin, Short-billed Dowitcher, Ring-billed Gull, Herring Gull, Gull-billed Tern (local; southern Florida), Caspian Tern, Sandwich Tern, Forster's Tern, Belted Kingfisher, Sedge Wren, Common Yellowthroat, Saltmarsh Sharp-tailed Sparrow (mainly Atlantic coast), Nelson's Sharp-tailed Sparrow (mainly northern and central Gulf coast), and Swamp Sparrow.

COASTAL STRAND includes beaches and dunes, one of the best-known of Florida landscapes and one responsible for attracting millions of tourists to the state annually. Beaches and associated dune systems extend along the entire Atlantic coast, and along the Gulf coast in the western Panhandle and from Tarpon Springs southward to Naples. They account for more than 750 miles of coastal frontage, mostly along chains of barrier islands a few miles out from the mainland. Today, beachfront development has obliterated coastal strand habitats along huge portions of the Atlantic coast and locally along the Gulf coast, especially from Clearwater southward. Sadly, large areas of the Panhandle coast, the most pristine coastline in Florida, are being developed currently or are planned for development.

Permanent residents: Brown Pelican, Double-crested Cormorant, Yellow-crowned Night-Heron, American Oystercatcher, Snowy Plover (local; Gulf coast), Wilson's Plover (local), Willet, Laughing Gull, Royal Tern, and Black Skimmer.

Summer resident: Least Tern.

Migrants: Semipalmated Sandpiper, Common Tern, and Black Tern.

Winter residents: Black-bellied Plover, Semipalmated Plover, Piping Plover (local, mainly Gulf coast), Ruddy Turnstone, Red Knot, Sanderling, Western Sandpiper, Least Sandpiper, Dunlin, Short-billed Dowitcher, Ring-billed Gull, Herring Gull, Great Black-backed Gull (mainly Atlantic coast), Lesser Black-backed Gull (local, mainly Atlantic coast), Caspian Tern, Sandwich Tern, and Forster's Tern. Pelagic species such as Northern Gannets and jaegers may sometimes be observed from Florida's beaches, primarily those on the Atlantic coast.

OPEN SALT WATER includes the Atlantic Ocean, Gulf of Mexico, Straits of Florida, and Caribbean Sea. Birds that occur here regularly are seabirds and other pelagic species. Except on days with strong winds blowing toward shore, trips on deep-sea fishing boats are usually required to observe these species. During spring (especially) and fall migrations, numerous landbirds may also be observed over open water. When birds are heavily stressed from strong winds or other factors, they may land on the boat.

Year-round visitors: Audubon's Shearwater (less common during winter), Masked Booby (uncommon), and Brown Booby (uncommon).

Summer visitors: Greater Shearwater, Cory's Shearwater, Wilson's Storm-Petrel, Bridled Tern, and Sooty Tern.

Migrant visitors: Common Tern and Black Tern.

Winter visitors: Northern Gannet (often seen from shore, especially along the Atlantic coast), Red-necked Phalarope, Red Phalarope, Pomarine Jaeger, and Parasitic Jaeger.

FRESHWATER HABITATS include wet prairies, marshes, lakes, and rivers. Wet prairies and freshwater marshes are areas flooded seasonally or permanently by anywhere from a few inches to a few feet of water. These wetlands are most abundant in the southern half of the Peninsula, where the land is extremely flat and poorly drained. The Everglades, which originally occupied over 7,500 square miles, is a freshwater marsh system unique in the world. Today, only about half of the Everglades remains in a semi-natural state, although an ambitious restoration plan is underway. Other marshland is created when agricultural fields are flooded after crops are harvested. Belle Glade (page 212), southeast of Lake Okeechobee, is a well-known birding site in late summer and early fall. A second site, former agricultural fields along the northern shore of Lake Apopka northwest of Orlando (the "Zellwood muck farms", page 147), was a premier fall-birding site that is now under restoration. This site hopefully will return to its former birding glory in the not-too-distant future. Lakes are numerous in Florida, especially in the northern two-thirds of the Peninsula. There are more than 7,800 lakes in the state of at least one acre in size. The largest is Lake Okeechobee (448,000 acres, or 700 square miles), which, after Lake Michigan, is the largest freshwater lake wholly within the United States. Florida's abundance of lakes is partially the result of the limestone base that underlies the state. As rainfall dissolves the limestone, a cavity forms. If the cavity becomes large enough, it may collapse to form a sinkhole, which quickly fills with water to form a lake. Rivers are also numerous in Florida, with more than 1,700 in the state if creeks, sloughs (pronounced *slewz*), and streams are included. Rivers in the Panhandle originate in the foothills of the Appalachian Mountains in Georgia or Alabama, while many other rivers are spring-fed. About 320 springs are found in Florida, which exceeds the number found in any other state and country. Twenty-seven of these are classified as "first magnitude", meaning that they each discharge a minimum of 64 million gallons of water per day.

Permanent residents: Black-bellied Whistling-Duck (local in the Peninsula, but increasing), Fulvous Whistling-Duck (very local; central and southern Peninsula), Muscovy Duck (areas of human habitation), Wood Duck, Mottled Duck (rare or absent in northern Florida), Mallard (feral individuals; areas of human habitation), Pied-billed Grebe

Great Blue Heron pair nesting in.
Brazilian Pepper (an invasive exotic!).

Arthur Morris/www.birdsasart.com

(more common during winter), Anhinga, Least Bittern (withdraws from the north during winter), Great Blue Heron, Great Egret, Snowy Egret, Little Blue Heron, Tricolored Heron, Green Heron, Black-crowned Night-Heron, White Ibis, Glossy Ibis (Peninsula), Wood Stork, Osprey, Bald Eagle, King Rail, Purple Swamphen (very local; increasing), Purple Gallinule (withdraws from northern Florida during winter), Common Moorhen, Limpkin (Peninsula), Sandhill Crane, Killdeer, Black-necked Stilt (local in the Panhandle and usually present only during spring and summer), Common Yellowthroat, Red-winged Blackbird, Common Grackle, and Boat-tailed Grackle.

Summer resident: Least Tern (local).

Migrants: Solitary Sandpiper (mostly spring), Spotted Sandpiper, Semipalmated Sandpiper, White-rumped Sandpiper (mostly spring), Pectoral Sandpiper (mostly fall), Stilt Sandpiper, Wilson's Phalarope (mostly fall), and Black Tern (mostly fall).

Winter residents: Green-winged Teal, Northern Pintail (local), Blue-winged Teal, Northern Shoveler, American Wigeon, Ring-necked Duck, Hooded Merganser, American Bittern, Northern Harrier, Virginia Rail, Sora, American Coot, Greater Yellowlegs, Lesser Yellowlegs, Western Sandpiper, Least Sandpiper, Long-billed Dowitcher, Wilson's Snipe, Laughing Gull (local), Ring-billed Gull, Forster's Tern, Caspian Tern (local), Belted Kingfisher, Sedge Wren, Marsh Wren, American Pipit (muddy shorelines), Swamp Sparrow, and Common Grackle.

D RY PRAIRIES in Florida are quite different from the rolling grasslands of the West. In Florida, dry prairies are flat, poorly-drained areas lying mostly west and north of Lake Okeechobee (see pages 168 and 209). They consist of treeless areas covered with bunch grasses and Saw Palmettos, mirroring the understory of pine flatwoods. Lightning fires historically burned dry prairies on perhaps an annual basis, which maintained the low, open cover of grasses and prevented invasion by woody shrubs and trees. Today, management of dry prairies usually is accomplished through prescribed burning. More than 80 percent of Florida's native dry prairies have been converted to human uses. Birds characteristic of prairies include four relict species that occur widely in the western plains or southwestern grasslands, but east of the Mississippi River are virtually or entirely limited to Florida: White-tailed Kite (local but increasing), Crested Caracara, Sandhill Crane, and Burrowing Owl. Florida Grasshopper Sparrow, an Endangered endemic race, is limited to a few prairies from Kenansville southwest to Avon Park. All prairie species except the sparrow can also be found in artificial prairie-like habitats such as cattle pastures, ball fields, golf courses, and other mowed areas; Burrowing Owls, in fact, are now virtually restricted in Florida to human-modified habitats (Bowen 2001). The following list emphasizes those species found in dry prairies and associated native habitats such as marshes and cypress heads.

Permanent residents: Wild Turkey, Northern Bobwhite, Great Blue Heron, Great Egret, Snowy Egret, Little Blue Heron, Cattle Egret, Black Vulture, Turkey Vulture, Red-shouldered Hawk, Red-tailed Hawk, Crested Caracara, Sandhill Crane, Killdeer (local), Mourning Dove, Common Ground-Dove, Burrowing Owl (local), American Crow, Fish Crow, Eastern Bluebird, Northern Mockingbird, Loggerhead Shrike, Bachman's Sparrow, Florida Grasshopper Sparrow (extremely local), and Eastern Meadowlark.

Summer residents: Swallow-tailed Kite, Common Nighthawk, and Eastern Kingbird.

Migrants: Barn Swallow, Bobolink.

Winter residents: Northern Harrier, American Kestrel, Wilson's Snipe, Barn Owl (less common during summer), Eastern Phoebe, Tree Swallow, Sedge Wren, Palm Warbler, Savannah Sparrow, Grasshopper Sparrow (eastern race), and Swamp Sparrow.

U RBAN and SUBURBAN HABITATS are increasing in Florida as human residents continue to invade the state in large numbers and alter vast amounts of native or agricultural habitats. Developed areas, especially from the central Peninsula southward, where mild winter temperatures allow tropical foliage to survive year-round, typically are landscaped with exotic vegetation. Exotic birds such as psittacids and finches that escape or are released usually find sufficient food resources outside of captivity. Several of these species have bred successfully and now maintain moderate to large populations in metropolitan areas; a few species are well established indeed. House Finches, which invaded the state from Georgia in the mid-1980s, are increasing south to the central Peninsula, invariably in urban or suburban areas. Another recent phenomenon linked to residential habitats is the movement east or southeast of western-breeding hummingbirds. Increasing numbers of these species are now wintering in Florida yards stocked with hummingbird feeders and/or honeysuckle or other flowering plants. Wintering hummingbirds are found throughout Florida, but western-breeding species are most frequent in the Panhandle, with diversity decreasing southward through the Peninsula. Rufous and Black-chinned Hummingbirds are now locally uncommon during winter, and several other species (including Allen's, Calliope, and Broad-tailed Hummingbirds) have been documented. In southern Florida, Ruby-throated Hummingbirds are uncommon, and Rufous Hummingbirds are expected in small numbers. Banding efforts continue to improve our knowledge of the status and winter distribution of hummingbirds in Florida.

Dozens of other native species can also persist in urban and suburban habitats, although Florida's most specialized landbirds (such as Hairy and Red-cockaded Woodpeckers, Florida Scrub-Jay, and Bachman's Sparrow) eventually are eliminated from developed areas. Wading birds—including Wood Storks—commonly forage in roadside ditches and stormwater retention ponds in developments. Waterfowl such as Ring-necked Ducks and American Coots are common in ponds and lakes, even in downtown areas. Purple Martins are virtually restricted to martin houses and hollowed-out gourds placed in yards. Granivorous species such as doves and icterids commonly visit bird feeders, and these in turn attract Sharp-shinned (winter) and Cooper's Hawks, and, in southeastern Florida, Short-tailed Hawks. Florida's state bird, Northern Mockingbird, is far more abundant in developed areas than in natural habitats.

Because birders rarely visit urban or suburban areas in search of native species other than vagrants, the following list is limited to exotic birds. Exotics typically are restricted to areas of human development (although there are a few exceptions such as Purple Swamphen), and all are permanent residents. Refer to the Birds of Particular Interest section (page 267) for information on specific locations for some of these species.

Permanent residents: Muscovy Duck, Mallard (feral), Purple Swamphen (non-countable; mainly Pembroke Pines but expanding northward and westward into natural areas), Rock Pigeon, Eurasian Collared-Dove, Budgerigar (declining; Hernando Beach and Bayonet Point), Rose-ringed Parakeet (non-countable; Fort Myers and Naples), Monk Parakeet (mainly central Gulf coast and southern Atlantic coast), Black-hooded Parakeet (ABA acceptance pending; mainly St. Petersburg to Sarasota), Blue-crowned Parakeet (non-countable; local), Mitred Parakeet (non-countable; local), Red-masked Parakeet (non-countable; local), Dusky-headed Parakeet (non-countable; Miami; rare), Chestnut-fronted Macaw (non-countable; Fort Lauderdale and Miami), White-winged Parakeet (Fort Lauderdale and Miami), Yellow-chevroned Parakeet (non-countable; Fort Lauderdale and Miami), Red-crowned Parrot (non-countable; Palm Beach, Fort Lauderdale, and Miami), Orange-winged Parrot (non-countable; Fort Lauderdale and Miami), Red-whiskered Bulbul (Kendall/Pinecrest), European Starling (more common during winter), Common Myna (non-countable; southern Atlantic coast), Hill Myna (non-countable; Miami), Spot-breasted Oriole (Fort Lauderdale to Miami), House Finch (range expanding southward), and House Sparrow.

WIDESPREAD NEOTROPICAL MIGRANTS

WIDESPREAD NEOTROPICAL MIGRANTS: Migrant landbirds can be found in of any of the above habitats, especially oak hammocks and swamps, plus mangrove forests, and others. Many of these birds are widespread breeders in parts of Florida (and a few winter widely), but all move through the state during spring and/or fall. Migration is limited mostly to the period from March to May, and then from August to October, although some migrants are moving through Florida during every month of the year.

Widespread Neotropical migrants include Yellow-billed Cuckoo, Ruby-throated Hummingbird, Eastern Wood-Pewee (mainly fall), Acadian Flycatcher (mainly fall), Great Crested Flycatcher, Eastern Kingbird, White-eyed Vireo, Yellow-throated Vireo (uncommon), Red-eyed Vireo, Northern Rough-winged Swallow, Bank Swallow (uncommon; mainly fall), Barn Swallow, Blue-gray Gnatcatcher, Veery, Gray-cheeked Thrush (uncommon), Swainson's Thrush, Wood Thrush (uncommon), Gray Catbird, Blue-winged Warbler (uncommon; mainly fall), Golden-winged Warbler (uncommon; mainly fall), Tennessee Warbler, Northern Parula, Yellow Warbler (mainly fall), Chestnut-sided Warbler (mainly fall), Magnolia Warbler (mainly fall), Cape May Warbler (mainly spring), Black-throated Blue Warbler, Black-throated Green Warbler (uncommon; mainly fall), Blackburnian Warbler (mainly fall), Yellow-throated Warbler, Prairie Warbler, Bay-breasted Warbler (mainly fall), Blackpoll Warbler (mainly spring), Cerulean Warbler (uncommon, mainly fall), Black-and-white Warbler, American Redstart, Prothonotary Warbler (near water), Worm-eating Warbler (uncommon; mainly fall), Ovenbird, Northern Waterthrush (near water), Louisiana Waterthrush (near water), Kentucky Warbler (uncommon), Hooded Warbler, Summer Tanager, Scarlet Tanager (uncommon), Rose-breasted Grosbeak, Blue Grosbeak, Indigo Bunting, Painted Bunting (uncommon), Bobolink, Orchard Oriole (mainly spring), and Baltimore Oriole (uncommon).

In Florida, the observation of Neotropical migrants depends upon three variables: season, location, and weather. Most spring migrants occur from mid-March through mid-May, but the first Purple Martins return in **mid-January**, while a few other species (e.g., Yellow-billed Cuckoo, Barn Swallow, and American Redstart) are still moving north in early June. "Fall" migration is similarly protracted. Purple Martins and Louisiana Waterthrushes begin southward migration by **late June**, and many species are still moving through in early November. Late fall migrants may be seen in early December. But most species are most common from late August through October. Although migrants can be found on any day during migratory periods, fallouts (observations of hundreds or occasionally thousands of birds) are typically storm-related. Because birds are reluctant to fly when headwinds or crosswinds are strong, they will land ahead of the storm and wait it out before continuing to migrate. Birds caught in the storm will fly until they see land, then will put down and wait until the storm passes. These fallouts are great for birders but bad for the birds; many hundreds or thousands unable to make landfall certainly drown at sea. During large fallouts (which are rare), it is often possible to see more than 20 species of warblers in a small area, along with many other colorful species.

Migrants winter in different regions south of Florida, so their distribution in the state varies geographically and seasonally. Migrants in the East are broken down into two primary categories: those that fly straight across the Gulf of Mexico from Mexico, Central America, or the West Indies to the northern Gulf coast, called *trans-Gulf migrants*, and those that fly around the Gulf of Mexico, called *circum-Gulf migrants*. The latter category can be further sub-divided into *western circum-Gulf migrants* that follow the Central American peninsula north through Texas and points beyond, and *eastern circum-Gulf migrants* that head north from or through the West Indies, then into or through Florida to points farther north. Western circum-Gulf and most trans-Gulf migrants winter in Central or South America, while Eastern circum-Gulf and a few trans-Gulf migrants winter in the West Indies.

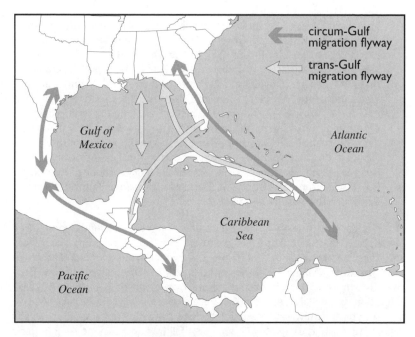

Strong winds can dramatically alter the distribution of north-bound migrants. Caribbean-wintering species, for instance, may be common along the Gulf coast of Florida after strong east winds, while trans-Gulf migrants may reach Florida during strong west winds. During fall, the routes of some species are similar to those taken during spring, while other species follow different routes at these two seasons. In general, the route of southbound trans-Gulf migrants falls a bit to the east of the northbound track (Stevenson 1957).

During spring, trans-Gulf migrants must cross hundreds of miles of water. For this reason, they typically land immediately (e.g., on the Florida coast) and refuel, unless weather conditions are favorable, in which case they may continue flying until they are many miles north of the state. As a result, most spring birding sites are located along the coasts. Although certain sites attract migrants dependably, *any coastal site can be good during spring, especially oak hammocks.* In contrast, fall migrants fly south over land to reach Florida, and the birds fan out throughout the state before most depart to spend the winter in Central or South America or the West Indies. Because of this, many fall migrant traps are located inland. An excellent source for information about weather effects on migrating landbirds is *Bird Migration, Weather, and Fallout: Including the Migrant Traps of Alabama and Northwest Florida* by Bob Duncan (1994). In addition to listing important migrant traps along the Panhandle coast, the book uses a series of weather maps to teach the reader how to predict good birding days by studying weather patterns.

Identifying migrants by their nocturnal flight calls is an increasingly popular side of birding, and may be helpful in monitoring populations of some species. For more information on this fascinating subject, go to <www.oldbird.org>.

Trans-Gulf migrants: Purple Gallinule, Black-billed Cuckoo, Yellow-billed Cuckoo, Common Nighthawk, Ruby-throated Hummingbird, Eastern Wood-Pewee, Acadian Flycatcher, Least Flycatcher, probably all other *Empidonax*, Great Crested Flycatcher, Eastern Kingbird, Yellow-throated Vireo, Warbling Vireo, Red-eyed Vireo, Bank Swallow, Veery, Gray-cheeked Thrush, Swainson's Thrush, Wood Thrush, Blue-winged Warbler, Golden-winged Warbler, Tennessee Warbler, Chestnut-sided Warbler, Blackburnian Warbler, Bay-breasted Warbler, Cerulean Warbler, Prothonotary Warbler, Swainson's Warbler, Ovenbird, Northern Waterthrush, Louisiana Waterthrush, Kentucky Warbler, Hooded Warbler, Summer Tanager, Scarlet Tanager, Rose-breasted Grosbeak, Blue Grosbeak, Indigo Bunting, Painted Bunting, Dickcissel, Orchard Oriole, and Baltimore Oriole.

Western circum-Gulf migrants: Mississippi Kite, Chimney Swift, Cliff Swallow, Black-throated Green Warbler, Mourning Warbler, Wilson's Warbler, Canada Warbler, Yellow-breasted Chat.

Eastern circum-Gulf migrants: Swallow-tailed Kite, Chuck-will's-widow, Black-throated Blue Warbler, Prairie Warbler, Palm Warbler, and Blackpoll Warbler.

PRECAUTIONS

Poisonous plants: **Poison Ivy** is common and widespread in moist wooded areas throughout Florida. **Poison Sumac** also occurs but is rare. Two poisonous tropical plants occur in southern Florida hammocks, especially in the Keys, and both have sap that causes a rash upon contact. **Poisonwood** is fairly common, and its fruit is a staple of the White-crowned Pigeon's diet. The sap causes a rash similar to that of Poison Ivy. The sap of **Manchineel** causes severe itching, and its fruits may be lethal if ingested in quantities. Because of this, Manchineel is removed from most areas of human habitation. The best way to avoid contact with either species is to stay on trails when walking through tropical hardwood hammocks.

Animal pests: With its subtropical climate and extensive wetlands, Florida has an abundance of **mosquitoes**, about 80 species. Visitors frequently are overwhelmed at the abundance and ferocity of these pests. Although mosquitoes are most abundant during summer, they can be bad year-round, especially during rainy years. Many of Florida's most widespread mosquitoes occur in saltwater habitats. Two areas (in)famous for their saltmarsh mosquitoes are Everglades National Park and some of the Lower Keys (e.g., Sugarloaf Key). In urban areas, mosquitoes are far less of a problem, because of eradication programs that cost millions of dollars annually. However, any oak hammock listed in this guide as a Neotropical migrant birding site during fall likely will have at least some mosquitoes. West Nile Virus invaded Florida in 2000 and now occurs nearly statewide, creating a new incentive to avoid mosquito bites. Other than staying out in the open (mosquitoes prefer shaded areas), the only defense against mosquitoes is to use a good insect repellent. Apply the repellent carefully because those that contain DEET can melt the rubber coating on binoculars.

Red Imported Fire Ants are small (2 mm) reddish ants native to Brazil that were released accidentally into the U.S. in the early 20th century. They now occur across most of the Southeast. Their sandy mounds, which may be up to a foot tall and contain 500,000 ants, are the easiest means of locating them. Fire ants are most common in dry, upland areas and are usually associated with areas of disturbance. Although they are tiny, the ants sting viciously when they are disturbed and can cause severe reactions in some people. **Deer Flies** are annoying half-inch-long flies with green, yellow, orange, or gray bodies. Their bite is mildly painful, but they are not known to carry diseases. They occur commonly during spring and summer. Deer flies have the habit of circling repeatedly (and noisily) before they land on you, giving you the opportunity to squash them before they bite. **Horse Flies** are larger (about an inch in length) and have black bodies. Their bite is more painful than that of deer flies, but fortunately these large flies are not nearly as numerous. **Sand Flies** are more popularly known as "no-see-ums" because of their size—so tiny they pass through window screens. Their bite is annoying but relatively painless. Sand flies are most common at dawn and dusk. They transmit malaria and other diseases in birds and some other animals, but are not known to carry human diseases in Florida. They are most common during fall and can be abundant along the coasts. **Ticks** are common in areas with a dense cover of grass or brush. Lyme Disease is very rare in Florida, but a few cases have been reported. Check yourself and your clothing after walking through grassy or brushy woodlands. **Chiggers** are extremely tiny red mites whose bites cause severe itching that may persist for many days. Common in grassy areas, chiggers can be avoided somewhat by not standing or sitting in one area for any length of time.

Spiders are a conspicuous part of Florida's oak hammocks and other forested habitats. Four species (Black Widow, Red Widow, Brown Widow, and Brown Recluse) are poisonous to humans, but the chance of encountering any of them is extremely remote. Two groups of spiders (Golden Orb-weavers and Banded Garden Spiders) are common in scrub and hammocks from July through October, when they build webs that may be five feet or more in diameter. Females of both species have body lengths of more than an inch, excluding the legs. These spiders are harmless to humans, but it is extremely annoying to walk face-first into a web. The webs are so strong that small birds have been caught in them on occasion. **Lovebugs**, also known as March flies, are harmless, slow-moving, black flies that swarm mainly during May and September. Native to central-southern North America, lovebugs moved eastward as forests were cleared and they reached the Florida Panhandle in the 1940s. They now occur virtually statewide. Males and females remain mated for about 12 hours, which gives lovebugs their popular name. They are attracted to chemicals found in exhaust fumes, and thus are abundant in grassy areas around roadways. Driving though a swarm causes thousands of the insects to become smeared on the windshields, grilles, and hoods of vehicles. If not removed quickly, chemicals in the bodies of Lovebugs can dissolve the paint from vehicles. There are thousands of species of **bees and wasps** in Florida, and a large majority is harmless to humans. But females of many social species sting if their nests are disturbed. The nests of many species are communal, and may be built underground, in tree cavities, in palmettos, or under protected surfaces such as picnic shelters or gazebos. The stings of bees and wasps are painful for a few minutes, but are not serious, except to those who are strongly allergic to the venom. So far, Africanized (aka "killer") honeybees have not invaded Florida. **Scorpions** (1½–2 inches) are widespread in Florida but are seldom seen because they spend most of their lives under leaf litter. Nonetheless, one may still encounter scorpions anywhere in the state—even the campground at Dry Tortugas National Park. Florida scorpions are not dangerous to humans; their sting is painful, but the pain usually subsides within a few minutes.

Florida is home to six species of poisonous snakes. Except possibly for the Cottonmouth, none is likely to be encountered while birding. Should you (be lucky enough to) find a snake, *do not kill it*. The **Coral Snake** is found throughout the state and is inconspicuous and docile. This beautiful animal is easily distinguished from the harmless Scarlet Kingsnake and Scarlet Snake by its black snout and wide red bands surrounded on both sides by narrow yellow bands. The two harmless species have red snouts and red bands bordered by black. (Remember the rhyme, "Red touch yellow kills a fellow; red touch black won't hurt Jack".) The **Copperhead** is restricted to the Panhandle. It is nocturnal and not aggressive. The **Cottonmouth** (or **Water Moccasin**) is common in freshwater habitats throughout the state, even on barrier islands. They often are confused with non-poisonous water snakes. When provoked, Cottonmouths gape, exposing their fangs and the white interior of their mouths (hence their name). The **Eastern Diamondback Rattlesnake** is among the largest snakes in North America, reaching a length of eight feet (and occasionally larger, at least formerly). Once widespread in Florida's pinewoods and prairies, this magnificent animal is declining due to habitat destruction and needless persecution. The **Timber (or Canebrake) Rattlesnake** is limited to north-central Florida. It is not aggressive. The **Dusky Pygmy Rattlesnake** is a small species, averaging 15 to 20 inches in length. It is widespread in moist habitats in the state, including dry prairies and oak hammocks. It, too, is nonaggressive.

The **American Alligator**, once hunted relentlessly in Florida, now numbers over one million individuals, and limited hunting is again legal. Alligators can attain lengths of over 12 feet but average about six to eight feet. Although they appear slow-moving and docile, alligators are capable of surprising speed for short distances on land. It is illegal to feed alligators, because this practice causes them to lose their fear of humans. ("Nuisance" alligators are killed rather than relocated.) When near alligators on land, keep your distance and do not provoke them. Attacks on humans are very rare and usually are the result of mistaken identity (although 'gators readily attack and eat dogs). Since the state began keeping records in 1948, more than 300 people have been attacked by alligators in Florida, 14 of them fatally. The **American Crocodile** is an Endangered species restricted to the extreme southern Peninsula and Upper Keys. It avoids humans and is seen by only a few lucky birders. For years, an individual exceeding eight feet in length has been seen around the boat-launch facility east of the Flamingo Lodge at Everglades National Park.

Lightning: Along with central Africa and the Amazon River basin, Florida is one of the lightning capitals of the world. About 25 cloud-to-ground strikes *per square mile* are recorded annually in Central Florida! Most lightning occurs from May through August, when afternoon thunderstorms can be an almost daily occurrence. Nonetheless, human injuries from lightning are rare; you should be safe if you take the usual precautions, such as avoiding taking shelter under single, isolated trees. (But be aware that summer thunderstorms can form quickly and may catch you unprepared.)

Hunting is a major activity in Florida, primarily for waterfowl, Northern Bobwhite, Wild Turkeys, White-tailed Deer, and Feral Hogs. All public lands in Florida except for state and national parks are open to hunting. Hunting season begins during fall and continues through spring. Most sites allow hunting on selected days, alternating with days without hunting. Some sites are closed to non-hunters during hunting season, while other sites remain open—though you may be required to wear a blaze-orange vest or cap. To be safest, avoid areas that are being hunted.

Crime: Florida is a state with more than 16 million residents and is visited by more than 40 million tourists annually. It is also a major drug-smuggling area and has experienced its share of racially-motivated violence, although not in the past several years. Most of the sites in this guide (e.g., state parks or national forests) are publicly owned sites at which violent crime is virtually unknown. However, especially when in major metropolitan areas (e.g., small city parks, or walking city streets in Fort Lauderdale or Miami looking for exotics), exercise typical precautions such as locking your car with valuables out of sight. Needless to say, single birders, especially women, should always be especially cautious, especially in remote areas. Previous editions of this guide included a few secluded sites where crimes against birders had been committed or where they seemed likely to occur. Those sites have been deleted from this edition of the guide. While one cannot rule out becoming the victim of random violence, all of the sites in this book should be safe during daylight hours.

BIRDING ETHICS

Private property: *Do not trespass in Florida.* Many Florida landowners rigidly enforce trespass laws. Nearly every birding site in this guide is in public ownership, in an effort to help birders avoid trespassing. Privately-owned birding sites in this book are clearly marked as such.

The use of tapes: It is well known that many species of landbirds respond to recordings (or whistled imitations) of Eastern Screech-Owl calls; birds mob the tape thinking a real owl is present. Tapes are used to attract migrant landbirds during fall, and secretive species and passerines on Christmas Bird Counts. Disturbance during these events is minor; the birds fly away from an Eastern Screech-Owl tape after five or 10 minutes of failing to find the "owl". During spring and summer, however, playing of tapes of conspecifics to attract breeding birds needs to be done carefully to avoid causing excessive stress. *This is especially true with Mangrove Cuckoo, whose U.S. range is limited to southern Florida.* Birders are expected to be especially cautious when using tapes to lure Mangrove Cuckoos during the breeding season. Several sites in Florida *prohibit the use of all tapes:* Everglades National Park, National Key Deer Refuge, Corkscrew Swamp Sanctuary, and J.N. "Ding" Darling National Wildlife Refuge. Birders should scrupulously observe any such prohibitions. Other activities, such as trampling fragile habitats, pruning vegetation to better observe or photograph nesting birds, or dragging ropes or chains to flush secretive birds such as rails, violate birding ethics and should be avoided at all times—some of these activities may even be illegal unless for permitted scientific research.

Readers of this guide are expected to follow at all times the *ABA Code of Birding Ethics* on page 400.

WHERE TO STAY

Florida probably has more motel rooms than any other state; it is hard to find a spot without one. However, during peak tourist season, all rooms may be booked. Reservations made weeks (or months) in advance are recommended, especially in major tourist areas. Rooms are usually much more expensive on barrier islands than on the mainland, although many convention-type hotels in large cities are also quite expensive. Motel rooms in Homestead are much cheaper than those in the Keys. A new feature of this edition of *A Birder's Guide to Florida* is the inclusion of brief camping information, if available, for each site described.

Tourism and Florida are synonymous, and Orlando is the top tourist destination in the world. More than 40 million tourists visit Florida annually, and this number continues to increase. Nearly everything in the state is geared to tourism, and motels, restaurants, novelty shops, roadside attractions, and theme parks are widespread. U.S. Route 192 in Kissimmee is a classic example of how tacky Florida can become when it caters to tourist dollars; drive the road at night for the most dramatic (i.e., worst) effect. Consider also that much of the area was home to Brown-headed Nuthatches, Bachman's Sparrows, and possibly Red-cockaded Woodpeckers, fewer than 40 years ago.

Travel by air: Seven international airports serve central and southern Florida, and nearly all birders who arrive in the state by air will come through one of these gateways. Several smaller airports in the region serve commuter traffic, and major airports are also located in Jacksonville, Pensacola, and Tallahassee.

- Fort Lauderdale/Hollywood International Airport, 320 Terminal Drive, Fort Lauderdale, Florida 33315; 954-359-1200; <www.broward.org/airport.>.
- Miami International Airport, P.O. Box 592075, Miami, FL 33159; <www.miami-airport.com>.
- Orlando International Airport, One Airport Boulevard, Orlando, FL 32827-4399; <www.orlandoairports.net/goaa/main.htm>.
- Palm Beach International Airport, 1000 Turnage Boulevard, West Palm Beach, FL 33406; <www.pbia.org>.
- St. Petersburg/Clearwater International Airport, 14700 Terminal Boulevard, Suite 221, Clearwater, FL 33762; <www.fly2pie.com>.
- Southwest Florida International Airport, 16000 Chamberlin Parkway, Suite 8671, Fort Myers, FL 33913; <www.lcpa.com>.
- Tampa International Airport, 5503 Spruce Street, Tampa, FL 33607-1475; <www.tampaairport.com>.

Travel by car: Public transportation in Florida is poor; to get around, you will need your own vehicle. Fortunately, car-rental outlets are abundant in metropolitan areas and can be found even in most small towns. The average cost for a small four-passenger car is about $25 to $30 per day, and there often is no limit on mileage. During weekdays, try to avoid major highways in metropolitan areas inbound during early morning, and outbound during late afternoon, when at least partial gridlock is common. Rush-hour times vary, but the worst periods are roughly 7:00 to 9:30 AM and 4:00 to 6:30 PM. Traffic is bad in all major metropolitan areas, but perhaps no road compares to Interstate 4 between Walt Disney World and downtown Orlando. Outside the big cities, traffic on the Interstates, Florida's Turnpike, and other major expressways flows well most of the time. Speed limits on most expressways are 65 or 70 mph. A few sites in this guide, especially state and national forests, feature unpaved roads. These can be hazardous under certain conditions: mud or clay roads can be extremely slippery when they are wet, and it is easy to get stuck on some sand roads when they are dry. Exercise caution when driving on unpaved roads in Florida.

WEATHER

Florida has a subtropical climate, and all regions but the Panhandle experience two primary seasons: a hot, wet season from May through September, and a cool, dry season from October through April. Rain in the Panhandle occurs more frequently during winter and early spring than elsewhere in the state. Temperatures increase from north to south and as one travels inland (i.e., away from sea breezes). Daytime temperatures are in the high 80s Fahrenheit by early April and may reach into the low 90s by the end of that month. Nighttime temperatures tend to be 20 or so degrees cooler. Ninety-degree temperatures are the daytime rule from May until September or October, when temperatures again drop into the 80s. During winter, daytime temperatures vary regionally, and rain usually is absent. Cold fronts frequently cause temperatures to drop briefly into the 20s in North Florida, the 30s in the central Peninsula, and the 40s or 50s farther south. Only the Keys are free from the threat of freezing temperatures. Snow in Florida occurs only a few times each decade, usually limited to tiny amounts in the extreme north.

Temperatures are only one part of Florida's weather; let's not forget the humidity, which typically is in range of 70–90 percent during spring and summer. Such conditions make 90 degree temperatures feel 15–20 degrees higher. Those not used to such stifling humidity should avoid prolonged exposure to the sun and should drink plenty of fluids. Air conditioning is a standard feature of motel rooms and rental cars. Florida's hot and humid climate requires that comfortable clothing be worn out of doors. Tennis shoes and loose-fitting clothing are ideal. Shorts may feel great during spring and summer, but long pants should be worn to protect your legs from the sun, biting insects, and vegetation. Long-sleeved shirts may be worn by those especially sensitive to the sun and where biting insects are abundant. Many birders wear a cap or visor to keep the sun out of their eyes—and, of course, don't forget to apply sunscreen, ideally 35 SPF or higher.

Florida receives almost 60 inches of rain a year, mostly from May to August, when (typically brief) afternoon thundershowers boost the humidity to 100 percent. These storms usually contain lightning, discussed in the "Precautions" section, above. Fog is another effect of Florida's high humidity. Fog is most prevalent at night and early in the morning and forms most commonly from late fall through early spring. Use caution when driving through dense fog, and turn on your vehicle's headlights for additional safety.

Hurricanes begin as tropical depressions that form over water, intensifying into powerful tropical storms. A storm is not officially a hurricane until its sustained winds exceed 74 miles per hour. Florida's hurricane season lasts from 1 June through 30 November. Besides delivering heavy rainfall, hurricanes spawn frequent tornadoes, and the hurricane itself creates extremely high winds, and often tidal surges along the coasts. Hurricanes are grouped into five categories according to their intensity. Category 1 hurricanes are the weakest, while Category 5 hurricanes are the most intense. Hurricane *Andrew*, a Category 5 storm that struck the Homestead/Florida City area in August 1992, and Hurricanes *Charley, Frances, Ivan,* and *Jeanne*, which all made landfall in Florida during August or September 2004, were among the most destructive hurricanes ever to strike the United States.

ORGANIZATIONS AND GOVERNMENTAL AGENCIES

The **Florida Ornithological Society**, with, surprisingly, only about 400 members, is *the* statewide birding and ornithological group in Florida. FOS publishes *Florida Field Naturalist*, an excellent quarterly journal and the primary outlet for scholarly publications about Florida birds. FOS also produces the *FOS Newsletter*, which contains notices and announcements about upcoming events, requests for information, assistance in research projects, and a listing of Christmas Bird Count dates, locations, and compilers. FOS holds two conventions each year (during spring and fall) at varying locations throughout Florida (and occasionally in neighboring states or West Indian countries). Membership in FOS is essential for all serious birders in Florida. Subscription rates are $20 per year. For more information, go to the FOS website at <www.fosbirds.org>.

Federal properties comprise some of the most significant conservation areas in Florida, and several of these offer excellent birding. Florida contains three **national parks** (Biscayne, Dry Tortugas, and Everglades), three **national forests** (Apalachicola, Ocala, and Osceola), and 28 **national wildlife refuges**. Together, these areas conserve over three million acres of land. The respective national websites are <www.nps.gov>, <www.fs.fed.us>, and <www.refuges.fws.gov>.

Florida claims to have the finest state park system in the country. The Florida Department of Environmental Protection manages more than 150 sites statewide, totaling more than 750,000 acres. Most of these are **state parks**, while others are state recreation areas, preserves, or greenways and trails. The state park website is <www.floridastateparks.org>. The Florida Division of Forestry manages 31 **state forests** in the state, encompassing nearly one million acres of land. The state forest website is <www.fl-dof.com>. The Florida Fish and Wildlife Conservation Commission manages more than 1.2 million acres, but the primary human use for most sites is hunting. Nonetheless, several **wildlife management areas** are listed in this book for their birding opportunities. The Commission's website is <www.floridaconservation.org>.

Water Management Districts were created by the Florida Legislature to regulate water resources in the state. The Districts have purchased vast amounts of wetland and upland recharge habitats. Because most WMD properties lack facilities, are accessible only to those on foot or horseback, and allow hunting in season, they are not listed in this guide. For information, contact the individual districts: **Northwest Florida Water Management District**, 81 Water Management District Drive, Havana, FL 32333; 850-539-5999 <www.nwfwmd.state.fl.us>; **Suwannee River Water Management District**, 9225 County Road 49, Live Oak, FL 32060; 386-362-1001; <www.srwmd.state.fl.us>; **St. Johns River Water Management District**, P.O. Box 1429, Palatka, FL 32178-1429; 386-329-4500 <www.sjrwmd.com>; **Southwest Florida Water Management District**, 2379 Broad Street, Brooksville, FL 34609-6899; 800-423-1476 <www.swfwmd.state.fl.us>; and **South Florida Water Management District**, P.O. Box 24680, 3301 Gun Club Road, West Palm Beach, FL 33416-4680; 800-432-2045 <www.sfwmd.gov>.

HOW TO USE THIS GUIDE

A *Birder's Guide to Florida* is written primarily for serious, knowledgeable birders. It is specifically geared to those who seek the maximum number of target species within a short time, but will be useful to birders of all skill levels. The state is divided into five regions: the Panhandle, Northern Peninsula, Central Peninsula, Southern Peninsula, and the Florida Keys. The Panhandle is subdivided into eastern and western halves. Each of the peninsular regions is subdivided into Gulf coastal, inland, and Atlantic coastal thirds. The Keys are subdivided into upper, middle, and lower thirds. Good birding spots are given for all regions, with the least emphasis on the Panhandle and Northern Peninsula, which lack nearly all of the Florida specialties that are sought by most birders. Nearly all sites in this guide are easily accessible to the public during daylight hours. Hunting is prohibited in most sites, and those that do allow hunting are clearly identified. I have tried to restrict the sites included in this guide to those that are truly worth birding at one or more seasons, but I have retained a few generally unremarkable sites that may interest birders for scenic or other reasons. Not included are hundreds of publicly-owned birding sites that typically contain only common, widespread species. Many municipal, county, and state parks, water management district lands, and other properties are therefore excluded from this guide.

- The names of all birding sites in this guide are listed in **bold type**. Sites that have exemplary birding opportunities are listed in **UPPER CASE**. Capitalization will help visitors with limited time to choose which sites to visit. Sites with names listed in regular type may be skipped if time is a factor or if the primary emphasis is finding Florida specialties. Some sites listed in regular type (such as Ocala National Forest, Corkscrew Swamp Sanctuary, and Big Cypress National Preserve) represent some of the most outstanding natural areas remaining in Florida. These sites are worth visiting solely to gain an appreciation of how the rest of the state once looked, even if their birding opportunities are limited relative to many other sites.

- All birding sites in this guide include specific directions from road intersections. Most road junctions are followed by a number in parentheses, e.g., (6.2). This indicates the mileage *from the last point so marked*. Keep in mind that vehicle odometers vary somewhat, so mileages listed in this guide may differ slightly from what you find in the field. (Birders from Canada who are driving cars with metric odometers will have to convert all mileages to kilometers). Turns are generally presented as either "left" or "right" rather than as compass directions, for clarity. If approaching a site from a direction opposite that presented in this guide, you will of course have to transpose right and left turns.

- The various types of roads in Florida are given standard abbreviations followed by a hyphen and the road number: Interstate Highway (e.g., I-75); Federal Highway (e.g., US-19); State Road (e.g., SR-52); County Road (e.g., CR-1), and Forest Road (e.g., FR-9). Many of these roads also have a name (e.g., Little Road), which in this guide follows the road number. Major roads in urban areas are frequently given a second number by the city; in these cases, the local number follows the road name in parentheses. As in the rest of the United States, roads that are oriented north-south are usually odd-numbered (e.g., I-75, US-19), while those oriented east-west are even-numbered (e.g., I-10, SR-70). The Florida Department of Transportation recently completed renumbering all Interstate exits to a system based on mileage. Exit numbers increase from south to north, and from west to east. Highway signs will display both the old and new exit numbers for the next few years, but only the new numbers are listed in this guide.

Many birding sites in this guide are state parks. Almost all have an entrance fee of $3.25 per vehicle (up to eight people), but some state parks charge $4.00 or $5.00 per vehicle. Individual annual passes may be purchased for $43.40 per year, which allows for unlimited visitation to all Florida state parks; see <www.floridastateparks.org/annualpass>. Many federal parks and wildlife refuges charge similar fees, and these are specifically listed. All state parks open at 8:00 AM and close at sunset. Most other natural areas with facilities follow a similar schedule. Undeveloped sites (i.e., those with few or no amenities) are often accessible anytime.

In recent years, local birdfinding guides have been published for the western Panhandle, Bay County (Panama City area), Tallahassee, Gainesville, Hernando County (Brooksville/Weeki Wachee areas), Pasco County (New Port Richey area), Manatee and Sarasota Counties (Bradenton and Sarasota areas), and the Keys. Although the quality of these guides varies greatly, they all contain many local birding sites that are not included here. Additionally, the Great Florida Birding Trail <www.floridabirdingtrail.com> is being established, scheduled for completion in 2006. Guidebooks for some regions of the trail are available, but birders should keep in mind that many of the sites contain only widespread, common species, and specific birdfinding information is not provided for any site.

Florida birds on the Internet: The Internet revolution has provided birders with a way to be informed instantly about rarities, a way to post photos of unknown species to be identified or rare species to be documented, and disk space for the creation of virtually countless personal websites related to birds and birding. Birding listserves are very popular, and several serve Florida (see below). However, all Florida listserves are unmoderated, with the result that some contain a horrifying amount of misinformation or misidentifications. Some of the birding lists require membership in order to view the archives, but most do not. Two superb websites—<www.birdingonthe.net>, by Jack Siler, and <www.fatbirder.com>, by "Bo" Beolens—contain thousands of bird-related URLs worldwide.

- **Rare Bird Alert**: <http://listserv.admin.usf.edu/archives/flrba.html>.
- **Statewide, but emphasizing Tampa Bay**: <http://listserv.admin.usf.edu/archives/brdbrain.html>; the posting of photos is permitted.
- **Statewide**: <http://groups.yahoo.com/group/FlaBirding>.
- **Statewide**: <http://www.lists.ufl.edu/archives/floridabirds-l.html>.
- **Northern Florida**: <http://groups.yahoo.com/group/nflbirds>.
- **Central Atlantic coast**: <http://groups.yahoo.com/group/Space CoastAudubon>.
- **Atlantic coast**: <http://groups.yahoo.com/group/Eastbirders>; this list has very few posts, and the archives are available only to members.
- **Southern Gulf coast**: <http://groups.yahoo.com/group/SWFL Birdline>.
- **Southern Atlantic coast**: <http://www.tropicalaudubon.org/tasboard/index.html>; lots of information on psittacids and other exotics, mainly in the Miami area.

Citations: Articles and notes published in peer-reviewed journals constitute the heart of ornithology. For the benefit of those readers who wish to learn more about topics addressed in this guide, I have provided literature references throughout. Citations are most common in the section on Birds of Particular Interest (page 267), but are peppered throughout the Introduction, too. Mostly, these papers are published in *Florida Field Naturalist* or *North American Birds* and its predecessors. All references are fully cited in a Literature Cited section toward the end of this guide (page 393).

Route for Those in a Hurry: The most difficult part of planning a birding trip is picking the route that allows you to see the maximum number of target species in the minimum amount of time. It is worthwhile to look over the Birds of Particular Interest section (page 267) and the bar graphs (page 342) to better plot the locations for the species you are seeking. *If you are visiting Florida for the first time and wish to see the maximum number of Florida's specialties, spend a week or more in late April or early May in the southern half of the Peninsula and the Keys, including a boat trip to Dry Tortugas National Park. All of Florida's specialties can be seen south of a line drawn from Brooksville to Titusville. If searching for Florida specialties is the sole purpose of a birding trip to the state, there is no need to travel north of the Central Peninsula.*

Birders visiting Florida in the winter months will find excellent birding throughout the state. Because all but one of the South Florida specialties depart the state to winter in the Caribbean or Neotropics, a trip to the Keys is not a necessity during winter. (The exception is the Mangrove Cuckoo, which is secretive and difficult to locate at this season.) In fact, the farther north one goes in Florida during winter, the more abundant waterfowl and many other species become. The Panhandle in particular has many fairly common wintering species that are rare or absent elsewhere in the state, and these are avidly sought by Florida's resident birders. In Central Florida, Merritt Island National Wildlife Refuge (page 174) may support the most diverse waterfowl assemblage, and Merritt Island, Honeymoon Island State Park (page 122) and Fort De Soto Park (page 131) all are superb sites for shorebirds and larids. Fort Lauderdale and Miami are musts for the multitude of exotics they support, and Short-tailed Hawks are easiest to find at Everglades National Park.

History of *A Birder's Guide to Florida*: During the 1970s, the late Jim Lane wrote the original *A Birder's Guide to Florida*, one of seven books in his groundbreaking *A Birder's Guide* series. More than 200 sites were included in his first edition, including dozens of sites that offered only fair birding opportunities. In a letter to Gloria Hunter written in 1980, Lane explained his reasoning for including so many lesser sites in his 1981 book:

> *The hardest part of writing this guide has been to find the best format. I started working on this book in 1972, and I still have not found the right way to present the material. The first decision I made was to write the book for the visiting birder rather than for the resident birder. But in Florida, some of the visitors stay for months. The 10-day visitor is looking for birds only and is not particularly interested in areas. The three-month visitor soon becomes interested in finding a new area to visit. I have listed many spots that are not particularly good for unusual birds, but they are pretty places to spend the day.*

Lane's guide was reprinted as a second edition three years later. This edition was nearly identical to the 1981 edition, with some minor changes made by Lane's friend and collaborator, Harold Holt. The third edition of the guide was published in 1989, two years after Lane's death. This edition contained some updated information, but a majority of the book remained unchanged from Lane's first edition written ten or more years earlier.

In 1994, the American Birding Association, which had assumed responsibility for updating the "Lane guides", offered me the opportunity to update *A Birder's Guide to Florida*, and I gratefully accepted the challenge. With help from dozens of other birders and ornithologists, I rewrote the book, retaining Lane's original format but little else. The ABA's Cindy Lippincott and Bob Berman professionally produced the maps and bar graphs, which added greatly to the book's visual appeal. The fourth edition of the guide was published in April 1996 and contained just over 250 birding sites. It was reprinted in December 1997 with revised text and the addition of several new sites.

This fifth edition was written sporadically between October 2002 and September 2005. During this time, the entire fourth edition text was carefully reviewed—and in most cases rewritten. Many new sites have been added, while several others have been dropped. I chose to rewrite the book rather than simply update sections of it because both my knowledge of Florida's birds and my writing skills have improved over the years. In cases where local birders were not available to update some sites included in the previous edition, I opted to remove the sites rather than retain them with potentially outdated or erroneous information. Revision of the birdfinding section took place between May 2003 and September 2005, and all information was current at the time of writing. However, *information can quickly become out of date in Florida, including telephone area codes, website addresses, and the locations of some birds (especially exotics)*. Website addresses (URLs) are especially short-lived; the links to all websites mentioned in this guide were active through September 2005. Use this book as a site guide only. New roads are constantly being built, and some roads in service in the next few years may not be present on maps in this guide. Also, the state's land-acquisition programs are constantly adding new public lands that may become excellent birding sites in the future. *It is always wise to contact local birders in areas you plan to visit*. As Jim Lane discovered almost three decades ago ago, ideas regarding the best way to present information in this guide continue to evolve. Your comments are welcomed to improve future editions of *A Birder's Guide to Florida*.

Even though maps are included that show nearly every site mentioned in this guide, it is recommended that visitors obtain a state map of Florida (maps may be downloaded from <www.flausa.com>). Visitors who plan to travel extensively in Florida should consider purchasing a copy of DeLorme Publishing's *Florida Atlas and Gazetteer*. Although it is becoming dated (e.g., hundreds of secondary roads built in the past 10 or so years are not mapped), this excellent atlas contains 103 large-scale maps covering the entire state and identifying many parks, historical sites, and other points of interest. The atlas and gazetteer costs about $20 and is available at most Florida bookstores and through ABA Sales. It can also be ordered from DeLorme Mapping at <www.delorme.com>.

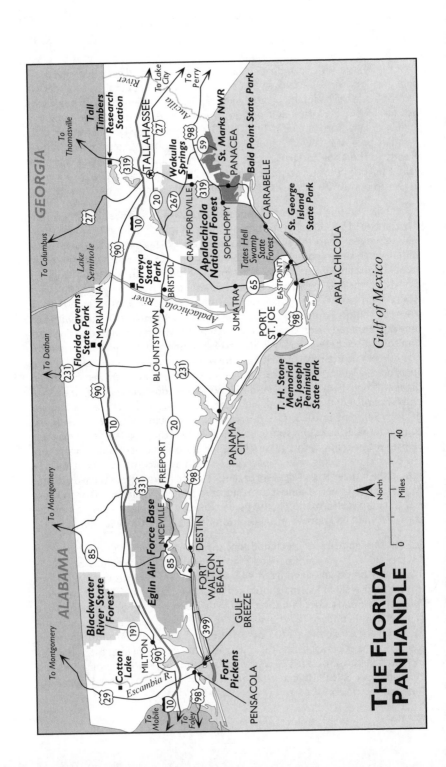

THE FLORIDA PANHANDLE

Gulf of Mexico

North

Miles

0   40

THE PANHANDLE

For the purposes of this book, the Panhandle is considered to be that part of Florida west of the Aucilla River, which flows south from Georgia to the Gulf of Mexico east of Tallahassee. The Panhandle is divided into western and eastern portions by the Apalachicola River, a division that also pertains to time zones: the western Panhandle lies within the Central Time Zone, where the time is one hour earlier than in the rest of the state. The Panhandle's hilly terrain is partly a result of rivers and streams depositing sediments from erosion of the Appalachian Mountains to the north. The highest point in Florida (345 feet above sea level) is located near Lakewood, on the Alabama border. The reddish clay soils of the northern portion of the Panhandle, covered with a mixture of hardwoods and pines, are an extension of those in Alabama and Georgia.

The Panhandle is the least populated region of Florida, although parts are under severe threat of development, especially coastal areas with their magnificent beaches and dunes. Timber production is one of the most important industries in the area, along with the production of oysters from Apalachicola Bay, a highly productive estuary and a recognized International Biosphere Reserve. There are many large publicly owned areas in the Panhandle; those described in this guide include Blackwater River State Forest, Eglin Air Force Base, and Apalachicola National Forest. These three sites in particular are vital refuges for the Red-cockaded Woodpecker—in fact, Apalachicola National Forest contains the largest population remaining in the world. Many of the coastal sites included in this guide can be excellent for migrant landbirds during spring.

The Apalachicola River, with bluffs rising as much as 150 feet above the river, is unique in Florida. Ravines cut into the bluffs contain many endemic plant species and many other plants common in the Appalachian Mountains but found nowhere else in Florida. In fact, the Apalachicola River watershed is believed to contain more plant and animal species per unit area than any other region in temperate North America. Fortunately, the river is relatively undeveloped, and the state of Florida and various conservation organizations have preserved most of the lands along it. The vast Tates Hell Swamp area on the east side of the river (adjacent to Apalachicola National

Bald Eagle, adult.   Arthur Morris/www.birdsasart.com

Forest to the north) contains more than 190,000 acres, most of which has recently been publicly purchased at a cost exceeding $108 million.

The Apalachicola area marks the normal westward breeding range in Florida for Bald Eagle, American Oystercatcher, Gray Kingbird, Marsh Wren, and Boat-tailed Grackle. (A few individuals of some of these species also breed in the Pensacola area, and eagles are increasing rapidly in the western Panhandle.) Scott's Seaside Sparrow, a subspecies endemic to the Florida Gulf coast, also reaches its western limit in the Apalachicola area (at St. Vincent National Wildlife Refuge), although other subspecies breed farther west.

The relatively few birders who live in the Panhandle are clustered around the larger cities, mostly Fort Walton Beach, Pensacola, and Tallahassee. Birders in the western Panhandle are allied much more closely to Alabama than to the rest of Florida. Although the Panhandle offers excellent birding opportunities, it is seldom visited by out-of-state birders because it is far from the major tourist destinations and lacks most of Florida's specialty species. For the most part, birds that do occur in the Panhandle are species found throughout eastern North America, along with a few western breeders straying east during fall and winter.

Birders from the rest of Florida visit the Panhandle to chase western strays or to search for wintering species that are rare or absent in the peninsula. These include waterfowl such as Tundra Swan(irregular), Snow Goose, American Black Duck, Mallard, Greater Scaup, all three scoters, Common Goldeneye; Golden Eagle (rare), Groove-billed Ani (rare), western-breeding hummingbirds (primarily Buff-bellied, Black-chinned, and Rufous Hummingbirds), Red-breasted Nuthatch (irruptive), Brown Creeper, Winter Wren, Golden-crowned Kinglet, Sprague's Pipit (extremely local), Henslow's, Le Conte's, and Fox Sparrows, Dark-eyed Junco, Rusty Blackbird, Purple Finch (irruptive), and Pine Siskin (irruptive). Breeding species more or less restricted to the Panhandle and generally difficult to find during other seasons elsewhere in the state include Canada Goose (exotic resident), Mississippi Kite, Broad-winged Hawk, White-breasted Nuthatch (resident), Swainson's Warbler, Kentucky Warbler, and Yellow-breasted Chat. House Finches remain most common within Florida in parts of the Panhandle, but this species now occurs into the central peninsula, as well.

Panhandle sites are generally listed west to east, and most sites in this chapter are coastal locations.

GULF BREEZE TO PENSACOLA

FORT PICKENS (1,742 acres; $8.00/vehicle; 200 campsites at $20.00/day; opens at 8:00 AM) is a part of the **Gulf Islands National Seashore** (28,976 acres in Florida). Although heavily damaged by Hurricane *Ivan*—with many oaks destroyed and some roads damaged—the park remains the favorite location of local birders seeking migrant landbirds. To reach the Fort from Pensacola (see map on next page), head south across Pensacola Bay on US-98. Proceed through Gulf Breeze and continue south toward the barrier island on SR-399. (*Note: SR-399 was still under repair in June 2005, but was expected to re-open soon after this guide went to press.*) Cross Santa Rosa Bay and turn right at the T-intersection (traffic light). The park is ahead (3.2 miles). From November to April, numbers of Northern Gannets may be seen from the beach road, while Snowy Plovers occur year-round. Continue past the Ranger Station (the red-roofed building, 4.0) and turn right

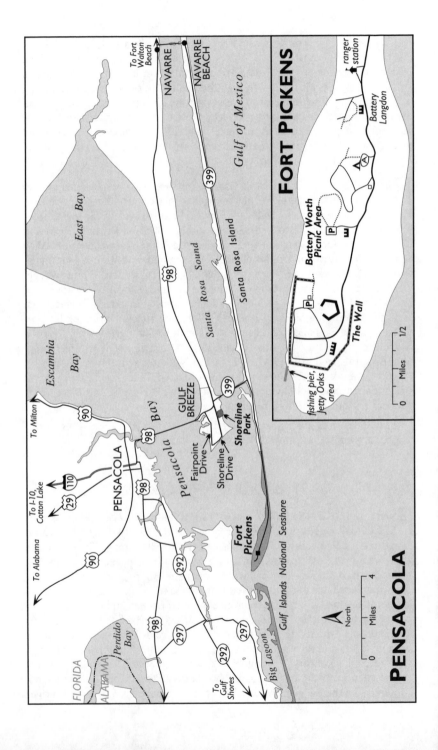

FORT PICKENS

ranger station

Battery Langdon

Battery Worth Picnic Area

The Wall

fishing pier, Jetty Oaks area

0   1/2
Miles

PENSACOLA

FLORIDA
ALABAMA

To Alabama

To Milton

Escambia Bay

East Bay

Gulf of Mexico

To Fort Walton Beach

NAVARRE

NAVARRE BEACH

Santa Rosa Sound

Santa Rosa Island

Gulf of Mexico

To I-10, Cotton Lake

PENSACOLA

Pensacola Bay

GULF BREEZE

Fairpoint Drive

Shoreline Drive

Shoreline Park

Fort Pickens

Gulf Islands National Seashore

Perdido Bay

Big Lagoon

To Gulf Shores

North

0   4
Miles

PENSACOLA

into **Battery Langdon** (0.3). From the parking lot, note the large oak near the northeast corner of the battery. This tree should be searched for migrants from late March through April. Walk the shell bicycle path to the west and turn left onto a sand trail just past the maintenance building road on the right. This trail returns you to the battery.

Return to the main road and continue west to **Battery Worth Picnic Area** (0.6), considered the premier birding hotspot of the park and possibly of the western Panhandle. Begin birding the oaks around the picnic tables. Then, from the east side of the parking area, walk a trail (about 1,000 feet long) that loops around a marshy area which should be checked for migrants. This trail goes by individual campsites, so take care not to disturb campers. At the small bridge, check both sides of the ditch for Louisiana and Northern Waterthrushes. The oaks west of the bridge can also be excellent for migrant landbirds. The trail returns you to the parking lot.

Continue west on the main park road to the western end of the island (0.9). At the "Fort Information" sign, turn right onto a narrow road that leads to a small white building and the entrance to the fort. Park here and walk east down the shell bicycle trail. The concrete wall on your left is known locally as **The Wall**, and vegetation in this area can be productive for migrant landbirds. On the sloped grassy area behind the fort, watch for Bobolinks during spring, sparrows during fall and winter, and vagrant flycatchers during both migrations. Continue along the path to the wooden bridge. Between here and the parking area, check the brushy edges for Groove-billed Anis in October and November, when they are rare but fairly regular. Return to the parking lot and continue west toward the end of the island. Beyond the fishing pier, check the cluster of Live Oaks, known as the **Jetty Oaks**, on the left just before the road turns back toward the park entrance. These isolated oaks often contain migrant landbirds.

Contact: Gulf Islands National Seashore, 1801 Gulf Breeze Parkway, Gulf Breeze, FL 32561; 850-934-2600; <www.nps.gov/guis>.

To reach **Cotton Lake**, a hardwood swamp along the Escambia River, go north on US-98 across Pensacola Bay and into Pensacola. Go north on I-110 until it ends at I-10. Head west and exit (#10B) onto US-29 (2.0), heading north. Cross over Pine Barren Creek (20.0) and turn right onto the first sand road (0.3). From here to the river (1.8), look for breeding species such as Swallow-tailed and Mississippi Kites, Barred Owl (resident), Acadian Flycatcher, and Swainson's, Kentucky, and Hooded Warblers. During wet weather, parts of the road may be inundated, so drive with caution.

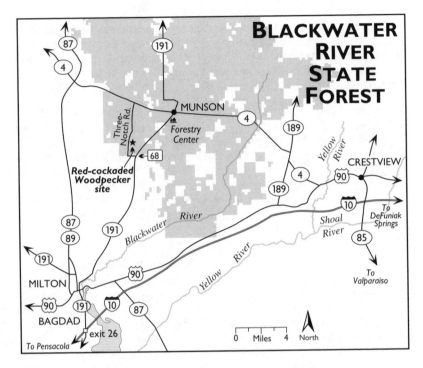

MILTON

Blackwater River State Forest (183,381 acres; no fee; more than 130 campsites at four campgrounds at $10.00–$13.00/day; accessible any-time) is composed mostly of pinewoods and sandhills, but extensive hard-wood forests grow along streams, and oak woodlands cover hillsides. Birding is best during spring and summer, when breeding species are active and vocal. To reach the forest from the west, exit from I-10 (Exit #26) onto SR-191 and head north toward Milton through picturesque Bagdad. Turn left onto US-90 (Caroline Street; 3.6), then right onto Stewart Street (SR-87) at a Burger King (0.2). Head north and turn right onto SR-191 at the Blackwater River State Forest sign across the street from Milton High School (0.7). Turn left onto Buddy Hardy Road (FR-68, at the Forestry Service sign; 13.5), then take the first right onto unpaved Three Notch Road (0.5). An active Red-cockaded Woodpecker cluster is along this road (0.7), with cavity trees banded with white paint. There are other woodpecker clusters along Three Notch Road. For other currently active clusters, contact forest management. At 5.4 miles, Three Notch Road intersects with SR-4, which provides access to this area from the north and intersects SR-191 in Munson, permitting a loop route. Brown-headed Nuthatches and Bachman's Sparrows are common through-out the flatwoods.

Contact: Blackwater River State Forest, 11650 Munson Hwy., Milton,FL 32570; 850-957-6140; <www.fl-dof.com/state_forests/ blackwater_river.html>.

EGLIN AIR FORCE BASE

One of the largest and most significant conservation areas in Florida is **EGLIN AIR FORCE BASE** (463,448 acres; $5.00/person; annual permit required; no camping; opens two hours before sunrise; *military operations*; *seasonal hunting*), which occupies about 725 square miles south of I-10 between Pensacola Bay and Choctawhatchee Bay. Eglin's bird list of 327 species ranks second in the state behind Everglades National Park, but the base is seldom visited except by locals. Most of the acreage is composed of Longleaf Pine sandhills with resident Red-cockaded Woodpeckers, Brown-headed Nuthatches, and Bachman's Sparrows. Most importantly, Eglin supports the fourth-largest population of Red-cockaded Woodpeckers remaining in the world, with more than 300 clusters active in 2003. Eglin contains more than 1,150 miles of streams and rivers, and these riparian areas are good for breeding species such as Prothonotary and Swainson's Warblers. Access requires a permit, which can be obtained at the Jackson Guard office at Niceville. To reach Eglin Air Force Base from the west (Gulf Breeze), head east on US-98 toward Fort Walton Beach, then head north on SR-85 toward Niceville (see map on next page). The base office is on the east side of CR-85 just north of SR-20 (John Sims Parkway) and is open Monday–Thursday 7:00 AM–4:30 PM, Friday 7:00 AM–6:00 PM, and Saturday 7:30 AM–12:30 PM. The office is closed on Sunday. After paying the recreation fee, you must watch a brief safety video; then you will be provided with a detailed Outdoor Recreation map. Parts of Eglin are used for live-fire bombing and gunnery practice, so *stay out of all closed areas*. Inquire at the Jackson Guard office for current locations for Red-cockaded Woodpeckers and other sought-after species.

Along the north side of Fort Walton Beach, on Eglin property leased to Okaloosa County, are a landfill and three wastewater treatment facilities that can provide excellent birding opportunities. Although an Eglin permit is not required to bird these areas, access is facilitated with a permit. To reach the **FORT WALTON BEACH SPRAY FIELD** (no fee, no camping; accessible anytime) from Niceville, head southwest on CR-85 (Government Avenue/Eglin Parkway) to CR-189 and turn right. At Beal Street Extension (3.2), turn right to its end. The spray fields are on the right. From US-98 West, head north on Mary Esther Boulevard to SR-189 (Beal Parkway; 1.8) and continue north. Just beyond Green Acres Road on the left (2.5), continue north on Beal Street Extension and proceed as above. Park across from the office on the left, and ask for permission to drive the perimeter road. A sightings book and bird checklists are available in the office. *The Eglin Recreation Permit is not required to visit the Spray Field or the Okaloosa Holding Ponds and Landfill.*

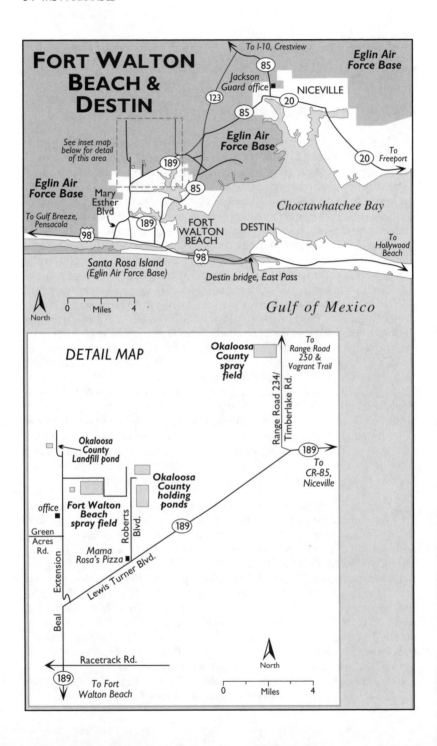

During wet summers, the holding pond and spray field attract many wading birds, ducks, and shorebirds. Glossy and White-faced Ibises have been seen here irregularly in recent years, and Black-necked Stilts have begun breeding. One or two Eared Grebes are seen during fall in most years. Various ducks, including Hooded Mergansers, winter on the pond, and numerous sparrows winter in the weedy fields. Besides common species, look for Grasshopper, Le Conte's, White-crowned, and, occasionally, Lark Sparrows. Mississippi Kites are regular during spring and summer, and Swallow-tailed Kites appear occasionally.

Just northwest of the spray field office is the **Okaloosa County Landfill pond** that is always worth a look when the landfill is open (7:00 AM–3:30 PM, Monday–Saturday). Show your binocular at the weigh station for permission to enter. The south end of what is known locally as **Vagrant Trail** can be accessed by driving north on the clay road to the bend, then shifting 50 feet to the right, and parking under the powerline. *Be careful to avoid getting locked inside.* The trail is good for landbirds, especially during fall migration and winter. One or more Ash-throated and Vermilion Flycatchers have wintered here recently, and other rarities have been observed.

Along the eastern edge of the spray field are the **Okaloosa County holding ponds** (no fee; no camping; usually opens 8:00 AM, *Monday–Friday only*). To reach the ponds from the spray field, go back to SR-189 (Lewis Turner Boulevard) and turn left. Proceed to Roberts Boulevard (0.8) and turn left just past Mama Rosa's Pizza. The ponds are ahead (0.5). The perimeters of the ponds on the right may be walked, but *do not enter the spray field from here*. Be careful to avoid getting locked inside. Sixteen species of ducks have been reported here, and one or two Eared Grebes usually are present from October through December. Baird's Sandpipers occasionally are seen in April and September.

Return to CR-189 and head east to Range Road 234 (Timberlake Road; 2.0). Turn left to the **Okaloosa County Spray Fields** on the left (1.0). *Scan the ponds from the road only.* Continue north past the powerlines to Range Road 250 (0.9) and turn left to its end (0.6). Park here and walk south 0.3 mile on the northern end of **Vagrant Trail**, which leads to the landfill and spray field mentioned above. The Eglin Recreation Permit is required to visit this site.

For coastal species, head east from Fort Walton Beach on US-98 and cross the Intracoastal Waterway to **Santa Rosa Island**. Continue east to Eglin property (1.0). From here to the bridge over East Pass several miles to the east, the beaches and dunes support breeding populations of Snowy Plovers and Least Terns (spring and summer). During winter, check the marshes at the extreme eastern end of the island for Nelson's Sharp-tailed Sparrows, and scan the Gulf for Northern Gannets, Common Loons, and sea ducks. A walk along the beach to the jetty may produce shorebirds, including Snowy

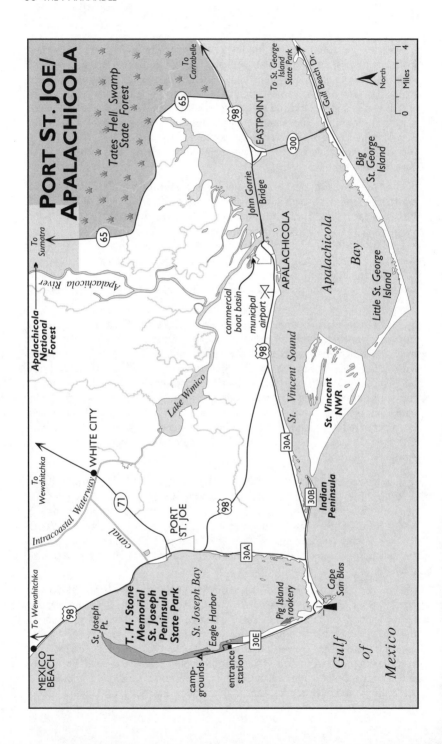

PORT ST. JOE/
APALACHICOLA

Plovers. During spring and summer, Least Terns and Black Skimmers breed near the east end of the bridge.

Contact: *Eglin Air Force Base, Jackson Guard, 107 Route 85 North, Niceville, FL 32578; 850-882-4164; <www.eglin.af.mil>.*

PORT ST. JOE

B eaches and dunes at **T. H. STONE MEMORIAL ST. JOSEPH PENINSULA STATE PARK** (2,516 acres; $4.00/vehicle; 119 camp-sites at $20.00/day; opens at 8:00 AM) provide breeding habitat for Snowy and Wilson's Plovers, and for wading birds and larids year-round. Wooded areas should be checked for migrant landbirds; impressive fallouts have occurred here in the past, usually during spring. Migrant landbirds may also be prevalent during fall, but raptors are the main attraction during that season. The most common species are Sharp-shinned and Broad-winged Hawks and American Kestrels. During heavy flights, as many as 1,500 Sharp-shinned Hawks and 200 American Kestrels have been seen, but daily totals usually are in the range of 200 or 300 hawks. Eagle Harbor, where the peninsula is most narrow, is the best place to observe raptors, but any place with an unobstructed view of the peninsula from Gulf to bay is good. An interesting feature of the fall raptor migration here is dictated by the shape of the land: raptors fly *north* up the peninsula to St. Joseph Point and then cross the few miles of water before continuing west along the mainland Gulf coast.

To reach the narrow, northward-pointing St. Joseph Peninsula, turn from US-98 onto CR-30A, about two miles south of the town of Port St. Joe. (This town was the site of Florida's first constitutional convention, in 1838.) At CR-30E (6.6), turn right onto the St. Joseph Peninsula and the park entrance (8.5). The shoreline and marshes around Eagle Harbor are good spots for wintering shorebirds and Nelson's Sharp-tailed Sparrows, and the harbor may contain sea ducks. Productive spots for migrant landbirds during spring and fall are around the campgrounds and the picnic area. Brown-headed Nut-hatches and Yellow-throated Warblers may be found in the taller pines throughout the park. The paved park road ends about two miles past the entrance, but park property continues for another seven miles to St. Joseph Point. It is permissible to hike into this "wilderness preserve", which harbors large numbers of nesting sea turtles during late summer.

Contact: *T. H. Stone Memorial St. Joseph Peninsula State Park, 8899 Cape San Blas Road, Port St. Joe, FL 32456; 850-227-1327; <www.floridastateparks.org/stjoseph>.*

APALACHICOLA

T his historic town, the center of Florida's oyster industry, is situated at the mouth of the Apalachicola River. Specialties of the area include Least Bit-

Least Tern on nest.   Arthur Morris/www.birdsasart.com

tern, Bald Eagle, Mississippi Kite, Marsh Wren, and Boat-tailed Grackle. Eurasian Collared-Doves are common in town and are joined by a few White-winged Doves moving east during fall. Several pairs of Gray Kingbirds and a single pair of Painted Buntings (unique in the Panhandle) are other local breeding specialties. In the mid-1990s, Vaux's Swifts roosted during winter in the chimney of the town hall.

The point of land at the mouth of the river in Apalachicola and the causeway of the **John Gorrie Bridge** (US-98) are good sites from which to observe vagrant birds blown onshore during tropical storms or hurricanes. The most common vagrant is Magnificent Frigatebird, but various larids may also be seen. Storms may also blow local birds onshore in large numbers, including White-rumped Sandpipers and Sandwich, Common, and Black Terns. The docks and oyster-shell piles at the commercial **boat basin** at the end of Market Street (the easternmost road in Apalachicola north of the US-98 traffic light downtown) are good for both night-herons and larids; North America's only record of Gray-hooded Gull was found here in December 1998. A pair of Gray Kingbirds usually breeds in this area each year. Once on the US-98 causeway heading east, pull over and scan the tidal flats for shorebird and larid flocks. Species to search for include American Golden-Plover (spring and fall), White-rumped Sandpiper (late spring–early summer), Red Knot (spring and fall), Piping Plover (fall through spring), Gull-billed Tern (spring and summer), Lesser Black-backed Gull (winter), and Franklin's Gull (late fall–winter).

Apalachicola Municipal Airport, worth checking for grassland birds during winter, is located about two miles west of town. Drive north from US-98 to the terminal's parking area (0.7). For the past several years, grassy areas around the runways have been the most reliable spot in Florida for wintering Sprague's Pipits (one to three individuals winter). Also likely to be present are American Pipits and sparrows such as Henslow's and Vesper. You must first check in at the office (open 7:00 AM–7:00 PM) before birding the airport. *Please stay off the runways at all times, and keep aware of planes taking off or landing.*

Contact: *Apalachicola Municipal Airport, 8 Airport Road, Apalachicola, FL 32320; 850-653-2222.*

To reach **Indian Peninsula**, go west from Apalachicola on US-98, bear left onto CR-30A, and then turn left sharply onto CR-30B. Marshes near the bridge on CR-30B are good during winter for Clapper Rails, Marsh Wrens, and Seaside Sparrows. Follow this road to the boat ramp at the end. The peninsula is a good, easily accessible spot for wading birds, shorebirds, larids, and other species. Walk north from the boat ramp several hundred yards to scope the western part of St. Vincent Sound. Black-crowned Night-Herons and American Oystercatchers (as many as 50 may be present, but only three or four pairs breed) are regular here. The telephone wires along the peninsula are good places for tyrannids; Scissor-tailed Flycatchers and Western Kingbirds are regular during fall.

St. George Island is a barrier island nearly 30 miles long. To reach it from Apalachicola, go east on US-98 across the John Gorrie bridge to Eastpoint and turn right onto SR-300 (6.2). The former causeway to the island has been converted to artificial islands that support an important larid rookery for Laughing Gulls and Royal, Sandwich, and Least Terns. Much of St. George Island is undergoing rapid residential development, but the eastern end of the island has been preserved, and this section of the island contains some of the most pristine dune systems remaining in Florida. To reach **DR. JULIAN D.**

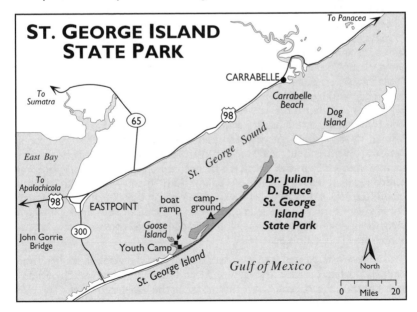

BRUCE ST. GEORGE ISLAND STATE PARK (1,962 acres; $4.00/vehicle; 60 campsites at $8.00–$14.00/day; opens at 8:00 AM), turn left onto East Gulf Beach Drive and proceed to the entrance (4.0). Once inside the park, the road continues for about eight miles before ending near the island's eastern end. The best place for migrant landbirds is the **Youth Camp area** on the left (0.7); several notable vagrants have been found here. The small borrow ponds along the road are good places to search for American Bittern during winter, and Groove-billed Anis have been seen here from late fall through winter. At the boat ramp at the end of the road, scan for sea ducks during winter and American Oystercatchers year-round. Return to the main road and turn left to the first of two boardwalks on the left. Check the beaches here for Northern Gannets (often seen from shore from late fall through early spring), wading birds, shorebirds, larids, and wintering sea ducks (including Common Goldeneye and scoters). The boardwalks lead to St. George Sound, which may also contain sea ducks and other wintering waterbirds. At the campground between the two boardwalks, check the trees for migrant and wintering landbirds and brushy areas for sparrows during winter. Gray Kingbirds breed here. Dunes near and beyond the end of the park road support small numbers of Snowy Plovers.

Contact: Dr. Julian D. Bruce St. George Island State Park, 1900 East Gulf Beach Drive, St. George Island, FL 32328; 850-927-2111; <www.floridastateparks.org/stgeorgeisland>.

A PALACHICOLA NATIONAL FOREST (569,596 acres; $3.00/vehicle at day use areas, other areas free; 50 campsites in five campgrounds at $3.00–$5.00/day; accessible anytime; *seasonal hunting*) is the largest of the three national forests in Florida. It extends from the Apalachicola River about 35 miles east to the Ochlockonee River. The four resident specialties of pine flatwoods and savannas—Red-cockaded Woodpecker, Brown-headed Nuthatch, Pine Warbler, and Bachman's Sparrow —occur widely in the forest. Apalachicola National Forest contains the largest population of Red-cockaded Woodpeckers remaining in the world. In 1999, the forest contained 611 clusters. Other birds of interest are breeding species such as Swallow-tailed and Mississippi Kites, Broad-winged Hawk, Red-headed Woodpecker, Eastern Wood-Pewee, Acadian Flycatcher, Wood Thrush, and Swainson's, Kentucky, Prothonotary, and Hooded Warblers. Another feature of the forest is Henslow's Sparrow, which is a fairly common to common migrant and winter resident from mid-October to mid-April in pinewoods with a grassy ground cover, and in open savannas (prairies or bogs in pine flatwoods). These savannas may also contain other grassland species from late fall through early spring, including Yellow Rail (rare), Sedge Wren (common), and Grasshopper and Le Conte's Sparrows.

The forest is divided into two ranger districts: the Apalachicola and the Wakulla. Habitats are more diverse and less disturbed in the Apalachicola district, but the largest sandhills tract is located in the Wakulla district. The U.S.

Forest Service currently burns about 30,000 acres annually to maintain fire-adapted plant communities. An emphasis on uneven-aged pine forests also furthers the goal of integrated ecosystem management. Detailed publications and maps are available from either ranger district office or from the supervisor's office in Tallahassee. Particularly useful publications and maps are Recreation Guide R8-RG16 for National Forests in Florida, Recreation Area Directory (free), and the Apalachicola National Forest map ($3.00), which is essential.

The following route traverses pine flatwoods and savannas in the Apalachicola ranger district. (A shorter and less scenic birding route in the Wakulla ranger district is on page 69). The village of Sumatra is an excellent starting point to reach prime habitats in the area. From Eastpoint, go east on US-98 to SR-65 (3.0) and turn left. At the Sumatra Grocery Store at SR-379 (26.9), turn left onto **APALACHEE SAVANNAS SCENIC BY-WAY**. An eight-mile section of the byway from here to FR-180 offers a variety of habitats and traverses the heart of open savannas that are dominated by

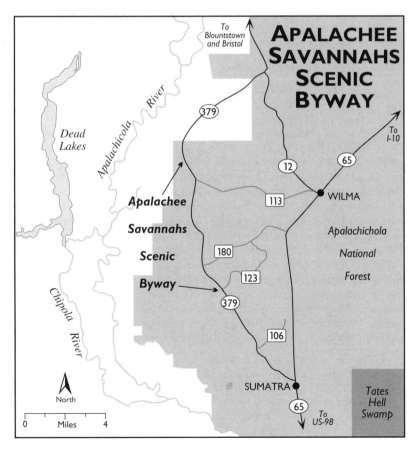

grasses, sedges, and herbs. Other pristine habitats located along or adjacent to the route are mature Longleaf Pine/Wiregrass woods and Swamp Titi shrub-swamp, cypress strands, and bayheads picturesquely interwoven with the pinewoods and savannas. Red-cockaded Woodpeckers, Brown-headed Nuthatches, and Bachman's Sparrows are all common in this area year-round (but, like elsewhere, the sparrow is difficult to locate when not singing). During winter, Sedge Wrens and Henslow's Sparrows are also common in the savannas. Particularly good for Henslow's Sparrows are two savannas and adjacent forest at the junction of SR-379 and FR-123, northwest of Sumatra (6.2). Two forest roads also provide a loop of 6.2 miles around one large semi-continuous savanna. Follow FR-123 east from CR-379 to FR-180, turn left, and loop back to SR-379. (FR-106, closer to SR-65, is another short 1.7-miles road through typical savanna habitat.)

Contacts: *Supervisor's Office, National Forests in Florida, Woodcrest Office Park, 325 John Knox Road, Suite F-100, Tallahassee, FL 32303; 850-942-9300; Apalachicola Ranger District Office, Florida Highway 20, P.O. Box 579, Bristol, FL 32321; 850-643-2282, Wakulla Ranger District Office, U.S. Highway 319, Route 6, Box 7860, Crawfordville, FL 32327; 850-926-3561; <www.southernregion.fs.fed.us/florida>.*

Directions for coastal areas to the east continue on page 95.

MARIANNA–BLOUNTSTOWN

One of the unique natural areas in the state is **FLORIDA CAVERNS STATE PARK** (1,319 acres; $4.00/vehicle; 38 campsites at $17.00/day; cave tours at $6.00/person; opens at 8:00 AM). To reach it from I-10 westbound, exit (#142) at SR-71 and go north to US-90 (1.9). Turn left to CR-166 (Jefferson Street; 3.1) and turn right to the entrance is on the left (2.8). From I-10 eastbound, exit (#136) at Kynesville Road (CR-276) and go northeast to its end at SR-73 (Jefferson Street; 3.0). Turn left (the road becomes CR-166) to the park entrance on the left (3.0). During spring and summer, Swallow-tailed and Mississippi Kites, Broad-winged Hawk, Eastern Wood-Pewee, Acadian Flycatcher, Wood Thrush, Swainson's, Kentucky, and Hooded Warblers, and Summer Tanager all breed in the park. During winter, look for Red-breasted Nuthatch (irruptive), Winter Wren, Golden-crowned Kinglet, Fox and White-throated Sparrows, Dark-eyed Junco, and Rusty Blackbird. Winter Wrens are often found near the spot where the Chipola River disappears underground, and elsewhere along the river.

Contact: *Florida Caverns State Park, 3345 Caverns Road, Marianna, FL 32446; 850-482-9598; <www.floridastateparks.org/floridacaverns>.*

Along the east side of the Apalachicola River River in an out-of-the-way area is picturesque **Torreya State Park** (3,115 acres; $2.00/vehicle; 30 campsites at $12.00/day; opens at 8:00 AM). To reach it from I-10, exit (#166)

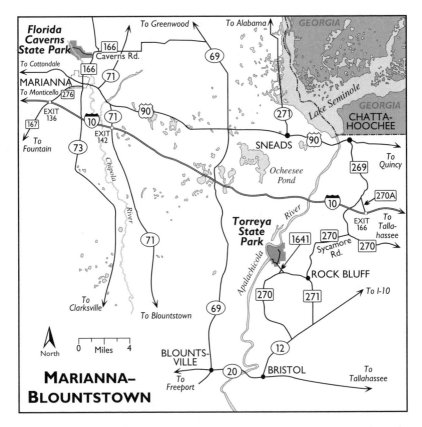

Florida
Caverns
State Park

To Greenwood

To Alabama

GEORGIA

To Cottondale

166 Caverns Rd.

166

69

71

MARIANNA
To Monticello 276

EXIT
136

167

To
Fountain

73

10 71

EXIT
142

Chipola

90

River

271

Lake Seminole

GEORGIA
CHATTA-
HOOCHEE

SNEADS

90

Ocheesee
Pond

269

To
Quincy

10

270A

EXIT
166

To
Talla-
hassee

Torreya
State
Park

River

71

1641

270

Sycamore
Rd.

270

Apalachicola

ROCK BLUFF

To
Clarksville

To Blountstown

69

270

271

To I-10

North

0   Miles   4

MARIANNA–
BLOUNTSTOWN

BLOUNTS-
VILLE

To
Freeport

20

12

BRISTOL

To
Tallahassee

onto CR-270-A (Flat Creek Road) and head *north* toward Chattahoochee. At its end at CR-269 (1.2), turn left. At Sycamore Road (CR-270; 4.0) turn right to the hamlet of Rock Bluff (6.1). Turn right onto CR-1641 to the park ahead (2.5). To reach the park from SR-71 in Blountstown, go east on SR-20 to SR-12 in Bristol (4.5) and turn left. At CR-1641 (6.5), turn left to the park ahead (6.4). From the coast west of Apalachicola, take SR-71 north to Blountstown. From Eastpoint or Carrabelle, take SR-65 north to SR-20, then west to Bristol. Proceed as above. Two endangered endemic trees, Florida Torreya (*Torreya taxifolia*) and Florida Yew (*Taxus floridana*), are main attractions of the park. Swallow-tailed and Mississippi Kites can be seen during spring and summer from the Gregory House, a majestic pre-Civil-War house moved across the Apalachicola River to its present location in the park. The view from the house is spectacular; on clear days, you can see west for 30 miles. Pines at the campground contain Brown-headed Nuthatches and Pine Warblers, which may be joined during winter by Brown Creeper and Golden-crowned Kinglet. The nature trail from the Gregory House down the bluff to just above the river is good for Winter Wrens during winter, and during spring and summer for many breeding species, including Louisiana

Waterthrush. Other trails begin from the picnic area. A trail on the left just inside the park entrance leads to a geologic overlook. Red-headed Woodpeckers, Eastern Bluebirds, and Bachman's Sparrows breed along the trail.

Contact: *Torreya State Park, 2576 Northwest Torreya Park Road, Bristol, FL 32321; 850-643-2674; <www.floridastateparks.org/torreya>.*

TALLAHASSEE REGION

The state capital of Florida, Tallahassee is located at the eastern edge of the Panhandle in a region known as the Red Hills. This physiographic region, which extends northeast to Thomasville, Georgia, is named for its red clay soils and rolling topography. The Red Hills originally supported an extensive Longleaf Pine/Wiregrass community, but this habitat was cleared and used for agriculture by Indians and then by early settlers. The fields later regenerated and returned to a semi-natural state, dominated by Loblolly Pines. Following the Civil War, the region was converted to large plantations owned by wealthy industrialists who established Northern Bobwhite hunting reserves. Today, many of these plantations remain intact, and the region continues to support remnants of the original Longleaf Pine community. The Red Hills contain the largest population of Red-cockaded Woodpeckers remaining on private property anywhere (although the birds are located mostly in Georgia), and this region is the last stronghold in Florida for White-breasted Nuthatch.

A nonprofit organization is working to preserve the Red Hills in perpetuity by purchasing conservation easements whereby development rights are given up, but sustainable practices such as hunting and limited logging continue. To date, more than 71,500 acres of Red Hills plantations have been protected from development in this manner. For more information on this effort, contact Tall Timbers Research Station (see below), or go to <www.ttrs.org/rhcp.htm>.

Tallahassee has a small but active birding community, served by a southern Georgia/northern Florida birding Internet list at <http://groups.yahoo.com/group/nflbirds>. Sites in this section are organized roughly from north to south.

North of town and immediately south of the Georgia state line is **TALL TIMBERS RESEARCH STATION** (4,000 acres; no fee; no camping; trail opens at 8:30 AM; *restricted access*). Tall Timbers is a private ecological research and conservation institute that is working actively to preserve Red Hills habitats by securing conservation easements on local plantations. To reach Tall Timbers from I-10 in Tallahassee, go north on US-319/SR-61 (Thomasville Road) to CR-12 (13.3), and turn left (a brown sign along US-319 marks the road). Head west to Henry Beadel Drive on the left (2.5), just before the TV tower on the right. (Before the tower was lowered, it was source

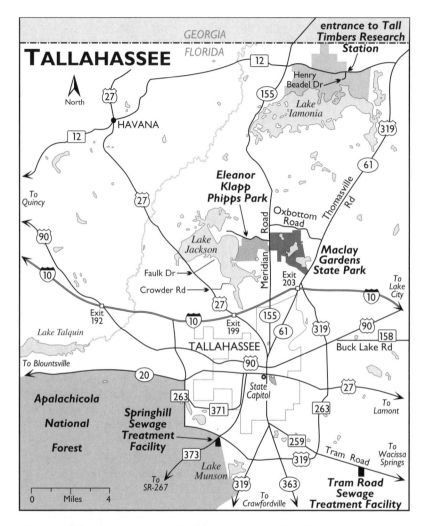

of tower-kill data used to study nocturnal migration of numerous species. The most amazing bird recorded from here occurred the night of 10–11 September 1964, during Hurricane *Dora*, when a Black-capped Petrel hit the tower!)

Bear left at the T-intersection at the top of the hill to the Wade Research Center, the largest brick building on the right (0.4). *You must check in here before birding the property.* The station contains a variety of habitats including hardwood forest, fields, lakes and ponds, and mixed pine forests. An 1,800-foot nature trail traverses these habitats and offers the chance to observe one of Florida's most restricted permanent residents, White-breasted Nuthatch. Other residents that may be seen are Wild Turkey, Hairy Woodpecker, Brown-headed Nuthatch, and Bachman's and Field Sparrows. During spring and summer, look for breeding species such as Eastern Wood-Pewee, Prothonotary and Kentucky Warblers, and Yellow-breasted Chat. The nature trail begins to the west of the group of buildings and is open to the public from 8:30 AM to 4:30 PM Monday through Friday and at other times by prior arrangement. The trail also has a bird window overlooking Gannet Pond. The station maintains an archive for photographs of rare Florida birds and an excellent regional bird specimen collection. These collections and the research buildings are available to the public by appointment.

Contact: *Tall Timbers Research Station, Inc., 13093 Henry Beadel Drive, Tallahassee, FL 32312; 850-893-4153 (ext. 249 to arrange for weekend visits); <www.ttrs.org>.*

Another birding area north of Tallahassee is **Lake Jackson**, a shallow, 4,000-acre lake surrounded by low hills. A variety of waterbirds, such as wading birds and waterfowl (mainly during winter), may be seen. To reach one access point, exit I-10 (Exit #199) onto US-27 and head northwest. At Crowder Road (1.7), turn right to the parking lot (1.2). To reach a second access point, return to US-27 and turn right. At Faulk Drive (1.1), turn right to the small turnaround (1.3).

To reach **Alfred B. Maclay Gardens State Park** (1,179 acres; $4.00/vehicle; no camping; opens at 8:00 AM) from the Capitol, go north on SR-61 (Monroe Street) and bear right onto SR-61 (now called Thomasville Road; 1.0). Pass by the junction of US-319 on the right (5.0) to the park entrance on the left (0.6). Mississippi Kites (spring and summer), Purple Gallinules (mostly spring and summer), and White-breasted Nuthatch (resident) breed in the park. With the addition of recently purchased land, this park now extends west to SR-155 (Meridian Road).

Contact: *Alfred B. Maclay Gardens State Park, 3540 Thomasville Road, Tallahassee, FL 32309; 850-487-4556; <www.floridastateparks.org/ maclay gardens>.*

Adjacent to Maclay Gardens to the west is **Elinor Klapp Phipps Park** (670 acres; no fee; no camping; opens at 8:00 AM). Fronting Lake Jackson, the park is managed by the City of Tallahassee and is a diverse landscape of open fields, upland mixed pine/oak/hickory forest, loblolly flats, and swamp forests. To reach the park from Maclay Gardens, continue north on US-319/SR-61 (Thomasville Road) to Oxbottom Road (1.2) and turn left. At the T-intersection at SR-155 (Meridian Road; 4.0), turn left to the park entrance on the right (1.3). Breeding species include White-breasted Nuthatch, Kentucky Warbler (spring and summer), Yellow-breasted Chat (spring and summer), and Field Sparrow.

Canada **Geese** were formerly abundant winter residents in the Tallahassee/St. Marks area, but the geese now winter north of Florida. (Land-use changes farther north now allow the geese to forage in agricultural fields rather than having to migrate farther south to Gulf coastal marshes.) In the late 1960s, the former Florida Game and Fish Commission released many geese of the non-migratory race *Branta canadensis maxima*, the Giant Canada Goose, into the Tallahassee area. Geese can now be found in many areas around the city year-round. To reach the best area from downtown, go northeast on US-90 (Mahan Drive). After crossing US-319 (Capitol Circle), continue to CR-158 (Buck Lake Road) (0.7) and turn right. For the next three to five miles, you should see Canada Geese and other waterbirds (including Wood Storks) in the many lakes and ponds.

Three small city parks within a short distance of downtown Tallahassee offer fair birding possibilities. **Myers Park** (47 acres; no fee; no camping; opens at sunrise) is fewer than five blocks from the Capitol. It attracts the usual spring and fall migrants and supports breeding pairs of Barred Owls, Yellow-throated Vireos, and Summer Tanagers. To reach the park from the Capitol, head east on Apalachee Parkway (US-90/27) to Myers Park Drive

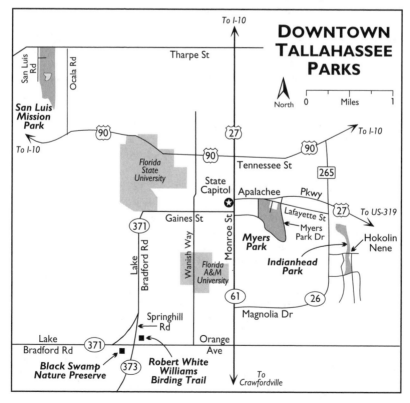

(0.6) and turn right. The park is one block ahead. **Indianhead Park** (32 acres; no fee; no camping; opens at sunrise) is also visited frequently by local birders. During fall, migrant landbirds can be numerous. Breeding species include Mississippi Kite, Broad-winged Hawk, White-breasted Nuthatch (resident), and sometimes Louisiana Waterthrush and Kentucky Warbler. To reach the park from the Capitol, take Apalachee Parkway (US-90/27) east to CR-265 (Magnolia Drive, the first major intersection; 1.2) and turn right. At Hokolin Nene (0.9) turn left and proceed two blocks to where the road crosses a creek. A footpath on the left parallels the creek on both sides and runs through the center of the park. It is acceptable to park on the street. Be sure to depart the area the same way you entered; it is easy to get lost amid this district's circuitous streets with strange names.

To reach **San Luis Mission Park** (69 acres; no fee; no camping; opens at sunrise) from the Capitol, head north on US-27 (North Monroe Street) to Tharpe Street (1.8) and turn left. At San Luis Road (2.5), turn left to the park entrance on the left (0.2). The best birding is usually along Lake Esther, a small pond near the parking area. A variety of migrant or wintering landbirds may be seen from the boardwalk; 28 species of warblers have been seen here.

Other birding opportunities are found south of the city. From the Capitol on SR-61 (Monroe Street), head west on CR-362 (Gaines Street). At CR-371 (Lake Bradford Road; 1.5), turn left. Bear left onto CR-373A (Springhill Road; 1.1), which soon becomes CR-373. At SR-373 (Orange Avenue; 0.4), turn left onto an unpaved, unmarked road (0.1) that leads to the **Robert White Williams Birding Trail** (no fee; no camping; opens at sunrise), which is the land bordering a stormwater drainage ditch. The trail is a small but productive riparian oasis surrounded by development. From the parking area, walk south around a locked gate. The short trail (500 yards) can be good for migrant landbirds during spring and fall, and Hooded Warblers breed here. *Because this site is near an urban area, birders should take appropriate precautions.*

From the Williams Birding Trail, return to SR-373 and head west to another unmarked road on the left (0.3). Park on the grass to the left of a small brick building to enter **Black Swamp Nature Preserve** (67 acres; no fee; no camping; opens at sunrise). The preserve features the sole remaining swamp of significant size within the Tallahassee city limits. An embankment enables birders to access the swamp. From the parking lot, walk south to a locked metal gate. Walk around it and proceed 100 yards to a sharp bend to the left. Another 200 yards or so brings you to the end of the trail. During fall and winter, Black Swamp hosts Winter Wrens and several species of sparrows. Watch for Rusty Blackbirds roosting among Red-winged Blackbirds. Wading birds and Limpkins may be seen year-round.

Two sewage treatment facilities can be good for migrant shorebirds and are popular birding spots (see Tallahassee map). The first of these is the Thomas P. Smith Water Reclamation Facility (colloquially known as

SPRINGHILL ROAD SEWAGE TREATMENT FACILITY; no fee; no camping). To reach it, return to Orange Avenue (SR-373) and head east to Springhill Road (0.4). Turn right and go past CR-263 (Capitol Circle Southwest; 1.7) to the facility on the left (0.1). Obtain permission from the plant office (open 24 hours a day, year-round) to walk around the holding ponds. *Do not drive on the dikes separating the ponds.* Nearby and lending itself to a brief stop for wintering waterfowl is **Lake Munson**. Return to CR-263 (Capitol Circle Southwest) and turn right. At US-319 (Crawfordville Road; 2.2), turn right to Munson Boat Landing Road (0.6). Turn right to the lake (0.2).

To reach the Southeast Farm Wastewater Reuse Facility (known locally as the **TRAM ROAD SEWAGE TREATMENT FACILITY**; no fee; no camping), return to CR-263 (Capitol Circle) and turn right to CR-259 (Tram Road; 3.5). Turn right to the facility on the right (2.8); look for the corn silos. Check in at the office, *usually open only on weekdays, 8:00 AM–4:00 PM*). To obtain permission to enter on weekends and holidays, call 850-891-1295 in advance. It is permissible to drive south on Farm Road (the paved road to the spray fields), *on Thursdays only* (8:00AM–4:00PM), but *do not drive any of the gravel side roads.* During winter, the holding ponds near the office usually contain hundreds of waterfowl (mostly Bufflehead and Lesser Scaup). Shorebirds can be common at the ponds during migration and winter. Fields south of the ponds contain many sparrows during winter.

A**PALACHICOLA NATIONAL FOREST** is detailed on page 60, but a section close to Tallahassee should produce Red-cockaded Woodpeckers and other species. A good loop trip into the Wakulla Ranger District

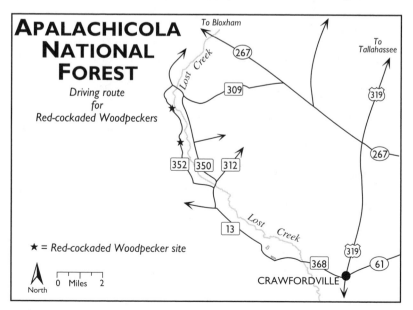

APALACHICOLA NATIONAL FOREST

Driving route for Red-cockaded Woodpeckers

To Bloxham

Lost Creek

267

To Tallahassee

309

319

352 350 312

267

★ = Red-cockaded Woodpecker site

Lost Creek

13

368 319

61

CRAWFORDVILLE

0 Miles 2

North

begins between Tallahassee and Crawfordville. From US-319 in Tallahassee, turn west onto SR-267 (9.0 south of Capitol Circle). You are now in the forest. Drive to the "Entering Leon County" sign (4.5) and turn left onto FR-309 (this is opposite CR-267A, Helen Guard Station Road). Cross FR-350 (4.8), then Lost Creek (0.6), and turn left onto FR-352 (0.3). Along this road are six woodpecker clusters that were active in 2004; look for trees painted with white bands. Brown-headed Nuthatches and Bachman's Sparrows (mainly spring and summer, when males are singing) should also be present. Listen for Swainson's Warblers during spring and summer around the junction of FR-312 (5.9). To exit the area, turn left and cross Lost Creek (0.2) to FR-350 (0.2). Then turn left to return to FR-309. Alternatively, you may turn right onto FR-312 to FR-13 (0.8). Turn left to reach US-319 in Crawfordville (7.2).

> **Contacts:** *Supervisor's Office, National Forests in Florida, Woodcrest Office Park, 325 John Knox Road, Suite F-100, Tallahassee, FL 32303; 850-942-9300, Apalachicola Ranger District Office, Florida Highway 20, P.O. Box 579, Bristol, FL 32321; 850-643-2282, Wakulla Ranger District Office, U.S. Highway 319, Route 6, Box 7860, Crawfordville, FL 32327; 850-926-3561; <www.southernregion.fs.fed.us/florida>.*

WAKULLA SPRINGS—ST. MARKS

South of Tallahassee is one of the best and most scenic birding sites in the area. The entrance to **EDWARD BALL WAKULLA SPRINGS STATE PARK** (5,952 acres; $4.00/vehicle; no camping; opens at 8:00 AM) is just east of the junction of SR-61 and CR-267. More than 125 feet deep, Wakulla Springs is one of the largest and deepest springs in the world. It releases about 850 million gallons of water every day. The park contains extensive hardwood forests that support numerous landbirds, but the main attractions are the waterbirds. The best way to see them is to take the 30-minute "Jungle Cruise" glass-bottom-boat ride or the riverboat tours ($6.00/person) from the Wakulla Springs Lodge (27 rooms at $75.00–$100.00/day). Besides American Wigeon and others ducks that winter at the springs, you should see Anhinga, wading birds, and Purple Gallinule (rare during winter). For decades, Wakulla Springs was a reliable spot for Limpkin, but the birds have largely disappeared from the area, possibly the result of an invasion of *Hydrilla*, an exotic plant. During spring and summer, Yellow-crowned Night-Heron nests may be visible from the boat. Because the birds are accustomed to humans, the cruise provides excellent photographic opportunities. (Birders on the right side of the boat have a view of the shore, while those on the left view the water.) A short woodland path next to the entrance booth can be good for migrant and wintering landbirds.

> **Contact:** *Edward Ball Wakulla Springs State Park, 550 Wakulla Park Drive, Wakulla Springs, FL 32327; 850-224-5950; <www.floridastateparks.org/wakullasprings>.*

After leaving Wakulla Springs, turn right onto CR-267, continue to its end at US-98, and turn left. Just before the bridge over the St. Marks River (0.4), turn left onto unpaved **Old Plank Road**. All the land here is privately owned, so *bird only from the road*. During spring and summer, look for breeding Swainson's and Kentucky Warblers and Yellow-breasted Chats in brushy areas for the next mile. (Stop at the point where you can smell the sulphur springs.) Swallow-tailed and Mississippi Kites also breed here.

Return to US-98 and, just across the river to the east, turn right (south) onto SR-59 to **ST. MARKS NATIONAL WILDLIFE REFUGE** (67,623 upland and 32,000 submerged acres; $4.00/vehicle; no camping; opens at sunrise; Visitor's Center opens at 8:15 AM Monday–Friday, 10:00 AM Saturday and Sunday), one of the best birding areas in Florida. During winter,

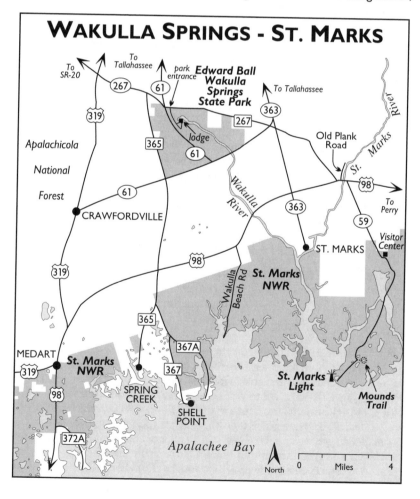

a large variety of waterfowl is found here. The woodlands around the visitor center on the right can be good for migrant and wintering landbirds. For the next five miles, the main refuge road (SR-59) offers access to many birding sites. The numerous impoundments offer excellent birding during winter for ducks and other waterbirds, and the woodlands can be good for wintering and migrant landbirds. **Mounds Pool Nature Trail** on the left is worth hiking. Shorebirds (including Long-billed Dowitchers and Stilt Sandpipers) can be common along the dikes, and this is one of the most reliable spots in Florida for wintering Snow Geese. Black Rails have been heard in the pools but probably occur here only irregularly. Vermilion Flycatchers are regular during fall, and one or more have wintered along the back dike of Stoney Bayou #2 for many years. During winter, many shorebirds roost near the tower on Mounds Pool. Wintering and migrant landbirds can be found in the oaks near the restrooms.

Around the **ST. MARKS LIGHTHOUSE** at the end of SR-59, scan the bay for loons, grebes, and bay ducks such as Common Goldeneye, Redhead, Greater Scaup, Bufflehead, and scoters. Walk the dike to the right to look for ducks and shorebirds. Take the path down the beach (*sometimes posted off-limits, in which case stay out*) to the left past the lighthouse for about 0.1 mile to the palms and cut through to a dry section of the saltmarsh. Marsh Wrens (resident), Nelson's Sharp-tailed Sparrows (winter), and Scott's Seaside Sparrows (resident) are found here. Check the mudflats for Wilson's Plover, Whimbrel, and Gull-billed Tern in season. The oaks around the lighthouse and shrubbery around Lighthouse Pond can be good for migrant and wintering landbirds. During low tide, the **Wakulla Beach** section of the refuge has shorebirds and other waterbirds. To reach this area from Newport, go west on US-98, cross SR-363 and the Wakulla River (2.4), and turn left onto the first unpaved road (1.2). The beach is at the end of the road (4.0). Resident Marsh Wrens and Scott's Seaside Sparrows, and wintering Nelson's Sharp-tailed Sparrows are found in the marshes.

Contact: *St. Marks National Wildlife Refuge, P.O. Box 68, St. Marks, FL 32355; 850-925-6121; <www.fws.gov/saintmarks>.*

SOPCHOPPY—ST. JAMES ISLAND

Areas west of St. Marks contain several good birding stops. From St. Marks or Wakulla Springs, head west on US-98. From Tallahassee or the eastern portion of Apalachicola National Forest, travel south on CR-319. At Medart, go south on US-98 to visit coastal areas, or head west on US-319 to visit **Ochlockonee River State Park** (392 acres; $3.00/vehicle; 30 campsites at $15.00/day; opens at 8:00 AM), which is good for pinewoods species. From Medart, go west on US-319 to the hamlet of Sopchoppy, then continue on US-319 south to the park on the left (4.0). From US-98 along the coast, head north on US-319 to the park on the right (7.0). For those not traveling farther north, Ochlockonee (pronounced *Ok-LOK-nee*) offers chances to see Red-cockaded Woodpeckers, Eastern Wood-Pewees (spring and summer), Brown-headed Nuthatches, Bachman's Sparrows (primarily spring and summer), and Summer Tanagers (spring and summer). As elsewhere, woodpecker cavity trees are marked with white paint. During winter, Henslow's Sparrows may be found in wet areas of short grass in recently burned pinewoods and under the powerlines across the main park road.

Contact: *Ochlockonee River State Park, P.O. Box 5, Sopchoppy, FL 32358; 850-962-2771; <www.floridastateparks.org/ochlockoneeriver>.*

To reach coastal sites from Medart, head south on US-98. Just prior to reaching Ochlockonee Bay (7.7), turn left onto CR-372 (Mashes Sands Road) to **Mashes Sands County Park** (50¢/vehicle during summer; no camping; accessible anytime) at the end of the road (2.6). Marsh Wrens and Seaside Sparrows are resident in the marshes and are joined during winter by Nelson's Sharp-tailed Sparrows. At low tide, shorebirds and larids can be common during migration and winter, especially on days with few sunbathers.

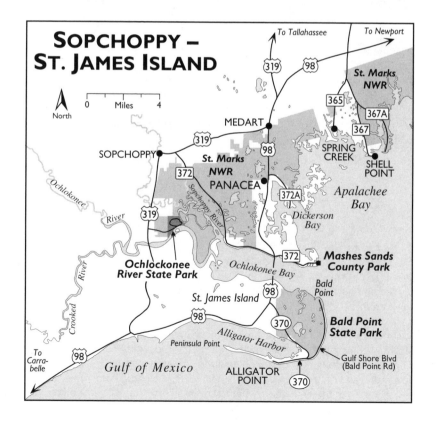

Black-crowned Night-Heron, adult.   Arthur Morris/www.birdsasart.com

During spring and summer, Gray Kingbirds should be seen perched on powerlines along the road.

Return to US-98 and continue south. After crossing Ochlockonee Bay, you enter St. James Island, which is really a peninsula. At SR-370 (Alligator Drive; 1.3), turn left. At the T-intersection (3.7), turn right (in other words, remain on Alligator Drive) to the community of **Alligator Point**. *Virtually the entire peninsula is private property, so bird only from the road.* On the right at 2.0 is the southernmost tip of land on the peninsula. This perhaps is the best spot to set up a scope and scan the Gulf, although Hurricane *Dennis* destroyed part of the road in 2004. Rebuilding of the road and ongoing construction have made parking along the road problematic at times; be aware of any construc- tion traffic and do not block any private access. Alligator Point is one of the few spots along the Gulf coast where scoters winter annually. All three species occur here (Black is most common, White-winged is rarest), along with other waterfowl such as Redhead, Lesser and Greater Scaup, Common Goldeneye, and Bufflehead. Also search for Red-throated Loons, which can winter here in numbers; Common Loons should be numerous. Occasionally, Pacific Loon is reported. Scan **Alligator Harbor** (north of the road); scoters and other sea ducks are often found here during winter, and larids frequently perch on the docks. Several pairs of Gray Kingbirds breed in the area during spring and summer and are frequently seen perched on powerlines.

Turn around and backtrack to the T-intersection. Turn right onto Gulf Shore Boulevard and head north. **BALD POINT STATE PARK** (1,391 acres; $3.00/vehicle; no camping at present; opens at 8:00 AM) is a recent state acquisition that consists of magnificent dunes and beaches, wet flatwoods, hammocks, and marshes. Facilities are planned for the future. In the meantime, several trails to the west offer access to pine flatwoods, scrub, ponds, and marshes, while beach and dune access is provided to the east. The peninsula attracts a diversity migrant landbirds; local rarities such as Western Kingbird, Scissor-tailed Flycatcher, and Lark Sparrow are regular during fall. White-winged Doves are increasing as migrants, and several species of waterfowl, including Bufflehead and Common Goldeneye, are present during winter.

Contact: *Bald Point State Park, 146 Box Cut, Alligator Point, FL 32346; 850-349-9146; <www.floridastateparks.org/baldpoint>.*

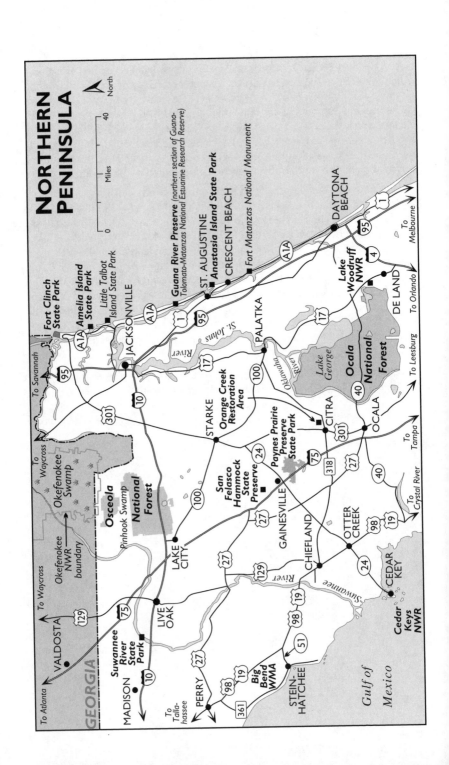

NORTHERN PENINSULA

North

Miles
0   40

GEORGIA

To Atlanta

To Savannah

To Waycross

VALDOSTA

MADISON

Okefenokee NWR boundary

Okefenokee Swamp

Suwannee River State Park

129

75

95

301

10

LIVE OAK

Osceola National Forest

Pinhook Swamp

To Waycross

Fort Clinch State Park

Amelia Island State Park

Little Talbot Island State Park

JACKSONVILLE

A1A

A1A

1

95

St. Johns River

River

Guana River Preserve (northern section of Guana-Tolomato-Matanzas National Estuarine Research Reserve)

ST. AUGUSTINE
Anastasia Island State Park

CRESCENT BEACH

Fort Matanzas National Monument

A1A

PALATKA

17

100

Oklawaha River

Orange Creek Restoration Area

STARKE

301

San Felasco Hammock State Preserve

24

Paynes Prairie Preserve State Park

CITRA

301

75

318

27

40

OCALA

Ocala National Forest

Lake George

To Leesburg

Lake Woodruff NWR

DE LAND

4

95

DAYTONA BEACH

1

To Orlando

To Melbourne

To Tampa

40

To Crystal River

GAINESVILLE

27

100

LAKE CITY

27

129

River

CHIEFLAND

129

OTTER CREEK

98

19

24

CEDAR KEY

Cedar Keys NWR

Suwannee River

19

98

51

STEIN-HATCHEE

Big Bend WMA

19

98

361

PERRY

27

To Talla-hassee

10

Gulf of Mexico

NORTHERN PENINSULA

The northern part of Florida is similar in many ways to neighboring Georgia. Many uplands contain mixed forests of Longleaf Pine, Turkey Oak, Live Oak, and other hardwoods, while Longleaf Pine flatwoods once covered other areas. Many uplands have been converted to Slash Pine plantations; paper production is one of the most important industries in the region. Extensive riparian habitats contain Bald Cypress, Tupelo, and other hardwoods. Along the Atlantic Coast, a sandy ridge that represents a former shoreline extends south all the way to Miami. This ridge formerly was covered with scrub vegetation and supported a large population of Florida Scrub-Jays that has been largely extirpated by oceanfront development. Along the Gulf coast, gently sloping topography offshore has resulted in the formation of extensive saltmarsh communities, rather than beaches and dunes. As a result, most of the area has been spared from the ravages of coastal development. In fact, virtually the entire Gulf coast between St. Marks National Wildlife Refuge and Port Richey—a stretch of more than 170 linear miles—is now in public ownership.

Most of the breeding species of the Panhandle also occur in the northern peninsula; the exceptions are Snowy Plover and White-breasted Nuthatch, and possibly also Swainson's Warbler and Louisiana Waterthrush. Species that reach their southern breeding limits in the region include Mississippi Kite, Broad-winged Hawk, Eastern Wood-Pewee, Wood Thrush, Gray Catbird, Prairie Warbler (eastern race), Hooded Warbler, Field Sparrow, and Orchard Oriole. Although Painted Buntings occur locally along the Atlantic coast south to about Merritt Island, they are easiest to find during spring and summer in the Jacksonville and St. Augustine areas. But brood parasitism by Brown-headed Cowbirds seems to have begun reducing Florida's Painted Bunting population in recent years. Breeding species of the peninsula that reach their northern limits in this region are Glossy Ibis, Mottled Duck, Short-tailed Hawk, Limpkin, Sandhill Crane, Burrowing Owl (except for a small isolated colony at Eglin Air Force Base in the western Panhandle), and Florida Scrub-Jay.

NORTHERN PENINSULA—GULF COAST

KEATON BEACH TO STEINHATCHEE

The northern peninsular Gulf coast is part of the Big Bend region of Florida, which extends west to the Alligator Point area in the eastern Panhandle. Because of the shallowness of the water offshore, wave action is insufficient to create sand beaches. Rather, coastal areas are covered extensively by *Juncus* (needle-rush) and *Spartina* (cordgrass) saltmarshes that contain populations of Black Rails (local), Clapper Rails (abundant), Marsh Wrens (common), and Seaside Sparrows (locally common). Just above the high-tide line are extensive hammocks that commonly contain Cabbage Palms, Florida's state tree (even though palms technically are not trees!) A die-off of hammocks in some coastal areas appears to be due to increased soil salinity caused by rising sea levels. Most of the Big Bend is sparsely inhabited and relatively unexplored.

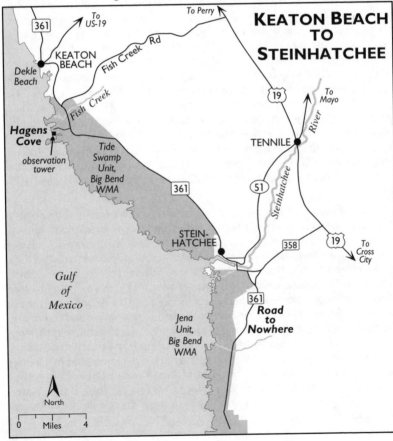

The few towns are small fishing and shellfishing villages on the Gulf, or old logging towns in a mix of light agriculture and Slash Pine silviculture inland. The state has purchased large portions of the coastal hardwood hammocks in the Big Bend, but most of these areas are inaccessible to birders in passenger vehicles. The two birding sites listed below are small and mostly lack facilities; both are part of **Big Bend Wildlife Management Area** (72,447 acres; no fee; *seasonal hunting*).

Hagens Cove (50 acres; no fee; no camping) is a non-hunted portion of Big Bend Wildlife Management Area south of Keaton Beach. The cove features a natural sand beach, rare in the region. To reach this area from US-19 south of Perry (4.5 miles from US-98), go southwest on CR-361 and turn right to Hagens Cove Road. To reach Hagens Cove from US-19 northbound, head west on SR-51 in Tennille to CR-361 in Steinhatchee and go north about 12 miles. An observation tower south of the end of the road offers a view of the surrounding marshes and mudflats. During winter, numerous ducks, shorebirds, and larids are present, and marshes contain Nelson's Sharp-tailed Sparrows. Wading birds can be common; Hagens Cove is one of the most dependable locations for Reddish Egrets in northern Florida. Impressive shorebird concentrations may be seen during fall migration. Low to mid-tide is best for observing wading birds and shorebirds. Hammocks in the area can be great for migrant landbirds during fall.

South of Steinhatchee (pronounced *STEEN-hach-ee*) is the southern terminus of **CR-361**, affectionately known as the "Road to Nowhere" because the road simply ends in a saltmarsh after traversing marshes and hammocks for about 12 miles. Most of the land along the road is part of the Wildlife Management Area. Marsh Wrens and Seaside Sparrows are common breeding residents of the marshes, and these are joined during winter by Sedge Wrens and Nelson's Sharp-tailed Sparrows. In the past, Black Rails have been found reliably in the upper marsh east of the end of the road, but some of this marsh is private property.

CEDAR KEY

Located about 20 miles southwest of US-19 at the end of SR-24 (see map on next page), Cedar Key is out of the way but worth a visit. In 1867, John Muir spent three months here after completing his famous "thousand-mile walk to the Gulf." Birders from Gainesville visit Cedar Key regularly, as it offers their nearest coastal birding. The causeway between the mainland and the islands attracts wading birds, shorebirds, and larids at low tide. During winter, numerous other species such as American White Pelican and sea ducks are present. Offshore is **Cedar Keys National Wildlife Refuge** (800 acres; no fee; no camping; *very limited access*), consisting of 12 small keys that support one of the largest wading bird rookeries in Florida. An average of 10,000 pairs nests here annually. The keys also support the northernmost roost of Magnificent Frigatebirds in Florida (300 or more birds), and during spring or summer some frigatebirds may be viewed by telescope from the airstrip, or may be seen gliding over town. To protect the birds, the interiors of the keys are off-limits year-round.

Contact: *Cedar Keys National Wildlife Refuge, 16450 NW 31st Place, Chiefland, FL 32626; 352-493-0258; <www.fws.gov/cedarkeys>.*

Return to the mainland and bear left onto CR-347 (1.0). For the next mile, land on both sides of CR-347 is part of **Cedar Key Scrub State Reserve** (5,028 acres; no fee; *seasonal hunting*), but most of the reserve is not accessible to passenger vehicles. The mainland north of Cedar Key marks the northernmost area along the Gulf coast that still supports Florida Scrub-Jays. Unfortunately, decades-long fire suppression has caused the oak scrub to become severely overgrown, and the scrub-jay population has plummeted as a consequence. Much-needed habitat restoration is taking place in the reserve, and the scrub-jay population should recover. Call the reserve for more information.

Contact: *Cedar Key Scrub State Reserve, P.O. Box 187, Cedar Key, FL 32625; 352-543-5567; <www.floridastateparks.org/cedarkeyscrub>.*

Continue north on CR-347 to CR-326 (2.2) and turn left. At the end of the road (3.5) is a large shell mound, created over hundreds of years as local Indians dumped oyster shells here. The mound is covered by large Live Oaks and is part of **Lower Suwannee National Wildlife Refuge** (52,935 acres; no fee; no camping; *seasonal hunting*), which also is largely inaccessible to passenger vehicles. The one-quarter-mile **Shell Mound Trail** (*non-hunted*) traverses hammocks that can be excellent for migrant landbirds, especially during spring. The mudflats visible from the mound may contains large numbers of wading birds and shorebirds at low tide. Huge numbers of American Oystercatchers winter in the Cedar Key area—more than 1,000 individuals in some years!—and many of these can be seen from the Shell Mound.

Contact: *Lower Suwannee National Wildlife Refuge, 16450 NW 31st Pl., Chiefland, FL 32626; 352-493-0258; <www.fws.gov/lowersuwannee>.*

Several miles inland from the coast is a large area of pine flatwoods that was purchased by the state in 1992 for $65 million. It is now known as **Goethe** (pronounced *GO-thee*) **State Forest** (53,398 acres; $1.00/person; no camping; accessible anytime; *seasonal hunting*) and supports a large population of Red-cockaded Woodpeckers. To reach the office from US-19 south of SR-24, turn northeast onto CR-121 at Lebanon (simply a sign; no town). At

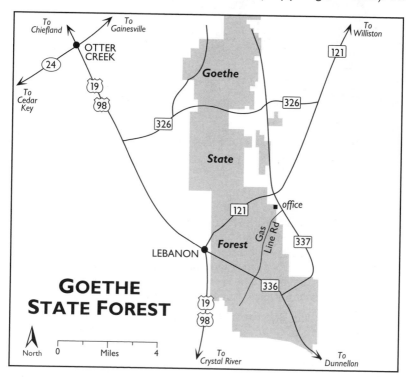

Color-banded Red-cockaded Woodpecker at its nest   Darcy Stumbaugh
in an artificial cavity implanted into a living Longleaf Pine.

CR-337 (4.9), turn right to the office on the right (0.5). Maps are available at the office. The forest contains 32 active Red-cockaded Woodpecker clusters, and cavity trees are banded with white paint. Two clusters are along Gas Line Road (a limerock road passable to all vehicles) between CR-337 and CR-336. Other species likely to be seen include Swallow-tailed Kite and Summer Tanager (spring and summer), and Brown-headed Nuthatch (year-round) and Bachman's Sparrow (mainly spring and summer).

Contact: *Goethe State Forest, 9110 Southeast County Road 337, Dunnellon, FL 34431; 352-465-8585; <www.fl-dof.com/state_forests/ Goethe.html>.*

Gulf coastal areas continue on page 110.

NORTHERN PENINSULA—INLAND

LIVE OAK AND LAKE CITY

Suwannee **River State Park** (1,858 acres; $3.00/vehicle; camping $15.00/night; opens at 8:00 AM) can be good for breeding and migrant landbirds, especially during fall. To reach it from US-129 in Live Oak, head northwest on US-90 to CR-132 (12.0). Turn right into the park. From I-10, exit at US-90 (Exit #275) and head west as above (5.0). The most productive areas are found along Limestone Spring Trail and in the portion of the park located west of the river. Bachman's Sparrows are commonly heard during spring and summer in open Longleaf Pine flatwoods.

> **Contact:** *Suwannee River State Park, 20185 County Road 132, Live Oak, FL. 32060; 386-362-2746; <www.floridastateparks.org/suwanneeriver>.*

Alligator **Lake Recreation Area** (1,000 acres; no fee; no camping; opens at 8:00 AM Saturday–Sunday, closed Monday–Tuesday, opens at 11:00 AM Wednesday–Friday) offers an easily accessible freshwater marsh surrounded by a three-mile dike (see map on next page). To reach it from US-441 in Lake City, head east on US-90 (Duval Street) to CR-133 (Old Country Club Road; 1.7). Turn right to the entrance on the right (1.7). The dike provides views of wading birds year-round and waterfowl and raptors during winter. During winter, walking along the edge of the marsh may produce Sora, Sedge Wren, and Grasshopper and Le Conte's Sparrows, while the swamps attract landbirds year-round.

> **Contact:** *Alligator Lake Recreation Area, 1498 SW Country Club Road (CR-133), Lake City, FL 32025; <www.columbiacountyfla.com/ParksandRecreation.asp>.*

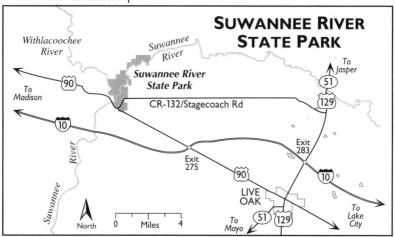

SUWANNEE RIVER STATE PARK

Withlacoochee River

Suwannee River

Suwannee River State Park

To Jasper

To Madison

CR-132/Stagecoach Rd

Exit 283

Exit 275

To Mayo

LIVE OAK

North   0   Miles   4

Suwannee River

To Lake City

OSCEOLA NATIONAL FOREST

Pinhook Swamp

To Fargo and
Athens, Georgia

Osceola

National

Forest

Big Gum
Swamp
Wilderness

To
Taylor

250

441

Exit
303

To
I-75

10

250

250A

268

10

241

207

To
Jacksonville

25A 441

250

278

216

250A

Still Rd

Ocean
Pond

278

215

241

90

100

90

241

national
forest
headquarters

OLUSTEE

LAKE
CITY

To
Live
Oak

441

10A

rest stop &
interpretive
trail

Olustee
Battlefield
Historic
State Park

245

100

133

To I-75 and
High Springs **Alligator
Lake
Recreation
Area**

Country
Club Rd

North

0

Miles

4

Northeast of Live Oak is **OSCEOLA NATIONAL FOREST** (198,484 acres; no fee; 67 campsites at Ocean Pond at $8.00–$18.00/day; accessible anytime; *seasonal hunting*), which contains some of the most extensive pine flatwoods remaining in the region. Characteristic species include Red-cockaded Woodpecker (66 clusters in 2000), Red-headed Woodpecker, Brown-headed Nuthatch, Eastern Bluebird, Eastern Wood-Pewee, Pine Warbler, and Bachman's Sparrow. The headquarters (open Monday through Friday, 7:30 AM–4:00 PM) are located on the south side of US-90 in Olustee about 12 miles east of US-441. Here you can obtain a Forest Service map that shows the locations of some of the Red-cockaded Woodpecker clusters. For a popular birding route, head west from the headquarters on US-90 to Still Road (7.7, or 4.4 miles east of US-441) and turn north. At FR-278 (2.0), turn right. Many Red-cockaded Woodpecker cavity trees (marked with white paint) are along this road, and Brown-headed Nuthatches and Bachman's

Sparrows are common throughout. At FR-215 (5), turn right to return to US-90 at the Mount Carrie rest stop, which has a one-mile interpretive trail. An alternate route from US-90 is to drive north on FR-215 to FR-216 (1.7). Turn right to FR-241 (2.4) and turn left onto (paved) CR-250A (2.9). At (paved) FR-268 (0.3), turn right to Ocean Pond, a large natural pond that may contain wintering ducks and other species. The woods surrounding the pond are good for landbirds at all seasons. Ocean Pond may also be reached from US-90 by heading north on CR-250A and turning left onto FR-268 (4.0). To exit the forest, return to US-90. Head east to access I-10 toward Jacksonville, or go west to reach US-441 and I-10 at Lake City.

History buffs may be interested in the **Olustee Battlefield Historic State Park** (no fee; no camping; opens at 8:00 AM), which commemorates the largest Civil War battle fought in Florida. The Battle of Olustee, 20 February 1864, resulted in more than 2,700 (mostly Union) casualties among an estimated 10,000 troops. Trails in the park are good for Red-cockaded Woodpecker and Bachman's Sparrow. A service road leads from the restrooms to a woodpecker cluster in about 0.25 mile. Sparrows may be heard from March to August throughout the flatwoods, including along the Battle of Olustee interpretive trail that begins near the restrooms.

> **Contacts:** *Osceola National Forest, P.O. Box 70, Olustee, FL 32072; 386-752-2577; <www.southernregion.fs.fed.us/florida/recreation/index_osc.shtml>*
> *Olustee Battlefield Historic State Park, P. O. Box 40, Olustee, Fl 32072; 386-758-0400; <www.floridastateparks.org/olustee>.*

North of Osceola National Forest is **Okefenokee National Wildlife Refuge** (396,000 acres, no access to the Florida acreage), located almost entirely in Georgia. Between the refuge and the forest is Pinhook Swamp, *240 square miles* of cypress swamp, wet pinewoods, and other habitats. Public purchase of this vast area, home to numerous Threatened or Endangered species, has been one of the top priorities of the state of Florida for several years. To date, more than 110,000 acres have been protected, at a cost of $60 million. Lands are added to Osceola National Forest as they are acquired.

GAINESVILLE

PAYNES PRAIRIE PRESERVE STATE PARK (20,958 acres; 50 campsites at $15.00/day; opens at 8:00 AM), a National Natural Landmark, is one of the most popular birding sites in northern Florida. William Bartram visited this wet prairie in 1774, when a large Seminole settlement was located along the shores of Alachua (pronounced *a-LA-chu-a*) Lake. Evidence shows that other Indians had lived here at least 9,000 years ago. During the Spanish years of the 1600s, the state's largest cattle ranch occupied the site. From late November to mid-February, many birders come to see the few

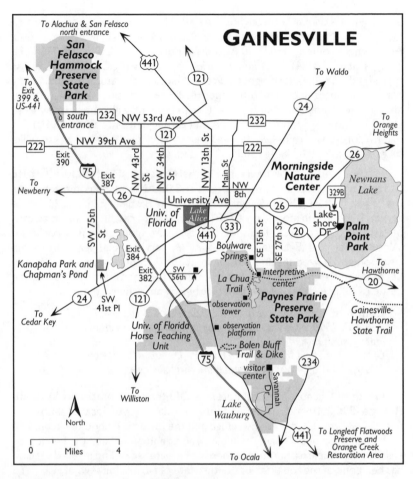

thousand wintering Greater Sandhill Cranes. In addition, the park hosts small reintroduced populations of American Bison and wild horses. On warm days in February and March, dozens of American Alligators bask on the canal banks along La Chua Trail. Visitors during spring and fall may be treated to a dazzling display of wildflowers.

La Chua Trail, on the north side of the prairie, offers the best birding in the park (although portions of this trail and the Bolen Bluff Trail were flooded during the 2004 hurricanes, and remained inaccessible in August 2005). To reach the trail from US-441 in Gainesville, go east on SR-26 to SE 15th Street (2.1) and turn right. Where the road turns sharply left (2.4), continue straight ahead onto the driveway (Camp Ranch Road) and park across from the headquarters building (0.5). Walk past the Interpretive Center and follow the path to the prairie. This entrance is open 8:00 AM–5:00 PM, Monday–Friday. Weekend visitors can reach La Chua Trail via the Gainesville–Hawthorne State Trail, which is accessed from the back of Boulware Springs Water Works, a city park located 0.5 mile north on SE 15th Street. Ranger-led tours are conducted on weekend mornings, November–April. Destinations alternate between La Chua Trail and a "Rim Ramble" to otherwise off-limits Persimmon Point, which is notable for its frequent sightings of Henslow's Sparrows during winter. Call 352-466-4100 for reservations.

La Chua Trail is a 1.3-mile-long levee trail that parallels a canal through open fields, extensive cattail marshes, and a lotus pond before ending at an observation tower on the shore of Alachua Lake. The best birding here is during late fall and winter, when Bald Eagles, Sandhill Cranes (hundreds or thousands may be observed from the observation tower), and many other species are likely to be seen. American Bitterns and Grasshopper, Lincoln's, and White-crowned Sparrows are rare but regular. During spring and summer, Least Bitterns and Purple Gallinules breed on the lake, Mississippi Kites are often seen overhead, and Blue Grosbeaks and Indigo Buntings breed in brushy areas.

To reach other parts of the park from Gainesville, go south on US-441 until you see extensive marshes on both sides of the road. Look for a 200-foot-long observation platform on the left. During winter afternoons, this is a good spot for watching the flocks of cranes and wading birds fly in to roost. Continue south on US-441 to the **Bolen Bluff Trail** parking area on the left (1.3). From here, a 1.3-mile loop leads through a mixed hardwood forest to a levee that extends 3,000 feet into the prairie. The trail can be very good during fall migration; more than 15 species of warblers have been reported here on some days, with Blue-winged, Golden-winged, Cerulean, Worm-eating, and Kentucky Warblers all regular. Thrushes are also seen frequently. The levee offers good winter birding for Sedge and Marsh Wrens and sparrows.

Farther south along US-441 is the park's **main entrance** ($4.00/vehicle) on the left (3.5). Follow Savannah Drive to the Lake Wauberg turn-off (1.1) and turn left onto the Lake Wauberg Road. This road can be good for Wild Turkeys, especially during winter. The road passes Puc Puggy campground before leading to the lake. (Puc Puggy was the Seminole name given to William Bartram; it meant "Flower Hunter".) During winter, Bald Eagles should be seen over the lake, and Orange-crowned, Yellow-throated, and other wintering warblers are fairly common in woods around the parking lot.

Return to Savannah Drive, turn left, and continue to the **visitor center** parking lot. The woods here, including the short Wacahoota Trail and the picnic area, can be good for migrant landbirds. This area is also the access point for the Cones Dike Trail. This four-mile trail should produce King Rails year-round and Soras and Marsh Wrens during winter. The most distant portion can be excellent for Least Bitterns and Purple Gallinules during spring and summer, and for sparrows during winter; it is the best spot in the park for Lincoln's Sparrow. The trail offers your best chance for spotting Sandhill Cranes during spring and summer, and bison and wild horses year-round.

Contact: Paynes Prairie Preserve State Park, 100 Savannah Boulevard, Micanopy, FL 32667; 352-466-3397; <www.floridastateparks.org/ paynesprairie>.

SAN FELASCO HAMMOCK PRESERVE STATE PARK (6,927 acres; $2.00/vehicle, $1.00/bicycle or pedestrian; no camping; opens at 8:00 AM) is located northwest of Gainesville. To reach the **south entrance** from SR-26, go north on US-441 to CR-232 (NW 53rd Avenue; 3.7), and turn left. Continue west to the parking area on the left (7.6). Mosquitoes can be a nuisance, so bring repellent. Acadian Flycatchers, Wood Thrushes, and Hooded Warblers breed in the hardwood forests. During fall, migrant landbirds are a special attraction. About 20 miles of trails are located in the hammock north of the road, including two loop trails of about five and six miles in length, respectively. The six-mile Spring Grove Loop has breeding Eastern Wood-Pewees and Yellow-throated Vireos. To reach the park's **north entrance**, exit I-75 (#399) at US-441 and head south to Progress Boulevard (2.8). Turn right to the gate (0.7). The 20-plus miles of trails were established for cyclists and equestrians, but the Cottontail Loop and Cellon Creek Trail can provide excellent birding for migrant landbirds and typical breeding species.

Contact: San Felasco Hammock Preserve State Park, 4732 Millhopper Road, Gainesville, FL 32653; 352-955-2008; <www.floridastateparks.org/ sanfelascohammock>.

Lake Alice (200 acres; no fee; no camping; accessible anytime), located on the campus of the University of Florida, is an excellent downtown birding spot. To reach it from SR-26 (University Avenue), travel south on US-441 to Museum Drive (0.5) and turn right into the campus. The parking area for the gardens and lake is on the left (1.0). To reach the lake from SR-24, go north on SR-121 to Radio Road (1.0) and turn right. At Museum Drive (0.5), turn left to the garden parking lot on the right (0.5). The gardens and surrounding areas can be good for migrant landbirds during spring and fall. Bobolinks are annual in late April and early May. A small boardwalk offers a view of the lake, where Least Bitterns and Purple Gallinules breed. Limpkins have occurred here but are sporadic.

Morningside Nature Center (278 acres; no fee; no camping; 9:00 AM–5:00 PM daily) is a good spot for Brown-headed Nuthatches and a few Eastern Wood-Pewees, along with other pinewoods species. From US-441, go east on SR-26 to the entrance on the left (3.7). Other birds likely to be seen here are Eastern Bluebirds and Pine Warblers and, during spring and summer, Summer Tanagers. There are 7.5 miles of trails in the park.

Sandhill Crane with colt.   Arthur Morris/www.birdsasart.com

From Morningside Nature Center, head east on SR-26. Where the road veers left (1.1), continue straight ahead on CR-329B (Lakeshore Drive) to Newnans Lake. At the lake, turn right, then left after a few hundred feet. Continue to **Palm Point Park** (2.0), watching carefully for the parking lot on the left. Bird the oaks and cypresses at the point, then return to the parking lot and walk north along Lakeshore Drive. This area contains breeding Bald Eagles and Prothonotary Warblers. During fall migration, the area can be excellent for landbirds, with Blue-winged, Golden-winged, Tennessee, and Ce-rulean Warblers, both waterthrushes, and Scarlet Tanager among the species observed regularly. Newnans Lake has produced some amazing finds during hurricanes, including Black-capped Petrel, Magnificent Frigatebird, Pomarine and Parasitic Jaegers, Sooty Tern, and American Oystercatcher.

Mississippi Kite is a fairly common breeding species (late April–mid-August) on the north rim of Paynes Prairie and throughout Gainesville. The birds often can be seen by simply driving city streets, especially from mid-July to mid-August. Your best bets are east-west thorough-fares in the northwest part of town as well as SW 75th Street, where Kanapaha Park at the corner of SW 75th Street and SW 41st Place offers a good vantage point. Black-bellied Whistling-Duck is a recent colonizer from the south at Chapman's Pond along SW 41st Place on the east side of Kanapaha Park. During spring and summer, dozens may also congregate around a small pond at the University of Florida's Horse Teaching Unit. From I-75 exit (#387) at SR-121 and go east to SW 34th Street (0.2; first traffic light). Turn right to SW 56th Avenue (0.25; sand road) and turn left. Continue to the signs for the Horse Teaching Unit; the pond is on the right just before the road turns left (1.3).

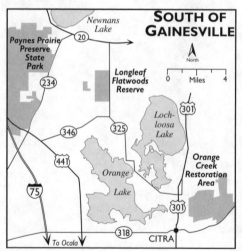

South of Gainesville are two additional sites worth a visit. The first, **Longleaf Flatwoods Reserve** (1,388 acres; no fee; no camping), is a newly-opened area of high-quality flatwoods and oak uplands. Red-headed Wood-pecker and Bachman's Spar-row are fairly easy to find along the White loop, and other pinewoods species such as Brown-headed Nuthatch, Yellow-throated Vireo (spring and summer), Summer Tana-ger (spring and summer), and Eastern Towhee are also present. **Orange Creek Restoration Area** (3,512 acres, no fee; no camp-ing) is composed of former agricultural lands being restored to wetlands. To reach it from US-301 at Citra, go east on CR-318 to the entrance on the left (3.1); the gate may be false-locked. Levees offer good views of the marshes. Trails along the north and south edges of the marsh are good for wrens, spar-rows, and other brush-loving species during winter. Wetlands and adjacent habitats support waterfowl, American Bitterns, and Marsh Wrens during win-ter, and Mottled Ducks, Purple Gallinules, Blue Grosbeaks, and Indigo Buntings during spring and summer. The area is closed irregularly during hunting seasons; the hunting schedule is available at <www.myfwc.com/hunting>.

Contact: *St. Johns River Water Management District, 4049 Reid St., Palatka, FL 32178; 386-329-4404; <www.sjrwmd.com>.*

Birders who are planning an extended visit to the Gainesville area should consider purchasing the excellent regional guide, *A Birdwatcher's Guide to Alachua County, Florida* by Rex Rowan and Mike Manetz. A revised edition is anticipated in 2006.

OCALA

Ocala **National Forest** (382,664 acres; no fee), established in 1908, is the southernmost national forest in the continental U.S. and was the first to be established east of the Mississippi River. Species of interest in the forest include Swallow-tailed Kite, Red-cockaded Woodpecker, Florida

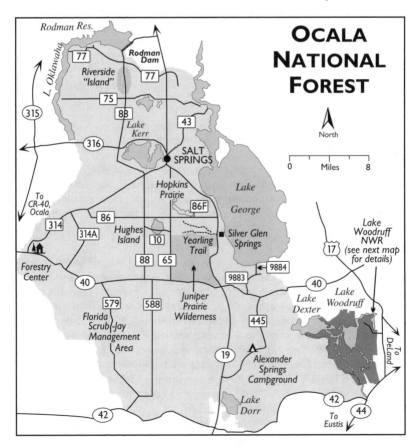

Scrub-Jay, and Bachman's Sparrow. Ocala National Forest is devoted mostly to the cultivation of Sand Pines, which are clear-cut and used as pulpwood. The pines are endemic to xeric (extremely well-drained) sandy soils. Ocala National Forest contains the most extensive patch of xeric oak scrub remaining in the world: more than 200,000 acres. Other habitats include are Longleaf Pine "islands", oak hammocks, and Slash Pine flatwoods. Prairie lakes are found in scattered locations, and bottomland hardwood forests grow along the St. Johns and Ocklawaha Rivers, Lake George, and around several springs. Most of the roads in the forest are unpaved but graded regularly.

Florida Scrub-Jays are common in areas clear-cut from four to 15 years previously, especially in the "Big Scrub", which is approximately 10 miles wide and runs north-south through the middle of the forest. In 2003, there were between 750 and 800 groups of scrub-jays in the forest, the largest population remaining in the world. Because forestry practices here discourage long-term occupancy by scrub-jays, sites are ephemeral, each supporting a population for about 10 years before the birds must move to more suitable sites. Search for areas with oak cover from three to seven feet tall interspersed with patches of open sand, and with little to no pine overstory. Scrub-jays can be found along most roads west of SR-19 (except in the westernmost parts of the forest). Two areas currently good for finding jays are Yearling Trail on the west side of SR-19 (5.1 miles north of SR-40) and the Florida Scrub-Jay Management Area on FR-579 (3.7–5.7 miles south of SR-40). Scrub-jays should persist at these locations through at least 2015.

The forest also supports at least 25 clusters of Red-cockaded Woodpeckers. The most accessible site is Riverside Island, an "island" of Longleaf Pines surrounded by scrub. From SR-19 at Salt Springs, drive west on CR-316 to FR-88 (6.1). Turn right and watch for the white-banded trees beginning at FR-75 (4.4). Several woodpecker clusters occur along the next three miles of FR-88. As with other sites, be at a cavity before dawn or dusk and watch from a non-intrusive distance. These flatwoods also support Bachman's Sparrows (conspicuous when males are singing, in spring and summer) and Brown-headed Nuthatches year-round.

A few other species of interest are found in scrub habitats. The Southeastern American Kestrel is a common permanent resident, owing to a successful nest-box program. Kestrels are found primarily in recently clear-cut scrub with scattered mature pines and snags. (Note that wintering northern American Kestrels occur throughout the forest from about October to mid-April). Red-headed Woodpeckers also are found year-round but are most common spring through fall. Yearling Trail is a good spot at present. Elsewhere, watch for Swallow-tailed Kites (March–July) virtually anywhere, but mostly around the Juniper Prairie Wilderness Area and near the Ocklawaha River at the northern end of the forest. Mixed-species flocks of wintering landbirds sometimes numbering in the hundreds of individuals (mostly Pine Warblers) are found in mature Sand Pine stands. Golden-crowned Kinglets, rare so far south, occasionally accompany these flocks. Yellow Palm Warblers reach the southern limit of their winter range here and are nearly as common as the western subspecies. Also during winter, red-eyed Eastern Towhees mingle with the resident pale-yellow-eyed subspecies.

Ocala National Forest contains two of Florida's 27 first-magnitude springs—Alexander Springs (76 million gallons/day) and Silver Glen Springs (70 million gallons/day)—along with 20 smaller springs. These springs are interesting to see, but the areas around them contain few birds not found elsewhere in the forest. Among the "springs specialties", Ruby-throated Hummingbirds and Red-eyed Vireos are regular during spring and summer. Acadian Flycatchers and Hooded and Prothonotary Warblers may also be seen, but all are more common along the Ocklawaha River. Of the four developed springs, Alexander Springs (5.1 miles east of SR-19 on CR-445) has the best birding possibilities. There is a mile-long nature trail near the swimming area, which can produce Limpkins year-round and migrant landbirds during fall. Short-tailed Hawks have been seen soaring over CR-445 near the entrance road during summer.

The forests surrounding Rodman Reservoir at Rodman Dam (perhaps soon to be eliminated as part of the Oklawaha River restoration, although the dam has powerful political allies) contain numerous Bald Eagle nests. To reach the reservoir, go northeast on SR-19 to FR-77 and turn left. At FR-88 (4.0) turn right to the dam (1.0). Numerous ducks usually winter on the lake, and Swallow-tailed Kites are found during spring and summer. Lake George is another area good for waterbirds, and it contains one of the highest densities of nesting Bald Eagles in the United States, with about 80 active nests in 2003. To reach the lake from Salt Springs on SR-19, go northeast on CR-43 to the lake (7.0). To reach another part of the lake from the south, go east on SR-40 to FR-9883 (Blue Creek Road). Turn left to unmarked FR-9884 (2.5) and turn left to the lake (1.0).

> **Contacts:** *Ocklawaha Visitor Center, 3199 Northeast Highway 315, Silver Springs, FL 34488; 352-236-0288. Pittman Visitor Center, 45621 State Highway 19, Altoona, FL 32702; 352-669-7495.*
> *Salt Springs Visitor Center (9:00 AM–5:00 PM, closed on holidays, 14100 North State Highway 19, Salt Springs, FL 32134; 352-685-3070.*
> *<www.southernregion.fs.fed.us/florida>.*

DELAND

Lake **Woodruff National Wildlife Refuge** (21,599 acres; no fee; no camping; *seasonal hunting*) is a good spot for waterbirds, primarily during winter. To reach it from Lake George, travel east on SR-40 and turn right onto US-17. At West Retta Street in DeLeon Springs (6.9), turn right. After one block, turn left onto CR-4053 (Grand Avenue) to Mud Lake Road (0.6). Turn right to the Visitor's Center (open Monday–Friday, 8:00 AM–4:30 PM; *closed weekends*) on the right (0.1), or continue west to the entrance (0.5). From the

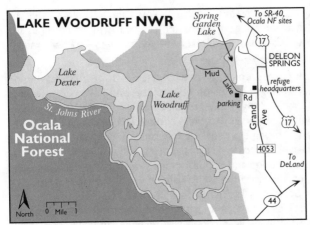

east or south, exit I-4 (#118) at SR-44 and head west. At CR-4053 (Grand Avenue; 7.7). turn right to Mud Lake Road (5.7), then turn left to the entrance. Much of the refuge is composed of wetlands. Most birders head to the impound- ments at the end of the road, where wading birds and alligators are numerous. An observation tower on the opposite side of the impoundments offers a good view of the area.

Wintering waterfowl are dependent on water levels, but Blue-winged Teal should be common and often are joined by Northern Shovelers, American Wigeon, and Green-winged Teal. Ring-necked Ducks and Lesser Scaup frequent the larger water bodies such as Spring Garden Lake. Wood Ducks are resident. Wading birds can be found year-round, and American Bitterns are regular winter residents. The refuge contains what is currently the second-largest Swallow-tailed Kite roost in the U.S., with as many as 500–600 kites present during July and August. The location of the roost is not publicized (to avoid disturbance), but kites can be seen over most of the refuge during the day; they often feed on the abundant dragonflies.

The refuge has widespread habitat suitable for Black Rail, and the species has been heard on a few occasions. Search marshes with water present in shallow pools that are not completely flooded. Use tapes sparingly to avoid harassing the rails excessively. Limpkins are resident. Shorebirds can be common during migration when water levels are favorable; Black-necked Stilts may breed in the impoundments. Landbird diversity is low around the impoundments, but hammocks can be good for migrant landbirds during fall. Barred Owls are fairly common residents. During winter, flocks of Tree Swallows may number in the hundreds of thousands of individuals, and these can be seen near dusk over the marshes. Marsh Wrens, Sedge Wrens, and Swamp Sparrows can be found during winter in grassy fields or brushy thickets around the impoundments.

Contact: *Lake Woodruff National Wildlife Refuge, P.O. Box 488, Mud Lake Road, DeLeon Springs, FL 32130-0488, 386-985-4673; <http:// lakewoodruff.fws.gov>.*

Inland areas continue on page 142.

NORTHERN PENINSULA—ATLANTIC COAST

AMELIA ISLAND

Across the St. Marys River from Cumberland Island, Georgia, is Amelia Island. Although Florida's northernmost barrier island is undergoing rapid development, several birding sites have been preserved. At the very northern tip of the island is **FORT CLINCH STATE PARK** (1,119 acres; $5.00/vehicle; 62 campsites at $22.00/day; opens at 8:00 AM). Fort Clinch had its origin in 1847 as one of a series of fortifications along the southern Atlantic coast. During the Civil War, it allowed the Union Army to control the adjacent Georgia and Florida coastlines. To reach the park, exit I-95 (#373) onto SR-200/A1A (Buccaneer Trail) and head east across the Amelia River. Once on Amelia Island, continue north on SR-A1A through the town of Fernandina Beach, bearing right onto Centre Street (which shortly changes to Atlantic Avenue). The park is on the left (1.5). From the south, simply follow (another section of) SR-A1A north from Jacksonville; Atlantic Avenue is 17 miles north of Little Talbot Island State Park, which is described in the next section, Jacksonville. **Willow Pond Nature Trail** on the west side of the main road (north of the road to the beach) is good for migrant and wintering landbirds. Painted Buntings breed here during spring and summer. The fishing pier probably is the most reliable spot in Florida for Purple Sandpiper; several winter here every year. During high tide, they often sit on the seawall with Ruddy Turnstones. The pier is a good spot from which to scan for sea ducks and larids, primarily during winter.

Contact: *Fort Clinch State Park, 2601 Atlantic Avenue, Fernandina Beach, FL 32034; 904-277-7274; <www.floridastateparks.org/fortclinch>.*

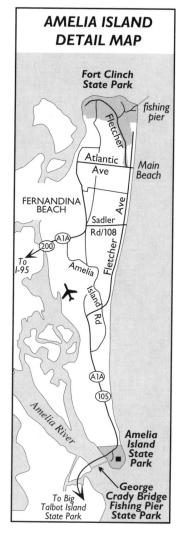

AMELIA ISLAND DETAIL MAP

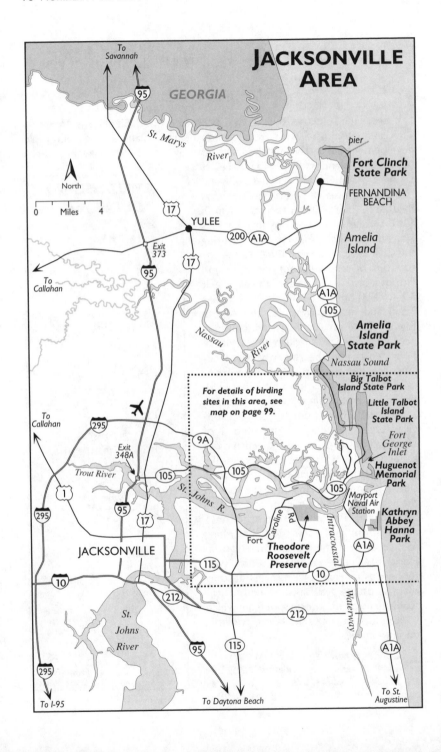

JACKSONVILLE AREA

To Savannah

GEORGIA

95

St. Marys River

North

0 Miles 4

17

YULEE

200 A1A

Exit 373

17

95

To Callahan

Nassau River

pier

Fort Clinch State Park

FERNANDINA BEACH

Amelia Island

A1A

105

Amelia Island State Park

Nassau Sound

Big Talbot Island State Park

Little Talbot Island State Park

For details of birding sites in this area, see map on page 99.

To Callahan

295

Exit 348A

Trout River

105

9A

105

1

295

95

17

JACKSONVILLE

115

St. Johns R.

Caroline Rd

Fort

Theodore Roosevelt Preserve

Fort George Inlet

Huguenot Memorial Park

Mayport Naval Air Station

Kathryn Abbey Hanna Park

A1A

10

212

10

St. Johns River

212

95

115

Intracoastal

Waterway

A1A

295

To I-95

To Daytona Beach

To St. Augustine

The section of SR-A1A between Fernandina Beach and Jacksonville is known as Buccaneer Trail. This scenic drive offers many oceanside spots from which to scan for Red-throated Loons, all three scoters (but predominantly Black Scoters), and Pomarine and Parasitic Jaegers from late fall through winter. Because you will be viewing the birds from ocean-level, it is best to pick days with calm or moderate winds (windy days create distortion that hampers viewing). The first of these coastal spots as you work south is **Main Beach**. To reach it from Fort Clinch, return to Atlantic Avenue and head east. Follow this until it intersects SR-A1A and continue straight ahead to the parking area (0.2). This is a good vantage point to scan the ocean; you may also walk the beach in either direction, scanning the ocean as you go. The next spot south is **Sadler Road** (CR-108; 2.0). A small public parking lot on the beach is a great place to observe migrating or wintering seabirds. There are several other well-marked beach access spots on Amelia Island, among the ever-growing number of shops and private gated subdivisions. The entrance to **Amelia Island State Park** (230 acres; $1.00/person; camping; open 24 hours, beach driving only during daylight hours) is on the left (8.6). This site is best during winter, when seabirds, ducks, and shorebirds may be seen. Larids roost at the south tip of the island. The old SR-A1A bridge has been converted to a fishing pier and is now a state park—**George Crady Bridge Fishing Pier State Park** ($1.00/person; no camping; open 24 hours). The entrance is through Amelia Island State Park. This mile-long pier, with access to the sound, is an excellent place to look for ducks, loons, and larids.

Contacts: *Amelia Island State Park, 12157 Heckscher Drive, Jacksonville, FL 32226; 904-251-2320; <www.floridastateparks.org/ameliaisland>. George Crady Bridge Fishing Pier State Park, 12157 Heckscher Drive, Jacksonville, FL 32226; 904-251-2320; <www.floridastateparks.org/ nassausound>.*

JACKSONVILLE

With a population approaching 900,000, a busy commercial seaport, a major airport, and two naval stations, Jacksonville is a major financial, transportation, and business center. It is also Florida's most expansive city; the whole of Duval County lies within the Jacksonville city limits. The city is divided by the St. Johns River, Florida's longest, which flows north from near Vero Beach to the Atlantic Ocean just east of Jacksonville's industrial center. Birding sites are found on both sides of the river, and those to the north extend to Amelia Island (described above). Because most birders will be approaching this area from the west (as opposed to from the north), the sites are organized here beginning from the St. Johns River and continuing *north-*

ward to the Nassau River. Sites lying south of the St. Johns River are listed after these, and follow the more conventional north-to-south arrangement.

From downtown Jacksonville, exit I-95 (#348A) onto SR-105 (Heckscher Drive) and head east. Pass the St. Johns River Ferry crossing (15.3) to Fort George Road (0.5). Turn left and follow the signs to **Kingsley Plantation** (no fee; no camping; opens at 9:00 AM) on **FORT GEORGE ISLAND**. This site is one of several within the National Park Service's **Timucuan** (pronounced *TIM-a-kwan*) **Ecological and Historic Preserve** (46,000 acres); sites are listed here individually. The 18th-century Kingsley Plantation House is the oldest such structure existing in Florida. If you have time, a tour offers insights into the plantation era of Florida. Fort George Island is best for migrant landbirds during spring and fall, and for Painted Buntings, which are common breeders in the woods and along marsh edges during spring and summer. Summer Tanagers also breed here. From Kingsley, turn left at the front gate and continue birding along the 4.4-mile loop road. The recently restored **Ribault Club Visitor Center** (1.1) has exhibits about the island's history. Pick up a map that shows the location of trails on the former golf course, which is reverting to native habitats. You can park and walk along the loop road, but use care, as parts of the road are narrow and winding. Most of the loop road winds through state-owned land on Fort George Island.

Contacts: *Kingsley Plantation, 11676 Palmetto Avenue, Jacksonville, FL 32226; 904-251-3537, <www.nps.gov/timu>.*

The best spot locally for shorebirds and larids is **HUGUENOT MEMORIAL PARK** (449 acres; 50¢/person; camping $5.00–7.00 plus tax/day; opens at 8:00 AM), a sandspit that juts out from the mouth of the St. Johns River into Fort George Inlet. To reach the park from Kingsley Plantation, return to Heckscher Drive and turn left. At the blinking light (0.8), turn right to the entrance station ahead. To reach the best areas of the park, follow the paved road and then turn left just before the pavement ends. Head to the inlet beach area, park above high tide level, and walk north. Most of the shorebirds are found along the mudflats and sandbars of Fort George Inlet. During migration and winter, a dozen or more species may be found here; low tide is best. Reddish Egrets are often seen from late summer through fall. During spring and summer, the beach supports a sizable larid colony, with thousands of Laughing Gulls, hundreds of Royal Terns, and smaller numbers of Gull-billed and Least Terns. During fall migration, hundreds of Common and Black Terns roost on the flats. From here you can either walk or drive the beach road cut through the dune to the ocean. To look for Purple Sandpipers (a few are usually found every winter), head south to the north jetty area; high tide is best. Lapland Longspurs have been seen in the dunes the past few winters. Watch for sea ducks, loons, and jaegers offshore.

Other spots for roosting shorebirds and larids are the sandspit between the jetty and the St. Johns River, or the north end of the dunes. These are the

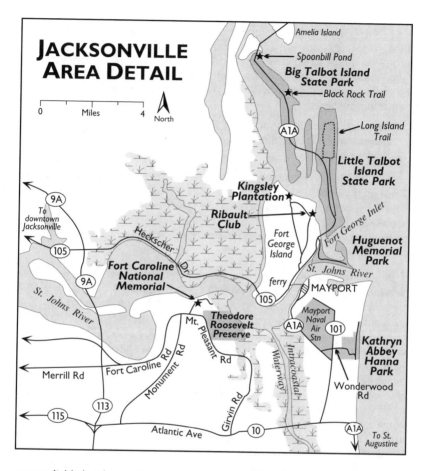

JACKSONVILLE AREA DETAIL

0 Miles 4

North

Amelia Island

Spoonbill Pond

Big Talbot Island State Park

Black Rock Trail

A1A

Long Island Trail

Little Talbot Island State Park

Kingsley Plantation ★

Ribault Club

Fort George Island

Fort George Inlet

Huguenot Memorial Park

9A

To downtown Jacksonville

105

Heckscher Dr

St. Johns River

Fort Caroline National Memorial

9A

St. Johns River

ferry

MAYPORT

105

Mayport Naval Air Stn

A1A

101

Theodore Roosevelt Preserve

Kathryn Abbey Hanna Park

Mt. Pleasant Rd

Intracoastal Waterway

Wonderwood Rd

Merrill Rd

Fort Caroline Rd

Monument Rd

Girvin Rd

113

115

Atlantic Ave

10

A1A

To St. Augustine

most reliable local spots for "white-winged" and "black-backed" gulls. Lesser Black-backed Gulls are most easily found during October but should be looked for year-round. Great Black-backed Gulls are common, and one or two Glaucous Gulls are observed almost annually. During migration, the shrubs and small trees between the entrance station and the park restrooms can be excellent for landbirds; note that the trails leading into these areas are primitive. This is also an excellent area for wintering sparrows.

Contact: *Huguenot Memorial Park, 10980 Heckscher Drive, Jacksonville, FL 32226; 904-251-3335; <www.coj.net/Departments/Parks+and+ Recreation/Recreation+Activities/oceanfront+parks.htm>.*

To reach **LITTLE TALBOT ISLAND STATE PARK** (2,500 acres; $4.00/vehicle; 40 campsites at $19.00/day; opens at 8:00 AM) return to Heckscher Drive (SR-A1A) and go north across the Fort George River to the park on the right (3.6 from Huguenot). The extreme north end of the beach may contain large numbers of shorebirds and an assortment of larids from fall through spring. Recently, a Snowy Plover has wintered in this area. A good spot from which to observe loons and grebes is the beach boardwalk at the first parking area. In November and December, scoters, mergansers, and other ducks pass by in numbers. The nature trail can be good for migrant and wintering landbirds.

Contact: Little Talbot Island State Park, 12157 Heckscher Drive, Jacksonville, FL 32226; 904-251-2320; <www.floridastateparks.org/littletalbotisland>.

Continue north on SR-A1A to the trailhead parking area of **Long Island Trail** on the right (0.6). The trail traverses the edges of the marsh and maritime hammock, and a variety of waterbirds and landbirds can be observed, especially Seaside (resident) and sharp-tailed (winter) sparrows. Conditions of the trail are subject to tide levels and some parts may be impassable; boots are recommended.

Return to SR-A1A and continue north. The entrance to Black Rock Trail (no fee), a part of **BIG TALBOT ISLAND STATE PARK** (1,708 acres; $1.00/person; no camping; opens at 8:00 AM), is on the right (2.5). This fairly short trail leads through wind-pruned oaks to the ocean. During migration, warblers and other landbirds can be found feeding at eye-level. The main entrance to Big Talbot is farther north (0.9). Besides having one of the most scenic beaches in northeastern Florida, the park's maritime hammock on old ocean bluffs serves as a trap for migrant landbirds. Trails are located both east and west of SR-A1A; use care when crossing the highway. The beach and mudflats at Big Talbot are good for shorebirds, primarily during low tide. To reach a spot known to locals as Spoonbill Pond, continue north to the boat ramp (0.7; $1.00/vehicle). The pond, which is across the road, is a reliable spot for wading birds year-round, wintering ducks, and migrant and wintering shorebirds. You may view the pond from a closed pull-off along the pond's edge, but *do not park your vehicle here.*

Contact: Big Talbot Island State Park, 12157 Heckscher Dr., Jacksonville, FL 32226; 904-251-2320; <www.floridastateparks.org/bigtalbotisland>.

Continuing northward on SR-A1A leads to the Nassau River and Amelia Island; see the previous section.

The south bank of the St. Johns River also provides good birding opportunities. The woodlands of **Fort Caroline National Memorial** (no fee; no camping; opens at 9:00 AM) and **Theodore Roosevelt Preserve** (600 acres; no fee; no camping; opens at 6:00 AM)—both part of **Timucuan Ecological and Historic Preserve** (46,425 acres)—can produce migrant and wintering landbirds. To reach the memorial from Heckscher Drive (SR-105), take SR-9A south across the impressive Napoleon Broward Bridge (known locally as Dames Point Bridge). Stay in the right lane, exit onto Southside

Laughing Gull on Brown Pelican.

Arthur Morris/www.birdsasart.com

Connector (first exit), and continue to the traffic light. At Merrill Road (0.8), turn left. Head east on Merrill Road, which merges with Fort Caroline Road (0.7). Continue to the memorial on the left (4.0). Fort Caroline was built by French Huguenots in 1564, but no part of the fort survives today. The National Park Service has built a two-thirds-scale replica of the fort, which may be walked. The nature trail and the trail by Spanish Pond (across the road) are the best areas to search for birds. Adjacent to the memorial to the east and located on St. Johns Bluff is **Theodore Roosevelt Preserve**. The preserve contains several miles of trails that lead through a hardwood hammock to saltmarshes and tidal creeks. Maps are available at the Fort Caroline visitor center. From the memorial entrance, turn right and return to Fort Caroline Road. Turn left (the road name changes to Mount Pleasant Road) and then left onto the road signed for Trailhead Parking (1.1).

Contacts: *Fort Caroline National Memorial and Theodore Roosevelt Preserve, 12713 Fort Caroline Road, Jacksonville, FL 32225; 904-641-7155; <www.nps.gov/foca>.*

Across the Intracoastal Waterway is **Kathryn Abbey Hanna Park** (450 acres; $1.00/person; nearly 300 campsites at $13.00–18.00 plus tax/day; opens at 8:00 AM), a city park adjacent to Mayport Naval Station. To reach it from Heckscher Drive, take the ferry across the St. Johns River and continue south on SR-A1A. At Wonderwood Road (2.3), turn left to the park at its end (1.2). From Fort Caroline or Roosevelt Preserve, head east on Mount Pleasant

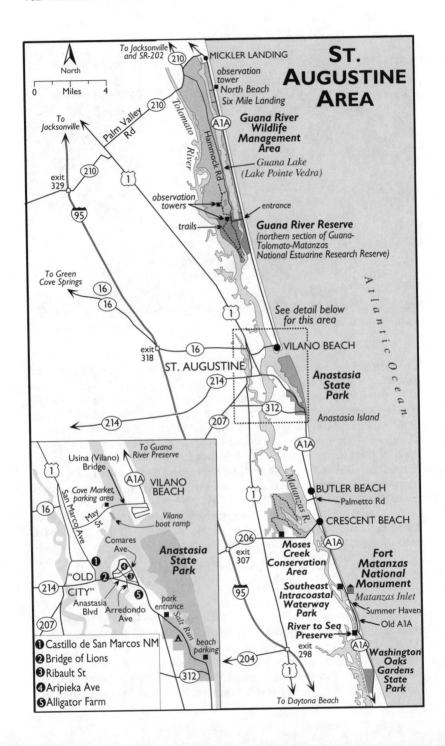

North

0 Miles 4

To Jacksonville
and SR-202

MICKLER LANDING

*observation
tower*
North Beach
Six Mile Landing

**ST.
AUGUSTINE
AREA**

**Guana River
Wildlife
Management
Area**

*Guana Lake
(Lake Pointe Vedra)*

*observation
towers*

entrance

trails

Guana River Reserve
*(northern section of Guana-
Tolomato-Matanzas
National Estuarine Research Reserve)*

To Jacksonville

Palm Valley Rd

Tolomato River

Hammock Rd

exit
329

To Green
Cove Springs

To
Daytona Beach

A t l a n t i c   O c e a n

See detail below
for this area

VILANO BEACH

**Anastasia
State
Park**

Anastasia Island

ST. AUGUSTINE

exit
318

To Guana
River Preserve

Usina (Vilano)
Bridge

San Marco Ave

Cove Market,
parking area

May St

VILANO
BEACH

*Vilano
boat ramp*

Comares
Ave

**Anastasia
State
Park**

"OLD
CITY"

Anastasia
Blvd

Arredondo
Ave

*park
entrance*

Salt Run

*beach
parking*

❶ Castillo de San Marcos NM
❷ Bridge of Lions
❸ Ribault St
❹ Aripieka Ave
❺ Alligator Farm

Matanzas R.

BUTLER BEACH
Palmetto Rd

CRESCENT BEACH

**Moses
Creek
Conservation
Area**

exit
307

**Southeast
Intracoastal
Waterway
Park**

**River to Sea
Preserve**

exit
298

**Fort
Matanzas
National
Monument**

Matanzas Inlet

Summer Haven

Old A1A

**Washington
Oaks
Gardens
State
Park**

Road, which turns southward and becomes Girvin Road (2.9 from Fort Caroline Road). At SR-10 (Atlantic Avenue; 3.0), turn left and cross the Intracoastal Waterway. At Mayport Road (SR-A1A0, turn left toward Mayport Naval Station. At Wonderwood Road (3.3), turn right to the park ahead (0.1). There are several miles of trails through maritime hammocks that can be excellent for migrant landbirds such as thrushes and warblers during spring and fall. The best trails are at the far south end of the park. Painted Buntings are fairly common breeders. During migration and winter, scan the ocean from the numerous beachfront pavilions for sea ducks, loons, and larids.

Contact: Kathryn Abbey Hanna Park, 500 Wonderwood Drive, Jacksonville, FL 32233; 904-249-4700; <http://www.coj.net/Departments/Parks+and+Recreation/Recreation+Activities/oceanfront+parks.htm>.

To visit Guana River Reserve or other St. Augustine coastal areas, continue south along the coast on SR-A1A.

ST. AUGUSTINE

About 20 miles south of Mayport and eight miles north of St. Augustine on SR-A1A is **Guana River Reserve** (2,398 acres; $3.00/vehicle; no camping; trails open at sunrise). The reserve—part of the larger Guana-Tolomato-Matanzas National Estuarine Research Reserve—protects more than four miles of ocean frontage, one of the longest stretches of undisturbed beach habitat remaining in Florida. Adjacent to the reserve and to the north is **Guana River Wildlife Management Area** (9,815 acres; no camping; *seasonal hunting from mid-October to mid-December*). This area is not accessible without prior permission except on foot or by bicycle, so birding opportunities are limited. Nearly all of the following text refers to the reserve. To reach the reserve from I-95 southbound, head east onto SR-202 (J. Turner Butler Boulevard, Exit #344) to its end at SR-A1A (12.5). Turn right to the reserve entrance on the right (10.0), just before the GateTrading Post convenience store. Straight ahead is Guana Lake (also known as Lake Ponte Vedra), an artificial impoundment created when the Guana River was dammed.

The dam marks the boundary between the WMA to the north and the reserve to the south, and should have waterfowl (mainly winter), wading birds, larids, and other waterbirds. Migrant raptors can be observed from the causeway in September and October. Areas of the park west of the causeway are currently closed to vehicles, but access is being considered. Walk west to the woods, where you should sign in and pick up a map and checklist. Bring your water, sunscreen, and insect repellent. There are five well-marked hiking trails, which offer miles of hiking through oak hammocks and pinewoods. (Some of these trails enter the Wildlife Management Area.) A bit west of where the main trail hits Hammock Road is an observation platform that overlooks a freshwater marsh. This can be a good area for landbirds (Painted Buntings breed in the area), but the trail may be flooded during summer and fall. Outside of the hunting season, hike into the Wildlife Management Area another mile to an observa-

Wood Stork family in the rain.   Arthur Morris/www.birdsasart.com

tion tower overlooking Capo Creek. The oak hammock before the tower can be good for migrant landbirds during spring and fall. Deer Flies, ticks, and chiggers can be bad here during spring and summer. Farther north along SR-A1A is the **NORTH BEACH USE AREA** parking area on the left (7.0). Cross the road to reach an observation platform on top of the dunes, which offers views of the Atlantic Ocean and Guana Lake. In September and October, the platform is an excellent spot to view the raptor migration (mainly falcons). There are several other parking areas with beach access and platforms.

> **Contact**: *Guana River Reserve, 505 Guana River Road, Ponte Vedra Beach, FL 32082; 904-823-4500; <www.dep.state.fl.us/coastal/sites/ gtm/guana_river.htm>.*

From the reserve, continue south on SR-A1A to a traffic light (7.2). Heading right will take you over the Usina Bridge. But, if you are interested in beach birding, instead continue south through this intersection to the stop sign at Vilano Road (0.1). Turning right leads to the old Vilano Bridge, which is now a fishing pier. Turning left leads to the beach at the Vilano boat ramp. Beach driving is permitted during summer, but it is best to park and walk the beach. During fall and winter, shorebirds and larids roost here and across the St. Augustine Inlet at Anastasia State Park (see below).

It was in this general area that Ponce de Leon is said to have begun his search for the Fountain of Youth in 1513. Founded in 1565, St. Augustine is the second-oldest continuously occupied city in the U.S. By the time St. Augustine was ceded to Great Britain in 1763, it already had served as the seat of government for Spain's Florida possessions and the center for thirty missions.

The following directions to birding sites will take you into parts of St. Augustine's "Old City". Return to SR-A1A and cross the Tolomato River via the Usina Bridge (known locally as the Vilano Bridge). Just beyond where the bridge meets the mainland, on the north side, is a parking area (opposite the Cove Market). During fall and winter, birding this area can be good for wading birds (including Roseate Spoonbill), ducks, shorebirds (including Whimbrel), and marsh sparrows. On the opposite side is the Vilano boat ramp, which is also an excellent spot when there are not too many boaters parked there.

Continue on SR-A1A (now called May Street) to San Marco Avenue (traffic light; 1.0) and turn left to head into downtown St. Augustine. (This street can be very congested.) This area is good for Gray Kingbirds (spring and summer), and may also offer looks at psittacids. Monk, Rose-ringed, and Black-hooded Parakeets are found in this area, and Mitred Parakeet formerly occurred here. History buffs will want to visit **Castillo de San Marcos National Monument** (25 acres; $6.00/person; no camping; opens at 8:45 AM; metered parking) on the left (0.9). The fort can be a good place to bird, time permitting. The perimeter of the fort and grounds can be walked (no fee); you may see psittacids or Gray Kingbirds (spring and summer).

Contact: *Castillo de San Marcos National Monument, 1 South Castillo Drive, St. Augustine, FL 32084; 904-829-6506; <www.nps.gov/casa>.*

ANASTASIA ISLAND

From downtown St. Augustine, continue south on SR-A1A then head east across the Bridge of Lions. On the island, the road name changes to Anastasia Boulevard. Head east to Comares Street (0.6) then turn left to another area for Rose-ringed and Black-hooded Parakeets (roll down your car windows to listen for the birds). At Ribault Street (0.4), turn left to its end at Arredondo Avenue. Turn right to Arpieka Avenue (0.2). Shortly after dawn and before dusk are best for the parakeets; House Finches may also be found in this neighborhood.

Return to Anastasia Boulevard (SR-A1A) and note the **St. Augustine Alligator Farm Zoological Park** on the right (0.6). The farm is a tourist facility ($17.95/person; opens at 9:00 AM) with a wading-bird rookery that may be worth a visit from mid-April through mid-May. A boardwalk allows close views of the hundreds of nesting birds, which may include Roseate Spoonbill and Wood Stork; be sure to bring your camera. At other times of the year, hundreds of wading birds roost here nightly.

Contact: *St. Augustine Alligator Farm Zoological Park, 999 Anastasia Boulevard, St. Augustine, FL 32084; 904-824-3337; <www.alligatorfarm. com>.*

A short distance beyond the alligator farm is the entrance to **Anastasia State Park** (1,500 acres; $5.00/vehicle; 139 campsites at $25.00/day; opens at 8:00 AM) on the left. Proceed to the canoe outpost on the left, which is a good spot to park and scan Salt Run. Farther south, pull off the road and scan for wintering loons, ducks, and shorebirds. During summer, Roseate Spoonbills may be seen. Continue on to the picnic area just beyond the campground. This area can be good during spring and fall for migrant landbirds. A boardwalk at the beach parking area provides views of the ocean. Northern Gannets are regularly observed from shore during late fall and winter. Peregrine Falcons and other raptors are seen in September and October. During spring and summer, Painted Buntings breed near the northern end of the parking area. Beach driving is no longer permitted at the park, so the large larid flocks that roost at the north end of the island (four miles from the entrance) are accessible only by foot or bicycle.

Contact: *Anastasia State Park, 1340A State Road A1A South, St. Augustine, Florida 32084; 904-461-2033; <www.floridastateparks.org/ anastasia>.*

CRESCENT BEACH TO MATANZAS INLET

From Anastasia State Park, return to SR-A1A and head south to **Palmetto Road** on the right (6.5). Drive west to the boat ramp (0.5). At high tide during migration and winter, large numbers of shorebirds roost on the docks to the north. (*The docks are private, so view them only from the road.*) Look for local specialties such as American Oystercatcher, Whimbrel, and Marbled Godwit. During the same seasons, scan oyster bars at low tide in the Intracoastal Waterway for American White Pelicans and Bald Eagles, and watch for Hooded Mergansers. Return to SR-A1A and continue south to SR-206 (1.5). Turn right to **Moses Creek Conservation Area** (2000 acres; no fee; primitive camping by permit; open anytime) on the right (1.7), which preserves one of the few undeveloped tidal creeks in the region. Vehicles are prohibited, but several trails offer access to maritime hammock, Sand Pine scrub, and saltmarsh. The conservation area can be excellent for migrant landbirds during spring and fall. Yellow-throated Warblers and Summer Tanagers breed here, and a few Northern Rough-winged Swallows nest in sandy bluffs along Moses Creek. Clapper Rails and Marsh Wrens are found year-round in the saltmarsh. Biting insects and Chiggers can be numerous during summer and fall.

Return to SR-A1A and head south to **Southeast Intracoastal Waterway Park** (114 acres; no fee; no camping) on the right (3.9). This new park includes coastal hammock with trails throughout, and should be great for migrant landbirds. **Fort Matanzas National Monument** (300 acres; no fee; no camping; opens at 9:00 AM) on the right (0.2). In addition to the small Spanish fort, which was completed in 1742, the monument contains a 0.5-mile boardwalk through a remnant maritime hammock that can be excellent for migrant landbirds during spring and fall. The boardwalk (wheelchair-accessible) also affords a view of the Intracoastal Waterway, which can have shorebirds and larids at low tide. Gray Kingbirds and Painted Buntings breed in the area during spring and summer.

Contact: *Fort Matanzas National Monument, 8635 SR-A1A South, St. Augustine, FL 32080; 904-471-0116; <www.nps.gov/foma>.*

Continue south on SR-A1A to **Matanzas Inlet** (no fee; no camping; accessible anytime). Parking is available on the north side of the inlet on both sides of SR-A1A. Least Terns and Willets nest in the dunes here; *stay out of roped-off areas.* Large numbers of larids winter here. In addition to flocks of Black Skimmers, look for Bonaparte's, Great Black-backed, and Lesser Black-backed Gulls. Piping Plovers also winter here. During fall, watch for migrant Peregrine Falcons and other raptors. To access the beach on the southeast side of the inlet (Summer Haven), cross the inlet and bear left onto SR-A1A (0.1) to the beach parking area on the left (0.3). During winter, hundreds of Northern Gannets may be seen feeding close to shore, and a few sea ducks such as scoters and mergansers can be present. During fall and winter, jaegers may pass by in singles or small flocks. From here, you may walk north along the seawall to the inlet. At low tide, coquina rocks near the bridge are often exposed, and one or two Purple Sandpipers usually winter here. (These rocks are inundated during high tides.)

Return to SR-A1A and continue south to another section of **Guana-Matanzas-Tolomato National Estuarine Research Reserve** on the right (3.2). A small upland part of the reserve is now the **River to Sea Preserve**, just opened to the public. Roads in the old campground offer easy access throughout a large maritime hammock that can be excellent for migrant landbirds during spring and fall. An area across SR-A1A offers additional parking and an excellent boardwalk for scanning the beach and ocean.

Farther south along SR-A1A is **WASHINGTON OAKS GARDENS STATE PARK** (425 acres; $4.00/vehicle; no camping; opens at 8:00 AM) on the right (2.2). There are several trails and parking areas (including one east of A1A with ocean access) that should be searched for migrant landbirds during spring and fall. Much of the park is beautifully landscaped, and the gardens are a special treat.

Contact: *Washington Oaks Gardens State Park, 6400 North Oceanshore Boulevard, Palm Coast, FL 32173; 386-446-6780; <www.floridastateparks.org/washingtonoaks>.*

Atlantic coastal areas continue on page 170.

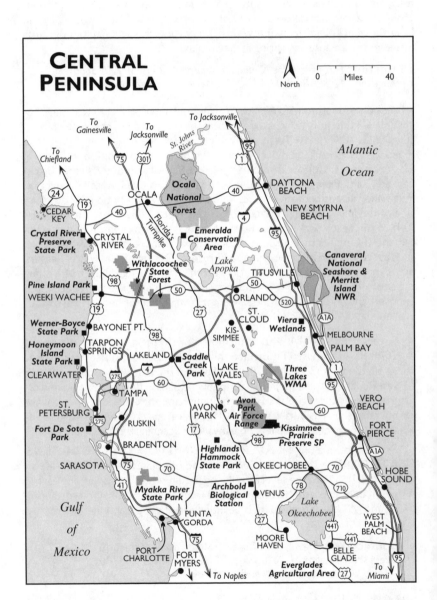

CENTRAL PENINSULA

North

0   Miles   40

To Gainesville

To Jacksonville

To Jacksonville

To Chiefland

St. Johns River

To Jacksonville

Atlantic

Ocean

75

301

95

1

24

19

Ocala National Forest

40

DAYTONA BEACH

CEDAR KEY

OCALA

40

4

NEW SMYRNA BEACH

Crystal River Preserve State Park

CRYSTAL RIVER

Florida's Turnpike

Emeralda Conservation Area

95

Canaveral National Seashore & Merritt Island NWR

Lake Apopka

TITUSVILLE

Withlacoochee State Forest

98

50

50

ORLANDO

520

Pine Island Park

WEEKI WACHEE

19

27

ST. CLOUD

Viera Wetlands

A1A

MELBOURNE

Werner-Boyce State Park

BAYONET PT.

KIS-SIMMEE

PALM BAY

Honeymoon Island State Park

TARPON SPRINGS

98

LAKELAND

Saddle Creek Park

LAKE WALES

Three Lakes WMA

1

CLEARWATER

275

4

60

95

ST. PETERSBURG

TAMPA

AVON PARK

Avon Park Air Force Range

VERO BEACH

60

Fort De Soto Park

275

RUSKIN

17

98

Kissimmee Prairie Preserve SP

FORT PIERCE

BRADENTON

Highlands Hammock State Park

A1A

SARASOTA

75

70

OKEECHOBEE

70

HOBE SOUND

41

Myakka River State Park

Archbold Biological Station

VENUS

78

Lake Okeechobee

710

WEST PALM BEACH

Gulf

of

Mexico

PUNTA GORDA

75

27

MOORE HAVEN

441

441

95

PORT CHARLOTTE

FORT MYERS

BELLE GLADE

To Miami

To Naples

Everglades Agricultural Area

27

CENTRAL PENINSULA

Home of the St. Petersburg/Tampa and Greater Orlando metropolitan areas and the Kennedy Space Center complex on Merritt Island, the Central Peninsula is the top tourist destination in the world. The region has witnessed an incredible increase in human residents in the past 50 years, which has resulted in severe habitat loss in many areas. Nonetheless, the region continues to support a large and diverse avifauna, primarily the result of the establishment of several large, publicly-owned conservation areas. The subtropical influence for which Florida is famous becomes apparent here, with extensive mangrove forests along the coasts and the increased presence of Cabbage Palms in wet areas throughout. The birdlife, too, shows more tropical influence, with breeding species such as Reddish Egret, Roseate Spoonbill, Fulvous and Black-bellied Whistling-Ducks, Snail Kite, Short-tailed Hawk, Mangrove Cuckoo, and Black-whiskered Vireo. In fact, the Central Peninsula contains the greatest diversity of native breeding species in Florida, at 126 species. The region also shows more of an exotic influence than areas to the north, with several species of breeding psittacids, primarily along the Gulf coast. The last remnants of the once-substantial Budgerigar population are found in residential areas at Hernando Beach and Bayonet Point, while other psittacids are increasing in range and numbers. Monk and Black-hooded Parakeets are locally common along the Gulf coast (and Monks occur sporadically elsewhere in the region).

Many other native "specialty" species occur in the Central Peninsula, such as Magnificent Frigatebird (mostly spring through fall), Wood Stork, Mottled Duck, Swallow-tailed Kite (spring and summer), Sandhill Crane, Purple Gallinule, Limpkin, Snowy Plover, Wilson's Plover, Piping Plover (fall through spring), American Oystercatcher, Burrowing Owl, Red-cockaded Woodpecker, Gray Kingbird (spring through fall), Florida Scrub-Jay, Bachman's Sparrow, Florida Grasshopper Sparrow (endemic to the region), and Seaside Sparrow. Other species reach their southernmost breeding limits in the state: Southeastern American Kestrel, Acadian Flycatcher, Carolina Chickadee, Marsh Wren, Yellow-throated Vireo, Yellow-throated Warbler, Blue Grosbeak, Indigo Bunting, Painted Bunting, and Seaside Sparrow (except the Cape Sable race).

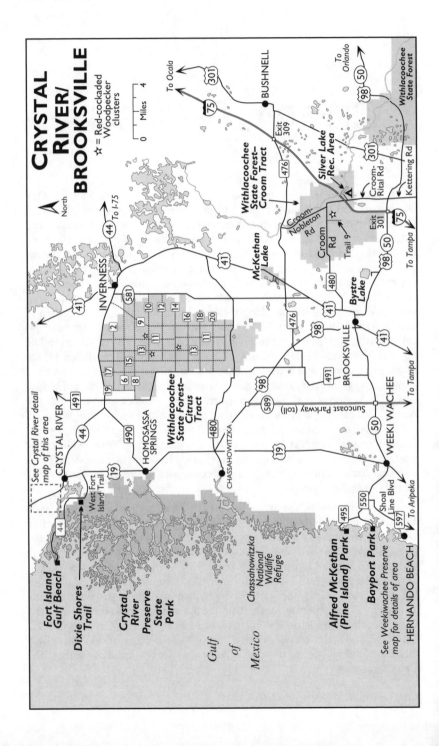

CENTRAL PENINSULA—GULF COAST

CRYSTAL RIVER AREA

Crystal River Preserve State Park (30,000 acres; no fee; no camping; opens at 8:00 AM) extends from the Withlacoochee River south through Chassahowitzka. To reach the **EcoWalk**, a 2.3-mile loop through a diversity of habitats, head west from US-19 onto State Park Street (north of the Days Inn) at the north edge of Crystal River. At Tallahassee Road (0.15), turn right to the park entrance on the left (2.1).

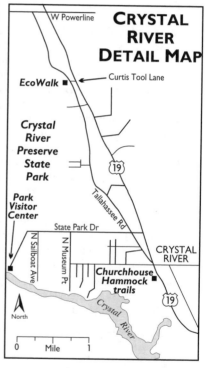

Pass through the gate and park in the first parking area. The signage suggests walking the trail counterclockwise, but the light will be more favorable in the morning if the trail is walked in a clockwise direction. Species that may be found along the trails include Blue Grosbeak and Summer Tanager (spring and summer), and Sedge Wren and Swamp Sparrow (winter).

There are several other trails in the state park. The entrance to one, **Churchhouse Hammock**, is located on the west side of US-19 opposite Crystal River Mall, 2.8 miles south of the EcoWalk. There is a 0.3-mile loop boardwalk and a 0.75-mile trail that loops back to the boardwalk. An extension over the marsh to the river is planned for the future. The trail traverses dense coastal hammock that may be good for wintering and migrant landbirds.

Contact: *Crystal River Preserve State Park, 3266 North Sailboat Avenue, Crystal River, FL 34428; 352-563-0450; <www.floridastateparks.org/ crystalriverpreserve>.*

CR-44 (Fort Island Trail) runs west from US-19 nine miles to the Gulf. The **Dixie Shores Trail**, through another part of Crystal River Preserve State Parkl, is on the left at the entrance to the Dixie Shores development (2.5). The trail is mowed and leads to the saltmarsh where Marsh Wrens and Seaside Sparrows breed, and where Sedge Wrens and Nelson's Sharp-tailed

Sparrows winter. Migrant and wintering landbirds may be found in the hammock between the road and the marsh.

Fort Island Gulf Beach (15 acres; no fee; no camping; opens at sunrise) lies at the end of Fort Island Trail. At the small beach, look for wading birds, shorebirds, and larids. At low tide, look for American Oystercatchers feeding on the exposed oyster bars, and scan offshore for wintering Common Goldeneye, Hooded Merganser, Common Loon, American White Pelican, and other species. A small wooded area between the beach and the boat ramp can be good for migrant landbirds; Gray Kingbirds may be found during spring and summer. Nelson's Sharp-tailed Sparrows winter in the small *Spartina* marsh.

About half of **WITHLACOOCHEE STATE FOREST** (160,000 acres in six tracts; no fee; 219 campsites at $5.00–13.00/day at 8 sites; *seasonal hunting*) is composed of Longleaf Pine/Turkey Oak sandhills that support a fairly large population of Red-cockaded Woodpeckers (55 families in 2003; cavity trees are marked with white paint), as well as Hairy Woodpecker (uncommon), Brown-headed Nuthatch, Yellow-throated Vireo (spring and summer), Yellow-throated and Pine Warblers, and Bachman's Sparrow. To reach the **Citrus Tract** from Crystal River, head east on SR-44 (Gulf to Lake Highway) and turn right onto Trail 13 at the Citrus Wildlife Management sign (11.3). The forest is gridded by unpaved roads at roughly one-mile intervals; those that run north-south are odd-numbered, while east-west roads are even-numbered. Many of these roads are too rough for two-wheel drive vehicles, but the following roads should be passable, and all lead to Red-cockaded Woodpecker clusters active in 2004. Head south on Trail 13 to Trail 10 (3.8) and turn left. After crossing Trail 11 (0.9), look for the woodpecker cavity trees on the left (0.1). Other woodpecker clusters are located at the southwest corner of Trails 10 and 13 (350 yards west on a hiking trail), and on the east side of Trail 13 south of the westbound section of Trail 14. From the latter site, you may continue southbound to CR-480 (Stage Coach Trail; 4.9). To return to U S-19 via US-98, turn right (9.0).

Contact: Withlacoochee Forestry Center, 15019 Broad Street, Brooksville, FL 34601; 352-754-6896; <www.fl-dof.com/state_forests/ withlacoochee.html>.

BROOKSVILLE

The **Croom Tract** of **Withlacoochee State Forest** supports a population of Red-cockaded Woodpeckers in 14 clusters. To reach a cluster active in 2004, head north from Brooksville on US-41 to CR-480 (Croom Road) and turn right. Once in the forest (4.4), the road surface is unpaved but well-graded. At Trail 9 (3.5, or 7.9 miles from US-41), turn right to the cavity trees on the right (0.3), which are marked with white paint. To reach an area

Yellow-throated Warbler, yellow-lored race.

Lyn S. Atherton

reliable for singing Yellow-throated Vireos and Bachman's Sparrows (mainly March–August), head back to Croom Road and proceed west for 1.1-1.6 miles; the north side of this stretch of road is more productive than the south side. Three campgrounds are found at Silver Lake, which is simply a wide portion of the Withlacoochee River. Continue east on Croom Road, veering right at the fork, to the campgrounds on the left (3.1). To reach Silver Lake from the SR-50, go north on Croom-Rital Road (one mile east of I-75 and three miles west of US-301; traffic light) to the area on the right (3.6).

McKethan Lake (opens at 8:00 AM; $2.00/vehicle), in another tract of the forest, contains extensive oak hammocks. From SR-50A at Brooksville, go north on US-41 to the entrance on the left (7.5). To reach McKethan Lake from Silver Lake, turn right onto Croom-Rital Road to Croom-Nobleton Road (2.0) and turn right. When the road becomes pavement (3.3), its name changes to Edgewater Avenue. At CR-476 (Lake Lindsey Road; 0.8), turn left. At US-41 (4.9), turn right to McKethan Lake on the left (0.5). There is a two-mile nature trail through the hammocks, which can be good for migrant landbirds during fall.

Bystre Lake east of Brooksville usually has American White Pelicans and a few species of ducks during winter. To reach it from SR-50, go north on Clayton Road (2.7 miles east of SR-50A and 5.6 miles west of I-75). At the end of the road (0.5), turn right into a grassy field owned by the county. *Stay off adjacent private property.*

WEEKI WACHEE

To visit two small coastal parks that are most productive during winter, travel west from US-19 on CR-550. At CR-495 (4.9), turn right to **PINE ISLAND (ALFRED McKETHAN) PARK** (3 acres; $2.00/vehicle, except free 15 November–14 February; no camping; opens at 8:00 AM), the best local site to observe wintering waterbirds. From the park look for sea ducks, Common Loons, wading birds, shorebirds (including American Oystercatchers), and larids. The shorebirds and larids are best viewed early in the morning or just before dark; at other times, the birds are constantly harassed by beach-goers. Check the wintering larid flocks carefully for Gull-billed Terns, which have been seen here on rare occasions in recent years. Return to CR-550 and turn right to **Bayport Park** (4 acres; no fee; no camping) at the end of the road. This small park is worth a quick stop to search for wintering loons and grebes, American Oystercatchers (at low tide), and larids.

> **Contact:** Hernando County Parks and Recreation Department, 20 North Main Street, Room 260, Brooksville, Florida 34601; 352-754-4027; <www.co.hernando.fl.us/parks_rec/parks>.

To look for **Budgerigars** at **Hernando Beach**, one of their two remaining sites, return to CR-550 and head east to CR-597 (Shoal Line Boulevard; 3.2). Turn right to Companero Entra (4.8). This and the next few roads to the north (as far as Eagle Nest Drive) should be carefully searched; drive around with your car windows open to listen for the Budgie's distinctive chittering. The flock moves around somewhat, but birds usually can be found along Flamingo Boulevard, Gulf Coast Drive, Gulfview Drive, or Gulf Winds Circle (left from the end of Gulfview Drive). *The entire area is within a quiet residential development, so please be respectful of people and property.*

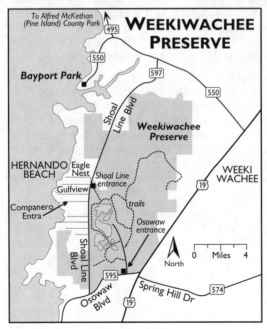

Weekiwachee Preserve (9,000 acres; no fee; no camping; opens at sunrise) protects a large area of hammock and river floodplain west of US-19 between the Weeki Wachee River and Osowaw Boulevard (CR-595). The park is best visited during fall migration and winter, when landbirds are most common. Many miles of hiking trails traverse wooded areas and open fields. There are two entrances. To reach the south end of the preserve from US-19, turn west opposite Spring Hill Drive onto CR-595 (Osowaw Boulevard; traffic light). Go a short distance to the T-intersection, and turn left to the parking area on the right (0.5 from US-19). This entrance is 1.1 mile east of the intersection of Shoal Line Boulevard and Osowaw Boulevard. Birding is best along the first trail to the left, 0.2 mile inside the gate. Hundreds of wading birds and icterids roost in a lake just beyond the end of the paved road. On the second Saturday of each month, the Osowaw gate is open, and you may drive close to the lake. Otherwise, walk through the gate to a fenceline (1.2) and go through it to the lake on the right (0.1). Weekiwachee Preserve may also be accessed from the east side of Shoal Line Boulevard, 3.0 miles north of Osowaw Boulevard.

Contact: *checklists may be obtained from the Southwest Florida Water Management District, 2379 Broad Street, Brooksville, FL 34609; 1-800-423-1476; <www.swfwmd.state.fl.us/recguide/recguide.htm>.*

Birding Sites in Hernando County was updated in 2003 by the Hernando Audubon Society. In addition to listing birding sites in the area, it includes a bird checklist for the county. It may be ordered free of charge from the Hernando County Tourist Development, 30305 Cortez Boulevard, Brooksville, FL 34602, 1-800-601-4580 or 352-754-4405.

ARIPEKA TO ANCLOTE

Crews Lake County Park (113 acres; no fee; free tent camping; opens at sunrise) can be an excellent spot for migrant landbirds during fall, and for waterbirds year-round (see map on next page). To reach it from US-19, turn east onto CR-578 (County Line Road; traffic light) to Shady Hills Road (5.5). Turn right to Lenway Road, just after toll road bridge (4.6). Turn left, and then right into the park (0.2). From Brooksville or other points north, go south on US-41 or the Suncoast Parkway to County Line Road and turn right. At Shady Hills Road (5.3 from US-41 or 3.8 from the Parkway), turn left and proceed as above. From Bayonet Point, travel east on SR-52, pass CR-587 (Moon Lake Road), then turn left onto Shady Hills Road (3.8; traffic light). At Lenway Road (2.9) turn right. From I-75, head west on SR-52, cross US-41 (10.0), turn right onto Shady Hills Road (2.4), and proceed as above. The park contains oak hammocks, sandhills, cypress swamps, and frontage along Crews Lake. Trails through the woodlands can be great during fall for migrant landbirds. An observation tower affords views of the lake, which can be extensive or just a few puddles, depending on recent rainfall. Many locally rare birds may be found, including Roseate Spoonbill (late summer), Fulvous Whistling-Duck, Purple Gallinule (mostly spring and summer), Limpkin, Black-necked Stilt, and Black

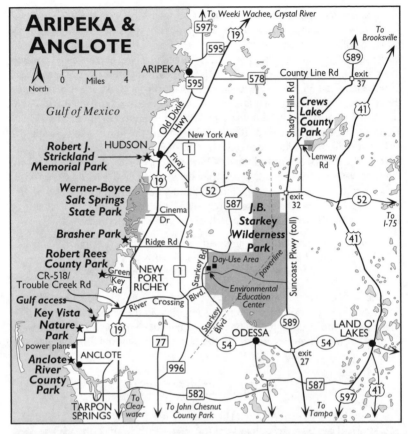

ARIPEKA & ANCLOTE

Gulf of Mexico

Tern. Waterfowl may be present in numbers during winter if water levels are high, while shorebirds may be common when levels are low. Grassy edges along the lake shore may contain large numbers of wintering Sedge Wrens.

Contact: *Crews Lake County Park, 16739 Crews Lake Drive, Spring Hill, FL 34610; 727-861-3038; <www.pascocountyfl.net/menu/index/ parkindex.html>.*

Return to US-19 and turn south to Hudson. Beyond the traffic light at Fivay Road, turn right onto Clark Street (0.3). Follow Clark Street to its end at **Robert J. Strickland Memorial Park** (6 acres; no fee; no camping; opens at sunrise). Scan the gulf for sea ducks, Common Loons, and Horned Grebes during winter. A few Budgerigars may still be seen in the trees in the parking lot, while Monk Parakeets may be found along Clark Street and adjacent streets.

Return to US-19 and head south. At SR-52 (2.0) turn right into the shopping center on your right. From here, scan for Budgerigars, which often perch on the power lines along the west side of US-19 prior to roosting in the oaks and sycamores lining the **Perkins Restaurant** parking lot. About 30 Budgies still frequented the site as of summer 2004. Arrive about an hour before dusk and keep alert; several thousand European Starlings, Red-winged Blackbirds, and grackles gather along the same powerlines before heading to roost, making it easy to overlook the parakeets.

Return to US-19 and continue south. At Cinema Drive (1.8), turn right, cross Scenic Drive (0.2), and enter **WERNER–BOYCE SALT SPRINGS STATE PARK** (3,400 acres, no fee at present; no camping at present; opens at 8:00 AM). This is a recent state acquisition with facilities still under development. The park contains breeding populations of Black Rails, Marsh Wrens, and Seaside Sparrows, but they are in areas not currently accessible. The half-mile trail that originates from the parking lot can be great for migrant landbirds, especially during fall. The trail is equipped with benches, but the middle section of the trail can be quite muddy. Proposed trails and boardwalks will offer access to other areas of the park in the future.

> **Contact:** *Werner–Boyce Salt Springs State Park, P.O. Box 490, Port Richey, Florida 34673; 727-816-1890; <www.floridastateparks.org/werner-boyce>.*

Return to US-19 and continue south. At Ridge Road (2.0), turn right to its end (0.1) then turn left. Go one block and then turn right onto Bay Boulevard. At Old Post Road (0.2), turn right to the entrance of **Brasher Park** (1 acre; no fee; no camping; opens at sunrise) on the left (0.4). This is an area of *Juncus* marshes and mangrove forests. Gray Kingbirds, Marsh Wrens, and Florida Prairie Warblers breed here. Numerous wading birds and some shorebirds and larids can be found here at low tide. Hooded Mergansers and Horned Grebes can be common in the estuaries during winter. To return to US-19 southbound, head south on Old Post Road to its end at Grand Boulevard. Make a left, then a quick right to US-19.

At **GREEN KEY ROAD** (1.3; between Carpet USA and ValuLodge; 0.2 north of the light at Main Street), turn right. This area is excellent at low tide for wading birds (including Reddish Egrets) and wintering waterfowl, shorebirds, and larids. At low tide, check all the estuaries before entering **Robert K. Rees County Park** (45 acres, no fee, no camping; opens at sunrise). At the entrance gate for the first two hours after dawn on spring mornings, large numbers of migrant warblers and other landbirds may be seen, especially following strong east winds. As many as 800 birds per hour have been seen flying east, and most of these are at or below eye level. (Note that many of the birds cannot be identified because of very brief views or poor lighting.) At the end of Green Key Road (1.5), check the small beach for shorebirds and larids, including local rarities such as Wilson's Plover, Bonaparte's Gull, and Gull-billed Tern. Scan the gulf for waterbirds; Hooded Mergansers commonly winter here. During spring and summer, Gray King-

Long-billed Curlew.   Arthur Morris/www.birdsasart.com

birds, Marsh Wrens, and Florida Prairie Warblers breed in the mangroves, and may be observed from the boardwalk to the north.

Return to US-19 and head south to CR-518 (Trouble Creek Road; 2.0). Turn right and continue through a curve in the road, where the road's name changes to **Strauber Memorial Highway**. The road winds through mangrove forests, with a canal on the right side. Wading birds, including Yellow-crowned Night-Herons, are frequently seen here. Watch the salt barrens on the left during summer for Roseate Spoonbills. A small gap in the mangroves on the right (1.5) offers a view of the gulf. At low tides, shorebirds and larids may be found here; a telescope is helpful.

Continue south; the road name again changes, this time to Baileys Bluff Road. Pass Pineview Drive on the right (1.5), then turn right into **Key Vista Nature Park** (103 acres, no fee; no camping; opens at sunrise). The park contains two miles of trails and boardwalks and an observation tower that overlooks the gulf. Wading birds (including Reddish Egrets, and Roseate Spoonbills during summer), shorebirds, and larids may be seen. Gull-billed Terns sometimes hunt for fiddler crabs on the beach. Migrant and wintering landbirds can be common along the trails.

Contact: *Key Vista Nature Park, 2700 Baileys Bluff Road, Holiday, FL 34690; <www.pascocountyfl.net/pubser/deptp/parks.html>.*

Anclote River County Park (29 acres, no fee; no camping; opens at sunrise) is farther south on Baileys Bluff Road, just beyond the power plant. Magnificent Frigatebirds often are seen overhead during spring and summer. At Anclote Boulevard (0.2), turn left to reach Alternate US-19 (2.0). From there, turn left toward US-19 in Holiday, or turn right toward Tarpon Springs.

East of Port Richey is **JAY B. STARKEY WILDERNESS PARK** (19,500 acres; no fee; camping at $5.00–15.00/day; opens at sunrise), an excellent birding spot. The park, which doubles as a well field, preserves perhaps the largest and highest-quality Longleaf Pine flatwoods remaining in the Tampa Bay region. It also supports several other habitats such as sandhills, hardwood hammocks, Sand Pine scrub, marshes, and cypress swamps along the Pithlachascotee and Anclote Rivers. To reach the park from the north, go south on CR-1 (Little Road), cross the Pithlachascotee River, and turn left onto River Crossing Boulevard. At Starkey Boulevard (0.4), turn left to Wilderness Road (1.9), then turn right to the entrance. From SR-54, go north on CR-1 to River Crossing Boulevard (1.4), turn right, and proceed as above. Once inside the park, stop first at the Environmental Education Center on the left, which contains a short boardwalk (closed when school is in session) to the Pithlachascotee River. Barred Owls and Red-eyed and Yellow-throated Vireos breed here during spring and summer. American Woodcocks may be seen at dawn or dusk during winter as they fly between the riverine swamp and the pasture. The woodland trails in the Day Use Area north of the main parking lot can be excellent for landbirds, especially during fall migration and winter. During spring and summer, Yellow-throated Vireos and Summer Tanagers breed here.

The remainder of the well field is closed to automobiles, but birders can either walk or bicycle the main well field road that heads east for nearly seven miles and connects with the bicycle path along the Suncoast Parkway. At or beyond the powerlines (2.75), you should find Yellow-throated Vireos (spring and summer), Brown-headed Nuthatches, Eastern Bluebirds, Yellow-throated Warblers, Summer Tanagers (spring and summer), and Bachman's Sparrows. Wild Turkeys may be seen anywhere in the park around dawn and dusk, and Hairy Woodpeckers may be found in recently burned flatwoods. During winter, you should see sparrows in grassy or brushy areas under the powerlines; among the many Savannah Sparrows, look also for Grasshopper, Bachman's, and Swamp Sparrows. The park also supports a fantastic diversity of butterflies, including several species of the state's rarest grass skippers.

Contact: Jay B. Starkey Wilderness Park, 10500 Wilderness Road, New Port Richey, FL 34655; 727-834-3247; <www.pascocountyfl.net/pubser/deptp/parks.html>.

TARPON SPRINGS

Fred Howard Park (155 acres; no fee; no camping; opens at 7:00 AM) is a worthwhile spot for wintering shorebirds and migrant landbirds (see next map). To reach it from US-19 in Tarpon Springs, go west on CR-582 (Tarpon Avenue) to Alternate US-19 (1.0) and turn left. At Meres Boulevard (0.6), turn right to Florida Avenue (1.6). Turn right to Sunset Drive (1.0), and turn left to the entrance (0.2). The main park road leads to an artificial island that contains the beach. Check the causeway and the beach for wading birds, shorebirds, gulls, and terns. Woodlands in the park can be very good for migrants, especially during fall.

Contact: *Fred Howard Park, 1700 Sunset Drive, Tarpon Springs, FL 34689; 727-943-4081; <www.pinellascounty.org/park/06_Howard.htm>.*

The hammocks and swamps of **JOHN CHESNUT, SR. PARK** (255 acres; no fee; no camping; opens at 7:00 AM) can be excellent for migrant landbirds during fall, and offer good birding at other seasons, as well. To reach the park from US-19 in Tarpon Springs, go east on CR-582 (Tarpon Avenue). At CR-611 (East Lake Road, 3.0), turn right to the entrance on the right (4.3). To reach the park from the south, travel north from SR-752 (Tampa Road) on CR-611 to the entrance on the left (2.0). There are three nature trails through hardwood forests, cypress swamps, and along the lakeshore. At the Y-intersection in the park road, bear right, cross a bridge, and turn right. Cross another bridge and turn left into the parking lot. Walk back across the road to the boardwalk on the left. This trail goes through a mixed cypress/hardwood swamp that can be excellent for migrants during fall. The trail ends at another parking lot. To return to your vehicle, follow the road to the left.

Return to the main park road. Just before the Y-intersection, turn right into the parking lot. A trail that begins to the right of the restrooms ends at the park boat ramp and passes a tower overlooking Lake Tarpon. The third trail, the Peggy Park Trail (named in honor of a slain wildlife officer), is a loop trail 3,000 feet long. It is located to the left of the Y, a bit past the boat ramp on the right. Limpkins are seen occasionally along the canal on the right, but the trail is most noted for migrant landbirds during fall.

Contact: *John H. Chesnut, Sr. Park, 2200 East Lake Road, Palm Harbor, FL 33685; 727-669-1951; <http://www.pinellascounty.org/park/04_Chesnut.htm>.*

OLDSMAR

Return to CR-611 and turn right. Go over SR-752, where the road name changes to McMullen-Booth Road. To visit **Harbor Palms Nature Park and Estuary Preserve** (35 acres; no fee; no camping), continue south to the traffic light at SR-586 (Curlew Road, 0.7) and turn left. At SR-752 (1.0),

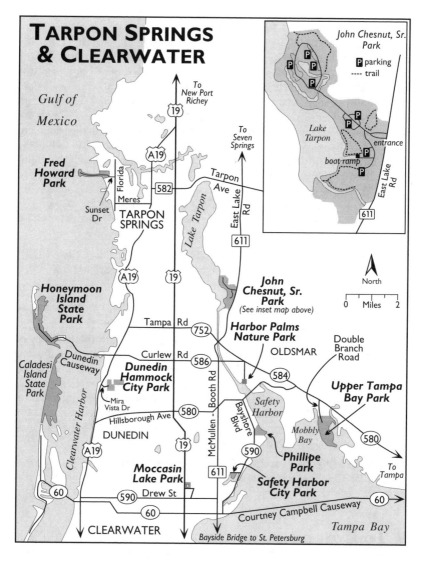

TARPON SPRINGS & CLEARWATER

Gulf of Mexico

To New Port Richey

19

To Seven Springs

A19

Fred Howard Park

582

Tarpon Ave

East Lake Rd

611

Florida

Meres

Sunset Dr

TARPON SPRINGS

Lake Tarpon

John Chesnut, Sr. Park

19

John Chesnut, Sr. Park
(See inset map above)

Harbor Palms Nature Park

Honeymoon Island State Park

A19

Tampa Rd

752

OLDSMAR

Double Branch Road

Caladesi Island State Park

Dunedin Causeway

Curlew Rd

586

584

Upper Tampa Bay Park

Dunedin Hammock City Park

Booth Rd

Safety Harbor

Mira Vista Dr

580

Hillsborough Ave

DUNEDIN

McMullen - Booth Rd

Bayshore Blvd

Mobbly Bay

580

A19

19

Moccasin Lake Park

611

590

Phillipe Park

To Tampa

60

590

Drew St

Safety Harbor City Park

Clearwater Harbor

60

60

CLEARWATER

Courtney Campbell Causeway

60

Bayside Bridge to St. Petersburg

Tampa Bay

Inset (top right):

John Chesnut, Sr. Park

P parking
---- trail

Lake Tarpon

entrance

boat ramp

East Lake Rd

611

North

0   Miles   2

---

turn right to Oak Leaf Boulevard (0.2). Turn right to Maple Leaf Boulevard (0.9) and turn right again into the park (0.1). The park contains a boardwalk through a hardwood hammock and a mangrove forest. From the viewing platform on the bay, look north to view an active Bald Eagle nest.

Contact: *Harbor Palms Nature Park and Estuary Preserve, 1820 Maple Leaf Boulevard, Oldsmar, FL 34677.*

Upper Tampa Bay Park (2,144 acres; $1.00/vehicle; no camping) contains a boardwalk along a mangrove shoreline, saltmarshes, estuaries, and pine flatwoods. From CR-611, go east on SR-752 or SR-586 (Curlew Road) to SR-584. Continue east to Double Branch Road (3.8) and turn right to the park on the right (0.5). (SR-584 merges with SR-58 about one mile before Double Branch Road). From Tampa, go west on SR-580 (Hillsborough Avenue), cross SR-589 (Sheldon Road) to Double Branch Road (6.2) on the left, and proceed as above. The best trails are the boardwalk that begins from the nature center, and the trail that heads west from the park road to Mobbly Bay. At low tide, the flats in Mobbly Bay can have numerous wading birds (including Reddish Egrets), shorebirds (including American Oystercatchers), and larids. When the tide is in, look for Lesser Scaup and other saltwater species. The oak hammock at the beginning of the trail can be great for migrant and wintering landbirds. An active Bald Eagle nest is located just northwest of the park; the birds are often seen overhead.

Contact: *Upper Tampa Bay Park, 8001 Double Branch Road, Tampa, FL 33615; 813-855-1765; <www.hillsboroughcounty.org/parks/parkservices/regionalparks.cfm>.*

Return to the junction of SR-586 (Curlew Road) and CR-611 and head south. At SR-580 (1.6; traffic light), turn left onto SR-590 (Bayshore Boulevard; 1.0). Follow SR-590 as it turns right and proceed to the entrance of **Philippe Park** (122 acres; no fee; no camping; opens at 7:00 AM) on the left. Located on the west shore of Safety Harbor, this is another park that can be good for migrant and wintering landbirds. The main park road ends at a tidal lagoon surrounded by a small area of mangroves and saltmarsh. Look here for Yellow-crowned Night-Herons. Scope the water from along the shore for wintering ducks and other waterbirds. During winter, a few Spotted Sandpipers can usually be found roosting along the seawall.

Contact: *Philippe Park, 2525 Philippe Parkway, Safety Harbor, FL 34695; 727-699-1947; <www.pinellascounty.org/park/11_Philippe.htm>.*

DUNEDIN

HONEYMOON ISLAND STATE PARK (408 acres; $5.00/vehicle; no camping; opens at 8:00 AM) is one of the outstanding birding locations on Florida's Gulf coast, especially for shorebirds and larids. From the entrance station, follow the main park road for just a couple hundred feet to a small parking area on the right, then walk along a very short trail that ends at an observation point overlooking extensive mudflats and oyster beds. At low tide, this area often contains a wide variety of shorebirds and good numbers of wading birds. After this, continue north to the second road after the toll booth and turn left. Park in the southern parking area, where a trail leads to the Pet Beach. The area around the small pond may support ducks, Virginia Rail, Sora, and Marsh and Sedge Wrens during winter. The Pet Beach itself often holds good numbers of shorebirds when people and their dogs are absent (usually early in the morning). In September, there are often impressive concentrations of several thousand terns in this area, including large numbers of migrant Common Terns.

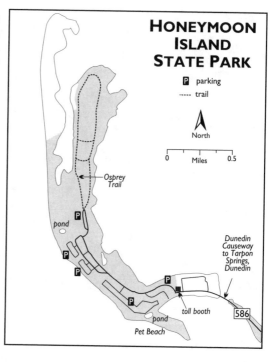

HONEYMOON ISLAND STATE PARK

🅿 parking
----- trail

North

0 Miles 0.5

Osprey Trail

pond

Dunedin Causeway to Tarpon Springs, Dunedin

toll booth

586

pond

Pet Beach

At the north end of the second parking lot is another small pond that is excellent for Virginia Rail and Sora during winter. Continue on the park road to the northernmost parking lot. Park at the picnic area (0.9) and follow the hiking trail (Osprey Trail) to the north end of the island. The Slash Pine woods here can be excellent for passerine migrants and a sprinkling of raptors during spring and fall. Gray Kingbirds and Florida Prairie Warblers breed here, as well as an occasional pair of Black-whiskered Vireos. Mangrove Cuckoos have occurred rarely during late spring. There are at least 20 active Osprey nests in the pines, and a pair of Great Horned Owls nests annually in an abandoned Osprey nest.

From the north end of Osprey Trail, walk west along the shoreline, checking the small *Spartina* (cordgrass) marshes for wintering Nelson's Sharp-tailed Sparrows. Return to your car and drive to the northernmost beach parking lot. Walk north along the beach, watching both the ocean and the lagoon for seabirds and other waterbirds. The far north end of the sand spit (a walk of over a mile) has one of the greatest shorebird concentrations in Florida for much of the year. This area, which will be partially submerged at high tide, is also one of the most important wintering sites in Florida for Piping Plovers; as many as 100 winter here and on nearby Three Rooker Island to the north and Caladesi Island to the south. *Many areas of the beach and dunes are roped off to protect critical nesting and roosting areas for shorebirds and larids; under no circumstances should birders enter these areas.*

Contact: *Honeymoon Island State Park, 1 Causeway Blvd., Dunedin, FL 34698; 727-469-5942; <www.floridastateparks.org/honeymoonisland>.*

Limpkin.   Arthur Morris/www.birdsasart.com

DUNEDIN HAMMOCK PARK (85 acres; no fee; no camping; opens at sunrise) can be excellent for migrant landbirds during fall, and is worth a visit at any season. To reach the park from Honeymoon Island, go east on Curlew Road to Alternate US-19 and turn right. At Mira Vista Drive (1.3), turn left, then left again onto Douglas Avenue (0.2). Turn right onto Buena Vista Drive (0.2) to the park. A boardwalk that ends in a brackish marsh can be reached via a bridge over the canal that leads east from the parking area. During winter, rails, Marsh Wrens, and Swamp Sparrows may be observed from the boardwalk or the observation tower. To bird the hammock for migrant landbirds, follow the many "unmanicured" trails east or south from the parking lot. Although these trails are unmarked, they are all loops that return to the parking lot; some may be flooded in places during summer and fall. Mosquitoes are usually plentiful during fall, so bring repellent.

> **Contact:** *Dunedin Hammock Park, 605 Buena Vista Drive North, Dunedin, FL 34698; 727-298-3286; <www.dunedingov.com/home.aspx? page=departments/leisureServices/parks&title=Parks>.*

CLEARWATER

Safety Harbor City Park (no fee; no camping) contains a wading bird rookery that is active during spring and summer. It is also good year-round for Limpkins and Monk Parakeets. From Philippe Park (page 122), continue south on SR-590 to 7th Street (2.0) and turn right. Go west a few blocks to the park on the left. A boat ramp at the west end offers views of Alligator Lake; this is the best spot in the park for Limpkins. Monk Parakeets nest in the light poles of the baseball field. The heronry is located on the island in the middle of the lake.

   Contact: *Safety Harbor City Park, 940 7th Street S., Safety Harbor, FL; 727-724-1545; <www.cityofsafetyharbor.com/marina_parks.htm>.*

   Moccasin Lake Park(51 acres; $3.00/person; no camping; closed Mondays, opens at 9:00 AM Tuesdays–Fridays and 10:00 AM on weekends) may also be worth a quick stop. To reach it, continue south on SR-590 to SR-60 and turn right. At CR-611 (McMullen-Booth Road; 0.25), turn right. At Drew Street (0.4), turn left to Fairwood Avenue (0.8), then turn right. Cross the railroad tracks (0.6) and turn left onto Park Trail to the park entrance (0.2). To reach Moccasin Lake Park from US-19, go east on Drew Street (0.4 miles north of SR-60) to Fairwood Avenue (0.3), turn left, and proceed as above. The park contains hammocks and swamps that are traversed by trails and boardwalks. Limpkins may be seen along the lakeshore year-round, but the park is best during fall, when migrant landbirds can be common.

   Contact: *Moccasin Lake Park, 2750 Park Trail Lane, Clearwater, FL 33759-2602; 727-462-6024; <www.clearwater-fl.com/gov/depts/ parksrec/facilities/mlnp.asp>.*

S R-60 is one of three highways across Tampa Bay linking Clearwater/St. Petersburg with Tampa. The shoreline of **Courtney Campbell Causeway**, which is the portion of SR-60 that crosses Tampa Bay, can be excellent for a variety of waterbirds, especially during winter. From McMullen-Booth Road (CR-611), travel east and pull off onto the causeway to an unpaved parking area (0.2). Scan the bay for flocks of wintering waterfowl. Afterward, walk west to the sewage-treatment facility. During winter, a sandbar there can be covered with shorebirds at low tide, and there are usually a few Bonaparte's Gulls in the area.

LARGO–SEMINOLE

T hree small parks between Clearwater and St. Petersburg can be excellent for migrant landbirds during spring and fall. At each of these parks, more than 30 species of wood-warblers have been seen; Golden-winged, Cerulean, and Swainson's Warblers are regular. (See map on next page.)

   To reach **JOHN R. BONNER NATURE PARK** (22 acres; no fee; no camping; opens at 7:00 AM standard time, 8:00 AM daylight savings) from US-19, head west on SR-688 (Ulmerton Road, which becomes Walsingham Road). At 143rd Street (7.6), turn right to the park ahead (0.5). As you enter the gate, note the shell path on your right, and walk back to it after parking.

This minimally-maintained path circles a hammock and crosses a stream. A second path, which is paved, starts at the parking lot and loops through an oak hammock. *Park managers request that tapes not be used.*

Contact: *John R. Bonner Nature Park, 14444 143rd Street North, Largo, FL 33774; 727-518-3047.*

To search for Monk and Black-hooded Parakeets, return to SR-688 (Walsingham Road) and head east. At the traffic light, where Walsingham meets Ulmerton Road (1.3), turn right (downhill) onto Walsingham Road. At 125th Street (0.2), turn right again to an **electrical substation** that contains several Monk Parakeet nests. Continue south to the **ball field** (0.1) and check the wires and light poles for Black-hooded Parakeets.

Return to Walsingham Road, turn right, and continue to the north entrance of **Walsingham Park** (354 acres; no fee; no camping; opens at 7:00 AM) on the right (0.3). The park contains more than three miles of paved paths that travel past a Red Maple swamp, through pine flatwoods and oak scrub, and loop around a reservoir. Drive the main road to the Y-intersection (0.3), turn right, and continue to the entrance to shelters 3 through 6 (0.2). Turn right and park beyond shelter 6. Cross the main road bearing left, and turn right on the path that heads to the maple swamp (the trail begins under the first large oak). This path connects with short, unmarked fire lanes. Bird the swamp perimeter counterclockwise. At the paved road, turn left and bird this road to complete the swamp loop. Return to the parking lot and walk behind the shelters to scan for Limpkins, which may be found anywhere along the shore of the reservoir. Continue south on the main park road to the south bridge (1.3). Turn right and park at the north end of the lot beyond shelter 8 (0.4). Paved paths head north and south; the north path leads past an island where wading birds roost. By returning east to the main road, you can exit the park onto 102nd Avenue North.

Contact: *Walsingham Park, 110601 125th St. North, Largo, FL 33778; 727-549-6142; <www.pinellascounty.org/ park/22_Walsingham.htm>.*

Boca Ciega Millennium Park (184 acres; no fee; no camping; opens at 7:00 AM) lies along the eastern shore of Boca Ciega Bay. To reach it from Walsingham Park, head east on 102nd Avenue North to 125th Street (0.1). Turn right, watching for Black-hooded or Monk Parakeets along the wires. Cross CR-694 (Park Boulevard; 1.6) to 74th Avenue North (0.2). Turn left to the park entrance on the right (250 feet). Drive to the parking lot for shelter

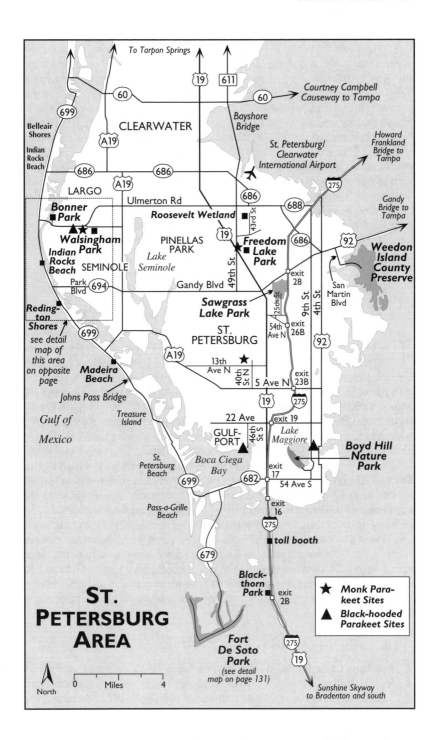

To Tarpon Springs

Courtney Campbell
Causeway to Tampa

CLEARWATER

Bayshore
Bridge

St. Petersburg/
Clearwater
International Airport

Belleair
Shores

Indian
Rocks
Beach

Howard
Frankland
Bridge to
Tampa

Gandy
Bridge to
Tampa

LARGO

Ulmerton Rd

Bonner
Park

Roosevelt Wetland

Walsingham
Park

PINELLAS
PARK

Freedom
Lake
Park

Weedon
Island
County
Preserve

Indian
Rocks
Beach

SEMINOLE

Lake
Seminole

Gandy Blvd

exit
28

San
Martin
Blvd

Park
Blvd

Sawgrass
Lake Park

Reding-
ton
Shores

ST.
PETERSBURG

54th
Ave N

exit
26B

see detail
map of
this area
on opposite
page

Madeira
Beach

13th
Ave N

5 Ave N

exit
23B

Johns Pass Bridge

Gulf of

Mexico

Treasure
Island

22 Ave

exit 19

GULF-
PORT

Lake
Maggiore

Boyd Hill
Nature
Park

St.
Petersburg
Beach

Boca Ciega
Bay

exit
17

54 Ave S

Pass-a-Grille
Beach

exit
16

toll booth

Black-
thorn
Park

exit
2B

Monk Para-
keet Sites

Black-hooded
Parakeet Sites

ST.
PETERSBURG
AREA

Fort
De Soto
Park
(see detail
map on page 131)

Sunshine Skyway
to Bradenton and south

North

0   Miles   4

5 (0.9) and turn right. Before parking, note the path on the right before the phone booth. Walk this path and bear right, cross the paved road, and begin the quarter-mile nature trail. Mosquitoes are frequently abundant, so bring repellent. The second half of the loop, which follows a stream, offers the best opportunity for migrant landbirds in season. You can also walk north of the nature trail (0.1) along unmarked fire lanes to another oak hammock. After birding the hammock, return to the parking lot and enter the paved path on the south side of the lot. This leads to a boardwalk with a 35-foot-tall observation tower that overlooks mangroves, mudflats, and the Intracoastal Waterway. Wadings birds such as Reddish Egret and Roseate Spoonbill may be seen at low tide. From the tower, walk the east boardwalk until it ends (0.2) at an overlook for wading birds. The west loop of the boardwalk passes through oaks (check for migrants) before arriving back at the shelter 5 parking lot. Other areas to check for migrant landbirds include woodlands around shelters 1, 3, and 7.

Contact: Boca Ciega Millennium Park, 12410 74th Avenue North, Seminole, FL 33772; 727-588-4882; <www.pinellascounty.org/park/ 03_Boca_Ciega.htm>.

INDIAN ROCKS BEACH–JOHNS PASS

The beaches from Indian Rocks Beach to Johns Pass can be productive for waterbirds, shorebirds, and larids. Offshore species such as Northern Gannet, Lesser Scaup, all three scoters (rare), and Pomarine and Parasitic Jaegers (rare) may be seen from shore. To avoid glare, it is best to scan the gulf before 10:00 AM. To reach the beaches, head west on CR-694 (Park Boulevard) across Boca Ciega Bay to SR-699 (Gulf Boulevard). Turn right to 1st Avenue and turn left into the **Indian Rocks Beach** parking lot (2.5). Eleven parking spaces are available (no fee) for non-residents. To reach other areas, head south on Gulf Boulevard to 182nd Avenue and park at the **Redington Shores Beach Access** ($1.00/hour) on the right (3.3). Limited (free) street parking is also available. After scanning the Gulf here, continue south to the north side of **Redington Long Pier** (1.0) and park on Gulf Boulevard. The area just north of the pier is the best location for resting larids, including Great and Lesser Black-backed Gull s, Sandwich Tern, and Black Skimmer. Farther south is a parking lot at **Madeira Beach**, on the northwest side of the Johns Pass Bridge (25¢/15 minutes; 4.0) at mile marker 8. Bonaparte's Gulls usually are found here during winter. Limited free parking is also available on the southeast side of the bridge; walk underneath the bridge to get to the beach.

ST. PETERSBURG

Freedom Lake Park(40 acres; no fee; no camping; opens at sunrise) offers fair birding. From US-19, head east on 49th Street. At Lake Boulevard (0.2), turn right and then make an immediate right onto 102nd Avenue. The park is on the right (0.2). To reach the park from I-275, exit (#28) onto SR-694 (Gandy Boulevard) and head west. At US-19, turn right to 49th Street (1.8), turn right and proceed as above. Monk Parakeets nest at the top of the tall communication tower and often are found foraging on the ground around the lake or perched in the oaks. A few Limpkins persist at the park, despite the city's efforts to "clean up" the lake by removing all emergent vegetation. Muscovy Ducks are common year-round.

Contact: Freedom Lake Park, 9990 46th Street North, Pinellas Park, FL 33782; <www.pinellas-park.com/Departments/Recreation/ freedomlake.asp>.

Nearby is the **Roosevelt Wetland** (no fee; no camping; accessible anytime), a series of shallow wetlands created for flood control. To reach it from 49th Street two blocks north of US-19 (and one block north of Freedom Lake Park), head east on Lake Boulevard to 43rd Street North (0.6). Turn left to the unpaved parking area on the right (0.2). The preserve contains open water and marshes surrounded by a levee that can be walked. Birds that may be seen include Mottled Duck (year-round), Least (year-round) and American (winter) Bitterns, wading birds, and Limpkin, which is more reliable here than at Freedom Lake Park. Black-necked Stilts bred here in 2003.

SAWGRASS LAKE PARK (400 acres; no fee; no camping; opens at sunrise) is an excellent birding spot during fall and winter (although during some winters, very few birds are found). To reach it from Freedom Lake Park, return to US-19, go south to 62nd Avenue North, and turn left. Just before an overpass (0.6), turn left onto 25th Street, and proceed to the park entrance ahead (0.4). From I-275 northbound, exit (#26B) onto 54th Avenue North and go northwest. Angle right onto Haines Road (0.3), turn right sharply onto 62nd Avenue North (0.8), and turn left onto 25th Street just before the overpass (0.5). The park contains Red Maple swamps, oak hammocks, a large portion of Sawgrass Lake, and other habitats. Two miles of trails wind through the forests, with more than a mile of elevated boardwalk, including an observation tower overlooking the lake. The state removed most of the vegetation from the lake, and since then, Sawgrass Lake has been generally sterile and often birdless. The park is most productive for migrant landbirds between mid-August and mid-September. The best areas are around the parking lot and in the oak hammock reached from the Maple Trail boardwalk (past Marker 6). After returning to the boardwalk, continue around the loop and return to the parking lot by walking along the canal. In a typical fall season, 30 or more warbler species are reported here, along with many other migrants.

Contact: Sawgrass Lake Park, 7400 25th Street North, St. Petersburg, FL 33702; 813-527-3814.

Weedon Island County Preserve (1,300 acres; no fee; no camping; opens at sunrise) is the largest natural area remaining in St. Petersburg.

Birding opportunities are limited because the preserve consists mostly of mangrove forest, making access difficult. However, in summer, Mangrove Cuckoos and Gray Kingbirds can be found. From I-275, go east on SR-694 (Gandy Boulevard), cross SR-92, and turn right onto San Martin Boulevard (1.1) just beyond Derby Lane Dog Track. At Weedon Drive (0.9), turn left. The entrance and Interpretive Center are on the left (1.0). From the center, walk the Bay Boardwalk any time from mid-May through the end of June for your best chances of finding the cuckoos. This is the northernmost known breeding site for Mangrove Cuckoos in the United States, and *birders should not use tapes here.* Cuckoos may also be found along the Tower Boardwalk and the Boy Scout trail leading to Lookout Point.

Contact: *Weedon Island County Preserve, 1500 Weedon Island Drive, St. Petersburg, FL 33702; 727-579-8360.*

Monk **Parakeets** are locally common throughout the greater St. Petersburg area. One reliable spot is an **electrical substation** on 13th Avenue North west of US-19 and I-275. To reach it from the Interstate, exit (#23B) onto SR-595 (5th Avenue North) and head west. At US-19 (34th Street North; 1.1), turn right to 13th Avenue North (0.5). Turn left to the substation on the right just beyond 40th Street North (0.5; address is 4055 13th Avenue North). Several parakeet nests are built on substation structures, and the birds can easily be seen from outside the fenced area. Eurasian Collared-Doves should also be seen here.

Black-hooded Parakeets, recently ratified as an established exotic by the Florida Ornithological Society Records Committee (but not yet ABA-countable), are also common in parts of St. Petersburg. One reliable spot is **Gulfport Municipal Marina**. To reach it from I-275, exit (#19) onto 22nd Avenue South (Gulfport Boulevard) and head west. At 46th Street South (1.0), turn left to its end at 29th Avenue South (0.5). Turn right to the marina just ahead on the left. Nearly 200 parakeets have been seen here at once; early morning and evening are the best times.

Boyd Hill Nature Park (245 acres; $1.00/person; no camping; opens at 9:00 AM Tuesday through Saturday, 11:00 AM Sunday, closed Monday) is worth a stop during fall, when migrant landbirds can be common. The park has several oak hammocks along the south side of Lake Maggiore (pronounced *ma-GOR-ee*) in southern St. Petersburg. To reach the park from US-19 or I-275 (Exit #17), go east on 54th Avenue South (SR-682). At 9th Street South (M.L. King Street; 2.0) turn left, then make another left onto Country Club Drive South (0.6). The park is on the right. In the past 10 years, 33 species of warblers have been found here. The park is a dependable spot for Cerulean Warblers in August and September.

Contact: *Boyd Hill Nature Park, 1101 Country Club Way South, St. Petersburg, Florida 33713; 727-893-7326; <www.stpete.org/fun/parks/ ayboyd3.htm>.*

FORT DE SOTO PARK (1,136 acres; no fee; 233 campsites at $27.75/day; opens at sunrise) is one of the most famous migratory stop-over sites in Florida, and one of the state's most popular birding spots. It is also popular with recreationists, attracting more than 2.7 million visitors annually. The park is situated at the mouth of Tampa Bay between St. Petersburg and Anna Maria Island. Fort De Soto Park and several other nearby islands, such as Egmont Key National Wildlife Refuge, Passage Key National Wildlife Refuge, Pinellas National Wildlife Refuge, and Shell Key Preserve are among the most important sites in Florida for breeding wading birds, shorebirds, larids, and Neotropical migrants. The park's location as the first landfall for trans-Gulf migrants, its large size and varied habitats, and its near-daily coverage by some of the state's best birders all contribute to its large and diverse bird list of more than 300 species. Rarities seen in the past 10 years have included Heermann's Gull, Elegant Tern, Long-billed Murrelet, Sulphur-bellied Flycatcher, several Tropical Kingbirds (apparently post-breeding dispersers from the Yucatán Peninsula), Yellow-green Vireo, Kirtland's Warbler, Bananaquit (perhaps also from the Yucatán), and Lazuli Bunting.

History buffs will also find plenty to enjoy. Construction of the fort began in March 1899 and was completed the following year. It was named in honor of Hernando de Soto, the Spanish explorer who landed at Tampa Bay in 1539. Today, the fort displays the only four 1890-model, 12-inch rifled seacoast mortars that remain in the continental United States. Additionally, two 1898-model, 6-inch Armstrong rapid-fire rifled guns from nearby Fort Dade (on Egmont Key) have been repositioned outside Fort De Soto. In 1977, Fort De Soto was added to the National Register of Historic Places. A newly reconstructed Quartermaster Storehouse Museum provides a history of the area.

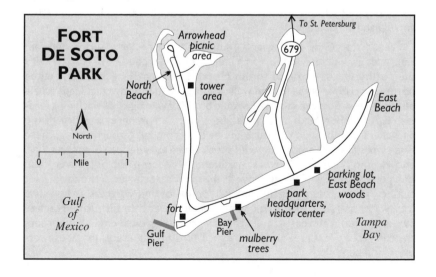

To reach the park from US-19 (34th Street) or I-275 (Exit #17) in St. Petersburg, drive west on State Road 682 (Pinellas Bayway; 54th Avenue South). After the 50¢ toll booth (1.0), watch for Monk or Black-hooded Parakeets on the wires along the road. At State Road 679 (1.3), turn left. You will reach the park ahead (5.0) after encountering another toll booth (35¢). Head straight to the park headquarters at the T-intersection to pick up a bird list. Then head east to the parking lot for what are known locally as the **East Beach woods** (0.2). From the east end of the parking lot, enter the woods on the left just before the beach. These woods, composed of Australian-pines and mangroves, are one of the best areas in the park for migrant landbirds. Note that the unmarked trails may be flooded in places and can harbor lots of mosquitoes. Although numerous landbirds can be found in the Australian-pines (many of which are being removed by park staff because this species is an invasive exotic), the East Beach woods also are good for lower- and mid-story species such as thrushes, Hooded and Swainson's Warblers, and both waterthrushes. Cross the small creek at the end of the trail to return along another woods trail, or walk along the beach back to the parking area.

Return to the main road and continue east to its end at **East Beach turnaround** (1.5), where wading birds, shorebirds, and larids should be found. Afterward, turn around and head west past the T-intersection. At the Bay Pier on the left (0.9), park in the parking lot and walk east around the ranger's house (*stay outside the fence!*) to a **grove of mulberry trees**. Hummingbird feeders and a fountain built specifically for birds are also here. The fountain is named after Larry Hopkins, a well-known local birder who died several years ago. In the spring, the fruiting trees, feeders, and the fountain attract many migrants. Black-hooded Parakeets have also been seen here in recent years. Next, stop at the **Gulf Pier** (0.8) to scan the Gulf and to check the trees for migrants in the picnic area and around the fort. During spring and fall, check the grassy fields in this area for American Golden-Plovers and Buff-breasted and Upland Sandpipers.

Watch for Gray (spring and summer) and Western (spring and fall) Kingbirds as you head to the north end of the park road (2.6). Turn left into the northernmost entrance to the **North Beach** parking lot. Park at the northwest corner of the lot and walk west to the foot bridge that leads to the beach. At low tide, the sand flats should be full of wading birds (including Reddish Egrets), shorebirds, and larids. Be sure to arrive here early before the picnickers and their dogs disturb the birds. From fall through spring, these flats offer superb shorebirding, with species such as American Oystercatcher, Snowy and Wilson's Plovers (resident breeders), Piping Plover, and Long-billed Curlew. The oak grove at the northeast corner of the parking lot can be excellent during spring and fall for vireos and warblers. There is a freshwater pond and a large oak hammock (accessed by trails) that is reached by walking south and east around the mangrove-vegetated ditch that borders the oak grove. This area also can be good for migrant vireos, thrushes, warblers, and buntings.

Wilson's Plover in breeding plumage.   Arthur Morris/www.birdsasart.com

Across the main park road from North Beach Concession is **Arrowhead Picnic Area**, another excellent area for migrant landbirds. The road winds through an oak hammock before ending at the picnic area. Unmarked paths cross this area; all are excellent for birds during migration. Marked trails through adjacent woods are also productive. The **Tower Area** to the south can be reached via these picnic area trails. During spring and fall, this area can also support numbers of thrushes, warblers, and buntings. Single-day counts of more than 25 warbler species have been made here after the passage of weather fronts.

> **Contact:** *Fort De Soto Park, 3500 Pinellas Bayway South, Tierra Verde, FL 33715; 727-582-2267; <www.pinellascounty.org/park/05_Ft_DeSoto. htm>.*

Depart St. Petersburg southbound on I-275 via the impressive **Sunshine Skyway bridge** ($1.00/vehicle). The Sunshine Skyway is the longest cable-stayed concrete bridge in the world, 29,040 feet long and 193 feet above the water at its center. The causeways on both sides of the bridge can be excellent for wading birds, shorebirds, and larids, especially at low tide. From the north toll booth leaving St. Petersburg, check out the first scenic view (1.2). Continue to Exit #2B (1.0) to the North Skyway Fishing Pier and rest area. Turn right just before **U.S.C.G. Blackthorn Park** (which honors a Coast Guard crew that perished when their cutter collided with a tanker and sank just offshore) onto a road curving back north along the shoreline. You can bird along here for about a half-mile. Among numerous common species, look for Magnificent Frigatebird (mostly spring and summer), American White Pelicans (winter), Reddish Egret, American Oystercatchers, and other shorebirds and larids, predominantly during winter. Lesser Black-backed Gulls have begun to winter here. Farther along are other birding sites along the causeway. (On the *northbound side* of the causeway, a hiker-biker trail allows access for the causeway's entire length. It starts on Pinellas Point Drive and 34th Street South, just east of I-275 at Exit #3 [northbound] of the highway).

After you cross over the bridge, you will be in Manatee County and may choose to bird a few sites in Bradenton (see page 138).

TAMPA

Lettuce Lake Park (240 acres; $1.00/vehicle; no camping; opens at 8:00 AM) is located on the north side of CR-582A (Fletcher Avenue) 1.0 mile west of I-75. The park's main attraction is a 3,500-foot boardwalk, including a 35-foot-tall observation tower, along the Hillsborough River. During low water levels, numbers of wading birds, including Roseate Spoonbills and both species of night-herons, can be seen from the boardwalk. Ospreys are common, and Limpkins and Barred Owls also occur. During spring and summer, Prothonotary Warblers breed along the river. A one-mile nature tail and a paved bicycle path also provide good birding opportunities. The portion of the paved path to the right of the boardwalk entrances can produce numerous wintering landbirds and migrants (especially during fall). Short-tailed Hawks are reported fairly frequently during spring and fall.

Contact: *Lettuce Lake Regional Park, 6920 East Fletcher Avenue, Tampa, FL 33592; 813-987-6204; <www.hillsboroughcounty.org/ parks/parkservices/regionalparks.cfml>.*

Northeast of the city is a vast expanse of pine flatwoods, sandhills, and other habitats that serves as a regional well field. Known collectively as **WILDERNESS PARK** (15,897 acres; no camping; opens at 8:00 AM), the area is divided into six units. Four of these units are described here, and each has an entrance fee of $1.00/vehicle. Three of the sites are along SR-579 (Morris Bridge Road—the continuation of Fletcher Avenue east of I-75), while the fourth site is to the east, along US-301. **Trout Creek Park** lies along the north side of Morris Bridge Road about 0.5 miles northeast of I-75 (Exit #266). A small boardwalk along the river and several other nature trails can be good for landbirds year-round; Swallow-tailed Kites are often seen overhead during spring and summer. **Morris Bridge Park** is located on both sides of Fowler Avenue/Morris Bridge Road 3.7 miles northeast of I-75. The portion of the park north of SR-579 has a 1,500-foot boardwalk and a trail along the river, which can be good for migrant landbirds during fall. The southern portion of the park contains a 4,000-foot tram road that ends at the

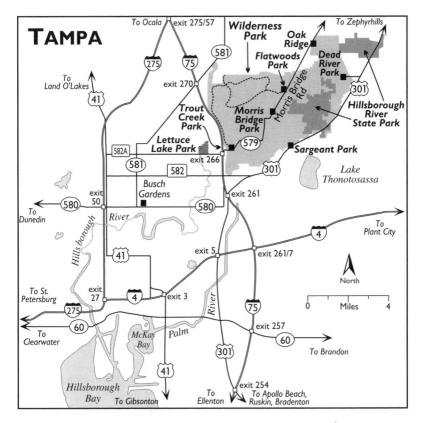

site of an old railroad bridge on the river, where Barred Owls are frequently seen. The entrance to **Flatwoods Park** is on the west side of Morris Bridge Road, 1.5 miles northeast of Morris Bridge Park. The park contains a nine-mile paved bicycle path and three 2,000-foot interpretive trails, all of which can all be good for fall migrants. Yellow-throated Vireo (spring and summer), Carolina Chickadee, Eastern Bluebird, and Bachman's Sparrow are fairly common along the bicycle path. **John B. Sargeant, Sr. Memorial Park** is on the west side of US-301, three miles northeast of SR-582 (Fowler Avenue; I-75 Exit #265). The park has a short circular boardwalk along the Hillsborough River that may produce Limpkins (year-round) and Prothonotary Warblers (spring and summer).

Contact: *Wilderness Park, Hillsborough County Parks and Recreation Administrative Office, 1101 East River Cove Street, Tampa, FL 33604; 813-975-2160; <http://www.hillsboroughcounty.org/parks/parkservices/regionalparks.cfm>.*

H illsborough River State Park (3,383 acres; $4.00/vehicle; 108 camp-sites at $13.00/day; opens at 8:00 AM) contains extensive hammock and riparian habitats that are good for landbirds during winter and fall migration. Continue on US-301 to the entrance on the left (six miles from Sargeant Park or nine miles from SR-582). From SR-54 West at Zephyrhills, head south on US-301 to the entrance on the right (7.2). The best birding is on the nature trail along the river, which begins at the small set of rapids. Two nature trails across the river can also be productive. Mosquitoes are often plentiful, so bring repellent.

Contact: Hillsborough River State Park, 15402 US-301 North, Thonotosassa, FL 33592; 813-987-6771; <www.floridastateparks.org/hillsboroughriver>.

APOLLO BEACH–RUSKIN

T ampa Electric Company offers winter visitors a chance to observe West Indian Manatees at their **Big Bend power plant**. The plant, located north of Apollo Beach, is visible for a considerable distance. To reach it, exit I-75 (Exit #246) at Big Bend Road (CR-672) and head west to the viewing center on the right, at the junction of Dickman Road (2.5). The viewing center is open from 1 December through 31 March (but is *closed on Mondays*) from 10 AM–5:00 PM. A boardwalk offers access to part of Hillsborough Bay; watch for Reddish Egrets here during low tide.

Contact: Tampa Electric Company Manatee Viewing Center, 813-228-4289; <www.tampaelectric.com/TEEVMVCLearning.cfm>.

E.G. Simmons Park (469 acres; $1.00/vehicle) offers a view of eastern Tampa Bay with its wintering Common Loons, American White Pelicans, larids, and other species. To reach it from US-41 in Ruskin, head west onto 19th Avenue NW (traffic light) to E.G. Simmons Parkway (2.0). Turn right to the park ahead. To reach the beach and boat ramp areas, turn left at the T-intersection once inside the park.

Contact: E.G. Simmons Park, 2410 19th Avenue NW, Ruskin, FL 33570; 813-671-7655; <www.hillsboroughcounty.org/parks/parkservices/regionalparks.cfm>.

C ockroach Bay Road offers varied birding opportunities for breeding Mangrove Cuckoos and Gray Kingbirds, and migrant shorebirds during fall. To reach it from 19th Avenue NW, head south on US-41 and turn west (4.7). A sod farm immediately to the right is worth checking during fall (August and September). Continue to another sod farm on the right (1.4–1.9), which is reliable for Pectoral Sandpipers and which may support Upland Sandpipers as well. Breeding Gray Kingbirds may be seen anywhere along the road from April through August; watch the power lines. The boat ramp at the end of the road (1.2) is often crowded with boaters, but the mangroves in this area

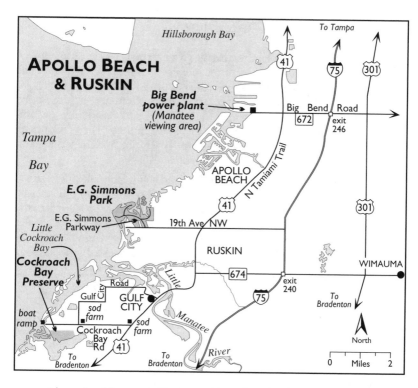

APOLLO BEACH & RUSKIN

Hillsborough Bay

To Tampa

41 • 75 • 301

Big Bend power plant (Manatee viewing area)

Big Bend Road
672 • exit 246

Tampa Bay

APOLLO BEACH

N Tamiami Trail

E.G. Simmons Park

41

E.G. Simmons Parkway

19th Ave NW

301

Little Cockroach Bay

RUSKIN

WIMAUMA

Cockroach Bay Preserve

674 • exit 240 • 75

To Bradenton

Gulf City Road

GULF CITY

sod farm

boat ramp

sod farm

Cockroach Bay Rd

41

Little

Manatee

River

To Bradenton

To Bradenton

North

0   Miles   2

support breeding Mangrove Cuckoos. From late April through July, cuckoos may be lured out with the *judicious* use of tapes. Another area for the cuckoos is accessed from the gated trail on the right as you head back east from the boat ramp (0.3). This path is part of the **Cockroach Bay Preserve** (875 acres; no facilities; no camping) and is open to foot traffic during daylight hours. The trail is sparingly maintained but should still be visible. It leads to open salt barren surrounded by mangroves on the right.

The Gulf coast between Tampa Bay and the Fort Myers area is heavily developed and contains few worthwhile birding sites. The exceptions are listed below, and even these can be bypassed if time is a factor. (However, Myakka River State Park is a beautiful spot, and Black-bellied Whistling-Ducks are most abundant in Florida around Sarasota). If time is short, it is best to drive through the area from St. Petersburg or Tampa on I-75. To visit Fort Myers, Sanibel Island, or the lower east coast, continue south on I-75. To bird the central prairies for Glossy Ibis, Crested Caracara, Burrowing Owl, and Florida Scrub-Jay, exit I-75 at either SR-70 (#217) or SR-72 (#205), which joins SR-70 near Arcadia. Those wishing to look for Black-bellied Whistling-Ducks should exit I-75 at SR-780 (#210; Fruitville Road). To visit Myakka River State Park, exit I-75 at SR-72 (#205); see page 141.

BRADENTON

To reach the **Palma Sola Causeway**, go south on US-41 to SR-64 (Manatee Avenue), turn right, and proceed west to the causeway (5.0). The causeway bisects Palma Sola Bay, which often has Reddish Egrets, Yellow-crowned Night-Herons, and other coastal species. Continue west to Perico Island. Bird the shore before you get to the bridge (1.9). In addition to common species, look for Reddish Egrets and Roseate Spoonbills here. Continue west on SR-64 to its end, at **Manatee County Public Beach**. Monk Parakeets nest in the palms around the restrooms.

To reach **Longboat Key** from SR-64, head south from the public beach on CR-789 (Gulf Drive). After crossing over the Longboat Key bridge (4.0), turn right onto Broadway (0.5) to the parking area. Take the boardwalk to the beach. It is best to get here early, because the beach is usually crowded with people except in the early morning. A few pairs of Snowy and Wilson's Plovers still nest on the beach, along with Least Terns and Black Skimmers. **Beer**

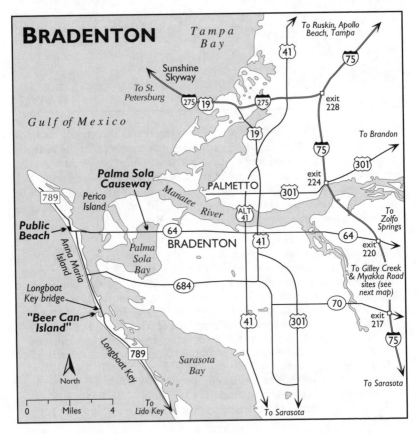

Can Island, which is really the northern tip of Longboat Key, can be good for migrant landbirds in spring. Wading birds including Reddish Egret and Roseate Spoonbill, and shorebirds such as American Oystercatchers can be found in the lagoon east of the "island." Magnificent Frigatebirds roost on nearby islands and may be seen overhead during spring and summer.

The portion of Manatee County east of I-75 offers locations for Black-bellied Whistling-Duck (local), Swallow-tailed Kite (spring and summer), Purple Gallinule, Burrowing Owl (local), and Bachman's Sparrow (see next map, for Sarasota). Purple Gallinules are dependable during summer below the bridge crossing **Gilley Creek**, northeast of Lake Manatee, on CR-675. From I-75, exit (#220) onto SR-64 and head east to CR-675 (10). Turn left to Gilley Creek (1.5). Park just beyond the bridge and walk back. Purple Gallinules may be found in the marsh to the west, and Barn and Northern Rough-winged Swallows nest under the bridge during spring and summer. Burrowing Owls are occasionally seen sitting on fence posts about 0.5 mile north of the bridge.

Birders with additional time to explore may wish to drive **Myakka Road** between SR-64 and SR-70 for wetland and prairie/pasture species (see Sarasota map). From CR-675, Myakka Road is about 13.5 miles east along SR-64, or about 9.5 miles east along SR-70 (it's the blinking light at the hamlet of Myakka City). Birds along this 10-mile route can include Glossy Ibis, Wild Turkey, Sandhill Crane, and Eastern Bluebird. About halfway along the route is a small bridge across Long Creek; park beyond the bridge and walk back. In addition to common wading birds, the creek may produce Black-crowned Night-Heron, Black-bellied Whistling-Duck, and Mottled Ducks.

SARASOTA

OSCAR SCHERER STATE PARK (1,382 acres; $4.00/vehicle; camping at $11.00–$16.50/day; opens at 8:00 AM) contains the largest protected population of Florida Scrub-Jays along Florida's Gulf coast. To reach the park from I-75 southbound, exit (#200) onto SR-681 and head southwest (see map on next page). At US-41, turn right to the entrance on the right (1.0). To reach the park from I-75 northbound, exit (#193) onto Jacaranda Boulevard and head south to Venice Avenue (0.7). Turn right to US-41 (3.0), and turn right to the park entrance on the right (5.8). About 35 groups of Florida Scrub-Jays are resident in this park (mostly the northeastern portion), and many of the birds are tame, but *feeding the jays is against park policy*. The park also contains several Bald Eagle nests.

Contact: *Oscar Scherer State Park, 1843 South Tamiami Trail, Osprey, FL 34229; 941-483-5956; <www.floridastateparks.org/oscarscherer>.*

Ackerman Park (no fee; no camping) can be great for wintering waterfowl and other species. To reach it from I-75, exit (#210) onto Fruitville

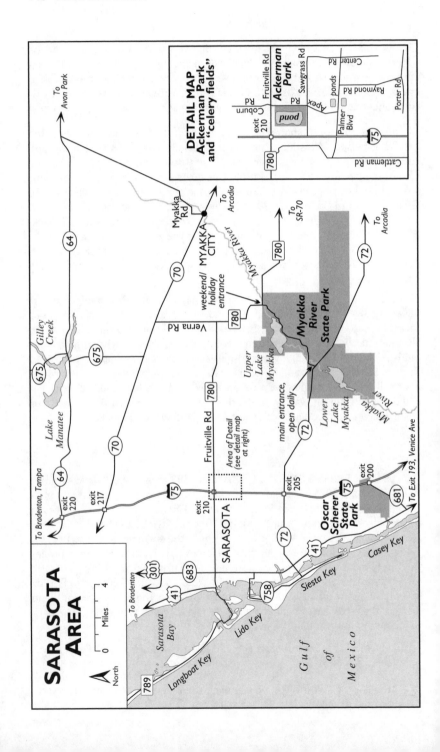

Road and head east to Coburn Road (0.5; first right). Turn right (the road name changes to Apex Road) to the park on the right (0.5). In addition to wintering ducks, look for Wood Stork, Glossy Ibis (mainly winter), Sandhill Crane (resident), and migrant and wintering shorebirds. Limpkins are seen occasionally, and Monk Parakeets may be found in palms in the park.

Recently, an area dubbed the **SARASOTA CELERY FIELDS** by local birders has proven to be another excellent birding spot. To reach it from Ackerman Park, continue south on Apex Road to its dead end at Palmer Boulevard (0.6). Turn left and park at the gazebo on the left (0.5). Ponds on both sides of Palmer Road consistently host Black-bellied Whistling-Ducks and can be excellent for wintering sparrows (13 species were found during 2002–2003). When water levels are suitable, shorebirds may be found during migration and winter; Black-necked Stilts breed during spring and summer. Barn Owls have been seen at dusk from the gazebo. A bit farther east is Center Road. Turn left and park where possible. Bird the shrubby areas and fencerows for wintering sparrows.

MYAKKA RIVER STATE PARK (28,875 acres; $5.00/vehicle; 76 campsites at $22.00/day; opens at 8:00 AM) southeast of Sarasota is an excellent birding spot. To reach it from I-75, exit (#205) onto SR-72 and go east to the entrance on the left (9.0). From Arcadia, the park is on the north side of SR-72 in about 27 miles. On weekends and holidays, a second entrance is available—head east from I-75 (Exit #210) on Fruitville Road to Verna Road (11) and turn right to the entrance on the right (3.7); scan the marshes at the Myakka River bridge for Black-bellied Whistling-Ducks. During spring and summer, watch the skies for Swallow-tailed Kites. East of the park entrance on SR-72, the marshes visible from bridges over the Myakka River and Clay Gully can host large numbers of wading birds, wintering waterfowl, and migrant and wintering shorebirds, depending on water levels. Fulvous and Black-bellied Whistling-Ducks have both been seen here. The park contains extensive oak and palm hammocks that can be good for fall migrant and wintering landbirds, but the main attractions are waterbirds. Over 12 miles of Myakka River frontage are contained in the park, and the extensive marshes and lakes attract wading birds including Glossy Ibis, Wood Stork, and Roseate Spoonbill (late summer), waterfowl (mainly during winter, but Mottled Duck is resident), Limpkin (resident), Sandhill Crane, and a few shorebirds (White-rumped Sandpiper occurs in late May and early June when water levels are low). Purple Gallinules also occur here but are difficult to find in the heavy vegetation. During winter, various ducks are usually present on Upper Myakka Lake and can best be viewed from the bird observation boardwalk north of the marina and store.

Contact: *Myakka River State Park, 13207 State Road 72, Sarasota, FL 34241-9542; 941-361-6511; <www.floridastateparks.org/myakkariver>.*

Gulf coastal areas continue on page 188.

CENTRAL PENINSULA—INLAND

LEESBURG–EUSTIS

EMERALDA MARSH CONSERVATION AREA (7,089 acres; no fee; no camping; opens at 8:00 AM; *seasonal hunting*) comprises mostly former agricultural land acquired in the early 1990s to improve water quality in adjacent Lake Griffin. The conservation area, consisting primarily of wetlands with scattered "islands" of hammocks and fields, is noted for concentrations of wading birds year-round and waterfowl and landbirds during fall and winter. It is accessible from levee roads. A 4.3-mile, one-way driving route (opens at 8:00 AM Fridays–Sundays) is open to motor vehicles *from the third weekend in February through May only*. But the road may be walked or biked year-round. There are several entrances into the area; this description focuses on Emeralda Island Road, which offers the greatest diversity of birds and habitats. Take CR-44 east from Leesburg or west from Eustis to the village of Lisbon. Head north on Lisbon Road to the T-intersection at Emeralda Island Road (0.75). Turn left to

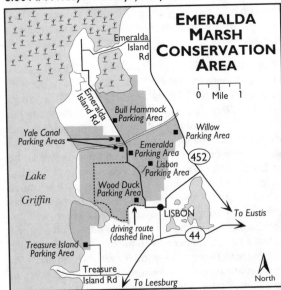

the entrance to Wood Duck parking lot on the left (0.5). Other entrances are 0.3, 0.9, and 1.3 miles farther north, as well as along CR-452, 5.8 and 6.4 miles north of CR-44, and along Treasure Island Road, which intersects CR-44 approximately seven miles west of Eustis.

Colonial waterbird rookeries that contain Glossy Ibises and numerous other species are located along the border of Lake Griffin. The rookeries are active from January through June. Black-bellied Whistling-Ducks, Least Bitterns, Purple Gallinules, and Limpkins breed in the adjacent marshes. During summer, Yellow-breasted Chats can be found in shrubby areas. Fall migrant landbirds can be abundant; Yellow Warblers are especially numerous along wetland edges and in willow thickets during August–September. Watch for flocks of Bobolinks in April or May.

B ird diversity and abundance peak during winter. Waterfowl, Wood Storks, and American Coots are usually abundant, and several hundred American White Pelicans may also be present. The most common ducks are Blue-winged Teal and Ring-necked Duck; Fulvous Whistling-Ducks are sporadic. Willow thickets bordering the Yale Canal between Emeralda Island Road and CR 452 are good for landbirds. Among wintering species, Orange-crowned Warbler is fairly common, and Least Flycatcher and Painted Bunting are present in small numbers. Rarities that are found in most winters are Ash-throated Flycatcher, Wilson's Warbler, and Yellow-breasted Chat. Fields along the northern section of the driving route contain large numbers of sparrows during winter. Savannah and Swamp Sparrows are common, and White-crowned, White-throated, Field, Lincoln's, Grasshopper, and Song Sparrows are regular in smaller numbers. In the fields northeast of the Bull Hammock parking area, Sedge Wrens are common, and Le Conte's and Henslow's Sparrows have been found on occasion.

Contacts: *Emeralda Marsh Conservation Area, St. Johns River Water Management District; 1-386-329-4404; <www.sjrwmd.com/programs/ operations/land_mgmt/trail_guides/pdfs/Emeralda_Drive_TG.pdf>, <www.stetson.edu/~pmay/emeralda/emindex.htm>.*

GREATER ORLANDO

B irding sites in the Greater Orlando area fall into three regions: downtown Orlando in the center, and areas to the northwest and east. Because of the number of birding sites listed and the distances between them, traveling from one of these areas to another may be difficult. Study the maps and directions carefully to determine your best route. Remember that traffic on most major roads in the area can be horrendous during rush hours (7:30–9:30 AM and 4–6:00 PM). Also, note that directions on road signs along I-4 are listed as east and west, even though the Interstate runs roughly north-south through Orlando. To go north, follow directions *east* (toward Daytona Beach); to head south, go *west* (toward Tampa). See Orlando maps on next page.

DOWNTOWN ORLANDO

T wo small parks in the downtown area are worth visits for common resident species and for migrant landbirds during fall. The first of these is **Harry P. Leu Botanical Gardens** (50 acres; $5.00/person; no camping; opens at 9:00 AM) located on Lake Rowena. To reach it from I-4, exit (#85) onto Princeton Street and head east to its end at US 17/92 (Mills Avenue; 0.7). Turn right to Nebraska Street (0.3), then turn left. At North Forest Avenue (0.4), turn left into the gardens via the mansion-style visitor center (0.1). Sprawling Live Oaks cover much of the grounds and provide excellent cover for migrant and resident landbirds. Resident species include Wood Duck,

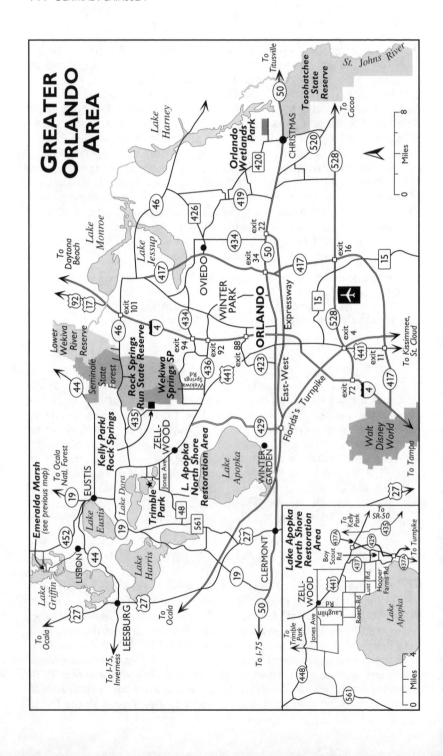

Limpkin, and Pileated Woodpecker. Check the butterfly garden for hummingbirds. A tour through the historic Harry P. Leu home is worthwhile.

Contact: Harry P. Leu Botanical Gardens, 1920 North Forest Avenue, Orlando, FL 32803; 407-246-2620; <www.leugardens.org>.

The other city park worth a visit is **MEAD GARDEN** (55 acres; no fee; no camping; opens at sunrise) in Winter Park. To reach it from Leu Botanical Gardens, return to Mills Avenue (US-17/92) and turn right. Mills Avenue becomes Orlando Avenue in Winter Park. At Orange Avenue (1.3), turn right to South Denning Avenue (0.3). Turn right to the entrance on the left (0.3). A stream along the park's eastern boundary is lined with Bald Cypress and attracts wading birds and Limpkins. Much of the uplands in the park are oak hammocks, which can be excellent for fall migrant landbirds. As many as 23 species of warblers have been reported here in a fall season. Breeding birds include Barred Owl and Yellow-throated Warbler. A butterfly garden in the north portion of the park attracts hummingbirds year-round.

Contact: Mead Garden, 1300 South Denning Drive, Winter Park, FL 32789; 407-599-3334; <www.ci.winter-park.fl.us/2005/depts/parks/meadgarden.shtml>.

NORTHWEST ORLANDO

To protect a regional population of Black Bears, a system of large, contiguous preserves has been established along the Wekiva River basin northwest of Orlando. Because most of the area is not accessible to passenger vehicles, only two of the sites are included here. **WEKIWA SPRINGS STATE PARK** (8,140 acres; $5.00/vehicle; 60 campsites at $20.00/day; opens at 8:00 AM) is closer to downtown and offers more access. To reach it, go north on I-4 and exit (#92) onto SR-436 (Semoran Boulevard). Head west to Wekiwa Springs Road (0.9) and turn right to the entrance on the right (4.1). From US-441, go east on SR-436 to Wekiwa Springs Road (1.6) and turn left to the entrance on the left (2.9). The park contains eight miles of frontage along Rock Springs Run, where Limpkins may be found. The park can be excellent for migrant landbirds, especially during fall.

Contact: Wekiva Basin State Parks, 1800 Wekiwa Circle, Apopka, FL 32712; 407-884-2008; <www.floridastateparks.org/wekiwasprings>.

North of the state park is **Rock Springs Run State Reserve** (13,850 acres; $2.00/vehicle; no camping; opens at 8:00 AM; *seasonal hunting*). To reach it from I-4, head west on SR-46 and turn left into the reserve at CR-433 (1.9). From the usually unmanned entrance booth, you may either continue south or immediately turn left onto an unpaved road that leads to a horse-riding concession. Beyond this point, the road is very rough and not passable by passenger cars, but the track can be walked. Birding here can be very good for migrant landbirds during fall. More than 20 miles of trails and old roads offer birding access throughout the reserve, but most are open only to foot traffic. At the end of the pavement (1.8), stop and look for Florida Scrub-Jays in the oak scrub west of the road. Swallow-tailed Kites are observed frequently during spring and summer, and Sandhill Cranes are resident. As you return to SR-46, notice the fence along both sides of the road. The fence was constructed to prevent Black Bears from crossing the road by funneling them to an underpass below the road. This area of Florida, north to Ocala National Forest, has the highest incidence of vehicle-caused bear mortality in the state.

Contact: Rock Springs Run State Reserve; same address and phone number as Wekiwa Springs; <www.floridastateparks.org/rockspringsrun>.

Kelly Park/Rock Springs (248 acres; $1.00/person; 23 campsites; opens at 8:00 AM November–March, 9:00 AM April–October) is adjacent to Wekiva Springs State Park but is not accessible from it. From Rock Springs Run State Reserve, travel west on SR-46 to SR-435 (St. Andrews Drive, which becomes Mount Plymouth Road; 4.5). Turn left to its end at Kelly Park Drive (4.0), then turn left. Continue through the sharp turn to the left (3.8) to the entrance on the right (0.1). From the south, take US-441 to Apopka, then head north on CR-435 (called North Park Avenue at this point, but it later becomes Rock Springs Road). At its dead-end at Kelly Park Drive (6.0), turn right and proceed as above. From the north, take US-441 to Zellwood, then head east on Poncan Road (0.3 south of Jones Avenue). At CR-435 (Rock Springs Road; 5.4), turn left to its end at Kelly Park Drive (1.8) and proceed as above. Wild Turkeys often are seen in the parking lot before crowds arrive. Mixed forests of hardwoods and pines offer good birding for fall migrant landbirds.

Contact: Kelly Park/Rock Springs, 400 East Kelly Park Road, Apopka, FL 32712; 407-836-6280.

From the 1960s through 1998, one of Florida's premier birding sites from late summer through fall was the flooded agricultural fields along the northeast shore of Lake Apopka, informally known to birders as the **Zellwood Muck Farms**. For over 50 years, these farms discharged billions of gallons of polluted water into the lake as part of routine farming operations. By the late 1990s, Lake Apopka was the state's most polluted body of water, and a major effort was undertaken to restore it. The primary means of cleaning up Lake Apopka was to buy out the farms to prevent continued discharge of polluted water. By late 1998, all of the farms had been purchased, at a cost exceeding $100 million. This 20,000-acre area now is known as **LAKE APOPKA NORTH SHORE RESTORATION AREA**. Many fields, flooded during summer 1998 for weed control, remained flooded through the winter; these fields attracted well over 100,000 waterbirds. During this time, the restoration area was visited by birders on a weekly basis to view the incredible numbers and diversity of species. Unfortunately, pesticide residues were present in at least one field, and a significant die-off of large fish-eating birds (primarily American White Pelicans) occurred. By February 1999, all the fields had been drained, and they remained unflooded through 2004. The U. S. Fish and Wildlife Service conducted a criminal investigation into the bird die-off, and the area remains off-limits to the public (although birders have been granted special access when rarities have been found). Through extensive soil sampling, it was discovered that an 11-acre "hotspot" was the primary source of the toxins. Soil at the "hotspot" was removed, and the area now is believed to be free of pesticide residues.

Since August 1998 from , Harry Robinson of De Land has conducted more than 650 surveys of the restoration area and has observed more than 300 species of birds. Included among these are several notable high counts and significant species, such as the first verifiable Florida records for Rough-legged Hawk and Eurasian Kestrel, as well as the first state breeding record for Dickcissel. It seems likely that the restoration area will be opened to birders within the next few years. It is located along US-441 (Orange Blossom Trail) at Zellwood, a small community 4.8 miles south of SR-46 and about 20 miles northwest of SR-50. From the traffic light at Jones Avenue, head west to unpaved Laughlin Road (0.25) and turn left. To reach the southeastern portion of the restoration area from Orlando, head north on SR-429 from SR-50 or Florida's Turnpike. At CR-437A (Exit #30; Ocoee–Apopka Road, about 7 miles north of SR-50), turn left. Go north to Boy Scout Road (0.8) and turn left to its end at CR-437 (South Binion Road; 1.2). To reach Lust Road, head north and then turn left (0.5); to reach Hooper Farms Road, head south and then turn right (0.5). Each road ends at a locked gate in less than a mile, but the road edges and fields can be good for wintering sparrows and other species of shrubby habitats; watch also for raptors overhead. (*Bird only from the roads.*) During winter evenings, there usually is a large tyrannid roost along Hooper Farms Road; more than 70 birds, mostly Western Kingbirds, have been seen at peak times. Watch also for Scissor-tailed Flycatchers and one or two Cassin's Kingbirds or Tropical Kingbirds.

Contact: Lake Apopka North Shore Restoration Area, St. Johns River Water Management District, P.O. Box 1429, Palatka, FL 32178; 321-676-6614; <www.sjrwmd.com/programs/outreach/pubs/recguide/pdfs/ lapopka.pdf>.

A few miles north of Zellwood is **Trimble Park** (71 acres; no fee; campsites at $18.00/day; opens at 8:00 AM). To reach it from the traffic light at Jones Avenue in Zellwood, go north on US-441 to CR-448 (Sadler Avenue; 1.6; traffic light) and turn left. At Dora Drive (1.6), turn right to Earlwood Avenue (1.2). The park is ahead on the right. There are two entrances; drive past the first one to the main entrance and turn left to the camping area. Follow this road to the lake, which has a short boardwalk along Lake Beauclair. Look for Black-crowned Night-Herons, Bald Eagles, and Limpkins here. At the end of the road, an oak hammock can be excellent for fall migrant landbirds and for breeding Yellow-throated Vireos during spring and summer.

Contact: Trimble Park, 5802 Trimble Park Road, Mount Dora, FL 32757; 352-383-1993.

EAST ORLANDO

ORLANDO WETLANDS PARK (1,650 acres; no fee; no camping; opens 30 minutes after sunrise; *closed 1 October–20 January*) is a facility that removes excess nutrients from treated wastewater by filtering the water through many ponds. It offers good to excellent birding for waterbirds year-round. To reach the park, drive east on SR-50 from SR-520. At CR-420 (Fort Christmas Road, 4.1), turn left to Wheeler Road (2.3), then turn right into the park (1.0). Check in and out at the visitor kiosk (0.5), where maps and checklists are available. Motorized vehicles are prohibited in the park's interior, but hiking, biking, or horseback riding is allowed on the berm roads. Birding is best in late winter and early spring, when American Bitterns and many waterfowl and shorebirds join the resident wading birds. Breeding species include Black-bellied Whistling-Duck, Mottled Duck, Least Bittern and other wading birds, Swallow-tailed Kite, Bald Eagle, King Rail, and Limpkin; Snail Kites have bred in the past. Unusual in Florida are the Purple Martins that nest in natural cavities in dead Cabbage Palms.

Contact: Orlando Wetlands Park, 25155 Wheeler Road, Christmas, FL 32709; 407-568-1706; <www.cityoforlando.net/public_works/parks/ cityparks/Owetlands/OWetlands.htm>.

South of SR-50 is **William Beardall Tosohatchee State Reserve** (34,000 acres; $3.00/vehicle; primitive camping at $4.00/person *seasonal hunting*), good for pine flatwoods species. To reach it from Orlando Wetlands

Park (see Orlando map on page 144), return to SR-50 and turn left to Taylor Creek Road (0.3). Turn right to the reserve on the left (2.8). Sign in and out at the kiosk at the entrance. Tosohatchee contains pine flatwoods, freshwater marshes, cypress swamps, hardwood and palm hammocks, and 19 miles of frontage along the St. Johns River. Vehicle access is limited to the middle portion of the reserve, and all roads are unpaved. In summer, many roads may be closed due to flooding. Characteristic breeding birds include Swallow-tailed Kite, Bald Eagle, Wild Turkey, Brown-headed Nuthatch, Eastern Bluebird, Prothonotary Warbler, and Bachman's Sparrow. Along Power Line Road, Osprey nests are prevalent on the metal supports; one of these nests is used by Bald Eagles. Although rare here, Henslow's Sparrows have been found during winter in the pine flatwoods.

Contact: *William Beardall Tosohatchee State Reserve, 3365 Taylor Creek Rd, Christmas, FL 32709; 407-568-5893; <www.floridastateparks.org/Tosohatchee>.*

To reach Merritt Island or other Atlantic coast birding sites from Orlando, go east on SR-50 or SR-520. Descriptions of those sites begin on page 170.

KISSIMMEE

For birders visiting Disney World or Orlando, Kissimmee (pronounced *ki-SIM-ee*) and St. Cloud offer many excellent birding spots within a half-hour drive of the city. In particular, Lake Tohopekaliga (usually shortened to *Toho*) in Kissimmee, East Lake Tohopekaliga (called *East Lake Toho*) in St. Cloud, and the extensive flatwoods and prairies to the south are popular birding areas (see next map). To reach the area from Orlando, head south on any of the following roads: US-17/92, US-441, SR-91 (Florida's Turnpike), or SR-15. From the west, exit I-4 (#64A) at US-192 and go east to Kissimmee.

On Lake Tohopekaliga at Kissimmee, **Brinson Park** (no fee) is a good spot for various waterbirds. To reach it from US-192 (Vine Street), drive east to US-17/92 (Main Street), then head south. At Drury Avenue (0.6), turn left to its end at Lakeshore Boulevard (0.3). Turn left to its end at CR-525 (Neptune Road; 0.2), then turn right to the parking lot on the left. During winter, flights of wading birds and Sandhill Cranes can be impressive. A walk along Lakeshore Boulevard to **Kissimmee Lakefront Park** to the south may produce Black-necked Stilts during spring and summer, and rafts of ducks and American Coots during winter. The **power substation** at the junction of Lakeshore Boulevard and Ruby Avenue (0.4 miles south of Drury) contains numerous Monk Parakeet nests, and the birds often forage in the park.

Contacts: *Brinson Park, 600 Neptune Road, Kissimmee, FL 34741; 407-518-2501; <www.kissimmeeparksandrec.com/maplocator.html>; Kissimmee Lakefront Park, 69 Lakeshore Boulevard, Kissimmee, FL 34741; 407-518-2501.*

From US-441/17/92 (Orange Blossom Trail) in Kissimmee, go west on US-192 to CR-525 (John Young Parkway; 0.8) and turn left. At CR-531 (Pleasant Hill Road; 3.4), turn left. At Poinciana Boulevard (7.5), turn left to (private) **Southport Park Marina and Campground** ($1.00/person; 37 campsites at $12.00–$23.00/day) on the south shore of Lake Tohopekaliga. Ask for permission to bird the campground and picnic areas; the oaks in these areas can be good for migrant landbirds during fall. A pair of tame Sandhill Cranes is often found near the office, and Crested Caracaras may be seen along the road, especially during winter. An active Bald Eagle nest is located in a cypress in the northwest corner of the park. Snail Kites are seen regularly around the lake.

Contact: *Southport Park Marina and Campground, 2001 West Southport Road, Kissimmee, FL 34746; 407-933-5822; <www. southportpark.com>.*

Return to Pleasant Hill Road and turn left to Scrub Jay Trail (1.2) on the left to enter **Disney Wilderness Preserve** (12,000 acres; $3.00/person; no camping; opens at 9:00 AM; *closed on weekends July–September*). The preserve contains a great expanse of Longleaf Pine flatwoods, oak scrub, and wetlands that was purchased to mitigate for development projects by the Walt Disney Company, Orlando International Airport, and others. The preserve is owned and operated by The Nature Conservancy. Characteristic flatwoods species such as Red-headed Woodpecker, Brown-headed Nuthatch, Pine Warbler, Bachman's Sparrow, and Summer Tanager (spring and summer) occur here. The preserve also supports 17 Bald Eagle nests, 15 pairs of Sandhill Cranes, and 11 Florida Scrub-Jay groups. A Wood Stork colony of more than 100 nests may be observed from a trail at Lake Russell. Most of the property is not easily accessible to the public, but nature trails of up to 4.7 miles in length start at the Conservation Learning Center. During prescribed burns, the preserve may be closed; it is advisable to call in advance.

Contact: *Disney Wilderness Preserve, 2700 Scrub Jay Trail, Kissimmee, FL 34759; 407-935-0002; <www.nature.org/wherewework/northamerica/ states/florida/preserves/art5523.html>.*

St. Cloud

To bird the St. Cloud area from US-441/192 (Space Coast Parkway), go north on CR-523 (Vermont Avenue) to Lakeshore Boulevard (0.9) and turn right. **Kaliga Park** (no fee), a small park on East Lake Tohopekaliga, is on the left (0.6). This is a good spot for Mottled Duck, Least Bittern, Glossy Ibis, Limpkin, and Sandhill Crane. The main attraction is Snail Kite, which is resident here but easiest to find during winter. If you don't find kites here, travel along Lakeshore Boulevard both east and west of Ka Park and scan the lake. Another good spot for Snail Kites is near the wastewater treatment facility to the west (1.0). A boat ramp at St. Cloud Canal (0.7 mile farther west) offers another view of the lake where kites may be seen.

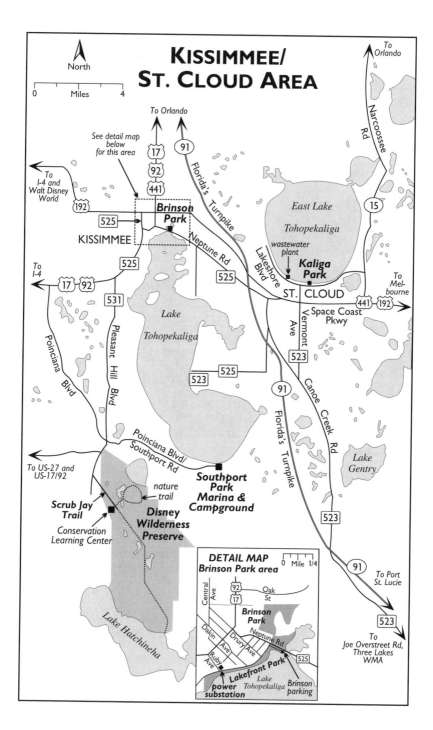

KISSIMMEE/ ST. CLOUD AREA

North

0 Miles 4

To Orlando

To Orlando

See detail map below for this area

17
92
441

To I-4 and Walt Disney World

192

525

Brinson Park

KISSIMMEE

Florida's Turnpike

Neptune Rd

91

Narcoossee Rd

East Lake Tohopekaliga

15

wastewater plant

Kaliga Park

ST. CLOUD

To I-4

17 92

531

525

525

Lakeshore Blvd

441 192

To Melbourne

Space Coast Pkwy

Lake Tohopekaliga

Pleasant Hill Blvd

Poinciana Blvd

523

525

Vermont Ave

523

91

Canoe Creek Rd

Lake Gentry

Poinciana Blvd/ Southport Rd

To US-27 and US-17/92

nature trail

Scrub Jay Trail

Conservation Learning Center

Disney Wilderness Preserve

Southport Park Marina & Campground

Florida's Turnpike

523

91

Lake Hatchineha

To Port St. Lucie

523

To Joe Overstreet Rd, Three Lakes WMA

DETAIL MAP
Brinson Park area

0 Mile 1/4

Central Ave

92
17

Oak St

Brinson Park

Dakin Ave

Drury Ave

Neptune Rd

525

Ruby Ave

Lakefront Park

Lake Tohopekaliga

power substation

Brinson parking

Crested Caracara adult with fully-engorged crop.　　　　Lyn S. Atherton

Return to US-192 westbound and turn south onto CR-523 (Vermont Avenue), which quickly becomes **Canoe Creek Road** (see previous map). Canoe Creek Road parallels Florida's Turnpike for about 35 miles. On the drive from St. Cloud, you will probably see Bald Eagles, Crested Caracaras, and Sandhill Cranes. This region of Florida retains its abundance of Wild Turkeys, seen most often shortly after dawn or before dusk in pastures near oak hammocks and swamps. Since January 1993, more than 100 Whooping Cranes have been released southeast of St. Cloud in an attempt to establish a non-migratory population in central Florida.

After about 20 miles, turn right onto unpaved **JOE OVERSTREET ROAD** (see map opposite) to look for wading birds, Crested Caracaras, Wild Turkeys, and Eastern Bluebirds. Overstreet Road ends at Lake Kissimmee (1.8). Scan the marshes and water for ducks, wading birds (including Least Bittern and Glossy Ibis), Snail Kite, Bald Eagle, Whooping Crane, Limpkin, and Purple Gallinule.

Return to CR-523 and continue southeast to the entrance of **THREE LAKES WILDLIFE MANAGEMENT AREA** (61,845 acres; $3.00/person or $6.00/vehicle; primitive camping; accessible anytime; *seasonal hunting*) on the right (3.7). Three Lakes Wildlife Management Area contains Longleaf Pine flatwoods, dry prairies, lakes, marshes, and hammocks and is a vital regional conservation area. All of the roads within the management area are unpaved; those shown on the map usually can be driven in passenger vehicles. Pine flatwoods species are common here, including Northern Bobwhite, Red-

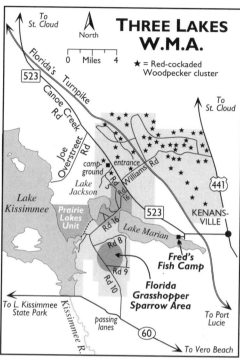

cockaded Woodpecker, Brown-headed Nuthatch, Eastern Bluebird, Pine Warbler, and Bachman's Sparrow. Ten or more Bald Eagle nests are present on the property, with more than 30 others in the surrounding region. As of 2003, there were 51 active Red-cockaded Woodpecker clusters on the property—roughly 130–140 adults. All the birds are color-banded, and cavity trees are painted with white bands. One cluster is within the **campground** at the entrance off Canoe Creek Road, with another just to the southwest, along the south side of Road 5. Other clusters are visible along Canoe Creek Road south of the entrance, and east of Canoe Creek Road along Williams Road, which continues east to meet US-441.

The **Prairie Lakes Unit** offers a five-mile wildlife drive and access to Lake Jackson. To reach this area, return to Canoe Creek Road and head south to Road 16 on the right (2.0). The trail traverses flatwoods, oak hammocks, and palmetto prairies. An observation tower that overlooks the southern end of Lake Jackson is reached by a 0.5-mile trail at the end of the road. Farther south, extensive dry prairie habitat supports about 100 pairs of Florida Grasshopper Sparrows, a nonmigratory, endemic subspecies, visible mainly when males are singing during early mornings, mostly late March to mid-July. This area is accessed from Road 16 by turning left onto Road 10 and heading south, or by heading north on Road 10 from SR-60. This southern entrance to the Wildlife Management Area is 5.0 miles east of the Kissimmee

River, or, from the east, just before the beginning of the westbound passing lane. This graded road is marked by a large sign, but note that this is a *sharp* right-angle turn with very little shoulder. With the abundance of traffic on SR-60, be extremely careful when turning onto this road. Once inside the management area, the road becomes Road 10. Florida Grasshopper Sparrows may be found along either side of Road 10 between Roads 8 and 9. Bachman's Sparrows are common in the same prairies. Road 10 continues north all the way to Canoe Creek Road.

Contact: *Three Lakes Wildlife Management Area, 1231 Prairie Lakes Road, Kenansville, FL 34739; 407-436-1818.*

Return to CR-523 and continue southeast for about five miles to a small restaurant (closed Mondays) on the right as the roads curves left. Turn right here onto Arnold Road, which ends at a quiet community on Lake Marian (0.5); *please be respectful of residents.* One or two Limpkins may be seen here; also watch for Snail Kites over the marshes. Turn around and then turn left onto Lakeshore Boulevard (0.2), which ends at **Fred's Fish Camp** (0.5). A Snail Kite often perches just offshore here, and Limpkins can be seen in the canals. Return to Canoe Creek Road, which ends at US-441 in about four miles. By turning right at US-441, you can reach Florida's Turnpike or SR-60 at Yeehaw Junction (14). If returning to the Kissimmee/St. Cloud area, you may wish to take US-441 back north, which ends at US-192. Then turn left to reach St. Cloud (13.0). This road is also good for observing Bald Eagles, Wild Turkeys, and Sandhill Cranes.

LAKELAND

From August through October, **SADDLE CREEK PARK** (740 acres; no fee; 32 campsites) can be an excellent spot for fall migrants. The park is also a reliable spot for Limpkins if you arrive before most park visitors. To reach the park from I-4, take SR-33 (Exit #38) south to SR-659 (1.7) and turn left. At US-92 (4.8), turn left and proceed to the entrance on the left (1.6). Upon entering the park, head north to the T-intersection with Morgan Combee Road to the left (1.0). Turn right here and park in the lot in front of the wooden observation tower (0.1). Walk to the start of the trail by the tower. The trail winds along a levee for about a mile, then ends. You must return via the same levee, but there are many side trails to explore. Bring along insect repellent. Lake Region Audubon Society <www.lakeregion.net> sponsors "warbler walks" every Saturday from mid-August through October, starting at the observation tower at 8:00 AM.

Contact: *Saddle Creek Park, 3716 Morgan Combee Road, Lakeland, FL 33801; 863-499-2613.*

Circle B Bar Reserve (1,267 acres; no fee; no camping; opens at 5:00 AM) along Lake Hancock east of Lakeland hosts large concentrations of Bald

Eagles (thanks to an adjacent landfill). To reach the reserve from the east, exit I-4 (#41) at the Polk Parkway (SR-570). Then head south to SR-540 (Winter Lake Road; Exit #14; 11.0). Turn left to the entrance on the left (2.6). From the west, exit I-4 at the Polk Parkway (SR-570; Exit #27) and head east to US-98 (10.0). Head south to CR-540 (Winter Lake Road; traffic light; 0.1) and turn left to the entrance on the right (1.1). A three-mile trail runs along the lakeshore and through oak hammocks. Wetlands restoration efforts are improving habitat for resident wading birds, shorebirds during migration, and American White Pelicans and ducks during winter. Uplands are good for Red-headed Woodpeckers and other landbirds.

Contact: *Polk County Natural Resources, 4177 Ben Durrance Road, Bartow, FL 33830; 863-534-7377; <www.polk-county.net>.*

Northwest of Lakeland is **Gator Creek Reserve** (1,086 acres; no fee; no camping; opens at 5 AM), which features a series of loop trails through varied habitats in the Green Swamp, a vast wetland of critical statewide importance. To reach the reserve from I-4, head north on US-98 (Exit #32) to the entrance on the right (6.4). Trails through pine flatwoods, hammocks, and cypress swamps offer views of Wild Turkey, Carolina Chickadee, Yellow-throated Warbler, and Summer Tanager (spring and summer). Migrant and wintering landbirds may be common in the hammocks.

Contact: *Polk County Natural Resources, 4177 Ben Durrance Road, Bartow, FL 33830; 863-534-7377' <www.polk-county.net>.*

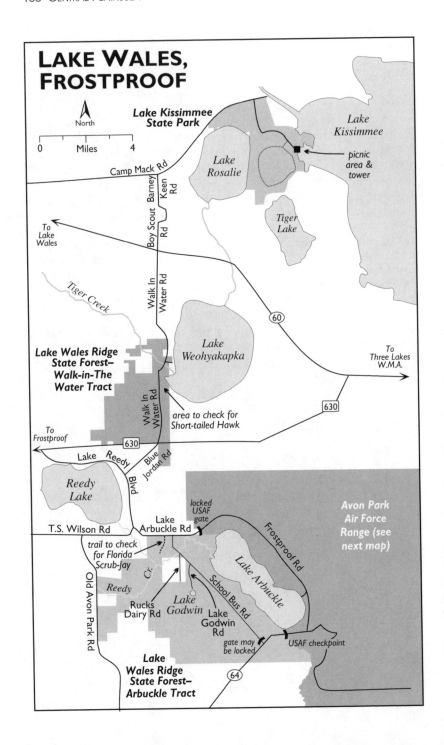

LAKE WALES, FROSTPROOF

North

0 — Miles — 4

Lake Kissimmee State Park

Lake Rosalie

Lake Kissimmee

picnic area & tower

Camp Mack Rd

Boy Scout Rd

Barney Rd

Keen Rd

To Lake Wales

Tiger Lake

Tiger Creek

Walk In Water Rd

Lake Weohyakapka

60

To Three Lakes W.M.A.

Lake Wales Ridge State Forest– Walk-in-The Water Tract

Walk In Water Rd

area to check for Short-tailed Hawk

630

To Frostproof

630

Lake Reedy Blvd

Blue Jordan Rd

Reedy Lake

T.S. Wilson Rd

Lake Arbuckle Rd

locked USAF gate

Frostproof Rd

Avon Park Air Force Range (see next map)

trail to check for Florida Scrub-Jay

Old Avon Park Rd

Reedy

Cr.

Rucks Dairy Rd

Lake Godwin

Lake Godwin Rd

School Bus Rd

Lake Arbuckle

gate may be locked

USAF checkpoint

Lake Wales Ridge State Forest– Arbuckle Tract

64

LAKE WALES–FROSTPROOF

Lake **Kissimmee State Park** (5,930 acres; $4.00/vehicle, 60 campsites at $17.00/day; opens 8:00 AM) is a picturesque park along Lake Kissimmee. To reach the park from Lake Wales, go east on SR-60 to Boy Scout Road (15.0) and turn left. (Toward its north end, the road name changes to Barney Keen Road.) At Camp Mack Road (3.7) turn right to the entrance on the right (5.6); watch for Crested Caracaras along the way. A few groups of Florida Scrub-Jays are found around and south of the entrance. Other species present in the park include Bald Eagle (one nest is visible from the Buster Island Loop Trail), Crested Caracara, Wild Turkey, Limpkin, Sandhill Crane, Red-headed Woodpecker, and Bachman's Sparrow (open flatwoods throughout). During spring and summer, watch for Swallow-tailed Kites overhead and Summer Tanagers in the pines. There are 13 miles of trails in the park, and those that traverse oak hammocks can be good for landbirds during fall migration and winter. An observation tower at the picnic area overlooks Lake Kissimmee, where Snail Kites can sometimes be seen.

> **Contact:** *Lake Kissimmee State Park, 14248 Camp Mack Road, Lake Wales, FL 33853; 863-696-1112; <www.floridastateparks.org/lake kissimmee>.*

Lake **Wales Ridge State Forest** (26,487 acres ; $1.00/person; camping at $5.00/day; open anytime; *seasonal hunting*) can be a worthwhile stop for pinewoods and scrub species, and offers a rare reliable spot for Short-tailed Hawks during spring and summer. There are two main tracts, Arbuckle and Walk-In-The-Water, which are located a few miles apart; each has multiple entrances. To reach the best area for Short-tailed Hawks (in the **WALK-IN-THE-WATER TRACT**) from SR-60 east of Lake Wales , head south on Walk In Water Road (opposite Boy Scout Road). Cross Tiger Creek (5.1), then park on the road shoulder after another 1.2 miles. (For those approaching this spot from CR-630 east of Frostproof, the distance north of CR-630 is 2.4 miles.) One or more pairs of Short-tailed Hawks breeds in the swamp between the road and Lake Weohyakapka to the east (March–July). Birds may be seen over the road at any time during the day, but are most reliable once thermals develop and the birds can begin foraging (around 8:30 or 9:00 AM). Check all soaring birds carefully, because vultures and other raptors will also be present.

The Walk-In-The-Water Tract is closed to vehicles (except for the small campground), so head south to the Arbuckle Tract to continue birding. Cross CR-630 (2.4) (the road name changes from Walk-In-The-Water to Blue Jordan Road). At the end of the road (1.7; blinking light), turn left. At Lake Arbuckle Road (1.6), again turn left. To search for Florida Scrub-Jays, park on the shoulder of the road at an unmarked sand trail on the right (1.1). Several scrub-jay groups are found along this trail for the next half-mile, and most are tame. *Do not lure the scrub-jays to Lake Arbuckle Road with peanuts, as this may encourage them to feed near the road, putting them at risk for getting hit by vehicles.* Return to your car and continue east. At Rucks Dairy Road (0.4, unpaved), turn right. After crossing Reedy Creek (0.7), bear left onto School Bus Road (0.1, unpaved). At Lake Godwin Road (1.0, unpaved; *no sign from the south*), turn right and follow the road to the lake (0.8)—this road is "tiled", but parts will be flooded after recent rains. There is no further vehicle access, so park here and walk around. The road that heads east just south of the parking area is good for typical pinewoods species such as Eastern Bluebird, Pine Warbler, Summer Tanager (spring and summer), and Bachman's Sparrow (mainly March–July). Brown-headed Nuthatch also occurs, but in lower density. After you return to School Bus Road, turn right to reach CR-64 (3.7). From here, you can head east (left turn) to visit Avon Park Air Force Range (1.1), or head west to access US-27 in Avon Park (9.4). *Note that the southern entrance to School Bus Road may be gated when prescribed burns are planned.*

Contact: *Lake Wales Ridge State Forest, Florida Division of Forestry, 851 County Road 630 East, Frostproof, Florida 33843; 863-635-8589; <www.fl-dof.com/state_forests/Lake_Wales_Ridge.html>.*

AVON PARK

AVON PARK AIR FORCE RANGE (106,110 acres; *permit required*: $6.00/weekend or $28.00/year; primitive camping at three campgrounds; *restricted access*; *military operations*; *seasonal hunting*; Outdoor Recreation office opens on Thursday at 12:00 PM, Friday–Sunday at 6:00 AM or earlier, and Monday at 7:30 AM, as military missions allow) is an active military reservation east of Avon Park. It is used for ground exercises and live-fire bombing and gunnery missions. To reach the range from US-27, head east on CR-64 to the entrance (10.5); the main road becomes South Boulevard. At the checkpoint, explain that you wish to go to the Outdoor Recreation office (the log cabin) on the left at the intersection of Frostproof Grade and Jennings Memorial Drive (1.5). You must sign in, get a permit, pick up a map, and receive a safety briefing. You will be informed about any areas that are closed to public use. The range has a variety of habitats, including extensive Longleaf Pine flatwoods, oak and Sand Pine scrub, dry prairies, riverine and hardwood forests, and freshwater marshes. Only a few sites away from active ranges are included here, and these concentrate on the range specialties. Those with more time can explore any of several graded roads (passable in regular automobiles) for additional birding opportunities. Note that food and fuel are not available on-site. The range is open year-round *from Fridays through Sundays only* except from the last week of October to mid-December, when the range is closed to birding because of heavy hunting activity. A recorded message tape gives more information about access; call 863-452-4119, extension 5. *Because military schedules may change abruptly, birders should call in advance of any visit to ensure that the range is open to recreation. Furthermore, beginning in 2006,*

AVON PARK

★ = Red-cockaded Woodpecker cluster

▲ = Florida Scrub-Jay site

the range may be closed to all access during and following Navy bombing activities—for up to 100 days per year.

Several sought-after species are regularly observed, including Wild Turkey (year-round), Swallow-tailed Kite (spring and summer; overhead virtually anywhere), Bald Eagle (mostly around Lake Arbuckle; rare during summer), Short-tailed Hawk (spring through fall, mainly near Arbuckle Creek), Crested Caracara (rare), Sandhill Crane (year-round), Red-cockaded Woodpecker (about 20 clusters; cavity trees are marked with white paint, and the birds are color-banded and under study), and Florida Scrub-Jay (about 150 birds, all color-banded and under study). Florida Grasshopper Sparrows formerly were common in dry prairies, but their numbers have plummeted, from uncertain causes. All remaining sparrows occur on active bombing or gunnery ranges, where public access is prohibited at all times. Pine flatwoods and plantations support Hairy Woodpeckers (fairly common, especially in recent burns), Eastern Kingbirds (spring and summer), Brown-headed Nuthatches (year-round), Eastern Bluebirds (common; a nest-box trail is established), Bachman's Sparrows (primarily spring and summer, when males are singing), and Summer Tanagers (spring and summer). Oak hammocks throughout the range can be good for migrant and wintering landbirds.

The **Lake Arbuckle Nature Trail** can be excellent for landbirds, especially during fall. To reach it from the log cabin, head north on Frostproof Road to the sand road on the left (1.1). The parking area is ahead (0.3). The trail traverses an oak hammock, a cypress swamp, and a small part of the lake. An observation tower (watch your head near the top!) provides views of the lily pads; watch for Purple Gallinules here (mainly spring and summer). Lake Arbuckle (4,300 acres) is the largest lake remaining in Florida with a shoreline almost entirely in public ownership. More than 20 Osprey nests ring the lakeshore, and a few are close to the tower.

To reach an active Red-cockaded Woodpecker cluster, return to Frostproof Road and turn left. At **Bravo Road** (0.6), turn right to the stand of Longleaf Pines (1.2). Cavity trees are found both north and south of the road, but in 2005 all active trees were to the north. Another cluster can be reached by continuing east on Bravo Road to the gate to Bravo Range (0.5; *off-limits at all times*). (Watch for Florida Scrub-Jays here.) Turn left onto Billig Grade. At the T-intersection (0.4), turn right and proceed to the north fenceline (3.3). Turn right and park at the gate in the fence (0.4). *Stay out of the private properties to the north.* The woodpeckers often approach from the south and fly over the fenceline en route to their cavities, which are mostly north of the fence.

An area with several Florida Scrub-Jay groups is found to the southeast. Return to the Outdoor Recreation office and turn left onto Jennings Memorial Drive. At Smith Grade (0.5), turn left to its end at **Old Bravo Road** (4.4). Turn right, and watch from here to (paved) Kissimmee Road (3.2) for scrub-jays in the oak scrub. *Stay out of posted sites in this area.* As you return to the Outdoor Recreation office, it is worth a stop along **Morgan Creek** (1.6) to look for migrant landbirds during fall; campgrounds are located at all four corners of the creek and Kissimmee Road.

Contact: *Avon Park Air Force Range, 29 South Boulevard, Avon Park Air Force Range, FL 33825-5700; 863-452-4254; <www.avonparkafr.com>.*

SEBRING

With its extensive oak hammocks, **HIGHLANDS HAMMOCK STATE PARK** (4,694 acres, $4.00/vehicle; 60 campsites at $18.00/day; opens at 8:00 AM) can be excellent for landbirds during fall migration and winter. Swallow-tailed Kites may be seen overhead throughout the day from March through mid-July. To reach the park from US-27, drive west on CR-634. The park is straight ahead (2.6). Purchased in 1931, before the state park system was established, Highlands Hammock was preserved by a group of conservationists who feared that the hammock would be cleared for agriculture. The park preserves one of the few virgin hardwood hammocks remaining in Florida, and some of the huge, ancient oaks and hickories must be seen to be believed. Other habitats here include cypress swamp, Slash Pine

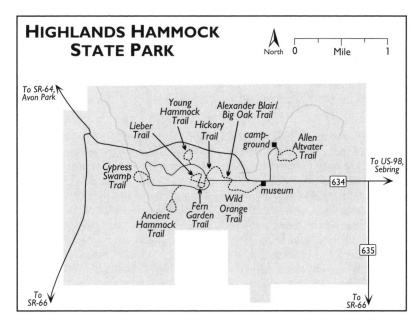

**HIGHLANDS HAMMOCK
STATE PARK**

North 0   Mile   1

To SR-64,
Avon Park

Young
Hammock
Trail
Alexander Blair/
Big Oak Trail
Lieber
Trail
Hickory
Trail
camp-
ground ■
Allen
Altvater
Trail
Cypress
Swamp
Trail
To US-98,
Sebring
634
museum
Wild
Orange
Trail
Fern
Garden
Trail
Ancient
Hammock
Trail
635
To
SR-66
To
SR-66

flatwoods, and oak and Sand Pine scrub. Mosquitoes are usually plentiful on the hammock trails, so bring along insect repellent.

There are nine trails through the park (five are connected), and these can be walked in about four or five hours. Just beyond the entrance station, turn right onto the road to the campground. At the small sign that points to campground lots 105 to 138, turn right, then make an immediate left. The entrance to **Allen Altvater Trail** is on the right, opposite lot 114. *Park out of the way of campers.* The trail, which may be flooded in late summer or fall, is a short loop through Slash Pine flatwoods where Pine Warblers and other common woodland species may be found. Migrants are most common in the oaks just before the small bridge, or in the campground.

Return to the main park road; turn right to unpaved CR-634 (0.2), and again turn right. The road traverses cypress swamps and Slash Pine flatwoods. In the latter, look for Pine Warblers and Summer Tanagers (spring and summer). The area around the bridge over **Charlie Bowlegs Creek** can be great for migrant landbirds such as Acadian Flycatchers, Prothonotary Warblers, and both waterthrushes . There is no parking area here, and the road shoulder is narrow and may be soft if it has rained recently; use care in pulling off here. The park ends at Hammock Road (0.5), so turn around, return to the main park road, and turn right to continue birding.

The other trails pass through oak hammocks that contain a few oaks and hickories that are more than 1,000 years old and as much as 38 feet (!) in circumference. In the 1930s, "surgery" was performed on a few of these trees to extend their lives. A cavity was cut into the side of a tree to remove the dead, rotted wood from the interior. Afterward, the cavity was filled with concrete and terra-cotta tile reinforced with iron rebar. At the entrance to Lieber Memorial Trail, a large limb of one of the old oaks blew down several years ago. The broken-off portion of the limb remains (it probably weighs a few tons!) and allows for close inspection of the amazing "construction" of the tree's interior.

The first hammock trail, **Wild Orange Trail** (named for the many naturalized *sour* citrus trees present), begins just west of the museum on the south side of the park entrance road; *this is east of CR-634*. It crosses the park road and becomes **Alexander Blair/Big Oak Trail**. If you don't have time to bird all the trails in the park, do not skip this one; the magnificent old oaks and hickories should not be missed. Big Oak Trail quickly becomes Hickory Trail, with a narrow catwalk through a maple swamp. Just beyond the catwalk, turn right to remain on the trail. Hickory Trail ends at the park road. Cross the road to bird **Fern Garden Trail** and **Lieber Memorial Trail**. Both trails include boardwalks through bay and cypress swamps, where waterthrushes and other migrant landbirds are found regularly during fall. At the end of Lieber Memorial Trail, walk *right* to return to your vehicle.

Drive to the fork in the road (0.1) and bear right. Past Lieber Memorial Trail is **Young Hammock Trail**, a loop trail through pine flatwoods that are succeeding, in the absence of fire, to an oak/bay hammock. Return to your vehicle and drive to the west side of the park loop to reach **Cypress Swamp Trail**, with its extensive boardwalk through a cypress swamp bordering Charlie Bowlegs Creek. This trail may be somewhat crowded with people (the others tend to be vacant), but it can be good for migrant landbirds during fall. Limpkins, Barred Owls, and American Alligators may be found on quiet days. The last trail, **Ancient Hammock Trail**, is another loop trail through a dense virgin hammock.

Contact: *Highlands Hammock State Park, 5931 Hammock Road, Sebring, FL 33872; 863-386-6094; <www.floridastateparks.org/ highlandshammock>.*

LAKE PLACID–VENUS

The Lake Placid–Venus area offers excellent birding for many sought-after species. From Miami, it provides easily accessible sites for Crested Caracara, Sandhill Crane, Florida Scrub-Jay, and Bachman's Sparrow. Venus is a hamlet with almost no facilities, but restaurants and motels are available in nearby Lake Placid. From the junction of US-27 and SR-70, Lake Placid is about six miles north, while Venus is about five miles south. (See next map.)

The region marks the southern end of the Lake Wales Ridge, a system of sand dunes that formed two to three million years ago when sea levels were much higher than they are presently. At times, the Lake Wales Ridge was a series of islands that represented nearly all of the southern Florida peninsula that was above water! The ridge stretches about 100 miles to the north and is 25 miles wide at its widest point. Around Lake Placid, however, the ridge is less than six miles wide, and it is even narrower at Venus. Since the early 1900s more than 85 percent of scrub habitats on the Lake Wales Ridge have been destroyed, mostly by the citrus and development industries. In the early 1990s, the State of Florida, The Nature Conservancy, and the U.S. Fish and Wildlife Service jointly committed to purchase all significant remaining parcels of scrub remaining along the Lake Wales Ridge, representing over 43,000 acres. As of 2002, nearly half of this amount had been purchased at a cost exceeding $40 million.

On SR-70 one mile west of US-27, turn left onto Old SR-8 (CR-17) to reach **Archbold Biological Station** (8,800 acres; no fee; no camping; opens at 8:00 AM Monday through Friday, *closed on weekends*) on the right (1.8). This independent biological research station preserves one of the largest patches of xeric oak scrub remaining on the Lake Wales Ridge. Much of what is known about this critically endangered ecosystem has been learned through research conducted at Archbold. Although scientists at Archbold are studying many aspects of the scrub and its inhabitants, one project in particular has made the station famous ornithologically. Since 1969, Glen Woolfenden, John Fitzpatrick, Reed Bowman, and their colleagues have

Banded Florida Scrub-Jay, adult.
Many populations on public lands are banded and under study.

J. Andrew Boyle

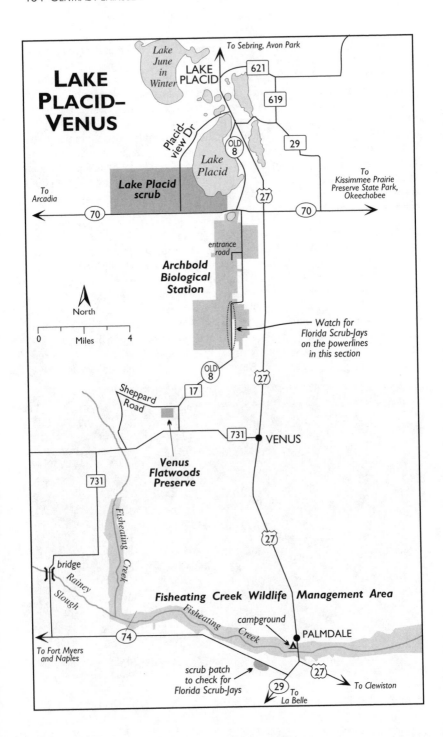

LAKE PLACID–VENUS

Lake June in Winter

LAKE PLACID

To Sebring, Avon Park

621

619

Placid-view Dr.

OLD 8

29

Lake Placid

To Kissimmee Prairie Preserve State Park, Okeechobee

To Arcadia

70

Lake Placid scrub

27

70

entrance road

Archbold Biological Station

Watch for Florida Scrub-Jays on the powerlines in this section

North

0   Miles   4

OLD 8

17

Sheppard Road

731

VENUS

Venus Flatwoods Preserve

731

Fisheating Creek

bridge

Rainey Slough

Fisheating Creek Wildlife Management Area

Fisheating Creek

campground

PALMDALE

74

To Fort Myers and Naples

scrub patch to check for Florida Scrub-Jays

29 To La Belle

27

To Clewiston

closely studied a color-banded population of Florida Scrub-Jays on the station. Because of ongoing research, most of the station is off-limits to the public, but a self-guided nature trail is provided; a "virtual tour" is available at <www.archbold-station.org/abs/trail/trail/index.html>. Brochures and maps are available at the visitor kiosk in the parking lot at the west end of the main drive. The trail winds through recently burned oak scrub and Slash Pine flatwoods, where Red-headed and Hairy Woodpeckers and Florida Scrub-Jays may be found. *Remember that the station is not a public facility; please respect the privacy of the staff and interns.* After leaving the main grounds of Archbold, continue south on Old SR-8 to where the road crosses the railroad tracks (3.0). Watch for Florida Scrub-Jays perched on powerlines along the right side of the road for the next two miles.

    Contact: *Archbold Biological Station, P.O. Box 2057, Lake Placid, FL 33862-2057; 863-465-2571; <www.archbold-station.org>.*

    From the railroad crossing mentioned above, continue south to Sheppard Road (5.6) and turn right. Proceed to **Venus Flatwoods Preserve** (98 acres; *no interior access*) on the left (0.3). Birders can no longer walk into this tract of old-growth Longleaf Pine flatwoods and seasonal ponds, but it may be worth a brief stop. Many of the birds—Eastern Kingbirds and Bachman's Sparrows during spring and summer, and Red-headed Woodpeckers, Eastern Bluebirds, and Pine Warblers year-round—are often seen from the road. Brown-headed Nuthatches may be found year-round but are erratic. The isolated family of Red-cockaded Woodpeckers that made this site popular in the past died out several years ago.

Return to Old SR-8 and head south to CR-731 (1.0). Turn right and proceed to the fork in the road (3.8). Bear left and continue south through citrus groves, wetlands, and Slash Pine plantations before reaching **Rainey Slough** (7.3), a nearly undisturbed wetlands system. The slough and adjacent uplands are now part of **Fisheating Creek Conservation Easement** (41,523 acres), in which the land remains in private ownership but the state owns the development rights. *Bird only from the road and bridge.* Around dawn and dusk, many wading birds fly to or from roosts to the west. There usually is a small roost of Black-crowned Night-Herons in bushes along the bridge. The slough is a fairly dependable spot for Limpkins and Purple Gallinules (mainly spring and summer). King Rails are resident and can be heard calling before dawn, and they are joined during winter by Soras. Also during winter, watch for Marsh Wrens and Swamp Sparrows on the west side of the road. American Bitterns usually are rather easy to observe during this season around dawn or dusk as they fly around the marsh.

    Adjacent to the conservation easement is **Fisheating Creek Wildlife Management Area** (18,272 acres; no fee except in campground; camping at $10.00–25.00/day; boat rentals; *seasonal hunting*), which extends for more than 40 miles along Fisheating Creek, the only undammed tributary that flows into Lake Okeechobee. Access by vehicle is extremely limited because most of the management area is composed of wetlands, but the Palmdale Campground is along the west side of US-27 just north of the bridge over the creek.

Contact: *Fisheating Creek Wildlife Management Area;*
<www.myfwc.com/recreation/fisheating_creek>.

CR-731 ends at SR-74 (2.7), where you can turn right to reach Fort Myers or Naples on the Gulf coast, or turn left to return to US-27. SR-74 is another prairie road that is good for finding Mottled Duck, Glossy Ibis, Sandhill Crane, and Crested Caracara. Small numbers of Florida Scrub-Jays persist in the scattered patches of oak scrub along the road; the best patch is 1.3–2.0 miles west of SR-29. Lack of habitat management (fire or roller-chopping) is causing the oak scrub to become overgrown, and as a result, extirpation of these scrub-jays can be expected over the next several years. A few pairs of Short-tailed Hawks breed regularly along Fisheating Creek, and birds can sometimes be seen from SR-74 as they soar over the creek during spring and summer.

Depending on your travel plans, you might consider returning north to the intersection of SR-70 and US-27. Examples of wet prairies remain east and west of the Lake Wales Ridge (although all are impacted by ditching and cattle grazing), and SR-70 offers quick access to these areas. East of US-27, where the prairies are wetter, SR-70 is narrow, and it is dangerous to pull over and stop. Consequently, birders may choose to drive the side roads off SR-70, or to bird the portion of SR-70 lying west of US-27. Because the birdlife is similar on both sides of US-27, one's destination after leaving the area may be the key factor in deciding which direction to drive on SR-70. To reach the Tampa Bay area, Fort Myers, or Naples, drive west; to reach Lake Okeechobee or the West Palm Beach/Miami coastal strip, head east.

There are no specific birding sites along SR-70 or any of the other roads in the prairie region. Generally, most birds of interest are large enough so that you can spot them while driving. Pull over only when it is safe to do so. Characteristic birds of the region include Mottled Duck, Glossy Ibis, Wood Stork, Swallow-tailed Kite (spring and summer), Sandhill Crane, and Crested Caracara. Scattered sightings of White-tailed Kites have occurred recently, mostly during fall and winter.

BASINGER

The largest contiguous expanse of Florida dry prairie remaining in the state is protected in **KISSIMMEE PRAIRIE PRESERVE STATE PARK** (53,760 acres; no fee at present, 35 campsites at $12.00/day; opens at 8:00 AM). There are *110 miles of trails* for hiking, mountain biking, or horseback riding. To reach the preserve from Sebring and points north, take US-98 east

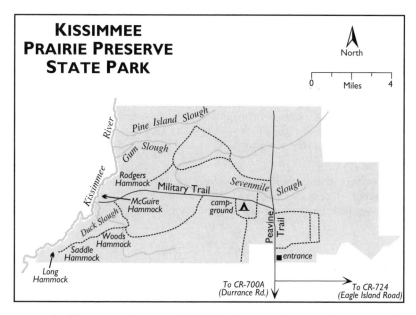

KISSIMMEE
PRAIRIE PRESERVE
STATE PARK

North

0 — Miles — 4

Kissimmee River

Pine Island Slough

Gum Slough

Rodgers Hammock

Military Trail

McGuire Hammock

Sevenmile Slough

camp-ground

Peavine Trail

Duck Slough

Woods Hammock

Saddle Hammock

Long Hammock

■ entrance

To CR-700A
(Durrance Rd.)

To CR-724
(Eagle Island Road)

across the Kissimmee River to CR-700A (Durrance Road; 3.6) and turn left. At its end at CR-724 (Eagle Island Road; 5.7), turn left and follow the signs to the preserve (6.0). From Lake Placid and points south, head east on SR-70 from US-27. At CR-721 (17.6), turn left to its end at US-98 (8.6). Turn right and proceed as above. From Okeechobee, head northwest on US-98 from SR-70 to CR-700A (14.2), turn right, and proceed as above. From the Atlantic coast, head west to US-441 and go north or south to CR-724 (Eagle Island Road; 1.0 north of SR-68). Head west and follow the signs to the preserve (18.0).

Just beyond the entrance, Burrowing Owls are present *on private property* in the pastures to the west—*stay out of this area.* Around dusk, the owls often hunt along the main preserve road between the front gate and the campground. The preserve supports the largest remaining population of the endangered Florida Grasshopper Sparrow—probably several hundred pairs. The best time to observe them is from dawn to about 9:30–10:00 AM from late March through mid-July. Prairies just north and east of the campground contain many sparrows. Birders may assist preserve staff with sparrow research (point-counts and mist-netting); contact the office in advance. Bachman's Sparrows are abundant year-round in the same prairies, and several others sparrows winter here, including Henslow's (40 were banded here during winter 2002–2003), Le Conte's (rare), Vesper, Swamp, and Savannah. Other dry-prairie species found in the preserve include White-tailed Kite (at least four pairs nested in 2002), Crested Caracara, and Sandhill Crane (hundreds of Greater Sandhill Cranes winter, and many pairs of Florida Sandhill Cranes are resident). A Black-crowned Night-Heron rookery at a willow pond approximately 1,000 feet north of the intersection of Peavine Trail and Military Trail is also used as a year-round roost by other wading birds. Oak hammocks are good for migrant landbirds (primarily during fall), while flooded pastures may support migrant shorebirds in July and August. During summer and fall, the preserve may be the best site in Florida for butterfly-watching, with 80 species reported, including large numbers of Palmetto, Aaron's, and Berry's Skippers. Because the preserve is large and remote, interested birders should contact the office prior to visiting for up-to-date information of bird locations and trail conditions. Much of the preserve may be flooded during summer or fall.

Contact: *Kissimmee Prairie Preserve State Park, 33104 NW 192nd Avenue, Okeechobee, FL 34972, 863-462-5360; <www.floridastateparks.org/kissimmeeprairie>.*

OKEECHOBEE

The small town of Okeechobee is located at the junction of US-441 and SR-70. It takes its name from the huge lake just to the south, well known for its immense ecological value. Historically, the lake was part of the vast

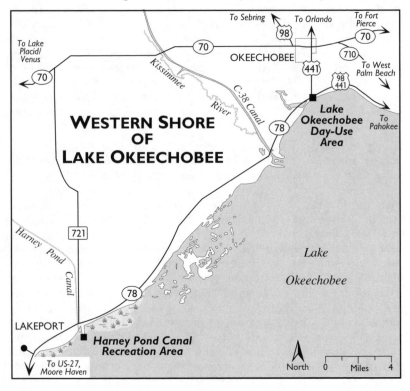

Kissimmee River–Everglades wetlands system. Water from the chain of dozens of interconnected lakes in Central Florida flowed north (beginning with tiny Lake Annie at Archbold Biological Station) all the way to Orlando. The water then flowed south through another chain of lakes before flowing into the Kissimmee River. The river meandered slowly southward before emptying into the northwest corner of Lake Okeechobee. Along its 102-mile length, the Kissimmee River nourished 35,000 acres of wetlands; its floodplain was up to five miles wide. During years of high water, Lake Okeechobee overflowed its southern banks, and the water would flow slowly south through the Everglades and eventually into Florida Bay, more than 100 miles to the south.

Although Lake Okeechobee is the second-largest freshwater lake entirely within in the U.S. (about 700 square miles, second only to Lake Michigan), it is quite shallow (its deepest part is only 20 feet deep). In the 1920s, two hurricanes passed over the lake. The tidal surges from the storms killed over 2,000 residents of Clewiston and Moore Haven. The 35-foot tall and 140-mile long Herbert Hoover Dike was built in the 1930s to prevent future flooding. But the dike isolated the lake from the Everglades—and it remains isolated today. In the 1960s, the Kissimmee River was converted to the C-38, a box-cut canal 300 feet wide, 30 feet deep, and 56 miles long. As the river floodplain was drained, predominately for cattle ranching, vast ecological harm was incurred (populations of wading birds and wintering waterfowl were reduced by 90 percent).

Lake Okeechobee is now used predominately as a source of drinking water for the 5.1 million people who live along Florida's southeast coast, and as an irrigation source for the Everglades Agricultural Area (EAA) on the lake's southern shore. The EAA is composed of 1,100 square miles of drained marshland now grown to sugar cane, rice, and vegetables. Water levels in the lake are therefore maintained for human uses, not for wildlife. In drought years, when water is needed most in the Everglades, it is kept instead in the lake to avoid water shortages for humans. In flood years, when wildlife is already stressed from high water levels, additional water is released into the Everglades to prevent flooding in agricultural and other developed areas. This water-management scheme has caused serious disruptions to the Everglades ecosystem in the past three decades.

Another serious problem plaguing the Everglades is exotic plants, especially Japanese and Old World Climbing-Ferns, Brazilian Pepper, and Australian Punk Tree. Control of these noxious plants is currently insufficient, and they continue to invade additional areas. It has been estimated that over one million acres of the southern peninsula contain Punk Trees.

Fortunately, a major reclamation project is (slowly) being implemented to allow the present-day Everglades to function more like the historic ecosystem. Among the ambitious plans in the project are filling in much of the C-38 Canal and returning flow to the Kissimmee River, filling in several other drainage canals, building impoundments in the EAA to filter phosphorus out of the agricultural wastewater before its discharge into the Everglades, and restoring farmland east of the present-day Everglades to marshland so that a more natural water regime will influence Everglades National Park and Florida Bay. Plans are to restore 43 miles of the Kissimmee River and almost 30,000 acres of wetlands. Given the current political climates in Washington and Tallahassee, however, this $8-billion, 30-year project may never be realized adequately to accomplish its goals. Time will tell.

B ecause of the dike, vast Lake Okeechobee is, ironically, not visible from the ground except from a few public access points. Four of these access points are listed here; one is south of the city of Okeechobee, two are along the northwest and west shores of the lake, and the last is west of Belle Glade on the southeast side of the lake. Two areas along the west side of Lake Okeechobee are worth quick stops, although the birding opportunities at both are limited. From SR-70 in Okeechobee, drive south on US-441. Cross SR-78 (3.2) to **Lake Okeechobee Day Use Area** (no fee; no camping). A non-breeding flock of Black Skimmers often loafs during the day in the first parking lot, and Purple Gallinules and Limpkins may be found at the east end of the road.

Continue southwest on SR-78 to Lakeport Plaza on the left (16.0; look for the BP gas station opposite CR-721). From the plaza parking lot, take the access road to the right to **Harney Pond Canal Recreation Area** (no fee; no camping). An elevated boardwalk at the far end of the parking lot offers a rare ground-level view of Lake Okeechobee. This site, too, may provide views of Purple Gallinules.

From Harney Pond Canal, you have several choices. To reach the Lake Placid/Venus area, go north on CR-721 to SR-70, then go west. (CR-721 is a lightly traveled road good for Crested Caracaras). Continuing south on SR-78 leads to US-27 in Moore Haven. About six miles south of town, turn west on SR-80 to reach Corkscrew Swamp Sanctuary (via SR-29 in Immokalee) or the Fort Myers/Naples area. Traveling east on SR-80 brings you to the Belle Glade area (great for shorebirds from July to September if you can find an accessible site), and after about 30 more miles, the West Palm Beach area.

Inland areas continue on page 207.

CENTRAL PENINSULA—ATLANTIC COAST

NEW SMYRNA BEACH

P once de Leon Inlet forms the northern terminus of the Indian River Lagoon, one of the most diverse estuaries in the world. There is no bridge over the inlet, so you must return to the mainland to travel between Daytona Beach and New Smyrna Beach. Parks are located on the north and south sides

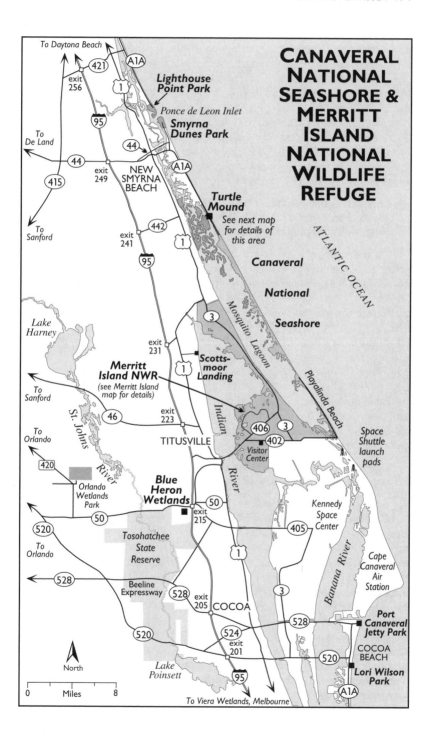

CANAVERAL NATIONAL SEASHORE & MERRITT ISLAND NATIONAL WILDLIFE REFUGE

To Daytona Beach

421

A1A

exit 256

1

Lighthouse Point Park

Ponce de Leon Inlet

Smyrna Dunes Park

95

To De Land

44

44

A1A

NEW SMYRNA BEACH

exit 249

415

To Sanford

Turtle Mound

See next map for details of this area

442

1

exit 241

95

Canaveral

National

Seashore

ATLANTIC OCEAN

Mosquito Lagoon

3

Lake Harney

exit 231

Scotts-moor Landing

1

Merritt Island NWR
(see Merritt Island map for details)

To Sanford

46

exit 223

Playalinda Beach

To Orlando

St. Johns River

Indian River

406

3

402

TITUSVILLE

Space Shuttle launch pads

420

Orlando Wetlands Park

Blue Heron Wetlands

Visitor Center

50

exit 215

50

520

To Orlando

Tosohatchee State Reserve

Kennedy Space Center

405

1

528

Beeline Expressway

528

exit 205

COCOA

3

Cape Canaveral Air Station

Banana River

520

524

exit 201

528

Port Canaveral Jetty Park

COCOA BEACH

North

Lake Poinsett

520

Lori Wilson Park

95

A1A

0   Miles   8

To Viera Wetlands, Melbourne

of the inlet and provide access to lagoon marshes, dunes, and beaches. Winter offers the best birding, when numbers of Northern Gannets may be feeding just offshore, larids such as Great and Lesser Black-backed Gulls are regular, and a few Purple Sandpipers should be frequenting the jetties on both shores of the inlet. During fall, watch overhead for Peregrine Falcons and other migrant raptors. On the north side of the inlet is **Lighthouse Point Park** (55 acres; $3.50/vehicle; no camping; opens at sunrise). To reach it from I-95, exit (#256) onto SR-421 (Dunlawton Avenue) and head northeast, crossing the Halifax River (watch for roosting flocks of shorebirds and larids along the causeway). At its end at SR-A1A (5.2), turn right to the park ahead (5.6).

Contact: *Lighthouse Point Park, 5000 Robert Merrill Parkway South Atlantic, Ponce Inlet, FL 32127; 386-756-7488 ; <http://volusia.org/parks/lighthouse.htm>.*

On the south side of Ponce Inlet is **SMYRNA DUNES PARK** (250 acres; $3.50/vehicle; no camping; opens at sunrise). To reach it from Lighthouse Point Park, return to the mainland and then head south on US-1. At SR-A1A (9.7), turn left and cross the Halifax River. At Peninsula Avenue (1.5), turn left to the park ahead, next to the U.S. Coast Guard station. From I-95, exit (#249A) onto SR-44 (Canal Street) and head east. At the junction with SR-44 Business Route (3.0) bear right onto Lytle Avenue. Cross US-1 (3.9) and proceed as above; Lytle Avenue becomes SR-A1A east of US-1. The park contains a 1.5-mile-long boardwalk through a remnant coastal hammock and over dunes. The hammock and dune scrub may support numbers of migrant landbirds during spring and fall. After parking, take the boardwalk north. Several exits lead to the beach, which may have shorebirds (including Purple Sandpiper) and larids (Great and Lesser Black-backed Gulls) at low tide, especially before crowds arrive.

Contact: *Smyrna Dunes Park, 2995 North Peninsula Drive, New Smyrna Beach, FL 32169; 386-424-2935; <www.volusia.org/birding/smyrna.htm>.*

South of town is **Apollo Beach**, which is the northern access point to **CANAVERAL NATIONAL SEASHORE** (57,662 acres; $5.00/vehicle; primitive camping at $10.00/day; opens at 6:00 AM). The seashore's 24 miles of beaches and dunes represent the longest undeveloped stretch remaining in Florida. To reach it from Ponce Inlet, return to the junction of SR-A1A and Peninsula Avenue and continue south (8.1). The seashore offers the best sea-watching opportunities in Florida; one of these sites is **Turtle Mound**, located just inside the park between Parking Areas 1 and 2. *When a high-pressure system is located off the Carolinas in late fall, watch for movements of pelagics off Florida.* Turtle Mound was created by Indians, who deposited oyster shells here for over 600 years (800–1400 AD). As the highest point in the area (it is 35 feet tall), it has served as a landmark for mariners since the 1500s. Similarly, its height makes Turtle Mound great for birding; it contains two viewing platforms. One overlooks the Atlantic Ocean and the other overlooks Mosquito Lagoon. During fall, migrant raptors (especially falcons) can be numerous. Check the vegetation on the mound for migrant landbirds, mainly during spring. Parking Area 2 has a raised platform, which gives good views of the ocean, but the best site is the platform at **PARKING AREA 5**. (*An unofficial clothing-optional beach begins a short distance beyond Parking Area 5.*) Along the beaches, about 4,000 sea turtle nests are dug from late April through early September;

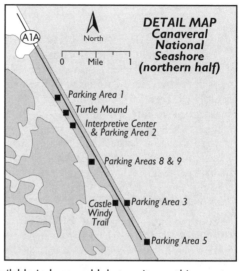

DETAIL MAP
Canaveral
National
Seashore
(northern half)

North

0   Mile   1

Parking Area 1
Turtle Mound
Interpretive Center
& Parking Area 2

Parking Areas 8 & 9

Castle ■ ■ Parking Area 3
Windy
Trail

■ Parking Area 5

night-time guided walks are available in June and July to witness this event.

During late fall 1991 (23 October–29 November), Harry Robinson conducted several sea-watches from Parking Area 5 and reported remarkable numbers of jaegers and other pelagic species from shore. Harry counted a total of 6,171 jaegers: 4,579 Pomarine, 1,591 Parasitic, and one Long-tailed . The following year, he counted 2,226 Pomarine and 4 Parasitic Jaegers on *just one day*, 9 November 1992. His pelagic list from Apollo Beach in 1991–1992 included 20 species: five shearwaters (Cory's, Greater, Sooty, Manx, and Audubon's), two boobies (Brown and Red-footed), all three jaegers, Northern Gannets, Red and Red-necked Phalaropes, South Polar Skua, Black-legged Kittiwake, Sabine's Gull, and Arctic Tern! Days with strong east or northeast winds are best, and a quality high-powered scope is essential

The seashore also affords other birding opportunities. **Castle Windy Trail**, opposite Parking Area 3, winds through a maritime hammock that can be good for migrant landbirds. The end of the trail overlooks Mosquito Lagoon, which may have waterfowl during winter. Opposite Parking Area 5 is a boat ramp to Mosquito Lagoon. Walk south along the lagoon to mudflats that are exposed during strong east winds; this area can be good for shorebirds. South of the Interpretive Center between Parking Areas 1 and 2 is a one-way loop road that heads west from the main road. The best opportunities are around Parking Areas 8 and 9, especially the half-mile trail that starts at Parking Area 9. When birding the hammocks, bring insect repellent: Mosquito Lagoon is aptly named! *Birders need to arrive early, because Parking Area 5 is small and fills up quickly.* You will be ticketed if you park on the side of the road.

Contact: *Canaveral National Seashore, 308 Julia Street, Titusville, FL 32796-3521; 386-321-1110; <www.nps.gov/cana>.*

TITUSVILLE

About 7 miles north of the city is **Scottsmoor Landing** (3 acres; no fee; no camping; opens at sunrise), a tiny passive recreation area that offers views of the Indian River Lagoon (see map on page 171). It is a good place to see wading birds year-round and waterfowl during winter. To reach it from the north, exit I-95 (#231) onto CR-5A and head northeast. At US-1 (0.9), turn right to Huntington Avenue (1.3), then turn left to the park ahead (1.9). From SR-46 and points south, head north on US-1 to Huntington Avenue (7.0), turn right, and proceed as above. Large numbers of Lesser Scaup and other waterfowl stage here before migrating north. Citrus groves along Dixie Way (one mile west of the park) contain Painted Buntings year-round. Males are conspicuous from late April through July, when singing from powerlines and other tall perches. *The groves are private property; bird only from along the road.*

Southwest of Titusville is **BLUE HERON WETLANDS TREATMENT FACILITY** (292 acres; no fee; no camping; opens at 7:00 AM), which filters treated wastewater before it is discharged into a tributary of the St. Johns River. It features earthen dikes that are drivable by private vehicle, and is a good spot for water birds, including Least Bittern (common year-round), Purple Gallinule (common, mainly spring and summer), and Gull-billed Tern (rare but regular during winter). To reach the facility, exit I-95 (#215) onto SR-50 and head west. When you see the huge white arch of the Great Outdoors RV park on the left (0.5), turn around and drive into the plant just east of the arch. On weekdays, the gate will be open. Sign in and get a vehicle pass at the office. During weekends, press the buzzer on the left side of the road and the gate will open automatically. Drive through the plant to the impoundments. There are seven cells: three shallow marsh cells, one deep-water cell, and three deep marsh cells. The dikes must be driven in a counter-clockwise direction only. The main dikes are wide enough to allow cars to pass, but interior dikes are more narrow.

Contact: *Blue Heron Wetlands Treatment Facility, 4800 Deep Marsh Road, Titusville, FL 2780; 321-383-5642.*

MERRITT ISLAND—CAPE CANAVERAL

MERRITT ISLAND NATIONAL WILDLIFE REFUGE (83,796 acres; no fee; no camping; opens at sunrise; *seasonal hunting. Portions are closed during Space Shuttle launches.* Visitor Center hours: 8:00 AM–4:30 PM Monday–Friday, 9:00 AM–5:00 PM weekends; *closed Sundays April–October*) is one of the best birding sites along Florida's Atlantic coast, especially during winter. The refuge supports large populations of wintering waterfowl, shorebirds, and larids, as well as 21 Threatened and Endangered animals, more than any other U.S. refuge outside Hawaii. When combined with Canaveral National Seashore, the refuge contains the world's second-largest population of Florida Scrub-Jays (second to Ocala National Forest). Insect repellent is

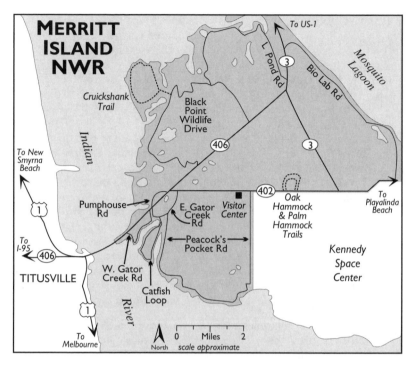

needed in much of the refuge during spring through fall. Refuge lands were purchased by the U.S. Government to develop the Kennedy Space Center. Non-essential parts of the property became the refuge; most of Kennedy Space Center is off limits to the public due to NASA and military launches and other activities. *It is best to call the refuge prior to visiting to learn if any areas are temporarily closed.*

Shortly after the government acquired the property in the 1950s and 1960s, miles of dikes were built along the edges of the saltmarshes. Once diked, the marshes were filled with water to prevent mosquitoes from laying eggs in the marsh soil. Converting the marshes to shallow pools greatly reduced mosquito populations and greatly increased the bird diversity of the area, but at terrible ecological cost: mosquito-control activities directly caused the extirpation of the endemic Dusky Seaside Sparrow from Merritt Island. (Other human activities on the adjacent mainland tragically caused its extinction a few year later). From an estimated 2,000 pairs, the sparrow population occupying Merritt Island had decreased to 600 pairs by 1957 and just 30 pairs by 1963. The last Dusky on the island was observed in 1977. Today, a stuffed specimen of a Dusky Seaside Sparrow at the refuge Visitor Center offers mute testimony of how short-sighted human endeavors affect the world around us.

To reach the refuge from US-1 in Titusville, head east on SR-406, crossing the Indian River. Upon reaching the island, turn right onto unpaved **West**

Gator Creek Road, which circles an impoundment for 1.6 miles. Before reaching SR-402, turn sharply right onto unpaved **Catfish Loop** to circle a second impoundment for 1.4 additional miles. These two impoundments can be excellent for wading birds, waterfowl, and shorebirds during migration and winter. At **East Gator Creek Road**, turn right, across from Pumphouse Road. This excellent birding loop will bring you back to SR-402 west of SR-406. To return to three impoundments on the north side of SR-406 along unpaved **Pumphouse Road**, turn left onto SR-402 back to SR-406, and then turn right onto Pumphouse Road (0.8). Park at the gate to bird the road on foot. Follow the water's edge on the right to the pumphouse and check the impoundments behind it. Return to SR-406 to the entrance of **BLACK POINT WILDLIFE DRIVE** on the left (1.6). This 6.3-mile long, one-way driving loop (unpaved but well maintained) travels in a clockwise direction and goes through one of the most productive parts of the refuge. Wading birds, waterfowl, shorebirds, and larids can all be abundant during migration and winter. About halfway through the wildlife drive is an observation tower and parking lot at the beginning of the 5-mile . The trail honors the late conservationist, birder, and wildlife photographer Allan D. Cruickshank, who lived in the area and strongly influenced the establishment of the refuge. To reach another road from the wildlife drive, see the section on L Pond Road, below.

After completing the wildlife drive, you return to SR-406 and have a choice. To reach the refuge Visitor Center, turn right to and return to the intersection with SR-402. Turn left to the center on the right (3.0). Alternatively, to head to the beach, turn left at SR-406 and go northeast to SR-3 (Kennedy Parkway; 1.7). Turn right, watching powerlines and oaks for perched Florida Scrub-Jays. To continue on to **Playalinda Beach** in the southern part of **Canaveral National Seashore** (57,662 acres; $5.00/vehicle; *primitive* camping at $10.00/day; opens at 6:00 AM), stay on SR-3 to SR-402 (traffic light; 3.2) and turn left. Parts of the seashore are closed on the day of a Space Shuttle launch and the preceding three days; call NASA at 321-867-2805 for information on shuttle launch dates. The road to the beach is only a few miles from the Space Shuttle launch pads; look for Gray Kingbirds in summer. After a few miles, the road heads north along the beach for about 6.5 miles before ending at a NASA camera pad. There are several parking areas and boardwalks over the dunes to view the Atlantic Ocean. *As at Apollo Beach to the north, an unofficial clothing-optional beach is found here, just beyond the north-ernmost Parking Area (# 13) at Playalinda.* Although the beach contains wading birds year-round, and migrant and wintering shorebirds, scoters, and larids (including Great Black-backed Gulls), the main draws here are the same as for Apollo Beach: migrant pelagics (mainly Northern Gannets and Pomarine and Parasitic Jaegers) and raptors (especially Merlins and Peregrine Falcons). The **Eddy Creek crossover** between Parking Areas 7 and 8 also affords a good view of Mosquito Lagoon to the west, which is worth a look for waterfowl (during winter), wading birds, or shorebirds (when water levels are low).

Return to SR-402 and cross SR-3 to the parking lot on the right (1.7). Two trails through a hardwood hammock originate here. **Oak Hammock Trail** (a half-mile walk) is usually more productive than Palm Hammock Trail. Return to SR-402 and turn right to the **Visitor Center** on the left (1.3), which offers restrooms, displays, and a small bookstore. There is also a boardwalk trail that originates from behind the center. The portion of SR-402 west of the Visitor Center has several pull-offs to allow for birding opportunities. From late fall through winter, waterfowl and American Coots are usually abundant in the marshes and impoundments here. This is one of the best sites in Florida for finding numbers of Northern Pintails. Scan the duck flocks carefully; one or two Eurasian Wigeons are found here almost annually, and Cinnamon Teals occur occasionally. Some of the larger shorebirds (such as yellowlegs) may also be here in numbers, depending on water levels.

L Pond Road begins on the left just beyond Marker 11 on Black Point Wildlife Drive. At the first impoundment, the road splits. The left road is better overall and it traverses about five miles before ending at SR-3. Turn right to return to SR-402. **Bio Lab Road** travels along the west side of Mosquito Lagoon. The road is located on SR-3 north of its junction with L Pond Road (0.6), and follows Mosquito Lagoon south to SR-402. During winter, waterfowl, shorebirds, larids, and other waterbirds can be common here.

Contacts: Merritt Island National Wildlife Refuge, P.O. Box 6504, Titusville, FL 32782; 321-861-0667; <http://merrittisland.fws.gov>. Canaveral National Seashore, 308 Julia Street, Titusville, FL 32796; 321-267-1110; <http://www.nps.gov/cana>. Kennedy Space Center, Kennedy Space Center, FL 32899; 321-867-5000; <www.ksc.nasa.gov>, <www.kennedyspacecenter.com>.

Just outside the Merritt Island/Cape Canaveral complex is Port Canaveral, which serves triple duty as a port facility for military vessels (including Trident submarines), cruise ships, and commercial shrimping or fishing boats. The southeastern point of the Port is **JETTY PARK** (35 acres; $5.00/vehicle; 150 campsites at $18.00–31.00/day; open 24 hours/day), which offers good birding opportunities from fall through spring (see map on page 171). To reach it from I-95, exit (#205) onto SR-528 (Beeline Expressway; the road that helped exterminate the Dusky Seaside Sparrow) and head east. Cross US-1 (4.2), then the Indian River, Merritt Island, and finally the Banana River onto the barrier island. As you approach the port facilities, turn left onto the "B" entrance and take George J. King Boulevard to its end at Park Road. Turn left to Jetty Drive (0.1) and turn right to the park. The maritime hammock, traversed by a trail along the south side of the park road, should be checked for migrant landbirds during spring (especially) and fall. A flock of psittacids, primarily Blue-crowned Parakeets but often with one or more Red-masked or White-eyed Parakeets, frequents the large sea grape tree along the south side of the restroom building. Large numbers of larids are usually found along the beach south of the jetty. In addition to common species, Great

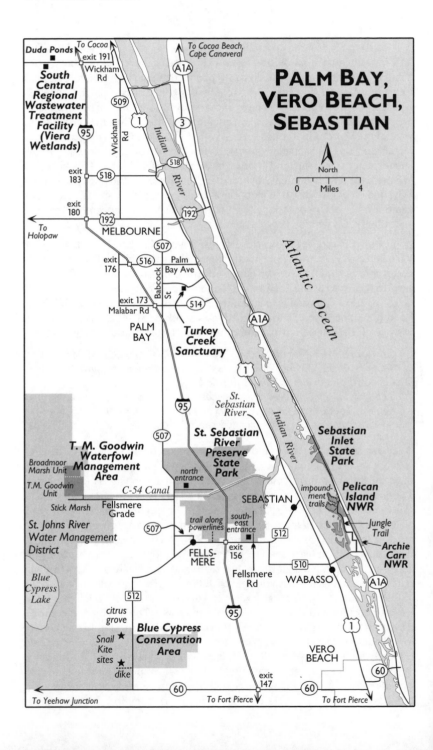

PALM BAY, VERO BEACH, SEBASTIAN

North

0 Miles 4

Duda Ponds

To Cocoa
exit 191
Wickham Rd

South Central Regional Wastewater Treatment Facility (Viera Wetlands)

95

509

1

Wickham Rd

To Cocoa Beach, Cape Canaveral

A1A

3

518

Indian River

exit 183
518

exit 180
192

To Holopaw

MELBOURNE

192

Atlantic Ocean

507

exit 176
516

Palm Bay Ave

Babcock St

exit 173
Malabar Rd

514

PALM BAY

Turkey Creek Sanctuary

A1A

1

St. Sebastian River

95

507

St. Sebastian River Preserve State Park

Sebastian Inlet State Park

T. M. Goodwin Waterfowl Management Area

Broadmoor Marsh Unit

T.M. Goodwin Unit

Stick Marsh

C-54 Canal

north entrance

Fellsmere Grade

SEBASTIAN

Indian River

impound-ment trails

Pelican Island NWR

St. Johns River Water Management District

507

trail along powerlines

south-east entrance

512

Jungle Trail

Archie Carr NWR

Blue Cypress Lake

FELLS-MERE

exit 156

Fellsmere Rd

510

WABASSO

A1A

512

citrus grove

Blue Cypress Conservation Area

95

1

Snail Kite sites

dike

60

VERO BEACH

60

To Yeehaw Junction

exit 147
60

To Fort Pierce

To Fort Pierce

Black-backed and Lesser Black-backed Gulls are regular in winter. Northern Gannets are often seen from shore, and a few Purple Sandpipers frequent the jetty in winter.

Contact: *Jetty Park, 400 East Jetty Park Drive, Cape Canaveral, FL 32920; 321-783-7111; <www.portcanaveral.org/funport/parks.htm>.*

To reach **Lori Wilson Park** (32 acres; 50¢ parking; no camping; opens at 8:00 AM), a small oceanfront park in Cocoa Beach, go south on SR-A1A, pass by SR-520 (Merritt Island Causeway; 3.5), to the park on the left (1.5, just south of the Hilton Hotel; see map on page 171). The park preserves a remnant wind-pruned maritime hammock that can be good for migrant landbirds during spring and fall. Painted Buntings frequent the feeder near the start of the trail. One family of Florida Scrub-Jays inhabits the northern part of the park. The Johnnie Johnson Nature Center honors Florida's late pioneer of pelagic trips, who lived in the area.

Contact: *Lori Wilson Park, 1500 North Atlantic Blvd., Cocoa Beach, FL 32931; 321-455-1380; <www.brevardparks.com/nature/loriwilson.htm>.*

MELBOURNE—PALM BAY

A newly created site that has attracted lots of attention recently is the **SOUTH CENTRAL REGIONAL WASTEWATER TREATMENT FACILITY** (140 acres; no fee; no camping; opens at sunrise) north of Melbourne. Informally known as Viera Wetlands, it consists of five cells that filter wastewater before its release into the St. Johns River. Good birds seen in this vicinity have included Greater White-fronted Goose, White-cheeked Pintail (of unknown provenance), Masked Duck, Eared Grebe, Ruff, and, in 2002, the first North American record of the Mangrove Swallow. To reach the facility from I-95, exit (#191) onto CR-509 (Wickham Road) and head west. Watch for Crested Caracaras around the sod farms on the drive in. The treatment facility office is on the left (2.3). Sign in before heading to the ponds, then drive west a short distance to the parking area. The main dikes may be driven, and observation towers are available. In addition to common wetland species, breeders include Least Bittern and Purple Gallinule, and Black-bellied Whistling-Ducks are seen on occasion. Wading birds are present year-round, and waterfowl can be common during winter. When water levels are suitable, migratory and wintering shorebirds will be present.

On the other side (north) of Wickham Road are the **Duda Ponds**, another part of the facility. After signing in at the office, head east on Wickham and turn left onto the first unpaved road (at the powerlines; about 300 feet), make a quick left and then a quick right to the gate, which should be unlocked. You are permitted to drive around the two ponds, but not on the dike that separates them. Depending upon water levels, migratory or wintering shorebirds can be common in the north pond. The south pond is usually too flooded for shorebirds but should have wintering waterfowl. Scan the sod farms east of the facility—*from the road or ponds only; they are private property*—for upland shorebirds such as American Golden-Plover and Pectoral, Upland, and Buff-breasted Sandpipers; mid-August through early September is best.

Contact: *South Central Regional Wastewater Facility, 10001 North Wickham Road, Viera, FL 23940; 321-255-4329.*

T URKEY CREEK SANCTUARY (138 acres; no fee; no camping; opens at 7:00 AM) can be excellent for migrant landbirds (especially warblers), primarily during fall. Thirty or more species of warblers are seen here annually from mid-August through mid-October. To reach the sanctuary from I-95, exit (#176) onto CR-516 (Palm Bay Road NE) and head east. At CR-507 (Babcock Street; 2.1), turn right to Port Malabar Boulevard (1.1) and turn left. The park is ahead on the right (1.1). The entrance is behind the Community Center, next to the library. From the south, exit I-95 (#173) onto SR-514 (Malabar Road NE) and head east. At CR-507 (Babcock Street; 0.5), turn left to Port Malabar Boulevard (1.4). Turn right and proceed as above. Nearly two miles of trails traverse hammock, Sand Pine scrub, and riparian areas.

Contact: *Turkey Creek Sanctuary, 1502 Port Malabar Boulevard, Palm Bay, FL 32905; 1-800-276-9130; <www.palmbayflorida.org/Departments/ Parks&Rec/turkey_creek_sanctuary.htm>.*

SEBASTIAN—FELLSMERE

A site that can be excellent for waterbirds is **T.M. Goodwin Waterfowl Management Area** (3,870 acres; no fee; no camping; opens 9:00 AM *Mondays and Thursdays only; seasonal hunting November–February*) northwest of Sebastian. To reach it from the north, exit I-95 (#173) onto SR-514 (Malabar Road NE) and head east. At CR-507 (Babcock Street, 0.5), turn left and head south. Cross over the C-54 Canal (12.6), and make an immediate right onto Fellsmere Grade. The management area is ahead on the right (6.3). From the south, exit I-95 (#156) onto CR-512 (Fellsmere Road) and head west. In Fellsmere, turn right onto CR-507 (Broadway Street, 3.0), Follow Broadway north, then west to SR-507. Turn left to Fellsmere Grade and proceed as above. As you drive in along Fellsmere Grade, you will pass by **Stick Marsh** to the south, good for ducks and American White Pelicans in winter. Black-bellied Whistling-Ducks sometimes nest in the dead palm snags, and the boat ramp usually has Limpkins around dawn or dusk.

The dikes at the management area to the north are open to driving on a limited basis, but they may be walked anytime during daylight hours—it is advisable to avoid walking the dikes during hunting season. The area is a wetlands restoration project within the Upper St. Johns River floodplain. Waterfowl winter here in numbers, and Black-bellied Whistling-Ducks may be seen at any time. Ponds with low water levels attract large numbers of wading birds year-round, and migratory shorebirds during spring and fall. Migrant landbirds can be common in the hammocks primarily during fall; bring along insect repellent for the mosquitoes. Also during fall, look for migrant swallows and Bobolinks. Contiguous with the waterfowl management area to the north is the **Broadmoor Marsh Unit** (2,400 acres; no fee; no camping; *seasonal hunting*), another marsh restoration project that provides good birding opportunities.

> *Contact:* T.M. Goodwin Waterfowl Management Area; 321-726-2862; <http://myfwc.com/duck/Check_Stations/Goodwin/t.m.goodwin.htm>.

S t. Sebastian River Preserve State Park (22,705 acres; no fee; primitive camping at $4.00/day; opens at 8:00 AM), a fairly recent state acquisition, supports all birds associated with pine flatwoods and oak scrub, including Red-cockaded Woodpeckers, Florida Scrub-Jays, and Bachman's Sparrows. To reach the park from Goodwin Waterfowl Management Area, return to SR-507 and turn left. Cross the canal and turn right onto Buffer Preserve Drive (0.3). The visitor's center for the **north entrance** is on the left (0.7). Park in the parking lot and walk north into the open flatwoods, which contains Bachman's Sparrows and one group of Florida Scrub-Jays. Continue east on Buffer Preserve Drive to the parking lot at Scrub Jay Road (1.5). Several Florida Scrub-Jays are found in the oak scrub near the beginning of the road to the north. To search for Red-cockaded Woodpeckers, continue east to the road to Pine Camp (1.0) and walk north. Turn east on the Blue/Yellow trail; woodpecker cavity trees are painted with white bands. Buffer Preserve Drive ends at the S-157 water control structure, with its viewing platform for West Indian Manatees. The park is a significant wintering site for manatees; as many as 100 animals have been seen during peak periods. Florida Scrub-Jays are common near the **southwest entrance**. From I-95, head west on CR-512 to the trail on the right, which parallels the powerlines (0.9). You should encounter Florida Scrub-Jays within 0.2 mile. East of this trail, watch for Swallow-tailed Kites roosting (early mornings and late afternoons, mid-March to mid-July) in dead pines along CR-512. To reach the **southeast entrance**, head east on CR-512 to WW Ranch Road on the left (1.9 from I-95). This section of the park contains open grasslands surrounded by pine flatwoods and scrub. Sandhill Cranes are usually seen along the road. When the fields are flooded from heavy rainfall, they attract wading birds year-round, ducks during winter, and occasionally shorebirds during migration.

> *Contact:* St. Sebastian River Preserve State Park, 1000 Buffer Preserve Drive, Fellsmere, FL 32948; 321-953-5006; <www.floridastateparks.org/stsebastian>.

S ebastian Inlet State Park (578 acres; $5.00/vehicle; 51 campsites at $23.00/day; accessible anytime) often is crowded with sunbathers, but it can still be good for birds. To reach it from I-95, exit (#156) onto CR-512 (Fellsmere Road) and head east. At CR-510 (2.4), turn right. Remain on this road through a turn to the east, cross US-1 and then the Indian River Lagoon before ending at SR-A1A on the barrier island. Turn left to Sebastian Inlet and cross the bridge (7.3) that divides the park into two sections. The entrance is on the left. At low tide, check the cove west of the parking area under the bridge for wading birds (including Reddish Egrets and Roseate Spoonbills), shorebirds, and larids. Wooded areas and the large grassy field may be good for migrant landbirds during spring and fall. The oceanside fishing jetty is a good spot to scan offshore for Northern Gannets, scoters, and jaegers from late fall through winter, especially on days with strong east or northeast winds. Also during winter, look for Purple Sandpipers on the jetty. Return to SR-A1A and head south over the bridge. Turn right onto the southern entrance road. Show your fee receipt at the toll booth, then continue west to the end of the road at the Indian River. Scan the shoreline and exposed sand-bars for wading birds, shorebirds, and larids. Sea turtles nest along the park's three miles of beaches; call the park (before May) to make reservations for a night-time guided tour. Information on boat trips to Pelican Island may also be obtained.

Contact: *Sebastian Inlet State Park, 9700 South SR-A1A, Melbourne Beach, FL 32951; 321-984-4852; <www.floridastateparks.org/sebastianinlet>.*

Pelican Island National Wildlife Refuge (5,413 acres; no fee at present; no camping; opens at 7:00 AM) was the first area set aside by the federal government, in 1903, for the protection of birds. Additional land acquisitions and several amenities have recently been added as part of the refuge's centennial celebration. Pelican Island itself is off-limits to protect the Brown Pelicans, herons, and other waterbirds that roost and nest there, but other parts of the refuge are accessible. To reach the refuge from Sebastian Inlet, simply head south on SR-A1A to Historic Jungle Trail on the right (3.5). From I-95, follow the directions for Sebastian Inlet State Park, but proceed north along SR-A1A to the entrance at Historic Jungle Trail on the left (3.8). Park in the lot beyond the hammock, then walk back to **Bird's Impoundment Trail**. Beyond a gate, it extends 2.5 miles around a mosquito-control impoundment. Farther south along Jungle Trail is the **Pelican Island Viewing Area** (0.5), which contains two trails. The half-mile Centennial Trail to the left leads to an 18-foot observation tower that provides a view of Pelican Island. **Pete's Impoundment Trail** is also 2.5 miles long around mosquito impoundment dikes; wading birds and shorebirds can be common along the impoundment trails when water levels are suitable. American White Pelicans, waterfowl, and other species are found in the Indian River Lagoon during winter. Future amenities to the refuge will include an additional trail and a half-mile wildlife drive through restored habitats.

Contact: *Pelican Island National Wildlife Refuge, 1339 20th Street, Vero Beach, FL 32960-3558; 772-562-3909; <www.fws.gov/pelicanisland>.*

Across SR-A1A from the refuge is one segment of **Archie Carr National Wildlife Refuge** (248 acres; no fee; no camping; opens at sunrise; see previous map). The refuge is essential for the preservation of nesting sea turtles—it is the second-most important site in the world for Loggerhead Sea Turtles, supporting 25 percent of the world's nesting population. The 20-mile stretch of beach and dunes from Melbourne Beach south to Wabasso Beach may contain more than 200 nests per mile! Overall, 13,000–15,000 nests are dug annually; most by Loggerhead Sea Turtles, but Atlantic Green Turtles and even a few Leatherback Sea Turtles nest here, as well. There is no public parking, and birding opportunities are quite limited. For a tour of nesting sea turtles, call Sebastian Inlet State Park, above.

Contact: *Archie Carr National Wildlife Refuge, same information as above for Pelican Island NWR; <www.fws.gov/archiecarr>.*

Blue Cypress Water Management Area (part of **Blue Cypress Conservation Area**; 54,458 acres; no fee; primitive camping; accessible anytime; *seasonal hunting*; see previous map) west of Vero Beach is a reliable site for Snail Kites when water levels are suitable. Exit I-95 (#147) at SR-60 and head west to CR-512 (7.5). *Turn right and drive with caution; large citrus trucks are a potential hazard.* Watch for a small sand road over the dike on the left (1.5), used by boaters to reach the St. Johns River. The dike may be walked west for about two miles. Snail Kites are seen here regularly, especially in early morning and before dusk. Look also for Fulvous Whistling-Duck, Mottled Duck, wading birds (including Least Bittern), King Rail, Purple Gallinule, and Limpkin. Another access point for Snail Kites is 2.5 miles farther north on CR-512, just before the citrus groves. Park off the road and walk in past the spillway.

Contact: *Blue Cypress Conservation Area, St. Johns River Water Management District, P.O. Box 1429, Palatka, FL 32178; 321-676-6614; <http://www.sjrwmd.com>.*

FORT PIERCE—PORT ST. LUCIE

Some of the best local birding spots are on North Hutchinson Island north of Fort Pierce (see map on next page). From I-95 (Exit #129) or Florida's Turnpike, go east on SR-70 to US-1 (4.0). For sites on North Hutchinson Island, turn left to SR-A1A North (3.2). Turn right and cross the Indian River Lagoon, checking the mangroves and mudflats for wading birds and shorebirds. Turn into **Fort Pierce Inlet State Park** (340 acres; $3.25/vehicle; no camping; opens at 8:00 AM) on the right (1.4). Turn right onto the first paved road to Dynamite Point. Look here for wading birds, shorebirds, and larids. Low tide is best. A telescope is helpful, because most of the birds will be across the channel on Coon Island. Back at the main park road, turn right and then left to the north end of the parking lot. The half-mile-long **Coastal Hammock Nature Trail** can be good for migrant landbirds.

Contact: *Fort Pierce Inlet State Park, 905 Shorewinds Drive, Fort Pierce, FL 34949; 772-468-3985; <www.floridastateparks.org/fortpierceinlet>.*

FORT PIERCE TO PORT ST. LUCIE

Return to SR-A1A and turn right. At the traffic light, turn left to **Jack Island Preserve State Park** (958 acres; no fee; no camping; opens at 8:00 AM) on the left (1.4). Cross the footbridge and pick up a trail map. The island is mostly mangroves, with patches of tropical hardwood hammock. It is criss-crossed by mosquito-control dikes. The **Marsh Rabbit Trail** (one mile long) contains an observation tower that overlooks the Indian River Lagoon. Roseate Spoonbills are present in summer, and Florida Prairie Warblers breed here. During winter, ducks and other species may be found.

To reach South Hutchinson Island, return to US-1 and head south. At SR-A1A South (Seaway Drive; 1.1), turn left to the coast (2.6). Continue east to the paved **jetty**, which is good for observing seabirds such as Northern Gannets and jaegers , especially during strong east winds. Return to SR-A1A and head south to **Bear Point Sanctuary** (13 acres; no fee; no camping) on the right (2.4). A dike trail at the north end of the parking lot ends at a pier and an observation platform that provides a view over the mangroves of wading birds and other coastal species. A dike trail that begins at the south end of the parking lot can be good for migrant landbirds during spring and fall.

Return to US-1 and head south beyond SR-70. At Savanna Road (0.6), turn left to a remnant patch of scrub between the city compound and the railroad tracks (0.7) that contains Florida Scrub-Jays.

R eturn to US-1 and head south to SR-712 (Midway Road; 3.7). Turn left to **Savannas Recreation Area** (550 acres; $1.00/vehicle; 34 campsites at $10.00–$20.00/day) on the right (1.4). The Savannas is an extensive area of freshwater marshes and wet prairies, a remnant of a system that once extended along much of Florida's Atlantic coast. The roads may be walked, but waterbirds are best viewed from a canoe ($4.00/hour rental). The marsh supports a rookery that is used by Anhingas and wading birds. Least Bitterns, King Rails, and Purple Gallinules are resident, and waterfowl occur during winter.

Contact: *Savannas Recreation Area, 1400 East Midway Road, Fort Pierce, FL 34982; 772-464-7855 or 1-800-789-5776; <www.stlucieco.gov/leisure/savanna.htm>.*

Head back west on SR-712 across US-1. At SR-615 (25th Street or St. James Drive; 1.5), turn left to **Oxbow Eco-Center** (220 acres; no fee; no camping; trails open at sunrise) on the left (1.7). The center was built in an environmentally sensitive manner and contains exhibits about the area's natural history. (If the center is closed, you may still walk the trails). Loop trails cross several habitats: pine flatwoods, scrubby flatwoods, floodplain forest, slough, and depression marsh. Limpkins are frequently seen along the canal banks.

Contact: *Oxbow Eco-Center, 5400 Northeast St. James Drive, Port St. Lucie, FL 34983; 772-785-5833; <www.stlucieco.gov/erd/oxbow>.*

R eturn to US-1 and head south to Walton Road (5.6). Turn left to **Savannas Preserve State Park** (5,100 acres; $3.25/vehicle; no camping; opens at 8:00 AM) on the left (1.9). The park, which stretches for more than 10 miles north to south, features an extensive freshwater marsh, along with pine flatwoods and oak scrub. Again, if the nature center is closed, the trails may still be walked. An unpaved road to the left off Walton Road leads to a canoe launch. This road can be birded by vehicle to a marsh overlook where nesting Bald Eagles and Sandhill Cranes and a variety of wintering waterfowl may be seen. Pine flatwoods contain several groups of Florida Scrub-Jays, as well as Brown-headed Nuthatches and Bachman's Sparrows.

Contact: *Savannas Preserve State Park, 2541 Walton Road, Port St. Lucie, FL 34952; 772-398-2779; <www.floridastateparks.org/savannas>.*

Atlantic coastal areas continue on page 213.

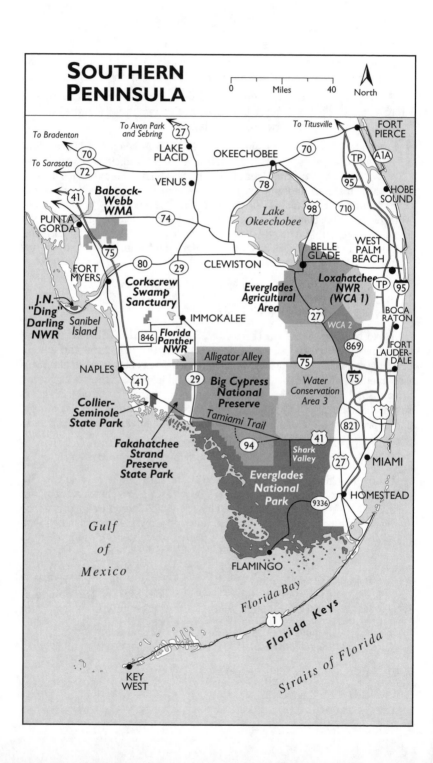

SOUTHERN
PENINSULA

One of the few truly subtropical regions in North America, mainland South Florida contains several species and subspecies of birds that cannot be found elsewhere in the ABA Area. The Cape Sable Seaside Sparrow is endemic to the region, which also supports the only reliable ABA-area sites for Greater Flamingo and Smooth-billed Ani (now rare and very local). Although more abundant in the Keys, White-crowned Pigeons can be reliably found in the Southern Peninsula. Additionally, many West Indian vagrants have been found in the region or the Keys, and several of these are becoming regular. La Sagra's Flycatcher, Bahama Mockingbird, and Western Spindalis now occur annually or nearly so, while others, such as Masked Duck, Key West Quail-Dove, Cuban Pewee, Thick-billed Vireo, and Bananaquit occur less frequently. White-cheeked Pintails are occasionally found, but this species is common in waterfowl collections—for all recent observations, the provenance of the birds involved has been considered suspect. Another species currently of uncertain provenance is Red-legged Honeycreeper, six of which were observed during 2003–2005. Several coastal parks from West Palm Beach southward can be excellent for migrant raptors during fall, and for migrant landbirds during spring and fall. During fall, migrant shorebirds are abundant in shallowly-flooded fields in the Everglades Agricultural Area southeast of Lake Okeechobee. And of course, there is Everglades National Park, the most diverse birding site in Florida, teeming with wading birds, migrant and wintering landbirds, and wintering waterfowl, shorebirds, and larids.

For birders seeking exotics, there is no more rewarding region in North America than the southeastern peninsula of Florida. Urban and suburban areas in the region—especially the vast Fort Lauderdale and Miami metropolitan areas—support a remarkable array of exotic birds from tropical areas of the world (but mainly the American tropics). These metropolitan areas have often been called open-air zoos due to the abundance and diversity of exotic birds, primarily psittacids. Three countable exotics are limited within the ABA Area to southern Florida: White-winged Parakeet (Miami; apparent hybrids are found at Fort Lauderdale), Red-whiskered Bulbul (Kendall/Pinecrest only), and Spot-breasted Oriole (Fort Lauderdale and Miami metropolitan areas). The Yellow-chevroned Parakeet, which is on the ABA Checklist, has not been accepted by the FOSRC, so the species is *not* ABA-countable in Florida. Muscovy Ducks and Monk Parakeets are widespread and locally common in the region, though both species occur elsewhere in Florida, as well.

Non-countable exotic species breeding in the region currently include Purple Swamphen (predominantly Pembroke Pines but dispersing widely north and west), Rose-ringed Parakeet (Fort Myers and Naples), Black-hooded Parakeet (mainly Fort Lauderdale, but also in Miami; *countable populations are found along the central Gulf coast*), Blue-crowned Parakeet (Fort Lauderdale and Miami, with a few at Naples), Green Parakeet (uncommon; Fort Lauderdale and Miami), Mitred Parakeet (Fort Lauderdale and Miami), Red-masked Parakeet (Fort Lauderdale and Miami, with a few at Naples), White-eyed Parakeet (uncommon; Fort Lauderdale and Miami, a few at Naples), Dusky-headed Parakeet (uncommon; Miami Springs only), Chestnut-fronted Macaw (uncommon; Fort Lauderdale and Miami), Blue-and-yellow Macaw (rare; Miami), Yellow-chevroned Parakeet (Miami metro area; apparent hybrids are found at Fort Lauderdale), White-fronted Parrot (uncommon; Fort Lauderdale and Miami), Red-crowned Parrot (Palm Beach and Fort Lauderdale, with some at Miami), Orange-winged Parrot (Fort Lauderdale and Miami), Common Myna (predominantly the Miami metropolitan area, but the species may occur throughout), and Hill Myna (southern Miami). Several of these species may be candidates for future establishment (and therefore ABA countability) if current population trends continue and if adequate research is conducted.

The best birding spots in the region are Everglades National Park (year-round, depending upon species sought), Greater Miami/Pembroke Pines (for exotics; year-round), the Fort Myers/Sanibel Island area (primarily winter), and the Everglades Agricultural Area (summer and fall). These areas can be birded easily in about a week, often including Corkscrew Swamp Sanctuary, Big Cypress National Preserve, Fakahatchee Strand Preserve State Park, or other excellent sites (such as the Keys or any of several nearby sites in the Central Peninsula).

SOUTHERN PENINSULA—GULF COAST

PUNTA GORDA

East of Punta Gorda is **FRED BABCOCK–CECIL M. WEBB WILDLIFE MANAGEMENT AREA** (69,727 acres; $3.00/person or $6.00/vehicle; annual pass available; all roads are unpaved; *seasonal hunting and a shooting range*). Much of the area has Slash Pine flatwoods with breeding birds such as Sandhill Crane, Eastern Kingbird (spring and summer), Brown-headed Nuthatch, Pine Warbler, and Bachman's Sparrow. The big at-

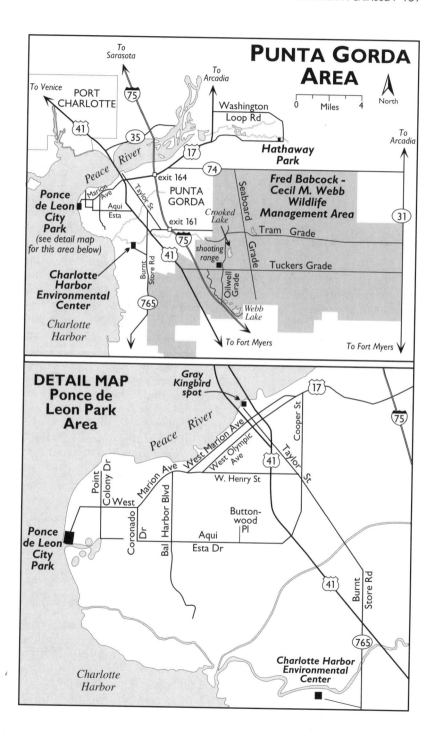

PUNTA GORDA AREA

To Sarasota

To Venice

PORT CHARLOTTE

75

41

35

17

Peace River

Marion Ave

Taylor St

Aqui Esta

To Arcadia

Washington Loop Rd

Hathaway Park

exit 164

PUNTA GORDA

74

Crooked Lake

exit 161

75

41

Burnt Store Rd

765

shooting range

Seaboard Grade

Fred Babcock – Cecil M. Webb Wildlife Management Area

Tram Grade

Tuckers Grade

Oilwell Grade

Webb Lake

To Arcadia

31

To Fort Myers

Ponce de Leon City Park
(see detail map for this area below)

Charlotte Harbor Environmental Center

Charlotte Harbor

To Fort Myers

0   Miles   4   North

DETAIL MAP
Ponce de Leon Park Area

Gray Kingbird spot

17

75

Peace River

West Marion Ave

West Olympic Ave

Cooper St

Taylor St

41

Point West

Colony Dr

Coronado Dr

Marion Ave

Bal Harbor Blvd

W. Henry St

Button-wood Pl

Aqui Esta Dr

Ponce de Leon City Park

41

Burnt Store Rd

765

Charlotte Harbor Environmental Center

Charlotte Harbor

traction is the Red-cockaded Woodpecker, with 27 clusters on-site (cavity trees are marked). To reach the management area from US-41 or I-75 (Exit #158), head east on Tuckers Grade to the entrance at its end. (Tuckers Grade is 3.1 miles south of SR-765 on US-41 at a flashing yellow light).

A recreation area (11,000 acres) at the west entrance offers about 15 miles of unpaved roads usually passable in regular vehicles. Three Red-cockaded Woodpecker clusters occur here, along with common flatwoods species. Stop at the self-pay fee station on your right at the two big ponds near the entrance. Maps are available here. In this area, watch for typical wetland species, and the huge numbers of Tree Swallows that may roost in nearby marshes during the winter. Just beyond the fee station, Tuckers Grade heads south along Babcock Lake and provides access to marshy areas beyond the campground that can produce views of King Rails, other marsh birds, and American Alligators.

Continuing east on Tuckers Grade, you will come to a small lock at the north end of Webb Lake. Limpkins may be found in the canal to the left. Just beyond the cattle guard (steel pipes laid perpendicular to the road that cattle won't willingly cross), check the grassy road shoulders for wintering sparrows, including Grasshopper Sparrows. As you continue east, the habitat changes: Slash Pine becomes more prevalent near the entrance to the shooting range on your left (0.6). Between here and the next intersection (**Oilwell Grade**; 0.5), begin searching for flatwoods species such as Hairy Woodpecker, Brown-headed Nuthatch, Eastern Towhee, and Bachman's Sparrows. Because most flatwoods species are gregarious, stop frequently to search for feeding flocks. During winter, these groups will be comprised largely of Pine and Palm Warblers, but woodpeckers (including Red-cockaded at times), Eastern Bluebirds, and Brown-headed Nuthatches usually are present as well. The nuthatches often are located by listening for their distinctive, high, squeaky calls. Bachman's Sparrows generally do not join these flocks and are very difficult to view during winter. However, during spring and summer, singing males are easily located.

Most birders visit Babcock–Webb to search for the Endangered Red-cockaded Woodpecker (*follow all birding ethics; tapes are not needed for this species*). Two clusters are marked on wildlife management area maps that are available at the fee station. To reach one woodpecker cluster, turn left onto Oilwell Grade. Bachman's Sparrows occur commonly throughout this area as well. At the cluster site (0.8), note the orange flagging on the trees on both sides of the road. There is also a sign here that reads "RCW". It is best to visit the clusters in the evening, because the birds typically return and work the area a bit before going to roost. During the day, your best bet for finding Red-cockadeds is to follow feeding flocks of landbirds, which may contain the woodpeckers. The two roads that lead to Crooked Lake (0.2 and 0.6) are very good areas to check for feeding flocks, and for Glossy Ibis, Wood Stork, and other wading birds, Sandhill Crane, Brown-headed Nuthatch, Eastern Bluebird, and Bachman's Sparrow. A second cluster is located at the intersection of Oilwell Grade and Tram Grade (0.6), an area that also supports the other species mentioned above. To reach a third woodpecker cluster (the second cluster marked on the WMA map), turn right onto Tram Road to the marked trees and another "RCW" sign on the left (0.4).

A bit farther down Tram Road is Seaboard Grade (0.7), which is a narrower, generally less-traveled road that may have vegetation growing on it. Less adventurous birders may wish to turn around here, but the road is passable in standard vehicles (although it requires slower speeds, and meeting an oncoming vehicle poses a challenge). If you choose to continue, turn right onto Seaboard Grade. Along both sides of the road is marsh habitat that is good for Anhingas, wading birds, and rails (King Rail year-round, Virginia Rail and Sora during winter), along with alligators and other reptiles. You can take this road back to Tuckers Grade, then turn right to return the entrance. The section of Tuckers Grade from Seaboard to Oilwell Grade contains pockets of flatwoods separated by freshwater marshes that may contain American Bitterns and rails during winter, along with numerous wading birds year-round.

Contact: *Fred Babcock–Cecil M. Webb Wildlife Management Area, 29200 Tuckers Grade, Punta Gorda, FL 33955; 941-639-1531; <www.wildflorida.org/hunting/wma/SW_Region/webb-web.pdf>.*

To visit other sites around Punta Gorda, head west on Tuckers Grade to US-41 (Tamiami Trail) and turn right. At CR-765 (Burnt Store Road; 3.1), turn left briefly stop at the Alligator Creek portion of **Charlotte Harbor Environmental Center** on the right (1.1). The center has numerous trails, a nature center, bird observation blind, and Bald Eagle nests.

Contact: *Charlotte Harbor Environmental Center, 10941 Burnt Store Road, Punta Gorda, FL 33955; 941-575-4800.*

If you wish to head to Cape Coral to search for the Burrowing Owls and Monk Parakeets (next page), continue south on CR-765. Otherwise, head back north to US-41 and turn left. At Aqui Esta Drive (1.8), turn left. During winter, check out the ponds at Buttonwood Place (0.8) and behind the plaza at Bal Harbor Boulevard (1.0; drive behind the plaza to view the pond). The latter pond attracts a huge roost of more than 1,000 Hooded Mergansers, and other ducks are often present. At the T-intersection with Coronado Drive (0.4), turn right to West Marion Avenue (0.5). Turn left, cross a short, tall bridge, and immediately turn right onto Colony Point Drive (0.4). Look for **Burrowing Owls** along this road; most burrows are marked by short T-perches, stakes, and flagging. The best area is 0.3–0.4 mile from West Marion Avenue, but this situation may change as the area continues to be developed. The north end of Colony Point Drive has a circular turnaround where you can head back south.

Return to West Marion Avenue and turn right to **Ponce de Leon Park** on the left (0.2). The park contains trails through mangroves, and a wildlife rehabilitation facility. Most birders come here to search for Mangrove Cuckoos, which breed here in small numbers. The cuckoos are vocal from late March through July; *the use of tapes here is seldom necessary and should be avoided*. Sometimes the birds nest close to the boardwalk trail and may be easily located, while during other years, they may be farther back in the mangroves. Florida Prairie Warblers also breed here; in winter look for Common Loons, Horned Grebes, and other waterbirds.

To search for Gray Kingbirds during spring and summer, return to West Marion Avenue, bearing left, then right, then left again. At **Taylor Street** (3.5), turn left and proceed to the end of the road; park in the parking area on the right. As many as four pairs of kingbirds nest in trees in the two-block area around the parking lot.

Head back south on Taylor Street and backtrack one block to West Olympia Avenue. Turn left; the road becomes US-17 once you cross US-41. Continue east from I-75 and turn right onto the northern portion of **Washington Loop Road** (5.8). This road runs for more than 10 miles before rejoining US-17, and it offers opportunities to see several species of interest. Check the wires along the first few miles for White-winged Doves. Florida Scrub-Jays may be found near the intersection of Blackjack Circle on the left (2.4). At Shell Creek (2.3), look for Black-bellied Whistling Ducks shortly after dawn and before dusk, and for Limpkin throughout the day. Just around the corner you will find the entrance to **Hathaway Park**, which has a few short trails where Limpkins and Barred Owls can be found. Farther along Washington Loop Road, look for Red-headed Woodpeckers in pastures with scattered pines. Swallow-tailed Kites (spring and summer) and Sandhill Cranes may be seen at several spots along the loop.

FORT MYERS

Fort Myers is an excellent base from which to bird the southern Gulf coast and western Everglades. Interstate 75 and Southwest Florida Regional International Airport are within a few miles of the city and provide convenient road and air access. Within the city, CR-869 (Summerlin Road) provides a bypass around congested downtown areas.

Many Burrowing Owls inhabit the city of **Cape Coral**, west of Fort Myers. From I-75, exit (#131) at Daniels Road and head west. Daniels Road becomes Cypress Lake Drive west of US-41. At Summerlin Road (5.8), turn right and proceed to College Parkway (0.7; the second light), then turn left. After you cross the Cape Coral Bridge ($1.00/vehicle), the road name changes to Cape Coral Parkway. To drive a loop with chances for Burrowing Owls and Monk Parakeets, go west to Pelican Boulevard (2.8), turn right, and continue to the ballfields on your left (0.8). Monk Parakeets nest in the light structures and surrounding palms and trees. Check the southern perimeter of the park (along SW 42nd Terrace) for Burrowing Owls. For more owls, turn left onto Pelican Boulevard to Mohawk Parkway (0.2). Turn left to the four-way stop at Skyline Boulevard (0.5). Continue straight to the first street on your right (0.3) and turn right. At SW 39th Terrace (0.1), turn left. A number of owl bur-

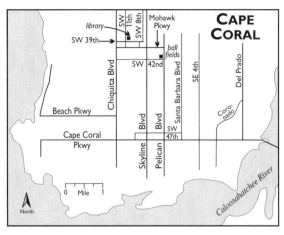

rows, which are roped-off areas to protect them from mowing tractors, are found along this street. Also check the library property, as owls are beginning to move away from development that is continuing along SW 39th Terrace. Continue to SW 11th Place (0.3) and turn left to return to Mohawk Parkway. To reach other owl burrows, turn left to return to the four-way stop at Skyline Boulevard (0.4). Turn right and continue to SW 47th Terrace (0.9; the last left before the traffic light at Cape Coral Parkway), and turn left again. Check the marked burrows along this street until you reach Pelican Boulevard (0.5), where you turn right to reach Cape Coral Parkway. Turn left to return to Fort Myers.

Lakes **County Park**(279 acres; parking $0.75/hour; no camping) is good for wading birds year-round and migrant landbirds during fall, although Hurricane *Charley* damaged some of the park's trees in 2004 . To reach the park from Summerlin Road (see map on next page), go east on Gladiolus Drive (1.8 south of Daniels Road) to the entrance on the left (1.0). The park contains a variety of habitats, including shallow lakes, a cypress swamp, and pinewoods. Trails access the woodlands and a boardwalk provides views of the lake. A large heronry of egrets, herons, and ibises is along the lake edge at the east side of the park. The boardwalk provides excellent views of the birds. The Fragrance Garden located in the northeast corner of the park is the best area to find migrant and wintering landbirds, including hummingbirds. Also check the area around the small bridge and amphitheater east of the Fragrance Garden along the paved path.

> **Contact:** *Lakes County Park, 7330 Gladiolus Drive, Fort Myers, FL 33907; 239-432-2000; <www.leeparks.org/facility_info.cfm? Project_Num=0101>.*

Six **Mile Cypress Slough Preserve** (2,200 acres; parking $0.75/hour; no camping) is a county park with a 1.2-mile elevated boardwalk that is fully

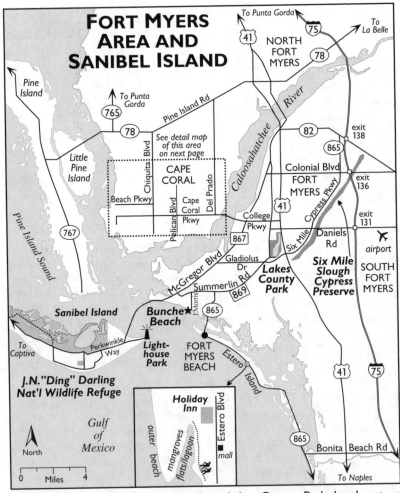

wheelchair accessible. To reach it from Lakes County Park, head east on Gladiolus Drive. Cross US-41 (0.4), where the road name changes to Six Mile Cypress Parkway. The entrance to the preserve is on the right (5.0). From I-75, exit (#136) onto Colonial Boulevard and head west to Six Mile Cypress Parkway (0.6). Turn left to the preserve entrance on the right (3.0). The slough has wading birds and an occasional Limpkin, and can be good for migrant landbirds during fall, particularly in October. Check the vegetation and trees around the parking area as well. The preserve is also one of the few remaining local sites that still supports Hairy Woodpeckers.

Contact: *Six Mile Cypress Slough Preserve, 7751 Penzance Crossing, Fort Myers, FL 33912; 239-432-2042.*

SANIBEL ISLAND

To reach **Sanibel Island**, return to Summerlin Road and head south to the Sanibel Causeway toll plaza. *Summerlin Road merges with McGregor Boulevard just before the causeway.* The mudflats beside the Sanibel toll plaza area and the causeway to Sanibel Island are great for wading birds (including Roseate Spoonbill), shorebirds, and larids, especially during winter. Wintering shorebirds may include Whimbrel, Long-billed Curlew, and Marbled Godwit. Parking is available on the left just before the toll booth. Check the extensive area to the left at low tide. After passing the toll station ($6.00/vehicle), pull off anywhere on the two causeway islands. Wilson's Plovers are resident. Flocks of larids usually contain a few Sandwich Terns. Again, low tide is best.

Upon reaching Sanibel Island, continue to Periwinkle Way (3.5 miles from the toll booth) and turn right. At Tarpon Bay Road (2.8), turn right, then left onto Sanibel-Captiva Road (0.3). The entrance to the main portion of **J.N. "DING" DARLING NATIONAL WILDLIFE REFUGE** (6,315 acres; $6.00/vehicle; no camping) is on the right (2.0). *The use of tape recordings is prohibited.* The refuge was established in 1945 and was renamed in 1967 to honor Jay Darling, the Pulitzer Prize-winning political cartoonist, conservationist, creator of the Federal Migratory Bird Hunting and Conservation Stamp ("Duck Stamp") program, and head of the U.S. Biological Survey during Franklin D. Roosevelt's administration. The visitor center is open 9:00 AM to 4:00 PM Monday through Thursday and Saturday but is *closed on Fridays*. The most popular birding attraction is the five-mile **Wildlife Drive**, open at 7:30 AM but also *closed on Fridays*. This excellent one-way drive traverses hammocks, mangrove forests, mosquito-control impoundments, and coastal estuaries. Although Hurricane *Charley* damaged some parts of the refuge in 2004, it is still one of the most-visited birding spots in Florida. The wildlife drive is best from October to early March, when wintering ducks, American White Pelicans, shorebirds, and landbirds augment the resident wading birds. Many

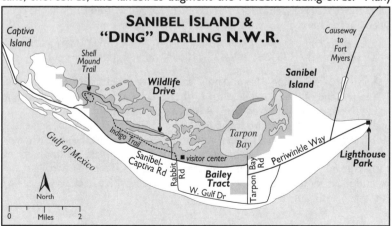

birds are tame and allow close approach for observation and photography. Reddish Egrets, Roseate Spoonbills, and Ospreys usually are easy to find year-round. Be sure to bring insect repellent during spring and summer.

During spring and summer, three Florida specialties breed in the refuge. Gray Kingbirds and Black-whiskered Vireos usually are easy to find, but Mangrove Cuckoo is much more of a challenge. A few cuckoos should be present along the wildlife drive, where they may be heard calling in early morning during spring and early summer, but the birds are very secretive. Walk the roadside through the dense mangrove forests, especially near Red Mangrove Overlook, the white point-count markers R1/7 to R1/8, and from miles 2.5 to 4.0 (measured from the entrance gate). *Again, you may not use tapes to attract Mangrove Cuckoos anywhere in the refuge.*

Shell Mound Trail on the left (0.3 before the end of the wildlife drive) allows access into a tropical hardwood hammock growing on an old Indian shell midden. The hammock (although damaged by Hurricane *Charley*) still includes plants of West Indian origin, including Gumbo Limbo and Spanish Stopper. This trail can be very good for migrants during spring and fall, but mosquitoes may be a problem. Wintering landbirds may also be seen. Shell Mound Trail can also be reached from Sanibel-Captiva Road via Wulfert Road (3.4 miles west of the refuge entrance), and is open even on Fridays when the rest of the refuge is closed.

Another trail accessible when the rest of the refuge is closed is **Indigo Trail**, which can be good on early spring mornings for Mangrove Cuckoo. The trail begins on the west side of the visitor center and follows a dike for two miles through mangrove forests. The trail continues to the wildlife drive via Cross Dike, but the latter two trails are *closed on Fridays.* The **Bailey Tract** (100 acres; no fee) is a small separate portion of the refuge. To reach it from Periwinkle Way, travel south on Tarpon Bay Road to the entrance on the right (0.4). The area contains thickets, marshes, and ponds, all reached by many short trails. Black-necked Stilts, Gray Kingbirds, and Black-whiskered Vireos breed here.

Contact: *J. N. "Ding" Darling National Wildlife Refuge, #1 Wildlife Drive, Sanibel, FL 33957; 239-472-1100; <http://dingdarling.fws.gov>.*

Return to Periwinkle Way and head east. Drive past Causeway Boulevard to the end of the road (1.4) into **Lighthouse Park** (5 acres; $2.00/hour parking; no camping) at Point Ybel. A boardwalk that begins at the parking lot leads to the lighthouse. The trail traverses a hammock that can be excellent for fall migrant raptors and landbirds as they are funneled to the southeastern tip of the island. Spring can be very productive when the weather drives trans-Gulf migrants to the coast. Pileated Woodpeckers are easy to find and exceptionally tame here. To return to the mainland, drive back to Causeway Boulevard and turn right.

Roseate Spoonbill.

Bruce Hallett

Once you return to the mainland, **Bunche Beach/San Carlos Bay Preserve** (800 acres; no fee; no camping) is an easily reached county park at the end of John Morris Road. From the Sanibel toll plaza, travel northeast on McGregor Boulevard, bear right onto Summerlin Road, and turn right onto John Morris Road (2.8 miles from the toll plaza or 1.5 miles west of San Carlos Boulevard). The park, at the end of the road (1.2), is good for wading birds, shorebirds, and larids during migration and winter. Wilson's, Piping (winter), and Snowy Plovers, and Long-billed Curlews (winter) are usually present. Low tide is best.

LITTLE ESTERO LAGOON (<10 acres; no fee; no camping) at Fort Myers Beach is excellent for migrant and wintering shorebirds and larids. To reach it, go south on SR-865 (San Carlos Boulevard) from Summerlin Road (4.3 from the toll plaza, or 1.5 from John Morris Road). To reach this junction from the north, go southwest from Daniels Road on Summerlin Road and turn left onto SR-865 (5.8). Once on the barrier island, San Carlos Boulevard continues southeast as Estero Boulevard. (*Traffic on the island during winter and spring can move very slowly.*) You may park at the Holiday Inn on the right (4.4), but *you must receive permission from the manager*, and you may have to pay a fee. Access to the lagoon area is around the south side of the hotel to the beach. *If the hotel parking lot is crowded or your request to park there is denied, drive another 0.1 mile farther south and park in the shopping mall lot on the left. Then walk back to the Holiday Inn.*

Wading birds (including Reddish Egrets and Roseate Spoonbills) and many shorebirds can be viewed closely by following the footpath along the edge of the lagoon to the flats south of the mangroves. August through October is best. Many of the birds present cannot be viewed well from the inside of the lagoon; for the best views, cross the lagoon to the outer beach. This is not advised at high tide, but is easy at low tide. Other options include walking back to the Holiday Inn and going around the mangroves to the outer beach, or by-passing the inside of the lagoon and proceeding straight to the outer beach. Walk south to the end of the mangroves (0.5). The outer beach is dynamic, and new inlets to the lagoon appear periodically, which may prevent full access to the area. Various shorebirds use the beach as a migratory staging area, and many species winter here as well. In addition to common species, look for Wilson's (resident), Piping (winter), and Snowy (uncommon resident) Plo-vers, American Oystercatcher (resident), Whimbrel, Marbled Godwit, and large numbers of Red Knots. Gulls, terns, and other waterbirds are also com-mon. Large numbers of Herring Gulls roost on the flats and outer beach in February and March, and a few Lesser Black-backed Gulls are often found among them. More than 100 Black Skimmers may be seen year-round, along with Royal and Sandwich Terns. As with the other sites, low tide is best.

Birders wishing to visit the Naples area or Corkscrew Swamp Sanctuary should continue south on SR-865, which turns east (becoming Bonita Beach Road) and connects with I-75. Those visiting Corkscrew will exit I-75 (#111) at CR-846, the first exit south of SR-865, in about 3.5 miles).

NAPLES

Southwest Florida is one of the fastest-growing areas in the United States, yet two-thirds of Collier County is in public ownership. These preserves support critical habitats for a number of Endangered and Threatened taxa, such as three species of sea turtles, West Indian Manatees, Florida Black Bears, Florida Panthers, Bald Eagles, and Red-cockaded Woodpeckers. Sev-eral of these sites also provide good to excellent birding opportunities, as well as the chance to explore some of the most remote areas in Florida. Before visiting these areas, however, there are several worthwhile sites within Na-ples city limits. The **North County Water Reclamation Facility** can be good for wading birds year-round, ducks during winter, and shorebirds during migration and winter. To reach the facility, exit I-75 (#111) onto CR-846 (Immokalee Road) and head west. At Goodlette– Frank Road (3.0), turn left to the facility entrance on the left (0.4). If the office is open, stop in to ask for permission to access the area. Otherwise, proceed 0.5 miles south for scope views of the treatment ponds from the bridge.

Several species of psittacids have recently been discovered in downtown Naples. A population of Rose-ringed Parakeets numbers over 100 individuals, with a few Blue-crowned, Red-masked, or White-eyed Parakeets also being seen. As is typical with psittacids in Florida, the birds can be difficult to find, and the locations of communal roosts may change unpredictably. Places to search include the area around **Tin City** (10th Street and 6th Avenue South), the **Naples Pier** (Gulf Shore Boulevard South and 12th Avenue South), and **Lowdermilk Park** (Gulf Shore Boulevard North and Banyan Boulevard).

Away from the breeding season, the parakeets may roost in the Royal Palms around the CVS Drug Store at US-41 and 3rd Avenue South, along Gulf Shore Boulevard North between Harbour Drive and Park Shore Drive (3–4 miles to the northwest), or in the Port Royal development (about 2–3 miles to the south).

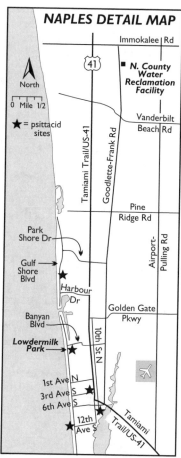

NAPLES DETAIL MAP

Immokalee Rd

■ **N. County Water Reclamation Facility**

North

0 Mile 1/2

★ = psittacid sites

Vanderbilt Beach Rd

Tamiami Trail/US-41

Goodlette-Frank Rd

Pine Ridge Rd

Airport-Pulling Rd

Park Shore Dr

Gulf Shore Blvd

Harbour Dr

Golden Gate Pkwy

Banyan Blvd

10th St N

Lowdermilk Park

1st Ave N
3rd Ave S
6th Ave S

12th Ave S

Tamiami Trail/US-41

Eagle Lakes Mitigation Site (90 acres; no fee; no camping; opens at sunrise) contains a trio of water retention ponds surrounded by a pine flatwoods conservation area (see map on next page). To reach the park from I-75, exit (#101) onto CR-951 (Collier Boulevard) and head south. At US-41 (6.9), turn right to the park on the right (1.3). A path between the ball fields provides access to trails that encircle the ponds. The eastern pond tends to hold more water than the other two ponds. Purple Gallinules and Black-necked Stilts breed here during spring and summer. High water levels in winter attract wading birds and ducks, while mudflats exposed during spring attract migrant shorebirds. Shiny or Bronzed Cowbirds may be seen along the ponds during winter.

Contact: *Collier County Parks and Recreation Administrative Office, 3300 Santa Barbara Boulevard, Naples, Fl. 34104, 239-353-0404; <www.colliergov.net/parks/colliercountyp/parks/index.html>, or Collier County Audubon Society, <www.collieraudubon.com/birding/spots.html>.*

Rookery Bay National Estuarine Research Reserve (110,000 acres; no fee; primitive camping) extends along the coast from Naples to Everglades National Park. The majority of the reserve is estuary and mangrove forests, inaccessible to vehicles. A newly constructed Environmental Learning Center is a good source for information. The entrance to the center is on the west side of CR-951, 0.7 miles south of US-41. To access the reserve, continue south to unpaved (but scheduled for paving) Shell Island Road (2.0) on the right. The upland area (0.5 to 1.5 miles) contains two groups of Florida Scrub-Jays that were released here in 1989 as part of a translocation experiment. This population has twice been supplemented with additional birds in

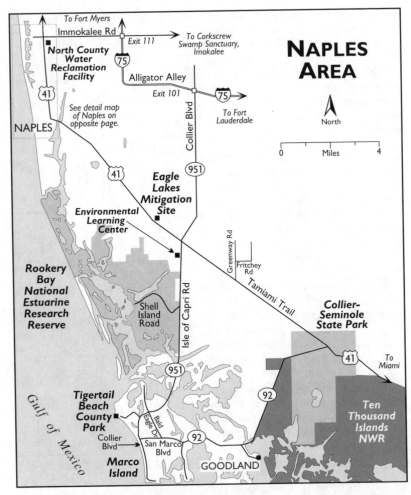

To Fort Myers
Immokalee Rd
Exit 111
To Corkscrew
Swamp Sanctuary,
Imokalee

**NAPLES
AREA**

North County
Water
Reclamation
Facility

Alligator Alley
Exit 101

Collier Blvd

To Fort
Lauderdale

North

0   Miles   4

NAPLES

See detail map
of Naples on
opposite page.

Eagle
Lakes
Mitigation
Site

Environmental
Learning
Center

Greenway Rd
Fritchey
Rd

Tamiami Trail

Rookery
Bay
National
Estuarine
Research
Reserve

Shell
Island
Road

Isle of Capri Rd

Collier-
Seminole
State Park

To
Miami

Gulf of Mexico

Tigertail
Beach
County
Park

Bald Eagle Dr

Ten
Thousand
Islands
NWR

Collier
Blvd

San Marco
Blvd

GOODLAND

Marco
Island

order for it to persist. (The Florida Scrub-Jays in this unsustainable and artificial population *are not ABA-countable.*) A trail to the south winds through uplands, while other trails at the end of the road (3.6) traverse mangrove forests that contain Mangrove Cuckoos, Black-whiskered Vireos, and Florida Prairie Warblers, mainly during spring and summer.

Contact: *Rookery Bay National Estuarine Research Reserve, 300 Tower Road, Naples, FL 34113; 239-417-6310; <www.rookerybay.org>.*

After exploring Rookery Bay, continue south on CR-951 to **TIGERTAIL BEACH COUNTY PARK** (31 acres; $4.00/vehicle; no camping; opens at sunrise). As you approach Marco Island, mangroves become more prominent, and Mangrove Cuckoo, Black-whiskered Vireo, and Florida Prairie Warbler (especially the latter two species) may be encountered along CR-951. As you cross the bridge to Marco Island, the three small islands to the east—named the ABC Islands—support the most significant wading bird rookery and roost in southwest Florida. Magnificent Frigatebirds are present year-round; as many as 1,600 roost here during the summer. On Marco Island, the road name changes to Collier Boulevard. Continue through the third traffic light (Bald Eagle Drive) to Tigertail Court (0.5), and turn right. At Hernando Drive (0.3), turn left to the park ahead (0.5). Tigertail Beach is arguably the most important site in southwestern Florida for wintering shorebirds, especially for Piping Plovers. Although the configuration of the lagoon and beach changes annually in response to currents, the best areas typically are along the mudflats and emergent sandbars that extend one mile to the north. Reddish Egrets are present year-round, as are other wading birds. Wilson's and Snowy Plovers, Least Terns, and Black Skimmers all breed here. *Some areas are roped off year-round as part of the Big Marco Pass Shoal Critical Wildlife Area; under no circumstances should these areas be entered.*

Contact: *Tigertail Beach County Park, 239-353-0404; <www.co.collier.fl. us/parks/colliercountyp/beach/beachparks/tigertail.html>, or Collier County Audubon Society, <www.collieraudubon.com/birding/spots.html>.*

Despite rampant development, there are a substantial number of Burrowing Owls on **Marco Island**, with 92 active burrows recorded in 2003. They can be found in the remaining vacant lots that are scattered along the many side roads. The following locations are all within a few blocks of Tigertail Beach: Hernando Drive between Kendall Drive and Lewis Court; Kendall Drive between Hernando Drive and Diplomat Court; the south side of Clifton Court; the southeast corner of Spinnaker Drive and Blackmore Court; and the northeast corner of Spinnaker Drive and Hunkin Court.

From Tigertail Beach, return to Collier Boulevard and turn right to San Marco Boulevard (1.0). Turn left, and once you are clear of the development (4.0), there is a good stretch of mangrove forest for the next five miles in which Mangrove Cuckoos, Black-whiskered Vireos, and Florida Prairie Warblers can be found. This stretch is one of the best road-accessible places in southwest Florida to find Mangrove Cuckoo, as is the first 0.7 miles along the road to Goodland (4.7). Looking east from the Goodland Bridge offers a scenic view of the Ten Thousand Islands National Wildlife Refuge (next section). Wading birds and shorebirds frequent the mudflats exposed at low tide at the east end of the bridge. CR-92 ends at US-41 (Tamiami Trail) in about six miles. At this point, you may turn left toward Naples, or turn right to continue east toward Big Cypress National Preserve, Everglades National Park, and the Miami area.

Limpkins and Snail Kites frequent the ditches and fields along US-41 (Tamiami Trail) between CR-951 and CR-92. Specific areas to search are the north side of US-41 3.9 miles east of CR-951 or 4.0 miles west of CR-92, and

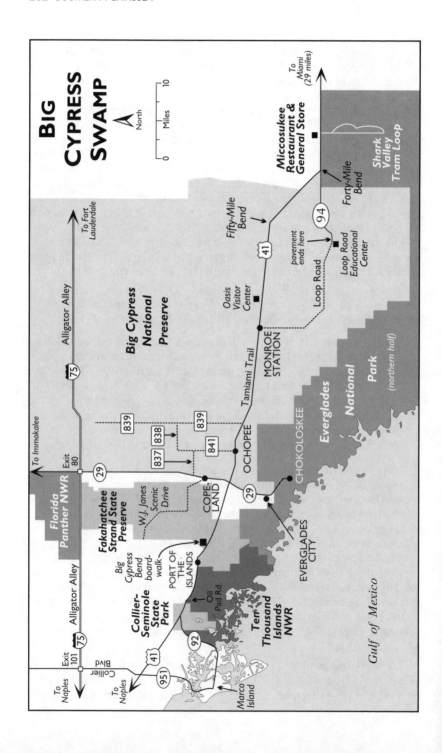

the south side of US-41 5.3 miles east of CR-951 or 2.6 miles west of CR-92. Turning north onto Greenway Road (3.3 from CR-951 or 4.6 from CR-92) and then turning right onto **Fritchey Road** (0.5) leads to abandoned fields that may contain substantial numbers of wading birds. During winter, Western Kingbirds have been found along Greenway Road.

BIG CYPRESS SWAMP

This vast area (close to 1,000,000 acres) of immense ecological value is located between the Gulf coast and the Everglades. Situated on slightly higher ground than the Everglades to the east, this region is composed mostly of cypress swamps (the "big" refers to the size of the swamp, not necessarily to the size of the trees themselves), tropical hardwood hammocks, pine flatwoods, and, closer to the Gulf, mangrove forests and shallow estuaries. In the 1970s, the Big Cypress region was targeted for development as an international airport and a massive urban area. Fortunately, this plan was scrapped when it was documented that the development of Big Cypress Swamp would destroy Everglades National Park, located immediately south (and downstream). The entire Big Cypress Swamp later was preserved by the federal government, but not until after construction of a three-mile long runway was completed. This "Dade–Collier Jetport" continues to be used by airline pilots who practice take-offs and landings. Off-Road Vehicle (ORV) use of the swamp has been substantial—*23,000 miles of trails* are estimated to exist within Big Cypress National Preserve! A management plan that was recently enacted will limit ORVs to 400 miles of trails. Several other equally important conservation areas buffer the preserve to the west. Fakahatchee Strand Preserve State Park, Picayune Strand State Forest, and Florida Panther National Wildlife Refuge are absolutely critical for maintaining populations of the Florida Panther in the southeastern United States. More than 80 panthers survived as of 2003, an increase from an estimated 30-50 animals just 10 years earlier.

The entrance to **Collier–Seminole State Park** (6,500 acres, $4.00/vehicle, camping $18.00/day; opens at 8:00 AM) is just east of the junction of CR-92 and US-41. Because the park overlaps the southern edge of Big Cypress Swamp and the northern edge of the mangrove forest, it contains an impressive array of habitats, such as saltmarsh, tropical hardwood hammock, and pine flatwoods. A 0.75-mile nature trail near the boat ramp winds through a hammock (good for wintering landbirds and sometimes containing White-crowned Pigeons) and ends at a marsh overlook. Another hiking trail on the north side of US-41 traverses pine flatwoods where Brown-headed Nuthatches can be found. Mosquitoes can be troublesome throughout the park during spring and summer.

Contact: *Collier–Seminole State Park, 20200 East Tamiami Trail, Naples, FL 34114; 239-394-3397; <www.floridastateparks.org/collier-seminole>.*

F arther east along US-41 is **Ten Thousand Islands National Wildlife Refuge** (35,000 acres; no fee; primitive camping; opens at sunrise; *seasonal hunting*), established in 1998. The refuge, which is largely inaccessible to vehicles, protects the northern Ten Thousand Islands area, named for the hundreds of mangrove keys located just off the mainland. Oil Pad Road offers the only upland access into the refuge; it is on the south side of US-41, 2.5 miles east of the entrance to Collier–Seminole State Park. It is one mile long and leads through brackish marshes before ending at what was, in the mid-1970s, the deepest exploratory oil well drilled in Florida. The trail is open only to foot traffic during daylight hours. Waterbirds occur year-round with especially large concentrations during October–December, when water levels drop rapidly. Mangrove Cuckoos and Florida Prairie Warblers breed in the mangroves at the end of the trail.

> **Contact:** *Ten Thousand Islands National Wildlife Refuge, 3860 Tollgate Boulevard, Suite 300, Naples, FL 34114; 239-353-8442; <www.southeast. fws.gov/TenThousandIsland>.*

Another 2.5 miles to the east brings you to **Port of the Islands**, a development built in the 1970s, coincident with the creation of the Faka Union Canal. Although the canal has wreaked havoc on natural drainage patterns of Big Cypress Swamp, the boat basin immediately south of US-41 is an important wintering area for as many as 300 West Indian Manatees. Gray Kingbirds can be found at the resort during spring and summer, and boats may be rented to explore the mangrove forests of the Ten Thousand Islands National Wildlife Refuge, located three miles to the south.

S till farther east along US-41 is **FAKAHATCHEE STRAND PRE- SERVE STATE PARK** (75,000 acres; no fee; no camping; opens at 8:00 AM). A "strand" is an elongated swamp aligned with water flow; Fakahatchee is the largest strand forest remaining. The park protects the largest Royal Palm hammock in the United States. Facilities are limited, but one of the most accessible portions of the preserve is the boardwalk at **Big Cypress Bend**, located on the north side of US-41, two miles east of Port of the Islands. The trail is 2,000 feet long and extends into a swamp with huge virgin Bald Cypresses. Birds that may be encountered here include Limpkin, Barred Owl, Pileated Woodpecker, and other swamp species. The trail can also be good for migrant and wintering landbirds. *Big Cypress Bend is especially recommended to those who do not plan to visit Corkscrew Swamp Sanctuary.* Farther along US-41 is an old gravel pit on the right (1.6), where wading birds breed and roost.

To reach another accessible portion of the preserve, continue east on US-41 to SR-29 and turn left. The first road on the left (2.6) is the start of **W. J. Janes Scenic Drive**. Proceed to the stop sign and turn right. The park office is next to the fire tower (0.9). For the next 11 miles, the drive passes through the heart of Fakahatchee Strand. A side road to the south (4.5) and a pullout on the north side (2.0) allow some access into the swamp. The road continues to SR-846 through the Southern Golden Gate Estates unit of **Pica-yune Strand State Forest** (69,975 acres; no fee; primitive camping), a massive unbuilt development under public acquisition (from 17,000 owners!) and planned for restoration. However, because of the maze of unmarked and occasionally flooded roads, it is recommended that you turn around at the west boundary of the state park and return to SR-29. From here you can go south to Everglades City (bordering Everglades National Park) and return to US-41 east to visit Big Cypress National Preserve or the Miami area; alternatively, you can continue north on SR-29 to Immokalee.

> **Contacts:** Fakahatchee Strand Preserve State Park, P.O. Box 548, Copeland, FL 34137; 239-695-4593; <www.floridastateparks.org/fakahatcheestrand>.
> Picayune Strand State Forest, 2121 52nd Avenue South, Naples, FL 34117; 239-348-7552; <www.fl-dof.com/state_forests/picayune_strand.html>

Adjacent to Fakahatchee Strand on the north side of I-75 is **Florida Panther National Wildlife Refuge** (26,000 acres; no fee; no camping; *very limited access*). The refuge was purchased in 1989 to preserve essential habitat for the critically Endangered Florida Panther. To avoid disturbance to the panthers, the refuge is closed to most public use except for a recently opened nature trail west of SR-29 and just north of I-75. (The fences along I-75 and the numerous animal overpasses along the highway through Big Cypress Swamp were constructed to prevent panthers from being killed while crossing the highway.)

> **Contact:** Florida Panther National Wildlife Refuge, 3860 Tollgate Boulevard, Suite 300, Naples, FL 34114; 239-353-8442; <www.fws.gov/floridapanther>.

The northwest corner of **EVERGLADES NATIONAL PARK** encompasses the southern Ten Thousand Islands area. This portion of the park can be visited only by boat. Tours of the Ten Thousand Islands ($16.00/person) or to the "Backcountry" rivers and bays ($25.00/person) are available at the Gulf Coast Ranger Station in Everglades City. Wading birds, including Roseate Spoonbills, are the highlight of the boat trips. The Ranger Station (open daily) is located south of Everglades City on SR-29 about five miles south of US-41. Other portions of Everglades National Park are described on pages 207 and 237.

> **Contact:** Everglades National Park, Gulf Coast Ranger Station, P.O. Box 120, Everglades City, FL 33939; 239-695-3311; <www.nps.gov/ever>.

Most of **Big Cypress National Preserve** (720,566 acres; no fee; five campgrounds, four primitive and one with campsites at $16.00/day; *seasonal hunting*) is inaccessible to passenger vehicles, but a few well-maintained gravel roads offer a 17-mile driving tour through the western section. From SR-29, go east on US-41 to CR-841 (Birdon Road; 3.5) and turn left. From Janes Scenic Drive and Fakahatchee Strand State Preserve, you may choose to

Snail Kite, color-banded female.   Arthur Morris

go north on SR-29 to CR-837 (Wagon Wheel Road; 1.0) and turn right. At the junction with Birdon Road, turn left. Beyond Wagon Wheel Road, the road turns to the right before ending at CR-839 (Turner River Road). Stop frequently along this road to look for wading birds, including both night-herons and American Bitterns (winter), Snail Kites, and Purple Gallinules. At CR-839, turn right to return to US-41.

Continue east on US-41 to Monroe Station and the western end of **Loop Road** (SR-94) on the right (10.5). Loop Road is a 26-mile scenic drive through the southern part of Big Cypress National Preserve. The southernmost breeding Red-eyed Vireos, Northern Parulas, and Prothonotary Warblers in North America can be found along this section during spring and summer, primarily in the strands three to seven miles south of US-41. Road conditions have improved considerably since the National Park Service took over maintenance. The Oasis Visitor Center is 4.4 miles east of Monroe Station, and the Clyde Butcher Gallery (with displays of the famous photographer's images) another 0.8 mile farther east. The eastern end of Loop Road is accessed 20 miles east of Monroe Station (from Miami, it is 28 miles west of Florida's Turnpike) at Forty-Mile Bend. The easternmost eight miles of Loop Road are paved, up to an environmental education center on the left. On the right opposite the center is a short nature trail through a West Indian hardwood hammock.

Contact: *Big Cypress National Preserve, HCR 61, Box 110, 33100 Tamiami Trail East, Ochopee, FL 34141; 239-695-2000; <www.nps.gov/bicy>.*

From Forty-Mile Bend, continue east on US-41 to the **MICCOSUKEE GENERAL STORE** (3.6) and the **MICCOSUKEE INDIAN RESTAURANT** (0.2), both on the left. An active Snail Kite roost is located in the marsh just north of this area, and the birds are easily viewed shortly after dawn and before dusk. During the day, the kites forage extensively and may be encountered wherever views of the marshes from the road are not hampered by vegetation. **SHARK VALLEY**, just east of the restaurant (0.1), is the northernmost access point to Everglades National Park ($8.00/vehicle; opens at 8:30 AM). A 15-mile paved loop road is available for hiking, biking (rentals are available), or via a two-hour guided tram ($12.00/person), but it cannot be driven by private vehicle. The road ends at a 65-foot-tall observation tower that overlooks the great River of Sedge ecosystem. Anhingas, wading birds, Snail Kites, Limpkins, American Alligators, and other wildlife may be seen from the trail. Call the Visitor Center (305-221-8776) or the tram reservation and bike rental (305- 221-8455) for more information. To reach Shark Valley from the east, go west on US-41 (Tamiami Trail) from either Florida's Turnpike (23.0) or Krome Avenue(18.0).

Contact: *Everglades National Park; 305-221-8455; <www.nps.gov/ever>.*

Several other areas to look for Snail Kites are at the commercial airboat operations over the next six miles of US-41, where good views of the marsh to the north can be obtained. *The speed limit along US-41 through the Miccosukee Indian Reservation is strictly enforced!*

SOUTHERN PENINSULA—INLAND

IMMOKALEE

Immokalee (pronounced *im-MOK-a-lee*) is a small farming community located in the northwestern Everglades. The following 65-mile loop that begins and ends in town is a good way to sample the local birdlife (see map on next page). Most of the property along this route is privately owned, so *bird only from the roads*. Look for Mottled Duck or other puddle ducks (winter), wading birds (including Glossy Ibis and Wood Stork), Swallow-tailed Kite (spring and summer), Crested Caracara, Purple Gallinule, Limpkin, and Sandhill Crane. Watch for Short-tailed Hawks overhead during spring and summer. From CR-846 in town, go north on SR-29 to Lake Trafford Road (CR-890; 1.8) and turn left to **Lake Trafford Park** (3 acres; no fee; no camping; open during daylight hours) at the end (2.9). Lake Trafford's 1,500 acres in size are slated for restoration. American Alligators, wading birds, Bald Eagles, Purple Gallinules, and Limpkins can be found year-round, and waterfowl and Northern Rough-winged Swallows may be found during winter.

Return to SR-29 and continue north to CR-832 (Keri Grade; 11.7) and turn right. This lightly traveled road traverses pine flatwoods, Cabbage Palm hammocks, Okaloacoochee Slough, marshes, and pastures for about 20 miles before ending at CR-833. The recently acquired **Okaloacoochee Slough State Forest and Wildlife Management Area** (32,039 acres; no fee; camping; opens at dawn; *seasonal hunting*; 3.8) extends for about five miles on

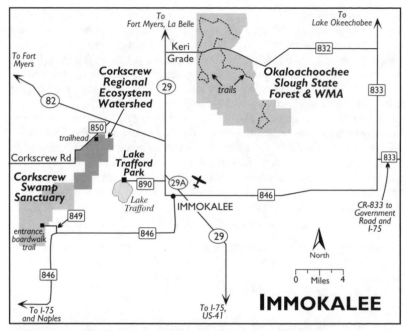

both sides of this road. An extensive network of trails offers access into the management area. The sugar cane fields on the right (10.8) and left (11.9) frequently contain huge roosts of Tree Swallows during winter and early spring. In February and March, when the cane is tall, *more than one million* swallows have roosted here in the past. At CR-833 (20.7), turn right and continue straight on CR-846 (10.4) then turn right to Immokalee (check the airport for Burrowing Owls). Alternatively, you can turn left (10.4) on CR-833 to **Government Road** and I-75 (Exit #49). This 31-mile stretch of road has yielded Scissor-tailed Flycatcher, Ash-throated Flycatcher, Western Kingbird, and Vermilion Flycatcher in recent winters.

Contact: *Okaloacoochee Slough State Forest and Wildlife Management Area, 863-612-0776; <www.myfwc.com/recreation/cooperative/ okaloacoochee_slough.asp>.*

National Audubon's **Corkscrew Swamp Sanctuary** (10,720 acres, $10.00/person; no camping; opens at 7:00 AM) preserves the largest remaining virgin Bald Cypress forest in North America; some trees are more than 500 years old. The sanctuary is worth a visit solely to view the huge trees. To reach the sanctuary from SR-29 in Immokalee, travel west on CR-846 to CR-849 (Sanctuary Road; 14.8. turn right and follow this road to the sanctuary (1.6). From the Gulf coast, exit I-75 (#111) onto CR-846 (Immokalee Road) and go east. At CR-849 (15.7), turn left and continue to the park. *The use of tape recordings in the sanctuary is prohibited.*

The main attraction is the 2.25-mile boardwalk that loops through a variety of habitats, including Slash Pine flatwoods, cypress swamp, lettuce lakes, and wet prairie. Corkscrew is home to a Wood Stork rookery that is often the largest in the nation; a few nests are usually visible from the boardwalk. The storks nest in late winter and early spring, and parts of the boardwalk may be closed to avoid disturbance to the colony. Breeding success is highly variable, depending on local water levels that determine food supply. Storks require lowering water levels that concentrate fish and other prey. During either drought years or years with excessive rainfall, storks cannot find sufficient food to feed their nestlings, and colonies may experience complete nesting failure. Other birds of special interest at Corkscrew include Swallow-tailed Kite (spring and summer), Limpkin, and Pileated Woodpecker. Barred Owls are often cooperative here. These species and American Alligators are all accustomed to people on the boardwalk. As a result, they are tame and may allow close study. Painted Buntings are fairly common winter residents and visit the feeders near the gift shop and in the picnic area regularly. Short-tailed Hawks occasionally are seen overhead during spring and summer.

Contact: *Corkscrew Swamp Sanctuary, 375 Sanctuary Road, Naples, FL 34120; 239-348-9151; <www.audubon.org/local/sanctuary/corkscrew>.*

The state is purchasing land surrounding the sanctuary as part of the **Corkscrew Regional Ecosystem Watershed (CREW)** project (26,000 acres; no fee; primitive camping; sunrise to sunset). Eventually , a corridor may link the sanctuary through Lake Trafford to the Florida Panther National Wildlife Refuge to the south. The easiest place to access CREW lands is the **Corkscrew Marsh Trail System**, south of CR-850 (Corkscrew Road). The trailhead can be reached from I-75 (18.0 miles east of Exit 126, Corkscrew Road) or Immokalee (north on SR-29, west on SR-82 4.7 miles, west on CR-850 1.5 miles).

Contact: *CREW Land and Water Trust, 23998 Corkscrew Road, Estero, FL 33928; 239-657-2253; <http://www.crewtrust.org>.*

SOUTHERN LAKE OKEECHOBEE

For birders traveling around the southern end of Lake Okeechobee, several birding sites are worthwhile, especially for migrant shorebirds during fall. They are presented here from Clewiston in the west to Belle Glade in the east; see map on next page. *All sites are privately owned or are accessible only under escort,* but they can offer superb birding opportunities when timing and water levels are ideal (two to four inches deep during August and September).

The small town of **Clewiston** has supported a small population of (not yet ABA-countable) Common Mynas since the mid-1980s. The most reliable spots to find the birds seem to be on the north side of US-27/SR-80, between

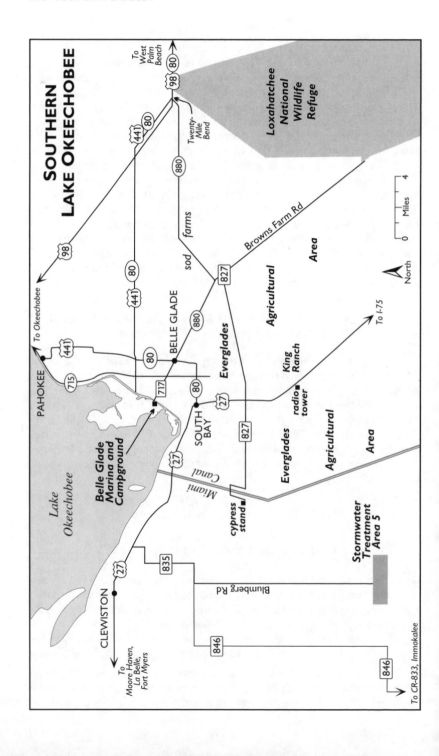

SOUTHERN LAKE OKEECHOBEE

Wal-Mart and McDonald's. The mynas nest in artificial cavities in buildings, signs, and streetlights.

About 20 miles south of Clewiston is **Stormwater Treatment Area 5** (5,120 acres; no fee; no camping; *seasonal waterfowl hunting*), one of six sites recently constructed to remove excess phosphorus from agricultural runoff before its discharge into the Everglades. *This site is owned and managed by the South Florida Water Management District, and is accessible to foot traffic only, and only while under district escort.* Tropical Audubon Society in Miami coordinates field trip dates with the district; check the society's website <www.tropicalaudubon.org> for more information. *Do not enter this site on your own.* To reach STA-5 from US-27 in Clewiston, head south on CR-835, which makes several turns before continuing south. At the point where CR-835 heads west (11.0), stay south on Blumberg Road. The treatment area is ahead (11.0). From Immokalee, head east on CR-846 to CR-833 (17.7) and turn left. Go north to another section of CR-846 (1.9) and turn right. The road turns right (5.8), then left (1.9) before again turning left onto CR-846 (2.9). The road again turns right (12.8) before intersecting with Blumberg Road (4.0). Turn right and proceed as above.

> **Contact:** *South Florida Water Management District; 1-800-432-2045; <www.sfwmd.gov>.*

From July through early September, harvested vegetable fields in the (private) **EVERGLADES AGRICULTURAL AREA** (100,000-plus acres) near the farming towns of Belle Glade and South Bay are flooded to prevent subsidence and to kill nematodes (microscopic worms that feed on plant roots). During this time, wading birds and migrant shorebirds and larids gather by the thousands. In addition to common species, look for Upland and Buff-breasted Sandpipers, Wilson's Phalarope, and Black Tern. Breeding species include Mottled Duck, Black-bellied and Fulvous Whistling-Ducks, King Rail, Black-necked Stilt (common), and Gull-billed Tern (rare). Some flooded fields also may contain huge numbers of wading birds. In recent years, flocks of hundreds or thousands of egrets, Glossy Ibises, and Wood Storks have been reported, and Roseate Spoonbills can be common. Most fields in this area are private property and are off limits to the public. Many farmers prohibit access because of past vandalism of equipment or because of liability concerns. Because most of the roads are unpaved and unmarked, it is difficult to distinguish between public and private roads, but most are private. *Under no circumstances should you drive through an open gate—you are trespassing, and you may get locked inside a farm.*

To reach some of the fields from Clewiston, head east on US-27/SR-80 to South Bay, then continue south on US-27 (*watch your speed*) to a **radio tower** on the right (11.0). The fields to the west can be good for shorebirds, if water levels are suitable. Turn around and return north on US-27 to **King Ranch** on the right, which contains thousands of acres of farm and sod fields. (These fields are accessible *solely* from a road that parallels US-27 just to the east, and which is reached via bridges over the canal between the roads, at 0.4, 2.6, 5.3, and 6.8 miles north of the turn-around.) When water levels are ideal, the agricultural fields can contain large numbers of wading birds and migrant shorebirds and Black Terns. Gull-billed Terns may be found in smaller numbers, and Fulvous or Black-bellied Whistling-Ducks and American White Pelicans may also be present. The sod farms at the north end of the ranch have consistently produced Upland Sandpipers in August and early September for the past few years; a spotting scope is usually essential.

To reach an area reliable for roosting Barn Owls, head west on CR-827 (1.0 mile from the north bridge to King Ranch, or 3.5 miles south of South Bay) to its end at the Miami Canal (7.9). Turn right to a bridge over the canal (1.0), cross it, then head back south to the remnant **cypress stand** on the right (1.0; *some local birders refer to this site as the "cedar grove," though the trees here are cypresses, not cedars*). As many as 30 Barn Owls have been observed using the trees as a diurnal roost, and Black-crowned Night-Herons should also be present. Migrant landbirds such as Yellow Warblers are regular in August and September. *The cypress stand is on private property, and the numerous fallen branches make walking difficult, so birders should stay on the levee.* Return to CR-827 and head east back to US-27, then head north.

From South Bay, head east on SR-80 to Belle Glade. In town, turn west onto CR-717 (West Canal Street North) to the levee (2.0). Drive up the levee road and cross the one-lane bridge to the **Belle Glade Marina** (*private; no fee; camping*), which is located on an island within Lake Okeechobee and Campground. Park at the community building or marina and walk the road to look for Indigo Buntings, Painted Buntings, Blue Grosbeaks, and Orchard Orioles, which have all wintered here. Check in at the entrance for admission to the campground area, and *be respectful around campsites.* A walkway through wetlands provides views of ducks, American (winter) and Least Bitterns, Purple Gallinules (numerous and almost tame here), Limpkins, and other species; Purple Swamphens have been seen here.

Contact: *Belle Glade Marina and Campground; 561-996-6322.*

BROWNS FARM ROAD (CR-827) provides public access to thousands of acres of agricultural fields, although only a few fields will be flooded at any time. The road heads south from CR-880 about five miles east of Belle Glade. To reach the road from the east, head west on SR-80 to Twenty-Mile Bend and veer left onto SR-880 (13.8 from Florida's Turnpike), then turn left onto Browns Farm Road (13.0). As you look for shorebirds, watch the roadside shrubbery for Barn Owls. A stretch of often productive **sod farms** is located on CR-880 about three miles east of Browns Farm Road. Upland and Buff-breasted Sandpipers have been seen here reliably in the past few years during August and September.

SOUTHERN PENINSULA—ATLANTIC COAST

HOBE SOUND

Jonathan Dickinson State Park (11,486 acres; $3.25/vehicle; 135 camp-sites at $14.00–$17.00/day; opens at 8:00 AM) contains the largest diversity of habitats remaining along Florida's southeast coast (see map on next page). The entrance is on the west side of US-1 about 3.5 miles north of Jupiter Inlet, or 4.7 miles south of CR-708 in Hobe Sound. Although not directly on the ocean, the park's acreage represents the largest protected coastal area between Hobe Sound and Miami, about 90 miles to the south. The park contains two miles of frontage along the Loxahatchee River, part of which is designated a National Wild and Scenic River. Habitats include Slash Pine flatwoods, Sand Pine scrub, cypress domes, sloughs, wet prairies, and floodplain and riverine wetlands. Bachman's Sparrows may be heard in spring and summer from the numerous sand roads through the flatwoods, but most of the Florida Scrub-Jays that previously occurred in the park are no longer present. The tower at the top of Hobe Mountain (a natural sand ridge) offers a panoramic view of the park.

Contact: Jonathan Dickinson State Park, 16450 Southeast Federal Highway, Hobe Sound, FL 33455; 772-546-2771; 32<www.floridastateparks.org/jonathandickinson>.

Royal Tern in breeding plumage.   Arthur Morris/www.birdsasart.com

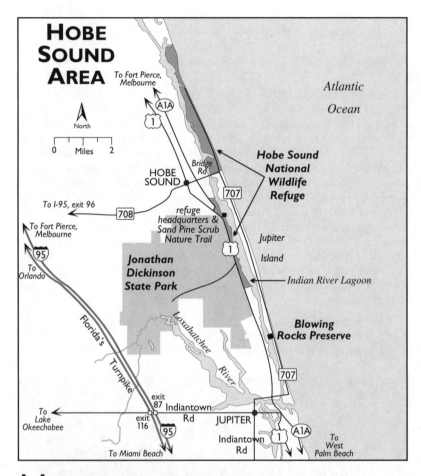

HOBE SOUND AREA

To Fort Pierce, Melbourne

North

0 Miles 2

Atlantic Ocean

Hobe Sound National Wildlife Refuge

HOBE SOUND

Bridge Rd

707

To I-95, exit 96

708

refuge headquarters & Sand Pine Scrub Nature Trail

Jupiter Island

To Fort Pierce, Melbourne

95

To Orlando

Jonathan Dickinson State Park

Indian River Lagoon

Loxahatchee River

Florida's Turnpike

Blowing Rocks Preserve

707

exit 87 Indiantown Rd

To Lake Okeechobee

exit 116

95

JUPITER

1 A1A

To Miami Beach

Indiantown Rd

To West Palm Beach

obe Sound National Wildlife Refuge (968 acres; $5.00/vehicle or $1.00/pedestrian) is located between Jonathan Dickinson State Park and the Intracoastal Waterway. There are two main access points to the refuge. The first is on the mainland on the east side of US-1, 2.4 miles north of the entrance to Jonathan Dickinson State Park. The refuge headquarters and Hobe Sound Nature Center are located here. There is no fee at this entrance, which features the Sand Pine Scrub Nature Trail (0.5-mile long), where Florida Scrub-Jays may be found. The trail winds along a dune ridge overlooking the Indian River Lagoon and is especially good for viewing migrant landbirds. The second part of the refuge is a few miles north on the barrier island. It features dunes, ocean frontage, and mangrove forests bordering the Indian River Lagoon. From the nature center, drive north on US-1 to CR-708 (Bridge Road; 2.3) and turn right. At CR-707 (Beach Road; 1.3), turn left to the refuge ahead (1.8). The beach, closed nightly, is a major sea turtle nesting area from April through September. As many as 100,000 turtle hatchlings may be produced in good years.

Contact: *Hobe Sound National Wildlife Refuge, P.O. Box 645, Hobe Sound, FL 33475; 772-546-6141; Hobe Sound Nature Center, 772-546-2067; <www.fws.gov/hobesound>.*

On the barrier island east of the park is **Blowing Rocks Preserve** (73 acres; $3.00/person; opens at 9:00 AM), owned by The Nature Conservancy. To reach it, follow CR-707 east and then north about 2.5 miles from US-1 in Jupiter. The small parking lot on the east side of the road is used primarily for beach access; a larger parking lot on the west side of the road is adjacent to the Hawley Education Center. The preserve is named for its unusual rocky Anastasia limestone shoreline, which shoots plumes of water into the air during extremely high wave action. Trails run north-south along the restored shoreline of the Indian River Lagoon and along the crest of the ocean dunes. Trails through the hammocks can be good for migrant landbirds.

Contact: *Blowing Rocks Preserve; 574 South Beach Road, Hobe Sound, FL 33455; 561-744-6668; <http://nature.org/wherewework/ northamerica/states/florida/preserves/art5522.html>.*

PALM BEACH TO BOCA RATON

John D. MacArthur Beach State Park (225 acres; $3.25/vehicle; no camping; opens at 8:00 AM) is visited mostly for migrant landbirds; see map on next page. To reach it from US-1 southbound in Palm Beach Gardens, head east (left) on CR-786 (PGA Boulevard) to SR-A1A (0.6) and follow the road south and east. The entrance is on the left. From the south, go east (right) on CR-708 (Blue Heron Boulevard) to SR-A1A (Ocean Drive; 1.8) and turn right into the park (2.0). Satinleaf Trail at the north end of the park and the area around the entrance station are the best places to search for migrants. West Indian vagrants are always a possibility; La Sagra's Flycatcher, Thick-billed Vireo, and Western Spindalis have all been seen here. Wading birds (including Roseate Spoonbills) and shorebirds can be seen during low tide from Burnt Bridge, just south of the park entrance.

Contact: *John D. MacArthur Beach State Park, 10900 State Road 703 (A1A), North Palm Beach, FL 33408; 561-624-6950; <www.floridastateparks.org/macarthurbeach>.*

In Palm Beach Gardens, **Frenchman's Forest Natural Area** (149 acres; no fee; no camping) contains Slash Pine flatwoods, a cypress strand, marshes, and oak scrub. It can be excellent for migrant landbirds during spring and fall. To reach it from US-1, head west on PGA Boulevard to Prosperity Farms Road (0.6). Turn right to the entrance on the left (0.7).

Contact: *Frenchman's Forest Natural Area, 12201 Prosperity Farms Road, Palm Beach Gardens, FL 33410; <www.co.palm-beach.fl.us/ erm/stewardship/french.asp>.*

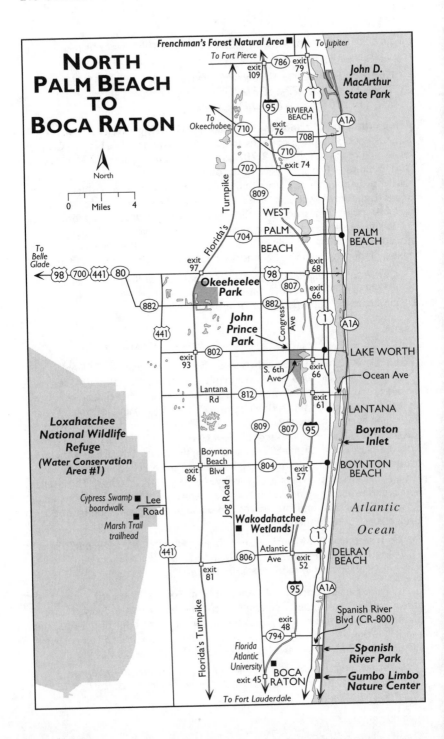

NORTH
PALM BEACH
TO
BOCA RATON

North

0   Miles   4

Frenchman's Forest Natural Area
To Jupiter
To Fort Pierce
exit 109
786
exit 79
1
John D. MacArthur State Park
95
RIVIERA BEACH
A1A
To Okeechobee
710
exit 76
708
710
exit 74
702
809
WEST
704
PALM
PALM BEACH
BEACH
exit 68
To Belle Glade
98 700 441 80
exit 97
Okeeheelee Park
98
807
exit 66
882
882
441
John Prince Park
Congress Ave
1
A1A
802
exit 93
LAKE WORTH
S. 6th Ave
exit 66
Ocean Ave
Lantana Rd
812
exit 61
LANTANA
Loxahatchee National Wildlife Refuge
(Water Conservation Area #1)
809
807
95
Boynton Inlet
Boynton Beach Blvd
804
exit 57
BOYNTON BEACH
exit 86
Jog Road
Atlantic Ocean
Cypress Swamp boardwalk
Lee Road
Marsh Trail trailhead
Wakodahatchee Wetlands
441
806
Atlantic Ave
exit 52
1
DELRAY BEACH
exit 81
95
A1A
exit 48
794
Spanish River Blvd (CR-800)
Florida's Turnpike
Florida Atlantic University
exit 45
BOCA RATON
Spanish River Park
Gumbo Limbo Nature Center
To Fort Lauderdale

John Prince Park (726 acres; no fee; 266 campsites at $15.00–$18.00/day; opens at sunrise) on Lake Osborne in Lake Worth is an excellent spot for Limpkins and can be good for migrant landbirds. To reach the park from I-95, exit (#63) onto 6th Avenue South and go west to SR-807 (Congress Avenue; 0.8; the second traffic light). Turn left to the entrance on the left (0.8). At the crossroads (0.2) turn right, then left, to follow the road along the canal. Check the lake on the left for Limpkins. Look also for Black-crowned Night-Herons and Purple Gallinules. From the parking lot, walk back to the canal and cross the foot-bridge to check the other lakes. Because of the crowds of people that use the park on weekends, it is best to visit on a weekday.

Contact: *John Prince Park, 4759 South Congress Ave. Lake Worth, FL 33461; 561-966-6600; <www.co.palm-beach.fl.us/parks/locations/central/jprince.htm>.*

Feeders around the nature center at **Okeeheelee Nature Center and Park** (900 acres; no fee; no camping; opens at sunrise) in West Palm Beach are visited by Indigo and Painted Buntings. Trails wind through the 90-acre pine flatwoods, where typical landbirds may be seen. To reach the park from I-95 exit (#66) onto SR-882 (Forest Hill Boulevard) and head west to the entrance on the right (6.0). Follow the signs to the nature center.

Contact: *Okeeheelee Nature Center and Park, 7715 Forest Hill Boulevard, West Palm Beach, FL, 33413; 561-233-1400; <www.co.palm-beach.fl.us/parks/locations/central/okeeheelee.htm>.*

BOYNTON INLET (no fee; no camping), near Boynton Beach, is worth a quick stop. From the mainland, head east on SR-812 (Lantana Road) to US-1 (Federal Highway) and turn right. At Ocean Avenue (0.15), turn left and cross the Intracoastal Waterway to the end of Ocean Avenue at SR-A1A (0.8). Turn right to the inlet (2.7). Jaegers and other pelagic species may be seen here, especially during east winds. It is one of the better seawatching spots in southeastern Florida, with peak movements in October. Although south of its regular range, Purple Sandpiper has occasionally been seen on the jetty. "Beer Can Island" on the northwest corner has a sheltered cove that hosts wading birds, including Reddish Egret. Black-hooded Parakeets frequent the Sea Grapes near the picnic area.

WAKODAHATCHEE WETLANDS (56 acres; no fee; no camping; opens at sunrise) is a wastewater treatment facility in Delray Beach. To reach it from I-95, exit (#52B) onto Atlantic Avenue and head west to Jog Road (3.8). (From Florida's Turnpike, take Exit #81 eastbound on Atlantic Avenue for 1.6 miles to Jog Road). At Jog Road, turn north to the wetlands entrance on the right (1.7). Wakodahatchee (pronounced *wa-KO-da-HATCH-ee*) is a series of landscaped settling ponds that filter some two million gallons of highly treated wastewater daily. The wetlands also serve as wildlife viewing area by means of a quarter-mile boardwalk through three ponds. Habitats include open water, emergent marshes, shrubby islands, and forested wetlands. Breeding species include Least Bittern, Mottled Duck, Limpkin, and Purple Gallinule. American Bitterns, Soras, and Virginia Rails (occasional) are found during winter.

Contact: Wakodahatchee Wetlands, 13026 Jog Road, Delray Beach, FL 561-434-5372; <www.pbcwater.com/wakodahatchee>.

ARTHUR R. MARSHALL LOXAHATCHEE NATIONAL WILDLIFE REFUGE (147,392 acres; $5.00/vehicle or $1.00/pedestrian; no camping; *seasonal hunting in areas far from the Visitor Center and impoundments*) contains the only natural habitats remaining in the northern Everglades. *Do not miss the gate closing at sunset, or you will risk a fine.* Much of the refuge is off limits to the public, with some areas accessible only by motorboat, but an excellent section west of Boynton Beach is accessible by passenger vehicle. To reach it from either I-95 (Exit #57) or Florida's Turnpike (Exit #86), travel west on SR-804 (Boynton Beach Boulevard) to US-441 and turn left. At Lee Road (2.0), turn right to the entrance just ahead. The visitor center is on the right (9:00 AM–4:00 PM daily from mid-October to mid-April, *otherwise closed Mondays and Tuesdays*).

The refuge has two nature trails. The **Cypress Swamp boardwalk** begins next to the visitor center. It is 2,000 feet long and traverses a cypress swamp. The **Marsh Trail** on the south side of Lee Road is 4,000 feet long and circles ten impoundments. Since water levels vary between impoundments, all should be searched. In or around the impoundments, look for Fulvous Whistling-Ducks, Mottled Ducks, Anhingas, wading birds, King Rails, Purple Gallinules, Limpkins, and Black-necked Stilts (mainly spring and summer). American Alligators are numerous. During winter, ducks and shorebirds can be common when water levels are favorable, and Painted Buntings may be found in shrubbery along Marsh Trail. During summer 2002, several Snail Kites roosted in the cypress head along the Marsh Trail south of the parking area, but the birds also use the interior of the refuge, where higher water levels are maintained. In winter, Lesser Nighthawks can be seen regularly at dusk hunting over the impoundments.

Contact: Arthur R. Marshall Loxahatchee National Wildlife Refuge, 10216 Lee Road, Boynton Beach, FL 33437-4796; 561-734-8303; <http://loxahatchee.fws.gov>.

The barrier island between West Palm Beach and Fort Lauderdale is heavily developed, with little natural vegetation remaining. However, two small parks in Boca Raton provide oases of habitat, and as a result, can offer excellent landbirding. **SPANISH RIVER PARK** (94 acres; $10.00–$12.00 parking fee; no camping; opens at 8:00 AM) can be great in spring for migrant landbirds and West Indian strays. This city park is very popular, so it is best to arrive early. Parking inside the park is expensive, but limited free parking is available along Spanish River Boulevard west of SR-A1A. To reach the park, exit (#48A) I-95 onto SR-794 (Yamato Road) and go east. At US-1 (0.8), turn right to CR-800 (Spanish River Boulevard; 0.6). Turn left, cross over the Intracoastal Waterway (0.5), and park on the right. Walk south through the Australian-pines into the park. West Indian vagrants seen in the park have included Bahama Mockingbird, Cuban Pewee (the first North American record), Thick-billed Vireo, Bananaquit, and Western Spindalis. Connecticut Warblers are seen nearly annually during the second week of May.

Contact: *Spanish River Park, 3001 North State Road A1A, Boca Raton, FL 33432; 561-393-7820; <www.ci.boca-raton.fl.us/parks/Spanishriver.cfm>.*

Red Reef Park (67 acres; no fee; no camping; opens at 8:00 AM), specifically the 20-acre **Gumbo Limbo Nature Center**, is the other park on the barrier island that is good for migrant landbirds in spring. It is located on the west side of SR-A1A, 1.25 miles south of Spanish River Boulevard. Short trails travel through a hardwood hammock both north and south of the center.

Contacts: *Red Reef Park, 1400 North State Road A1A, Boca Raton, FL 33432; <www.ci.boca-raton.fl.us/parks/redreef.cfm>. Gumbo Limbo Nature Center, 1801 North State Road A1A, Boca Raton, FL 33432; 561-338-1473; <www.gumbolimbo.org>.*

POMPANO BEACH–FORT LAUDERDALE

The **POMPANO BEACH LANDFILL** is closed to the public, but lakes to the north and east provide excellent opportunities for studying gulls from fall through spring when the landfill is operating (sometimes Monday through Friday only). To reach the area, exit (#39) I-95 at SR-834 (Sample Road) and go west; see next map. At SR-845 (Powerline Road; 1.7), turn right. Between SR-834 and SR-869 (Sawgrass Expressway; SW 10th Street; 2.0), check the lakes and open areas for gulls. The lake on the west side of Powerline Road just north of the landfill usually contains many thousands of gulls. A specialty is Lesser Black-backed Gull; more than 50 individuals have been seen here at times. Rarities that have been found in the area include Franklin's, Thayer's, Great Black-backed, Glaucous, and Iceland Gulls.

Fern Forest Nature Center (243 acres; no fee; no camping; opens at 8:00 AM) provides excellent birding for landbirds during migration and winter. To reach it, exit I-95 (#36B) or Florida's Turnpike at Atlantic Boulevard and head west. At Lyons Road, continue across the intersection and make a U-turn back to Lyons; the entrance is on the right (250 feet). The fruiting trees attract migrants during spring and fall, and Cedar Waxwings and warblers during winter. The Cypress Creek Trail is a 0.5-mile elevated boardwalk through a cypress and maple swamp that is good for migrant landbirds during spring or fall, and for warblers in winter. The one-mile Prairie Overlook Trail travels through oak and mixed woodlands and prairie. During winter, the woodland edge around the prairie usually has a mixed flock of warblers, often including Black-throated Green. A few Broad-winged Hawks also are found here each winter.

Contact: *Fern Forest Nature Center, 201 Lyons Road South, Coconut Creek, FL 33063; 954-970-0150; <www.broward.org/parks/nature. htm#ff>.*

HUGH TAYLOR BIRCH STATE PARK (180 acres; $4.00/vehicle; no camping; opens at 8:00 AM) is the best local spot for migrants and West Indian vagrants. From I-95 exit (#29A) onto SR-838 (East Sunrise Boulevard) and go east to the park on the left (just past the Intracoastal Waterway). The park road traverses a tropical hardwood hammock for about a mile. The hammock can be an excellent for migrant landbirds during spring and fall. Key West Quail-Dove, Ruddy Quail-Dove, La Sagra's Flycatcher, Bahama Mockingbird, Bananaquit, and Western Spindalis are among the rarities that have been found here.

Contact: *Hugh Taylor Birch State Park, 3109 East Sunrise Boulevard, Fort Lauderdale, FL 33304; 954-564-4521; <www.floridastateparks.org/ hughtaylorbirch>.*

John U. Lloyd Beach State Park (251 acres; $4.00/vehicle; no camping; opens at 8:00 AM) is also worth exploring for migrants and West Indian strays. To reach the park from US-1 in Dania, drive east on SR-A1A (Dania Beach Boulevard) and follow the signs north to the entrance (2.2). During winter, Northern Gannets, Magnificent Frigatebirds, and Great Black-backed Gulls (rare) may be observed from the jetty at the northernmost tip of the park. Barrier Island Nature Trail is good for migrants and West Indian strays. La Sagra's Flycatcher, Bahama Mockingbird, and Bananaquit have all occurred in the park in recent years.

Contact: *John U. Lloyd Beach State Park, 6503 North Ocean Drive, Dania, FL 33004; 954-923-2833; <www.floridastateparks.org/ lloydbeach>.*

Tree Tops County Park (356 acres; $1.00/person weekends and holidays; no camping; opens at 8:00 AM) contains a 1,000-foot boardwalk through a freshwater marsh. It also contains the Pine Island Ridge, which represents the highest natural point in Broward County, at 29 feet above sea level. To reach the park, exit I-95 (#23) at SR-818 (Griffin Road) and go west. At SW 100th Avenue (7), turn right to the entrance on the right (0.5). Follow the road to the boardwalk sign (0.6) and park. During winter, several species of warblers may be observed along the oak hammock trails, and Broad-winged Hawks are sometimes present in the woods around the visitor center. A La Sagra's Flycatcher wintered near the visitor center in 1994–1995.

Contact: *Tree Tops County Park, 3900 SW 100th Avenue, Davie, FL 33328; 954-370-3750; <www.broward.org/parks/parklist.htm>.*

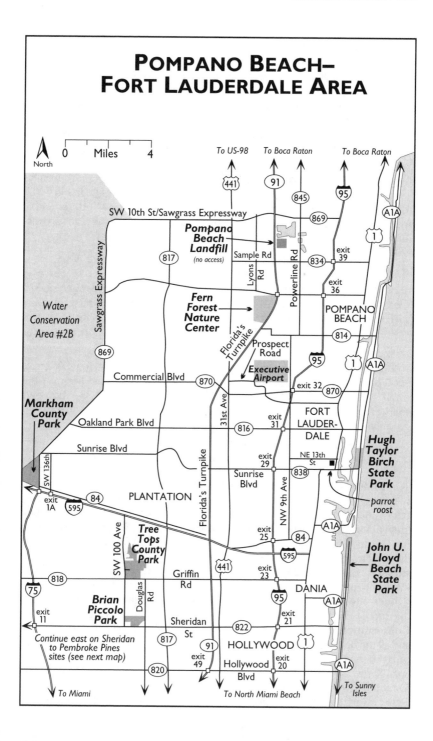

POMPANO BEACH–
FORT LAUDERDALE AREA

North
0 Miles 4

To US-98
To Boca Raton
To Boca Raton

441
91
845
95
A1A

SW 10th St/Sawgrass Expressway

869
1

Pompano Beach Landfill
(no access)

Sample Rd

817

Lyons Rd

Powerline Rd

834

exit 39

exit 36

POMPANO BEACH

Water Conservation Area #2B

Fern Forest Nature Center

Florida's Turnpike

869

Prospect Road

814

Executive Airport

95
1
A1A

Commercial Blvd
870

exit 32
870

31st Ave

Markham County Park

Oakland Park Blvd

exit 31

FORT LAUDER-DALE

816

Hugh Taylor Birch State Park

Sunrise Blvd

NE 13th St

838

parrot roost

SW 136th

exit 29

Sunrise Blvd

NW 9th Ave

exit 1A
595
84

PLANTATION

Florida's Turnpike

exit 25
84

A1A

John U. Lloyd Beach State Park

Tree Tops County Park

SW 100 Ave

595

818

Griffin Rd

441

exit 23

DANIA

75

Douglas Rd

95

A1A

exit 11

Brian Piccolo Park

Sheridan St

exit 21

822

817

91

HOLLYWOOD
1

Continue east on Sheridan to Pembroke Pines sites (see next map)

820

exit 49

Hollywood Blvd

exit 20

A1A

To Miami

To North Miami Beach

To Sunny Isles

Since the 1970s, a flock of (non ABA-countable) *Amazona* parrots has roosted in **downtown Fort Lauderdale**. The large majority are Red-crowned Parrots, with lesser numbers of Orange-winged Parrots. A few individuals of several other species may also be seen, such as Blue-fronted or Yellow-naped Parrots. The roost is generally in the area of the southwest corner of US-1 and NE 13th Street, but the specific location changes somewhat as vegetation is pruned or the birds are disturbed. The parrots typically fly into the area about 30 minutes before dusk and mass on powerlines and in Australian-pines before they all fly off to roost. Numbers of parrots are greatest following the breeding season (September to February), when begging juveniles are common; more than 200 parrots were using the roost regularly in 2002. Low-light conditions hamper viewing, but it's still quite a show—the sound of dozens of parrots can be almost deafening. During the day, the birds are dispersed over a considerable area, and sightings are hit-or-miss.

Two areas in Fort Lauderdale still contain Burrowing Owls. One site is **Fort Lauderdale Executive Airport**, which has active burrows marked with plastic perches. To reach the airport, exit (#32) I-95 at SR-870 (Commercial Boulevard or NW 50th Street) and go west. At 31st Avenue (2.1), turn right to Prospect Road (0.5). Turn right, then left onto Executive Airport Perimeter Road (0.1). Turn right after entering the airport and park at a viewing area on the left. The burrows are in the field ahead.

Burrowing Owls are also found in **Brian Piccolo Park** (180 acres; $1.00/person; no camping; opens at 8:00 AM), a recreational park on the north side of SR-822 (Sheridan Street) 6.5 miles west of I-95. Burrows (marked with wooden stakes and flagging tape) are located near the park entrance and office and around the ball fields.

Contact: Brian Piccolo Park, 9501 Sheridan Street, Cooper City, FL 33024; 954-437-2600; <www.broward.org/parks/parklist.htm>.

MARKHAM COUNTY PARK (666 acres; $1.00/person; 80 campsites at $17.00–$23.00/day; opens at 8:00 AM) borders Water Conservation Area 2B, where Snail Kites can usually be observed year-round (depending on water levels). To reach the park, exit I-595 (#1A) at SW 136th Avenue and immediately turn left onto SR-84 (Weston Road), which parallels the Interstate to the north. The park is on the right (1.9). Turn left immediately past the entrance building and drive to the nature trail on the left (0.2). Walk through the Australian-pines until you reach a canal, then head to the right. A short distance after the canal curves to the right is an access point to the top of the L-35, a levee that separates the current Everglades (Water Conservation Area 2B) from the former Everglades (Markham County Park and all the development that surrounds it). You may walk this levee either left or right; the elevated view allows you to scan the marshes for a great distance. Snail Kites, Limpkins, and Purple Gallinules may be seen here; a few Purple Swamphens recently have been found here, as well. During periods of low water levels, spectacular concentrations of wading birds may be seen as they

Adult gray-headed Purple Swamphen at Pembroke Pines.   Kurt Radamaker

feed on fish concentrated in isolated pools. The nature trail is good for migrant and wintering landbirds.

Contact: *Markham County Park, 16001 West State Road 84, Sunrise, FL 33326; 954-389-2000; <www.co.broward.fl.us/parks/parklist.htm>.*

PEMBROKE PINES

This suburban area at the eastern edge of the Everglades is the primary site for **Purple Swamphens** in southern Florida. The species currently does not occur elsewhere in the ABA Area. The birds apparently escaped from one or two aviculturists in the early to mid-1990s; they were discovered outside of captivity around December 1996. Swamphens have colonized nearby wetlands, and several individuals have dispersed dozens of miles from Pembroke Pines. Purple Swamphens are not yet ABA-countable, but they show strong signs of becoming established (providing that no government agency attempts an eradication program, which might in any case be futile). To get to the two best ponds (see map on next page), exit I-75 (#11B) at Sheridan Street and head west to Jaguar Way (1.3; traffic light). Turn right into the parking lot of **Southeast Regional Library** in Academic Village. Park near the mitigation pond on the right and walk the boardwalk. Several pairs of swamphens usually are resident in the pond, along with Mottled Ducks, Pied-billed Grebes, Least Bitterns, and Purple Gallinules. Black-bellied Whis-

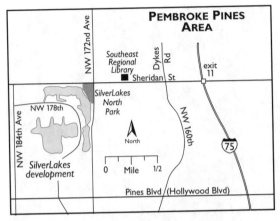

tling-Ducks have been seen from time to time, and at least two male Masked Ducks graced the ponds in May 2001.

The main lake in the **SilverLakes** development, which begins just past the traffic light at NW 172nd Avenue (0.3), is the other reliable site for Purple Swamp-hens. Numbers declined dramatically in 2004, perhaps due to high water levels. You can park either in the SilverLakes North Park at the southwest corner of Sheridan Street and NW 172nd Avenue, or pull off on the extensive shoulder along the south side of Sheridan Street anywhere between NW 172nd and NW 184th Avenues. Swamphens are usually easy to find in the marshy portions of the lake. To reach Pembroke Pines from Florida's Turnpike, exit onto Pines Boulevard (also called Hollywood Boulevard) and go west to NW 172nd Avenue. Turn north to Sheridan Street (1.5 miles) and follow the directions as above. From US-27, simply head east on Sheridan Street (traffic light) to the lake (2.8–3.5). Numerous other wetland species can be seen here; a wading bird roost is located on the islands just off the North Park parking lot. Mottled Ducks, Least Bitterns, and Purple Gallinules are resident, and are joined in winter by several species of waterfowl, American Bitterns, and other common species. Snail Kites have been seen when water levels are low.

GREATER MIAMI

Miami-Dade County, the home of the heavily urbanized Greater Miami area, is laid out as a grid, a system that allows most sites to be located easily. Streets (16 to the mile) run east-west, and avenues (10 to the mile) run north-south. Most of the streets and avenues are numbered using the junction of Flagler Street (just north of US-41; 8th Street) and Miami Avenue (between I-95 and US-1) as the center point. Streets and avenues are numbered outward from this point; thus 3rd Street is close to Flagler Street, while 162nd Street would be 10 miles away. Streets and avenues to the northwest of this intersection are labeled NW, those to the southwest are labeled SW, and so on. Because the intersection of Flagler Street and Miami Avenue is so near the coast, most of the streets and avenues in the area bear either NW or SW designations. A few communities (e.g., Coral Gables, Homestead) use their own street numbering systems. During rush-hour (mainly 7:00–9:30 AM and

4:00–6:30 PM), traffic can be terrible on most of the main highways, such as SR-826 (Palmetto Expressway), SR-836 (Dolphin Expressway), 1-95, Florida's Turnpike, SW 40th Street (Bird Road), and SW 88th Street (Kendall Drive).

Birding sites within the Greater Miami area are scattered widely, so for the purposes of this guide the area has been divided into five regions. Areas north of US-41 (Tamiami Trail) are listed as North Miami. Areas south of US-41 are split into four areas: Key Biscayne, South Miami, Kendall/Pinecrest, and Homestead/Florida City. Greater Miami comprises many suburban towns and unincorporated areas (e.g., Hialeah, Coral Gables, Opa-Locka, Kendall) that were once separated by pinelands but which are now combined as one continuous, sprawling region. The divisions used in this guide are merely for the sake of convenience; visitors will notice little or no difference from one area to the next. US-41 (Tamiami Trail) offers direct access to Shark Valley (Everglades National Park), Big Cypress National Preserve, Fakahatchee Strand Preserve State Park, and points farther west (see page 205). A reliable Snail Kite site is located near the Miccosukee Indian Restaurant on US-41.

Tropical Audubon Society operates the Miami Bird Board, an Internet bulletin board for local observations, often emphasizing exotics: <www. tropical audubon.org/tasboard/index.html>. The same website offers additional information on birding sites and where to find local specialties. Birders who will be spending several days in the Miami area should also consult the Miami chapter in *A Birder's Guide to Metropolitan Areas of North America*, edited by Paul Lehman (2001).

NORTH MIAMI

Many psittacids can be found along Curtiss Parkway in **MIAMI SPRINGS**, a residential area just north of Miami International Airport (see map on next page). From SR-826 (Palmetto Expressway), exit onto NW 36th Street and go east to the light at Curtiss Parkway (2.0). Turn left and follow the road as it curves to the right through the Miami Springs Golf Course. Park on Navarre Drive at the **Fair Haven Nursing Home** on the right (1.0). Bird the block around the nursing home first, then walk the median of Curtiss Parkway back to the golf course. Dozens of Monk Parakeets nest in the *Melaleuca* trees on the nursing-home grounds, and other psittacids also occur regularly. Curtiss Parkway is a divided roadway with a wide, landscaped median between the lanes. Check the oaks, figs, and other trees in the median for psittacids, Spot-breasted Orioles, and wintering and migrant landbirds. Psittacids that have occurred here include Chestnut-fronted Macaw, Maroon-bellied, Black-hooded, Mitred, Red-masked, White-winged, and Yellow-chevroned Parakeets, and Red-crowned, Blue-fronted, Orange-winged, and Yellow-headed Parrots. Gray Kingbirds may be present during spring and summer.

To visit a nearby area that usually is good for psittacids, go south on Navarre Drive one block to Morningside Drive, turn right, and follow it across Curtiss Parkway. Morningside Drive curves to the right and becomes Prospect Street. Turn left onto Westward Drive (0.4) to Apache Drive (0.8, the first traffic light) and turn right. Go two blocks to the house on the southwest corner of Apache Drive and Falcon Avenue, which may have feeders visited by many parakeets. Monk Parakeets are the most common, but sometimes also present are Mitred, Red-masked, White-eyed, Dusky-headed, Yellow-chevroned, Maroon-bellied, Green-cheeked, Blue-crowned, Green, Scarlet-fronted, and Orange-fronted Parakeets. This area is also a good spot for Spot-breasted Orioles.

A few pairs of Burrowing Owls inhabit grassy areas in the southern part of **Miami International Airport**. From Curtiss Parkway, return to NW 36th Street and turn right. At NW 72nd Avenue (Milam Dairy Road; 1.5), turn left to NW 12th Street (1.6), which becomes Perimeter Road. Turn left again and continue to the parking area on the right (1.3). From here, walk the airport fence east to NE 57th Avenue (Red Road). Owls should be seen between the fence and the runway. To return to a major roadway from the

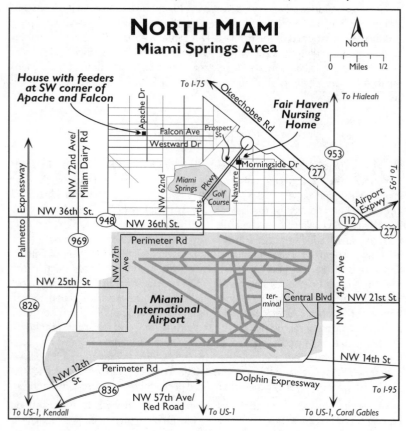

NORTH MIAMI
Miami Springs Area

North

0   Miles   1/2

House with feeders at SW corner of Apache and Falcon

To I-75

Okeechobee Rd

Apache Dr

To Hialeah

Fair Haven Nursing Home

Falcon Ave

Prospect St.

Westward Dr

953

Morningside Dr

27

To I-95

NW 72nd Ave/ Milam Dairy Rd

NW 62nd

Miami Springs

Navarre

Curtiss Pkwy

Golf Course

Airport Expwy

Palmetto Expressway

NW 36th St.

948

NW 36th St.

112

27

969

Perimeter Rd

NW 67th Ave

NW 25th St

826

Miami International Airport

ter-minal

Central Blvd

42nd Ave

NW 21st St

NW

NW 14th St

NW 12th St

Perimeter Rd

Dolphin Expressway

To I-95

836

NW 57th Ave/ Red Road

To US-1, Kendall

To US-1

To US-1, Coral Gables

parking lot, travel east on Perimeter Road to NW 57th Avenue (0.4) and turn right to reach SR-836. (Airport officials are considering building a new runway in the area that contains most of the owl burrows.)

KEY BISCAYNE

Head south on I-95 through downtown Miami (see map on next page), following the signs to Key Biscayne via Rickenbacker Causeway ($1.00/vehicle). Pass Virginia Key to Key Biscayne, where the road name changes to Crandon Boulevard (see map on next page). Upon entering the key, pull into the marina on the right to look for Common Mynas. Return to Crandon Boulevard and turn left into **Crandon Park** (960 acres; $3.50/vehicle; no camping; opens at sunrise). Park in the north parking area and walk the beach north. The park contains almost 3.5 miles of ocean frontage, and shorebirding here may produce Wilson's and Piping Plovers, Whimbrel, and other species (especially along the southern part of the beach). There is a nature center at the north end of the northernmost parking lot. The trails are good for migrants and have produced La Sagra's Flycatcher; in winter, look for Short-tailed Hawks overhead. Another good birding area is Crandon Gardens at the south end of the park. The gardens occupy the site of the former Crandon Park Zoo, which may have been responsible for the releases of many exotic birds in the area (Black-bellied Whistling-Duck, Great Black-Hawk, and Red-crested Cardinal are three examples). Some of these birds may no longer occur, but Green Iguanas native to the Neotropics are still present, and there is a waterfowl collection. Migrant landbirds can be common here during spring and fall, and a Western Spindalis was seen here in spring 2002.

Contact: Crandon Park, 4000 Crandon Boulevard, Key Biscayne, Florida 33149; 305-361-5421; <www.miamidade.gov/parks/Parks/crandon_beach.asp>.

After leaving Crandon Park, continue south (2.6) to the end of Key Biscayne to **BILL BAGGS CAPE FLORIDA STATE PARK** (425 acres; $5.00/vehicle; no public camping; opens at 8:00 AM). Since Hurricane *Andrew* destroyed the park's largely exotic vegetation in August 1992, the area has been replanted with native species, and native habitats have been restored. Cape Florida can be excellent for migrant landbirds, particularly during days with east winds. Caribbean strays such as Key West Quail-Dove, Zenaida Dove, Bahama Mockingbird, La Sagra's Flycatcher, and Western Spindalis have been observed, as has Red-legged Honeycreeper. Both the interior trail and the bike path provide good birding. During fall, the south end of the park is good for migrant raptors, including Merlins and Peregrine Falcons.

Contact: Bill Baggs Cape Florida State Park, 1200 South Crandon Boulevard, Key Biscayne, FL 33149; 305-361-8779; <www.floridastateparks.org/capeflorida>.

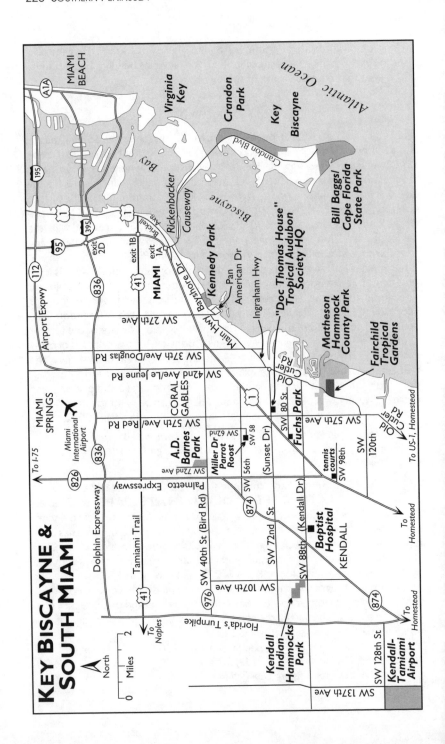

KEY BISCAYNE & SOUTH MIAMI

SOUTH MIAMI

From Rickenbacker Causeway, go south on US-1 (Brickell Avenue) to South Miami Avenue (0.2) and turn left (this road soon becomes South Bayshore Drive). **Kennedy Park** (no fee; no camping; opens at sunrise) in Coconut Grove is on the left (1.4). A flock of 25 to 30 White-winged and Yellow-chevroned Parakeets sometimes occurs here, and other psittacids may also be present. **Miami City Hall**, at the end of Pan American Drive on the left (0.3 mile past Kennedy Park), may also have psittacids and Hill Mynas.

South Bayshore Drive ends a few blocks past Pan American Drive at McFarlane Avenue. Turn right, go one block, then turn left onto Main Highway, which ends at SW 37th Avenue (1.0). Turn left onto SW 37th Avenue, then turn right onto Ingraham Highway (0.2). Ingraham Highway ends at SW 42nd Avenue (LeJeune Road), where you turn left. Go halfway around the circle to Old Cutler Road, then continue south for 1.8 miles to **MATHESON HAMMOCK PARK** (100 acres; no camping; opens at sunrise). At the light, turn left toward the beach and marina. Park on the left and check the picnic area for White-crowned Pigeons, Blue-and-yellow Macaws, White-winged and Yellow-chevroned Parakeets, and Hill Mynas. Check the palm snags in the park for nesting psittacids and Hill Mynas along with native species such as Eastern Screech-Owl and Pileated Woodpecker. The picnic area is especially good for migrant and wintering landbirds and has had its share of rarities. Mangrove Cuckoos may occur, especially during spring and fall, and Short-tailed Hawks are seen regularly during fall and early winter. Across Old Cutler Road from the south end of the picnic area, an undeveloped section of the park preserves a West Indian hardwood hammock. Besides the birds mentioned above, look for migrant and wintering landbirds and Black-whiskered Vireos, which have bred here during spring and summer. Farther into the park (after the fee station, $3.50/vehicle), the road forks. The left fork leads to the marina and the right one to an impressive Red Mangrove forest. Florida Prairie Warblers breed here, and other warblers winter. At the end of the road, wading birds and shorebirds (including a few Piping Plovers) frequent the beaches, especially at low tide.

Contact: *Matheson Hammock Park, 9610 Old Cutler Road, Miami, FL 33156; 305-666-6979.*

Continue south on Old Cutler Road to the T-intersection with SW 57th Avenue (Red Road). To bird inland sites in South Miami, drive north to SW 40th Street and turn left.

A.D. ("Doug") Barnes Park (no fee; no camping; opens at sunrise) contains a hardwood hammock and pine rocklands that are best during migration and winter. To reach the park from SW 40th Street (Bird Road), drive north on SW 72nd Avenue to the entrance on the right (0.2). At the T-intersection just past the entrance, turn left to a group of buildings on the left (0.2) and park on the right. Behind the buildings is a mixed pine and hardwood hammock reached by a nature trail. (The hammock is fenced, but a gate north of the first building is usually left unlocked.) Check this area, especially during migration; more than 20 warbler species have been seen here during fall. Spot-breasted Orioles have bred here. To the right of the parking lot is a pineland picnic area. Return to the T-intersection and continue south to a hardwood picnic area for additional birding.

Contact: *A.D. Barnes Park, 3401 SW 72nd Avenue, Miami, FL 33155; 305-666-5883; <www.miamidade.gov/parks/Parks/ad_barnes.asp>.*

To reach a psittacid roost, exit SR-826 (Palmetto Expressway) at SW 56th Street (**Miller Drive**) and go east. At SW 62nd Avenue (1.5), turn right. After two blocks (0.1), turn right onto SW 58th Street. Just beyond the five-way intersection, the road crosses a canal (0.3). Park here and watch for the birds as they come to roost about a half-hour before dark. The psittacids roost in large *Ficus* and *Poinciana* trees south of the canal. You may have to walk around the neighborhood a bit to find them. White-crowned Pigeons also occur in this area during spring and summer. *Some birders may not feel safe in this neighborhood.* Another, smaller psittacid roost is located near **Fuch's Park** (pronounced *fyewks*) on the southeast corner of SW 80th Street and US-1. *(Note that the same birds use both roosts, moving from one to the other. Sometimes both roosts are in use simultaneously; at other times, all the birds use just one of the roosts.)* Check the area near the apartment buildings just northeast of the park, starting about a half-hour before dusk. The nightly cast varies, but Red-masked Parakeets and Orange-winged and White-fronted Parrots usually are most common; Blue-fronted and Lilac-crowned Parrots are less frequent, and many other species are possible.

The **Doc Thomas House** is the headquarters of the Tropical Audubon Society, an active local birding chapter. It is located on the south side of SW 72nd Street (Sunset Drive) just east of SW 57th Avenue (Red Road) in South Miami. The offices and a small shop are open 9:00 AM to 4:00 PM daily, but birders should call ahead before visiting. On the grounds, Monk, Yellow-chevroned, and White-winged (least common) Parakeets are observed almost daily, Red-whiskered Bulbuls are nearby, and Spot-breasted Orioles nest here in most years. Native species are also represented, with Gray Kingbirds breeding in the area. Check the trees for migrant and wintering landbirds.

Contact: *Tropical Audubon Society, 5530 Sunset Drive, Miami, FL 33134; 305-666-5111; <www.tropicalaudubon.org>.*

KENDALL–PINECREST

This suburban district of Greater Miami is known among birders as the home of the Red-whiskered Bulbul, which became liberated from a "bird farm" in August 1960. The species is marginally established in the Kendall/ Pinecrest area, although its range remains limited to a small section of the district. The bulbul popula-

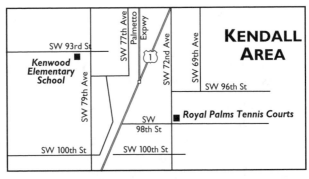

tion numbered about 250 birds in early 1970, but has not been studied at all since that time. Current numbers and distribution are, therefore, unknown, although bulbuls can still be found rather easily in their core range. The birds are most common within the triangle created by US-1 on the north and west, SW 57th Avenue (Red Road) on the east, and SW 120th Street on the south, but bulbuls occur south to SW 186th Street and west to SW 100th Avenue. Bulbuls currently are fairly easy to find around the **Royal Palm Tennis Courts** at the northeast corner of SW 98th Street and SW 72nd Avenue, just east of US-1. Check the wires along SW 98th Street, the side streets to the south, and the entrance to the courts. Watch the treetops and wires; bulbuls often sit in exposed places. Drive around the area, and you should see one eventually. Early morning is best.

A couple of blocks north of the tennis courts is the home of Art and Betty Furchgott (6901 SW 96th Street), who are very friendly to visiting birders. Red-whiskered Bulbul, Spot-breasted Oriole, and several species of parakeets, such as Mitred, Red-masked, and Yellow-chevroned, are regular in the neighborhood. The area in and around **Kenwood Elemetary School** at 9300 SW 79th Avenue is another area good for bulbuls, Spot-breasted Orioles, and other landbirds during fall and winter.

A large Monk Parakeet colony is located on the grounds of **Baptist Hospital** on the south side of SW 88th Street (North Kendall Drive) just west of SW 87th Avenue. The parakeets are easiest to find in trees near the westernmost pond. Look in the *Melaleuca* trees for the nests. Other birds possible here include White-winged Parakeet, Red-whiskered Bulbul, and Hill Myna. Many of these species can also be found in the neighborhood across Kendall Drive. Check the hospital ponds for wading birds, Ring-necked Ducks (winter), and other waterbirds.

Kendall Indian Hammocks Park (105 acres; no fee; no camping; opens at sunrise) is a long, narrow park north of SW 88th Street (North Kendall Drive) between SW 107th and SW 114th avenues. To reach it from Kendall Drive, take SW 107th Avenue north to the entrance on the left at SW 84th Street (0.4). Park on the left next to the ball fields (0.6). A hardwood hammock on the right has trails through the hammock that can be good for migrant and wintering landbirds.

Contact: *Kendall Indian Hammocks Park, 11395 SW 79th Street, Miami, FL 33173; 305-596-9324; <www.miamidade.gov/parks/ Parks/kendall_ind_hammocks.asp>.*

Kendall-Tamiami Airport has a few Burrowing Owls. Take SW 128th Street west from SW 137th Avenue. Active burrows are marked with plastic cones; one pair of owls nests at the Wings over Miami Air Museum.

Contact: *Kendall-Tamiami Airport, 12800 SW 145th Avenue, Miami, FL 33186; 305-869-1700; <www.miami-airport.com/html/kendall-tamiami_facilities.html>.*

HOMESTEAD–FLORIDA CITY

Castellow Hammock Preserve (60 acres; no fee; no camping; opens at sunrise) boasts a nature center and an extensive hardwood hammock. To reach the park from US-1, drive west onto SW 216th Street (Hainlin Mill Drive). Turn left onto SW 162nd Avenue (Farm Life Road) to the entrance on the left (0.5). Feeders in front of the hammock may be visited by Painted Buntings during winter. The butterfly garden also attracts hummingbirds during winter, mainly Ruby-throated and Rufous. White-winged Doves are common year-round, and Swallow-tailed Kites and Black-whiskered Vireos may be found during spring and summer.

Contact: *Castellow Hammock Preserve and Nature Center, 22301 SW 162nd Avenue, Miami, FL 33170; 305-242-7688; <www.miamidade.gov/ parks/Parks/castello_hammock.htm>.*

Since at least 1987, West Indian Cave Swallows have nested under highway overpasses and bridges north of Homestead, at **Cutler Ridge**. To reach the largest colony, go east from US-1 on SW 216th Street (Hainlin Mill Drive) to Florida's Turnpike. Go under the overpass and turn left immediately onto the northbound service road that parallels the turnpike. Park on the grass strip on the right side of the road next to the canal. (*If you leave your car, be advised that there have been some auto break-ins here.*) Cave Swallows usually can be observed easily from this point. They are most obvious during the breeding season (April through July), but birds are virtually resident now. Cave Swallows only roost here during the non-breeding season, and may difficult to find except shortly after dawn or before dusk.

Continue south on US-1 to SW 248th Street (Coconut Palm Drive) and turn left. A power substation on the left (0.5) contains **Monk Parakeet nests**. Check at the turnpike overpass (2.3) in spring and summer for Cave Swallows, which have nested here in previous years. "**Mount Trashmore**",

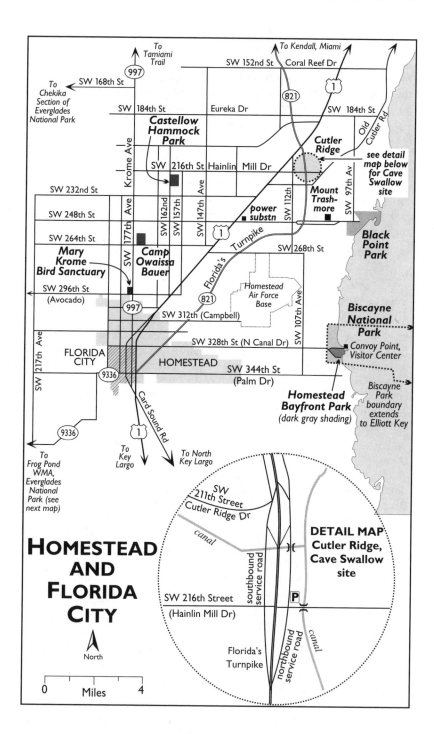

To Tamiami Trail

997

To Chekika Section of Everglades National Park

SW 168th St

SW 152nd St   Coral Reef Dr

To Kendall, Miami

821

1

SW 184th St   Eureka Dr   SW 184th St

Old Cutler Rd

Castellow Hammock Park

Cutler Ridge

see detail map below for Cave Swallow site

Krome Ave

SW 216th St   Hainlin   Mill Dr

SW 97th Av

SW 232nd St

SW 177th Ave

SW 162nd

SW 157th

SW 147th Ave

SW 112th

Mount Trash-more

power substn

Black Point Park

SW 248th St

SW 264th St

Mary Krome Bird Sanctuary

Camp Owaissa Bauer

Turnpike

SW 268th St

SW 296th St (Avocado)

997

SW 312th (Campbell)

821

Florida's Turnpike

Homestead Air Force Base

SW 107th Ave

Biscayne National Park

Convoy Point, Visitor Center

FLORIDA CITY

SW 217th Ave

HOMESTEAD

SW 328th St (N Canal Dr)

SW 344th St (Palm Dr)

9336

Homestead Bayfront Park (dark gray shading)

Biscayne Park boundary extends to Elliott Key

9336

1

Card Sound Rd

To Frog Pond WMA, Everglades National Park (see next map)

To Key Largo

To North Key Largo

HOMESTEAD AND FLORIDA CITY

North

0   Miles   4

SW 211th Street Cutler Ridge Dr

canal

southbound service road

DETAIL MAP Cutler Ridge, Cave Swallow site

P

SW 216th Street (Hainlin Mill Dr)

canal

Florida's Turnpike

northbound service road

a huge local landfill on the left (1.8), can be good for gulls and sometimes has Bald Eagles and shorebirds. The road ends (0.5 mile) at **Black Point Park** (no fee; no camping; opens at sunrise). Turn left before the parking lot, cross the bridge, turn right at the stop sign at the extension of SW 97th Avenue, and go to the small parking area. Walk along the channel that leads to the bay. At the end is a rock jetty that can be good for wading birds, shorebirds, and larids. Purple Sandpiper and Lesser Black-backed Gull have been seen here.

Return to Krome Avenue and turn left to SW 264th Street (Bauer Drive). Turn left to **Camp Owaissa Bauer** (119 acres; no fee; group camping in cabins only; opens at sunrise; 10.3 miles), which contains a large hammock that can be good for migrant and wintering landbirds. During spring and summer, look for Swallow-tailed Kites and Black-whiskered Vireos. During winter, check the feeders near the office for Painted Buntings.

Contact: Camp Owaissa Bauer, 17001 SW 264th Street, Miami, FL 33030; 305-247-6016; <www.miamidade.gov/parks/Parks/ owaissa_bauer_camp.asp>.

Return to SR-997 (Krome Avenue, SW 177th Avenue) and turn left. Drive south to SW 296th Street (Avocado Drive; 2.0). Park on Krome Avenue south of this intersection and walk back to small, unmarked **Mary Krome Bird Sanctuary** (3 acres; no fee; no camping; opens at sunrise) at the northwest corner of Krome Avenue and Avocado Drive. *Avoid the avocado and mango groves to the west and north; they are private property.* Ruby-throated Hummingbirds are regular from fall through spring, and Rufous Hummingbirds have also occurred frequently. The park may also contain other wintering and migrant landbirds.

About four miles south of Black Point Park, at the east end of SW 328th Drive (North Canal Drive), are **Homestead Bayfront Park** and the Convoy Point Visitor Center for Biscayne National Park. (The visitor center is north of the road, and the county park is to the south.) Because most of **Biscayne National Park** (181,500 acres; no fee; key camping, $10.00/day, requires boat transportation) is offshore, a boat is needed to visit most of it. A private concession operates boat tours from Convoy Point (305-230-7275). A smaller visitor center is located on Elliott Key, about eight miles offshore. The key contains West Indian hardwood hammocks that can be good for landbirds; the first Florida record of La Sagra's Flycatcher occurred here in December 1982. Nearby Boca Chita Key hosted the first North American Red-legged Honeycreeper (possibly an escapee) in March 2003. The park also contains a coral reef that may be explored by a glass-bottom-boat tour or by snorkeling. (This park is far less crowded than John Pennekamp Coral Reef State Park on Key Largo.) The jetty at Convoy Point can be good for wading birds, shorebirds, and larids.

Contact: Biscayne National Park, 9700 SW 328th Street, Homestead, FL 33033-5634; 305-230-7275; <www.nps.gov/bisc>.

Swallow-tailed Kite.   Arthur Morris/www.birdsasart.com

Return to SR-997 (Krome Avenue) and go south through **downtown Homestead** to SR-9336 (Palm Drive; SW 344th Street; 3.0 miles). To search for Common Mynas (not yet ABA-countable), turn left and proceed to US-1. Just south of SW 344th Street, mynas often are found in the parking lots of the various fast-food restaurants, especially the Burger King. Otherwise, turn right onto SR-9336, which after several turns along the way (follow the signs), leads to Everglades National Park. However, there are a few birding sites before the park that may be worth a stop during winter and early spring.

At the **C-111E Canal** (5.2 miles from SR-997; see map on next page), wooded areas north of the road can produce a variety of sparrows and buntings, and the canal itself could have a few wading birds and perhaps Mottled Ducks or Limpkins. Continue past the canal to SW 209th Avenue (0.4; usually unmarked) and turn right. Make a loop by continuing north to a T-intersection (0.2), turning left at another T (0.2), then returning to SR-9336 (0.2) on SW 212th Avenue. Watch powerlines, fencelines, sprinkler heads, or dead limbs in this area from November to April for wintering Western Kingbirds and Scissor-tailed Flycatchers; Cassin's Kingbird may also be present. Check the blackbird flocks here and in the surrounding neighborhood for rarities such as Yellow-headed Blackbird, Shiny Cowbird, or Bronzed Cowbird. Other birds that may be present are raptors (including Swainson's Hawks) during winter, Upland Sandpipers and Bobolinks during fall, Painted Buntings from fall through spring, and various sparrows (including Clay-colored, Lark, Grasshopper, and White-crowned) during winter. Exploring the roads in this whole area could produce many good birds during the winter months. *But be sure to remain on the roadway: in this area trespassing on farmlands is not tolerated!*

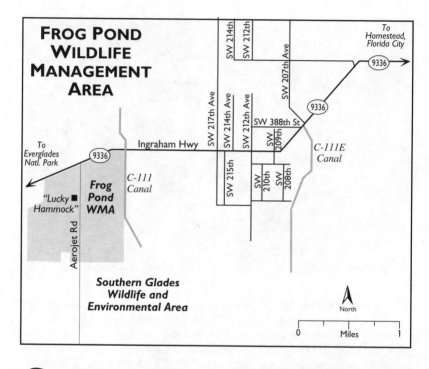

FROG POND
WILDLIFE
MANAGEMENT
AREA

SW 214th
SW 212th
SW 207th Ave

To
Homestead,
Florida City

9336

SW 217th Ave
SW 214th Ave
SW 212th Ave
SW 209th

9336

SW 388th St

To
Everglades
Natl. Park

9336

Ingraham Hwy

C-111E
Canal

Frog
Pond
WMA

C-111
Canal

SW 215th
SW 210th
SW 208th

"Lucky ■
Hammock"

Aerojet Rd

Southern Glades
Wildlife and
Environmental Area

North

0   Miles   1

Continue westward. Cross over the C-111 canal (8.0 from SR-997) to Aerojet Road (0.5; look for the sign for Southern Glades Youth Camp). Turn left to the small hammock on the right (called "Lucky Hammock" by locals; 0.25), a part of the **FROG POND WILDLIFE MANAGEMENT AREA** (480 acres; no fee; no camping; *seasonal dove hunting*). Bird the hammock, the adjacent fields (these, too, are in public ownership, and may be restored in the future), and the shrubby area on the east side of the road. All have been very productive, especially during migration and winter. In recent years Lucky Hammock has been reliable for wintering Yellow-breasted Chats, and the area around the hammock may support Swainson's Hawk, Lesser Nighthawk, Scissor-tailed Flycatcher, several species of sparrows, or Yellow-headed Blackbird during winter. Continue south to the sign for **Southern Glades Wildlife and Environmental Area** (32,299 acres; no fee). The area from the sign to the youth camp has also provided good birding; White-crowned Pigeons are sometimes seen here.

As you drive along SR-9336 toward Everglades National Park, you pass through some of the most valuable farmland in the U.S., supplying the country with the bulk of its winter vegetables. You will notice two unique characteristics about this region: the "soil" is composed of small pieces of rock, and the native vegetation has been almost totally obliterated. (You will know that you are approaching Everglades National Park by the line of Slash Pines visible from a great distance.) Most of southern Miami-Dade County is low-lying and was frequently inundated prior to drainage. Upland vegetation grows on outcroppings of limestone deposited about one million years ago. The limestone is at ground level or just a few inches below it. The "rock plow", a combination bulldozer and plow, was invented to break up the soft limestone into small pieces to allow farming.

The pinelands on these limestone outcroppings comprise a unique ecosystem called Miami Rockland. Although the pines are the same variety of Slash Pines that are found elsewhere in southern Florida, the Miami Rockland understory contains many shrubs of West Indian affinity, and the herbaceous layer contains several endemic species. Originally, 180,000 acres of Miami Rockland could be found in Miami-Dade County. Today, fewer than 4,000 acres remain outside Everglades National Park, a 98 percent reduction. Many pinelands that remain in private hands are small parcels that are heavily overgrown with exotic plants, especially Brazilian Pepper and Australian-pine.

EVERGLADES NATIONAL PARK

With so much written about the Everglades, many people have preconceived ideas about what is to be found there. First-time visitors are often amazed to discover that Everglades National Park is not what they thought it would be. Having heard about subtropical Florida, some come looking for jungles but find that the cypresses are stunted and grow in savannahs or on islands surrounded by marshes. Other people expect a great "river of grass", but find that during dry years there is almost no fresh water in the park. Almost no one is prepared for the flat terrain that stretches for miles with virtually no relief.

Dedicated in 1947 by President Harry S. Truman, Everglades was the first national park to be established at the mouth of a river rather than at its source. Since then, it has been designated an International Biosphere Reserve, a World Heritage Site, a Wetland of International Significance, and an Important Bird Area. Today, it is visited annually by more than one million people, of whom about a third arrive from outside the U.S. Although only a few Florida bird specialties are found here, Everglades National Park is one of the state's most visited birding spots. Without doubt, the park and the entire Everglades ecosystem are associated throughout the world with Florida and its wading birds. A book about the avifauna of Everglades National Park, written by Sonny Bass and the late Richard Cunningham, is planned for publication in 2005. It is expected to be the definitive book on one of the nation's most unique and diverse ecosystems.

The Seminoles called this area *Pa-hay-okee*, meaning "grassy waters". In her monumental book, Marjory Stoneman Douglas also refers to the Everglades as a great *River of Grass*. Unlike any other river, the Everglades is a vast, shallow expanse of water moving slowly south through sawgrass and cypress prairies. Sawgrass, the dominant plant of the Everglades, is not a grass

Short-tailed Hawk, dark morph adult in an Australian-pine.   Larry Manfredi
It is rare to find a Short-tailed Hawk perched away from a nest-site.

but a sedge, so, technically, the Everglades is a "River of Sedge". Because of the extreme flatness of the region, the "river" is 50 miles wide and only inches deep. The water drops only 15 feet over its 100-mile flow (less than two inches per mile) from the southern shore of Lake Okeechobee to Florida Bay. Less than 20 percent of the original Everglades is contained within the boundaries of Everglades National Park. (Another 30 percent is protected in other parks and water conservation areas, and about 50 percent has been destroyed.) At 1,506,309 acres, Everglades is the largest national park east of the Mississippi River, and it contains almost 150 miles of coastal shoreline (not even counting all the keys in Florida Bay).

Except for the Everglades City and Shark Valley regions described earlier in this guide, the only land access to the park is from SR-9336 in Florida City. From the park entrance station, it is 38 miles to the end of the main park road at Flamingo. *Make sure that your vehicle has sufficient fuel to complete the round-trip.* For the entire drive, the elevation of the road never exceeds six feet above sea level. In fact, the area is so flat and low that a sea-level rise of only a few feet would convert much of Everglades National Park to a shallow estuary, which could have dire consequences for many of the park's inhabitants, especially Cape Sable Seaside Sparrows.

Florida specialties to search for in the park include Greater Flamingos (mostly at high tide at Snake Bight), Short-tailed Hawks (fairly common over

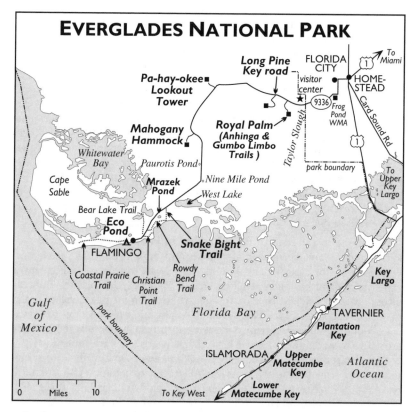

EVERGLADES NATIONAL PARK

Long Pine Key road –
Pa-hay-okee■ Lookout Tower
FLORIDA CITY
To Miami
visitor center
★ (9336) Frog Pond WMA
HOME-STEAD
Royal Palm (Anhinga & Gumbo Limbo Trails)
Mahogany Hammock■
Taylor Slough
Card Sound Rd
Whitewater Bay
Paurotis Pond●
park boundary
Cape Sable
Mrazek Pond
●Nine Mile Pond
West Lake
To Upper Key Largo
Bear Lake Trail
Eco Pond
Snake Bight Trail
FLAMINGO
Coastal Prairie Trail
Christian Point Trail
Rowdy Bend Trail
Key Largo
Gulf of Mexico
park boundary
Florida Bay
TAVERNIER
Plantation Key
ISLAMORADA
Upper Matecumbe Key
Atlantic Ocean
0 Miles 10
To Key West
Lower Matecumbe Key

uplands anywhere during winter), Painted Buntings (fairly common during winter in brushy areas throughout), and Cape Sable Seaside Sparrows (uncommon and secretive; most reliable south of the road to Mahogany Hammock). Small numbers of Lesser Nighthawks have recently begun to winter around Flamingo, and Whip-poor-wills (regular during winter) and Barn Owls (unpredictable year-round) may be seen along the main road at night. Wading birds, including Wood Storks and Roseate Spoonbills, are widespread year-round. Because Everglades National Park consists of sawgrass and cypress prairies, West Indian hardwood hammocks, and mangrove forests, visitors should expect mosquitoes, especially during summer. What most visitors are unprepared for is the sheer number of mosquitoes (and their ferocity), especially at places like Snake Bight Trail and Eco Pond. At times, venturing outside your vehicle is impossible without strong insect repellent, and even this defense only lessens the misery. *Be forewarned: parts of Everglades National Park may be unbearable during summer because of mosquitoes. At other seasons, mosquitoes are less often a problem, their numbers linked to recent rainfall (if any).*

Although lodging is found easily outside the park, there is only one motel (with 102 rooms and 24 cottages) inside the park, at Flamingo. The rates are most expensive from 15 December to 30 April and cheapest from 1 May to 31 October, when food service is minimal. For information, call the Flamingo Lodge at 941-695-3101. Additionally, Everglades National Park has three campgrounds, at Chekika, Long Pine Key, and Flamingo.

To reach the park from the Homestead/Florida City area, go west on SR-9336 (Palm Drive) from SR-997 (Krome Avenue), US-1, or SR-821 (Florida's Turnpike). *The Turnpike ends just north of SR-9336, so turn right imme-diately after merging with US-1.* Drive to the visitor center (8:00 AM–5:00 PM daily) on the right before the toll booth (0.6). The center contains a large se-lection of natural-history books, a 15-minute movie about the Everglades, and a logbook for recording interesting sightings. *The use of tape recordings is pro-hibited in the park.* Once inside the park ($10.00/vehicle), drive to the bridges over Taylor Slough (1.0). This site is good for wading birds; watch especially for American Bitterns during winter.

Continue to the road to **ROYAL PALM HAMMOCK** (0.5) and turn left. The most popular birding site here is **Anhinga Trail**, a 0.5-mile board-walk over Taylor Slough. The wooden boardwalk was destroyed by Hurri-cane *Andrew* and has been rebuilt, partially using recycled plastic. Because birds and other wildlife are accustomed to people on the boardwalk, the ani-mals have become extraordinarily tame. As a result, Anhinga Trail offers ex-cellent photographic and nature-study opportunities when water levels are attractive to wading birds. Some birds that may observed are American (win-ter) and Least Bitterns, both night-herons (Yellow-crowned is the more com-mon), and Purple Gallinules. American Alligators are common year-round. It will not take long for you to realize why this is called Anhinga Trail; these birds are numerous here, and in spring, nest within feet of the boardwalk. A few Great White Herons (mostly immatures) should also be present along the trail. During spring and summer, Swallow-tailed Kites may be seen overhead, and this is one of several areas in the park where Short-tailed Hawks may been seen from late fall through early winter.

Gumbo Limbo Trail enters the hammock from the south end of the Royal Palm Visitor Center. One-half-mile-long, it is named for the tree characterized by reddish, peeling bark. Like most other trees in the ham-mock, the Gumbo Limbo is of West Indian origin, restricted in the United States to South Florida. The trail can be good for tree snails and migrant and wintering landbirds. Wintering *Myiarchus* flycatchers should be examined closely, because Brown-crested Flycatchers occur here occasionally, in addi-tion to the resident Great Crested Flycatchers. Many warblers may be found along the trail during winter, including Black-throated Green, Worm-eating, and Magnolia. Also during winter, Short-tailed Hawks are often seen over the hammock; mid-morning (9:00–9:30 AM) is best. Where the trail crosses the grassy Old Ingraham Highway, you can walk about a mile from the visitor cen-ter area through excellent hammock habitat.

Return to the main park road and turn left. At the road to **Long Pine Key** (2.2), turn left. Long Pine Key is not a key in the true sense of the word, but an island of Miami Rockland pinewoods surrounded by sawgrass prairies. Pinelands Nature Trail (2.1 miles from the campground) on the right side of the main road can be good for migrants and wintering landbirds such as Barn Owls and Whip-poor-wills. Pine Warblers breed here, but five other characteristic species of Florida's pinewoods (Wild Turkey, Red-cockaded Woodpecker, Hairy Woodpecker, Brown-headed Nuthatch, and Eastern Bluebird) had become extirpated by the mid-1990s. In recent years, turkeys, nuthatches, and bluebirds have been re-established on Long Pine Key.

Pa-hay-okee Overlook on the right (6.3) is not particularly good for birds, but a 1,000-foot-long boardwalk and overlook offer views of the extensive sawgrass prairie community that dominated the original Everglades ecosystem. Sometimes a pair of Sandhill Cranes is present here. The Pa-hay-okee area is the start of the dwarf cypress forest. Many Pond-Cypresses in this region are stunted due to a shallow water level. Although the trees are only 10 to 20 feet tall, they may be well over a century old.

Mahogany Hammock (7.1), located to the right off the main road, is good for Barred Owls, Pileated Woodpeckers, and tree snails. During winter, the hammock is a good spot for White-crowned Pigeons, and it can be excellent for wintering warblers. There are usually a few Magnolia and Black-throated Green Warblers here, and Hooded Warblers have been found on rare occasions. The road to the hammock can have Western Kingbirds and Scissor-tailed Flycatchers during winter.

The best area in the park to search for **Cape Sable Seaside Sparrow** is a zone centered on the road to Mahogany Hammock. From about 1.5 miles before this road to about 1.5 miles beyond it, look for the sparrows in the marshes on both sides of the main park road. The best single site is located about 1.1 miles past the turn to Mahogany Hammock. The best time to find the birds is before 10:00 AM from March to July, when singing males are conspicuous. Otherwise, they are difficult to locate.

Paurotis Pond on the right (4.4 miles from the road to Mahogany Hammock) is the first of five roadside ponds. Wood Storks have nested here in late winter the past few years. **Nine Mile Pond** on the left (2.0) is worth a stop for Mottled Ducks (and other ducks during winter), wading birds, Swallow-tailed Kites (spring and summer), Limpkins, and White-crowned Pigeons. **West Lake** on the left (4.4) is not as productive as other sites, but the boardwalk along the Mangrove Trail may provide views of White-crowned Pigeons (mainly at dusk), Mangrove Cuckoos during spring and summer, and migrant and wintering landbirds.

The 1.8-mile **SNAKE BIGHT TRAIL** on the left (1.6) is the best of several trails in this area. The trail goes through a mangrove forest and ends at a boardwalk that provides a panoramic view of Snake Bight (a bight is a bay

Cape Sable Seaside Sparrow.   Drew Fulton

formed by a curved coastline). *Be aware that mosquitoes can be horrendous along the trail.* Mangrove Cuckoos occur here during spring and summer (and perhaps year-round). The boardwalk is very productive for shorebirds, especially at low tide, when extensive mudflats are exposed. Snake Bight is the most reliable site in the U.S. for Greater Flamingos (best at high tide). Brown-crested Flycatchers are sometimes found near the trailhead. You may find it preferable to ride a bicycle (rentals available at Flamingo) rather than to walk the trail. The mangroves leading to the bay support several species of warblers during winter—the birding can be good if the mosquitoes are light enough to allow you to stop and look at warblers.

Mrazek Pond on the left (1.6) can be disappointing from late spring through early winter, but from January to April—when the water level may be low, concentrating the fish—the pond attracts hundreds of wading birds, including Wood Storks and Roseate Spoonbills. Opportunities for nature study and photography then are excellent, but the peak of bird activity usually lasts for only a few days.

The 2.5-mile **Rowdy Bend Trail** (1.1) and the two-mile **Christian Point Trail** (1.9) cross coastal prairies and mangrove forests, but you will probably find more birds along the two-mile **Bear Lake Trail**, which starts from the end of Bear Lake Road (0.4). The trail goes through a tropical hardwood hammock that may have Mangrove Cuckoos, White-crowned Pigeons, and other landbirds. Swallow-tailed Kites breed here. During winter, watch for Scissor-tailed Flycatchers along the first few hundred feet of the trail.

Flamingo (0.4) is a small commercial area at the end of the park road, containing a visitor center, marina, motel, restaurant, and campground. From the restaurant, you can view a Bald Eagle nest (active during winter) in mangroves in the bay. At low tide, the mudflats south of the visitor center may feature numerous American White Pelicans, wading birds (including Great White Herons and Reddish Egrets), shorebirds, and larids. Check the tern flocks for Gull-billed Terns, which winter here in small numbers. Search the blackbird flocks for Shiny Cowbirds, and the Sea Grapes and other trees for migrant and wintering landbirds, including Ruby-throated Hummingbirds, Cape May Warblers, and Baltimore Orioles. Yellow-throated Warblers may be seen in the palms from fall through spring. In the canal behind the marina, you may be lucky enough to see an American Crocodile, an Endangered species. (Be aware that American Alligators may also be present. Recognize crocodiles by their dull greenish color and narrower snout.)

On the right toward the campground is **ECO POND**, a small pond once used to recycle treated wastewater. There is a short boardwalk and observation platform overlooking the pond, and trails around it. Several rarities have been seen here, including a Yellow-faced Grassquit in January–February 2001. White Ibises abound, and other wading birds, including Roseate Spoonbills, roost on the pond's island. During winter, watch for Short-tailed Hawks overhead, and Lesser Nighthawks over the pond around dusk. Least Bitterns are often seen year-round. Migrant and wintering landbirds (including Painted Buntings) are found in brushy areas around the water.

At the **campground**, watch for Scissor-tailed Flycatchers during winter. **Coastal Prairie Trail** begins off Campground Loop B and cuts through coastal marshes for seven miles. It can be a rough walk because of the vegetation and the mosquitoes, but Sedge Wrens and numerous Swamp Sparrows winter in the marsh. Also present during winter are sharp-tailed sparrows, reportedly Saltmarsh Sharp-tailed Sparrows. Very lucky birders have been rewarded with views of Yellow Rail during winter, but the species should not be expected. To search for marsh birds, it is often best to leave the trail and hike through the marsh.

Several boat trips start at the marina, but most are not particularly good for birding. Since these trips vary widely from season to season, it is wise to check with a park naturalist about which one to take. Greater Flamingos have been seen during winter on Sandy Key, about seven miles southwest of Flamingo. When they are present in the park but not found at Snake Bight, it may be possible to charter a boat from the marina to search for them.

Contact: *Everglades National Park, 40001 SR-9336, Homestead, FL 33034; 305-242-7700; <www.nps.gov/ever>.*

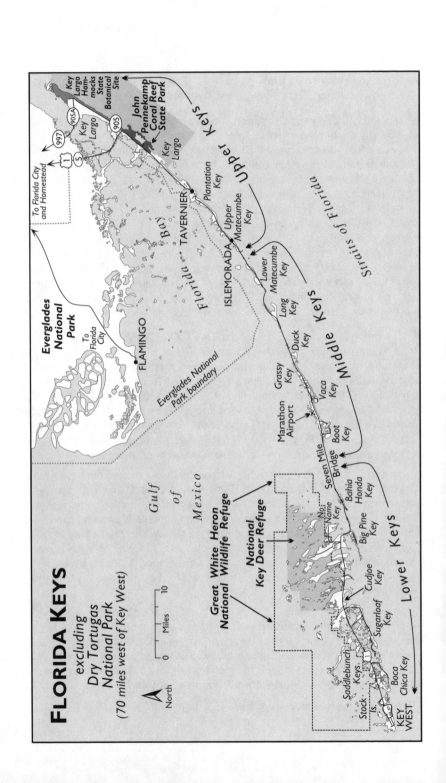

FLORIDA KEYS

The Florida Keys are among the few places in the ABA Area that feature native birds not seen easily elsewhere. Breeding birds in the Keys include Masked Booby (Dry Tortugas), Magnificent Frigatebird, Great White Heron, Reddish Egret, Roseate Tern (spring and summer), Bridled Tern (spring and summer), Sooty Tern (Dry Tortugas; spring and summer), Brown Noddy (Dry Tortugas; spring and summe), White-crowned Pigeon, Mangrove Cuckoo, Antillean Nighthawk (spring and summer), Gray Kingbird (spring through fall), Black-whiskered Vireo (spring and summer), and Cuban Yellow Warbler. Nearly all are relatively easy to find from April through July, provided that the Dry Tortugas are included in your trip. The cuckoo is the only one of these that is difficult to locate without effort (e.g., tape playback, patience, and mosquito bites). Other birds more or less restricted to the Keys are Brown Booby (Dry Tortugas; spring and summer; sometimes common), Red-footed Booby (Dry Tortugas; almost annual during spring and summer), Black Noddy (Dry Tortugas; at least one is found nearly every spring), West Indian Short-eared Owl (spring and summer), and Shiny Cowbird. All of these can be found at the Tortugas; the owl and cowbird also occur regularly during spring or summer at Key West. Pelagic trips into the Gulf Stream should produce Audubon's Shearwater, Brown Booby, Sooty and Bridled Terns, and perhaps several other species such as Cory's or Audubon's Shearwaters, Wilson's or Band-rumped Storm-Petrels, or Pomarine or Parasitic Jaegers. Migrant landbird fallouts may occur in any Keys hammock during spring or fall; recent banding projects have detected large numbers of Swainson's Warblers, which were not previously known to move through the region in numbers. The Florida Keys are one of the best places in North America to observe raptors (especially Sharp-shinned Hawks, Merlins, and Peregrine Falcons) during fall.

To date, 20 or 21 West Indian or Tropical American species have strayed to the Keys: Masked Duck, Least Grebe, Scaly-naped Pigeon, Zenaida Dove, White-tipped Dove (Yucatán subspecies), Key West Quail-Dove, Ruddy Quail-Dove, Antillean Palm Swift, La Sagra's Flycatcher, Fork-tailed Flycatcher, Cuban Martin, Southern Martin, Bahama Swallow, Bahama Mockingbird, Thick-billed Vireo, Bananaquit, Western Spindalis, Yellow-faced Grassquit, Black-faced Grassquit, Tawny-shouldered Blackbird, and perhaps Red-legged Honeycreeper. Most of these species are extremely rare, but La

Mangrove Cuckoo in mangroves.   Lyn S. Atherton

Sagra'sFlycatcher, Bahama Mockingbird, and Western Spindalis occur annually or nearly so. Other birds are represented by West Indian races, different
from those found elsewhere in North America: Mourning Dove, Short-eared
Owl, Cave Swallow, and Yellow Warbler. Other rarities found in the Keys include the only North American record of European Turtle-Dove (April 1990;
rejected by the ABA Checklist Committee), the first North American record
of Piratic Flycatcher (March 1991), and Florida's only Slaty-backed Gull (September 2002–May 2003) and Golden-crowned Sparrow (June 1990). "Florida
specialty" exotics are rather scarce in the Keys, although Monk,
Black-hooded, Mitred, Red-masked, and Blue-crowned Parakeets are found
on some of the Keys. Eurasian Collared-Doves are common, and Common
Mynas are increasing.

Access through the Keys is along US-1 (the Overseas Highway), which follows the bed of Henry Flagler's Overseas Railroad. A few abandoned
sections of the original railway bridges still remain, with the first highway, built
after the railroad, on top. The highway is 128 miles long and contains 43
bridges. The longest bridge is Seven Mile Bridge (now only 6.7 miles long) between Knight Key and Little Duck Key. While the Keys are heavily developed,
the two predominant upland habitats on the island chain—West Indian hardwood hammocks and mangrove forests—remain evident. Fortunately, public
acquisition of all remaining significant patches of West Indian hammocks in the
Keys, including the magnificent forests on Upper Key Largo, has been a state
priority since the mid-1980s. (Mangrove forests are largely protected from
development by wetland-protection laws.) In recent years, the reefs in the

Keys have experienced dramatic die-offs, paralleling similar events around the world. Increasing water temperature due to global warming is thought to be the primary cause.

The varied shapes of the keys—generally long, slender, and aligned northeast-to-southwest from Key Largo to Big Pine Key, but shorter, thicker, and aligned more north-to-south from Big Pine Key to Key West—reflect different formations of limestone outcroppings. The northern two-thirds of the Keys are composed of Key Largo limestone, while keys in the southern third consist of Miami limestone. The two formations meet at the southeast corner of Big Pine Key. For purposes of this guide, the Mainline Keys (those accessible by automobile) are divided into Upper, Middle, and Lower thirds. Except for the bulk of Upper Key Largo—the first key encountered from the mainland—much of the Upper Keys is developed, and birding spots are limited mostly to small parks. Development thins out as you travel "down" the Keys, until you reach Key West, the final Mainline Key, after about 115 driving miles. Key West is entirely developed and offers limited birding opportunities. Birders who are visiting the Upper Keys should note that motel prices at Homestead, on the mainland, are usually much cheaper than those in the Keys.

UPPER KEYS

From Homestead/Florida City, two parallel roads head south toward the Keys: US-1 and Card Sound Road, which splits off from US-1 about 0.9 mile south of SR-9336. US-1 is a wider two-lane road with passing zones, but Card Sound Road often offers better birding opportunities; this is the recommended route for birders (see map on next page). Head south to the toll booth ($1.00/vehicle) at the Card Sound Bridge (11.5). Cuban Yellow Warblers are heard frequently during spring and summer in the mangroves, particularly near the restaurant just before the toll booth. After you cross the bridge, you are on Upper Key Largo, which supports the largest stands of West Indian hardwood hammocks remaining in North America. Its immense ecological value has made Upper Key Largo a high priority for preservation by the state. Since 1993, 4,250 upland acres have been publicly acquired, at a cost of more than $73 million. Purchased sites have become **Crocodile Lake National Wildlife Refuge** (1,805 upland and 4,801 wetland and aquatic acres; *no access*) and **DAGNY JOHNSON KEY LARGO HAMMOCK BOTANICAL STATE PARK** (2,415 acres; $1.50/person; no camping; opens at 8:00 AM; *limited access*). Card Sound Road runs through mangrove forests and a series of shallow lagoons that now are part of the national wildlife refuge. At low tide, this area is used extensively by wading birds and shorebirds. West Indian hardwood hammocks represent a habitat that supports populations of several rare or endemic plants and animals, such as *Liguus* tree snails, Schaus's Swallowtail, American Crocodile, Key Largo Woodrat, and Key Largo Cotton Mouse. Because of the ecological value of these prop-

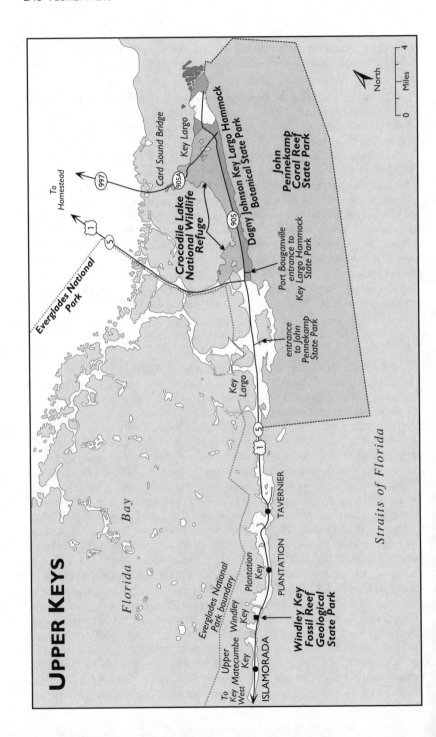

UPPER KEYS

John Pennekamp Coral Reef State Park

Dagny Johnson Key Largo Hammock Botanical State Park

Card Sound Bridge

Key Largo

Crocodile Lake National Wildlife Refuge

Port Bougainville entrance to Key Largo Hammock State Park

entrance to John Pennekamp State Park

Everglades National Park

To Homestead

Key Largo

Straits of Florida

Florida Bay

Everglades National Park boundary

Windley Key Fossil Reef Geological State Park

TAVERNIER

Plantation Key

PLANTATION

Windley Key

Upper Matecumbe Key

To West

ISLAMORADA

North

Miles

erties, much of the area is off limits at all times. Furthermore, areas are patrolled regularly by law-enforcement personnel who are looking for drug smugglers. *Under no circumstances should birders trespass into areas on Upper Key Largo that are posted off limits!*

At the junction of Card Sound Road and SR-905, continue ahead a very short distance to the dead end. This area is part of the state park and can support numbers of wading birds and shorebirds when the old roadbed beyond the barricade is flooded by tides. It can also be good a good spot for observing migrant raptors, and Short-tailed Hawks are often seen overhead during winter. Return to SR-905, turn left, and head southwest through the large West Indian hardwood hammock along both sides of the road (Crocodile Lake National Wildlife Refuge is on the right and Dagny Johnson Key Largo Hammock Botanical State Park is on the left). The Upper Keys support the greatest tree diversity in the United States. About 80 percent of the plants, such as Gumbo Limbo, Mahogany, Poisonwood, Manchineel, Strangler Fig, and Cupania, are of West Indian origin. Trees are festooned with bromeliads, orchids, and ferns. *Bird this area from the road only.* Florida Prairie Warblers are common year-round, and Black-whiskered Vireos are fairly common from mid-April through mid-August. White-crowned Pigeons are resident but are most common during spring and summer. Watch the treetops between here and Key West and you are bound to see pigeons eventually.

Access into the state park is through the failed Port Bougainville development on the left; look for the pink archway (8.6 miles from Card Sound Road or 0.4 from US-1). *Bird only from the paved roads and the marked nature trail; the remainder of the site is off limits without a permit.* (To reach other parts of the site, contact John Pennekamp Coral Reef State Park at 305-451-1202 and request a backcountry permit.) The state acquired this site after some development had been finished. In addition to the archway, there is a large fountain, roads and parking lots, and a few buildings—the latter are *off limits* for safety reasons. The roads and nature trail allow access into one of the best West Indian hardwood hammocks remaining. White-crowned Pigeons are present but wary—you will often hear their explosive flapping as they take off from within the canopy—and Florida Prairie Warblers are resident. Black-whiskered Vireos are fairly common breeders (April to August), and Mangrove Cuckoos are present but hard to find. Be alert for West Indian strays; Zenaida Dove, La Sagra's Flycatcher, Thick-billed Vireo, and Western Spindalis have been seen on Key Largo. During spring (especially) and fall, the hammocks can support large numbers of migrant landbirds.

Contacts: *Crocodile Lake National Wildlife Refuge, P.O. Box 370, Key Largo, FL 33037; 305-451-4223; <www.southeast.fws.gov/ CrocodileLake>; Dagny Johnson Key Largo Hammock Botanical State Park, P.O. Box 487, Key Largo, FL 33037; 305-451-1202; <www.floridastateparks.org/keylargohammock>.*

Black-whiskered Vireo.   Larry Manfredi

Once you depart the state park, turn left and continue southwest along SR-905. After US-1 enters on the right (0.4), look for Mile Marker 106. All directions along US-1 in the Keys are given in relation to these small green mile markers, a convenient system. The mile markers (abbreviated MM) begin at the County Courthouse in Key West and end in Florida City, for a total of 124 miles. Therefore, as you head toward Key West, the MM mileage *decreases*. Also, for mileage listed in tenths of a mile, you must *subtract the correct amount from the previous marker* (e.g., MM 82.3 is 0.7 miles beyond MM 83).

The entrance to **John Pennekamp Coral Reef State Park** (2,350 upland and 60,744 submerged acres; $4.00/vehicle; 47 campsites at $19.00/day; opens at 8:00 AM; four types of boat tours) is on the left (MM 102.4). The park, which is eight miles wide and 21 miles long, preserves the only living coral reef in the continental United States and receives more than two million visitors annually. Excellent displays, including a 30,000-gallon saltwater aquarium, introduce the coral reef environment to visitors. Glass-bottom-boat tours offer views of the reef; snorkeling equipment is also available. The reef contains more than 650 (!) species of fishes, 40 species of coral, and many other reef inhabitants. Two short nature trails offer access through mangrove forests and West Indian hardwood hammocks. Breeding birds include White-crowned Pigeon (resident), Gray Kingbird and Black-whiskered Vireo (spring and summer), and Cuban Yellow Warbler (resident). The hammock can host numerous migrant landbirds during spring. An observation tower near the marina can be good for watching migrant raptors and swallows.

Contact: *John Pennekamp Coral Reef State Park, P.O. Box 487, Key Largo, FL 33037; 305-451-1202; <www.floridastateparks.org/ pennekamp/default.cfm>.*

Windley Key Fossil Reef Geological State Park (31 acres; $1.50/person; no camping; opens at 8:00 AM, *Thursday–Monday only*) on the right (MM 85.2; just beyond the Snake Creek drawbridge) contains abandoned quarries where fossilized coral was mined as building material for Flagler's railway. The eight-foot tall quarry walls and floor show cross-sections of several coral species. The park has 1.5 miles of trails through West Indian hammocks, which contain migrant landbirds during spring and fall. Black-whiskered Vireos (spring and summer) and Florida Prairie Warblers breed here.

Contact: *Windley Key Fossil Reef Geological State Park, P.O. Box 1052, Islamorada, FL 33036; 305-664-2540; <www.floridastateparks.org/ windleykey>.*

MIDDLE KEYS

The Middle and Lower Florida Keys offer spectacular opportunities for observing raptor migration during fall. The season starts in early August, when Swallow-tailed Kites begin their journey from central Florida roosts to their South American wintering grounds. Raptor migration may last into early December, but peak numbers occur from the last week of September through mid-October. The primary sites are described below, but any spot with an unobstructed view of the sky can be rewarding. The following 14 raptors are regular migrants into or through the Keys during fall: Osprey (common), Swallow-tailed Kite (early migrant; departs before other raptors arrive), Mississippi Kite (rare), Bald Eagle (rare), Northern Harrier (uncommon), Sharp-shinned Hawk (common to abundant), Cooper's Hawk (uncommon), Red-shouldered Hawk (rare), Broad-winged Hawk (common to abundant), Short-tailed Hawk (rare), Swainson's Hawk (generally rare), American Kestrel (common to abundant), Merlin (uncommon), and Peregrine Falcon (common!). Daily totals of 10 or more species and 1,000-plus individuals have been recorded, and seasonal totals typically exceed 15,000 southbound individuals. It has been suggested that the middle Florida Keys offer the best sites in the world for observing migrant Peregrine Falcons. Additionally, more Swainson's Hawks are found here than at any other location east of the Mississippi River. (See map on next page.)

Long Key State Park (849 upland and 117 submerged acres; $3.50/person; 60 campsites at $29.00/day; opens at 8:00 AM) on the left (MM 67.5) offers a two-mile nature trail along the beach and a boardwalk through a

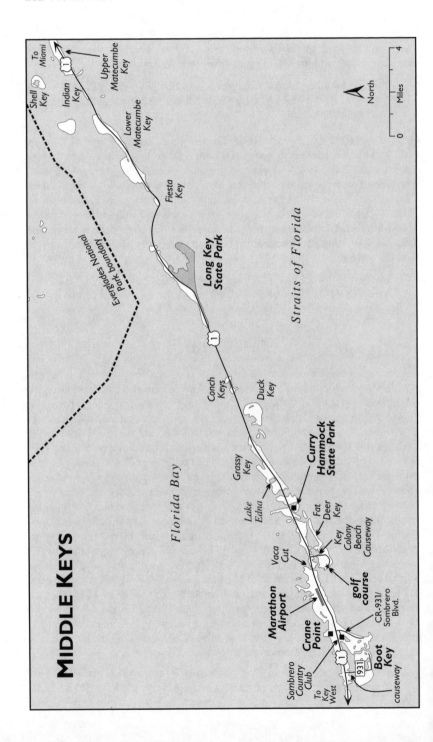

MIDDLE KEYS

mangrove-lined lagoon. The Australian-pines in the campground at the western end of the park are popular roosts for migrant raptors. The end of Long Key (MM 65.6) at the foot of the Dante Fascell bridge is also an excellent spot for watching raptor migration during fall.

Contact: *Long Key State Park, P.O. Box 776, Long Key, FL 33001; 305-664-4815; <www.floridastateparks.org/longkey>.*

Lake Edna on Grassy Key is one of the few places in the Keys that contains standing fresh water. To reach it, turn right onto Tropical Avenue (MM 57.9) to the ponds (0.2). Turn around and then turn right onto Crains Street, a partially paved road that parallels US-1. Turn right at the stop sign onto unmarked Peachtree Street (0.1) and the main ponds on the left. Continue to the end of Peachtree Street and turn left at Morton Street (0.4). At Kyle Avenue (0.3), turn left to reach the other side of the ponds. Reddish Egrets, shorebirds (including Wilson's Plovers and Black-necked Stilts), and Gray Kingbirds are reliably present during spring and summer, and many Least Terns roost here in late summer.

CURRY HAMMOCK STATE PARK (665 acres; $3.50/person; *no camping*; open 8:00 AM to sunset) has recently been established as the premier site in Florida for observing raptor migration during fall. An official hawkwatch takes place daily between 9:00 AM and 5:00 PM (8:00 AM to 4:00 PM after Daylight Saving Time ends) from 15 September to 7 November each year. The public is welcome to observe the raptor migration and banding activities. To reach the hawkwatch, turn left into the park (MM 56.1). Drive past the ranger's house to the restroom facilities building; the hawkwatch takes place from the deck of this building. More Peregrine Falcons have been counted at this site than from any other location in the world. Between 1999 and 2003, seasonal totals have averaged more than 1,950 individuals. The world record single-day total of 521 Peregrines was set on 1 October 2003—a rate of more than one Peregrine Falcon every minute of the eight-hour watch! The watch is not just about Peregrine Falcons—counts of other some other species approach or reach their national records. For more information about the Middle Keys hawkwatches, go to <www.hawkwatch.org/keysmigration>. During other seasons, Antillean Nighthawks may be found in spring and summer, and shorebirds can be found along the beach nearly year-round.

Contact: *Curry Hammock State Park, 56200 Overseas Highway, Marathon, Florida 33050; 305-289-2690; <www.floridastateparks. org/curryhammock>.*

Continue southwest on US-1 to the stoplight at MM 53.8. Turn left into Key Colony Beach Causeway. Follow the signs to the **municipal golf course**. Turn right at West Ocean Drive (0.7) and right again onto 8th Street (0.2). Check out the small golf course for Burrowing Owls, especially where the road loops around to become 7th Street, which returns you to West Ocean Drive.

Several **charter fishing boats** dock at Vaca Cut (MM 53.0), and their half-day trips may be worthwhile for pelagic birds if the boats reach deep water. Talk to the captains first to see which boats head to the Gulf Stream, beyond the edge of the continental shelf (about 10 miles out).

MARATHON AIRPORT on the right (MM 52.5-51.0) offers a reliable spot for Antillean Nighthawks around dusk from late April through mid-August. During winter, check the wires (especially toward the far end) for Western Kingbirds and Scissor-tailed Flycatchers. At MM 51.0, between the Disabled American Veterans building and the large orange windsock, is a retention pond. When it contains water, the pond may have ducks, wading birds, and shorebirds. Included among these may be species that otherwise are difficult to find in the Keys, such as Glossy Ibis, American Golden-Plover, Whimbrel, and Solitary, White-rumped, Pectoral, and Buff-breasted Sandpipers. Late August through September tends to be the most productive period.

Crane Point (63 acres; $5.00/person; opens at 9:00 AM Monday–Saturday, noon on Sunday) is a private facility that houses the Museum of Natural History and contains several miles of nature trails through West Indian hammocks. It is on the right, across from CR-931 (MM 50.5). A walk along the trails may produce Black-whiskered Vireos (spring and summer), migrant landbirds (spring or fall), and possibly Mangrove Cuckoos.

Contact: *Crane Point, 5550 Overseas Highway, Marathon, FL 33050; 305-743-9100; <www.cranepoint.org>.*

A short side trip to view Burrowing Owls is possible here by returning across US-1 from Crane Point and going south on CR-931 (Sombrero Boulevard). At Sombrero Beach Boulevard (0.1), turn right to travel the road around the Sombrero Country Club, where Burrowing Owls are frequently seen on the golf course. Return to U S-1 and turn left.

At MM 48.5, turn right to reach the **Marathon Government Center** at 2798 Overseas Highway. Roseate and Least Terns nest on the office roof from late April through July, and adults may be seen flying to or from the colony throughout the day. *Due to weekday traffic around the center, it is best to visit on weekends or holidays.*

Across the CR-931 drawbridge (MM 48.1) is **BOOT KEY**, one of the best raptor migration roosting sites in North America during fall (though not as good as Curry Hammock State Park). *Note that the entire key is private property, so bird only from the road.* Boot Key can be excellent during early mornings (until about 10 AM) and late afternoons (between 4:00 and 6:00 PM), when low-flying raptors leave or return to roosts. An evening visit to Boot Key in early October could yield sightings of up to 50 American Kestrels, 20 Merlins, and 10 Peregrine Falcons, which perch on the large cell tower just north of the bridge to Boot Key. On days with high winds, many raptors mill about over Boot Key before making the seven-mile overwater crossing to the Lower Keys. The best place on the island for raptor-watching is about 0.9 mile south of the bridge; bring along a lawn chair. Boot Key may also be birded *from the road* for migrant landbirds; one good spot is the patch of upland vegetation on the west side of the road just south of the bridge. The mangrove forest at the east end of the road can be good for Mangrove Cuckoos. A Key West Quail-Dove remained here for several months in 1987, and a Thick-billed Vireo was found in October 2004.

LOWER KEYS

Beyond the Seven Mile Bridge the traffic gets a little lighter and the birding better. Any of the numerous beaches host wading birds, shorebirds, and larids year-round. Magnificent Frigatebirds are usually seen overhead, especially during spring and summer. The first pair of keys beyond the long bridge (Little Duck and Missouri), and the bridges connecting them, can be good for migrant raptors during fall. Hawks crossing from Boot Key are often much lower and thus easier to see when they reach these keys (see map on next page).

After crossing the Missouri/Ohio channel onto **OHIO KEY** (also called Sunshine Key; MM 38.9), look to the left opposite the campground. This intertidal lagoon, now part of National Key Deer Refuge (see below), is a critical shorebird staging area in the Keys. Several Piping Plovers winter here, the only reliable site in the Mainline Keys for this species. The key is also a good spot for watching migrant raptors during fall.

Bahía Honda State Park (491 acres; $4.00/vehicle; 80 campsites at $19.00/day; opens at 8:00 AM) on both sides of the road (MM 36.8) has wading birds and shorebirds. During fall, raptor migration can be impressive, with large numbers of Peregrine Falcons. Silver Palm Nature Trail at the far eastern picnic area may have migrant landbirds during spring and fall. A variety of warblers winters in and around the campgrounds.

Contact: *Bahía Honda State Park, 36850 Overseas Highway, Big Pine Key, FL 33043; 305-872-2353; <www.floridastateparks.org/bahiahonda>.*

Big Pine Key has a mix of habitats such as West Indian hardwood hammocks, pinelands, mangrove forests, mudflats, and beaches. It is one of the few keys with a permanent source of fresh water. Around dusk and dawn, Antillean Nighthawks may be heard over much of the island during spring and summer. Upon entering the key, turn left onto Long Beach Road (MM 32.9), the first paved road to the left, past a private campground. After the road curves to the right (0.4), park at a gated trail on the left. Beyond the gate, bear

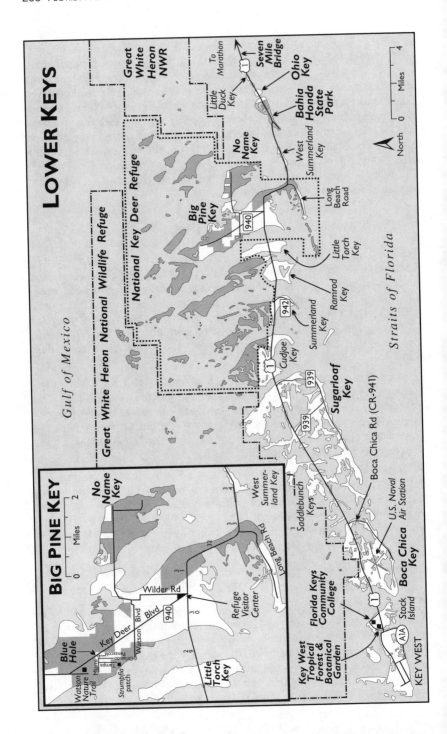

LOWER KEYS

Gulf of Mexico

Great White Heron National Wildlife Refuge

National Key Deer Refuge

Great White Heron NWR

To Marathon

Seven Mile Bridge

Ohio Key

Bahia Honda State Park

Little Duck Key

No Name Key

West Summerland Key

Big Pine Key

940

Long Beach Road

Little Torch Key

Ramrod Key

942

Summerland Key

Cudjoe Key

1

Straits of Florida

939

Sugarloaf Key

Boca Chica Rd (CR-941)

Saddlebunch Keys

939

U.S. Naval Air Station

Boca Chica Key

North

0   Miles   4

BIG PINE KEY

No Name Key

West Summer-land Key

0   Miles   2

Blue Hole

Watson Nature Trail

Orlando Pensacola
Miami
Tampa

Strumpfia patch

Key Deer Blvd

Watson Blvd

940

Refuge Visitor Center

Wilder Rd

Long Beach Rd

Little Torch Key

Key West Tropical Forest & Botanical Garden

Florida Keys Community College

Stock Island

A1A

1

KEY WEST

left onto a berm road that extends to the shore. Most of the land here is part of the **NATIONAL KEY DEER REFUGE** (8,542 acres; no fee; no camping; open daylight hours). The shoreline should have wading birds and shorebirds (at low tide). White-crowned Pigeons are resident, and Mangrove Cuckoos and Black-whiskered Vireos breed here (spring and summer). Watch overhead for migrant raptors during fall.

Other productive areas in the refuge can be reached by returning to US-1 and continuing west. At CR-940 (Key Deer Boulevard; MM 30.5), turn right. Watch the roadsides for Key Deer, a tiny, endemic race of the White-tailed Deer, about the size of a very large dog. The current population numbers 700–800 deer, with about 600 on Big Pine and No Name Keys, and 100–200 others elsewhere in the Lower Keys. *Do not feed the deer; it is illegal* because it encourages the deer to lose their fear of humans. Road kills account for 70 percent of Key Deer mortality, so drive carefully on Big Pine and No Name Keys.

The refuge visitor center is located in the Big Pine Shopping Plaza just north of US-1 between Key Deer Boulevard and Wilder Road. To reach the refuge headquarters (closed to the public) from US-1, head northwest on Key Deer Boulevard to Watson Boulevard (1.7). Turn left to Narcissus Avenue and the gate to the headquarters gate (0.6). Antillean Nighthawks are found here from late April through August. Turn around and head back east. Cross Key Deer Boulevard and continue to the stop sign at the T-intersection. Turn left, cross over a hump-backed bridge, then cross a larger bridge onto **No Name Key** (1.4). Much of No Name Key is part of the refuge and is open to foot traffic. Past the bridge (1.0), a sand road to the right (Paradise Drive) leads through a hardwood hammock that can be good for Mangrove Cuckoos and other landbirds. At the end of the pavement (0.4), a trail leads south for several hundred feet along the beach berm. This area also has Mangrove Cuckoos (mainly spring and summer) and a variety of warblers during winter.

Return to Key Deer Boulevard on Big Pine Key and turn right to **Blue Hole** on the left (1.2). An old quarry now filled with fresh water (rare in the Keys), Blue Hole supports several alligators and is important to the survival of Key Deer. Just beyond Blue Hole is 3,800-foot-long **Watson Nature Trail** (0.3). From early October through late November, kettles of vultures and raptors form in the morning around Blue Hole and soar over the pinelands. Broad-winged Hawks can be common, and Swainson's and Short-tailed Hawks are found regularly.

Turn around and turn right onto Higgs Lane (immediately south of Blue Hole), and quickly turn right onto Pensacola Road. At the stop sign, turn right onto Orlando Road, which soon curves left and becomes Miami Boulevard. Continue a short distance to Tampa Road and turn left to the end of the pavement (0.3). A short distance beyond, the road emerges from pinelands into a shrubby marsh known as the *Strumpfia* patch, named for a rare Bahamian shrub. Antillean Nighthawks (spring and summer) have bred here, and the marsh occasionally attracts local rarities such as Glossy Ibis and Wilson's Snipe (winter). Watch for raptors during fall migration.

Contact: *National Key Deer Refuge, 28950 Watson Boulevard, Big Pine Key, FL 33043-2239; 305-872-2239; <http://nationalkeydeer.fws.gov>.*

On the north side of US-1 between Marathon and Key West are dozens of keys that are part of **Great White Heron National Wildlife Refuge** (2,087 land acres; no fee). The refuge stretches from Marathon to Key West and covers an area of eight miles long and 40 miles wide. **Key West National Wildlife Refuge** (2,019 land acres; no fee) starts near Key West and stretches west through the Marquesas Keys. This refuge extends 15 by 25 miles in area. Neither refuge is accessible except by private boat.

On **Summerland Key** (MM 25.1), turn left onto East Shore Drive (the first road) to a salt pond on the right where wading birds can be found. At Margaret Street (0.1), turn right to Katherine Street (0.1). Turn left to a freshwater pond on the left. Watch for puddle ducks(during winter), Least Bittern, and White-crowned Pigeon.

On **Sugarloaf Key** turn left onto the western part of CR-939 opposite the Sugarloaf Lodge (MM 17.1). At the end of the road (2.6), turn right and go over the bridge to Saddlebunch Key. A well-known site for Mangrove Cuckoos is between the bridge and the end of the paved road (0.9). You can walk down the sand road past the gate, but only the first few hundred yards are good cuckoo habitat. Florida Prairie Warblers are common breeders, with lesser numbers of Cuban Yellow Warblers. Sugarloaf Key is also famous for its saltmarsh mosquitoes, so be sure to bring along a strong insect repellent. *Because this is one of the most visited sites for Mangrove Cuckoo, tapes should be used here only sparingly, if at all.*

From US-1 on Big Coppitt Key (MM 10.7), turn left onto Boca Chica Road (CR-941) to explore the road to **Boca Chica Key Beach** (no facilities; no fee; no camping). Reddish Egrets and Roseate Spoonbills are regular here, as are shorebirds during migration and winter. Watch for falcons and others raptors during fall migration. During spring and summer, the mangroves along the road harbor Mangrove Cuckoos and Black-whiskered Vireos; the bridges are convenient stopping places. At the end of the road, park (lock your car) and walk 0.5 mile to a salt pond that is excellent for waders, shorebirds, and terns through early March. *Note that birders have sometimes been harassed for "spying" on the planes at the adjacent Boca Chica Naval Air Station.*

On **Stock Island**, go past the golf course and turn right onto College Road, the last road before the bridge to Key West (MM 4.2). The **Key West Tropical Forest and Botanical Garden** (15 acres; no fee—ignore the requested donation; no camping; open 10:00 AM–4:00 PM but *closed Wednesdays and the month of September*) is on the right (0.2). The garden is a good spot for White-crowned Pigeons (year-round) and Black-whiskered Vireos

Gray Kingbird, adult.

Lyn S. Atherton

(spring and summer). During spring and fall migration, landbirds such as thrushes and warblers can be found. (If the park is closed, you may bird around the parking lot.) In March, check the trees and utility poles for Gray Kingbird and Scissor-tailed Flycatcher.

Contact: *Key West Tropical Forest and Botanical Garden, 5210 College Road, Key West, FL 305-296-1504; <www.keywestbotanicalgarden.org>.*

Continue east on College Road to **Florida Keys Community College** on the left (1.1), where Antillean Nighthawks may be heard around dusk during spring and summer.

KEY WEST

Over the short bridge at Stock Island is Key West, the southernmost city in the U.S. and the capital of the "Conch (pronounced *konk*) Republic". Just four miles long and two miles wide, the place is packed with historic homes and tourists. The atmosphere in Key West is decidedly laid-back. A little-known ornithological feature of the island is its well-established (but not yet countable) population of Red Junglefowl (i.e., chickens) that reportedly have been present since the early 1800s. The birds are found throughout quieter parts of the island and number about 2,000 individuals. A controversial

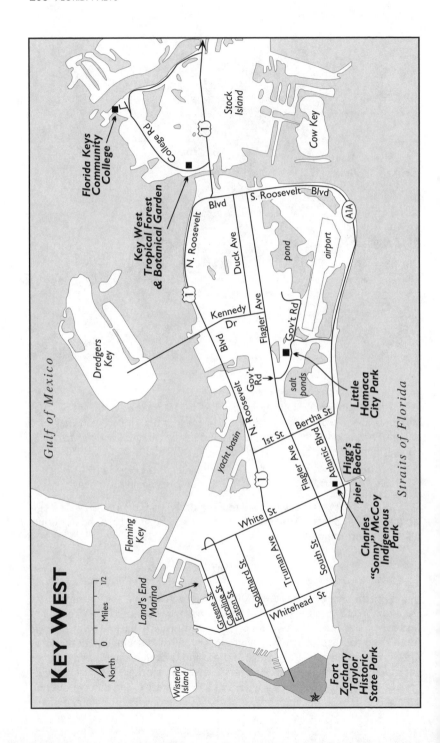

KEY WEST

North

0   Miles   1/2

Gulf of Mexico

Fleming Key

Wisteria Island

Dredgers Key

Land's End Marina

yacht basin

Greene St
Caroline St
Eaton St
Southard St
White St
Truman Ave
South St
Whitehead St

Flagler Ave

Atlantic Blvd

1st St

Bertha St

N. Roosevelt Blvd

Gov't Rd

Flagler Ave

Kennedy Dr

Blvd

N. Roosevelt Blvd

Duck Ave

S. Roosevelt Blvd

College Rd

Stock Island

Cow Key

airport

pond

salt ponds

Gov't Rd

A1A

Straits of Florida

Florida Keys Community College

Key West Tropical Forest & Botanical Garden

Little Hamaca City Park

Charles "Sonny" McCoy Indigenous Park

Higg's pier Beach

Fort Zachary Taylor Historic State Park

program to reduce the population by about half is underway. See <www. keywestchickens.com> for more information—as well as for chicken jokes and recipes!

Upon entering Key West, turn left onto SR-A1A (S. Roosevelt Boulevard) to Duck Avenue (0.15). Turn right and check the powerlines during winter for Western Kingbirds and Scissor-tailed Flycatchers. At the T-intersection with Glynn Archer Drive (traffic light; 1.0), turn left. At Flagler Avenue (0.1), turn right to Government Road (0.5), then turn left into **Little Hamaca City Park** (no fee; no camping). A series of mangrove-fringed pools—known locally as the Salt Ponds—on the right is good for wading birds year-round, shorebirds during migration and winter, and waterfowl during winter. During spring and summer, continue along the back side of Key West International Airport to search for Antillean Nighthawks. Shortly after the road curves left is a small parking lot (0.7). A nature trail and a boardwalk here pass through low hammock and mangrove habitats, good for migrant and wintering warblers and other landbirds as well as nesting White-crowned Pigeons. This park may be the last place in Key West that regularly has Mangrove Cuckoos. Return to Flagler Avenue and continue west to Bertha Street (0.4). Turn left to Atlantic Boulevard (0.3) then turn right. At White Street (0.5), an old **pier** extends into the ocean; check this for larids.

Just before White Street is **CHARLES "SONNY" McCOY INDIGENOUS PARK** (10 acres; no fee; no camping; open 7:00 AM–4:00 PM Monday–Friday, *closed weekends*) on the right. The park gates are closed during weekends, but the park can still be accessed during that time via the wildlife rehabilitation center within the park; the center's gate is about 50 yards on the left beyond the main gate. The park offers good birding year-round, and it can be excellent during fall for migrant landbirds; as many as 24 warbler species have been seen here on peak days. A Western Spindalis spent the winter of 2004–2005. The park is also a good spot for some of Key West's junglefowl.

> **Contact:** Charles "Sonny" McCoy Indigenous Park, 1801 White Street, Key West, FL 33045; 305-292-8157 or 305-292-8190.

Across the street is **Higg's Beach** (no fee; no camping), a good spot for larids; Florida's first Slaty-backed Gull spent eight months here during winter 2002–2003. Watch also for Common Mynas, which are increasing their range and numbers on Key West (and elsewhere in the Keys).

FORT ZACHARY TAYLOR HISTORIC STATE PARK (87 acres; $4.00/vehicle; no camping; opens at 8:00 AM) is worth a visit, especially during spring. Built during 1845–1866 as part of Florida's coastal defense system, it has armaments and other historic artifacts. The site, at the southwest corner of the island, is reached from White Street by turning west onto Southard Street to the entrance. In addition to common shorebirds, the park is a good place to see Roseate Terns offshore; they breed on nearby rooftops. One or two West Indian Short-eared Owls are found every spring. During migration—primarily during spring—the hammocks on the fort side of the parking lot can be excellent for landbirds, especially warblers. Swallows forage over the field, and Antillean Nighthawks are regular during spring and summer.

Contact: *Fort Zachary Taylor Historic State Park, P.O. Box 6560, Key West, FL 33041; 305-292-6713; <http://www.floridastateparks.org/forttaylor>.*

DRY TORTUGAS NATIONAL PARK

Perhaps the pinnacle of Florida birding is a spring visit to **DRY TORTUGAS NATIONAL PARK** (70 upland acres, 64,600 marine acres; $5.00/person; 11 campsites at $3.00/day; fort open during daylight hours). The park consists of five small keys (formerly seven; three of the keys have merged) in the Florida Straits about 70 miles west of Key West. Two of the keys are open to the public year-round but are accessible only by private boat or seaplane. Because there is no naturally occurring fresh water on the islands, and because insects and other prey are scarce, the Dry Tortugas support few landbirds during summer and winter. But during spring migration, the keys can be home to a dazzling assortment of migrant landbirds. (Fall migration may be equally impressive, but the park is seldom birded during that season.) Additionally, many West Indian or Tropical American species have strayed to the Dry Tortugas, including Ruddy Quail-Dove, White-tipped Dove (twice), Piratic Flycatcher, Bahama Swallow, Bahama Mockingbird, Thick-billed Vireo, Western Spindalis, Yellow-faced Grassquit, and Shiny Cowbird (annual). A Red-legged Honeycreeper found in the park during spring 2003 was probably a vagrant from Cuba. In addition to the Neotropical migrants and the vagrants, seabirds make the Tortugas a birding magnet. Besides the islands' breeding species (Magnificent Frigatebird, Masked Booby, Sooty Tern, and Brown Noddy), rarities such as White-tailed Tropicbird, Brown and Red-footed Boobies, and Black Noddy occur annually or nearly so, although the tropicbird has become scarce recently. Roseate Terns are fairly common during spring and summer but no longer breed in the park. And, as Jim Lane wrote in the first edition of this guide, "one can spend hours and hours just watching the dozens of frigatebirds drifting slowly back and forth over the fort."

GARDEN KEY is the arrival point for all visitors to the Tortugas. It is only 16 acres in size, but is the Tortugas' second-largest key. Most of the key is contained inside the remains of massive Fort Jefferson, begun in 1846 but never completed. More than 16 million bricks went into the fort's construction, with its three-storied walls as much as eight feet thick. The 19th-century architecture of the fort is truly impressive. From the Civil War to

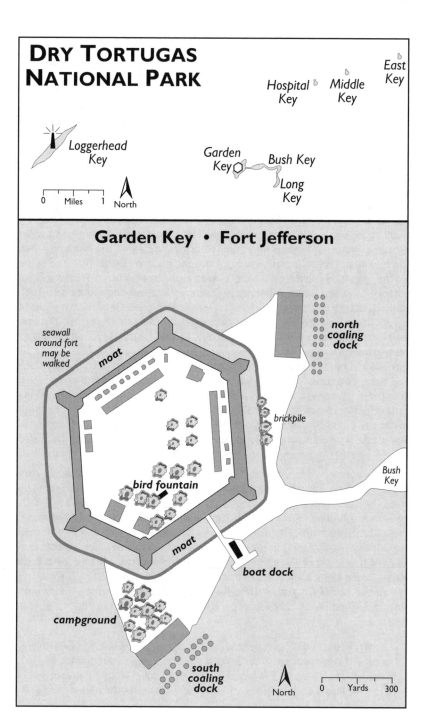

DRY TORTUGAS NATIONAL PARK

Hospital Key

Middle Key

East Key

Loggerhead Key

Garden Key

Bush Key

Long Key

0 Miles 1 North

Garden Key • Fort Jefferson

seawall around fort may be walked

moat

north coaling dock

brickpile

Bush Key

bird fountain

moat

boat dock

campground

south coaling dock

North

0 Yards 300

1874, the fort was used as a Federal prison. Its most famous prisoner was Dr. Samuel Mudd, who provided aid to John Wilkes Booth after Booth assassinated President Lincoln (Mudd had no knowledge of the murder, but was convicted as an accomplice nonetheless). Dr. Mudd was later pardoned after fighting a yellow fever epidemic that swept through the fort in 1867. Today, rooms in the fort contain living quarters for the park rangers, and a small interpretive center and store (these rooms are air conditioned). Most of the fort is accessible to birders during daylight hours—the top provides views of the keys and coral reefs—but is closed at night.

Inside Fort Jefferson is a large expanse of lawn with numerous trees, palms, cactuses, and shrubs, mostly of West Indian origin. Check all the vegetation for raptors, landbirds, and other migrants. The bird fountain installed inside a small copse to your left as you enter the fort is an excellent place to observe warblers and other birds as they come to drink and bathe. The fountain is also the spot to observe a famous Tortugas spectacle: Cattle Egrets that land at the Tortugas quickly discover that insects are scarce, so they turn to stalking small passerines at the water fountain. (Or the egrets visit the fountain to soak their avian prey to aid in swallowing.) Despite this improvisation, many Cattle Egrets that reach the Tortugas die of starvation. Outside the fort to the east are the remains of the north coaling docks. Brown Noddies rest on the pilings during the day. The noddies should be searched carefully because one or more Black Noddies may perch here, too. Between the north coaling dock and the fort entrance is a brickpile overgrown with shrubs and trees. This area often harbors thrushes, warblers, and other thicket-loving birds. West of the fort entrance is the small, primitive campground shaded by coconut palms and oaks. You must provide your own food and water, but restrooms, picnic tables, and cooking grills are provided. The trees and palms here also should be searched carefully for migrant landbirds.

Now connected to Garden Key by a narrow isthmus are **Bush and Long Keys**, which are off-limits from 1 March to 1 October to protect the tern and frigatebird colonies. An estimated 25,000 pairs of Sooty Terns and 2,000 pairs of Brown Noddies nest on Bush Key, and about 100 pairs of Magnificent Frigatebirds nest on Long Key. The Tortugas represents the only North American breeding ground for these species. Two to five miles northeast of Garden Key are three tiny sandbars known as **Hospital, Middle, and East Keys**. Since 1984, a few pairs of Masked Boobies have nested annually in late winter and early spring on Hospital Key, their only breeding colony in the continental United States. Middle Key washes over every summer but reappears during fall.

The last island in the Tortugas chain is the largest. **LOGGERHEAD KEY**, about three miles west of Garden Key, is conspicuous for its tall U.S. Coast Guard lighthouse. The key previously was covered by a dense forest of Australian-pines, but these were cut down and burned in the mid-1990s to en-

View of the Garden Key parade grounds from atop Fort Jefferson. Bill Pranty

courage the growth of native vegetation. The migrant landbirds that were previously attracted to the "pines"—and the raptors subsequently attracted to the migrants—are less prevalent now but still occur. The burned debris and subsequent regrowth of cactuses and agaves make parts of Loggerhead Key difficult to traverse.

> **Contact**: *Everglades and Dry Tortugas National Parks, 40001 State Road 9336, Homestead, Florida 33034-6733; 305-242-7700; <www.nps.gov/drto/index.htm>.*

As mentioned above, there are two ways of getting to the Tortugas: boat and seaplane. The seaplane flight offers impressive views of coral reefs, a shipwreck, the Marquesas Keys, and the Tortugas, but birders are restricted to Garden Key. Nesting Masked Boobies on Hospital Key can at best be seen very distantly with a high-powered telescope, as can buoy-roosting Brown Boobies and Roseate Terns. Birds on Loggerhead Key are completely inaccessible. The standard seaplane tour is brief: 40 minutes each way for the flight, with a bit more than two hours at the fort. Extended visits of any duration are possible, but the fee is almost doubled because the plane must make two round-trip flights. The standard tour costs about $189; a full-day tour (with about 6 hours on land) costs $325; and an extended visit (with a future scheduled pick-up) costs $329.

> **Contact:** *Seaplanes of Key West, Key West International Airport, 3471 South Roosevelt Boulevard, Key West, FL 33040; 1-800-950-2359; <www.seaplanesofkeywest.com>.*

Birders who choose a boat trip to the Tortugas have an additional choice to make: a single-day trip or an extended three-day trip as part of a guided birding tour. Single-day boat trips are offered by two companies, and both run similar schedules: a Key West departure at 8:00 AM, followed by about four hours at Fort Jefferson, then a return to Key West at 5:00 or 5:30 PM. Garden Key is the only key visited, and the boat does not visit the buoys and channel markers in the park for boobies and terns. But the trips out and back, effectively daytime pelagic trips, usually produce Audubon's Shearwaters and Bridled Terns in fair to good numbers. Several other species are possible, such as Masked and Brown Boobies, Band-rumped Storm-Petrels, Red and Red-necked Phalaropes, and Pomarine and Parasitic Jaegers . Single-day trips cost $110 (via the *Fast Cat II*) or $134 (via the *Yankee Freedom II*). If you wish to camp at Fort Jefferson, the *Yankee Freedom* offers a rate of $149 for the round-trip.

Contact: *Sunny Days Catamarans, 1-800-236-7937;*
<www.sunnydayskeywest.com/fastcat.htm>.
Yankee Freedom, 1-800-634-0939; <www.yankeefreedom.com>.

Birders who wish to visit the Tortugas as part of a three-day birding tour may choose among several companies that feature trips to the park in April and May. These extended trips offer several advantages over single-day seaplane or boat trips, but are considerably more expensive. Some trips depart Key West at midnight and arrive at dawn, while others leave at dawn and arrive around noon. The trips leave the Tortugas during the third morning and return to Key West in the afternoon. Most trips offer varied sleeping options: birders may sleep in (often tiny) bunks below deck, in sleeping bags on deck (the rainy season usually doesn't begin until mid-May), or, space providing, at the Garden Key campground.

The main advantage that three-day tours have over seaplane or single-day boat trips is access to the other Tortugas islands. The boat will visit Loggerhead Key for a few hours (often on multiple days), and will cruise the park's boundary to observe Brown Boobies and Roseate Terns roosting on the buoys and channel markers. One evening, the boat will anchor off Hospital Key to watch the Masked Boobies fly in to roost. Boat tours also supply a dinghy or Zodiac used for close-up views of Bush and Long Keys. These small boats offer the closest views possible of the nesting Magnificent Frigatebirds, Sooty Terns, and Brown Noddies, together with the opportunity to search for a Red-footed Booby or Black Noddy roosting on Bush Key. Because food is not available at the Tortugas, the boat will supply all of your meals. Three-day birding trips to the Tortugas cost at least $700. Many companies also provide an optional South Florida/Keys birding extension tour before or after the Tortugas trip for an additional fee.

FLORIDA BIRDS OF PARTICULAR INTEREST

L isted below are species likely to be of interest to birders visiting Florida. Because Florida often represents the first eastern state visited by birders, these accounts include dozens of species not normally considered Florida specialties (e.g., Pacific Loon, White-faced Ibis, Long-billed Murrelet, Sprague's Pipit, and House Finch). But European birders making their first visit to North America may be as interested in seeing Blue Jays as they are in finding Florida Scrub-Jays! All of the state's regular breeding or wintering species are included in this section. Also found here are all West Indian species that have strayed to Florida, many other vagrants, and several other species with interesting patterns of occurrence. Wholly migratory species, which are far less predictable in their appearance, are represented less thoroughly.

Also included here are accounts of many "non-countable" exotics not on the official Florida bird list maintained by the Florida Ornithological Society Records Committee (FOSRC). Some of these species (e.g., Purple Swamphen and Common Myna) number in the hundreds of individuals and are increasing in range, and might eventually be added to the state list once the necessary studies are conducted and the results published. Many other non-countable exotics (e.g., several parakeets, Hill Myna, various munias) are included because they are breeding in Florida at the present time, although populations of most are small and/or do not appear to be expanding. Finally, accounts are included for one native species recently removed from the FOSRC list and the ABA Checklist (Loggerhead Kingbird), and for four extirpated exotics (Black Francolin, Ringed Turtle-Dove, Blue-gray Tanager, and Java Sparrow) to alert birders that these species no longer occur in Florida (despite statements to the contrary that may be found in other sources).

B etween 2000 and 2002, major field guides were authored by David Sibley (2000) and Kenn Kaufman (2000), and two other guides were revised, those by the National Geographic Society (2002) and the late Roger Tory Peterson (2002). These guides differ in their inclusion of various species, both native and exotic, that occur in Florida. Where pertinent, differences among these four North American field guides are discussed. For West Indian species that stray to Florida, two additional guides—*A Guide to the Birds of the West Indies* by Herbert Raffaele et al. (1998) and *Birds of Cuba* by Orlando Garrido and Arturo Kirkconnell (2000)—may be cited. *Birds of the West Indies* by the late Bond...James Bond (1990) does not include color illustrations for several species, and its taxonomy is out-of-date; it is now of limited use. The superb *Guide to the Birds of Mexico and Northern Central America* by Steve Howell and Sophie Webb (1995) is helpful with Mexican species that may stray to the Gulf coast of Florida (e.g., Greater Flamingo, White-tipped Dove, Tropical Kingbird, Bananaquit, Red-legged Honeycreeper).

The number of accounts featured in this chapter of *A Birder's Guide to Florida* decreased from 147 in the first edition to 144 in the second edition and 141 in the third edition. The number of accounts increased to 212 in the fourth edition, and increased again in this fifth edition to 396, with more than 425 species discussed. Material contained in this chapter is based on information published in recent ornithological and birding publications. Literature sources for these accounts are contained in *The Birdlife of Florida* (Stevenson and Anderson 1994), *Florida Bird Species: An Annotated List* (Robertson and Woolfenden 1992), *The Atlas of the Breeding Birds of Florida* (Kale et al. 1992 and <www.wildflorida.org/bba>), *The Birds of Escambia, Santa Rosa, and Okaloosa counties, Florida* (Duncan and Duncan 2000), *The Important Bird Areas of Florida, 2000–2002* (Pranty 2002 and <www.audubon.org/bird/iba/florida>), various papers published in *Florida Field Naturalist*, *North American Birds* and its predecessors, other journals, and the Florida Ornithological Society's Field Observations Committee seasonal bird reports published quarterly in *Florida Field Naturalist*. Generally, citations are included in the following accounts only for papers that were published after the publication of Robertson and Woolfenden (1992) and Stevenson and Anderson (1994).

Following a distinction increasingly observed in the birding world, the term *report* is used here for any observation, while only those reports that are supported by archived verifiable evidence (i.e., a specimen, photograph, or audio or video tape) are called *records*. The term "spring and summer resident" denotes birds such as Chimney Swift, Common Nighthawk, and Prothonotary Warbler that migrate northward to breed in Florida, then return southward to winter in the Tropics, while the term "permanent resident" implies a breeding bird that remains year-round. The "Mainline Keys" refer to those keys between Key Largo and Key West that are traversed by US-1. Taxonomic sequence follows the seventh edition of the *American Ornithologists' Union Check-list of North American Birds* (AOU 1998), and supplements through the 46th supplement in the July 2005 edition of the *Auk*. The complete AOU bird list in current taxonomic order is available online at <www.aou.org/aou/checklist/index.php3>.

Waterfowl—Only four species of native waterfowl (Black-bellied and Fulvous Whistling-Ducks, Mottled Duck, and Wood Duck) breed regularly in

Florida (several exotic species also are regular breeders). But an additional 22 species winter annually in the state (a few of these breed irregularly), and 14 others occur less frequently. St. Marks National Wildlife Refuge is probably the best site in the state to observe wintering waterfowl, but Merritt Island National Wildlife Refuge and numerous other sites can also be excellent. A few species of migratory ducks return to Florida in August (Blue-winged Teal is typically the first arrival). But most waterfowl do not arrive until November, and most individuals depart in February or March. In addition to those listed below in separate accounts, the following species are regular during winter: **Snow Goose** (rare to uncommon; mostly in the Panhandle; the two morphs occur about equally), **Green-winged Teal** (uncommon to common throughout; there are two records of the Eurasian subspecies), **American Black Duck** (uncommon; mostly at St. Marks; *identify with care* in the peninsula), **Northern Pintail** (local; mostly at St. Marks or Merritt Island), **Northern Shoveler** (fairly common throughout), **Gadwall** (local; most common in the Panhandle), **American Wigeon** (fairly common throughout), **Canvasback** (local; mostly coastal), **Redhead** (local; mostly coastal), **Ring-necked Duck** (common throughout), **Black Scoter** (rare to locally common; mostly along the Panhandle and northern peninsular coasts), **Surf Scoter** (rare to uncommon; mostly along the Panhandle and northern peninsular coasts), **White-winged Scoter** (the rarest of the scoters in Florida; mostly along the Panhandle and northern peninsular coasts), **Common Goldeneye** (uncommon; mostly along the Panhandle coast), **Bufflehead** (mostly coastal; common in the Panhandle, uncommon south through the central peninsula), and **Ruddy Duck** (rare to locally common throughout). One or more **Cinnamon Teal** and **Eurasian Wigeons** are usually reported in Florida each year.

Black-bellied Whistling-Duck—An uncommon to locally abundant *and increasing* permanent resident of the peninsula. A small flock discovered near Sarasota in the early 1980s is believed to have dispersed from the Yucatán Peninsula. Since that time, Black-bellied Whistling-Ducks have undergone a dramatic population increase and range expansion. The population in Sarasota currently exceeds 700 individuals, with more than 100 others at Gainesville, and dozens of birds elsewhere in the central peninsula. A few have been seen in the Panhandle. As of 2005, the species seemed poised to colonize eastern Georgia. Further increases in Florida can be expected, and birds may be seen virtually anywhere in the state. A few Black-bellied Whistling-Ducks in the southeastern peninsula and the western Panhandle may be escapees or feral individuals.

Fulvous Whistling-Duck—An uncommon to common, *extremely local and often unpredictable* permanent resident of freshwater marshes and flooded farmlands in central and southern Florida. Rare and irregular in the Panhandle and in the Keys. Reliable sites from spring through fall include Emeralda Marsh Conservation Area, Lake Apopka Restoration Area, and the Everglades Agricultural Area. *Note that the chicks of Fulvous Whistling-Ducks have been misidenti-fied in Florida as female Masked Ducks.*

Cackling Goose (*Branta hutchinsii*)—Formerly considered a subspecies of Canada Goose, but upgraded to species status by the AOU (2004). Status currently under FOSRC review; apparently a casual winter resident from far-ther west. There seem to be only two verifiable records—both of Richard-son's Goose (*B. h. hutchinsii*)—three near St. Marks in January 1957 and two north of Sebastian in January 2003.

Canada Goose—Formerly an abundant winter resident in the St. Marks area but now rare or irregular. However, in the late 1960s, biologists of the former Florida Game and Fresh Water Fish Commission began releasing birds of the non-migratory subspecies *Branta canadensis maxima* (the Giant Canada Goose) into the state, predominantly in the Tallahassee area. Additional birds have been released by others, and Canada Geese have bred as far south as Hialeah Race Track at Miami. It is essentially impossible to distinguish wild wintering Canada Geese from permanent resident feral birds; the latter are locally common and presumably account for the vast majority of birds that now occur in Florida.

Muscovy Duck—Exotic, native from northern Mexico to South Amer-ica. An uncommon to locally abundant feral permanent resident of residential areas throughout, least common in the Panhandle, northern peninsula, and the Keys. Considered an established, countable exotic in the state by Robert-son and Woolfenden (1992) and the FOSRC (Bowman 2000). Muscovy Ducks in Florida bear little resemblance to their wild Mexican counterparts, ranging from all-white to all-black, and all combinations in between.

Wood Duck—A fairly common permanent resident of the mainland, lo-cal in the extreme southern peninsula and rare in the Keys. Seen most often in flight around dusk and dawn, as it travels between roosting and foraging areas. Some individuals in city parks may be semi-feral.

Mallard—An uncommon to fairly common winter resident of the Pan-handle and extreme northern peninsula, rare in the remainder of the penin-sula, and very rare in the Keys. Feral Mallards are uncommon to common, well-established permanent residents in most of the mainland but are rare in the Keys. Wild Mallards typically are found in freshwater habitats, while feral birds are often found in salt or brackish water. Feral Mallards often exhibit bi-zarre plumage combinations caused by inbreeding, or may appear as all-white ducks with orange bills and legs (i.e., Pekin Ducks).

Mottled Duck—An uncommon to common permanent resident of marshes, lakes, and other freshwater habitats in the peninsula from about Gainesville south to about Lake Okeechobee. Local in brackish bays and estu-aries. Johnson et al. (1991) estimated that the statewide population was stable at 14,000 pairs. However, hybridization with feral Mallards is a serious threat; Moorman and Gray (1993) reported that at least five percent of all Mottled

Ducks in Florida exhibited Mallard plumage characteristics. If action to eliminate feral Mallards is not undertaken soon and comprehensively—an effort that seems extremely unlikely to occur—then Mottled Duck may eventually become extirpated from Florida.

Blue-winged Teal—A common migrant in the western Panhandle, and a fairly common to abundant winter resident elsewhere; perhaps the most widespread wintering duck in Florida. A very rare and irregular breeder throughout the mainland.

White-cheeked Pintail—A very rare and irregular visitor from the West Indies, primarily to the southern half of the peninsula. Unfortunately common in captivity; all recent observations have been rejected by the FOSRC because of uncertain provenance. Avicultural color morphs may range from all-white to natural plumage.

Lesser Scaup—A common to abundant winter resident along the mainland coasts. Far less common inland, and irregular in the Keys. Florida's most abundant waterfowl, but apparently declining severely in the past few decades. None of the five breeding reports is verifiable.

Greater Scaup—Status uncertain due to difficulty in separating from Lesser Scaup. Believed to be an uncommon to fairly common coastal winter resident of the Panhandle, uncommon in the northern third of the peninsula, and rare but perhaps regular south into the central peninsula. Stevenson and Anderson (1994) question all reports south of Lake Okeechobee. Very rare and unverified inland. There is one non-verifiable breeding report.

Hooded Merganser—An uncommon to locally common winter resident throughout the mainland, decreasing southward. Found inland and in coastal estuaries. Very rare in the Keys. Breeds rarely but perhaps annually in the northern half of the peninsula, with occasional reports in the Panhandle.

Common Merganser—A very rare and irregular winter resident perhaps throughout, but the status of this species is uncertain because of potentially widespread misidentifications. There are only three known verifiable records (two at St. Marks National Wildlife Refuge and one at Tampa Bay), all, strangely for this freshwater species, from brackish estuaries. *Any sighting of this species in Florida should be documented.*

Red-breasted Merganser—A common migrant and winter resident along the coasts. Rare inland and during summer (non-breeding).

Masked Duck—A very rare and irregular visitor from the West Indies, mostly to the southern peninsula and Keys but with reports north to the Panhandle. First recorded in 1955, with about 32 subsequent observations. About half of all reports are from Loxahatchee National Wildlife Refuge; a purported breeding report from there in February 1977 was not accepted by the FOSRC. The two recent documented records involved two or three males at Pembroke Pines in May–June 2001, and a female at Viera Wetlands in

April 2005. *Note that the chicks of Fulvous Whistling-Ducks have been misidentified in Florida as female Masked Ducks.*

Black Francolin (*Francolinus francolinus*)—Exotic, native from southwest Asia to the Indian subcontinent. An introduction of 35 pairs of wild-trapped francolins released into the Everglades Agricultural Area in 1962 did not succeed, nor did other reported releases (Genung and Lewis 1982). The last known observation dates from 1976 (Robertson and Woolfenden 1992), although Genung and Lewis (1982) suggested that birds persisted into the early 1980s. *The statement in Peterson (2002) that Black Francolins are "locally established" in Florida was inadvertently retained from the 1980 edition of the guide.*

Common Peafowl—Exotic, native to the Indian subcontinent but introduced widely. Currently non-countable populations are found in numerous cities, towns, and rural areas from the central peninsula south into the Keys. Locally fairly common, and present at some areas for decades. No population has been studied in detail, so Common Peafowl has never been considered as being established. (*No site described in this guide is reliable for seeing Common Peafowl.*)

Wild Turkey—An uncommon to locally common permanent resident throughout, except absent from the region southeast of Lake Okeechobee and from the Keys. Recently re-established in eastern Everglades National Park. Perhaps most abundant in the extensive prairie/pasture region between Kissimmee and Lake Okeechobee. Prefers areas with a mix of pastures and hammocks or swamps. Wild Turkeys roost nightly in trees, and they are most active shortly after dawn and before dusk.

Northern Bobwhite—A rare to uncommon permanent resident of prairies, fields, and sparsely wooded areas throughout the mainland. Absent from the Keys. Most readily found during spring and summer, when males are calling.

Red-throated Loon—A rare but regular coastal winter resident, reported most often along the northern Atlantic coast and at Alligator Point in the eastern Panhandle. Occasionally seen in numbers migrating southward off the northeast coast during fall. Rare in the western Panhandle, and irregular inland and south to the Keys.

Pacific Loon— A rare but perhaps regular winter resident throughout the Gulf coast. Reported most often from the Panhandle, but documented south to the Keys. Reported much less frequently in the Atlantic. Some individuals in the Panhandle have lingered through summer. *Small Common Loons in Florida have been misidentified as Pacific Loons.*

Common Loon—An uncommon to locally common coastal migrant and winter resident south to the central peninsula; rare farther south. Also found inland on large lakes. Rare during summer (non-breeding).

Least Grebe—A casual straggler from the West Indies (perhaps Cuba, where common) to the southern peninsula and the Keys. There are four accepted reports (two of these verifiably documented), all of single birds: Miami

(November 1970 and April 1992), Big Pine Key (October 1988), and Marco Island (March–April 1990).

Pied-billed Grebe—An uncommon permanent resident throughout, mostly in freshwater habitats. Seemingly most widespread in the central peninsula during spring and summer. Numbers during winter, when flocks of dozens of birds may be seen, increase through the addition of northern breeders.

Horned Grebe—An uncommon to very common winter resident of the peninsula, rare and irregular in the Keys. Most common along the coasts, but locally common inland on larger lakes.

Eared Grebe— A rare to uncommon but *extremely local* winter resident of sewage treatment ponds and other artificial water bodies in the Panhandle and northern half of the peninsula; as many as 27 birds have been seen at once. Otherwise, a rare migrant and winter resident throughout the mainland, mostly along the Gulf coast. Not yet reported from the Keys.

Tubenoses (petrels, shearwaters, and storm-petrels)—Unlike some other coastal states, Florida has few regularly scheduled pelagic boat trips (other than those that are by-products of trips to Dry Tortugas National Park). The scarcity of organized trips (no more than a few per year) is due to two primary factors: first, pelagic birding in Florida is generally fair to poor—an hour or more may separate observations of *any* birds during some summer trips; and second, chartering a boat to specifically look for pelagics is expensive, with most day trips costing $75–125 per person. To reach deep water favored by pelagic birds, trips in the Gulf of Mexico must travel 50–80 miles offshore. Trips into the Atlantic vary in how far they must travel: the Gulf Stream is only about five miles off Palm Beach County, but it is more than 50 miles off Jacksonville. Pelagic trips from the Keys need to travel south into the Florida Straits 5–15 miles. Charter fishing boats operate out of nearly every marina in the state, and self-sufficient pelagic birders may choose to tag along (some boats charge less for passengers who do not fish, so talk to the captains first). Inexperienced birders should wait to participate in an organized offshore trip, since pelagic birding is an entirely different experience from land birding, and it takes many trips to become accustomed to the different birding elements. Another possibility is watching for pelagic species from shore at select, elevated spots on the Atlantic coast. As sites such as Guana River Reserve (page 103) or the south end of Apollo Beach (page 172), several species may be seen *with the aid of a high-powered telescope*—the birds may be hundreds of yards offshore. Pelagic birding from land from fall through spring may produce good counts of Red-throated Loons, Northern Gannets (sometimes by the hundreds), scoters, and jaegers. On some occasions, especially with strong east or northeast winds, shearwaters, storm-petrels, boobies, Red and Red-necked Phalaropes, Sabine's Gulls, or Arctic Terns have been seen by particularly skilled and tenacious sea-watchers.

Yellow-nosed Albatross—A casual vagrant off the Gulf coast and the Keys, represented by three verifiable records: St. Marks National Wildlife

Refuge (July 1983), Key Largo (May 1992; a moribund bird sitting in the median of US-1!), and about 30 miles off Tarpon Springs (May 2000). Several other reports exist, including birds off the western Panhandle and in the Atlantic.

Black-capped Petrel—A rare but regular visitor spring through fall in Gulf Stream waters in the Atlantic and off the Keys. Casual in the Gulf and inland after tropical storms.

Cory's Shearwater—A fairly common to occasionally abundant visitor off the Atlantic coast; generally rare in the Gulf. Occurs most commonly summer through fall.

Greater Shearwater—A rare to uncommon visitor off the Atlantic coast; less common in the Gulf. May be seen virtually year-round, but most frequent from May through October.

Sooty Shearwater—A rare, regular visitor off the Atlantic coast, generally very rare in the Gulf and off the Keys. There are two inland reports. Possible year-round, but typically found spring through fall.

Short-tailed Shearwater—One moribund bird found 25 miles off Sanibel Island in July 2000 was preserved as a specimen. This furnished the first record of Short-tailed Shearwater in the ABA Area away from the Pacific Ocean (Kratter and Steadman 2003).

Manx Shearwater—A rare visitor off the Atlantic coast; casual in the Gulf. Has occurred in all months except July, but most reports are during winter.

Audubon's Shearwater—An uncommon to locally common visitor offshore, mostly off the southeastern peninsula and the Keys. Rare to uncommon elsewhere off the peninsula but only casual off the Panhandle. Observed most frequently spring through fall, and seen on most spring boat trips between Key West and Dry Tortugas National Park.

Wilson's Storm-Petrel—Generally a rare to uncommon visitor off both coasts (mostly the Atlantic), but sometimes common.

Leach's Storm-Petrel—A rare visitor off the peninsular coasts, apparently more common in the Atlantic than in the Gulf. There are only two records from the western Panhandle, both of birds found on beaches. Weather systems in May 1991 and April–May 2001 forced dozens to hundreds of Leach's Storm-Petrels to Atlantic beaches, where many birds perished.

Band-rumped Storm-Petrel—Generally considered a rare and perhaps irregular visitor offshore, but Haney (1985) found it to be fairly common 45 to 60 miles off the Atlantic coast from Daytona Beach northward (especially off Jacksonville) from late April to early September. Recently reported fairly regularly on spring boat trips between Key West and Dry Tortugas National Park, and perhaps more common than Wilson's Storm-Petrel off the Panhandle coast during spring and summer (Duncan and Duncan 2000). There have been numerous reports off the central and southern Atlantic coast in recent years, but none of these is verifiable.

White-tailed Tropicbird—A rare and irregular spring and summer visitor to the Dry Tortugas, occurring there in six out of the past 13 years (1992–2004). Elsewhere, an irregular visitor off both coasts, mainly the Atlantic.

Red-billed Tropicbird—A casual vagrant offshore spring through fall, represented by 11 reports (six of these verifiable). One report was from the western Panhandle, one from the southern Gulf coast, three between Key West and Dry Tortugas National Park, and the remaining six off the Atlantic coast.

Masked Booby—An uncommon permanent resident at Dry Tortugas National Park, nesting annually since 1984; chicks are often seen during April and May. Elsewhere, a rare but regular visitor off both coasts nearly year-round; seen on many pelagic trips spring through fall. Unlike the Brown Booby, the Masked Booby does not perch on buoys and channel markers, but often sits on the water.

Brown Booby—An uncommon to sometimes common non-breeding resident at Dry Tortugas National Park; the record count is 145 individuals. Usually seen perched on buoys and channel markers. Elsewhere, rare but regular off both coasts, with two anomalous reports from Lake Okeechobee.

Red-footed Booby—A very rare but nearly annual non-breeding spring and summer visitor to Dry Tortugas National Park. Casual elsewhere along both coasts. The brown morph occurs in Florida.

Northern Gannet—An uncommon to abundant migrant and winter resident off both coasts. Often seen in numbers from shore along the Panhandle and Atlantic coasts; rare off the peninsular Gulf coast.

American White Pelican—An uncommon to abundant but *local* winter resident of the peninsula, numbering 10,000–12,000 birds annually. Occurs coastally and at several inland sites such as large lakes and flooded farm fields. In the Panhandle and Keys, found primarily during migration. Spectacular soaring flocks of American White Pelicans may be seen during migration and winter. Dozens to hundreds of birds, perhaps individuals too young to breed, remain into the summer months.

Brown Pelican—A common to abundant permanent coastal resident throughout, but less common in the Panhandle, especially during winter. Inland occurrences, primarily of juveniles, are increasing in the central peninsula, and a few pairs bred at Lake Okeechobee in the 1990s.

Double-crested Cormorant—A common to abundant permanent resident in most of Florida, breeding mostly along the coasts and inland in the central peninsula. Numbers are augmented by northern breeders during winter, when flocks of hundreds or thousands may be seen. A common to abundant winter resident of the western Panhandle, where breeding records are almost unknown.

Great Cormorant—A very rare but fairly regular winter visitor along the Atlantic coast; one or two are reported in most years. Casual along the Gulf coast, inland, and in the Keys.

Anhinga—A common permanent resident in the peninsula, but rare in the western Panhandle and the Keys. Most withdraw from the Panhandle during fall. Strongly prefers freshwater habitats. Anhingas soar to great heights, often in flocks of several dozen individuals, when they can present an identification challenge.

Magnificent Frigatebird—A common permanent resident at Dry Tortugas National Park; about 100 pairs nest annually at Long Key, the only breeding colony in North America. Elsewhere, frigatebirds are rare to locally common non-breeding residents of coastal areas, primarily along the Gulf coast. Roosts that may number in the hundreds of individuals are found from Cedar Key to Naples. Irregular in the western Panhandle, along the northern Atlantic coast, and inland, with most such records occurring after storms. Thus far, all frigatebirds identified in Florida have been Magnificent Frigatebirds, but observers should be alert to the possibility that other species may be present; Great Frigatebird (*Fregata minor*) breeds off Costa Rica and has strayed to California and Oklahoma, while Lesser Frigatebird (*F. ariel*) breeds off Brazil and has been recorded in coastal Maine (AOU 1998, ABA 2002).

Wading birds—Perhaps no other avian family represents the image of Florida to most people more clearly than its wading birds. Although current populations are greatly reduced from numbers that occurred up to about 1870, wading birds remain a highly visible and widespread component of all wetlands in the state, even stormwater retention ponds in urban areas. Most species are common year-round throughout the state, although numbers in the Panhandle diminish during winter. In many areas, truly spectacular numbers of wading birds can be seen. **Great Blue, Little Blue, and Tricolored Herons** and **Great and Snowy Egrets** are common to abundant permanent residents throughout. **White Ibises** are abundant in the peninsula but rare in parts of the Panhandle. **Green Herons** are uncommon throughout the mainland and rather rare in the Keys. **Black-crowned and Yellow-crowned Night-Herons** are uncommon to locally common permanent residents throughout (Yellow-crowned withdraws from the Panhandle during fall). Black-crowned is usually more common inland, while Yellow-crowned is more common coastally, especially along the Gulf coast.

American Bittern—An uncommon migrant and winter resident of marshes and other freshwater wetlands of the mainland; occasional in the Keys. Infrequently seen because of its secretive habits and generally inaccessible habitats. Rare during summer in the form of lingering non-breeders or possibly occasional breeders (there is no verifiable breeding record in Florida).

Least Bittern—An uncommon to locally common spring and summer resident of freshwater marshes throughout. Winters from the central peninsula southward. Less common in saltwater and brackish marshes and man-grove forests (Bowman and Bancroft 1989). Most common in Lake Okee-chobee and the Everglades, but virtually every cattail marsh in the peninsula contains Least Bitterns. In recent years it has been determined that Least Bit-terns give a call that sounds very similar to that of King Rails, but the bittern's call is a bit shorter.

Great White Heron—A fairly common permanent resident of the southern peninsula and the Keys, numbering about 800 pairs. Currently con-sidered to be a white morph of Great Blue Heron, it may deserve species sta-tus (which it has been granted in the past). Almost certain to be seen along US-1 from Key Largo to Key West, and fairly common also at Flamingo, Everglades National Park. During post-breeding dispersal from late summer to early fall, birds may occur anywhere along the coasts, and a few are found inland.

Wurdemann's Heron—Apparently a Great Blue Heron x Great White Heron hybrid; its appearance is like that of a Great Blue Heron but with the white head and neck and yellowish legs of a Great White Heron. Rare to un-common in southern Florida, predominantly the Keys, but individuals have strayed to the extreme northern peninsula.

Reddish Egret—A fairly common coastal permanent resident along the Gulf from Tampa Bay southward through the Keys, less common on the Atlan-tic coast north to Merritt Island. The statewide population numbers about 500 pairs and continues to increase as historic breeding grounds are re-colonized. Post-breeding dispersal carries birds, especially juveniles, northward increas-ingly to the eastern Panhandle and even inland. The dark morph is much more common than the white morph except in the Lower Keys, where the white morph predominates. Occurs regularly at Hagens Cove, Honeymoon Island State Park, Fort De Soto Park, Merritt Island National Wildlife Refuge, J.N. "Ding" Darling National Wildlife Refuge, Fort Myers Beach, Everglades Na-tional Park (Flamingo area), and along US-1 in the Keys.

Cattle Egret—A common to abundant permanent resident throughout the mainland. Rare to uncommon in the Mainline Keys, and solely a migrant at Dry Tortugas National Park, where it often becomes marooned. Wintering egrets withdraw partially from the Panhandle and northern third of the penin-sula. First reported in Florida in the early 1940s, Cattle Egret is now the most abundant wading bird in the state. Unlike other wading birds, Cattle Egrets forage primarily in upland sites such as pastures and fields, often following farm machinery ("Tractor Egrets").

Scarlet Ibis—Status uncertain. Specimens collected in 1874 and before 1883 may represent natural vagrants (Robertson and Woolfenden 1992, AOU 1998). However, the species shows little incidence of vagrancy, and the natu-ral population nearest to Florida—at Trinidad—is more than 1,200 miles away. Five reports from Cuba since the late 1950s (Raffaele et al. 1998) likely represent "vagrant escapees" from Florida rather than natural stragglers from

Trinidad or South America. Complicating matters greatly was an intentional introduction of Scarlet Ibises into Miami in 1961. At Greynolds Park, 22 Scarlet Ibis eggs that had been laid in Trinidad were placed into White Ibis nests, fledging 17 Scarlet Ibises. In subsequent years, the "pure" Scarlet Ibises hybridized with White Ibises, which produced offspring of various shades of pink. Scarlet Ibises are common in captivity in the state, and some captive individuals reportedly have escaped.

Recent observations of Scarlet Ibises in Florida are seldom documented adequately to rule out the possibility of hybrids. Most ibises observed in Florida are not *intense scarlet overall*, which characterizes "pure" adult Scarlet Ibises (juveniles are similar to juvenile White Ibises but have a pinkish tinge to the back and rump). However, Stevenson and Anderson (1994) point out that plumage coloration of escaped Scarlet Ibises may be diluted from "dietary changes", so plumage color may not be a good determinant for judging the "purity" of a Scarlet-type ibis. One or more pale pink ibises has roosted at Eco Pond, Everglades National Park, since 1994, and one or more red ibises has been present in the Fort Myers area since 1991. At Lakes County Park (page 193), red ibises are frequently seen in the heron roost, and one reportedly nested in 2001 and 2002. *Given the difficulty is determining "pure" Scarlet Ibises from potential hybrids, the term "Scarlet-type ibis" should perhaps be used when reporting any pink or red ibis in Florida.* Robertson and Woolfenden (1992) suggested that *all* Scarlet Ibises in Florida may be escapees rather than natural vagrants.

Glossy Ibis—An uncommon to common but *local* permanent resident of marshes and wet prairies throughout the peninsula, though generally rare in the Panhandle and Keys. The state's population numbers 2,000 to 3,000 pairs and is increasing. Usually easy to find in marshes along the St. Johns River west of Titusville, at Myakka River State Park, in the prairie region west of Lake Okeechobee, and in the Everglades Agricultural Area.

White-faced Ibis—A very rare non-breeding (?) resident, reported increasingly in Florida in recent years. There are two old breeding reports from the southern half of the peninsula (1886 and 1937). Recent observations are from Fort Walton Beach Spray Field, Lakeland, Lake Apopka, Lake City, and St. Marks National Wildlife Refuge. Probably overlooked; some juveniles cannot safely be distinguished from juvenile Glossy Ibises, and adults in nonbreeding plumage are distinguishable primarily by iris color.

Roseate Spoonbill—An uncommon to locally common coastal permanent resident in the southern half of the peninsula and the Keys. Rare in the northern half of the peninsula and casual in the western Panhandle. At least 1,000 pairs breed in the state, and this number is increasing. Nests north to Tampa Bay and Merritt Island, and inland breeding has occurred at Corkscrew Swamp and in the Everglades. Post-breeding dispersal carries the birds northward to the eastern Panhandle, along the entire Atlantic coast, and inland (mostly hatching-year birds). Reliable sites include Fort De Soto Park, Merritt

Island National Wildlife Refuge (Black Point Wildlife Drive), J.N. "Ding" Darling National Wildlife Refuge, Flamingo and other sites in Everglades National Park, and the Keys.

Wood Stork—An uncommon to locally abundant permanent resident of the peninsula, rare in the Panhandle and the Keys. Florida's population numbers about 5,000 pairs. Wood Storks breed during late winter and early spring, when nesting success (which depends upon receding water levels that concentrate fish and other prey) is highly variable. A large rookery is found at Corkscrew Swamp Sanctuar, and some nests may be visible from open portions of the boardwalk. Post-breeding dispersal carries birds throughout the state, and flocks of hundreds or even thousands of individuals may be seen when flooding conditions are ideal.

Black Vulture—An uncommon to common permanent resident throughout the mainland; rare in the Keys as a non-breeding visitor.

Turkey Vulture—A common to abundant permanent resident throughout the mainland. Uncommon in the Keys, except during fall migration, when locally abundant.

Greater Flamingo—Up to the late 19th century, a common to abundant winter resident at Florida Bay (within present-day Everglades National Park), from breeding colonies in the western Bahamas. This wintering population disappeared as the species' breeding range contracted eastward as a result of human persecution. In the 1930s, Greater Flamingos from Cuba were released at Hialeah Race Track near Miami in an attempt to establish a local breeding flock. The original birds were not pinioned, and many of them flew away. Eventually, a breeding population was established at Hialeah, and the birds continue to nest there. The Hialeah flamingos are not pinioned or banded, and all are capable of sustained flight; over 300 were present by 2003. Since the 1950s, there has been a flock of as many as 40 flamingos (often including juveniles) in the southwest portion of Everglades National Park, in the Snake Bight area. The birds often remain through summer but may be most numerous during fall and winter. (Perhaps surprisingly, the Snake Bight flamingo flock has never been studied in detail.) High tide is best for viewing, as it forces the flamingos closer to shore. (Florida Bay is extremely shallow; at low tide, the birds may forage several miles offshore.)

The provenance of the Snake Bight flamingo flock has been debated for decades. Some claim that the flock is composed entirely of wild birds from colonies in Cuba or the Bahamas, while others suspect that all the flamingos at Snake Bight are from Hialeah Race Track. Still others have suggested that both wild and escaped flamingos could be present. Part of the mystery was solved in October 2002, when a Greater Flamingo color-banded as a nestling at a colony on the Yucatán Peninsula in Mexico was photographed with several other flamingos at Snake Bight. Birds observed elsewhere in Florida outside of Snake Bight are usually presumed to be escapees, but some appear to be genuine vagrants. McNair and Gore (1998) documented that four of eight flamingo occurrences in the Panhandle—with three of these known to be of Greater Flamingos—followed tropical storms that passed over the Yucatán Peninsula or western Cuba before making landfall along the northern Gulf coast.

Lastly, note that *flamingos seen in Florida are not necessarily Greater Flamingos*. There are two reports of Chilean Flamingos (*Phoenicopterus chilensis*) in Florida, both presumed to be escapees. The presence of exotic flamingos in the state is probably under-reported, as most observers likely assume that all flamingos seen in Florida are Greater Flamingos.

Osprey—A locally common permanent resident throughout, occurring both coastally and inland. Most birds withdraw from northern Florida during fall. The large nests of Ospreys are frequently seen in trees and on man-made structures such as power poles, TV antennas, and specially constructed nesting platforms. This species is hard to miss in the peninsula, especially around large lakes. Lake Istokpoga east of Lake Placid hosts more than 225 *active nests*, believed to be the greatest density of Ospreys in the world (Mike McMillian, personal communication).

Swallow-tailed Kite—A rare to uncommon migrant and spring and summer resident throughout the mainland. Rather easy to find in the peninsula from March through June. By mid-July, most of the state's Swallow-tailed Kites are concentrated west of Lake Okeechobee, where they become locally abundant. The state's population is estimated at 500 to 800 pairs, which represents the bulk of the U.S. population. Kites roost communally in late summer before beginning migration. Roosts are found at Lake Woodruff National Wildlife Refuge, Corkscrew Swamp Sanctuary, and Fisheating Creek. The precise locations of the roosts are not disclosed to avoid disturbance, but kites should be seen throughout the general areas in July, especially along the west side of Lake Okeechobee. Fall migration begins in August, when kites head southwest across the Gulf of Mexico (often island-hopping through the Keys and Cuba) to wintering grounds in South America. A graceful and stunning species, the favorite bird of many Florida birders.

White-tailed Kite—A very rare and irregular migrant in the Panhandle and northern half of the peninsula, and a rare and local permanent resident in the southern half of the peninsula. Occurs in semi-native prairies, drained Everglades marshes, and other grassland habitats. White-tailed Kites have been increasing their range and numbers in the central and southern peninsula, following a rangewide increase noted since the 1980s. Kissimmee Prairie Preserve State Park (page 166) and various sites in and around Everglades National Park are current breeding locations.

Snail Kite—A locally common but *nomadic* permanent resident of freshwater wetlands of the central and southern mainland. Unknown in the western Panhandle and the Keys. The entire Florida population in the early 1960s was perhaps 20–25 birds—but today, at least 1,000 individuals are found in Florida! Snail Kites move around the southern half of the peninsula according to local water conditions, which affect the availability of their chief prey, Apple Snails (*Pomacea* species). Most Snail Kites inhabit inaccessible areas of the Everglades, but some birds are resident in the central peninsula, at Lakes Kissimmee, Tohopekaliga, and East Tohopekaliga (page 149). Snail Kites are also reliably seen from Markham County Park (page 222) and around the Miccosukee Indian Restaurant on US-41 (page 206).

Mississippi Kite—A rare migrant throughout and an uncommon to fairly common spring and summer resident of the Panhandle and northwestern peninsula. Breeds south to about Cedar Key and Gainesville. Not too difficult to find within the breeding range from mid-April through August. Most Mississippi Kites are west circum-Gulf migrants, but small numbers are seen in the Keys during fall. Their call resembles the final two notes of the Olive-sided Flycatcher's *Quick! Three beers!* song.

Bald Eagle—A fairly common and still recovering permanent resident throughout the eastern Panhandle and peninsula. Rare in the western Panhandle and uncommon in the Keys. Florida's population, the largest of any state outside Alaska, occupied more than 1,100 active territories by 2001, and this total has increased annually since surveys began in 1972. The greatest density of nesting eagles in the state is in the Lake Kissimmee area, with more than 100 active territories. From May through August or September, following the breeding season, eagles become scarce in Florida as many migrate northward out of the state. In other months, they are not hard to find in the peninsula. A truly majestic species.

Northern Harrier—A fairly common migrant and winter resident throughout. Four peninsular breeding reports from the early 1900s are not verifiable. Females and immatures compose the bulk of Florida's population; adult males are rare.

Sharp-shinned Hawk—A fairly common migrant and winter resident throughout. Breeding reports from the early 19th century were not documented and have been discounted by later authors. However, Sharp-shinned Hawks were discovered nesting at Conecuh National Forest in Alabama in 2001 and 2002, in each case fewer than 10 miles from the Florida state line (James Tucker, personal communication), so breeding may eventually be documented in Florida.

Cooper's Hawk—A rare to uncommon migrant and *increasing* permanent resident nearly throughout. Its breeding range has been expanding southward to Fort Myers, Archbold Biological Station, and Miami, and westward into the western Panhandle. The abundance in southern Florida of a suitable prey species, Eurasian Collared-Dove, is thought to have played a part in the recent range expansion of Cooper's Hawk in the state. Cooper's Hawks formerly were thought to be rare migrants in the Keys, but recent hawkwatches have recorded hundreds of birds during fall.

Common Black-Hawk (*Buteogallus anthracinus*) and/or **Great Black-Hawk** (*Buteogallus urubitinga*)—Status uncertain. Robertson and Woolfenden (1992) summarized "the black-hawk problem" as "a hardy perennial of Florida field ornithology." Basically, a few black-hawks were reported at Fort Lauderdale, Miami, and the Lower Keys between 1972 and 2005. Details for most observations are lacking, and only three individuals—all at Greynolds Park, Miami, in the 1970s—were photographed. Although the black-hawk photographed in Abrahamson (1976) was identified as a Common Black-Hawk, P. William Smith (*in* Pranty 1995) believes that all south Florida individuals were Great Black-Hawks that escaped from captivity and have "experienced very limited breeding".

Red-shouldered Hawk—A common permanent resident over most of the state, less common in the western Panhandle and the Keys. Florida's most widespread diurnal raptor, it is found in swamps and other wooded habitats and is often seen perched on powerlines. The southern Florida subspecies, *Buteo lineatus extimus*, is particularly pale and small. Vocal and virtually impossible to miss in the state.

Broad-winged Hawk—An uncommon to fairly common breeder in the Panhandle and northern peninsula, southeast to about Gainesville. Generally rare during migration, but common in the western Panhandle and the Keys during fall. Broad-winged Hawks winter regularly in the extreme southern peninsula and the Keys, often perching on powerlines. Reports north of these areas should be documented.

Short-tailed Hawk—A rare to locally uncommon permanent resident of the peninsula. Irregular in the eastern Panhandle and unreported farther west. Breeds sparingly throughout the peninsula in extensive areas of riparian woodlands and cypress swamps, especially near open habitats. Lake Wales Ridge State Forest (page 157) is a reliable breeding site. Winters nearly exclusively south of Lake Okeechobee, both on the mainland and in the Keys. Perhaps easiest to find during that season—one or two days in Everglades National Park between November and February should result in a few sightings. Northward migration begins in February. Characteristically aerial hunters and feeders, Short-tailed Hawks are seldom seen while perched (unless early in the morning, or near a nest, when they usually perch inside the canopy). Short-tailed Hawks do not perch on powerlines and very rarely perch on the tops of power poles. Like vultures, Short-tailed Hawks wait until thermals develop in mid-morning; when in an area known to be occupied by the hawks, watch for them as soon as the first soaring vultures appear. Two color morphs are present in Florida, and although mixed breeding pairs do occur, there are no intermediate plumages. Light morphs may be confused with Red-tailed Hawk, while dark morphs may recall Black Vulture. Dark morphs outnumber light morphs in Florida about 3 or 4 to 1. White-winged Doves and Eurasian Collared-Doves apparently constitute an important and increasing part of their winter diet in southern Florida, and the hawks may be moving into residential areas to exploit these abundant prey. Light-morph adults, especially, are spectacular birds.

Swainson's Hawk—Generally a rare to uncommon late fall migrant and winter resident in the extreme southeastern mainland and the Keys, but kettles of more than 100 birds have been reported. Very rare and irregular elsewhere, usually seen during migration. Both dark and light morphs have been observed in Florida, and many individuals appear to be juveniles.

Zone-tailed Hawk—A vagrant from the southwestern U.S. or Central America. The sole Florida record refers to presumably the same hawk seen over Big Pine Key and Boca Grande Key nine days apart in December 2000.

Red-tailed Hawk—A rare to uncommon permanent resident of open country in the mainland, but strictly a non-breeding visitor in the Keys. During winter, Red-tails occur throughout the state as northern breeders move southward into Florida. Commonly perches on the tops of power poles, but rarely if ever on powerlines. There are reports of the Harlan's (Blackshaw and Polisse 1990), Fuerte's (Norton and Ripple 1997), and Krider's Red-tailed Hawks in Florida. Additionally, eastern Red-tailed Hawks seem to exhibit leucism rather frequently, with some individuals appearing nearly all white.

Ferruginous Hawk—Perhaps a very rare and irregular winter resident of the Panhandle and peninsula, but there are only two verifiable records: 2 birds at Lake Apopka December 1983–March 1984, and one in the north-central Panhandle in March 1986.

Rough-legged Hawk—Perhaps a very rare and irregular winter resident throughout, with more than 25 reports. However, the only verifiable record refers to three birds (one light morph and two dark morphs) present at Lake Apopka from February to April 2000.

Golden Eagle—A rare but probably annual migrant and winter resident. Usually found in the Panhandle but reported south to Everglades National Park.

Crested Caracara—An uncommon to fairly common permanent resident of the prairies north and west of Lake Okeechobee. A few birds occur west to Myakka River State Park and north to SR-50 east of Orlando. Communal roosts that may exceed 25 caracaras, primarily non-breeding adults and juveniles, may be seen. The Crested Caracara is a Threatened species in Florida, with a population of 500 or more birds. Sure to be seen eventually if the following roads are driven: Canoe Creek Road south of Kissimmee, US-27 south of SR-70, SR-29, SR-70 east and west of US-27, SR-74, and SR-80, and CR-721, CR-832, and CR-833 in Glades, Hendry, and Highlands Counties.

American Kestrel—Two or three populations occur in Florida. The eastern subspecies (*Falco sparverius sparverius*) may be abundant along the Atlantic coast and the Keys during migration (primarily during fall) and is uncommon to locally common during winter throughout. The Southeastern American Kestrel (*F. s. paulus*) is a rare to uncommon *local* permanent resident of open pine forests and pastures primarily of the western Panhandle and the interior of the peninsula south to about Lake Okeechobee. The Cuban Kestrel (*F. s. sparverioides*) of Cuba, the Bahamas, and Jamaica occurs in distinctive light and dark morphs; color illustrations are found in *A Guide to the Birds of the West Indies* (Raffaele et al. 1998) and *Field Guide to the Birds of Cuba* (Garrido and Kirkconnell 2000). There have been several reports of Cuban Kestrels in the Keys, but apparently none of these is verifiable.

Merlin—An uncommon to locally common fall migrant along the Atlantic coast and in the Keys; rare along the Gulf coast and inland. Also a rare to uncommon spring migrant and winter resident throughout, mostly along the coasts.

Eurasian Kestrel—An accidental winter resident from Eurasia. One at Lake Apopka during February–March 2003 provided the first record for the southeast (Pranty et al. 2004).

Peregrine Falcon—An uncommon to locally common fall migrant along the Atlantic coast and in the Keys. Peak daily totals during early October often exceed 100 birds, and nearly 2,000 are thought to pass through the Keys every fall. Elsewhere, generally rare along the coasts during winter and spring, and rare inland at any season. Two subspecies are found in Florida: *Falco peregrinus anatum* and the paler *F. p. tundrius*.

Yellow Rai—Al scarcely seen but probably regular migrant and winter resident throughout. Favored habitats include dry prairies, marshes, fields, and other areas with short grass. Generally silent in Florida; *be aware that the call of the Cricket Frog (Acris gryllus) can sound very similar to the typical* tic-tic, tic-tic-tic *call of the Yellow Rail.*

Black Rail—A secretive and little-known permanent resident of scattered areas throughout the peninsula, rare to locally uncommon. Breeds in coastal marshes along the northern and central Gulf coast (south to at least Port Richey), in brackish marshes west and east of Titusville, and apparently in freshwater marshes inland at several sites in the peninsula. Migrants occur throughout the state, including the Keys, but are very rarely encountered. Winters from the central peninsula southward. Reliable sites include St. Marks National Wildlife Refuge (page 71), the end of CR-361 south of Steinhatchee (page 79), and Lake Woodruff National Wildlife Refuge (page 93). Black Rails respond well to tape recordings of their calls, *but birders should avoid overuse of tapes.* Black Rails are most easily located during the two hours or so before dawn and after dusk.

Clapper Rail—A common permanent resident of salt and brackish marshes and mangrove forests throughout. Rarely seen, but vocalizes frequently, often throughout the day.

King Rail—An uncommon but widespread permanent resident of freshwater marshes throughout the mainland. Occasional in the Keys during migration. Rarely seen, but vocalizes often, chiefly around dawn and dusk.

Virginia Rail—A rare to uncommon migrant and winter resident throughout the mainland, but very rare and irregular in the Keys. There is one documented breeding record from the northern peninsula in 1984.

Sora—A fairly common to common migrant and winter resident throughout the mainland; rare in the Keys.

Purple Swamphen (*Porphyrio porphyrio*)—Exotic, widespread in the Old World. A population (not yet countable) may be becoming widely established in the southern peninsula. Purple Swamphens were first noted in Florida around December 1996 at Pembroke Pines on the eastern edge of the Everglades. The birds apparently escaped from one or two nearby aviculturists who kept unpinioned birds in their collections. Individuals quickly colonized artificial wetlands in adjacent developments, and appear to be colonizing natural and artificial wetlands throughout the region. Among sites recently colonized are Emeralda Marsh, Lake Okeechobee, the Everglades, and Big Cypress Swamp—an area perhaps 6 million acres in extent! Swamphens breed readily in Florida (nearly year-round), and their population numbered 135 individuals in February 1999. All subsequent surveys have recorded fewer birds, perhaps the result of widespread dispersal away from Pembroke Pines. *Note that swamphens can be difficult to find during periods of high water levels.* Purple Swamphens are a highly variable species that Sangster (1998) suggested should be split into six separate species. If this recommendation were followed by the AOU, then (most of) the Florida individuals would be assigned to *P. [p.] poliocephalus*, the "Gray-headed Swamphen," which is native from Turkey east to southern Asia. A few Florida swamphens appear to have all-bluish heads (although head color and intensity varies somewhat according to viewing angle and lighting), and these blue-headed swamphens potentially could be considered a different species! The only North American field guide that illustrates Purple Swamphens is Sibley (2000), which shows a blue-headed adult with short legs, and a red-billed (rather than dusky-billed) juvenile—later editions of Sibley's guide may feature corrected illustrations. Pranty et al. (2000) and Pranty (2001a) provide additional information on the Florida population. Photographs of Purple Swamphens from Pembroke Pines appear as a photo quiz in the February and April 1999 issues of *Birding*, and in an article in the August 2004 issue of *Birding*.

Purple Gallinule—A rare to fairly common, *local* spring and summer resident nearly throughout; rare in the Keys. Migrants are found throughout, even at Dry Tortugas National Park. Winters locally from the central peninsula southward. Found in shallow freshwater wetlands covered with floating vegetation such as water lilies, water lettuce, and water hyacinth. Reliable breeding sites statewide are Edward Ball Wakulla Springs State Park (spring and summer only), Myakka River State Park, Lake Okeechobee, the Everglades Agricultural Area, Pembroke Pines, and Everglades National Park (especially Shark Valley). A few Purple Gallinules usually are present in the same ponds at Pembroke Pines that contain Purple Swamphens (above).

Common Moorhen—A common permanent resident of *vegetated* freshwater habitats throughout the peninsula; local and less numerous in the Panhandle. Absent as a breeder from the Keys except at Key West.

American Coot—A winter resident, common to abundant in the mainland, but uncommon in the Keys. Forms rafts of hundreds or thousands of individuals at favored wintering sites such as St. Marks National Wildlife Refuge, Merritt Island National Wildlife Refuge, Myakka River State Park, and Everglades National Park. Breeds regularly but rarely and unpredictably throughout the mainland.

Limpkin—Generally an uncommon permanent resident of marshes and swamps throughout much of the peninsula. Rare to absent in the Panhandle, southern Everglades, and the Keys. Extremely vocal, especially at night. Reliable sites include Roosevelt Wetland, Saddle Creek Park, Fred's Fish Camp, Corkscrew Swamp Sanctuary, Loxahatchee National Wildlife Refuge, John Prince Park, and Shark Valley in Everglades National Park.

Sandhill Crane—A fairly common permanent resident of pastures and marshes in the peninsula, much more common during winter due to an influx of breeders from the West. High-flying southbound flocks may be heard overhead in the latter half of November. Rare in the Panhandle and Everglades, and absent from the Keys (except for a few Dry Tortugas reports). About 2,000 pairs of the resident, nearly endemic race, Florida Sandhill Crane (*Grus canadensis pratensis*), breed in the peninsula, most commonly in the central portion. About 25,000 birds of the migratory race, Greater Sandhill Crane (*G. c. tabida*), winter in the peninsula, with numbers decreasing southward. There is one report of Lesser Sandhill Crane (*G. c. canadensis*) in Florida (Nesbitt 1992). A few thousand cranes winter at Paynes Prairie Preserve State Park, with other large flocks found in the prairie region northwest of Lake Okeechobee, from Avon Park to Moore Haven. Sandhill Cranes become surprisingly tame in some areas and are not hard to find in less-developed areas in the central peninsula.

Whooping Crane—Formerly an occasional winter visitor or an extirpated permanent resident in the peninsula, last recorded in 1927 or 1928. As part of a project to better secure the long-term survival of Whooping Cranes, biologists from several agencies and organizations are re-establishing two separate populations into the Florida peninsula. The first project, begun in 1993, involves releasing captive-reared juveniles into central Florida in the hopes of creating a non-migratory breeding population of at least 25 pairs by 2020. The second project, begun in 2001, is creating a migratory population that will breed in Wisconsin and winter in and around Chassahowitzka National Wildlife Refuge near Crystal River along Florida's north-central Gulf coast. As of January 2005, the resident population numbered nearly 90 individuals, and the wintering population contained nearly 50 individuals (Stephen Nesbitt, Florida Fish and Wildlife Conservation Commission, personal communication 1999). Nesting activity began in 2001 (Nesbitt and Folk 2000), and in 2002, one pair successfully fledged a juvenile at Leesburg (in the north-central peninsula), the first Whooping Crane to successfully fledge in the U.S. since the 1930s and the first known fledgling produced in Florida. Unlike Whooping Cranes elsewhere, which forage primarily in marshes, the birds released into Florida can spend much time foraging in pastures, a habit shared with Florida Sandhill Cranes. Birds are released while in juvenal plumage, which is molted into full adult plumage the following year. The cranes are color-banded, fitted with radio transmitters on both legs, and monitored carefully. Sightings of Whooping Cranes anywhere in the northern or central peninsula should not be surprising, but the birds rarely occur farther south.

Shorebirds—As might be expected in a state with thousands of miles of shoreline, Florida is a major migratory and wintering area for shorebirds. Important shorebird stopover and wintering areas mentioned in this guide include St. Marks National Wildlife Refuge, Honeymoon Island State Park, Fort De Soto Park, Merritt Island National Wildlife Refuge, Little Estero Lagoon, Tigertail Beach, Everglades National Park, and Ohio Key. During fall migration (mid-July to late October), flooded agricultural fields southeast of Lake Okeechobee and former agricultural areas now under restoration, such as Emeralda Marsh Conservation Area and Lake Apopka North Shore Restoration Area, may contain many thousands of shorebirds when water levels are ideal. Holding ponds at sewage treatment facilities provide additional habitat, especially inland. Of the 48 species of shorebirds verified in Florida, only seven breed in the state (all are listed below). Of the 41 non-breeding species, 33 occur more or less annually. The eight irregularly-occurring species (not discussed below) are Northern Lapwing, Mountain Plover, Black-tailed Godwit, Hudsonian Godwit, Bar-tailed Godwit, Surfbird, Sharp-tailed Sandpiper, and Curlew Sandpiper.

Some shorebirds are restricted to coastal habitats, but most occur inland as well, especially during migration. Shorebirds *not* found inland regularly are Snowy, Wilson's, and Piping Plovers, American Oystercatcher, Whimbrel, Long-billed Curlew, Red Knot, and Sanderling. Migrant species more or less restricted to inland (or at least upland) sites are American Golden-Plover, Upland, Pectoral, and Buff-breasted Sandpipers, Long-billed Dowitcher, and Wilson's Phalarope. During winter, few species of shorebirds are found inland; exceptions are Killdeer, Black-necked Stilt (local), both yellowlegs, Western and Least Sandpipers, Long-billed Dowitcher, Wilson's Snipe, and American Woodcock. A few individuals of other species (e.g., Dunlin, Short-billed Dowitcher, and Spotted Sandpiper) may also be found inland during winter. Except for Long-billed Dowitcher, Wilson's Snipe, American Woodcock, and Red-necked and Red Phalaropes (both pelagic), all of Florida's wintering shorebirds occur in brackish or saltwater habitats along the coasts. To observe the largest diversity of wintering shorebirds in the state, visit any of the coastal sites listed above, where one may observe up to 6 species of plovers, American Oystercatcher, and up to 13 species of sandpipers.

Snowy Plover—A rare to uncommon, *local* permanent resident of less-disturbed sandy beaches and flats along the Gulf coast. Not found regularly along the Atlantic coast or in the Keys, and there are no inland reports. Because of its tiny population size (311 individuals were found statewide during winter 2000–2001) and susceptibility to disturbance by humans and dogs, the Snowy Plover probably is Florida's most endangered bird. The largest numbers are found in the western Panhandle, but small numbers occur along the entire peninsular Gulf coast. Snowy Plovers can usually be found year-round at Fort Pickens, St. George Island State Park, Honeymoon Island State Park, Fort De Soto Park, Little Estero Lagoon, and Tigertail Beach.

Wilson's Plover—Generally an uncommon to fairly common permanent resident of sandy beaches and flats throughout, but rare in the western Panhandle. Most breeders in northern Florida winter in the southern half of the peninsula. Found at all sites listed above for Snowy Plover, and at other areas such as the Atlantic coast and the Keys. Virtually unknown inland.

Semipalmated Plover—A fairly common migrant and winter along the coasts. Rare during summer. Occurs regularly inland in small numbers during migration.

Piping Plover—A rare to uncommon, *local* winter resident of sandy, tidal flats on the Gulf coast and northern Atlantic coast; rare in the Keys. About 450 individuals were found statewide during winter 2000–2001. Fall migrants begin returning to Florida in August, and a few wintering plovers remain into May. Reliable sites include Fort Pickens, St. George Island State Park, Little Talbot Island State Park, Huguenot Memorial Park, Honeymoon Island State Park, Fort De Soto Park, Little Estero Lagoon, Tigertail Beach, and Bill Baggs Cape Florida State Park.

Killdeer—An uncommon to common permanent resident throughout the mainland; rare and local in the Keys. Numbers are augmented by northern breeders during winter, when Killdeers may be locally abundant in pastures, fields, and other open habitats.

American Oystercatcher—An uncommon to locally common permanent resident (about 400 pairs) along both coasts, but most common along the central Gulf coast. Rare in the western Panhandle, the extreme southern mainland, and in the Keys. Easy to find at Honeymoon Island State Park and Little Estero Lagoon. During winter, it becomes common in other areas, and is especially abundant at Cedar Key. Probably in response to disturbance from humans and their dogs, some oystercatchers have begun nesting on rooftops (Douglass et al. 2001).

Black-necked Stilt—A rare to uncommon migrant, and an uncommon to locally abundant spring and summer resident of the peninsula and Keys. Occurs throughout but is more common at inland sites such as flooded agricultural fields. Easy to find at the Everglades Agricultural Area during summer and early fall. Winters locally at a few sites in the central and southern peninsula. In the Panhandle (especially the western half), occurs chiefly as a migrant, but now breeds at a few sites.

American Avocet—A common but very local winter resident of the southern half of the peninsula. Merritt Island National Wildlife Refuge and the Flamingo area of Everglades National Park are two reliable wintering sites. As a migrant, rare to uncommon along both coasts, and inland at a few sites during fall. American Avocets may remain year-round at favored wintering sites, but breeding in Florida has not yet been documented.

Greater Yellowlegs—A fairly common to common migrant and winter resident throughout.

Lesser Yellowlegs—A common to abundant migrant and winter resident throughout. Outnumbers Greater Yellowlegs during winter and also often during migration.

Willet—The Eastern Willet (*Catoptrophorus semipalmatus semipalmatus*) is a fairly common permanent resident of coastal marshes and mudflats throughout. The species as a whole becomes locally abundant during winter with the arrival of breeders from farther west and north (including Western Willets, *C. s. inornatus*). Willets are regular inland in small numbers during fall at flooded agricultural fields.

Whimbrel—A rare to uncommon migrant and local winter resident of coastal areas throughout. Reliable wintering sites include Honeymoon Island State Park, Merritt Island National Wildlife Refuge, and Little Estero Lagoon. Casual inland.

Long-billed Curlew—A rare migrant and *very local* winter resident, primarily of the Gulf coast. One to three birds winter regularly at Honeymoon Island State Park, Fort De Soto Park, and Little Estero Lagoon. Casual inland.

Marbled Godwit—A local winter resident of the eastern Panhandle and peninsula, more common along the Gulf coast; irregular in the Keys. An irregular migrant through the western Panhandle, and regular inland to flooded fields during fall. Usually easy to find during winter at Honeymoon Island State Park, Fort De Soto Park, Merritt Island National Wildlife Refuge, and Everglades National Park (Flamingo and Snake Bight).

Ruddy Turnstone—A common to abundant migrant and winter resident along the coasts. Regular in small numbers inland, mainly during fall.

Red Knot—An uncommon to locally abundant but *rapidly declining* migrant and winter resident, especially along beaches of the central Gulf coast. Rare in the western Panhandle and the Keys. Found commonly at Honeymoon Island State Park, Fort De Soto Park, Merritt Island National Wildlife Refuge, Little Talbot Island, and Little Estero Lagoon. Casual inland.

Sanderling—A common to abundant migrant and winter resident of sandy beaches along the coasts. Very rare inland during migration.

Semipalmated Sandpiper—An uncommon to abundant migrant throughout, but local inland. Apparently rare to uncommon during winter in the extreme southern peninsula and the Keys, but few reports are verifiable.

Western Sandpiper—A common to abundant migrant throughout. During winter, common to abundant along the coasts and rare to uncommon inland.

Least Sandpiper—A common to abundant migrant throughout. During winter, common to abundant along the coasts and uncommon to common inland.

Pectoral Sandpiper—A common to locally abundant fall migrant of flooded agricultural fields and other muddy habitats throughout the mainland. Much less common during spring, and rare along the coasts. There is one verifiable winter record.

Purple Sandpiper—A rare to locally uncommon winter resident of jetties and rock or shell outcroppings along the northern Atlantic coast. Irregular south to Miami and along the Gulf coast. Reliable sites include Fort Clinch State Park, Matanzas Inlet, and Smyrna Dunes Park.

Dunlin—An uncommon to abundant migrant throughout. During winter, common to abundant along the coasts and rare inland.

Stilt Sandpiper—An uncommon to common migrant throughout, especially inland at flooded fields in the Everglades Agricultural Area during fall. A rare to locally uncommon winter resident in the southern half of the peninsula.

Ruff—A rare but regular migrant and very rare, irregular winter resident throughout the peninsula. Usually found in flooded agricultural fields during fall. Unreported from the western Panhandle and not known from the Keys except for one report at Dry Tortugas.

Short-billed Dowitcher—A common migrant throughout, and a common to abundant *coastal* winter resident. Apparently rare to locally uncommon (but seldom documented) inland during winter. At least two subspecies, *Limnodromus griseus hendersoni* and *L. g. griseus*, occur in Florida.

Long-billed Dowitcher—An uncommon to locally common migrant throughout the mainland, rare to locally common during winter. Strongly prefers freshwater habitats—especially during winter—but also found in brackish impoundments (e.g., at Merritt Island National Wildlife Refuge) during migration. Status in the Keys uncertain. Believed not to occur along the coasts during winter. Arrives later in fall than Short-billed Dowitcher.

Wilson's Snipe—An uncommon migrant and uncommon to locally common winter resident of shallow marshes and muddy lakeshores throughout the mainland. Rare in the Keys. Occasional during summer and in brackish marshes during winter.

American Woodcock—A rare to uncommon winter resident throughout the mainland; not known from the Keys. Active from dusk to dawn. Breeds during late winter and early spring south to at least north-central Florida, with a few reports south to Corkscrew Swamp Sanctuary and Everglades National Park.

Phalaropes—All three phalaropes occur in Florida. **Wilson's Phalarope** is an irregular spring migrant and a rare to uncommon fall migrant, mostly at flooded farmlands. *No winter report is verifiable.* **Red-necked and Red Phalaropes** are rare to uncommon migrants and winter residents offshore, and are seen on many Atlantic pelagic trips. Red Phalarope seems to be the more common of the two species. Red and Red-necked Phalaropes both occur irregularly inland, usually following storms.

South Polar Skua—Apparently a casual visitor off the Atlantic coast; reports off the Keys and the Gulf coast are not verifiable. All four documented records refer to birds found on beaches: Melbourne (June 1993), Fort Clinch State Park (October 1998), Smyrna Dunes State Park (November 1998), and Boynton Inlet (December 1998–January 1999).

Jaegers—As a group, jaegers are uncommon winter residents and spring migrants offshore. During fall migration, they are uncommon in the Gulf but may be common to abundant in the Atlantic, where many are observed from shore. The end of the road south of Apollo Beach (page 172), a part of Canaveral National Seashore, may be the best single spot in Florida to view jaegers from shore. Hundreds—occasionally thousands!—of jaegers have been seen from this spot from mid-October through November on days with strong east or northeast winds. *A high-powered telescope is essential. Adult jaegers are easy to identify if seen well, but juveniles remain among the most challenging of North American birds to identify.* **Pomarine Jaeger** is fairly common in Florida, **Parasitic Jaeger** is rare to uncommon, and **Long-tailed Jaeger** is rare, possibly irregular, and seldom seen from shore .

Gulls—Eighteen species of gulls have been recorded in Florida, although only one, Laughing Gull, breeds in the state. All other species are best thought of as winter residents or visitors, although individuals of many species remain through the summer. In addition to those discussed below, the following species occur in very small numbers in Florida annually or nearly so: **Franklin's Gull** (mostly Gulf coast), **Glaucous Gull** (mostly Atlantic coast), and **Black-legged Kittiwake** (mostly pelagic off the Atlantic coast). Irregular stragglers to Florida that are not featured below are **Little, Black-headed, Thayer's,** and **Iceland Gulls**. Most gull species are limited to coastal areas, but Laughing, Bonaparte's, Ring-billed, and Herring (rare) Gulls also occur inland at dairies, flooded agricultural fields, large lakes, and landfills.

Laughing Gull—A common to abundant permanent resident on the coast; locally uncommon to common inland (non-breeding) at landfills and large lakes. The second-most common and widespread larid in Florida, and the only gull that breeds in the state. *Laughing Gulls with reddish bills and legs are* *observed in Florida perhaps annually, so use care when identifying Black-headed Gulls in the state;* see the article and photographs in *Birding* (Patten 2000). Laughing Gulls are frequently seen landing on the head of a Brown Pelican to try to steal fish from the pelican's pouch! See photo on page 101.

Bonaparte's Gull—A variable migrant and winter resident, ranging from rare to locally abundant throughout. Found along the coasts as well as on large inland lakes.

Heermann's Gull—An accidental vagrant from the Pacific coast. One that arrived at Fort De Soto Park in October 2000 has yet to leave the state. This individual presumably has traveled along the Gulf coast from Choctawhatchee Bay in the western Panhandle to Sanibel and Captiva Islands to the south, but returns frequently to Fort De Soto Park.

Gray-hooded Gull (*Larus cirrocephalus*)—An accidental vagrant, presumably from the Pacific coast of South America. The sole record for the ABA Area was of an adult photographed at Apalachicola in December 1998 (McNair 1999).

Belcher's Gull (*Larus belcheri*)—Formerly a part of Band-tailed Gull. Native to the Pacific coast of Peru and Chile, and a casual or accidental visitor along the Florida Gulf coast. One that was captured at Pensacola in September 1968 was kept in captivity until its death in November 1983. Subsequent observations were made in the Naples area in June 1970, November 1974–January 1975, and January–February 1976, when two individuals may have been present (Stevenson et al. 1980).

Ring-billed Gull—A common to abundant migrant and winter resident throughout, occurring coastally as well as inland; Florida's most abundant and widespread larid. Uncommon during summer (non-breeding).

California Gull—A casual straggler from the western U.S. to the Gulf coast. There is only one unequivocal Florida record, one juvenile at Apalachicola in September 1998 (McNair 2000b).

Herring Gull—An uncommon to locally common migrant and winter resident along the coasts. Generally rare inland, usually at landfills.

Lesser Black-backed Gull—An *increasing* winter resident, rare to locally common along the Atlantic coast, rare and local along the Gulf coast, and irregular inland. Reliable sites along the Atlantic coast are Huguenot Memorial Park, Jetty Maritime Park, the Pompano landfill, and Bill Baggs Cape Florida State Park. Less common along the Gulf coast; try Little Estero Lagoon. Still rare and irregular in the interior of the state.

Great Black-backed Gull—An uncommon to common *but increasing* winter resident (year-round) of the Atlantic coast south to Merritt Island. Generally rare farther south, along the entire Gulf coast, and in the Keys. No inland report is verifiable.

Slaty-backed Gull—An accidental vagrant from eastern Asia. The only verifiable Florida record pertains to an individual at Key West (September 2002–May 2003).

Sabine's Gull—A very rare migrant along and off the Atlantic coast during fall; less frequent along the peninsular Gulf coast and at Dry Tortugas National Park. There are only one winter and two spring reports for the state. Many of the birds have been in juvenal plumage.

Gull-billed Tern—A rare to uncommon, *local* spring and summer resident at a few coastal and inland sites from Apalachicola eastward; many sites are ephemeral. During winter, often seen in Everglades National Park (Snake Bight and Flamingo), and elsewhere in the southern half of the peninsula, including Blue Heron Wetlands Treatment Facility. This is Florida's only white tern that does not typically dive for prey; rather, it picks prey off the surface of the water or land. Gull-billed Terns observed recently in Pasco County seem especially fond of fiddler crabs (Ken Tracey, personal communication).

Caspian Tern—Generally a rare to locally common permanent resident throughout the mainland, but withdraws from the western Panhandle during winter. Rare year-round in the Keys. Breeding was first documented in 1962, and all colonies have been on artificial dredged-material disposal islands. McNair (2000a) provides a summary of Caspian Tern breeding sites in the southeastern United States.

Royal Tern—An uncommon to locally abundant *coastal* permanent resident throughout, with numbers augmented during winter by northern breeders. Rare to uncommon and *very local* inland at phosphate-mine impoundments in the central peninsula. Breeds in scattered colonies along both coasts, with largest numbers at Tampa Bay.

Elegant Tern—First recorded in 1999 (Kwater 2001) and observed annually in the Tampa Bay area through 2004. One Elegant Tern apparently paired with a Sandwich Tern at a colony south of Tampa and produced a chick during summer 2002 (Paul et al. 2003)! Most often seen at Fort De Soto Park. "Elegant-type" terns recently have been observed in the Tampa Bay area, and another was photographed at Dry Tortugas National Park in spring 2003. These may represent Elegant x Sandwich Tern hybrids, or Cayenne Terns, variously treated as a subspecies of Sandwich Tern or a distinct species, which are found in the West Indies and South America and are intermediate in bill coloration between Elegant and (North American) Sandwich Terns. Photographs of several of these Elegant-type terns are posted to Lyn Atherton's website: <http://home.earthlink.net/~bonniedabird/FirstElegant.htm>.

Sandwich Tern—A rare to locally common *coastal* permanent resident throughout, except absent from the western Panhandle during winter. Overall more common along the Gulf coast than the Atlantic. Generally absent inland, except locally common at phosphate-mine impoundments in the central peninsula. Breeding colonies are scattered along both coasts, with the largest numbers at Tampa Bay.

Roseate Tern—An uncommon to fairly common spring and summer resident of the Lower Keys, numbering 300–350 breeding pairs annually. Roseate Terns usually are found resting on beaches, buoys, and channel markers at Dry Tortugas National Park, and on channel markers at Fort Zachary Taylor State Park in Key West. Pairs nest on the roof of the Marathon Government Center (page 254). Seen on most spring and summer pelagic trips in the Lower Keys. Rare elsewhere offshore and along the Atlantic coast. Stevenson and Anderson (1994) reject all reports from the Gulf coast and inland.

Common Tern—An uncommon to abundant coastal migrant throughout, more common during fall. A few pairs bred along the eastern Panhandle coast in the 1960s and 1970s, but there have been no subsequent reports. Very rare inland except after tropical storms. Very rare to rare during winter—Forster's Terns often are misidentified as Common Terns during this season, despite their lack of dark carpal bars.

Forster's Tern—An uncommon to locally abundant migrant and winter resident throughout the mainland; very rare in the Keys. Found inland as well as along the coasts.

Least Tern—A rare to uncommon migrant, and an uncommon to common spring and summer resident along both coasts, rare to locally uncommon inland. Roof-nesting is increasing as beach-nesting birds are heavily disturbed by humans and their dogs. Although reported annually during winter (usually on Christmas Bird Counts), *there is no verifiable record of a Least Tern in Florida from November through February.*

Bridled Tern—An uncommon to common offshore visitor from breeding colonies in the West Indies. Most numerous in the Gulf Stream off the southeastern coast and the Keys, especially from April to October. Less common elsewhere, and rare during winter. Seen on most spring boat trips between Key West and Dry Tortugas National Park. Since 1987, a very rare breeder (one–five pairs) at Pelican Shoal Critical Wildlife Area off the Lower Keys, the only known nesting colony in North America (Hoffman et al. 1993).

Sooty Tern—An abundant spring and summer resident on Bush Key at Dry Tortugas National Park, numbering 25,000 or more pairs. Elsewhere, rare during summer off both coasts, often blown ashore or inland following strong storms. The nasal, tri-syllabic call of this species, often rendered as *wide awake* and uttered incessantly day and night, is a characteristic sound of a spring trip to the Tortugas.

Black Tern—A non-breeding migrant, uncommon to common during spring, uncommon to abundant during fall. Found coastally as well as inland. There is at least one verifiable winter record.

Brown Noddy—An abundant spring and summer resident on Bush Key at Dry Tortugas National Park, numbering about 2,000 pairs. Otherwise, rare off both coasts (mainly summer), and occasionally blown ashore or inland following storms.

Black Noddy—A very rare but fairly regular non-breeding spring and summer visitor to Dry Tortugas National Park. Reported in eight of the past 13 years (1992–2004). During spring 1997, *seven* birds were present. Can usually be seen if one persistently scans the noddies that perch on the remains of the north coaling dock on Garden Key, which allows easy comparison with the larger and somewhat paler Brown Noddies. Unknown elsewhere in Florida except for a bird photographed at Clearwater in June 2003.

Black Skimmer—An uncommon to abundant permanent resident of coastal areas throughout the mainland; solely a winter resident in the Keys. Usually withdraws from the Panhandle during fall. Also occurs inland, at times abundantly (though rarely breeding) at flooded agricultural fields and around large lakes.

Long-billed Murrelet—Unknown in the state until December 1986, when one was found freshly dead at Honeymoon Island State Park (Hoffman and Woolfenden 1988). Another was found dead in Fort De Soto Park in December 1993, a third bird was observed at Cedar Key in March 1994 (Muschlitz 1995), and a fourth individual was captured off St. Petersburg in November 1994. Vagrants from Siberia, Long-billed Murrelets occur casually throughout North America, so the occurrence of four singles along the Florida Gulf coast—with three of these occurring during an 11-month period!—was astonishing.

Rock Pigeon—Exotic, native to the Old World. An uncommon to locally abundant permanent resident in cities, but generally absent from rural or natural areas. Birds often nest under highway overpasses. Racing-pigeon clubs are found throughout Florida, and color-banded Rock Pigeons often are found; <www.pigeon.org> provides contact information for owners of lost racing pigeons.

Scaly-naped Pigeon (*Patagioenas squamosa*)—An accidental vagrant to Key West, presumably from Cuba. There are only two North American records: single birds collected in October 1898 and May 1929. This is a large, dark-gray pigeon with a reddish-purple nape and breast, and red irides, orbital rings, and feet. Dark "scaling" on the nape gives it its English name. The Scaly-naped Pigeon is illustrated in Peterson (2002; head only), *A Guide to the Birds of the West Indies* (Raffaele et al. 1998) and *The Birds of Cuba* (Garrido and Kirkconnell 2002).

White-crowned Pigeon—A common to abundant spring and summer resident of the Keys and extreme southern mainland, numbering about 8,500 pairs. Usually easy to find in the Mainline Keys and along the main road through Everglades National Park. White-crowned Pigeons nest on raccoon-free islands, mostly in Florida Bay and travel to the Mainline Keys to feed on *Ficus* (fig), Poisonwood, and other fruiting hardwoods. Because these hammocks are vital to the survival of White-crowned Pigeons in the U.S., most remaining hammocks have been publicly acquired. Local during winter, when many birds migrate to Cuba or the Bahamas.

Ringed Turtle-Dove (*Streptopelia "risoria"*)—Exotic; believed to be a long-domesticated form of the African Collared-Dove (*S. roseogrisea*). Ringed Turtle-Doves are not countable anywhere in the ABA Area (ABA 2002). They are now extirpated from Florida, although some birds may persist at St. Petersburg, where several hundred individuals were found as recently as the early 1990s. Ringed Turtle-Doves are the white doves released during weddings and other events, so individuals may be turn up anywhere. The plumages of Ringed Turtle-Doves and (to a much lesser extent) Eurasian Collared-Doves vary because of avicultural morphs that may be present in a population, but there are several definitive differences between the two species. Turtle-Doves are slimmer than are Collared-Doves; the former suggests a Mourning Dove while the latter is reminiscent of a White-winged Dove. Eurasian Collared-Doves *generally* have darker plumage, with blackish primaries, and a distinctive white border around the black collar. Ringed Turtle-Doves are pale to white, with brownish or grayish primaries, and no contrasting border between the collar and the nape. Eurasian Collared-Doves sing a low, *hoo-hoo, HOO* that is uttered incessantly, while Ringed Turtle-Doves give a rollicking, *coo-coo-ka-REWWWW*, with the final syllable rolled.

European Turtle-Dove (*Streptopelia turtur*)— One photographed at Lower Matecumbe Key 9–11 April 1990 (Hoffman et al. 1990) furnished the first record in North America. This record was accepted by Robertson and Woolfenden (1992), the FOSRC, and the AOU (1998), but was not accepted by the ABA Checklist Committee.

Eurasian Collared-Dove—Exotic, native to India, Asia Minor, and the Balkans. Naturally colonized much of central and western Europe during the 20th century. Collared-doves apparently colonized the southeastern Florida coast and the Keys from a few dozen birds released in the Bahamas in 1974 (Smith 1987). Since that time, they have colonized much of the state, and their range and numbers continue to increase (collared-doves now occur west to the Pacific coast). Though still uncommon and local in rural areas, Eurasian Collared-Doves now are one of the most abundant urban birds in Florida. Their monotonous *hoo-hoo, HOO* call is heard year-round. For a history of the Eurasian Collared-Dove in North America, refer to Smith (1987), Romagosa and McEneaney (2000), Romagosa and Labisky (2000), and Romagosa (2002).

White-winged Dove—Two separate populations occur in Florida. Breeders from the western U.S. winter sparsely in peninsular Florida, and migrants from these populations are seen along the Gulf coast, primarily during fall. A separate, resident population is increasing explosively throughout the peninsula. The origin of the breeding birds is debated. Some (e.g., Fisk 1968, Saunders 1980) have claimed that the birds are exotics that were obtained from Mexico and were released into the Homestead area after 1959, while others (e.g., Aldrich 1981) felt that the plumage of these birds more closely resembled West Indian forms. Recent observations of White-winged Doves at Dry Tortugas National Park may (at least partially) support the theory of natural colonization from the West Indies. Whatever the origin of the Homestead birds, biologists from the former Florida Game and Fresh Water Fish Commission captured hundreds of them in the 1970s and released them into Central Florida (to provide hunters with another avian target!). This population is colonizing the entire peninsula—and may soon move into Georgia.

Zenaida Dove—A casual visitor from the West Indies to the Keys. Only three documented Florida records are known, with two of these occurring within the past 50 years: Plantation Key (two birds, December 1962–March 1963) and Key Largo (June 1988 and May 2002). John James Audubon claimed that Zenaida Doves bred on a few of the Keys in the 1830s, but there have been no subsequent breeding reports. For a recent summary see Smith and Smith (1989). *Zenaida Doves appear very chunky due to their short tail. You won't think of a Mourning Dove when you see one, despite the similarities in plumages.*

Mourning Dove—Ubiquitous throughout, abundant in urban and suburban areas but generally less common in natural habitats. Mourning Doves that breed throughout the mainland are of the widespread subspecies *Zenaida macroura carolinensis*, but those that breed in the Keys are of the Greater Antillean race *Z. m. macroura*.

Common Ground-Dove—An uncommon to fairly common permanent resident throughout, usually seen as family groups of two to four birds. As their name suggests, ground-doves are found on or close to the ground in open, sandy habitats such as fields, citrus groves, pine flatwoods, sandhills, and dunes. Common Ground-Doves are declining almost throughout their entire range and are becoming hard to find in many parts of Florida.

Key West Quail-Dove—A casual visitor from the West Indies to the southern mainland and the Keys, with about 22 accepted reports. Reported by John James Audubon to breed at Key West in the 1830s, but all subsequent observations have been of singles. There have been four reports since 1990, the most recent at Long Key State Park in June 2002.

Ruddy Quail-Dove—An accidental visitor from the West Indies to the Keys, with three verifiable records, the most recent at Dry Tortugas National Park in December 1977.

Psittacids—Through 2005, there have been 76 (!) species of exotic parrots reported outside of captivity in Florida, and the occurrence of 38 of these is verifiable from archived photographs or specimens. But only four psittacids (the Budgerigar, Monk Parakeet, Black-hooded Parakeet, and White-winged Parakeet) are on the official Florida bird list maintained by the FOSRC. Another 15 species are breeding (or are presumed to be breeding) currently, in populations that number in the dozens to low hundreds of individuals, while populations of a few other species have become extirpated. The remaining 50 or so species are represented by one or a few individuals that escaped or were intentionally released, and persisted briefly before dying out or being re-captured. Nearly all the psittacids that are breeding in Florida are native to the New World, the only exceptions being the Budgerigar (from Australia) and the Rose-ringed Parakeet (from India). This New World bias to Florida's psittacids is explained by importation patterns: most parrots brought into the U.S. since the 1960s have been imported from Argentina, Brazil, Mexico, or Peru. Between 1982 and 1988, an estimated *1.4 million* (!) wild-caught parrots entered the U.S. legally, with nearly half of these obtained from Argentina (Thomsen and Mulliken 1992). Tragically, such massive capture of wild psittacids has severely endangered numerous species in their native lands. Fortunately, the Wild Bird Conservation Act of 1992 enacted by the federal government has greatly reduced the trade of wild-caught parrots.

Most of Florida's psittacids have been reported in the Fort Lauderdale and Miami metropolitan areas, but some species occur elsewhere in the state. In most cases, these species—primarily Black-hooded, Blue-crowned, and Red-masked Parakeets—occur in several cities each, while other species are more limited in their distribution. Some, such as White-eyed Parakeet, occur in small numbers in several cities, but locations are unpredictable and can be short-lived. Observing parrots can be a frustrating experience for a number of reasons. When resting, parrots can be very quiet, and it can be surprisingly difficult to find them, even when they are perched in an isolated tree. Several species often occur together in fast-moving flocks. And the identification of species in several genera (primarily *Brotogeris, Aratinga,* and *Amazona*) is often difficult, although recent field guides (especially Sibley 2000) and other identi-fication aids (e.g., Pranty and Garrett 2003) have helped. Some birds encoun-tered may represent artificial (avicultural) color morphs (e.g., blue Rose-ringed Parakeets, or yellow Budgerigars) or wild- or captive-bred hy-brids that are not illustrated in any guides. Low-light conditions prevail at eve-ning roosts, obscuring field marks. And it often is difficult to follow birds as they fly around suburban neighborhoods or downtown areas. Additionally, some birders may not feel safe birding in some neighborhoods that contain parrot populations.

For all of these reasons, birders who wish to take on the challenge of searching for Florida's varied psittacids must be willing to be patient. During the day, the birds forage widely at feeders and in flowering or fruiting palms, trees, or shrubs, and finding them often is hit-or-miss. Some sites (e.g., yards with well-stocked feeders) may be reliable for years, while other hotspots may be very short-lived. Most psittacids are much easier to locate in the late afternoon as they return to communal roosts; the location of several are listed in this guide. However, some species do not join communal roosts, and the locations of roosts can be unpredictable because of disturbance, or from trimming or removing roosting vegetation. At other times, roosts are unaccountably abandoned, and may remain vacant for weeks or months, only to be suddenly reactivated. Some psittacids seem to have multiple roost sites that may be used alternately some nights, and in tandem on others. Roosting substrates vary, but nearly all are in exotic trees (especially Australian-pines for *Amazona* parrots) and palms, especially Cuban Royal Palms (most *Aratinga* and *Brotogeris* parakeets, as well as Rose-ringed Parakeets at Naples). Budgerigars roost in various deciduous trees planted in yards or parking lots, while Monk Parakeets roost nightly in their nest structures. Roosting substrates for Black-hooded Parakeets are not known.

Nearly all pairs of psittacids in Florida nest singly in cavities originally excavated by woodpeckers. Nests can be difficult to find, especially because local birders (primarily in the Fort Lauderdale and Miami areas) usually withhold the location of active nests out of fears that the nests will be raided by trappers who capture the birds to sell to the pet trade. (Because these psittacids are not native to Florida, such practices apparently are legal—although trappers often trespass to reach nests). Many psittacids select particular species of palms as nesting substrates, so knowledge of palm identification is helpful. Chestnut-fronted Macaws at Fort Lauderdale and Miami seem to favor large Royal Palm (*Roystonea regia*) snags, while White-winged and Yellow-chevroned Parakeets found in the same areas create nests by "burrowing" into the dry, fibrous material of dead fronds, especially those of Canary Island Date Palms (*Phoenix canariensis*). Black-hooded Parakeets in the St. Petersburg area nest mostly in Mexican Fan Palm (*Washingtonia robusta*) snags and telephone poles. *Amazona* parrots and *Aratinga* parakeets seem to be more general in their nesting substrate preferences, selecting cavities from a variety of living or dead palms or trees. Budgerigars breed in boat davits or nest-boxes built to their specifications. Monk Parakeets use any substrate—natural or artificial—that can support their often sizable stick nests. Some of the most commonly used Monk Parakeet nesting substrates in Florida are electrical substations, palms of several species (with Canary Island Date Palms a favorite in the St. Petersburg area and Coconut Palms [*Cocos nucifera*] and Royal Palms selected in the Fort Lauderdale and Miami areas), powerline towers, telephone poles (especially those with transformers), and Australian Punk Trees (such as at Miami Springs and Kendall Baptist Hospital).

The following accounts include the four countable psittacids, plus 15 other breeding species that currently occur in small to moderate numbers. Some of the latter species may be candidates for future establishment once (if) the necessary studies are conducted and the results published. Pranty and Garrett (2003) summarized the status and distribution of all psittacids found in Florida, with color photographs for 15 species, while Pranty and Epps (2002) summarized the psittacid fauna of Broward County (Fort Lauderdale–Hollywood areas) as it existed around 2000. All of the species mentioned below are included in recent field guides by Kenn Kaufman (2000),

David Sibley (2000), and the National Geographic Society (2002). The treatment of psittacids in Peterson (2002) was not updated from his 1980 edition and now is of little value.

For the identification of those psittacids not mentioned in standard North American field guides (e.g., White-eyed Parakeet), a birder has three book options. (There are innumerable Internet options available, of course, of varying reliability.) One choice is to purchase Volume 4 of the *Handbook of Birds of the World* series edited by Josep del Hoyo et al. (1997). Each volume in this monumental series costs $200 or more, but the text, photographs, and plates are all of the highest quality. Two much more affordable books are available, but the text is outdated in one book, and the illustrations are of lower quality in the other. *Parrots of the World* by Joseph Forshaw (1973) is out of print but usually available from rare-book dealers. *Parrots, a Guide to Parrots of the World* by Tony Juniper and Mike Parr (1998) is more recent, with much more information. The plates in Forshaw (1973) generally are of higher quality than those in Juniper and Parr, but the latter book often includes more illustrations per species. Both books rely heavily on non-standard English names, which can result in great confusion about what bird is being discussed. For instance, both books refer to Red-crowned Parrot as "Green-cheeked Amazon". With much effort given in recent decades to developing standard English names of birds, it is unfortunate that Juniper and Parr did not follow suit. (The names used in *Handbook of Birds of the World* are much closer to those used by the AOU and ABA.) Another limitation of the two parrot books is that identification hints are often left out by the authors because the native ranges of many species do not overlap. In Florida, however, one may encounter (and have to identify) similar species that have separate geographical origins, such as Crimson-fronted, Mitred, Red-masked, and Scarlet-fronted Parakeets. Finally, the illustrations in both books show mostly side views of psittacids perched at eye level, so that the *upperside* of the tails is shown. Birders usually see the *underside* of the tail of psittacids perched overhead on wires or vegetation. Needless to say, birders who encounter "unfamiliar" psittacids in Florida should take copious notes and ideally obtain photographs or videotapes.

Budgerigar—Exotic, native to Australia. ABA-countable only along the central Florida Gulf coast, where populations have declined severely since the late 1970s. At its peak, the population may have numbered or exceeded 20,000 individuals; one roost at Holiday contained as many as 8,000 birds. By the mid-1980s, the population had crashed, with perhaps fewer than 75 Budgerigars remaining in Florida as of December 2004. The primary causes of the decline apparently are nesting competition with European Starlings in natural cavities and House Sparrows in nest boxes, as well as a reduction in the number of nest-boxes available (Pranty 2001b). Currently, Budgerigars exist in small flocks at Hernando Beach (page 114) and Bayonet Point (page 115). Local escapees, often including white, blue, or yellow avicultural morphs, may found throughout Florida, but they do not survive long—*these are non-countable.*

Rose-ringed Parakeet—A non-countable exotic native to Africa and Asia; at least some of the birds in Florida are of the Indian subspecies *manillensis*. Flocks have been found in several cities since the 1950s or earlier, but populations seem unable to persist for long periods. Only three sites are known currently. The Naples flock (page 198) numbered at least 131 parakeets in November 2001, with 30 others at Fort Myers in December 2001. Smaller numbers apparently persist at St. Augustine, but there are few recent data. The Rose-ringed Parakeets formerly present at Miami have apparently been extirpated for more than 10 years.

Monk Parakeet—Exotic, native to southern South America. Countable populations exist in several cities in peninsular Florida. Moderate to large populations are found along the Gulf coast from Hudson south to Venice and along the Atlantic coast from West Palm Beach south to Homestead. Sites included in this guide include electrical substations at Port Richey, St. Petersburg, and Homestead. Small "colonies" at St. Augustine, Cape Canaveral, Kissimmee, and several other areas may be too small and/or have been monitored for too short a period to be considered established. A popular cage bird, Monk Parakeets may be found anywhere, and range expansion into new areas is likely.

Black-hooded Parakeet—Exotic, native to South America. Considered established by the FOSRC and probably soon to be added to the ABA Checklist. Established populations are found along the central Gulf coast from Bayonet Point to Sarasota, most commonly around St. Petersburg. Smaller populations are found in several other areas, such as St. Augustine, Fort Lauderdale, Miami, and the Upper Keys, but these are not considered established. Black-hooded Parakeets were first seen in Florida in 1969, and perhaps 900 birds were present by 2003 (Pranty and Lovell 2004). Gulfport Municipal Marina (page 130) is a reliable spot in the St. Petersburg area.

Blue-crowned Parakeet—A non-countable exotic, native to South America. Populations seem to be increasing in Florida. Flocks have been reported in the southern half of the peninsula and the Keys since the late 1980s. Several dozen birds currently are found at Fort Lauderdale, with smaller flocks present at St. Petersburg, Port Canaveral (page 177), and perhaps elsewhere.

Mitred Parakeet—A non-countable exotic, native to South America. Populations seem to be increasing in Florida. Apparently over 200 birds are present in the Miami area, with more than 50 others at Fort Lauderdale. Similar to Red-masked Parakeet but larger in direct comparison, and with little or no red on the leading edge of the wing.

Red-masked Parakeet—A non-countable exotic, native to South America. Populations seem to be increasing in Florida. Flocks of 30 or more are found in the Fort Lauderdale and Miami areas and at Upper Key Largo, with smaller numbers elsewhere in the southern half of the peninsula. Similar in plumage to Mitred Parakeets but noticeably smaller in direct comparison, with red on the leading edges of the wings.

White-eyed Parakeet (*Aratinga leucophthalmus*)—A non-countable exotic, native to northern and central South America. Found increasingly at Fort Lauderdale and Miami, perhaps now numbering 100 or more birds.

Dusky-headed Parakeet (*Aratinga weddellii*)—A non-countable exotic, native to central South America. Perhaps 50 individuals are present at Miami Springs (page 225).

Chestnut-fronted Macaw (*Ara severa*)—A non-countable exotic, native to Panama and northern South America. There are perhaps fewer than 100 individuals in the Fort Lauderdale and Miami areas. Breeds in palm snags.

Blue-and-yellow Macaw (*Ara ararauna*)—A non-countable exotic, native to northern South America and Trinidad. A few pairs breed in the Miami area, and others may be breeding at Fort Lauderdale.

White-winged Parakeet—A countable exotic, native to northern South America. Formerly considered conspecific with the Yellow-chevroned Parakeet, when both forms were known collectively as the Canary-winged Parakeet. Although present at Miami since the mid-1940s, populations were small until the late 1960s and early 1970s, when they exploded in size due to frequent escapees from captivity—at least 230,000 White-winged Parakeets were imported between 1968 and 1972 (Brightsmith 1999). By 1972, the Miami population alone was estimated at 1,500 to 2,000 birds, and White-winged Parakeets ranged north along the Atlantic coast to West Palm Beach and beyond. However, numbers and range had declined dramatically by the 1980s, corresponding with a cessation of importation. Currently, perhaps 200 or more White-winged Parakeets occur at Fort Lauderdale, with uncertain numbers at Miami. *Many White-winged and Yellow-chevroned Parakeets at Fort Lauderdale display plumage characteristics that suggest that they may be hybrids* (Pranty and Voren 2003).

Yellow-chevroned Parakeet—A non-countable exotic, native to central South America. Yellow-chevroned Parakeets first appeared in Florida sometime in the 1980s. As with White-winged Parakeet, populations are limited to the southeastern coast. The Miami population exceeds 400 individuals (Pranty and Garrett 2003), and others occur at Fort Lauderdale, where the possibility of hybrids with White-winged Parakeets confuses the issue (Pranty and Voren 2003). *Note: the Yellow-chevroned Parakeet was added to the ABA Checklist in 2003, but has not been placed on the official Florida list by the FOSRC. Therefore, the Yellow-chevroned Parakeet is not ABA-countable in Florida.*

White-fronted Parrot (*Amazona albifrons*)—A non-countable exotic native to Central America. Small numbers currently are breeding at Fort Lauderdale, with other birds (breeding status unknown) found at Miami. Does not roost communally with other *Amazona* parrots.

Red-crowned Parrot—A non-countable exotic endemic to Mexico. The Florida population numbers at least 400 individuals from Palm Beach to Miami, with the largest population at Fort Lauderdale, where there is a large and dependable roost (page 222). Breeding populations at Fort Lauderdale and possibly Miami (where now rare) have persisted for 30 years or more, but because no study has been conducted on the species in Florida, it is still considered to be non-established.

Blue-fronted Parrot (*Amazona aestiva*)—A non-countable exotic native to central South America. Small numbers are present at Fort Lauderdale and Miami. Roosts communally with other *Amazona* parrots.

Orange-winged Parrot (*Amazona amazonica*)—A non-countable exotic, native to northern and central South America. Perhaps 100 are found at Fort Lauderdale and Miami. Roosts with other *Amazona* parrots.

Yellow-headed Parrot (*Amazona oratrix*)—A non-countable exotic, native to Central America. Formerly present in numbers at West Palm Beach, Fort Lauderdale, and Miami, but apparently only a few individuals remain presently. Roosts with other *Amazona* parrots.

Yellow-naped Parrot (*Amazona auropalliata*)—A non-countable exotic, native to Central America. A few birds are breeding at Fort Lauderdale and Miami. Roosts with other *Amazona* parrots.

Yellow-billed Cuckoo—An uncommon migrant and uncommon to fairly common spring and summer resident throughout, heard much more frequently than it is seen. There are a few verifiable winter occurrences.

Mangrove Cuckoo—An uncommon and *inconspicuous* permanent resident of mangrove and West Indian hardwood hammocks of the southern mainland and the Keys. Rare but regular along the Gulf coast north to St. Petersburg, but infrequent along the Atlantic coast north of Miami. It is either less common or simply more difficult to find during fall and winter, when silent. Responds well to recorded Mangrove Cuckoo calls during spring and summer, *but tapes should be used sparingly, given the rarity of the species and the potential for disrupting nesting birds.* The use of tapes is prohibited altogether in J.N. "Ding" Darling National Wildlife Refuge, Everglades National Park, and National Key Deer Refuge. *Yellow-billed Cuckoos also breed in the same habitats as Mangrove Cuckoos, so flying cuckoos that show rufous flashes in the primaries are not necessarily Mangrove Cuckoos.*

Smooth-billed Ani—Now a rare, declining, and *unpredictable* permanent resident of the southern mainland and the Keys. Prefers fields overgrown with tall grasses and shrubs. Because sites are usually occupied for short periods, perhaps no place in Florida is now dependable. Birders seeking this species are advised to consult Internet websites for recent locations. Responds well to recorded Smooth-billed Ani calls, but *birding ethics may be violated if tapes are used repeatedly on the same few remaining birds.* Breeds communally, so typically found in small flocks that represent family groups. Mlodinow and Karlson (1999) is a good reference.

Groove-billed Ani—A rare but regular migrant and winter resident of the Panhandle, especially the western half. May be found throughout the peninsula, but occurrences are unpredictable. Fort Pickens and St. Marks National Wildlife Refuge are two fairly dependable sites. See Mlodinow and Karlson (1999) for more information.

Barn Owl—A rare to uncommon permanent resident of open habitats throughout the mainland. Rare in the Keys, apparently due to collisions with vehicles. More common during winter with the influx of northern breeders. Strictly nocturnal, but roosts in abandoned buildings, often communally. Perhaps easiest to see by driving farm roads after dark and watching for the birds perched on powerlines and poles, or on the ground. Barn Owls sometimes are fairly common along wooded portions of the main road through Everglades National Park. A roost is currently present in the Everglades Agricultural Area (page 212).

Eastern Screech-Owl—A fairly common permanent resident throughout, except absent from the Middle and Lower Keys. Occurs in all wooded areas, even in suburbs where trees have been retained. Responds well to recorded screech-owl calls, sometimes answering even during the day. Eastern Screech-Owls occur in two or three color morphs that range continuously from rufous to gray; the intermediate color is sometimes termed a brown morph. Rufous morphs tolerate warm temperatures better than other color morphs, and hence most Eastern Screech-Owls in Florida are of this morph.

Great Horned Owl—An uncommon but widespread permanent resident, absent only from the Keys. Prefers pinewoods or a mix of deciduous woods and pastures or fields. Most vocal during winter and spring, when breeding. In Florida, often nests in Bald Eagle or Osprey nests, occasionally after evicting the rightful owner.

Burrowing Owl—An uncommon to fairly common but *local* permanent resident of the peninsula and the Keys, represented by the endemic subspecies *Athene cunicularia floridana*. A highly isolated small population, discovered in 1993, is present at an inaccessible portion of Eglin Air Force Base in the western Panhandle. Burrowing Owls have significantly expanded their range in Florida in the past 100 years, coincident with widespread clearing of forests and draining of wetlands by humans. However, factors such as habitat loss and depredation by feral cats eventually eliminate Burrowing Owls from most developed areas. Small, isolated populations are especially ephemeral. A statewide survey in 1999, conducted primarily from public roadways, located 946 Burrowing Owl territories (Bowen 2001)—and not one of these was in natural habitats! Because Burrowing Owls now seem dependent on human-modified habitat, their prospects for long-term survival may be poor. Reliable sites include Cape Coral west of Fort Myers (page 191), near Lorida northeast of Lake Istokpoga (page 149), Fort Lauderdale Executive Airport (page 222), Miami International Airport (page 225), and a few sites near Marathon (page 254).

Barred Owl—A fairly common permanent resident of hardwood hammocks, swamps, and bayheads throughout the mainland; generally absent from the Keys. Responds well to tape recordings and imitations of its *Who-cooks-for-you, who-cooks-for-you-all* call. Because it is diurnal and becomes acclimated to humans where not persecuted, it can often be seen during the day in places such as Highlands Hammock State Park, Corkscrew Swamp Sanctuary, Everglades National Park (especially Mahogany Hammock), and similar areas. Usually fairly easy to locate with a tape, but *the use of tapes is forbidden in Corkscrew Swamp Sanctuary and Everglades National Park.*

Short-eared Owl—Represented in Florida by two populations with greatly differing patterns of occurrence. The North American subspecies (*Asio flammeus flammeus*) generally is a rare migrant and unpredictable winter resident of open areas of the Panhandle and northern half of the peninsula, irregular farther south. Owls from Greater Antillean populations (subspecies not yet determined; the taxonomy and nomenclature of Short-eared Owls in the region are confused and poorly documented) have expanded into Florida since the first documented observation in 1978. Antillean Short-eared Owls have been observed mostly in the Keys (especially Key West and the Dry Tortugas), but recently also north into the central peninsula. Most individuals observed have been juveniles that presumably have dispersed from their natal grounds, probably in Cuba, where the population is increasing since its discovery in 1981. Compared with birds from North America, those from the West Indies are somewhat smaller, have less streaking on the belly, and are buffier below. Hoffman et al. (1999) is an essential reference for Antillean Short-eared Owls in Florida.

Lesser Nighthawk— A rare and perhaps irregular migrant predominately along the Gulf coast, and an apparently regular winter resident (at least in recent years) in the southern peninsula, especially Frog Pond Wildlife Management Area (page 236) and Everglades National Park (either the Flamingo Campground or nearby Eco Pond). Concentrations of more than 75 (!) nighthawks have been reported at these sites. Lesser Nighthawks have never been known to vocalize in Florida, but their flight tends to be lower to the ground and more erratic than that of Common Nighthawks. Occasionally, the distinctive *buffy primary bars* of female Lesser Nighthawks have been noted in Florida.

Common Nighthawk—A fairly common spring and summer resident throughout, including the Keys. During fall migration, flocks of hundreds or even thousands can be seen heading south. *Despite many reports, there is no verifiable record of Common Nighthawk in Florida during the winter months.*

Antillean Nighthawk—An uncommon spring and summer resident of the Keys, primarily the Lower Keys. A few individuals have been observed at

Homestead and Florida City, and vagrants have been heard north into the central peninsula. From late April to August, Antillean Nighthawks usually are rather easy to locate by their calls around dusk at any of the following sites: the Key West airport (page 261), near the community college on Stock Island (page 258), on Big Pine Key (page 255), near the Marathon airport (page 254), and over open habitats elsewhere in the Lower Keys. Observed rarely but perhaps annually during spring at Dry Tortugas National Park; many of these birds are silent. Although slightly smaller and buffier than the Common Nighthawk, diagnostic identification is determined by voice; Antillean Nighthawk's one- to four-note pit calls (usually written as *killy-ka-dick* or *pittypit-pit*) bear no resemblance to the typical *peent* call of Common Nighthawk. Be aware, however, that Common Nighthawks, which also breed in the Lower Keys, may also utter a two-note call that sounds like *crick-et* or *pip-et*, and this call is very similar to that of the Antillean Nighthawk, although given only a few times.

Chuck-will's-widow—A fairly common spring and summer resident throughout the mainland, absent as a breeder from the Keys. Migrants occur throughout, and small numbers winter in the southern third of the peninsula and the Keys. Spring migration begins in late February, and singing is conspicuous from March through June or July. Its song, delivered at night, is characteristic of Florida's oak and pine woodlands.

Whip-poor-will—A rare to uncommon winter resident virtually throughout. Birds often sing in March before migrating northward. Often rather easy to find by driving roads in Everglades National Park at night. During winter, gives single-note *Whip!* calls around dawn and dusk, and whistled imitations of this call often induce birds to respond.

White-collared Swift—A casual straggler from two separate populations. A specimen found near Pensacola in January 1981 belonged to the subspecies *Streptoprocne zonaris mexicana* from Mexico. A second specimen, this one from Fort Lauderdale in September 1994, was of the West Indian subspecies *S. z. pallidifrons.*

Chimney Swift—An uncommon migrant throughout, and an uncommon to common spring and summer resident of cities and towns virtually throughout the mainland. Several hundred individuals may roost communally in chimneys. *There is no verifiable winter record in Florida.*

Vaux's Swift—A rare and perhaps irregular migrant and winter resident of cities and towns in the eastern Panhandle and the northern third of the peninsula, primarily Apalachicola, Tallahassee, and Gainesville. Unidentified *Chaetura* swifts observed elsewhere in the state may refer to Vaux's Swifts, but conclusive identification requires comparison of call-notes. *Any small grayish-brown swift observed in Florida from mid-November through February should be documented because Chimney Swifts are not known to occur in the state during winter.*

Antillean Palm Swift (*Tachornis phoenicobia*)—An accidental stray, probably from Cuba. The sole North American record refers to two birds at Key West in July–August 1972. Peterson's (2002) eastern guide is the only North American field guide that includes this species, although it also is included in *A Guide to the Birds of the West Indies* (Raffaele et al. 1998) and *Field Guide to the Birds of Cuba* (Garrido and Kirkconnell 2000). Smaller than Chimney Swifts, Antillean Palm Swifts have black upperparts with white rumps, and white underparts with conspicuous black breast bands and black undertail coverts.

Buff-bellied Hummingbird—A very rare winter resident; a few individuals are found annually or nearly so. Most frequently visits feeders in the western Panhandle, but birds have strayed south to Naples and Fort Lauderdale.

Bahama Woodstar—A casual visitor from the Bahamas to the southeastern coast, represented by only four verifiable records, the most recent at Homestead (July–August 1981). All sightings so far have been of females or immature males. Bahama Woodstars are illustrated in National Geographic Society (2002; adult male, adult female, and immature male), Peterson (2002; adult male and female), and Raffaele et al. (1998; adult male and female), but are not included in Kaufman (2000) or Sibley (2000).

Ruby-throated Hummingbird—A rare to uncommon spring and summer resident south into the central peninsula; more local in the southern mainland and absent from the Keys. Migrants occur throughout, sometimes commonly during spring. During winter, fairly common in the southern peninsula and the Keys, rare to uncommon farther north. Our knowledge of wintering hummingbirds in the Panhandle continues to improve with recent banding efforts.

Black-chinned Hummingbird—Recently detected as a rare to uncommon winter resident throughout, especially the Panhandle. Perhaps more likely to occur than Ruby-throated Hummingbird during winter in some areas from the central peninsula northward. Black-chinned Hummingbirds seem to have a behavioral trait that *helps* to distinguish them from Ruby-throated Hummingbirds. When hovering, Black-chinneds tend to bob their hind ends almost continuously, whereas Ruby-throateds tend to flick their tails only occasionally.

Anna's Hummingbird—A casual or accidental vagrant from the Pacific coast. There is only one Florida record: a female that wintered at Tallahassee (January–March 1988).

Calliope Hummingbird—A casual but perhaps increasing winter visitor to the Panhandle, with one record south to Lakeland. First identified in Florida in December 1989, but there have been five subsequent accepted reports.

Broad-tailed Hummingbird—A casual vagrant from the western U.S. There are two verifiable records: an immature male in Wakulla County (eastern Panhandle) during January–February 2000 and an immature female at Pensacola during November 2000–April 2001.

Rufous Hummingbird—A rare to uncommon winter resident throughout the mainland; not yet reported from the Keys. Perhaps most frequent in the Panhandle and extreme northern peninsula. Because all plumages except those of brown-backed adult males are indistinguishable in the field from Allen's Hummingbird, most non-banded *Selasphorus* hummingbirds in Florida should be identified solely to genus.

Allen's Hummingbird—Perhaps not field-identifiable in any plumage; conclusive identification seems to require measurements of outer tail feathers. Status uncertain, but there are at least two verifiable records: one male banded at Gainesville during winter 1996–1997, and an adult male banded at Pensacola in January 2002. Increased banding of wintering hummingbirds in Florida and elsewhere should improve our knowledge of the status of the Allen's Hummingbird in the Southeast.

Belted Kingfisher—Generally a fairly common winter resident throughout. Fall migration begins in July, and winter residents remain into mid-April. Kingfishers are rare and local breeders in river or stream banks in the Panhandle and northern third of the peninsula, and casual breeders farther south.

Red-headed Woodpecker—An uncommon to fairly common, *local* permanent resident of open pinelands, sandhills, and oak woodlands in the mainland. An irregular visitor to the extreme southern peninsula and the Keys, except at the Dry Tortugas, where it occurs annually or nearly so during spring. Withdraws during winter from some areas in northern Florida and may be irruptive elsewhere, with numbers varying considerably from year to year.

Golden-fronted Woodpecker—An accidental vagrant, presumably from Texas. The sole Florida record was of a male that spent 10 months (April 1981–February 1982) at Pensacola, bred with a female Red-bellied Woodpecker, and fledged two young. *Note that Red-bellied Woodpeckers can show yellow (rather than red) on their heads, and may be misidentified as Golden-fronted Woodpeckers.*

Red-bellied Woodpecker—A common permanent resident throughout, less common in the Keys. The most common and widespread woodpecker in Florida. "If you miss this one, you should turn in your binoculars" (Lane 1981).

Yellow-bellied Sapsucker—An uncommon migrant and winter resident of woodlands throughout.

Downy Woodpecker—A fairly common permanent resident of the mainland, found even in suburban yards. Absent from the Keys. Compared with Hairy Woodpeckers, forages more on the branches and twigs of trees than on trunks.

Hairy Woodpecker—A rare to uncommon, *local* permanent resident of the mainland. Virtually extirpated from the southern peninsula, and absent from the Keys. Perhaps the most difficult to find of Florida's woodpeckers. In the peninsula, Hairies are usually found in extensive, *fire-maintained* pine flatwoods and sandhills, and may be dependent on recently-burned areas with many dead and dying pines. Compared with Downy Woodpeckers, forages more on the trunks and larger branches of trees, and generally avoids small branches.

Red-cockaded Woodpecker—A rare to uncommon, *extremely local* permanent resident of mature, fire-maintained pine flatwoods and sandhills of the Panhandle and northern half of the peninsula. Rare south to the Big Cypress Swamp in southwestern Florida. In 1999, there were 1,226 Red-cockaded Woodpecker clusters (family groups) found on public lands in the state. Red-cockaded Woodpeckers are dependent upon mature (more than 60 years old) pines, usually Longleaf Pines, for cavity excavation. The birds laboriously excavate a cavity into a living pine infected with Red-heart (*Phellinus pini*), a fungal disease that attacks the tree's heartwood. Cavity excavation may take as much as three years to complete! The birds drill "resin wells" above and around the cavity entrance, which causes sap to flow down the trunk. These coatings of resin are believed to repel tree-climbing snakes that would otherwise prey on adults and nestlings. The resin also allows active cavity trees to be easily distinguished; sap on inactive trees ceases to flow and turns grayish. Most cavities face in a westerly direction, probably because the afternoon sun causes the greatest flow of resin. Red-cockaded Woodpeckers are colonial breeders, usually with one helper, typically a son from the previous breeding season, associated with each breeding pair. Each woodpecker roosts in its own cavity, and individuals may have alternate cavities. Most cavity trees on protected lands are painted with a band of white paint four or five feet above the ground. Because they forage widely during the day (average territories encompass 400 or more acres), Red-cockaded Woodpeckers are best viewed near their cavities. Cavity trees should be watched from a non-obtrusive distance—remember that the species is Federally Endangered—before dawn or an hour-and-a-half before dusk. The woodpeckers tend to remain nearby after departing their cavities in the morning, which may allow better viewing at this time. In the evening, the woodpeckers often fly directly into their cavities, allowing only brief views. However, because it is difficult to find active cavity trees in the dark, most birders arrive at a cluster site in the evening and wait around until the woodpeckers return to roost.

Because of their social nature, Red-cockaded Woodpeckers are a vocal species. Their call is a somewhat squeaky single *churrr!* note that is higher pitched than that of Red-bellied Woodpeckers. The male's red "cockade" for which the species is named is virtually impossible to see in the field, but the large white cheek patches of all Red-cockaded Woodpeckers are distinctive and conspicuous. Reliable sites include Apalachicola National Forest (page 60), Osceola National Forest (page 84), Ocala National Forest (page 91), Goethe State Forest (page 81), Withlacoochee State Forest (page 112), Avon Park Air Force Range (page 158), Three Lakes Wildlife Management Area (page 153), and Babcock-Webb Wildlife Management Area (page 188).

Northern Flicker—"Yellow-shafted" Flicker is a rare to uncommon permanent resident of the mainland and Upper Keys. Found primarily in large natural areas, it apparently cannot persist in developed areas. There are reports of "Red-shafted Flickers" or intergrades in Florida, but none of these is verifiable.

Pileated Woodpecker—A fairly common permanent resident of the mainland, occurring even in wooded suburban areas. Rare on Key Largo and absent elsewhere in the Keys. Vocal, especially in late winter, and usually not too hard to find. An impressive species when seen in flight.

Ivory-billed Woodpecker—The discovery of Ivory-billed Woodpeckers in eastern Arkansas in 2004–2005 stunned birders and ornithologists continentwide (and beyond). The discovery also suggested—albeit remotely—that Ivory-billeds may persist elsewhere in the southeastern United States, including the extensive riverine swamps of the Florida Panhandle or the vast Okefenokee Swamp area along the Georgia–Florida border. Needless to say, as perhaps the rarest bird in the world at present, any claim about the presence of Ivory-billed Woodpeckers in Florida or anywhere else needs to be unequivocally documented with photographs, videotapes, or audiotapes. Also, the location of any sighting should be disclosed solely to the proper authorities and not to the birding community at large. An online resource is <www.birds.cornell.edu/ivory/identifying>.

Western Wood-Pewee—An accidental vagrant from the western U.S. The only documented record in Florida involved a singing bird near Archbold Biological Station on 19 June 1995 (Woolfenden et al. 1996). Conclusive identification of the wood-pewees can be made only when they are singing their species-specific songs or when in-hand measurements are taken.

Eastern Wood-Pewee—An infrequently detected trans-Gulf migrant during spring, and an uncommon to fairly common fall migrant throughout (when it can be quite vocal). Breeds uncommonly in open pinewoods and sandhills in the Panhandle and the peninsula south to about Gainesville. *There are no documented winter records in Florida.*

Cuban Pewee (*Contopus caribaeus*)—Apparently a casual vagrant from the Bahamas or Cuba to the southeastern peninsula (and possibly the Keys). Through 2004, there was only one accepted record: one pewee videotaped at Spanish River Park in March–April 1995. Cuban Pewees are best distinguished by their rapid see-see-see-see calls that are distinct from vocalizations of all flycatchers of the eastern U.S. The only North American field guide that includes the Cuban Pewee is National Geographic Society (2002), but the species appears in Caribbean field guides such as *A Guide to the Birds of the West Indies* (Raffaele et al. 1998) and *Birds of Cuba* (Garrido and Kirkconnell 2000). Cuban Pewees are similar to Eastern Wood-Pewees but they have a partial eye-ring solely behind the eye (i.e., a crescent); at times they may appear slightly crested. Kaufman (1984) provides identification hints. **Commentary:** Raffaele et al. (1998) made the regrettable decision to rename Cuban Pewee as "Crescent-eyed Pewee." Field guides are not the place for undertaking nomenclatural changes that are at odds with those adopted by the American Ornithologists' Union. To make matters worse, Raffaele et al. (1998) do not mention the official name at all, which is sure to cause confusion among birders who cannot find the name Cuban Pewee in that guide.

Acadian Flycatcher—An uncommon to fairly common spring and summer resident of swamps and riparian forests of the Panhandle and northern half of the peninsula. A trans-Gulf spring migrant during spring; rare to uncommon along the Gulf coast and virtually unknown elsewhere. During fall, when it is usually vocal, it occurs fairly commonly throughout. *There are no documented winter records in Florida.*

Least Flycatcher—Occurs regularly during spring only in the Panhandle; a rare to uncommon fall migrant throughout. A rare but regular winter resident in southern Florida and the Keys, irregularly north to the northern half of the peninsula. *This is the only* Empidonax *verified to occur in Florida during winter, when it calls fairly frequently.*

Other *Empidonax* **flycatchers**—All five species of eastern *Empidonax* flycatchers are believed to have occurred in Florida, but no western-breeding species has yet been identified. Except for many Acadian Flycatchers, which are vocal during fall migration, fall-migrant empids in Florida tend to be silent and may be impossible to identify conclusively (despite observers' frequent claims to the contrary!). Northbound empids, in contrast, can be vocal. **Yellow-bellied Flycatcher** appears to be a rare migrant throughout, usually found during fall. **Alder and Willow Flycatchers** may be regular fall migrants and perhaps are irregular during spring, but separating the two species during migration is usually impossible—even many specimens can be identified only as "Traill's" Flycatchers. Because all verifiable records are of silent birds (i.e., specimens or banding records), the evidence supporting the occurrence of Alder Flycatchers in Florida "may be the weakest for any species admitted to the list of verifiable species" (Robertson and Woolfenden 1992). *Other than Least Flycatcher, there is no verifiable record of any* Empidonax *in Florida during winter.*

Eastern Phoebe—A fairly common winter resident throughout the mainland; irregular in the Keys. There are two confirmed breeding records in the western Panhandle near the Alabama border, in 1988 (Ware and Duncan 1989) and 1990. "If you miss this one, your life list must be under 100" (Lane 1981).

Vermilion Flycatcher—A rare but regular migrant along the Panhandle coast, and a rare winter resident, primarily of the peninsula from Gainesville southward. Unreported from the Keys. Prefers open habitats, typically with ponds or lakes nearby. Many wintering individuals appear to return to the same location for multiple years.

Ash-throated Flycatcher—Apparently a regular fall migrant and winter resident throughout the mainland, either increasing in frequency of occurrence or simply being correctly identified more often. Most frequent along the western Panhandle coast, at Gainesville, and at Lake Apopka. *Ten* Ash-throated Flycatchers were observed at Lake Apopka in February 2004.

Great Crested Flycatcher—A common spring and summer resident virtually throughout. Its loud, ringing *Wheep!* call is one of the most frequently heard avian sounds in Florida during spring. Increasingly observed during winter, especially south of Lake Okeechobee. Note that during this season, several other *Myiarchus* species may be found in the state.

Brown-crested Flycatcher—Apparently a very rare to rare, but regular winter resident. Found primarily in the extreme southern mainland and the Keys, but may winter north to Gainesville. Brown-crested Flycatchers are extremely similar to Great Crested Flycatchers (which occasionally have all-dark lower mandibles), but are easily distinguished by voice: a loud, clear *Whit* note.

Piratic Flycatcher (*Legatus leucophaius*)—An accidental vagrant from Tropical America to the southern U.S. The sole Florida record was an individual photographed at Dry Tortugas National Park on 15 March 1991 and originally identified as a Variegated Flycatcher (Bradbury 1992).

La Sagra's Flycatcher—First recorded in 1982 (Robertson and Biggs 1983) and now a rare but regular non-breeding visitor from Cuba or the Bahamas to the southeastern mainland and the Keys. Most reports have occurred during December–January and April–May, which may simply reflect peaks of observer activity. Illustrated in all major North American field guides. Compared with a Great Crested Flycatcher, La Sagra's is smaller, mostly white below and dull brown above, with an all-black bill. Feathers in the wings and tail may have an inconspicuous rusty tinge. The belly is pale, showing little or only faint yellow tones; the illustration in Peterson (2002) shows too much yellow below. Its voice is similar to the *Wheep!* of a Great Crested Flycatcher, but it is higher in pitch, lacks the burry quality, and is not as loud. An article by Smith and Evered (1992) contains much information and several color photographs.

Tropical and Couch's Kingbirds—Very rare but perhaps regular migrants and winter residents throughout; most frequently observed along the Gulf coast. Wintering individuals appear to return to the precisely same location for multiple years. There are more than 40 reports of Tropical/Couch's Kingbirds in Florida, but the only two verifiable records are both Tropical

Kingbirds (Snyder and Hopkins 2000). Summer occurrences along the central Gulf coast may represent post-breeding dispersal of Tropical Kingbirds from Mexico. Because Couch's Kingbird may plausibly stray to Florida, *call notes of all "Tropical-type" kingbirds in Florida should be tape-recorded if possible.*

Cassin's Kingbird—First reported in Florida in 1984 and first verified in 1988, but now reported annually or nearly so. Of the 15 reports through mid-2005, one was from the western Panhandle and the others were from Lake Apopka southward to Homestead and Florida City. Some individuals appear to return to winter in the same spot for multiple years.

Western Kingbird—A rare to uncommon winter resident in the southern half of the peninsula and the Keys; irregular farther north. May form surprisingly large roosts during winter; 72 were at Lake Apopka in January 2002. Migrants occur along both coasts, especially during fall, but are more frequent along the Gulf coast. *Yellow-bellied kingbirds in Florida should be scrutinized carefully, because Tropical and Cassin's Kingbirds may also be present, and other species may occur.*

Eastern Kingbird—An uncommon to common migrant throughout, especially during fall, when flocks of dozens or hundreds may be seen. Also a fairly common spring and summer resident of pinewoods, prairies, and pastures throughout the mainland. Despite annual reports on Christmas Bird Counts, there is only one verifiable record in Florida during winter: one at Lake Placid during December 1994–January 1995 (Bowman et al. 1995). *Wintering Eastern Kingbirds in Florida should be documented carefully, ideally by photograph or videotape.*

Gray Kingbird—An uncommon to locally common spring and summer resident along both coasts; easiest to find in the Mainline Keys. Breeds inland south of Lake Okeechobee, including suburban areas from West Palm Beach to Homestead, and throughout Everglades National Park. Local in the Panhandle and northeastern peninsula. In the Panhandle, it is found most frequently at Alligator Point, but a few pairs breed as far west as Fort Pickens. Wanders inland during migration, when flocks of 20 or more birds may be seen at favored coastal sites. There are several verifiable winter records in the southern peninsula. Note that some Gray Kingbirds have pale yellow underparts.

Loggerhead Kingbird (*Tyrannus caudifasciatus*)—For years, thought to be a casual visitor probably from Cuba to the southeastern coast and Keys, based on several observations in the 1970s. A recent re-examination of archived photographs (Smith et al. 2000) suggests that no report can be definitively identified as a Loggerhead Kingbird. The FOSRC and ABA Checklist Committee recently agreed with this assessment and removed the Loggerhead Kingbird from the Florida and North American lists. Smith et al. (2000) further suggested that the initial Florida observation, from Islamorada in December 1971, may represent a **Giant Kingbird** (*Tyrannus cubensis*), a native of Cuba. Identification of the Islamorada kingbird as a Giant Kingbird was rendered at the time by West Indian bird authority James Bond, but little value seems to have been placed on his assessment because some birders had already "identified" the bird as a Loggerhead Kingbird (Smith et al. 2000).

Scissor-tailed Flycatcher—A circum-Gulf migrant, rare along the Gulf coast, and a rare to locally uncommon winter resident in the southern half of the peninsula and the Keys. As many as 21 Scissor-tailed Flycatchers have been seen together at favored wintering sites. Reported in Florida in every month, but most common from October to April. Based on recent reports from elsewhere in the southeast, which suggest an expanding breeding range for this species, Scissor-tailed Flycatchers may eventually begin breeding at least occasionally in Florida.

Fork-tailed Flycatcher—An irregular straggler from South America, with all known reports from the southern half of the peninsula and the Keys. There have been about 19 reports (6 of these birds were photographed) since the first in 1952. Lockwood (1999) provides information on distribution and identification of Fork-tailed Flycatchers in the ABA Area.

Loggerhead Shrike—An uncommon to locally common permanent resident of open areas north of the Everglades, decidedly rare in the extreme southern peninsula and the Keys. Seemingly more common throughout during winter, with the addition of breeders from farther north. Although declining throughout their range, Loggerhead Shrikes are still easy to find in much of Florida.

White-eyed Vireo—A fairly common permanent resident virtually throughout. May be locally common during migration, especially at coastal areas during spring. Can be somewhat difficult to find during winter, when it is generally silent, but White-eyed Vireos respond well to pishing and Eastern Screech-Owl recordings. White-eyed Vireos include the calls of other birds in their songs—Hairy Woodpecker, Downy Woodpecker, White-breasted Nuthatch, Blue Jay, Florida Scrub-Jay, and Summer Tanager are some of the species mimicked by vireos in Florida.

Thick-billed Vireo—A casual straggler from the northern Bahamas to the southeastern coast and Keys. There apparently are only four verifiable records: birds at Bill Baggs Cape Florida State Park (September–October 1989), one at Hypoluxo Island, Palm Beach County (March–April 1991), one at Boot Key (October 2004), and one at Hollywood (May 2005). An article by Smith et al. (1990), which includes five color photographs of Thick-billed Vireos, should be consulted before reporting this species from Florida. Thick-billed Vireo is illustrated in Sibley (2000) and National Geographic Society (2002), but not in Kaufman (2000) or Peterson (2002).

Yellow-throated Vireo—A rare to uncommon migrant throughout, and an uncommon to fairly common spring and summer resident of sandhills and oak hammocks through the northern half of the peninsula. Also a rare but regular winter resident in the extreme southeastern mainland and the Keys; irregular elsewhere during winter. *Winter observations outside southern Florida* *often refer to misidentified Pine Warblers, which can occur miles from pinewoods outside the breeding season.*

Blue-headed Vireo—An uncommon migrant and winter resident throughout. **Plumbeous Vireo** has been reported in Florida several times but has not been verified.

Red-eyed Vireo—A fairly common migrant throughout, and an uncommon to common spring and summer resident of swamps, riparian areas, and moist woodlands of the mainland. Rare and local as a breeder south of Lake Okeechobee. *There are no documented winter records in Florida.*

Black-whiskered Vireo—A fairly common spring and summer resident of mangrove and hardwood hammocks from Sanibel Island and the Miami area south through the Keys. As recently as the early 1980s, this species occurred north to Clearwater and Merritt Island; brood parasitism by Brown-headed Cowbirds may be the cause of this range contraction. Very rare and irregular along the entire Gulf coast to Pensacola, usually during spring. Some of the Black-whiskered Vireos in the Panhandle have been of the subspecies *Vireo altiloquus altiloquus* (native to the Greater Antilles, wintering in South America), whereas Florida's breeding birds are *V. a. barbatulus.*

Blue Jay—A common permanent resident of wooded habitats throughout, except rare or absent in the Middle and Lower Keys. Numbers during winter are augmented by birds that breed north of Florida (the subspecies *Cyanocitta cristata bromia*). "Even five-year-old kids can identify this one" (Lane 1981).

Florida Scrub-Jay—The only bird species endemic to Florida under current taxonomy is generally a rare or uncommon, *very local* permanent resident of the peninsula. Florida Scrub-Jay populations have declined at least 90 percent over the past century due to destruction of scrub habitats for development and citrus groves, and from long-term fire exclusion. Further declines can be expected, especially where populations are small and isolated. Florida Scrub-Jays are cooperative breeders; young birds often remain with their parents for up to several years and help to defend the territory and to raise subsequent broods. Perhaps 10,000 Florida Scrub-Jays remain, with the largest populations found at Ocala National Forest (page 91), Merritt Island National Wildlife Refuge (page 157), and along the Lake Wales Ridge from Lake Wales to Venus (pages 157–165). Other dependable sites include Oscar Scherer State Park (page 139), and Avon Park Air Force Range (page 158). Ideal scrub-jay habitat is oak scrub 4–7 feet tall with patches of open sand and little or no tree canopy. A study of Florida Scrub-Jays has been conducted over more than 35 years at Archbold Biological Station (page 163), and several other populations are color-banded and under study. *Note that the few scrub-jays found near Naples (page 199) represent an unsustainable and experimental (i.e., introduced) population that is not ABA-countable.*

American Crow—An uncommon to common permanent resident of non-coastal habitats, especially ranchlands throughout most of the mainland.

Absent from the Keys and the region southeast of Lake Okeechobee, but curiously present at Flamingo, Everglades National Park.

Fish Crow—A common to abundant, largely coastal permanent resident of the mainland, even in cities. Absent from the Keys except for a small population at Key West. Except around large water bodies, Fish Crows are rare or absent from the interior, where American Crows dominate.

Purple Martin—An uncommon to abundant migrant throughout, and a local, uncommon to abundant spring and summer resident of the mainland. The first "spring" arrivals appear in mid-January, and "fall" migration may begin as early as late May; most breeding colonies are deserted in June. Gathers in huge summer roosts prior to migrating out of Florida. Breeds in natural cavities at Orlando Wetlands Park. Otherwise, perhaps limited to artificial nest-sites (gourds and martin houses). *Despite nearly annual reports on Christmas Bird Counts, there are no verifiable records in Florida during November or December.*

Cuban Martin—An accidental vagrant from Cuba. The sole North American record is one bird collected at Key West in May 1895. Other purported Cuban Martin specimens were re-examined recently and were determined to be Purple Martins (Banks 2000). Cuban Martins are common spring and summer residents throughout Cuba and the Isle of Youth. Males cannot be distinguished from male Purple Martins in the field. Females are said to be browner below than are female Purple Martins, but conclusive field identification perhaps is not possible.

Southern Martin—An accidental visitor from southern South America. One collected at Key West in August 1890 (but not identified correctly until 1963) constitutes the sole record for the ABA Area.

Tree Swallow—An uncommon to locally abundant migrant and winter resident throughout. Numbers fluctuate widely from year to year, and Tree Swallows can be hard to find locally during some winters. Roosts communally in huge assemblages in freshwater marshes; some flocks have contained *one million or more. Tree Swallows often are identified in August, but most of these likely refer to immature Barn Swallows, which have short tails and which can be nearly pure white below—any Tree Swallow in Florida before October is unusual.*

Mangrove Swallow—An accidental straggler from Mexico. The sole North American record is one bird at Viera Wetlands in November 2002 (Sykes et al. 2004).

Bahama Swallow—A casual visitor from the Bahamas to the southeastern peninsula and the Keys. There are 13 accepted Florida reports (Smith and Smith 1990), including an adult that spent five consecutive breeding seasons at a Cave Swallow colony at Cutler Ridge until April 1992. There have been no subsequent reports. Except for two winter reports, Bahama Swallows have been observed in Florida from March through mid-August. Some swallows (including the Cutler Ridge bird) have remained for many weeks after their initial discoveries. Breeding in the state is purely hypothetical; Bahama Swallows are pinewoods cavity-nesters. All plumages of Bahama Swallow have white underwing coverts, compared to dark underwings in all plumages of Tree Swallows. Juveniles in post-breeding dispersal may be overlooked in Florida. Smith and Smith (1990) provide a complete history of the Bahama Swallow in Florida, along with four color photographs—including juveniles, which are not featured in any North American field guide or in *A Guide to Birds of the West Indies* (Raffaele et al. 1998).

Northern Rough-winged Swallow—A rare to fairly common migrant throughout. Also a fairly common and widespread breeder in the western Panhandle and a rare to uncommon breeder throughout the peninsula. Flocks of dozens or hundreds of Northern Rough-winged Swallows often are seen during winter south of Lake Okeechobee.

Cliff Swallow—Generally a rare migrant throughout and a very rare, irregular breeder (Lewis and McNair 1998). There is one verifiable winter record.

Cave Swallow—Represented in Florida by two subspecies that may be candidates for full-species status (Smith et al. 1988). Since at least 1987, the Caribbean subspecies (*Hirundo fulva fulva*) has bred under highway overpasses across canals south of Miami (page 232), and the birds now are virtually year-round residents. Additionally, Cave Swallows have recently been found roosting under bridges and overpasses north to the Fort Lauderdale area, so the breeding population may be expanding northward. Elsewhere in Florida, Cave Swallows are rare, regular, but *unpredictable* migrants or vagrants throughout; they often are reported from Dry Tortugas National Park. Many (most?) of the Cave Swallows observed from the Panhandle and northern half of the peninsula, along with increasing reports from the southern peninsula, are said to involve the subspecies that breeds in the southwestern United States (*H. f. pelodoma*), which has been documented only once in the state.

Barn Swallow—An uncommon to abundant migrant throughout, and a rare to common *local* breeder throughout, with abundance decreasing southward. Fall migration begins in July and continues into December, but few winter reports are verifiable.

Carolina Chickadee—A permanent resident, common in the Panhandle, uncommon in the peninsula south to Tampa Bay, Lakeland, and Merritt Island, and essentially unknown farther south.

Tufted Titmouse—An uncommon to common permanent resident of the Panhandle and northern half of the peninsula. Rare to uncommon in the southwestern peninsula, and mostly absent in the southeastern peninsula and the Keys. Responds readily to pishing and Eastern Screech-Owl calls, and scolding titmice often attract other landbirds.

Red-breasted Nuthatch—An irruptive winter resident, often absent but sometimes fairly common. Most frequent in pine forests in the Panhandle and extreme northern peninsula, with irregular reports into the southern peninsula. *Carolina Wrens have been misidentified as Red-breasted Nuthatches in Florida on several occasions—habitat preferences of the two species differ, but plumage patterns and tree-climbing behavior are similar.*

White-breasted Nuthatch—A rare to uncommon permanent resident of oak/pine woodlands in the Red Hills region from Tallahassee northward. Very rare and unexpected elsewhere in Florida. Until the 1930s, White-breasted Nuthatches were fairly common and widespread permanent residents in the Panhandle and northern half of the peninsula, with winter reports south to Everglades National Park and Miami. Destruction of Florida's Longleaf Pine community following clear-cutting may have been responsible for the dramatic range contraction. Elinor Klapp Phipps Park (page 66) and Tall Timbers Research Station (page 64) are two reliable sites.

Brown-headed Nuthatch—An uncommon to fairly common permanent resident of pinewoods and plantations south through the central peninsula. Rare to uncommon farther south, and absent from the Keys. Responds well to Eastern Screech-Owl calls, and flocks with Tufted Titmice, Carolina Chickadees, Pine Warblers, and other small passerines. The high, squeaky "rubber ducky" calls of Brown-headed Nuthatches are distinctive.

Brown Creeper—A rare winter resident in the Panhandle and northern peninsula, very rare and irregular to the extreme southern peninsula. Not known from the Keys. Florida Caverns State Park is a reliable spot.

Carolina Wren—A common and widespread resident throughout the mainland. Absent from the Keys except for Key Largo. Its loud, variable, bi- or tri-syllabic song is one of the most common avian sounds of Florida. Their plumage and tree-climbing behavior have resulted in Carolina Wrens being misidentified as Red-breasted Nuthatches, despite different habitat preferences.

House Wren—A fairly common winter resident throughout, but less common in the Keys. This is one of the few wintering species that routinely sings while in Florida, primarily during spring and fall.

Winter Wren—A rare to locally uncommon winter resident of the Panhandle and extreme northern peninsula. Reports south of Gainesville do not inspire confidence. Prefers brushy areas along streams and rivers. Regularly found at Florida Caverns State Park.

Sedge Wren—A fairly common winter resident of grassy areas south through the central peninsula. Secretive but fairly easy to find once its distinctive *chip-chip* call is learned. Rare farther south, and very rare in the Keys. Sedge Wrens often remain to late May, and some birds have constructed nests, but there are no breeding reports in Florida.

Marsh Wren—A fairly common to common permanent resident of coastal marshes, represented by two breeding subspecies. **Marian's Marsh Wren** (*Cistothorus palustris marianae*) breeds along the Gulf coast from St.

Marks to New Port Richey, while **Worthington's Marsh Wren** (*C. p. griseus*) breeds along the Atlantic coast south to Jacksonville. Additionally, populations from at least five other subspecies (*dissaeptus, iliacus, palustris, thryophilus*, and *waynei*) that breed north of Florida winter throughout (Stevenson and Anderson 1994).

Red-whiskered Bulbul—An ABA-countable exotic, native to India. A few birds that escaped from a Miami "bird farm" in 1960 began breeding shortly afterward. The species is now established marginally in residential areas south of Miami at Kendall and Pinecrest. The population has not been censused since 1969–1970, when "about 250" bulbuls were thought to occupy "3.2 square miles" of suburbs (Carleton and Owre 1975). Red-whiskered Bulbuls are usually fairly easy to find in neighborhoods surrounding the Kendall tennis courts (page 231), and north of Kendall Baptist Hospital (page 231). Their song is a series of whistles that rise and fall.

Golden-crowned Kinglet—An irruptive winter resident, ranging from fairly common to absent. Occurs primarily in the Panhandle, with birds occurring south to central Florida during invasion years.

Ruby-crowned Kinglet—A fairly common migrant and winter resident of the Panhandle and northern half of the peninsula; less common farther south.

Blue-gray Gnatcatcher—A fairly common to very common migrant and winter resident throughout. Also an uncommon to fairly common spring and summer resident in most of the mainland, but largely absent as a breeder from the southern Atlantic coast. Does not breed in the Keys.

Northern Wheatear—A casual fall vagrant from Arctic Canada. There are five accepted reports in Florida: two along the Panhandle coast, one east of Naples, one at Miami, and one at Big Pine Key. All individuals were found between 21 September and 2 November, and all appear to represent the subspecies *Oenanthe oenanthe oenanthe* (Smith and Woolfenden 1995).

Eastern Bluebird—An uncommon to locally common permanent resident throughout most of the mainland. Local in the extreme southern peninsula, and absent from the Keys. Numbers during winter are augmented by breeders from farther north. Prefers pine flatwoods, pastures, and similar open areas with scattered trees. Eastern Bluebirds recently have been re-established into the Long Pine Key region of Everglades National Park, where they became extirpated in the 1960s.

Veery, Swainson's Thrush, and Gray-cheeked Thrush—Generally rare to uncommon migrants throughout; more common coastally during spring. *There are no verifiable wintering records in Florida for any of these three species.*

Bicknell's Thrush—Breeds in southeastern Canada and the northeastern United States, and winters in the West Indies (primarily the Dominican

Republic). Although morphological measurements *generally* are diagnostic for separating Bicknell's Thrush from Gray-cheeked Thrush, *conclusive* field identification of silent birds may be impossible (Sibley 2000, Rimmer et al. 2001). The status of Bicknell's Thrush in Florida is uncertain, although birds may migrate regularly along the Atlantic coast, especially during spring. Bicknell's Thrush specimens from Florida purportedly exist (Stevenson and Anderson 1994, Rimmer et al. 2001), and nocturnal flight calls of presumed Bicknell's Thrushes have been recorded over Cape Canaveral (Evans 1994). However, the species is not on the official Florida bird list (Bowman 2000, 2001) because the FOSRC is awaiting taxonomic clarity before it considers Florida reports. Although Bicknell's Thrush was granted species status in 1995, some ornithologists (e.g., Marshall 2001) still consider Bicknell's Thrush to be a subspecies of Gray-cheeked Thrush.

Hermit Thrush—A migrant and winter resident throughout, uncommon south to the central peninsula and rare farther south. Irregular in the Keys.

Wood Thrush—A rare migrant throughout, and an uncommon to fairly common spring and summer resident of the Panhandle and peninsula south sparingly to Gainesville. There are two verifiable winter records.

American Robin—An irruptive winter resident throughout the mainland, with numbers varying considerably from year to year. Generally rare in the Keys. Also a rare to uncommon, *local* spring and summer resident in the Panhandle, with occasional breeding reports south to Tampa.

Varied Thrush—A casual winter visitor from the West. There are four verifiable records: Lantana (October 1977), Panama City (January 1998 and November 2002), and Honeymoon Island (November 1996).

Gray Catbird—A fairly common to common migrant and winter resident throughout. As a breeder, rare and local in the Panhandle and northern third of the peninsula, irregular south through the central peninsula.

Northern Mockingbird—Generally a common to abundant, ubiquitous permanent resident throughout, although less common in undeveloped areas. Irregular at Dry Tortugas National Park. Some northern breeders migrate to Florida during fall, but these movements are largely obscured by the resident population. The state bird of Florida, mockingbirds are superb mimics, and the "talent" of some individuals is quite impressive.

Bahama Mockingbird—First noted in 1976 and now a regular visitor from the Bahamas to the southeastern coast and Keys, mostly during spring. One or more Bahama Mockingbirds built nests at Key West in 1991 and 1992, but reports of Bahama Mockingbirds nesting successfully with Northern Mockingbirds, or of Bahama Mockingbird x Northern Mockingbird hybrids, are not verifiable.

Brown Thrasher—A permanent resident throughout, common in the Panhandle and northern half of the peninsula, uncommon farther south. Very rare in the Keys. Numbers during winter are augmented by northern breeders.

European Starling—Exotic, native to Europe and Africa, but now nearly cosmopolitan. An uncommon to common permanent resident of urban areas throughout; rare or absent from large natural areas. Sometimes abundant during winter with the addition of northern breeders.

Common Myna—A non-countable *terrestrial* exotic, native to Asia but introduced into many areas. Much more common and widespread in Florida than Hill Myna. First noted at Miami in 1983, Common Mynas have been observed north to Lake Placid, Sanford (north of Orlando), and Cocoa Beach, with one at Jacksonville in spring 2004. A small population has been present at Clewiston (page 209) since the 1980s. The Florida population seems clearly to be established, but the FOSRC is awaiting publication of a formal study. Preferred habitats are fast-food restaurants and shopping centers, where mynas build nests in signs and other artificial "cavities." Rather easy to find at the junction of US-1 and SR-9336 (page 232), but perhaps equally common in much of the surrounding suburban areas of Florida City, Homestead, and elsewhere in southeastern Florida. Included in Kaufman (2000), Sibley (2000), and National Geographic Society (2002), but not in Peterson (2002).

Hill Myna—A non-countable *arboreal* exotic, native to India, Southeast Asia, and Indonesia. Hill Mynas were rather widespread along the southeastern coast in the 1970s and 1980s but are now restricted to the Miami metropolitan area, where they are locally uncommon. Hill Mynas in Florida seem to nest exclusively in natural cavities, primarily palm snags. Matheson Hammock Park (page 229) and Kendall Baptist Hospital (page 231) are two reliable sites.

American Pipit—A migrant and winter resident of muddy shorelines and recently plowed fields. Common in the Panhandle and northern peninsula, rare to uncommon in the central peninsula, and rare and irregular farther south.

Sprague's Pipit—A very rare and perhaps irregular winter resident of artificial shortgrass habitats (e.g., airport shoulders and road shoulders) along the Panhandle coast; casual elsewhere. Apalachicola Airfield (page 58) usually has one or more Sprague's Pipits each winter (McNair 1998).

Cedar Waxwing—An irruptive winter resident, with numbers varying considerably from year to year. May not arrive in numbers until December, and usually most numerous during late winter or early spring, when flocks of hundreds may be seen. Flocks often remain into May.

Wood-warblers—Only 12 species of wood-warblers breed regularly in Florida, but 42 species have been documented in the state. Excluding the probably extinct Bachman's Warbler (once a locally common migrant along the Gulf coast) and four irregularly-occurring species (Black-throated Gray, Townsend's, Golden-cheeked, and Kirtland's Warblers), 37 species occur in Florida annually or nearly so.

Orange-crowned Warbler—A rare to uncommon migrant and winter resident throughout.

Northern Parula—A common migrant throughout, arriving early in both spring (February) and fall (July). Also a generally common to very common spring and summer resident south through the central peninsula. Rare and local as a breeder south of Lake Okeechobee, and absent from the Keys. Small numbers winter in the southern half of the peninsula and the Keys.

Yellow Warbler—Represented in Florida by two groups that formerly were considered separate species. At least four subspecies of the widespread North American "Yellow Warbler" group have occurred in Florida. The eastern subspecies (*Dendroica petechia aestiva*) is an uncommon to fairly common fall migrant throughout (especially late July–early September) and is less frequent during spring. Yellow Warblers are very rare during winter in the southern half of the peninsula, and few observations are verifiable; bright Orange-crowned Warblers may be the source of many reports. Two other races, *D. p. amnicola* and *D. p. rubiginosa*, have occurred during migration (Stevenson and Anderson 1994). The subspecies *D. p. gundlachi* of the West Indian **"Golden Warbler"** group is a fairly common permanent resident (possibly with some withdrawal during winter) of mangrove forests of the extreme southern peninsula (mainly the southwestern side) and the Keys. Areas near the Card Sound Bridge toll booth (page 247), on Saddlebunch Key (page 258), and on Boca Chica Key (page 258) are reliable spots. Except for some bright male *D. p. gundlachi* that show a distinct chestnut cap, Yellow Warblers cannot be safely identified to subspecies in the field by plumage characters.

Yellow-rumped Warbler—**Myrtle Warbler** is a common to abundant winter resident throughout, although somewhat irruptive in the extreme south. **Audubon's Warbler** is a casual migrant or vagrant, with four verifiable records, all within the past 12 years.

Yellow-throated Warbler—A fairly common permanent resident of cypress or mixed pine/cypress forests in the Panhandle and northern half of the peninsula. Most birds move out of the western Panhandle during fall. Uncommon throughout during migration, with the first southbound birds arriving in mid-July. An uncommon winter resident of the southern half of the peninsula and the Keys.

Pine Warbler—A common permanent resident of pinewoods throughout the mainland; may be abundant during winter, when birds join flocks of Eastern Bluebirds, Tufted Titmice, Palm Warblers, and other species, *often far from pine habitats*; male Pine Warblers may often be misidentified as Yellow-throated Vireos. Irregular in the Keys, occurring mainly during winter

Prairie Warbler—Represented in Florida by two subspecies that have different seasonal and distributional patterns and habitat preferences. The widespread subspecies *Dendroica discolor discolor* is a rare to uncommon spring and summer resident of second-growth habitats in the Panhandle and the northern third of the peninsula. It is uncommon throughout during migration, with fall migration beginning in mid-July, and it winters uncommonly in the southern half of the peninsula and the Keys, rarely farther north. The endemic **Florida Prairie Warbler** (*D. d. paludicola*) is a permanent resident of mangrove forests from about Hudson and Merritt Island southward through the Keys. Its northern range limits have contracted since the early 1980s, perhaps due to brood parasitism by Brown-headed Cowbirds. The two races of Prairie Warbler cannot be safely identified in the field by plumage characters.

Palm Warbler—A common and *largely terrestrial* migrant and winter resident throughout. Two subspecies (along with an intermediate plumage) occur in Florida: the western-breeding **Western Palm Warbler** (*Dendroica palmarum palmarum*) and the eastern-breeding **Yellow Palm Warbler** *D. p. hypochrysea*. According to a review of specimens from Florida, the western subspecies predominates in the state, with Yellow Palm Warblers constituting fewer than 10 percent of the individuals found (Johnston 1976).

Black-and-white Warbler—An uncommon migrant and winter resident throughout, except rare in the western Panhandle during winter. Fall migration begins in mid-July.

American Redstart—An uncommon to common migrant throughout, and a rare to uncommon winter resident of the extreme southern peninsula and the Keys; irregular during winter farther north. Perhaps a regular breeder in the western Panhandle, but there seems to be only one confirmed breeding record: a pair feeding young at Laurel Hill (a few miles from the Georgia border) in June 1962.

Prothonotary Warbler—A fairly common spring and summer resident in the Panhandle, uncommon and local in the northern half of the peninsula, and rare farther south to Big Cypress Swamp. Also a rare to uncommon migrant throughout. There is one verifiable winter record.

Swainson's Warbler—A rare and *inconspicuous* migrant throughout, preferring moist, shady areas with abundant leaf litter; recently detected in the Keys through banding efforts. A rare to uncommon spring and summer resident of swamp edges and other wet forested areas in the Panhandle, rarely south to the Steinhatchee and Gainesville areas. There are two verifiable winter records.

Ovenbird—An uncommon to fairly common migrant throughout. Also an uncommon winter resident of moist deciduous woodlands and swamps in the southern half of the peninsula and the Keys; rare and irregular farther north.

Northern Waterthrush—An uncommon migrant throughout, especially during fall. Also a rare to uncommon winter resident in the southern half of the peninsula and the Keys; rare and irregular farther north.

Louisiana Waterthrush—An uncommon migrant throughout, being one of the first migrants to move north during spring (February) and south during fall (June). Also a rare spring and summer resident in the Panhandle and irregularly into the northwestern peninsula. A rare but perhaps regular winter resident of the extreme southern peninsula and the Keys, irregular farther north.

Kentucky Warbler—A rare to uncommon trans-Gulf migrant during spring, but found throughout during fall. Also an uncommon spring and summer resident of moist woodlands in the Panhandle and extreme northwestern peninsula. There is one verifiable winter record.

Common Yellowthroat—A fairly common permanent resident throughout the mainland, but does not breed in the Keys. Also an uncommon to abundant migrant throughout.

Hooded Warbler—An uncommon to fairly common spring and summer resident in the Panhandle and northern third of the peninsula. Also an uncommon to common migrant throughout. There is one verifiable winter record.

Yellow-breasted Chat—Breeds fairly commonly in the Panhandle, and locally in the peninsula (primarily the western half) south to Crystal River and Lake Apopka. Also a surprisingly rare migrant throughout, irregular at most sites. During winter, rare in the southern third of the peninsula and the Keys, irregular elsewhere.

Bananaquit—An occasional visitor from the Bahamas to the southeastern coast and the Upper Keys, with one record from Fort De Soto Park. There are about 35 accepted reports, with six of these occurring from 1992 through 2004. Bananaquits in southern Florida represent the white-throated subspecies *Coereba flaveola bahamensis* from the Bahamas. The Fort De Soto individual may plausibly have flown from the Yucatán Peninsula, as the Yucatán race (*C. f. caboti*) also is white-throated (Howell and Webb 1995).

Blue-gray Tanager—A non-countable exotic, native to Central and South America. Tiny "populations" at Hollywood, Dania, and Miami have been extirpated since 1975 or earlier. The highest count at any location was *three* individuals!

Summer Tanager—A rare to uncommon migrant throughout, and a fairly common spring and summer resident of oak hammocks, sandhills, and pine flatwoods south through the central peninsula. Rare or absent as a breeder south of Lake Okeechobee and absent from the Keys. A rare but regular winter resident in the southern half of the peninsula and the Keys, irregular farther north.

Western Spindalis—A rare but probably annual visitor from the Bahamas (and Cuba?) to the southeastern coast and the Keys, with a single observation near Bradenton. Nearly all observations have been of singles, but flocks of two, three, and even seven birds have been seen. Two-thirds of the birds have been males, possibly simply because their bright, distinctive plumage makes them easier to locate and identify. Spindalises have been seen in Florida in every month except July, with most observations in April, May, and December. Most verifiable records of males refer to *Spindalis zena zena*, the only spindalis with a black back, but a green-backed male at Key West during October 2004–January 2005 was photographed. The four subspecies of green-backed Western Spindalises are *townsendi* of the northern Bahamas, *pretrei* from Cuba, *benedicti* of Cozumel Island, Mexico, and *salvini* of the Cayman Islands. Field marks to distinguish the various green-backed Western Spindalises may tentatively have been worked out for males, but females probably cannot be identified to subspecies, except possibly by voice (Garrido et al. 1997). See Pranty and Smith (2001) for a thorough summary of the occurrence of Western Spindalises in Florida. Garrido et al. (1997) is the sole source for separating the various species and subspecies.

Red-legged Honeycreeper (*Cyanerpes cyaneus*)—Status uncertain; native to Central and South America. Honeycreepers in Cuba, Jamaica, and Bonaire are "probably based on escaped cage birds" (AOU 1998), but are considered native to Cuba by some Cuban authorities. Through August 2005, there have been six reports—all of adult males—in the Miami area or the Keys. So far, no report has been accepted by the FOSRC as a native vagrant due to uncertainty about the provenance of birds. While natural vagrancy from Mexico or Cuba is possible (even likely), the presence of Red-legged Honeycreepers in aviculture in Florida muddies the issue (although the locations of some of the honeycreepers—on islands within national parks—is a point in favor of vagrancy). Additional observations will be necessary to develop a pattern of occurrence before the possibility of escapees can be ruled out.

Yellow-faced Grassquit—A casual stray from the West Indies to the extreme southern mainland and Dry Tortugas National Park. There are five reports, all recent: Homestead (July 1990, photographed), Dry Tortugas National Park (April 1994, April 2000, and April 2002), and Eco Pond, Everglades National Park (January 2001, photographed). Two other Yellow-faced Grassquits seen at Miami in September 1992 were considered escapees. Smith et al. (1991) provide information on the first Florida record, along with extensive discussion on subspecific identification and importation patterns. Grassquits are kinglet-sized finches common in shrubby habitats in the West Indies and Central America. National Geographic Society (1999) is the only North American field guide that illustrates Yellow-faced Grassquit (a male only). *Field Guide to the Birds of Cuba* (Garrido and Kirkconnell 2000) and *A Guide to the Birds of the West Indies* (Raffaele et al. 1998) illustrate both sexes. Yellow-faced Grassquits are grayish-olive overall, with black eyes, bill, and legs. Males have an orange-yellow line above the eye that extends from the bill to the ear-patch, and an orange-yellow chin and throat, bordered by black. The breast is black, but the remainder of the underparts are olive. Females are mostly olive, with only a hint of the yellow on the face. The Central American subspecies that occurs in Florida aviculture has extensive black on the breast (extending to the belly), cheeks, and crown, compared with the West Indian subspecies described above.

Black-faced Grassquit—A casual stray from the West Indies to the southeastern coast and the Keys, with five verifiable records. Recent observations are from Homestead (March 1993), Key West (May 1993), and Everglades National Park (September 2003). Sibley (2000) and Kaufman (2000) do not include Black-faced Grassquit, but National Geographic Society (2002) and Peterson (2002) do, as do Raffaele et al. (1998) and Garrido and Kirkconnell (2000).

Cuban Grassquit (*Tiaris canora*)—Exotic; native to Cuba and the Isle of Youth. All 11 reports from southeastern Florida and the Keys are thought to represent escapees (Cuban Grassquits are very popular among Cuban expatriates who now live in the region.) The two most recent sightings were singles at Miami (April 1995 and December 2000). The only North American field guide that includes Cuban Grassquit is Peterson (2002), which illustrates a male. *A Guide to the Birds of the West Indies* (Raffaele et al. 1998) includes illustrations of both sexes, as does *Field Guide to the Birds of Cuba* (Garrido and Kirkconnell 2000). Cuban Grassquits are olive above, with a black breast and pale belly and undertail coverts. The nape and crown are olive, and the face is black, with a large yellow crescent that curves downward from behind the eye to the breast. The female is similar but has a rusty face and entirely pale underparts.

Sparrows—Only four species of sparrows breed regularly in Florida, but 17 additional species winter annually in the state, and several others occur irregularly. Most sparrows are typically found in open, weedy or grassy "sparrow fields". Some species prefer dry fields, others prefer wet areas, and still others may be found in either. Similarly, the height, thickness, and type of plant cover (grass, weeds, or shrubs) all affect the distribution of sparrows. Saltmarsh Sharp-tailed, Nelson's Sharp-tailed, and Seaside Sparrows are restricted to brackish or salt marshes.

Green-tailed Towhee—A casual vagrant from the west. There are two verifiable records, both in the central peninsula: Lake Alfred (January–February 1990) and Honeymoon Island State Park (February–March 2003).

Spotted Towhee—An accidental vagrant from the west, represented by a single record: one bird collected in the eastern Panhandle (December 1967).

Eastern Towhee—A common to abundant permanent resident throughout the mainland, but only a rare winter resident in the Keys. The race that inhabits the extreme western Panhandle, *Pipilo erythrophthalmus canaster*, has red irides. *P. e. rileyi*, also resident in the western Panhandle, has orange irides. Elsewhere in Florida, *P. e. alleni* has white or pale yellow irides. During winter, red- or orange-eyed towhees from northern breeding populations may be locally common in the peninsula. Towhees in the peninsula sing a variety of songs, and few or none of these sound like the *Drink your tea* song mentioned in most field guides; call notes also differ.

Bachman's Sparrow—A fairly common permanent resident of the Panhandle and northern two-thirds of the peninsula. Rare farther south in the peninsula during winter. Bachman's Sparrows are found in open pinewoods, pine plantations, and dry prairies. They are difficult to locate except from March (sometimes February) through July or August, when males are singing. The beautiful song is variable, but the most common variety is a single drawn-out whistle followed by a series of trills; it sounds like *He-e-e-e-e-re kitty, kitty, kitty, kitty*. Males typically sing from a perch (often a pine branch) five–20 feet above the ground (perch heights of sparrows inhabiting dry prairies are one–three feet). During winter, birds often respond to recorded Bachman's Sparrows songs (Cox and Jones 2004), usually by chipping excitedly; some may respond to an Eastern Screech-Owl tape. Bachman's Sparrows in Florida are known to escape danger by running into Gopher Tortoise burrows (Stevenson and Anderson 1994, Dean and Vickery 2002).

Chipping Sparrow—A winter resident, fairly common to common in the Panhandle and extreme northern peninsula, uncommon to rare farther south. Irregular in the Keys. There are three breeding reports from the Panhandle, the most recent in 1959.

Clay-colored Sparrow—A rare migrant throughout, and a rare winter resident of the peninsula.

Field Sparrow—A rare to uncommon permanent resident of the eastern Panhandle and northwestern peninsula. Also a winter resident of the mainland, uncommon to common in the Panhandle and northern peninsula but generally rare farther south. Not known from the Keys except for a single report from Dry Tortugas National Park.

Vesper Sparrow—A winter resident, fairly common in the Panhandle, uncommon south into the central peninsula, and rare south through the Keys.

Lark Sparrow—A rare migrant throughout, and a rare winter resident, primarily of the peninsula. Lark Sparrows typically are the first sparrow to arrive during fall; the earliest migrants are found in August.

Savannah Sparrow—The most common and widespread wintering sparrow in Florida, occurring throughout, even at Dry Tortugas National Park. Six subspecies have been collected in the state, and flocks often appear to contain two or more subspecies.

Grasshopper Sparrow—Represented in Florida by two subspecies. The **Eastern subspecies** (*Ammodramus savannarum pratensis*) is a rare to uncommon but widespread migrant and winter resident of grassy fields and dry prairies. The **Florida Grasshopper Sparrow** (*A. s. floridanus*) is a permanent resident endemic to dry prairies in south-central Florida; all remaining populations occur within 10 miles of the Kissimmee River in Highlands,

Okeechobee, and Osceola Counties. Formerly much more widespread, it is now restricted to Avon Park Air Force Range (nearly extirpated), Kissimmee Prairie Preserve State Park (page 166), Three Lakes Wildlife Management Area (page 153), and adjacent private properties. The total population of Florida Grasshopper Sparrows was thought to number about 1,000 individuals in 1998 (Delany et al. 1999), and populations have declined since that time. Note that despite what is written in field guides, *floridanus* and *pratensis* cannot be safely distinguished in the field—or even in the hand. The identification of Florida Grasshopper Sparrows can only be made when males are singing from March (ideally mid-May; *pratensis* may remain into early May) through July or August.

Henslow's Sparrow—A rare to uncommon winter resident of the Panhandle and peninsula south to Lake Okeechobee. Rare or absent farther south, and unknown in the Keys. Prefers wet grassy or shrubby areas such as pine savannas, pitcher plant bogs, dry prairies, fields, and powerline rights-of-way. Extremely secretive and easily overlooked. Perhaps most common at Apalachicola National Forest (page 60).

Le Conte's Sparrow—A rare winter resident of the Panhandle and northern half of the peninsula. Irregular or absent farther south and not reported from the Keys. Prefers dry fields with low stubble or grass. Extremely secretive and easily overlooked.

Nelson's Sharp-tailed Sparrow and **Saltmarsh Sharp-tailed Sparrow**—Fairly common winter residents of brackish and salt marshes south to about Port Richey on the Gulf coast and Merritt Island on the Atlantic coast. Generally rare farther south, although Saltmarsh Sharp-tailed Sparrows apparently occur annually around Cape Sable in Everglades National Park. Considered a single species until 1995, the distribution of the two sharp-tailed sparrow species in Florida is uncertain; even the published literature is contradictory. But generally, Nelson's Sharp-tailed Sparrows predominate on the Gulf coast (except apparently at Cape Sable), while Saltmarsh Sharp-tailed Sparrow are more common along the Atlantic. Location, though, is not necessarily sufficient to identify a sharp-tailed sparrow to species. A two-year study of wintering sharp-tailed sparrows near Cedar Key, on the Gulf coast of the northern peninsula, established that 96 percent of 162 banded birds were Nelson's Sharp-tailed Sparrows (nearly all from the population that breeds in north-central North America), while only four percent were Saltmarsh Sharp-tailed Sparrows (Post 1998). Further study of the two species in Florida is needed, especially along the Atlantic coast.

Seaside Sparrow—A fairly common permanent resident of marshes, represented by several subspecies. Along the Gulf coast, **Louisiana Seaside Sparrow** (*Ammodramus maritimus fisheri*) breeds east to Pensacola. **Wakulla Seaside Sparrow** (*A. m. juncicola*; a weakly differentiated race) is found from Choctawhatchee Bay to East Bay (Panama City), and **Scott's Seaside Sparrow** (*A. m. peninsulae*) occurs from Apalachicola to Port

Richey. Along the Atlantic coast, **MacGillivray's Seaside Sparrow** (*A. m. macgillivraii*) occurs south to Jacksonville. During winter, the migratory **Northern Seaside Sparrow** (*A. m. maritima*) winters in suitable habitat along the entire Atlantic coast. **Dusky Seaside Sparrow** (*A. m. nigrescens*), once considered a separate species, became extinct in 1987. Occurring only in salt and brackish marshes in Brevard County, it had the most restricted range of any bird in North America. Alteration of its habitat for mosquito control, construction of highways through its core area, and other human-related events caused its extinction. Sykes (1980) and Walters (1992) are good sources for the history of failed management by federal and state authorities that doomed the Dusky. **Cape Sable Seaside Sparrow** (*A. m. mirabilis*), also once considered a separate species, occurs in fresh and brackish marshes wholly within Everglades National Park and Big Cypress National Preserve. Cape Sable Seaside Sparrows are most easily found along Shark River Slough near the turn-off to Mahogany Hammock (page 241) from March to July, when males are singing. Post and Greenlaw (2000) is a good reference.

Fox Sparrow—A rare to uncommon winter resident of the Panhandle and extreme northern peninsula; irregular south to the central peninsula, and virtually unknown farther south.

Song Sparrow—An uncommon to fairly common winter resident of the Panhandle and northern third of the peninsula. Rare through the central peninsula, and irregular south into the Keys.

Lincoln's Sparrow—A rare migrant throughout. During winter, a rare resident of the southern half of the peninsula, irregular farther north and in the Keys.

Swamp Sparrow—A fairly common migrant and winter resident in the Panhandle and northern half of the peninsula. Uncommon in the southern mainland and rare in the Keys.

White-throated Sparrow—A fairly common winter resident of the Panhandle and northern peninsula, but rare and local farther south. There are a few reports from the Keys.

White-crowned Sparrow—Generally a rare to uncommon winter resident throughout. There are several documented records in Florida of the western subspecies *Zonotrichia leucophrys gambelii*, which has pale (rather than black) lores.

Golden-crowned Sparrow—An accidental vagrant from the western U.S. The only Florida record is of an individual found singing at Islamorada in the Keys—in late June 1990! (Hoffman et al. 1991).

Dark-eyed Junco—A winter resident, varying in abundance from year to year. Sometimes fairly common in the Panhandle and extreme northern peninsula, but very rare to absent in the central and southern peninsula.

There is one report for the Keys. Most juncos in Florida are **Slate-colored Juncos**, but **Oregon Junco** also has been verified in the state.

Snow Bunting—A casual winter resident primarily along the extreme northern Atlantic coast.

Northern Cardinal—A common and widespread permanent resident throughout, except only a vagrant to Dry Tortugas National Park.

Blue Grosbeak—An uncommon migrant throughout, and an uncommon to locally common spring and summer resident of abandoned agricultural fields and citrus groves, and other shrubby habitats south into the central peninsula. There are a few verifiable winter records throughout, all of them recent.

Indigo Bunting—An uncommon to locally common migrant throughout, and a fairly common spring and summer resident of abandoned agricultural land and other shrubby habitats south into the central peninsula. Perhaps increasing as a winter resident from the central peninsula southward, though still rare farther north.

Painted Bunting—An uncommon to fairly common but declining spring and summer resident of hammock edges, coastal scrub, and abandoned citrus groves along the Atlantic coast south to about Titusville. Breeds much less commonly inland in central Florida, and one or a few pairs breed annually or nearly so near Apalachicola. Elsewhere, a regular migrant along the Atlantic coast, rare or irregular inland and along the Gulf coast. Uncommon during winter (often at feeders), where locally fairly common in the southern half of the peninsula and the Keys, rare farther north.

Dickcissel—A rare migrant, mostly along the Gulf coast during spring but throughout during fall, and a rare winter resident throughout. In the past few years, singing male Dickcissels have been found during spring or summer in weedy fields from the western Panhandle south to the southern Everglades, and breeding was confirmed at Lake Apopka in 1999 (Pranty et al. 2002) and 2005.

Bobolink—A rare to abundant spring migrant throughout, with numbers varying widely. During fall, rare and perhaps irregular in the western Panhandle, but rare to sometimes common elsewhere. There is one verifiable winter record.

Red-winged Blackbird—A common to abundant, ubiquitous permanent resident of wetlands throughout. One of the most numerous and widespread birds in Florida. Wintering flocks are often segregated by sex.

Tawny-shouldered Blackbird (*Agelaius humeralis*)—An accidental visitor from Cuba to Key West, represented by a single verified record: two birds collected in February 1936. Peterson (2002) is the only North American field guide that illustrates Tawny-shouldered Blackbird (a male only). The species is illustrated also in *A Guide to the Birds of the West Indies* (Raffaele et al. 1998) and *Field Guide to the Birds of Cuba* (Garrido and Kirkconnell 2000). Tawny-shouldered Blackbirds are common residents throughout most of Cuba, and the plumage of males is *virtually identical* to male Red-winged Blackbirds. The sole distinguishing mark is the color of the lesser wing-coverts: red in Red-winged Blackbirds but brownish-orange in Tawny-shouldered. This field mark is difficult to see conclusively except under ideal conditions, and variation in the plumage of some Red-wingeds adds to the difficulty of identification. Females are virtually identical to males except that the wing patch is duller in color. Vocalizations may differ from Red-winged Blackbirds: one call is described by Raffaele et al. (1998) as *wiii-wiii-wiii* and by Garrido and Kirkconnell (2000) as *weee-weee*, while the most common call is either "a strong short *chic-chic*" or "a strong *cheek*, often repeated".

Eastern Meadowlark—An uncommon to common permanent resident throughout the mainland. Irregular in the Keys during migration and winter.

Western Meadowlark—Status uncertain. Reportedly a regular winter resident in the western Panhandle during the mid-1950s, but not reported from there after 1965. The last definitive record was from Tallahassee in 1977.

Yellow-headed Blackbird—A rare but regular migrant throughout, and a rare winter resident of the southern two-thirds of the peninsula. Usually found in flocks of other icterids.

Rusty Blackbird—Generally a rare to uncommon winter resident in the Panhandle and extreme northern peninsula, but locally common during some years. Rare and irregular farther south through the mainland; many reports do not inspire confidence. Found in swamps, riverine forests, and along lakes. *Female Red-winged Blackbirds (and Common Grackles?) apparently are often misidentified as Rusty Blackbirds in the southern half of the peninsula.*

Brewer's Blackbird—A rare to locally common, irruptive winter resident of the Panhandle and extreme northern peninsula, rare to casual south to the Keys. Apparently declining in the past 20 years, after colonizing Florida in the 1940s. Found in pastures, fields, and cattle feedlots; often seen foraging in manure. *Common Grackles are often misidentified as Brewer's Blackbirds.*

Common Grackle—A fairly common to abundant permanent resident throughout, except very rare at Dry Tortugas National Park. Numbers increase during winter with the addition of northern breeders. Interestingly, Common Grackles that breed in the Mainline Keys migrate *northward* to winter in the mainland. Florida's breeding subspecies is the **Purple Grackle** (*Quiscalus quiscula quiscula*), but **Bronzed Grackle** (*Q. q. versicolor*) has occurred during winter.

Boat-tailed Grackle—Generally a common to abundant permanent resident of the peninsula, found even in cities and towns. Rare to uncommon in the Panhandle, especially the western part and inland, and casual in the Keys. Three subspecies occur in Florida: *Quiscalus major alabamensis* (winter resident; has white irides) around Pensacola; *Q. m. torreyi* (permanent resident; also has white irides) along the Atlantic coast from the St. Johns River (Jacksonville) north to the Georgia line; and *Q. m. westoni* (permanent resident; has brown irides) throughout the remainder of the state. Leucistic Boat-tailed Grackles are seen frequently; some have just a few white flight or body feathers, while others are entirely whitish. Such individuals often are misidentified, sometimes badly so!

Shiny Cowbird—This resident of Trinidad, Tobago, and South America has been expanding its range for the past 100 years, due primarily to conversion of forests to grazing land. Shiny Cowbirds first appeared in Florida in 1985, after colonizing a succession of West Indian islands. In Florida, only about 25 Shiny Cowbirds are found annually, mostly in the Keys (Pranty 2000). Through 2004, breeding in Florida remains undocumented (despite statements to the contrary), although there is a verifiable record from coastal Georgia (Sykes and Post 2001). Small numbers usually are found during spring at Flamingo and Dry Tortugas National Park, and individuals appear to be resident at Key West. Shiny Cowbirds are quite rare inland. While males are readily identified if seen well, *the identification of females is extremely difficult, and perhaps should not be attempted in most cases.* Females average darker than female Brown-headed Cowbirds, with a more prominent pale supercilium, darker eye-stripe and auriculars, a darker and less contrasting throat, little or no streaking below, and an all-blackish bill. Juveniles seem to be buffy above with a bold buffy supercilium, and little or no streaking below (juvenile Brown-headed Cowbirds are brownish-gray overall with conspicuous dark streaking on the underparts). For more information, consult Smith and Sprunt (1987) and Pranty (2000); both articles feature color photographs of Shiny Cowbirds and other icterids.

Bronzed Cowbird—A rare to uncommon, *increasing* winter resident in the peninsula, but casual in the Panhandle and the Keys. Flocks of as many as 40 birds have been seen. Breeds as far east as Louisiana, and may eventually breed in Florida; individuals summered in the southern peninsula in 2004 and 2005.

Brown-headed Cowbird—A common permanent resident in the Panhandle and northern peninsula, rare to uncommon farther south, mostly along the coasts. Locally abundant during winter, when numbers swell with the addition of northern breeders. This brood parasite may be responsible for population declines and range reductions of Painted Buntings along the northern Atlantic coast, and of Black-whiskered Vireos and Florida Prairie Warblers along the central Gulf coast.

Orchard Oriole—A common spring and summer resident of the Panhandle, uncommon in the peninsula south to about Gainesville, rarely to Orlando. During spring, a circum-Gulf migrant seldom seen inland or on the Atlantic coast, but sometimes fairly common along the Gulf coast after westerly winds. Very rare throughout as an early fall migrant (beginning in July). There are at least three verifiable winter records.

Hooded Oriole—A casual or accidental vagrant from the west, with one verifiable record at Gulf Breeze (October 2002).

Spot-breasted Oriole—A countable exotic native to southern Mexico and northern Central America. First noted in Florida in Miami in the late 1940s, Spot-breasted Orioles had extended their range north along the Atlantic coast to Cocoa Beach by the 1970s. The population declined rapidly in numbers and range by the early 1980s (for unknown reasons), and birds now are restricted to areas from West Palm Beach south to about Cutler Ridge, Miami. The Spot-breasted Oriole has never been the subject of formal study in Florida, and little is known about its biology here. *Spot-breasted Orioles in Florida often are misidentified as Altamira, Hooded, or Scott's Orioles.*

Baltimore Oriole—An uncommon migrant and winter resident throughout, often found in citrus groves and at feeders that provide fresh fruit. There is one unverifiable breeding report from Key West in 1972!

Bullock's Oriole—Known to winter in the state, but its status is obscured due to confusion with female-plumaged Baltimore Orioles. Bullock's and Baltimore Orioles often flock together during winter, and such flocks are often found at feeding stations, in citrus groves, or at fruiting fig trees (in southern Florida). Photographs should be obtained for any Bullock's Oriole seen in Florida; there are only six verifiable records in the state.

Purple Finch—An irruptive winter resident of the Panhandle and extreme northern peninsula, ranging from absent to locally common. Very rare and irregular south through the mainland.

House Finch—An established exotic, native to western North America and Central America. A population that originated from a few birds released on Long Island, New York, in 1940 now occupies most of the eastern United States. Several House Finches wintered in Pensacola and Tallahassee in 1987–1988, and birds bred at Tallahassee in 1989. House Finches now are uncommon to locally common permanent residents of developed areas in the Panhandle and peninsula south locally to Tampa, Lake Wales, and Daytona Beach. They seem to be more common during winter, perhaps with the arrival of breeders from farther north. Eventual occupation of the southern half of the peninsula is likely, but range expansion in Florida has not been rapid. A small breeding population at Fort Lauderdale may be composed entirely of escapees. The plumage of males varies and may be yellow, orange, or red.

Red Crossbill—An accidental vagrant from farther north. Numbers invaded the northern third of the peninsula December 1906–January 1907. Subsequent undocumented reports, one as recent as 1975, are often dismissed.

Pine Siskin—An irruptive winter resident. Usually rare and restricted in Florida to the Panhandle, but has occurred in numbers south to Key West. Flocks with American Goldfinches and often visits bird feeders.

American Goldfinch—An irruptive winter resident nearly throughout, uncommon to locally abundant. Rare and irregular during migration at Dry Tortugas National Park. Commonly visits thistle-seed feeders.

Evening Grosbeak—A casual and *irruptive* winter visitor to the Panhandle and northern half of the peninsula, first recorded in 1968. In the past 13 years (1992–2004), there have been only three reports, the most recent at Havana in December 1998.

House Sparrow—A countable exotic, native to Eurasia and northern Africa, but now nearly cosmopolitan. A fairly common permanent resident throughout most developed areas, but rare or absent from the Everglades region and the Keys. In Florida, most common at cattle feedlots and shopping centers, where it nests in signs and other artificial cavities.

Java Sparrow—A non-countable exotic, native to the East Indies, with naturalized populations in Hawaii, Puerto Rico, and elsewhere. A population at Miami numbered at least 150 birds in 1969, but was observed last in 1977. Local escapees, including all-white avicultural morphs, may be seen anywhere.

Orange Bishop and **Red Bishop**—Non-countable exotics native to Africa. In recent years, individuals or small flocks of bishops have been found throughout the mainland, but they have not yet persisted. Orange Bishop is illustrated in Sibley (2000), National Geographic Society (2002), and Raffaele et al. (1998), but Red Bishop is not illustrated in any of these guides. Only adult males can be identified conclusively; other plumages are indistinguishable. Adult male Orange Bishops have a black cap that extends to the base of the lower mandible, but *the chin is orange*. In Red Bishop, the black cap extends downward *to include the chin*. All breeding-plumaged male bishops photographed in Florida have been Orange Bishops.

Munias (*Lonchura* species)—Non-countable exotics, native variously to Africa, Asia, New Guinea, and surrounding areas. Munias—also known as silverbills or mannikins (note spelling; not to be confused with *manakins* of the New World)—are small finches that are found in flocks in grassy or shrubby areas. The taxonomy is confusing and few species are illustrated in North American field guides. Sibley (2000), Peterson (2002), and National Geographic Society (2002) all include **Nutmeg Mannikin,** and Peterson also includes what is now known as **Tricolored Munia** (*L. malacca*)—the Chestnut Munia recently was split into **Chestnut Munia** (*L. atricapilla*) and Tricolored Munia (*L. malacca*). Nutmeg Mannikins, Chestnut Munias, and Tricolored Munias all have been observed in Florida in the past few years. Tricolored Munias are breeding in Cuba and elsewhere in the Caribbean, and recent sightings at Dry Tortugas National Park, Everglades National Park, and Big Cypress National Preserve may be natural colonizers from Cuba. However, munias also occur in aviculture, so distributional and temporal patterns of occurrence will need to develop to rule out local escapees as the source of Florida's munias. A Tricolored Munia at the Tortugas in June 1999 was not accepted by the FOSRC because of concerns about its provenance. *Because the identification of munias is difficult—impossible for many juveniles—photographs should be obtained for any individuals observed in the state.*

EXOTIC BIRDS OF FLORIDA

The following list includes the 104 species of exotic birds whose occurrence in Florida can be verified from archived photographic or specimen evidence. Scarlet Ibis is included here because all recent observations likely refer to escapees or hybrids. At least 55 of these species, marked with an **asterisk (*)**, reportedly have bred in the wild; breeding has been reported also for 14 other exotics that are unverifiable in Florida. Twelve verifiable breeding species considered **established** by the Florida Ornithological Society Records Committee are marked with an **E**. Brief distributional information is provided for all species known to have bred in Florida, those that have been reported recently in numbers, or those that potentially may be natural vagrants; see Pranty (2004) for more information and photographs of 20 species. AOU taxonomy and nomenclature are used for species that appear in the main list of the AOU *Check-list* (1998) and its supplements through 2005. For all other species, taxonomy and nomenclature follow that used in the fifth edition of *Birds of the World: A Checklist* (Clements 2000).

White-faced Whistling-Duck (*Dendrocygna viduata*)—several recent observations, with two of these supported by photographs (Pranty 2004). Native to Central and South America and a potential natural vagrant.

*Mute Swan (*Cygnus olor*)—Fairly common in waterfowl collections. Small breeding populations are found at Lakeland and Orlando, and perhaps elsewhere. Non-breeding individuals likely represent local escapees or releases rather than vagrants from expanding breeding populations north of Florida.

*Black Swan (*Cygnus atratus*)—small breeding populations are found at Lakeland and Orlando (Pranty 2004); escapees may be seen anywhere.

Whooper Swan (*Cygnus cygnus*)—two photographed at Clermont in 1992.

*Swan Goose (*Anser cygnoides*)—common on farms and in urban waterfowl collections; occasionally seen outside of captivity, often as the white domesticated variety.

*Greylag Goose (*Anser anser*)—common on farms and in urban waterfowl collections; occasionally seen outside of captivity, often as the white domesticated variety.

Orinoco Goose (*Neochen jubatus*)—singles photographed at Loxahatchee National Wildlife Refuge in 1989 and central Palm Beach County in 1999.

*Egyptian Goose (*Alopochen aegypticus*)—a small population formerly occurred at Tampa; other birds have bred sparingly elsewhere. All-white avicultural morphs have been observed in Florida.

Common Shelduck (*Tadorna tadorna*)—one photographed at Boca Raton in January 2004.

*Ruddy Shelduck (*Tadorna ferruginea*)—occasional sightings; an apparent family group was videotaped along the Kissimmee River in 2000.

*Muscovy Duck (*Cairina moschata*) **E**—see the account on page 270. A photograph appears in Pranty (2004)

Ringed Teal (*Callonetta leucophrys*)—more than 200 were reported near Loxahatchee National Wildlife Refuge in 1991 (Robertson and Woolfenden 1992), but there have been few subsequent Florida reports. Fairly common in waterfowl collections.

Philippine Duck (*Anas luzonica*)—one photographed at Pembroke Pines in 2000 (Pranty 2004).

Red-crested Pochard (*Netta rufina*)—one photographed at Bonita Springs in 2002.

Rosy-billed Pochard (*Netta peposaca*)—one photographed at Bonita Springs in 2002.

Chukar (*Alectoris chukar*)—several records from the peninsula.

*Black Francolin (*Francolinus francolinus*)—see the account on page 272.

*Red Junglefowl (*Gallus gallus*)—yes, these are the ancestors of barnyard chickens! A population of about 2,000 birds is established (but not countable) at Key West; others may be seen anywhere.

Golden Pheasant (*Chrysolophus pictus*) × **Lady Amherst's Pheasant** (*Chrysolophus amherstiae*)—one hybrid photographed at Miami in 2002 (Pranty 2004).

*Common Peafowl (*Pavo cristatus*)—see the account on page 272.

Pink-backed Pelican (*Pelecanus rufescens*)—one photographed at Naples in 2001 apparently had wandered from its owner in Fort Lauderdale.

*Sacred Ibis (*Threskiornis aethiopicus*)—several recent reports of 30 or more seen in the Miami and West Palm Beach areas, beginning in 2000 (Pranty 2004); one nesting pair found at Loxahatchee NWR in 2005.

Scarlet Ibis (*Eudocimus ruber*)—see the account on page 277. A photograph appears in Pranty (2004)

Abdim's Stork (*Ciconia abdimii*)—apparently three different individuals in scattered areas of southwestern Florida in 1998 and 1999; storks were photographed at Sanibel Island and Immokalee (Pranty 2004). Another was seen at Orlando in 2004.

Woolly-necked Stork (*Ciconia episcopus*)—one that escaped from Miami MetroZoo in 1992 (Smith and Smith 1995) was observed through 2005 and was photographed over Everglades National Park in 1999.

Crane Hawk (*Geranospiza caerulescens*)—one was captured at Miami in 1972 and kept in captivity until its death in 1973; the specimen now is at Archbold Biological Station. Some have suggested that this Central and South American species may be a potential natural vagrant to Florida.

Common Black-Hawk (*Buteogallus anthracinus*) and/or **Great Black-Hawk** (*Buteogallus urubitinga*—see the account on page 282.

*Sarus Crane** (*Grus antigone*)—one in central Pasco County from the late 1980s to 1994 reportedly bred successfully with a Sandhill Crane (Eliason 1992).

*Purple Swamphen** (*Porphyrio porphyrio*)—see the account on page 285. A photograph appears on page 223 of this guide and in Pranty (2004)

Southern Lapwing (*Vanellus chilensis*)—several observations (and two specimens) from southern Florida during 1959–1962, and two photographed in Columbia County in 2003 (Pranty 2004).

*Rock Pigeon** (*Columba livia*) **E**—see the account on page 295.

*Ringed Turtle-Dove** (*Streptopelia "risoria"*)—see the account on page 296.

*Eurasian Collared-Dove** (*Streptopelia decaocto*) **E**—see the account on page 296.

*Diamond Dove** (*Geopelia cuneata*)—a few recent records in the peninsula.

*Inca Dove** (*Columbina inca*)—a small population formerly present at Key West died out in 1980. The provenance of these birds was never determined, and natural vagrancy was a possibility.

Galah (*Eolophus roseicapillus*)—one photographed north of Tampa in 2000.

Tanimbar Cockatoo (*Cacatua goffini*)—one photographed at Plantation in 1999.

Cockatiel (*Nymphicus hollandicus*)—recent escapees may be seen throughout, but these survive for only short periods.

Red-rumped Parrot (*Psephotus haemantonotus*)—one photographed at Tampa in 1986 (Pranty 2004). A photograph appears in Pranty and Garrett (2003).

*Budgerigar** (*Melopsittacus undulatus*) **E**—see the account on page 300.

*Rose-ringed Parakeet** (*Psittacula krameri*)—see the account on page 301.

Plum-headed Parakeet (*Psittacula cyanocephala*)—one specimen from Miami in 1971.

Red-breasted Parakeet (*Psittacula alexandri*)—singles photographed at Fort Lauderdale in 2001 and Miami in 2004.

Peach-faced Lovebird (*Agapornis roseicollis*)—one found dead at Lake Placid in 1995 and one photographed at Port Richey in 1999.

Yellow-collared (Masked) Lovebird (*Agapornis personatus*)—two photographic records in 2004: one at Kendall in May, and two at Tallahassee in August.

*****Monk Parakeet** (*Myiopsitta monachus*) **E**—see the account on page 301.

*****Black-hooded Parakeet** (*Nandayus nenday*) **E**—see the account on page 301. Photographs appear in Pranty and Garrett (2003) and Pranty (2004).

*****Blue-crowned Parakeet** (*Aratinga acuticauda*)—see the account on page 301. Photographs appear in Pranty and Garrett (2003).

Scarlet-fronted Parakeet (*Aratinga wagleri*)—one photographed at Miami Springs in December 2004.

*****Green Parakeet** (*Aratinga holochlora*)—small numbers are present at Fort Lauderdale and Miami; note that juveniles of other *Aratinga* species may be all green. A photograph appears in Pranty and Garrett (2003).

Red-throated Parakeet (*Aratinga rubritorquis*)—one photographed at Fort Lauderdale in 2001.

*****Mitred Parakeet** (*Aratinga mitrata*)—see the account on page 301. A photograph appears in Pranty and Garrett (2003).

*****Red-masked Parakeet** (*Aratinga erythrogenys*)—see the account on page 301. Photographs appear in Pranty and Garrett (2003).

*****White-eyed Parakeet** (*Aratinga leucophthalmus*)—see the account on page 302.

*****Dusky-headed Parakeet** (*Aratinga weddellii*)—see the account on page 302. A photograph appears in Pranty and Garrett (2003).

*****Orange-fronted Parakeet** (*Aratinga canicularis*)—previously occurred in small numbers at Fort Lauderdale and Miami, but now apparently extirpated except for recent escapees.

Peach-fronted Parakeet (*Aratinga aurea*)—singles photographed at St. Petersburg in May 2004 and Miami Springs in November 2004.

Gray Parrot (*Psittacus erithacus*)—one photographed at Hollywood in 2000.

*****Chestnut-fronted Macaw** (*Ara severa*)—see the account on page 302. A photograph appears in Pranty and Garrett (2003).

Scarlet Macaw (*Ara macao*)—two photographed near Clermont in 2003.

***Blue-and-yellow Macaw** (*Ara ararauna*)—see the account on page 302.

***Green-cheeked Parakeet** (*Pyrrhura molinae*)—formerly bred in small numbers at Miami, but there have been no published reports since 1991. Escapees have been observed elsewhere.

***White-winged Parakeet** (*Brotogeris versicolurus*) **E**—see the account on page 302. A photograph appears in Pranty and Garrett (2003).

***Yellow-chevroned Parakeet** (*Brotogeris chiriri*)—see the account on page 302. A photograph appears in Pranty and Garrett (2003).

Scaly-headed Parrot (*Pionus maximillani*)—recently detected at Miami; one photographed at Matheson Hammock in April 2005. See photograph on back cover.

***White-fronted Parrot** (*Amazona albifrons*)—see the account on page 302.

***Red-crowned Parrot** (*Amazona viridigenalis*)—see the account on page 303. A photograph appears in Pranty and Garrett (2003).

Lilac-crowned Parrot (*Amazona finschi*)—singles photographed at Sarasota in 1999 and Fort Lauderdale in 2001.

***Red-lored Parrot** (*Amazona autumnalis*)—One photographed at Miami in the 1980s (Toops and Dilley 1986).

Mealy Parrot (*Amazona farinosa*)—one photographed at Fort Lauderdale in 1999.

***Blue-fronted Parrot** (*Amazona aestiva*)—see the account on page 303.

***Orange-winged Parrot** (*Amazona amazonica*)—see the account on page 303. A photograph appears in Pranty and Garrett (2003).

***Yellow-headed Parrot** (*Amazona oratrix*)—see the account on page 303.

***Yellow-crowned Parrot** (*Amazona ochrocephala*)—One photographed at Miami on an unknown date.

***Yellow-naped Parrot** (*Amazona auropalliata*)—see the account on page 303.

Eastern Yellow-billed Hornbill (*Tockus flavirostris*)—one photographed at Sanibel Island in October 2004.

African Gray Hornbill (*Tockus nasutus*)—one photographed near Brooksville during 1998–2000.

Wreathed Hornbill (*Aceros undulatus*)—two photographed on Manasota Key in 1994.

Silvery-cheeked Hornbill (*Ceratogymna brevis*)—one photographed at Miami in October 2004.

Abyssinian Ground-Hornbill (*Bucorvus abyssinicus*)—one that escaped from Sunken Gardens, St. Petersburg, in 1991 was photographed nearby.

Southern Ground-Hornbill (*Bucorvus leadbeateri*)—two photographed at McIntosh in May 2004.

Great Kiskadee (*Pitangus sulphuratus*)—one photographed at Fort Lauderdale in 1960–1961 was perhaps equally likely an escapee as a vagrant from the western U.S. or Mexico.

Asian Fairy-bluebird (*Irena puella*)—one photographed at St. Petersburg in 1967.

*****House Crow** (*Corvus splendens*)—two adults and a nest at Nokomis Beach during 2001–2004 were photographed (Pranty 2004).

White-necked Raven (*Corvus albicollis*)—one at Delray Beach in 2002–2003 was photographed.

Common Nightingale (*Luscinia megarhynchos*)—an introduction at Bok Tower Sanctuary, Lake Wales, in the 1920s or 1930s was not successful.

*****Red-whiskered Bulbul** (*Pycnonotus jocosus*) **E**—see the account on page 319.

Black Bulbul (*Hypsipetes madagascariensis*)—apparently the same banded individual was photographed at Merritt Island National Wildlife Refuge in April 1998 and Vero Beach in May 1998.

*****European Starling** (*Gracula religiosa*) **E**—see the account on page 321.

*****Common Myna** (*Acridotheres tristis*)—see the account on page 321. A photograph appears in Pranty and Garrett (2003).

*****Crested Myna** (*Acridotheres cristatellus*)—bred in small numbers at Miami in the 1980s, but now extirpated.

*****Hill Myna** (*Gracula religiosa*)—see the account on page 321. A photograph appears in Pranty (2004).

*****Blue-gray Tanager** (*Thraupis episcopus*)—see the account on page 324.

Red-legged Honeycreeper (*Cyanerpes cyaneus*)—see the account on page 325. A photograph appears in Pranty (2004).

*****Cuban Grassquit** (*Tiaris canorus*)—see the account on page 326.

Troupial (*Icterus icterus*)—one photographed at Sanibel Island in 1997 (Pranty 2004).

*****Spot-breasted Oriole** (*Icterus pectoralis*) **E**—see the account on page 333. A photograph appears in Pranty (2004).

*****House Finch** (*Carpodacus mexicanus*) **E**—see the account on page 333.

House Sparrow — no

*House Sparrow (*Passer domesticus*) **E**—see the account on page 334.

*Java Sparrow (*Padda oryzivora*)—see the account on page 334. A photograph appears in Pranty (2004).

Orange Bishop (*Euplectes franciscanus*)—see the account on page 334. A photograph appears in Pranty (2004).

Zebra Finch (*Taeniopygia subflava*)—photographs of three at Bayonet Point in 2000 and one at Ridge Manor in 2000.

Tricolored Munia (*Lonchura malacca*)—see the account on page 334.

*Chestnut Mannikin (*Lonchura atricapilla*)—see the account on page 334.

Pin-tailed Whydah (*Vidua macroura*)—singles photographed at Deltona in 1994 and Fort Lauderdale in 2002.

Bar Graphs of The Birds of Florida

Except for species now extinct or extirpated, the complete, official bird list of Florida is found in the following bar graphs. Also included are several species of uncertain provenance or currently non-countable exotics mentioned in the section of Florida Birds of Particular Interest. Non-ABA-countable species and those of unknown provenance lack a check-box before their names.

The bar graphs are based primarily on the actual abundance of a species rather than its "visibility." Therefore, small, less conspicuous species may require more effort to locate than large, conspicuous ones. Most landbirds are easiest to find during spring and summer, when males are singing from exposed perches; these same species may be difficult to locate at other seasons, especially during winter. *Note also that the graphs refer to the likelihood of finding a bird, which does not necessarily mean seeing it.* Some species (e.g., rails, owls, nightjars) obviously are heard much more frequently than they are seen.

The six abundance or frequency codes used in the graphs follow:

COMMON: Present in moderate to large numbers, and easily found in appropriate habitat at the right time of year.

FAIRLY COMMON: Present in small to moderate numbers, and usually can be found in appropriate habitat at the right time of year.

UNCOMMON: Present in small numbers, and sometimes—but not always—found with some effort in appropriate habitat at the right time of year.

RARE: Occurs annually in very small numbers. Not to be expected on any given day, but may be found with extended effort over the course of the appropriate season(s).

CASUAL: Occurs less than annually, but there tends to be a pattern over time at the right time of year in appropriate habitat.

ACCIDENTAL: Represents an exceptional occurrence that might not be repeated again for decades; there are usually fewer than 5 records.

When perusing the bar graphs, keep in mind the following points:

1.   The graphs were compiled by active, experienced Florida birders knowledgeable about the birds, habitats, and seasons. Beginning birders and out-of-state visitors may find it more difficult to locate some of these species.

2.   The Panhandle column is divided into two sections denoting the eastern and western sections, because of well-defined differences in the distribution of many species between Pensacola and Tallahassee (about 200 miles distant). Except for a few species with well-defined range-limits, none of the other four regions is similarly divided. The Keys column denotes only the Mainline Keys (Key Largo to Key West), so Dry Tortugas National Park is not represented in the graphs.

3.   The five regional and twelve monthly columns attempt to "average" many distributional variables present over a large area. The bars represent the range of species occurrence and (except for rarities) make no attempt to list all outlying regional and seasonal reports.

4.   For many rare, casual, or accidental species, only verified occurrences are reflected in the bar graphs (i.e., questionable or undocumented sightings are omitted).

5.   Some species are followed by dittoes and a second or third line. This is done when seasonal occurrence or abundance varies considerably among regions of the state. For example, Short-tailed Hawks are rare summer visitors in the Panhandle and northern Florida, rare to uncommon residents in the southern mainland, and uncommon migrants and winter residents in the Keys.

6.   Other species have dittoes and a second line because they have clearly identifiable races with different distributions.

The Status column may contain one of four letters, defined below:

B—Breeds regularly in at least part of the state. (Irregular breeders are not marked).

E—Exotic. These species are all residents; therefore, all breed in the state. Nearly all are restricted to areas of human development, and most have extremely limited ranges.

M—Migrant, wholly or in large part. Distribution of these species may vary greatly from day to day, depending on local weather conditions.

R—Documentation of these species is required by the Florida Ornithological Society Records Committee. For more information or to submit a report, go to the FOSRC's webpage at <www.fosbirds.org/RecordCommittee/GuidelinesforSubmitting.htm>. The official bird list for Florida is found at <www.fosbirds.org/RecordCommittee>.

A great deal of subjectivity is involved in producing the bar graphs; most Florida birders would have slightly different interpretations of how these graphs should look. Florida is a large and very diverse state. The distribution of birds can differ substantially along the coast as opposed to inland, and many coastal species have different patterns of occurrence between the Atlantic and Gulf coasts. Finally, not even the most comprehensive publications on Florida birds specify the abundance of every species for every region in the state on a *weekly* basis, as do these graphs.

Note those species marked "Unverified during winter". These are birds that reportedly have occurred in Florida during winter, often on Christmas Bird Counts, but for which verifiable documentation is not known. Should you observe any of these species in winter, please make every effort to obtain identifiable photographs or videotapes, or to alert other observers.

In 1998, Cornell Laboratory of Ornithology's Library of Natural Sounds released a cassette or CD that contains vocalizations of 112 characteristic Florida birds. An asterisk (*) in the following bar graph section indicates those species and subspecies featured in Bird Songs of Florida. Contact ABA Sales for information about ordering this CD or cassette.

F or the fifth edition of this guide, I chose to add new species, update records of rarities, and correct errors, but I did *not* examine most bar graphs. Indeed, while perusing some of them in 2004, I occasionally disagreed with decisions I made nine to ten years earlier about the status of species. But I realized that spending dozens of hours trying to revise the graphs would serve little point, since they are so subjective, even though I did make some changes. *Please use these bar graphs solely as a guide.*

	Panhandle	North Peninsula	Central Peninsula	South Peninsula	Mainline Keys		January	February	March	April	May	June	July	August	September	October	November	December
☐ Black-bellied Whistling-Duck Local, but range expanding						B												
☐ Fulvous Whistling-Duck " " Local						B												
☐ Greater White-fronted Goose																		
☐ Snow Goose																		
☐ Ross's Goose Beware of Snow Goose X Ross's Goose hybrids						R												
☐ Brant Coastal																		
☐ Cackling Goose						R												
☐ Canada Goose Most individuals are feral						E												
☐ Tundra Swan																		
☐ Muscovy Duck Urban and suburban areas						E												
☐ Wood Duck						B												
☐ Gadwall																		
☐ Eurasian Wigeon																		
☐ American Wigeon																		
☐ American Black Duck Identify carefully in the peninsula																		
☐ Mallard Most individuals are feral						E												
☐ Mottled Duck * Beware of Mottled Duck X Mallard hybrids						B												
☐ Blue-winged Teal Irregular breeder " " Irregular breeder																		
☐ Cinnamon Teal																		
☐ Northern Shoveler																		

Species	Panhandle	North Peninsula	Central Peninsula	South Peninsula	Mainline Keys	January	February	March	April	May	June	July	August	September	October	November	December
White-cheeked Pintail — Most individuals are probably escapees			⋮		R	R											
Northern Pintail																	
Green-winged Teal																	
Canvasback																	
Redhead																	
Ring-necked Duck — Several unverifiable breeding reports																	
Greater Scaup — Coastal; one unverifiable breeding report																	
Lesser Scaup — Several unverifiable breeding reports	⋮	⋮	⋮	⋮		R											⋮
King Eider — Coastal																	
Common Eider — Coastal																	
Harlequin Duck — Coastal																	
Surf Scoter — Mostly Panhandle and Atlantic coasts																	
White-winged Scoter — Mostly Panhandle and Atlantic coasts																	
Black Scoter — Mostly Panhandle and Atlantic coasts																	
Long-tailed Duck — Mostly Panhandle and Atlantic coasts																	
Bufflehead — Mostly coastal																	
Common Goldeneye — Coastal																	
Hooded Merganser — Irregular breeder south into the central peninsula																	

✔	Panhandle	North Peninsula	Central Peninsula	South Peninsula	Mainline Keys		January	February	March	April	May	June	July	August	September	October	November	December
☐ Common Merganser						R												
☐ Red-breasted Merganser Mostly coastal																		
☐ Masked Duck						R												
☐ Ruddy Duck Locally common																		
☐ Wild Turkey						B												
☐ Northern Bobwhite *						B												
☐ Red-throated Loon Coastal																		
☐ Pacific Loon Coastal																		
☐ Common Loon Mostly coastal																		
☐ Least Grebe						R												
☐ Pied-billed Grebe * " "						B B												
☐ Horned Grebe Mostly coastal																		
☐ Red-necked Grebe Coastal						R												
☐ Eared Grebe																		
☐ Western Grebe Coastal						R												
☐ Yellow-nosed Albatross Offshore						R												
☐ Northern Fulmar Atlantic coast						R												
☐ Black-capped Petrel Offshore Atlantic																		
☐ Cory's Shearwater Offshore																		
☐ Greater Shearwater Offshore																		
☐ Sooty Shearwater Offshore																		
☐ Short-tailed Shearwater						R												

	Panhandle	North Peninsula	Central Peninsula	South Peninsula	Mainline Keys		January	February	March	April	May	June	July	August	September	October	November	December
☐ Manx Shearwater Offshore Atlantic						R												
☐ Audubon's Shearwater Offshore																		
☐ Wilson's Storm-Petrel Offshore, mostly Atlantic																		
☐ Leach's Storm-Petrel Offshore																		
☐ Band-rumped Storm-Petrel Offshore																		
☐ White-tailed Tropicbird Mostly Dry Tortugas																		
☐ Red-billed Tropicbird Offshore						R												
☐ Masked Booby Offshore; breeds at Dry Tortugas						B												
☐ Brown Booby Offshore Atlantic; common at Dry Tortugas																		
☐ Red-footed Booby Mostly Dry Tortugas						R												
☐ Northern Gannet Offshore																		
☐ American White Pelican " "																		
☐ Brown Pelican Mostly coastal						B												
☐ Double-crested Cormorant						B												
☐ Great Cormorant Coastal																		
☐ Anhinga " "						B B												
☐ Magnificent Frigatebird Coastal; breeds at Dry Tortugas						B												
☐ American Bittern A few unverifiable breeding reports																		

	Panhandle	North Peninsula	Central Peninsula	South Peninsula	Mainline Keys	January	February	March	April	May	June	July	August	September	October	November	December

Least Bittern   *
  "   "

Great Blue Heron

Great White Heron
   Breeds coastally;
   some disperse inland

Great Egret

Snowy Egret

Little Blue Heron

Tricolored Heron

Reddish Egret
   Breeds coastally; some
   disperse inland

Cattle Egret
  "   "

Green Heron
  "   "

Black-crowned
Night-Heron
   More common inland

Yellow-crowned
Night-Heron
   Mostly coastal
  "   "
   Mostly coastal

White Ibis
   Mostly coastal
  "   "

Scarlet Ibis
   Probably all are
   escapees or hybrids

Glossy Ibis

White-faced Ibis

Roseate Spoonbill
  "   "
   Breeds coastally;
   some disperse inland

Wood Stork   *
   Locally abundant

✔	Panhandle	North Peninsula	Central Peninsula	South Peninsula	Mainline Keys		January	February	March	April	May	June	July	August	September	October	November	December
Black Vulture						B												
Turkey Vulture						B												
Greater Flamingo																		
Mostly Snake Bight area; elsewhere beware of escaped Chilean Flamingos																		
Osprey　　*						B												
"　　"						B												
Swallow-tailed Kite　*						B												
White-tailed Kite　*						B												
Local																		
Snail Kite　　*						B												
Mississippi Kite						B												
Bald Eagle　　*						B												
Northern Harrier																		
Sharp-shinned Hawk																		
Cooper's Hawk						B												
Non-breeder in the Keys																		
Northern Goshawk						R												
Red-shouldered Hawk　*						B												
Broad-winged Hawk						B												
"　　"																		
Short-tailed Hawk　*						B												
"　　"						B												
"　　"																		
Swainson's Hawk																		
Zone-tailed Hawk						R												
Red-tailed Hawk						B												
Non-breeder in the Keys																		
Ferruginous Hawk						R												
Rough-legged Hawk						R												
Golden Eagle																		
Crested Caracara　*						B												
Eurasian Kestrel						R												

	Panhandle	North Peninsula	Central Peninsula	South Peninsula	Mainline Keys	January	February	March	April	May	June	July	August	September	October	November	December
☐ American Kestrel						B											
" "																	
☐ Merlin																	
Mostly coastal																	
☐ Peregrine Falcon																	
Mostly coastal																	
☐ Yellow Rail																	
☐ Black Rail *						B											
Local																	
" "						B											
Local																	
☐ Clapper Rail *						B											
Coastal																	
☐ King Rail *						B											
☐ Virginia Rail																	
One breeding record																	
☐ Sora																	
Purple Swamphen						E											
Very local																	
but range expanding																	
☐ Purple Gallinule *						B											
" "																	
Local during winter																	
☐ Common Moorhen *						B											
☐ American Coot						B											
☐ Limpkin *						B											
☐ Sandhill Crane *						B											
Florida race																	
" "																	
Greater race																	
Whooping Crane																	
" "																	
Dispersing northward from																	
introduction sites;																	
some pairs now breeding																	
☐ Northern Lapwing						R											
☐ Black-bellied Plover																	
Mostly coastal																	

	Panhandle	North Peninsula	Central Peninsula	South Peninsula	Mainline Keys		January	February	March	April	May	June	July	August	September	October	November	December
☐ American Golden-Plover Mostly inland																		
☐ Snowy Plover Local; Gulf Coast						B												
☐ Wilson's Plover *						B												
Coastal																		
☐ Semipalmated Plover Mostly coastal																		
☐ Piping Plover Local, mostly Gulf Coast																		
☐ Killdeer *						B												
Mostly inland																		
☐ Mountain Plover	····			··		R									·		··	
☐ American Oystercatcher Coastal						B												
☐ Black-necked Stilt *						B												
Mostly inland																		
☐ American Avocet																		
☐ Greater Yellowlegs																		
☐ Lesser Yellowlegs																		
☐ Solitary Sandpiper						M												
☐ Willet *						B												
Mostly coastal																		
☐ Spotted Sandpiper Mostly coastal																		
☐ Upland Sandpiper Inland						M												
☐ Whimbrel Coastal																		
☐ Long-billed Curlew Local; Gulf Coast																		
☐ Black-tailed Godwit Coastal		··		··		R		········										
☐ Hudsonian Godwit																		
☐ Bar-tailed Godwit	··		····			R	········									········		
☐ Marbled Godwit Local; coastal					····													

	Panhandle	North Peninsula	Central Peninsula	South Peninsula	Mainline Keys	January	February	March	April	May	June	July	August	September	October	November	December
☐ Ruddy Turnstone — Mostly coastal																	
☐ Surfbird — Mostly Gulf Coast					R												
☐ Red Knot — Local, coastal																	
☐ Sanderling — Coastal																	
☐ Semipalmated Sandpiper — " "					M												
☐ Western Sandpiper — Rare during winter in the western Panhandle																	
☐ Least Sandpiper																	
☐ White-rumped Sandpiper					M												
☐ Baird's Sandpiper					M												
☐ Pectoral Sandpiper					M												
☐ Sharp-tailed Sandpiper					R												
☐ Purple Sandpiper — Mostly Atlantic coast																	
☐ Dunlin																	
☐ Curlew Sandpiper																	
☐ Stilt Sandpiper — Mostly inland; does not winter in the western Panhandle					M												
☐ Buff-breasted Sandpiper — Inland					M												
☐ Ruff — Mostly inland					M												
☐ Short-billed Dowitcher * — Coastal except during fall; rare during winter in the western Panhandle																	
☐ Long-billed Dowitcher * — Restricted to fresh water																	
☐ Wilson's Snipe — Inland																	

	Panhandle	North Peninsula	Central Peninsula	South Peninsula	Mainline Keys		January	February	March	April	May	June	July	August	September	October	November	December
✔																		
☐ American Woodcock Inland						B												
☐ Wilson's Phalarope Inland																		
☐ Red-necked Phalarope Mostly Atlantic						M												
☐ Red Phalarope Mostly Atlantic						M												
☐ South Polar Skua Atlantic coast						R												
☐ Pomarine Jaeger Mostly Atlantic																		
☐ Parasitic Jaeger Mostly Atlantic																		
☐ Long-tailed Jaeger Offshore; mostly Atlantic																		
☐ Laughing Gull Mostly coastal	*					B												
☐ Franklin's Gull																		
☐ Little Gull Mostly Atlantic coast						R												
☐ Black-headed Gull						R												
☐ Bonaparte's Gull																		
☐ Belcher's Gull Gulf coast						R												
☐ Heermann's Gull Gulf coast						R												
☐ Gray-hooded Gull						R												
☐ Ring-billed Gull																		
☐ California Gull						R												
☐ Herring Gull Mostly coastal																		
☐ Thayer's Gull Coastal						R												
☐ Iceland Gull Coastal						R												

✔	Panhandle	North Peninsula	Central Peninsula	South Peninsula	Mainline Keys		January	February	March	April	May	June	July	August	September	October	November	December

☐ **Lesser Black-backed Gull**
Mostly Atlantic coast; range expanding

☐ **Slaty-backed Gull** — R

☐ **Glaucous Gull**
Coastal

☐ **Great Black-backed Gull**
Mostly Atlantic coast

☐ **Sabine's Gull**
Mostly Atlantic and Dry Tortugas

☐ **Black-legged Kittiwake**
Offshore Atlantic

☐ **Gull-billed Tern** — B
Local; winters in the extreme south

☐ **Caspian Tern** — B
Does not winter in the Panhandle

☐ **Royal Tern**   * — B
Mostly coastal

☐ **Elegant Tern** — R
Gulf coast. One breeding record! Beware of "Elegant-type" terns

☐ **Sandwich Tern**   * — B
Coastal; rare in the Panhandle during winter

☐ **Roseate Tern** — B
Middle and Lower Keys; otherwise offshore

☐ **Common Tern**
Coastal; casual breeder; use care when identifying during winter

☐ **Arctic Tern** — M
Mostly Atlantic

☐ **Forster's Tern**

☐ **Least Tern** — B
Mostly coastal

☐ **Bridled Tern** — B
Offshore; breeds off Key West

✔	Panhandle	North Peninsula	Central Peninsula	South Peninsula	Mainline Keys		January	February	March	April	May	June	July	August	September	October	November	December
☐ Sooty Tern * Breeds at Dry Tortugas; otherwise offshore						B												
☐ Black Tern																		
☐ Brown Noddy * Breeds at Dry Tortugas; otherwise offshore						B												
☐ Black Noddy * Dry Tortugas																		
☐ Black Skimmer * Mostly coastal; has bred inland						B												
☐ Dovekie Atlantic coast																		
☐ Thick-billed Murre Atlantic coast						R												
☐ Razorbill Atlantic coast						R												
☐ Long-billed Murrelet Gulf coast						R												
☐ Atlantic Puffin						R												
☐ Rock Pigeon Urban and suburban areas						E												
☐ Scaly-naped Pigeon						R												
☐ White-crowned Pigeon * Coastal						B												
☐ Band-tailed Pigeon Gulf coast						R												
Ringed Turtle-Dove Identify carefully; no known extant population						E												
European Turtle-Dove Provenance uncertain						R												
☐ Eurasian Collared-Dove *						E												
☐ White-winged Dove * Gulf Coast " " Range expanding northward						E												
☐ Zenaida Dove Coastal						R												

Species	Regions (Panhandle · North Peninsula · Central Peninsula · South Peninsula · Mainline Keys)	Status	Months (Jan–Dec)
Mourning Dove	(all regions)	B	(year-round)
Common Ground-Dove *		B	
White-tipped Dove — Dry Tortugas		R	(April–May)
Key West Quail-Dove — Coastal			
Ruddy Quail-Dove — Coastal		R	(scattered)
Budgerigar — Hernando Beach and Bayonet Point; declining		E	
Monk Parakeet — Urban and suburban areas		E	(year-round)
Black-hooded Parakeet — Mostly central Gulf coast; urban and suburban areas		E	(year-round)
Green Parakeet — Fort Lauderdale and Miami		E	
White-eyed Parakeet — Fort Lauderdale and Miami		E	
White-winged Parakeet — Fort Lauderdale and Miami		E	
Yellow-chevroned Parakeet — Mostly Miami		E	
Blue-crowned Parakeet — Mostly Fort Lauderdale		E	
Mitred Parakeet — Fort Lauderdale and Miami		E	
Red-masked Parakeet — Suburban and urban areas		E	
Chestnut-fronted Macaw — Fort Lauderdale and Miami		E	
Rose-ringed Parakeet — Mostly Naples		E	
Orange-winged Parrot — Fort Lauderdale and Miami		E	
Red-crowned Parrot — Mostly Fort Lauderdale		E	
Black-billed Cuckoo		M	

	Panhandle	North Peninsula	Central Peninsula	South Peninsula	Mainline Keys		January	February	March	April	May	June	July	August	September	October	November	December
☐ Yellow-billed Cuckoo *						B												
☐ Mangrove Cuckoo * Coastal	··					B												
☐ Smooth-billed Ani * Unpredictable						B												
☐ Groove-billed Ani																		
☐ Barn Owl * " "						B												
☐ Flammulated Owl	··		··			R												·
☐ Eastern Screech-Owl *						B												
☐ Great Horned Owl *						B												
☐ Snowy Owl	··					R ··												···
☐ Burrowing Owl * Local and declining						B												
☐ Barred Owl *						B												
☐ Long-eared Owl	·····					R	·· · ·									·	·
☐ Short-eared Owl Northern race " " West Indian race																		
☐ Northern Saw-whet Owl	··	··		··		R ·										· ·	··
☐ Lesser Nighthawk																		
☐ Common Nighthawk *						B												
☐ Antillean Nighthawk *						B												
☐ Chuck-will's-widow * Rare during winter south of Lake Okeechobee						B												
☐ Whip-poor-will *																		
☐ White-collared Swift	··			··		R ·									·		
☐ Chimney Swift * Non-breeder in the Keys						B												
☐ Vaux's Swift	—	—				R												
☐ Antillean Palm-Swift	··					R								·····			
☐ Broad-billed Hummingbird	··														·		

	Panhandle	North Peninsula	Central Peninsula	South Peninsula	Mainline Keys		January	February	March	April	May	June	July	August	September	October	November	December

Buff-bellied Hummingbird

Bahama Woodstar
Atlantic coast — R

Ruby-throated
Hummingbird — B

" "
Non-breeder in the Keys — B

Black-chinned
Hummingbird

Anna's Hummingbird — R

Calliope Hummingbird — R

Broad-tailed Hummingbird — R

Rufous Hummingbird

Allen's Hummingbird — R
Identification requires
in-hand measurements

Belted Kingfisher — B

" "

Red-headed Woodpecker* — B

" "

Golden-fronted
Woodpecker — R
One breeding report!

Red-bellied Woodpecker* — B

Yellow-bellied Sapsucker

Downy Woodpecker   * — B

Hairy Woodpecker   * — B
Local; mostly fire-
maintained pinewoods

Red-cockaded   * — B
Woodpecker
Extremely local

Northern Flicker   * — B
Yellow-shafted race

Pileated Woodpecker   * — B

Olive-sided Flycatcher — M

Western Wood-Pewee — R
Identify with great care

	Panhandle	North Peninsula	Central Peninsula	South Peninsula	Mainline Keys		January	February	March	April	May	June	July	August	September	October	November	December

☑

☐ Eastern Wood-Pewee — B
    "   "
    Often mistaken for
    Empidonax — M

☐ Cuban Pewee — R

☐ Yellow-bellied Flycatcher — M
    Identify with care

☐ Acadian Flycatcher   * — B
    "   " — M
    Often vocal during fall

☐ Alder Flycatcher — M
    Only two accepted reports

☐ Willow Flycatcher — M
    Only two accepted records

  "Traill's Flycatcher" — M
    Specific identity usually
    impossible

☐ Least Flycatcher — M
    Often vocal during winter

☐ Black Phoebe — R

☐ Eastern Phoebe   *
    Two Panhandle breeding
    reports

☐ Say's Phoebe — R

☐ Vermilion Flycatcher

☐ Ash-throated Flycatcher

☐ Great Crested Flycatcher * — B
    "   " — B

☐ Brown-crested Flycatcher*

☐ La Sagra's Flycatcher
    Atlantic coast and Keys

☐ Sulphur-bellied Flycatcher — R
    Includes all Myiodynastes
    reports

☐ Piratic Flycatcher — R
    Dry Tortugas

☐ Tropical Kingbird — R
    Includes all
    Tropical/Couch's Kingbirds

✔	Panhandle	North Peninsula	Central Peninsula	South Peninsula	Mainline Keys		January	February	March	April	May	June	July	August	September	October	November	December
Cassin's Kingbird																		
Western Kingbird Gulf coast " "						M												
Eastern Kingbird * Non-breeder in the Keys						B												
Gray Kingbird * Mostly coastal						B												
Scissor-tailed Flycatcher Gulf coast " "						M												
Fork-tailed Flycatcher																		
Loggerhead Shrike * Non-breeder in the Keys						B												
White-eyed Vireo *						B												
Thick-billed Vireo Atlantic coast and Keys						R												
Bell's Vireo " "																		
Blue-headed Vireo																		
Yellow-throated Vireo * " " " "						B M M												
Warbling Vireo						M												
Philadelphia Vireo						M												
Red-eyed Vireo * Non-breeder in the Keys						B												
Yellow-green Vireo						R												
Black-whiskered Vireo * Gulf coast only outside the southern peninsula						B												
Blue Jay *						B												
Florida Scrub-Jay * Very local						B												
American Crow *						B												
Fish Crow *						B												

	Panhandle	North Peninsula	Central Peninsula	South Peninsula	Mainline Keys		January	February	March	April	May	June	July	August	September	October	November	December
Horned Lark																		
Purple Martin ✳						B												
" "																		
Cuban Martin						R												
Southern Martin						R												
Tree Swallow																		
Local during winter																		
Mangrove Swallow						R												
Bahama Swallow						R												
Atlantic coast and Keys																		
Northern Rough-winged Swallow						B												
" "						B												
Bank Swallow						M												
Cliff Swallow						M												
Cave Swallow ✳						B												
" " Extremely local; Homestead																		
Barn Swallow						B												
Carolina Chickadee ✳						B												
Tufted Titmouse ✳						B												
Red-breasted Nuthatch Irruptive																		
White-breasted Nuthatch						B												
Brown-headed Nuthatch ✳						B												
Brown Creeper Irruptive																		
Rock Wren						R												
Carolina Wren ✳						B												
Bewick's Wren 1995-2004 status only						R												
House Wren																		
Winter Wren																		
Sedge Wren Has built nests																		

	Panhandle	North Peninsula	Central Peninsula	South Peninsula	Mainline Keys		January	February	March	April	May	June	July	August	September	October	November	December
✔																		

□ **Marsh Wren** ∗ — B
　　Coastal only
　　" "

□ **Red-whiskered Bulbul** ∗ — E
　　Kendall-Pinecrest

□ **Golden-crowned Kinglet**
　　Irruptive

□ **Ruby-crowned Kinglet**

□ **Blue-gray Gnatcatcher** ∗ — B
　　Non-breeder in the Keys;
　　rare during winter in
　　north Florida

□ **Northern Wheatear** — R
　　Mostly coastal

□ **Eastern Bluebird** ∗ — B

□ **Mountain Bluebird** — R

□ **Veery** — M

□ **Gray-cheeked Thrush** — M
　　Status of Bicknell's Thrush
　　under review

□ **Swainson's Thrush** — M

□ **Hermit Thrush**

□ **Wood Thrush** — B
　　" " — M

□ **American Robin** — B
　　Irruptive
　　" "
　　Irruptive

□ **Varied Thrush** — R
　　Coastal

□ **Gray Catbird** — B
　　" "

□ **Northern Mockingbird** ∗ — B

□ **Bahama Mockingbird**
　　Atlantic coast and Keys;
　　has built nests

□ **Sage Thrasher** — R

□ **Brown Thrasher** ∗ — B

✔	Panhandle	North Peninsula	Central Peninsula	South Peninsula	Mainline Keys	January	February	March	April	May	June	July	August	September	October	November	December
☐ Curve-billed Thrasher						R											
☐ European Starling Urban and suburban areas						E											
Hill Myna Southern Miami area						E											
Common Myna Atlantic coast and Keys; range expanding						E											
☐ American Pipit																	
☐ Sprague's Pipit						R											
☐ Cedar Waxwing Irruptive																	
☐ Blue-winged Warbler " "						M M											
☐ Golden-winged Warbler						M											
☐ Tennessee Warbler						M											
☐ Orange-crowned Warbler																	
☐ Nashville Warbler						M											
☐ Northern Parula * " " " "						B B											
☐ Yellow Warbler Eastern race " " * Cuban race						M B											
☐ Chestnut-sided Warbler						M											
☐ Magnolia Warbler " "						M											
☐ Cape May Warbler " "						M											
☐ Black-throated Blue Warbler " " Winters in extreme south																	
☐ Yellow-rumped Warbler Myrtle race " " Audubon's race						R											

✔	Panhandle	North Peninsula	Central Peninsula	South Peninsula	Mainline Keys		January	February	March	April	May	June	July	August	September	October	November	December
☐ Black-throated Gray Warbler																		
☐ Golden-cheeked Warbler			••			R									•			
☐ Black-throated Green Warbler						M												
" "						M												
☐ Townsend's Warbler	••		••	••		•••••••••••									•			•••
☐ Blackburnian Warbler						M												
☐ Yellow-throated Warbler *						B												
Irregular during winter in the Panhandle																		
" "						M												
☐ Pine Warbler *						B												
☐ Kirtland's Warbler						R												•
Coastal																		
☐ Prairie Warbler *						B												
Eastern race																		
" "						M												
Eastern race																		
" "						B												
Florida race; coastal																		
☐ Palm Warbler																		
☐ Bay-breasted Warbler						M												
☐ Blackpoll Warbler						M												
☐ Cerulean Warbler						M												
☐ Black-and-white Warbler																		
☐ American Redstart						M												
Has bred in the western Panhandle																		
" "						M												
☐ Prothonotary Warbler *						B												
" "						M												
☐ Worm-eating Warbler						M												
Has bred in the western Panhandle																		
" "						M												
☐ Swainson's Warbler *						B												
" "						M												

	Panhandle	North Peninsula	Central Peninsula	South Peninsula	Mainline Keys		January	February	March	April	May	June	July	August	September	October	November	December
☐ Ovenbird						M												
" "						M												
☐ Northern Waterthrush						M												
" "						M												
☐ Louisiana Waterthrush						B												
" "						M												
☐ Kentucky Warbler						B												
" "						M												
☐ Connecticut Warbler						M												
Absent from the Gulf coast during fall																		
☐ Mourning Warbler						M												
☐ MacGillivray's Warbler						R												
☐ Common Yellowthroat *						B												
Non-breeder in the Keys																		
☐ Hooded Warbler *						B												
" "						M												
Casual during winter in the extreme south																		
☐ Wilson's Warbler						M												
☐ Canada Warbler						M												
☐ Yellow-breasted Chat *						B												
" "						M												
☐ Bananaquit																		
Atlantic coast and Keys																		
☐ Western Spindalis																		
Black-backed race; Atlantic coast and Keys																		
" " Green-backed race																		
☐ Summer Tanager *						B												
☐ Scarlet Tanager						M												
☐ Western Tanager																		
Red-legged Honeycreeper						R												
Perhaps vagrants from Cuba																		
☐ Yellow-faced Grassquit						R												
☐ Black-faced Grassquit						R												

✔

✔	Panhandle	North Peninsula	Central Peninsula	South Peninsula	Mainline Keys		January	February	March	April	May	June	July	August	September	October	November	December
☐ Green-tailed Towhee			··			R	·············											
☐ Spotted Towhee	··					R												·
☐ Eastern Towhee ∗						B												
" "																		
☐ Bachman's Sparrow ∗ Secretive when not singing						B												
☐ American Tree Sparrow	····					R			·						·			
☐ Chipping Sparrow Has bred in the western Panhandle " "																		
☐ Clay-colored Sparrow																		
☐ Field Sparrow " "						B												
☐ Vesper Sparrow																		
☐ Lark Sparrow																		
☐ Black-throated Sparrow	··					R	··											
☐ Lark Bunting	····	··	··			R	·········	····					·····					
☐ Savannah Sparrow Various northern races " " Ipswitch race; Atlantic coast	····						··········											·····
☐ Grasshopper Sparrow Eastern race " " ∗ Florida race; extremely local; generally indistin- guishable from eastern race by plumage						B												
☐ Henslow's Sparrow																		
☐ Le Conte's Sparrow																		
☐ Nelson's Sharp-tailed Sparrow Coastal																		
☐ Saltmarsh Sharp-tailed Sparrow Mostly Atlantic coast																		

	Panhandle	North Peninsula	Central Peninsula	South Peninsula	Mainline Keys		January	February	March	April	May	June	July	August	September	October	November	December
☐ Seaside Sparrow ∗ Coastal						B												
" " ∗ Cape Sable race; Everglades National Park						B												
☐ Fox Sparrow																		
☐ Song Sparrow																		
☐ Lincoln's Sparrow																		
☐ Swamp Sparrow																		
☐ White-throated Sparrow																		
☐ Harris's Sparrow						R												
☐ White-crowned Sparrow																		
☐ Golden-crowned Sparrow						R												
☐ Dark-eyed Junco Slate-colored race																		
" " Oregon race																		
☐ Lapland Longspur																		
☐ Chestnut-collared Longspur						R												
☐ Snow Bunting Mostly Atlantic coast																		
☐ Northern Cardinal ∗						B												
☐ Rose-breasted Grosbeak Winters in extreme south						M												
☐ Black-headed Grosbeak																		
☐ Blue Grosbeak ∗ " "						B M												
☐ Lazuli Bunting						R												
☐ Indigo Bunting " "						B M												
☐ Painted Bunting ∗ Mostly Atlantic coast " "						B M												
☐ Dickcissel Two breeding records																		

	Panhandle	North Peninsula	Central Peninsula	South Peninsula	Mainline Keys		January	February	March	April	May	June	July	August	September	October	November	December
☐ Bobolink						M												·
☐ Red-winged Blackbird ✳						B												
☐ Tawny-shouldered Blackbird				··		R	·											
☐ Eastern Meadowlark ✳						B												
☐ Western Meadowlark No report since 1993						R												
☐ Yellow-headed Blackbird																		
☐ Rusty Blackbird Identify carefully south of Gainesville																		
☐ Brewer's Blackbird Identify carefully south of Gainesville																		
☐ Common Grackle ✳						B												
" "						B												
☐ Boat-tailed Grackle ✳						B												
☐ Shiny Cowbird ✳ Mostly coastal; primarily Key West and Dry Tortugas																		
☐ Bronzed Cowbird																		
☐ Brown-headed Cowbird ✳						B												
☐ Orchard Oriole ✳						B	··											
" "						M												
☐ Hooded Oriole	··					R											·	
☐ Bullock's Oriole						R												
☐ Spot-breasted Oriole Urban and suburban areas along the Atlantic coast						E												
☐ Baltimore Oriole One breeding report																		
☐ Purple Finch Irruptive																		
☐ House Finch Local but range expanding; urban and suburban areas						E												
☐ Red Crossbill	····					R	····											····

✔	Panhandle	North Peninsula	Central Peninsula	South Peninsula	Mainline Keys		January	February	March	April	May	June	July	August	September	October	November	December
☐ Pine Siskin 　Irruptive													..					
☐ American Goldfinch																		
☐ Evening Grosbeak																		
☐ House Sparrow 　Urban and suburban areas					E													

LISTS OF
OTHER FAUNA

B ecause complete and definitive lists for other fauna of Florida are difficult to locate and often are contradictory, the following lists were compiled by local experts. John Epler complied the damselfly list and edited the dragonfly list, and Buck and Linda Cooper edited the butterfly list. The amphibian, reptile, and mammal lists have been revised from Internet resources posted to the University of Florida website. Meshaka et al. (2004) was used to update information about Florida's exotic herpetofauna.

DAMSELFLIES OF FLORIDA
(47 species)

___**Sparkling Jewelwing** (*Calopteryx dimidiata*)
___**Ebony Jewelwing** (*Calopteryx maculata*)
___**American Rubyspot** (*Hetaerina americana*)
___**Smoky Rubyspot** (*Hetaerina titia*)
___**Common Spreadwing** (*Lestes australis*)
___**Elegant Spreadwing** (*Lestes inaequalis*)
___**Slender Spreadwing** (*Lestes rectangularis*)
___**Antillean Spreadwing** (*Lestes spumarius*)
___**Blue-striped Spreadwing** (*Lestes tenuatus*)
___**Carolina Spreadwing** (*Lestes vidua*)
___**Swamp Spreadwing** (*Lestes vigilax*)
___**Blue-fronted Dancer** (*Argia apicalis*)
___**Seepage Dancer** (*Argia bipunctulata*)
___**Variable Dancer** (*Argia fumipennis*)
___**Powdered Dancer** (*Argia moesta*)
___**Blue-ringed Dancer** (*Argia sedula*)
___**Blue-tipped Dancer** (*Argia tibialis*)
___**Tail-light Damsel** (*Chrysobasis lucifer*)
___**Double-striped Bluet** (*Enallagma basidens*)
___**Familiar Bluet** (*Enallagma civile*)

___**Purple Bluet** (*Enallagma coecum*)
___**Cherry Bluet** (*Enallagma concisum*)
___**Attenuated Bluet** (*Enallagma daeckii*)
___**Sandhill Bluet** (*Enallagma davisi*)
___**Turquoise Bluet** (*Enallagma divagans*)
___**Atlantic Bluet** (*Enallagma doubledayi*)
___**Burgundy Bluet** (*Enallagma dubium*)
___**Big Bluet** (*Enallagma durum*)
___**Skimming Bluet** (*Enallagma geminatum*)
___**Pale Bluet** (*Enallagma pallidum*)
___**Florida Bluet** (*Enallagma pollutum*)
___**Orange Bluet** (*Enallagma signatum*)
___**Golden Bluet** (*Enallagma sulcatum*)
___**Slender Bluet** (*Enallagma traviatum*)
___**Vesper Bluet** (*Enallagma vesperum*)
___**Blackwater Bluet** (*Enallagma weewa*)
___**Citrine Forktail** (*Ischnura hastata*)
___**Lilypad Forktail** (*Ischnura kellicotti*)
___**Fragile Forktail** (*Ischnura posita*)
___**Furtive Forktail** (*Ischnura prognata*)
___**Rambur's Forktail** (*Ischnura ramburii*)
___**Eastern Forktail** (*Ischnura verticalis*)
___**Sphagnum Sprite** (*Nehalennia gracilis*)
___**Southern Sprite** (*Nehalennia integricollis*)
___**Tropical Sprite** (*Nehalennia minuta*)
___**Caribbean Yellowface** (*Neoerythromma cultellatum*)
___**Duckweed Firetail** (*Telebasis byersi*)

DRAGONFLIES OF FLORIDA
(121 species)

___**Gray Petaltail** (*Tachopteryx thoreyi*)
___**Amazon Darner** (*Anax amazili*)
___**Comet Darner** (*Anax longipes*)
___**Common Green Darner** (*Anax junius*)
___**Springtime Darner** (*Basiaeschna janata*)
___**Fawn Darner** (*Boyeria vinosa*)
___**Blue-faced Darner** (*Coryphaeschna adnexa*)
___**Regal Darner** (*Coryphaeschna ingens*)
___**Mangrove Darner** (*Coryphaeschna viriditas*)
___**Swamp Darner** (*Epiaeschna heros*)
___**Taper-tailed Darner** (*Gomphaeschna antilope*)
___**Harlequin Darner** (*Gomphaeschna furcillata*)
___**Twilight Darner** (*Gynacantha nervosa*)

___**Cyrano Darner** (*Nasiaeschna pentacantha*)
___**Malachite Darner** (*Remartinia luteipennis*)
___**Pale-green Darner** (*Triacanthagyna septima*)
___**Phantom Darner** (*Triacanthagyna trifida*)
___**Two-striped Forceptail** (*Aphylla williamsoni*)
___**Gray-green Clubtail** (*Arigomphus pallidus*)
___**Southeastern Spinyleg** (*Dromogomphus armatus*)
___**Black-shouldered Spinyleg** (*Dromogomphus spinosus*)
___**Eastern Ringtail** (*Erpetogomphus designatus*)
___**Blackwater Clubtail** (*Gomphus dilatatus*)
___**Cocoa Clubtail** (*Gomphus hybridus*)
___**Gulf Coast Clubtail** (*Gomphus modestus*)
___**Cobra Clubtail** (*Gomphus vastus*)
___**Clearlake Clubtail** (*Gomphus australis*)
___**Sandhill Clubtail** (*Gomphus cavillaris*)
___**Lancet Clubtail** (*Gomphus exilis*)
___**Hodges' Clubtail** (*Gomphus hodgesi*)
___**Ashy Clubtail** (*Gomphus lividus*)
___**Cypress Clubtail** (*Gomphus minutus*)
___**Westfall's Clubtail** (*Gomphus westfalli*)
___**Twin-striped Clubtail** (*Gomphus geminatus*)
___**Dragonhunter** (*Hagenius brevistylus*)
___**Tawny Sanddragon** (*Progomphus alachuensis*)
___**Belle's Sanddragon** (*Progomphus bellei*)
___**Common Sanddragon** (*Progomphus obscurus*)
___**Shining Clubtail** (*Stylurus ivae*)
___**Laura's Clubtail** (*Stylurus laurae*)
___**Russet-tipped Clubtail** (*Stylurus plagiatus*)
___**Yellow-sided Clubtail** (*Stylurus potulentus*)
___**Townes' Clubtail** (*Stylurus townesi*)
___**Twin-spotted Spiketail** (*Cordulegaster maculata*)
___**Arrowhead Spiketail** (*Cordulegaster obliqua*)
___**Say's Spiketail** (*Cordulegaster sayi*)
___**Florida Cruiser** (*Didymops floridensis*)
___**Stream Cruiser** (*Didymops transversa*)
___**Allegheny River Cruiser** (*Macromia alleghaniensis*)
___**Illinois River Cruiser** (*Macromia georgina*)
___**Royal River Cruiser** (*Macromia taeniolata*)
___**Prince Baskettail** (*Epitheca princeps*)
___**Stripe-winged Baskettail** (*Epitheca costalis*)
___**Common Baskettail** (*Epitheca cynosura*)
___**Mantled Baskettail** (*Epitheca semiaquea*)
___**Sepia Baskettail** (*Epitheca sepia*)
___**Robust Baskettail** (*Epitheca spinosa*)

___**Florida Baskettail** (*Epitheca stella*)
___**Selys' Sundragon** (*Helocordulia selysii*)
___**Alabama Shadowdragon** (*Neurocordulia alabamensis*)
___**Smoky Shadowdragon** (*Neurocordulia molesta*)
___**Umber Shadowdragon** (*Neurocordulia obsoleta*)
___**Cinnamon Shadowdragon** (*Neurocordulia virginiensis*)
___**Calvert's Emerald** (*Somatochlora calverti*)
___**Fine-lined Emerald** (*Somatochlora filosa*)
___**Coppery Emerald** (*Somatochlora georgiana*)
___**Mocha Emerald** (*Somatochlora linearis*)
___**Treetop Emerald** (*Somatochlora provocans*)
___**Clamp-tipped Emerald** (*Somatochlora tenebrosa*)
___**Red-tailed Pennant** (*Brachymesia furcata*)
___**Four-spotted Pennant** (*Brachymesia gravida*)
___**Tawny Pennant** (*Brachymesia herbida*)
___**Amanda's Pennant** (*Celithemis amanda*)
___**Red-veined Pennant** (*Celithemis bertha*)
___**Calico Pennant** (*Celithemis elisa*)
___**Halloween Pennant** (*Celithemis eponina*)
___**Banded Pennant** (*Celithemis fasciata*)
___**Faded Pennant** (*Celithemis ornata*)
___**Double-ringed Pennant** (*Celithemis verna*)
___**Scarlet Skimmer** (*Crocothemis servilia*)
___**Swift Setwing** (*Dythemis velox*)
___**Pin-tailed Pondhawk** (*Erythemis plebeja*)
___**Eastern Pondhawk** (*Erythemis simplicicollis*)
___**Great Pondhawk** (*Erythemis vesiculosa*)
___**Seaside Dragonlet** (*Erythrodiplax berenice*)
___**Little Blue Dragonlet** (*Erythrodiplax minuscula*)
___**Band-winged Dragonlet** (*Erythrodiplax umbrata*)
___**Metallic Pennant** (*Idiataphe cubensis*)
___**Blue Corporal** (*Ladona deplanata*)
___**Golden-winged Skimmer** (*Libellula auripennis*)
___**Bar-winged Skimmer** (*Libellula axilena*)
___**Yellow-sided Skimmer** (*Libellula flavida*)
___**Slaty Skimmer** (*Libellula incesta*)
___**Purple Skimmer** (*Libellula jesseana*)
___**Needham's Skimmer** (*Libellula needhami*)
___**Twelve-spotted Skimmer** (*Libellula pulchella*)
___**Painted Skimmer** (*Libellula semifasciata*)
___**Great Blue Skimmer** (*Libellula vibrans*)
___**Marl Pennant** (*Macrodiplax balteata*)
___**Hyacinth Glider** (*Miathyria marcella*)
___**Spot-tailed Dasher** (*Micrathyria aequalis*)

___**Three-striped Dasher** (*Micrathyria didyma*)
___**Elfin Skimmer** (*Nannothemis bella*)
___**Roseate Skimmer** (*Orthemis ferruginea*)
___**Blue Dasher** (*Pachydiplax longipennis*)
___**Wandering Glider** (*Pantala flavescens*)
___**Spot-winged Glider** (*Pantala hymenaea*)
___**Eastern Amberwing** (*Perithemis tenera*)
___**Common Whitetail** (*Plathemis lydia*)
___**Blue-faced Meadowhawk** (*Sympetrum ambiguum*)
___**Variegated Meadowhawk** (*Sympetrum corruptum*)
___**Yellow-legged Meadowhawk** (*Sympetrum vicinum*)
___**Garnet Glider** (*Tauriphila australis*)
___**Evening Skimmer** (*Tholymis citrina*)
___**Vermilion Saddlebags** (*Tramea abdominalis*)
___**Sooty Saddlebags** (*Tramea binotata*)
___**Striped Saddlebags** (*Tramea calverti*)
___**Carolina Saddlebags** (*Tramea carolina*)
___**Antillean Saddlebags** (*Tramea insularis*)
___**Black Saddlebags** (*Tramea lacerata*)
___**Red Saddlebags** (*Tramea onusta*)

BUTTERFLIES OF FLORIDA
(166 species)

___**Pipevine Swallowtail** (*Battus philenor*)
___**Polydamus Swallowtail** (*Battus polydamus*)
___**Zebra Swallowtail** (*Eurytides marcellus*)
___**Black Swallowtail** (*Papilio polyxenes*)
___**Giant Swallowtail** (*Papilio cresphontes*)
___**Schaus's Swallowtail** (*Papilio aristodemus*)
___**Bahamian Swallowtail** (*Papilio andraemon*)
___**Eastern Tiger Swallowtail** (*Papilio glaucus*)
___**Spicebush Swallowtail** (*Papilio troilus*)
___**Palamedes Swallowtail** (*Papilio palamedes*)
___**Florida White** (*Appias drusilla*)
___**Checkered White** (*Pontia protodice*)
___**Cabbage White** (*Pieris rapae*)
___**Great Southern White** (*Ascia monuste*)
___**Falcate Orangetip** (*Anthocharis midea*)
___**Orange Sulphur** (*Colias eurytheme*)
___**Southern Dogface** (*Colias cesonia*)
___**Cloudless Sulphur** (*Phoebis sennae*)
___**Orange-barred Sulphur** (*Phoebis philea*)
___**Large Orange Sulphur** (*Phoebis agarithe*)

___**Statira Sulphur** (*Phoebis statira*)
___**Lyside Sulphur** (*Kricogonia lyside*)
___**Barred Yellow** (*Eurema daira*)
___**Little Yellow** (*Eurema lisa*)
___**Mimosa Yellow** (*Eurema nise*)
___**Dina Yellow** (*Eurema dina*)
___**Sleepy Orange** (*Eurema nicippe*)
___**Dainty Sulphur** (*Nathalis iole*)
___**Harvester** (*Feniseca tarquinius*)
___**Atala** (*Eumaeus atala*)
___**Great Purple Hairstreak** (*Atlides halesus*)
___**Amethyst Hairstreak** (*Chorostrymon maesites*)
___**Silver-banded Hairstreak** (*Chlorostrymon simaethis*)
___**Coral Hairstreak** (*Satyrium titus*)
___**Banded Hairstreak** (*Satyrium calanus*)
___**King's Hairstreak** (*Satyrium kingi*)
___**Striped Hairstreak** (*Satyrium liparops*)
___**Oak Hairstreak** (*Satyrium favonius*)
___**Frosted Elfin** (*Callophrys irus*)
___**Henry's Elfin** (*Callophrys henrici*)
___**Eastern Pine Elfin** (*Callophrys niphon*)
___**Juniper Hairstreak** (*Callophrys gryneus*)
___**Hessel's Hairstreak** (*Callophrys hesseli*)
___**White-M Hairstreak** (*Parrhasius m-album*)
___**Gray Hairstreak** (*Strymon melinus*)
___**Martial Scrub-Hairstreak** (*Strymon martialis*)
___**Bartram's Scrub-Hairstreak** (*Strymon acis*)
___**Mallow Scrub-Hairstreak** (*Strymon istapa*)
___**Fulvous Hairstreak** (*Electrostrymon angelia*)
___**Red-banded Hairstreak** (*Calycopis cecrops*)
___**Gray Ministreak** (*Ministrymon azia*)
___**Eastern Pygmy Blue** (*Brephidium isophthalma*)
___**Cassius Blue** (*Leptotes cassius*)
___**Miami Blue** (*Hemiargus thomasi*)
___**Nickerbean Blue** (*Hemiargus ammon*)
___**Ceraunus Blue** (*Hemiargus ceraunus*)
___**Eastern Tailed-Blue** (*Everes comyntas*)
___**Spring Azure** (*Celastrina ladon*)
___**Little Metalmark** (*Calephelis virginiensis*)
___**American Snout** (*Libytheana carinenta*)
___**Gulf Fritillary** (*Agraulis vanillae*)
___**Julia Heliconian** (*Dryas iulia*)
___**Zebra Heliconian** (*Heliconius charitonia*)
___**Variegated Fritillary** (*Euptoieta claudia*)

___**Silvery Checkerspot** (*Chlosyne nycteis*)
___**Texan Crescent** (*Phyciodes texana*)
___**Cuban Crescent** (*Phyciodes frisia*)
___**Phaon Crescent** (*Phyciodes phaon*)
___**Pearl Crescent** (*Phyciodes tharos*)
___**Question Mark** (*Polygonia interrogationis*)
___**Eastern Comma** (*Polygonia comma*)
___**Mourning Cloak** (*Nymphalis antiopa*)
___**American Lady** (*Vanessa virginiensis*)
___**Painted Lady** (*Vanessa cardui*)
___**Red Admiral** (*Vanessa atalanta*)
___**Common Buckeye** (*Junonia coenia*)
___**Mangrove Buckeye** (*Junonia evarete*)
___**Tropical Buckeye** (*Junonia genoveva*)
___**White Peacock** (*Anartia jatrophae*)
___**Malachite** (*Siproeta stelenes*)
___**Red-spotted Purple** (*Limenitis arthemis*)
___**Viceroy** (*Limenitis archippus*)
___**Dingy Purplewing** (*Eunica monima*)
___**Florida Purplewing** (*Eunica tatila*)
___**Pale Cracker** (*Hamadryas amphichloe*)
___**Ruddy Daggerwing** (*Marpesia petreus*)
___**Florida Leafwing** (*Anaea floridalis*)
___**Goatweed Leafwing** (*Anaea andria*)
___**Hackberry Emperor** (*Asterocampa celtis*)
___**Tawny Emperor** (*Asterocampa clyton*)
___**Southern Pearly-Eye** (*Enodia portlandia*)
___**Appalachian Brown** (*Satyrodes appalachia*)
___**Gemmed Satyr** (*Cyllopsis gemma*)
___**Carolina Satyr** (*Hermeuptychia sosybius*)
___**Georgia Satyr** (*Neonympha areolata*)
___**Little Wood-Satyr** (*Megisto cymela*)
___**Common Wood-Nymph** (*Cercyonis pegala*)
___**Monarch** (*Danaus plexippus*)
___**Queen** (*Danaus gilippus*)
___**Soldier** (*Danaus eresimus*)
___**Mangrove Skipper** (*Phocides pigmalion*)
___**Zestos Skipper** (*Epargyreus zestos*)
___**Silver-spotted Skipper** (*Epargyreus clarus*)
___**Hammock Skipper** (*Polygonus leo*)
___**Long-tailed Skipper** (*Urbanus proteus*)
___**Dorantes Longtail** (*Urbanus dorantes*)
___**Golden Banded-Skipper** (*Autochton cellus*)
___**Hoary Edge** (*Achalarus lyciades*)

___**Southern Cloudywing** (*Thorybes bathyllus*)
___**Northern Cloudywing** (*Thorybes pylades*)
___**Confused Cloudywing** (*Thorybes confusis*)
___**Hayhurst's Scallopwing** (*Staphlyus hayhurstii*)
___**Florida Duskywing** (*Ephyriades brunneus*)
___**Sleepy Duskywing** (*Erynnis brizo*)
___**Juvenal's Duskywing** (*Erynnis juvenalis*)
___**Horace's Duskywing** (*Erynnis horatius*)
___**Zarucco Duskywing** (*Erynnis zarucco*)
___**Funereal Duskywing** (*Erynnis funeralis*)
___**Common Checkered-Skipper** (*Pyrgus communis*)
___**White Checkered-Skipper** (*Pyrgus albescens*)
___**Tropical Checkered-Skipper** (*Pyrgus oileus*)
___**Common Sootywing** (*Pholisora catullus*)
___**Swarthy Skipper** (*Nastra lherminier*)
___**Neamathla Skipper** (*Nastra neamathla*)
___**Three-spotted Skipper** (*Cymaenes tripunctus*)
___**Clouded Skipper** (*Lerema accius*)
___**Least Skipper** (*Ancyloxpha numitor*)
___**Southern Skipperling** (*Copaeodes minimus*)
___**Fiery Skipper** (*Hylephila phyleus*)
___**Dotted Skipper** (*Hesperia attalus*)
___**Meske's Skipper** (*Hesperia meskei*)
___**Baracoa Skipper** (*Polites baracoa*)
___**Tawny-edged Skipper** (*Polites themistocles*)
___**Crossline Skipper** (*Polites origenes*)
___**Whirlabout** (*Polites vibex*)
___**Southern Broken-Dash** (*Wallengrenia otho*)
___**Northern Broken-Dash** (*Wallengrenia egeremet*)
___**Little Glassywing** (*Pompeius verna*)
___**Sachem** (*Atalopedes campestris*)
___**Arogos Skipper** (*Atrytone arogos*)
___**Delaware Skipper** (*Atrytone logan*)
___**Byssus Skipper** (*Problema byssus*)
___**Zabulon Skipper** (*Poanes zabulon*)
___**Aaron's Skipper** (*Poanes aaroni*)
___**Yehl Skipper** (*Poanes yehl*)
___**Broad-winged Skipper** (*Poanes viator*)
___**Palmetto Skipper** (*Euphyes arpa*)
___**Palatka Skipper** (*Euphyes pilatka*)
___**Dion Skipper** (*Euphyes dion*)
___**Dukes' Skipper** (*Euphyes dukesi*)
___**Berry's Skipper** (*Euphyes berryi*)
___**Dun Skipper** (*Euphyes vestris*)

___**Monk Skipper** (*Asbolis capucinus*)
___**Dusted Skipper** (*Atrytonopsis hianna*)
___**Pepper-and-Salt Skipper** (*Amblyscirtes hegon*)
___**Lace-winged Roadside-Skipper** (*Amblyscirtes aesculapius*)
___**Common Roadside-Skipper** (*Amblyscirtes vialis*)
___**Dusky Roadside-Skipper** (*Amblyscirtes alternata*)
___**Eufala Skipper** (*Lerodea eufala*)
___**Twin-spot Skipper** (*Oligoria maculata*)
___**Brazilian Skipper** (*Calpodes ethlius*)
___**Salt-Marsh Skipper** (*Panoquina panoquin*)
___**Obscure Skipper** (*Panoquina panoquinoides*)
___**Ocola Skipper** (*Panoquina ocola*)
___**Yucca Giant-Skipper** (*Megathymus yuccae*)
___**Cofaqui Giant-Skipper** (*Megathymus cofaqui*)

AMPHIBIANS OF FLORIDA
(56 species)

SALAMANDERS

___**Alabama Waterdog** (*Necturus alabamensis*)—Streams in the Panhandle.
___**Two-toed Amphiuma** (*Amphiuma means*)—Wetlands throughout.
___**One-toed Amphiuma** (*Amphiuma pholeter*)—Streams in the Panhandle and along the Gulf coast to Hernando County.
___**Greater Siren** (*Siren lacertina*)—Wetlands throughout.
___**Lesser Siren** (*Siren intermedia*)—Wetlands throughout.
___**Northern Dwarf Siren** (*Pseudobranchus striatus*)—Hyacinth-covered waters throughout the mainland.
___**Mole Salamander** (*Ambystoma talpoideum*)—Moist woodlands in the Panhandle south to central Florida.
___**Marbled Salamander** (*Ambystoma opacum*)—Hammocks in the Panhandle and northern peninsula.
___**Flatwoods Salamander** (*Ambystoma cingulatum*)—Pinewoods in the Panhandle and northern peninsula.
___**Tiger Salamander** (*Ambystoma tigrinum*)—Moist woodlands in the Panhandle south to the central peninsula.
___**Eastern Newt** (*Notophthalmus viridescens*)—Quiet waters throughout the mainland.
___**Striped Newt** (*Notophthalmus perstriatus*)—Quiet waters south to the central peninsula.
___**Northern Dusky Salamander** (*Desmognathus fuscus*)—Streams in the Panhandle and a few sites in the central peninsula.
___**Apalachicola Dusky Salamander** (*Desmognathus auriculatus*)—Swamps south to the central peninsula.

___**Seal Salamander** (*Desmognathus monticola*)—Only in Canoe Creek, Escambia County.

___**Slimy Salamander** (*Plethodon glutinosus*)—Moist woodlands south to the central peninsula.

___**Four-toed Salamander** (*Hemidactylium scutatum*)—Bogs and other wetlands of two regions in the Panhandle.

___**Many-lined Salamander** (*Stereochilus marginatus*)—Bayhead swamps in the Okefenokee Swamp region.

___**Mud Salamander** (*Pseudotriton montanus*)—Shallow streams in the Panhandle south to the central peninsula.

___**Southern Red Salamander** (*Pseudotriton ruber*)—Small streams in the Panhandle.

___**Southern Two-lined Salamander** (*Eurycea cirrigera*)—Small streams in the Panhandle and the northwestern peninsula.

___**Long-tailed Salamander** (*Eurycea longicauda*)—Moist woodlands in the Panhandle.

___**Dwarf Salamander** (*Eurycea quadridigitata*)—Swamps south to the central peninsula.

___**Georgia Blind Salamander** (*Haideotriton wallacei*)—About 15 caves near Marianna.

TOADS AND FROGS

___**Eastern Spadefoot Toad** (*Scaphiopus holbrooki*)—Sandy woodlands throughout.

___**Southern Toad** (*Bufo terrestris*)—Most habitats throughout.

___**Woodhouse's Toad** (*Bufo woodhousei*)—Wetlands in the Panhandle.

___**Oak Toad** (*Bufo quercicus*)—Pinewoods and oak hammocks throughout.

___**Giant Toad** (*Bufo marinus*)—Exotic, native to Tropical America. Human-modified habitats from the central peninsula southward.

___**Greenhouse Frog** (*Eleutherodactylus planirostris*)—Exotic, native to the West Indies. Moist woodlands throughout.

___**Puerto Rican Coqui** (*Eleutherodactylus coqui*)—Exotic, native to Puerto Rico. Miami area.

___**Southern Cricket Frog** (*Acris gryllus*)—Wetlands throughout.

___**Northern Cricket Frog** (*Acris crepitans*)—Swamps in the Panhandle.

___**Spring Peeper** (*Hyla crucifer*)—Moist woodlands south to the central peninsula.

___**Pine Barrens Treefrog** (*Hyla andersonii*)—Swamps in the western Panhandle.

___**Green Treefrog** (*Hyla cinerea*)—Wetlands throughout.

___**Barking Treefrog** (*Hyla gratiosa*)—Woodlands throughout, except absent from the extreme south.

___**Pinewoods Treefrog** (*Hyla femoralis*)—Pinewoods and cypress swamps throughout, except absent from the extreme south.

___**Squirrel Treefrog** (*Hyla squirella*)—Moist woodlands throughout.

___**Cope's Gray Treefrog** (*Hyla chrysoscelis*)—Woodlands in the Panhandle and northern peninsula.

___**Bird-voiced Treefrog** (*Hyla avivoca*)—Swamps in the Panhandle.

___**Cuban Treefrog** (*Osteopilus septentrionalis*)—Exotic, native to Cuba. Woodlands and human-modified habitats from the central peninsula southward.

___**Upland Chorus Frog** (*Pseudacris triseriata*)—Moist woodlands along the upper Apalachicola River.

___**Southern Chorus Frog** (*Pseudacris nigrita*)—Wet prairies and pinewoods throughout, except absent from the extreme south.

___**Ornate Chorus Frog** (*Pseudacris ornata*)—Ponds south to the central peninsula.

___**Little Grass Frog** (*Pseudacris ocularis*)—Brushy wetlands throughout.

___**Eastern Narrowmouth Toad** (*Gastrophyne carolinensis*)—Wetlands throughout.

___**Bullfrog** (*Rana catesbeiana*)—Permanent waters south to the central peninsula.

___**River Frog** (*Rana heckscheri*)—Permanent waters south to the central peninsula.

___**Pig Frog** (*Rana grylio*)—Permanent waters throughout.

___**Carpenter Frog** (*Rana virgatipes*)—Okefenokee Swamp in Baker and Columbia Counties.

___**Bronze Frog** (*Rana clamitans*)—Wetlands in the Panhandle and northern peninsula.

___**Southern Leopard Frog** (*Rana utricularia*)—Wetlands throughout.

___**Pickerel Frog** (*Rana palustris*)—One old and possibly erroneous record from Pensacola.

___**Gopher Frog** (*Rana capito*)—Threatened. Gopher Tortoise burrows south to the southern peninsula.

___**Bog Frog** (*Rana okaloosae*)—An endemic species discovered in 1982. All 23 known localities are in small streams of the Yellow and East Bay Rivers in Okaloosa, Santa Rosa, and Walton Counties. All but three localities are within Eglin Air Force Base.

REPTILES OF FLORIDA
(123 species)

CROCODILIANS

___**American Crocodile** (*Crocodylus acutus*)—Endangered, with the Florida population numbering about 1,00 individuals. In the U. S., limited to extreme southern Florida, in mangrove systems from Cape Sable to southern Biscayne Bay, south to northern Key Largo. Non-breeding animals may be seen north to about Naples, and on the Lower Keys.

Compared to American Alligators, American Crocodiles are pale greenish in color, with a narrow snout. The fourth tooth of the lower jaw is visible "bulldog fashion" when the mouth is closed.

___**American Alligator** (*Alligator mississippiensis*)—Widespread in freshwater habitats throughout, but rare in salt water.

___**Spectacled Caiman** (*Caiman crocodilus*)—Exotic, native to Central and South America. Rare in freshwater canals in the Miami area, with a few reports north to Orlando.

Turtles

___**Common Snapping Turtle** (*Chelydra serpentina*)—Wetlands throughout.

___**Alligator Snapping Turtle** (*Macroclemys temminckii*)—Slow-moving waters in the Panhandle and the northwestern peninsula.

___**Stinkpot** (*Sternotherus odoratus*)—Wetlands throughout.

___**Loggerhead Musk Turtle** (*Sternotherus minor*)—Wetlands south to the central peninsula.

___**Mud Turtle** (*Kinosternon subrubrum*)—Shallow waters throughout.

___**Striped Mud Turtle** (*Kinosternon bauri*)—Wetlands throughout, except absent from the western Panhandle.

___**Spotted Turtle** (*Clemmys guttata*)—Wetlands in the northern and central peninsula.

___**Box Turtle** (*Terrapene carolina*)—Wooded areas throughout.

___**Diamondback Terrapin** (*Melaclemys terrapin*)—Saltmarshes and mangrove forests along both coasts.

___**Barbour's Map Turtle** (*Graptemys barbouri*)—Chipola and Apalachicola Rivers in the Panhandle.

___**Alabama Map Turtle** (*Graptemys pulchra*)—Escambia and Yellow Rivers in the western Panhandle.

___**Red-eared Slider** (*Trachemys scripta*)—Wetlands in the Panhandle and northern Florida; exotic in scattered locations in the Peninsula and the Keys.

___**River Cooter** (*Pseudemys concinna*)—Gulf coast streams and estuaries south to Tampa Bay.

___**Florida Cooter** (*Pseudemys floridana*)—Wetlands throughout, except absent from the extreme south.

___**Florida Redbelly Turtle** (*Pseudemys nelsoni*)—Endemic to wetlands in the peninsula.

___**Alabama Redbelly Turtle** (*Pseudemys alabamensis*)—Panhandle coast.

___**Chicken Turtle** (*Deirochelys reticularia*)—Wetlands throughout.

___**Gopher Tortoise** (*Gopherus polyphemus*)—Threatened. Well-drained areas throughout the mainland, except restricted to coastal areas south of Lake Okeechobee.

___**Atlantic Green Turtle** (*Chelonia mydas*)—Endangered, with only about 375 adult females in Florida. Oceanic; nests along virtually the entire Atlantic coast, but most numerous from Melbourne to Jupiter. Archie

Carr National Wildlife Refuge (page 182) in Brevard and Indian River Counties is currently being established to prevent the extirpation of Florida's nesting sea turtles.

___**Atlantic Hawksbill Turtle** (*Eretmochelys imbricata*)—Endangered; only 1–2 nests are found in Florida annually, along the central and southern Atlantic coast. A Caribbean species restricted in the U.S. to Florida.

___**Loggerhead Sea Turtle** (*Caretta caretta*)—Threatened. Oceanic; nests in Florida along sandy Gulf coast beaches, Dry Tortugas National Park, and most of the Atlantic coast. Nesting densities from Melbourne to Jupiter can exceed 200 nests per linear mile (a nest every 25 feet!), one of the densest nesting concentrations in the world.

___**Kemp's Ridley** (*Lepidochelys kempii*)—Endangered; does not normally nest in Florida. Adults are restricted to the Gulf of Mexico from Everglades National Park (Cape Sable) to the Yucatán Peninsula; a few have also been found along the Atlantic coast.

___**Leatherback Sea Turtle** (*Dermochelys coriacea*)—Oceanic; nests in Florida very rarely, predominately along the central Atlantic coast.

___**Smooth Softshell** (*Apalone muticus*)—In Florida, restricted to extreme northwest Escambia County in the western Panhandle.

___**Spiny Softshell** (*Apalone spinifera*)—Streams in the Panhandle.

___**Florida Softshell** (*Apalone ferox*)—Quiet waters throughout the mainland; introduced on Big Pine Key.

LIZARDS

___**Common Agama** (*Agama agama*)—Exotic, native to East Africa. Small colonies in Broward and Miami-Dade Counties.

___**Indochinese Bloodsucker** (*Calotes mystaceus*)—Exotic, native to the East Indies. Glades and Okeechobee Counties.

___**Asian House Gecko** (*Cosymbotus platyorus*)—Exotic, native to Indochina. Small colonies at Gainesville, Clearwater, Tampa, Fort Myers, and Homestead.

___**Tropical Gecko** (*Hemidactylus mabouia*)—Exotic, native to the Old World. Southern half of the peninsula, throughout the Keys.

___**Tropical House Gecko** (*Hemidactylus frenatus*)—Exotic, native to the Old World. Key West, Homestead, and Fort Myers.

___**Mediterranean Gecko** (*Hemidactylus turcicus*)—Exotic, native to the Old World. Declining from most of the peninsula.

___**Indo-Pacific Gecko** (*Hemidactylus garnoti*)—Exotic, native to the Old World. Central Florida southward, with scattered populations farther north.

___**Bibron's Thick-toed Gecko** (*Pachydactylus bibronii*)—Exotic, native to South Africa. Bradenton.

___**Ashy Gecko** (*Sphaerodactylus elegans*)—Exotic, native to Cuba. Lower Keys.

___**Reef Gecko** (*Sphaerodactylus notatus*)—Uplands in extreme southern Florida.

___**Ocellated Gecko** (*Sphaerodactylus argus*)—Exotic, native to the West Indies. Key West.

___**Ringed Gecko** (*Tarentola annularis*)—Exotic, native to Africa. Fort Myers and Homestead.

___**Yellow-headed Gecko** (*Gonatodes albogularis*)—Exotic, native to Central America. Key West.

___**Tokay Gecko** (*Gekko gekko*)—Exotic, native to Indonesia. Scattered populations throughout.

___**Green Anole** (*Anolis carolinensis*)—Woodlands throughout.

___**Brown Anole** (*Anolis sagrei*)—Exotic, native to the West Indies. Spreading throughout.

___**Jamaican Giant Anole** (*Anolis garmani*)—Exotic, native to Jamaica. Fort Myers and Miami.

___**Hispaniolan Green Anole** (*Anolis chlorocyanus*)—Exotic, native to Hispaniola. One small colony in Broward County.

___**Crested Anole** (*Anolis cristatellus*)—Exotic, native to Puerto Rico. Miami area.

___**Large-headed Anole** (*Anolis cybotes*)—Exotic, native to the West Indies. Fort Lauderdale and Miami.

___**Bark Anole** (*Anolis distichus*)—Exotic, native to the Bahamas. Southeast coast and Keys.

___**Knight Anole** (*Anolis equestris*)—Exotic, native to Cuba. Scattered locations in the southern peninsula and the Keys.

___**Cuban Green Anole** (*Anolis porcatus*)—Exotic, native to Cuba. Miami area.

___**Basilisk Brown** (*Basiliscus vittatus*)—Exotic, native to Tropical America. From Palm Beach south to Miami.

___**Green Iguana** (*Iguana iguana*)—Exotic, native to Tropical America. Scattered locations from Gainesville south.

___**Mexican Spinytail Iguana** (*Ctenosaura pectinata*)—Exotic, native to Tropical America. Miami.

___**Black Stinytail Iguana** (*Ctenosaura similis*)—Exotic, native from Mexico to Central America. Scattered colonies in the southern peninsula.

___**Eastern Fence Lizard** (*Sceloporus undulatus*)—Brushlands and pine flatwoods south to the central peninsula.

___**Florida Scrub Lizard** (*Sceloporus woodi*)—Threatened. Endemic to coastal and interior ridge systems in the southern half of the peninsula.

___**Texas Horned Lizard** (*Phrynosoma cornutum*)—Exotic, native to the western United States. Scattered reports throughout the mainland.

___**Northern Curly-tailed Lizard** (*Leiocephalus carinatus*)—Exotic, native to the West Indies. Southeast coast.

____**Red-sided Curly-tailed Lizard** (*Leiocephalus schreibersii*)—Exotic, native to Hispaniola. Broward and Miami-Dade Counties.

____**Six-lined Racerunner** (*Cnemidophorus sexlineatus*)—Well-drained soils throughout.

____**Giant Ameiva Whiptail** (*Ameiva ameiva*)—Exotic, native to Tropical America. Miami.

____**Rainbow Whiptail** (*Cnemidophorus lemniscatus*)—Exotic, native to Tropical America. Miami area.

____**Giant Whiptail** (*Cnemidophorus montaguae*)—Exotic, native to Central America. Miami-Dade County.

____**Brown Mabuya** (*Mabuya multifasciata*)—Exotic, native to Southeast Asia. Miami.

____**Ameiva** (or **Ground Skink**) (*Scincella lateralis*)—Woodlands throughout.

____**Five-lined Skink** (*Eumeces fasciatus*)—Woodlands in the Panhandle and northern half of the peninsula.

____**Broad-headed Skink** (*Eumeces laticeps*)—Woodlands in the Panhandle and northern half of the peninsula.

____**Southeastern Five-lined Skink** (*Eumeces inexpectatus*)—Woodlands throughout.

____**Southern Coal Skink** (*Eumeces anthracinus*)—Moist woodlands in the central Panhandle.

____**Mole Skink** (*Eumeces egregius*)—Well-drained soils throughout.

____**Sand Skink** (*Neoseps reynoldsi*)—Threatened. Endemic to ridge systems in interior of the central peninsula.

____**Eastern Glass Lizard** (*Ophisaurus ventralis*)—Moist woodlands and meadows throughout.

____**Slender Glass Lizard** (*Ophisaurus attenuatus*)—Grassy areas throughout.

____**Island Glass Lizard** (*Ophisaurus compressus*)—Well-drained uplands in the eastern Panhandle and peninsula.

____**Mimic Glass Lizard** (*Ophisaurus mimicus*)—Pinewoods in the Panhandle and extreme northeast Florida.

____**Florida Worm Lizard** (*Rhineura floridana*)—Endemic. Sandy areas in the peninsula south to Lake Okeechobee.

SNAKES

____**Brahminy Blind Snake** (*Ramphotyphlops braminus*)—Exotic, native to the Old World. Scattered populations from the central peninsula southward.

____**Florida Green Water Snake** (*Nerodia floridana*)—Marshes and swamps throughout.

____**Brown Water Snake** (*Nerodia taxispilota*)—Streams and rivers throughout.

____**Banded Water Snake** (*Nerodia fasciata*)—Shallow waters throughout.

____**Salt Marsh Snake** (*Nerodia clarkii*)—Brackish and saltmarshes throughout.

____**Swamp Snake** (*Seminatrix pygaea*)—Hyacinth-covered waters throughout.

___**Brown Snake** (*Storeria dekayi*)—Wetlands throughout.

___**Redbelly Snake** (*Storeria occipitomaculata*)—Woodlands south to the central peninsula.

___**Plain Watersnake** (*Nerodia erythrogaster*)—Wetlands in the Panhandle and northern peninsula.

___**Midland Watersnake** (*Nerodia sipedon*)—Escambia, Yellow, and Choctawhatchee Rivers in the extreme western Panhandle.

___**Queen Snake** (*Regina septemvittata*)—Streams in the Panhandle.

___**Glossy Water Snake** (*Regina rigida*)—Swamps in the Panhandle south to the central peninsula.

___**Striped Crayfish Snake** (*Regina alleni*)—Vegetated ponds in the extreme eastern Panhandle and peninsula.

___**Garter Snake** (*Thamnophis sirtalis*)—Wetland edges throughout.

___**Ribbon Snake** (*Thamnophis sauritus*)—Wetland edges throughout.

___**Smooth Earth Snake** (*Virginia valeriae*)—Deciduous forests in the Panhandle and northern peninsula, with scattered populations farther south.

___**Rough Earth Snake** (*Virginia striatula*)—Dry uplands south to the central peninsula.

___**Eastern Hognose Snake** (*Heterodon platirhinos*—Sandy areas throughout.

___**Southern Hognose Snake** (*Heterodon simus*)—Sandy areas south to the central peninsula.

___**Ringneck Snake** (*Diadophis punctatus*)—Moist woodlands throughout.

___**Pine Woods Snake** (*Rhadinaea flavilata*)—Moist woodlands south to the southern peninsula.

___**Mud Snake** (*Farancia abacura*)—Swamps throughout.

___**Rainbow Snake** (*Farancia erytrogramma*)—Moist areas south to the central peninsula.

___**Racer** (*Coluber constrictor*)—Uplands throughout.

___**Eastern Coachwhip** (*Masticophis flagellum*)—Uplands throughout.

___**Rough Green Snake** (*Opheodrys aestivus*)—Woodlands throughout.

___**Indigo Snake** (*Drymarchon corais*)—Uplands throughout.

___**Corn Snake** (*Elaphe guttata*)—Woodlands throughout.

___**Rat Snake** (*Elaphe obsoleta*)—Uplands throughout.

___**Pine Snake** (*Pituophis melanoleucus*)—Well-drained soils throughout the mainland, except absent south of Lake Okeechobee.

___**Kingsnake** (*Lampropeltis getulus*)—Woodlands throughout.

___**Scarlet Kingsnake** (*Lampropeltis triangulum*)—Woodlands throughout.

___**Mole Kingsnake** (*Lampropeltis calligaster*)—Fallow lands in the Panhandle, and scattered sites in the central peninsula.

___**Scarlet Snake** (*Cemophora coccinea*)—Sandy areas throughout.

___**Short-tailed Snake** (*Stilosoma extenuatum*)—Endemic to sandhills in the northern half of the peninsula.

___**Florida Crowned Snake** (*Tantilla relicta*)—Dry uplands throughout.

___**Rim Rock Crowned Snake** (*Tantilla oolitica*)—Endemic to woodlands in coastal Miami-Dade County and the Upper Keys.

___**Southeastern Crowned Snake** (*Tantilla coronata*)—Upland habitats in the Panhandle.

___**Coral Snake** (*Micrurus fulvius*)—Woodlands throughout.

___**Copperhead** (*Agkistrodon contortrix*)—Swamps in the Upper Apalachicola River.

___**Cottonmouth** (or **Water Moccasin**) (*Agkistrodon piscivorus*)—Wetlands throughout.

___**Pygmy Rattlesnake** (*Sistrurus miliarius*)—Wet prairies and moist woodlands throughout.

___**Timber Rattlesnake** (*Crotalus horridus*)—Wet woodlands in central northern peninsula.

___**Eastern Diamondback Rattlesnake** (*Crotalus adamaneus*)—Woodlands throughout.

___**Burmese Python** (*Python molurus*)—Exotic, native to Southeast Asia. Everglades National Park and Miami area.

MAMMALS OF FLORIDA
(106 species)

MARSUPIALS

___**Virginia Opossum** (*Didelphis virginiana*)—Woodlands throughout.

INSECTIVORES

___**Southeastern Shrew** (*Sorex longirostris*)—Moist woodlands in the northern half of the peninsula.

___**Southern Short-tailed Shrew** (*Blarina carolinensis*)—Uplands throughout.

___**Least Shrew** (*Cryptotis parva*)—Marshes and prairies throughout.

___**Eastern Mole** (*Scalopus aquaticus*)—Sandy areas throughout.

BATS

___**Southeastern Myotis** (*Myotis austroriparius*)—Caves in the Panhandle and northern peninsula.

___**Gray Myotis** (*Myotis grisescens*)—Mostly in caves near Marianna.

___**Little Brown Bat** (*Myotis lucifugus*)—Caves and buildings in the Panhandle and northern peninsula.

___**Indiana Bat** (*Myotis sodalis*)—One record at Florida Caverns State Park in 1955.

___**Eastern Pipistrelle** (*Pipistrellus subflavus*)—Caves south to the central peninsula.

___**Big Brown Bat** (*Eptesicus fuscus*)—Caves south to the central peninsula.

___**Red Bat** (*Lasiurus borealis*)—Woodlands in the Panhandle and northern peninsula.

___**Hoary Bat** (*Lasiurus cinereus*)—-Woodlands south to the central peninsula.

___**Northern Yellow Bat** (*Lasiurus intermedius*)—Woodlands throughout.

___**Seminole Bat** (*Lasiurus seminolus*)—Woodlands south to Lake Okeechobee.

___**Silver-haired Bat** (*Lasionycteris noctivagans*)—Woodlands in the Panhandle.

___**Evening Bat** (*Nycticeius humeralis*)—Buildings and woodlands throughout.

___**Rafinesque's Big-eared Bat** (*Plecotus rafinesquii*)—Woodlands south to the central peninsula.

___**Brazilian Free-tailed Bat** (*Tadarida brasiliensis*)—Caves, woodlands, and buildings throughout the mainland.

___**Mastiff Bat** (*Eumops glaucinus*)—Buildings near Miami.

___**Velvety Free-tailed Bat** (*Molossus molossus*)—Three colonies in the Middle and Lower Keys in 1995.

___**Jamaican Fruit-eating Bat** (*Artibeus jamaicensis*)—One colony in the Keys in 1995.

EDENTATES

___**Nine-banded Armadillo** (*Dasypus novemcinctus*)—Exotic; native to the southwestern U.S. and tropical America. Sandy woodlands throughout the mainland.

PRIMATES

___**Rhesus Monkey** (*Macaca mulatta*)—Exotic, native to India. A feral population lives in Silver Springs; the monkeys were released at this site, which was where the Tarzan television show was filmed in the 1950s!

___**Vervet Monkey** (*Cercopithecus aethiops*)—Exotic, native to Africa. Released into Dania (Broward County) in the 1950s and 1970s.

___**Man** (*Homo sapiens*)—Cosmopolitan. "This is a box animal. It lives in boxes, sleeps in boxes, hunts for food in boxes, and is buried in a box." Lane (1981).

LAGOMORPHS

___**Eastern Cottontail** (*Sylvilagus floridanus*)—Woodlands throughout the mainland.

___**Marsh Rabbit** (*Sylvilagus palustris*)—Marshes throughout.

___**Black-tailed Jackrabbit** (*Lepus californicus*)—Exotic, native to the western U.S. Miami International Airport (at least formerly).

RODENTS

___**Eastern Chipmunk** (*Tamias striatus*)—Along the Yellow River in the extreme western Panhandle.

___**Gray Squirrel** (*Scuirus carolinensis*)—Woodlands throughout.

___**Fox Squirrel** (*Scuirus niger*)—Woodlands throughout the mainland.

___**Red-bellied Squirrel** (*Scuirus aureogaster*)—Exotic, native to Mexico. Elliott Key and nearby keys in Biscayne National Park.

___**Southern Flying Squirrel** (*Glaucomys volans*)—Woodlands throughout.

___**Southeastern Pocket Gopher** (*Geomys pinetis*)—Sandy areas south to the central peninsula.

___**Beaver** (*Castor canadensis*)—Streams in the Panhandle.

___**Marsh Rice Rat** (*Oryzomys palustris*)—Marshes throughout.

___**Eastern Harvest Mouse** (*Reithrodontomys humulis*)—Fields and marshes south to Lake Okeechobee.

___**Oldfield** (or **Beach**) **Mouse** (*Peromyscus polionotus*)—Sandy areas south to the central peninsula.

___**Cotton Mouse** (*Peromyscus gossypinus*)—Thickets throughout. ___**Key Largo Cotton Mouse** (*P. g. allapaticola*) is endemic to northern Key Largo.

___**Florida Mouse** (*Podomys floridanus*)— Endemic to well-drained soils in the central peninsula.

___**Golden Mouse** (*Ochrotomys nuttalli*)—Thickets south to the central peninsula.

___**Hispid Cotton Rat** (*Sigmodon hispidus*)—Moist woodlands and marshes throughout.

___**Eastern Woodrat** (*Neotoma floridana*)—Thickets south to the central peninsula. **Key Largo Woodrat** (*N. f. smallii*) is endemic to Key Largo.

___**Meadow Vole** (*Microtus pennsylvanicus*)—Salt marshes in Levy County.

___**Pine** (or **Woodland**) **Vole** (*Microtus pinetorum*)—Pinewoods in the Panhandle and northern peninsula.

___**Round-tailed Muskrat** (*Neofiber alleni*)—Marshes in the peninsula.

___**Black Rat** (*Rattus rattus*)—Exotic, native to the Old World; now cosmopolitan. Human-modified habitats throughout.

___**Norway Rat** (*Rattus norvegicus*)—Exotic, native to the Old World; now cosmopolitan. Human-modified habitats throughout.

___**House Mouse** (*Mus musculus*)—Exotic, native to the Old World; now cosmopolitan. Human-modified habitats throughout.

___**Nutria** (*Myocastor coypus*)—Exotic, native to South America; widely introduced into the U.S. Freshwater wetlands locally throughout the mainland.

CARNIVORES

___**Dog** (*Canis familaris*)—Exotic; found throughout.

___**Coyote** (*Canis latrans*)—Uncommon but increasing throughout the mainland, with the southernmost report from Fakahatchee Strand; only Miami-Dade and Monroe counties now lack observations (Main et al. 2000). While some Coyotes have been released for "sport hunting", most of the population increase is probably due to the massive-scale conversion of forests to grasslands that allowed Coyotes to colonize Florida from the west. Colonization of Florida took about 40 years.

___**Red Wolf** (*Canis rufus*)—Extirpated; formerly occurred throughout. St. Vincent National Wildlife Refuge in the eastern Panhandle currently serves as an island propagation site for wolves being reintroduced into North Carolina and Tennessee.

___**Red Fox** (*Vulpes vulpes*)—Exotic, native to the Holarctic. Rare to uncommon throughout the mainland.

___**Gray Fox** (*Urocyon cinereoargenteus*)—Uncommon in open woodlands throughout the mainland.

___**Black Bear** (*Ursus americanus*)—Threatened. Rare to uncommon and local throughout the mainland.

___**Raccoon** (*Procyon lotor*)—Common in woodlands throughout.

___**Long-tailed Weasel** (*Mustela frenata*)—Rare to uncommon south to the central peninsula.

___**Mink** (*Mustela vison*)—Rare in woodlands throughout the mainland; near water.

___**Spotted Skunk** (*Spilogale putorius*)—Rare to uncommon in open woodlands and prairies throughout the mainland.

___**Striped Skunk** (*Mephitis mephitis*)—Rare to uncommon in open woodlands and prairies throughout.

___**River Otter** (*Lutra canadensis*)—Uncommon in wetlands throughout the mainland.

___**Harbor Seal** (*Phoca vitulina*)—1 record from Daytona Beach.

___**Hooded Seal** (*Cystophora cristata*)—2 records: Brevard County in 1917 and Fort Lauderdale in 1984. Its normal range is the North Atlantic.

___**Domestic Cat** (*Felis silvestris*)—A long domesticated form of the Wild Cat native to Africa and Asia. Feral individuals are found nearly throughout. There are probably hundreds of thousands or millions of cats in Florida, killing probably millions of birds annually. For information and links about feral cats in Florida, go to <www.abcbirds.org/cats/states/florida_intro.htm>.

___**Bobcat** (*Lynx rufus*)—Uncommon in woodlands throughout, south to the Upper Keys.

___**Florida Panther** (*Felis concolor coryi*)—Endangered, but recovering from near-extinction. Formerly found throughout the Southeast, populations of this endemic subspecies of the Mountain Lion declined severely due to hunting (now illegal) and habitat destruction. The current population, numbering about 80 animals, is largely restricted to the Big Cypress Swamp region of southwestern Florida, although panthers have been documented recently as far north as Avon Park. *The notion that panthers are found in the Everglades is false; panthers are limited to hammocks, cypress swamps, and other upland habitats mostly lying north and west of Everglades National Park.* Panther sightings are often claimed by the public, but most of these are misidentifications (or, in a few cases, are escapees of other subspecies).

Especially suspect are reports of black Florida panthers, which, quite simply, do not exist. Florida Panthers are extremely secretive and are rarely seen, even by panther researchers. The panther's survival depends on the willingness of Florida's government to regulate land use in a huge area from Fort Myers and Naples east to Lake Okeechobee—lands being converted rapidly to suburbia or citrus groves. Accessible sites that are occupied by panthers include Fakahatchee Strand Preserve State Park and Big Cypress National Preserve, but even at these sites your chances of seeing a panther are virtually nil. Panthers are nocturnal hunters, feeding mostly on White-tailed Deer and feral hogs. Maehr (1997) is an excellent reference.

___**Jaguarundi** (*Felis yagouaroundi*)—Presumed exotic, native to the southwestern U.S. south to South America. Scattered reports throughout the mainland.

CETACEANS

___**Rough-toothed Dolphin** (*Steno bredanensis*)—Oceanic.
___**Long-snouted Spinner Dolphin** (*Stenella longirostris*)—Oceanic.
___**Short-snouted Spinner Dolphin** (*Stenella clymene*)—Oceanic.
___**Striped Dolphin** (*Stenella coeruleoalba*)—Oceanic.
___**Atlantic Spotted** (or **Cuvier's**) **Dolphin** (*Stenella frontalis*)—Oceanic.
___**Spotted Dolphin** (*Stenella plagiodon*)—Oceanic.
___**Pantropical Spotted Dolphin** (*Stenella attenuata*)—Oceanic.
___**Saddle-backed Dolphin** (*Delphinus delphis*)—Oceanic.
___**Fraser's Dolphin** (*Lagenodelphis hosei*)—Oceanic.
___**Atlantic Bottle-nosed Dolphin** (*Tursiops truncatus*)—Oceanic, common off both coasts.
___**False Killer Whale** (*Pseudorca crassidens*)—Oceanic.
___**Killer Whale** (*Orcinus orca*)—Oceanic.
___**Pygmy Killer Whale** (*Feresa attenuata*)—Oceanic.
___**Risso's Dolphin** (or **Grampus**) (*Grampus griseus*)—Oceanic.
___**Short-finned Pilot Whale** (*Globicephala macrorhynchus*)—Oceanic.
___**Harbor Porpoise** (*Phocoena phocoena*)—Oceanic.
___**Pygmy Sperm Whale** (*Kogia breviceps*)—Oceanic.
___**Dwarf Sperm Whale** (*Kogia simus*)—Oceanic.
___**Sperm Whale** (*Physeter macrocephalus*)—Endangered. Oceanic.
___**Goose-beaked Whale** (*Ziphius cavirostris*)—Oceanic.
___**Dense-beaked Whale** (*Mesoplodon densirostris*)—Oceanic.
___**Antillean Beaked Whale** (*Mesoplodon europaeus*)—Oceanic.
___**True's Beaked Whale** (*Mesplodon mirus*)—Oceanic.
___**Fin Whale** (*Balaenoptera physalus*)—Endangered. Oceanic.
___**Minke Whale** (*Balaenoptera acutorostrata*)—Oceanic.
___**Sei Whale** (*Balaenoptera borealis*)—Endangered. Oceanic.
___**Bryde's Whale** (*Balaenoptera edeni*)—Oceanic.
___**Humpback Whale** (*Megaptera novaeangliae*)—Endangered. Oceanic.

___**Right Whale** (*Eubalaena glacialis*)—Endangered. Oceanic.

SIRENIANS

___**West Indian Manatee** (*Trichecus manatus*)—Endangered, ranging from the southeastern U.S. south to northern South America. Generally a rare resident of inland waterways and coastal estuaries and bays of both coasts, but locally common at favored sites, especially during winter. Least numerous along the Panhandle and northern peninsular Gulf coasts. During winter, this large, interesting, aquatic relative of the elephant moves into warmer waters of coastal streams, inland springs, and, recently, power-plant outlet canals. The Florida population, perhaps the largest one remaining, is thought to number between 2,000–3,000 manatees, but mortality is high—usually 10 percent or more are killed annually. Manatees have no natural enemies, but collisions with boats kill several dozen individuals per year. Extreme cold and "red tide" (caused by blooms of a microscopic marine organism) cause additional mortality. Without additional protection, the long-term outlook for manatees in Florida is poor. During winter, the Big Bend power plant south of Tampa (page 134) is a reliable site; directions to other sites can be found online. For more information, go to <www.savethemanatee.org> and <www.floridamarine.org>.

ARTIODACTYLS

___**Wild Boar** (**wild pig** or **feral hog**) (*Sus scrofa*)—Exotic, widely domesticated, native to Europe. Now occurs as a pest throughout the Panhandle and peninsula.

___**White-tailed Deer** (*Odocoileus virginianus*)—Woodlands throughout. **Key Deer** (*O. v. clavium*) is endemic to Big Pine Key and surrounding keys (page 255).

___**Sambar Deer** (*Cervus unicolor*)—Exotic, native to India, Sri Lanka, the East Indies, and Philippines. Introduced onto St. Vincent Island in Franklin County in 1908.

___**Axis Deer** (*Cervus axis*)—Exotic, native to Ceylon and India. Accidentally introduced into Volusia County in the 1930s.

___**Elk** (*Cervus elaphus*)—Exotic, native to northern and western North America. Introduced into Highlands County in the late 1960s.

___**American Bison** (*Bison bison*)—Extirpated, formerly found south to the central peninsula. Rare or absent from Florida until the late 1600s, when herds were observed commonly; bison possibly moved into the state due to deforestation. Apparently eliminated through hunting by the late 1700s. In 1975, 10 animals from Oklahoma were released into Paynes Prairie Preserve State Park outside Gainesville.

LITERATURE CITED

ABA [American Birding Association]. 2002. *ABA Checklist: Birds of the Continental United States and Canada*, 6th edition. American Birding Association. Colorado Springs, CO.

Abrahamson, I.J. 1976. The Black Hawk (*Buteogallus anthracinus*) in south Florida. *American Birds* 30: 661–662.

Aldrich, J.W. 1981. Geographic variation in White-winged Doves with reference to possible source of new Florida population. *Proceedings of the Biological Society of Washington* 94: 641–651.

AOU [American Ornithologists' Union]. 1998. *Check-list of North American Birds*, 7th edition. American Ornithologists' Union. Washington, D.C.

AOU [American Ornithologists' Union]. 2004. Forty-fifth supplement to the American Ornithologists' Union *Check-list of North American Birds*. *Auk* 121: 985–995.

Bailey, H.H. 1925. *The Birds of Florida*. Williams and Wilkins. Baltimore, MD.

Banks, R.C. 2000. The Cuban Martin in Florida. *Florida Field Naturalist* 28: 50–52.

Blackshaw, S.R., and P. Polisse. 1990. Harlan's Hawk over-winters in St. Lucie County, Florida. *Florida Field Naturalist* 18: 10–12.

Bond, J. 1990. *Birds of the West Indies*, 5th edition. Collins. London, UK.

Bowen, P.J. 2001. Demography and distribution of the Burrowing Owl in Florida. *Florida Field Naturalist* 29: 113–126.

Bowman, R. 2000. Thirteenth report of the Florida Ornithological Society Records Committee: 1996, 1997, 1998, 1999, and 2000. *Florida Field Naturalist* 28: 138–160.

Bowman, R. 2004. Fourteenth report of the Florida Ornithological Society Records Committee: 2001–2002. *Florida Field Naturalist* 32: 7–33.

Bowman, R., and G.T. Bancroft. 1989. Least Bittern nesting on mangrove keys in Florida Bay. *Florida Field Naturalist* 17: 43–46.

Bowman, R., P.W. Smith, and J.W. Fitzpatrick. 1995. First winter record of an Eastern Kingbird in Florida. *Florida Field Naturalist* 23: 62–64.

Bradbury, R.C. 1992. First Florida record of Variegated Flycatcher (*Empidonomus varius*) at Garden Key, Dry Tortugas. *Florida Field Naturalist* 20: 42–44.

Brightsmith, D. 1999. White-winged Parakeet (*Brotogeris versicolurus*) and Yellow-chevroned Parakeet (*Brotogeris chiriri*). *In* The Birds of North America, No. 386–387 (A. Poole and F. Gill, eds.). The Birds of North America, Inc., Philadelphia, PA.

Carleton, A.R., and O.T. Owre. 1975. The Red-whiskered Bulbul in Florida: 1960–1971. *Auk* 92: 40–57.

Clements, J.F. 2000. *Birds of the World: A Checklist*. 5th edition. Ibis Publishing. Vista, CA.

Cox, J.A., and S.R. Jones. 2004. Use of recorded vocalizations in winter surveys of Bachman's Sparrows. *Journal of Field Ornithology* 75: 359–363.

Dean, T.F., and P.D. Vickery. 2003. Bachman's Sparrows use burrows and palmetto clumps as escape refugia from predators. *Journal of Field Ornithology* 74: 26–30.

del Hoyo, J., A. Elliott, and J. Sargatal, editors. 1997. *Handbook of Birds of the World*, Volume 4: Sandgrouse to Cuckoos. Lynx Edicions. Barcelona, Spain.

Delany, M.F., P.B. Walsh, B. Pranty, and D.W. Perkins. 1999. A previously unknown population of Florida Grasshopper Sparrows on Avon Park Air Force Range. *Florida Field Naturalist* 27: 52–56.

Dinsmore, J.J. 1977. Notes on [American] avocets and [Black-necked] stilts in Tampa Bay, Florida. *Florida Field Naturalist* 5: 25–30.

Douglass, N.J., J.A. Gore, and R.T. Paul. 2001. American Oystercatchers nest on gravel-covered roofs in Florida. *Florida Field Naturalist* 29: 75–80.

Duncan, R.A. 1994. *Bird Migration, Weather, and Fallout, Including the Migrant Traps of Alabama and Northwest Florida*. Published by the author. Gulf Breeze, FL.

Duncan, R.A., and L.R. Duncan. 2000. *The Birds of Escambia, Santa Rosa, and Okaloosa Counties, Florida*, 2nd edition. Published by the authors. Gulf Breeze, FL.

Eliason, G.T. 1992. Exotic crane in Pasco County, Florida. *Florida Scientist* 55: 56–57.

Emslie, S.D. 1998. *Avian Community Change, Climate, and Sea-Level Changes in the Plio-Pleistocene of the Florida Peninsula*. Ornithological Monograph No. 50. American Ornithologists' Union. Washington, D.C.

Evans, W.R. 1994. Nocturnal flight call of Bicknell's Thrush. *Wilson Bulletin* 106: 55–61.

Fisk, E.J. 1968. White-winged Doves breeding in Florida. *Florida Naturalist* 41: 126.

Forshaw, J.M. 1973. *Parrots of the World*. Landsdowne Press. Melbourne, Australia. (*Reprinted by others several times subsequently, often with poorer quality plates*).

Garrido, O.H., and A. Kirkconnell. 2000. *Field Guide to the Birds of Cuba*. Cornell University Press. Ithaca, N.Y.

Garrido, O.H., K.C. Parkes, G.B. Reynard, A. Kirkconnell, and R. Sutton. 1997. Taxonomy of the Stripe-headed Tanager, genus *Spindalis* (Aves: Thraupinae) of the West Indies. *Wilson Bulletin* 109: 561–594.

Genung, W.G., and R.H. Lewis. 1982. The Black Francolin in the Everglades Agricultural Area. *Florida Field Naturalist* 10: 65–69.

Haney, J.C. 1985. Band-rumped Storm-Petrel occurrences in relation to upwelling off the coast of the southeastern United States. *Wilson Bulletin* 97: 543–547.

Hoffman, W. 1994. Yellow-nosed Albatross specimen from Key Largo. *Florida Field Naturalist* 22: 75–77.

Hoffman, W., and G.E. Woolfenden. 1988. A specimen of the Asiatic Marbled Murrelet from Florida. *Florida Field Naturalist* 16: 37–38.

Hoffman, W., R. Sawicki, C. Thompson, and M. Carrington. 1991. Golden-crowned Sparrow appears in Florida. *Florida Field Naturalist* 19: 19–21.

Hoffman, W., A. Sprunt IV, P. Kalla, and M. Robson. 1993. Bridled Tern breeding record in the United States. *American Birds* 47: 379–381.

Hoffman, W., G.E. Woolfenden, and P.W. Smith. 1999. Antillean Short-eared Owls invade southern Florida. *Wilson Bulletin* 111: frontispiece and 303–313.

Howell, A.H. 1932. *Florida Bird Life.* Coward–McCann. New York, NY.

Johnston, D.W. 1976. Races of Palm Warblers killed at a Florida TV tower. *Florida Field Naturalist* 4: 22–24.

Johnston, D.W. 2002. Additional 16th century bird reports from Florida. *Florida Field Naturalist* 30:1–8.

Jue, S., C. Kindell, and J. Wojcik. 2001. *Florida Conservation Lands 2001.* Florida Natural Areas Inventory. Tallahassee, FL.

Juniper, T., and M. Parr. 1998. *Parrots: A Guide to Parrots of the World.* Yale University Press. New Haven, CT.

Kale, H.W., II, B. Pranty, B.M. Stith, and C.W. Biggs. 1992. The Atlas of the Breeding Birds of Florida. Final Report submitted to the Florida Game and Fresh Water Fish Commission. Tallahassee, FL. Unpublished, but available on-line at: <http://www.wildflorida.org/bba>.

Kaufman, K. 1984. Identification of two potential Florida vagrants [Cuban Pewee and Bahama Yellowthroat]. *Birding* 16: 112–113.

Kaufman, K. 2000. *Birds of North America.* Houghton Mifflin. New York, NY.

Kratter, A.W., and D.W. Steadman. 2003. First Atlantic Ocean and Gulf of Mexico specimen of Short-tailed Shearwater. *North American Birds* 57: 277–279.

Kwater, E. 2001. First record of Elegant Tern in Florida. *Florida Field Naturalist* 29: 90–94.

Lane, J.A. 1981. *A Birder's Guide to Florida.* L & P Press. Denver, CO. Second edition published in 1984, and third edition (with revisions by H.R. Holt) published in 1989.

Lehman, P., editor. 2001. *A Birder's Guide to Metropolitan Areas of North America.* American Birding Association. Colorado Springs, CO.

Lewis, T.E., and D.B. McNair. 1998 Second breeding locality of Cliff Swallows in Florida. *Florida Field Naturalist* 26: 117–121.

Lockwood, M. 1999. Possible anywhere: Fork-tailed Flycatcher. *Birding* 31: 126–139.

Loftin, R.W., G.E. Woolfenden, and J.A. Woolfenden. 1991. *Florida Bird Records in American Birds and Audubon Field Notes (1947–1989): Species Index and County Gazetteer.* Florida Ornithological Society Special Publication No. 4. Gainesville, FL.

Maehr, D.S. 1997. *The Florida Panther: Life and Death of a Vanishing Carnivore.* Island Press. Washington, D.C.

Main, M.B., S.F. Coates, and G.M. Allen. 2000. Coyote distribution in Florida extends southward. *Florida Field Naturalist* 28: 201–203.

McKinley, D. 1985. *The Carolina Parakeet in Florida.* Special Publication No. 2. Florida Ornithological Society. Gainesville, FL.

McNair, D.B. 1998. Sprague's Pipit overwinters at Apalachicola, Franklin County, and an assessment of its winter status. *Florida Field Naturalist* 26: 21–23.

McNair, D.B. 1999. The Gray-hooded Gull in North America: first documented record. *North American Birds* 53: 337–339.

McNair, D.B. 2000a. The breeding status of Caspian Terns in the southeastern United States (Mississippi to Virginia). *Florida Field Naturalist* 28: 12–21.

McNair, D.B. 2000b. First certain record of California Gull (*Larus californicus*) in Florida. *Florida Field Naturalist* 28: 22–24.

McNair, D.B., and J.A. Gore. 1998. Occurrences of flamingos in northwest Florida, including a recent record of the Greater Flamingo (*Phoenicopterus ruber*). *Florida Field Naturalist* 26: 40–43.

Meshaka, W.E., Jr., B.P. Butterfield, and J.B. Hauge. 2004. *The Exotic Amphibians and Reptiles of Florida.* Krieger Publishing Co. Malabar, FL.

Mlodinow, S.G., and K.T. Karlson. 1999. Anis in the United States and Canada. *North American Birds* 53: 237–245.

Muschlitz, B.P. 1995. Asiatic Marbled Murrelet: first spring record in North America. *Florida Field Naturalist* 23: 30–32.

National Geographic Society. 2002. *Field Guide to the Birds of North America*, 4th edition. National Geographic Society. Washington, DC.

Nesbitt, S.A. 1992. A Lesser Sandhill Crane in Florida. *Florida Field Naturalist* 20: 15–17.

Nesbitt, S.[A.] and M.J. Folk. 2000. Reintroduction of the Whooping Crane in Florida. *North American Birds* 54: 248.

Norton, R.L., and J. Ripple. 1997. First report of Fuerte's Red-tailed Hawk from Florida. *Florida Field Naturalist* 25: 138–140.

Patten, M.A. 2000. Who's laughing now?—Comments on a colorful gull in Florida. *Birding* 32: 263–265.

Paul, R.T., B. Pranty, A.F. Paul, A.B. Hodgson, and D.J. Powell. 2003. Probable hybridization between an Elegant Tern and a Sandwich Tern in west-central

Florida: The first confirmed North American nesting record of Elegant Tern away from the Pacific coast. *North American Birds* 57: 280–282.

Peterson, R.T. 2002. *A Field Guide to the Birds of Eastern and Central North America*, 5th edition. Houghton Mifflin. Boston, MA.

Post, W. 1998. The status of Nelson's and Saltmarsh Sharp-tailed Sparrows on Waccasassa Bay, Levy County, Florida. *Florida Field Naturalist* 26: 1–6.

Post, W., and J.S. Greenlaw. 2000. The present and future of the Cape Sable Seaside Sparrow. *Florida Field Naturalist* 28: 93–110.

Pranty, B. 1995. Field observations spring report: March–May 1995. *Florida Field Naturalist* 23: 99–108.

Pranty, B. 2000. Possible anywhere: Shiny Cowbird. *Birding* 32: 514–526.

Pranty, B. 2001a. Purple Swamphens on the move. *Winging It* 13(7): 1, 6–7.

Pranty, B. 2001b. The Budgerigar in Florida: Rise and fall of an exotic psittacid. *North American Birds* 55: 389–397.

Pranty, B. 2002. *The Important Bird Areas of Florida, 2000–2002*. Tampa, FL. *Unpublished*.

Pranty, B. 2004. Florida's exotic avifauna: A preliminary checklist. *Birding* 36: 362–372.

Pranty, B., and P.W. Smith. 2001. Status, distribution, and taxonomy of the spindalis complex ("Stripe-headed Tanager") in Florida. *Florida Field Naturalist* 29: 13–25.

Pranty, B., and S. Epps. 2002. Distribution, population status, and documentation of exotic parrots in Broward County, Florida. *Florida Field Naturalist* 30: 111–131.

Pranty, B., and K.L. Garrett. 2003. The parrot fauna of the ABA Area: A current look. *Birding* 35: 248–261.

Pranty, B., and H. Voren. 2003. Variation and possible hybridization of *Brotogeris* parakeets at Fort Lauderdale, Florida. *Birding* 35: 262–266.

Pranty, B., and H.W. Lovell. 2004. Population increase and range expansion of Black-hooded Parakeets in Florida. *Florida Field Naturalist* 32: 129–137.

Pranty, B., Kim Schnitzius, Kevin Schnitzius, and H.W. Lovell. 2000. Discovery, origin, and current distribution of the Purple Swamphen (*Porphyrio porphyrio*) in Florida. *Florida Field Naturalist* 28: 1–11.

Pranty, B., G.D. Basili, and H.P. Robinson. 2002. First breeding record of the Dickcissel in Florida. *Florida Field Naturalist* 30: 36–39.

Pranty, B., E. Kwater, H. Weatherman, and H.P. Robinson. 2004. Eurasian Kestrel in Florida: First record for the southeastern United States, with a review of its status in North America. *North American Birds* 58: 168–169.

Raffaele, H., J. Wiley, O. Garrido, A. Keith, and J. Raffaele. 1998. *A Guide to the Birds of the West Indies*. Princeton University Press. Princeton, N.J.

Rimmer, C.C., K.P. McFarland, W.G. Ellison, and J.E. Goetz. 2001. Bicknell's Thrush (*Catharus bicknelli*). *In* The Birds of North America, No. 592 (A. Poole and F. Gill, editors). The Birds of North America, Inc., Washington, D.C.

Robertson, W.B., Jr., and C.W. Biggs. 1983. A West Indian *Myiarchus* in Biscayne National Park, Florida. *American Birds* 37: 802–804.

Robertson, W.B., Jr., and G.E. Woolfenden. 1992. *Florida Bird Species: An Annotated List*. Special Publication No. 6. Florida Ornithological Society. Gainesville, FL.

Rowan, R., and M. Manetz. 1995. *A Birdwatcher's Guide to Alachua County, Florida*. Published by the authors. Gainesville, FL.

Sangster, G. 1998. Purple Swamp-hen is a complex of species. *Dutch Birding* 20: 13–22.

Saunders, G.B. 1980. The origin of White-winged Doves breeding in south Florida. *Florida Field Naturalist* 8: 50–51.

Sibley, D.A. 2000. *The Sibley Guide to Birds*. Alfred A. Knopf. New York, N.Y.

Smith, P.W. 1987. The Eurasian Collared-Dove arrives in the Americas. *American Birds* 41: 1370-1379.

Smith, P.W, and A. Sprunt IV. 1987. The Shiny Cowbird reaches the United States. *American Birds* 41: 370-371.

Smith, P.W., and S.A. Smith. 1989. A Zenaida Dove in Florida, with comments on the species and its appearance here. *Florida Field Naturalist* 17: 67-69.

Smith, P.W., and S.A. Smith. 1990. The identification and status of the Bahama Swallow in Florida. *Birding* 22: 264–271.

Smith, P.W., and D.S. Evered. 1992. Photo Note—La Sagra's Flycatcher. *Birding* 24: 294-297.

Smith, P.W., and S.A. Smith. 1993. An exotic dilemma for birders: The Canary-winged Parakeet. *Birding* 25: 426-430.

Smith, P.W., and S.A. Smith. 1995. Determining the origin of non-native birds seen in the wild in Florida—A case study case [sic]: Woolly-necked Stork. *Florida Field Naturalist* 23: 10–12.

Smith, P.W., and G.E. Woolfenden. 1995. Status of the Northern Wheatear in Florida. *Florida Field Naturalist* 23: 93–96.

Smith, P.W., W.B. Robertson, Jr., and H.M. Stevenson. 1988. West Indian Cave Swallows nesting in Florida, with comments on the taxonomy of *Hirundo fulva*. *Florida Field Naturalist* 16: 86–90.

Smith, P.W., D.S. Evered, L.R. Messick, and M.C. Wheeler. 1990. First verifiable records of the Thick-billed Vireo from the United States. *American Birds* 44: 372-376.

Smith, P.W., S.A. Smith, and W. Hoffman. 1991. A Yellow-faced Grassquit in Florida, with comments on importation of this and related species. *Florida Field Naturalist* 19: 21–24.

Smith, P.W., G.E. Woolfenden, and A. Sprunt IV. 2000. The Loggerhead Kingbird in Florida: The evidence revisited. *North American Birds* 54: 235–240.

Snyder, L.F., and L.A. Hopkins. 2000. A record of Tropical Kingbird (*Tyrannus melancholicus*) in Florida. *Florida Field Naturalist* 28: 182–185.

Sprunt, A., Jr. 1954. *Florida Bird Life*. Coward-McCann. New York, NY.

Sprunt, A., Jr. 1963. Addendum to *Florida Bird Life* (1954). Published by the author.

Stevenson, H.M. 1957. The relative magnitude of the Trans-Gulf and Circum-Gulf spring migration. *Wilson Bulletin* 69: 39–77.

Stevenson, H.M., and B.H. Anderson. 1994. *The Birdlife of Florida*. University Press of Florida. Gainesville, FL.

Stevenson, H.M., L.E. Goodnight, and C.L. Kingsbery. 1980. An early record of the Band-tailed Gull in Florida. *Florida Field Naturalist* 8: 21–23.

Sykes, P.W., Jr. 1980. Decline and disappearance of the Dusky Seaside Sparrow from Merritt Island, Florida. *American Birds* 34: 728-737.

Sykes, P.W., Jr., and W. Post. 2001. First specimen and evidence of breeding by the Shiny Cowbird in Georgia. *Oriole* 66: 45-51.

Sykes, P.W., Jr., L.S. Atherton, M. Gardler, and J.H. Hintermister, V. 2004. The first Mangrove Swallow recorded in the United States. *North American Birds* 58: 4–11.

Thomsen, J.B., and T.A. Mulliken. 1992. Trade in Neotropical psittacines and its conservation implications. Pages 221–239 in *New World Parrots in Crisis: Solutions from Conservation Biology* (S.R. Beissinger and N.F.R. Snyder, editors). Smithsonian Institution Press, Washington, D.C.

Toops, C.M., and W.E. Dilley. 1986. *Birds of South Florida: An Interpretive Guide*. River Road Press. Conway, AR.

USFWS [United States Fish and Wildlife Service]. 2000. Technical/Agency Draft Revised Recovery Plan for the Red-cockaded Woodpecker (*Picoides borealis*). United States Fish and Wildlife Service. Atlanta, GA.

Walters, M.J. 1992. *A Shadow and a Song: The Struggle to Save an Endangered Species*. Chelsea Green Publishing Company. Post Mills, VT.

Ware, D.H., and R.A. Duncan. 1989. First record of the Eastern Phoebe nesting in Florida. *Florida Field Naturalist* 17: 22.

Webber, T., and C.T. Collins. 1995. Recordings verify that Vaux's Swifts visit Florida during winter. *Florida Field Naturalist* 23: 25–29.

Wood, D.A., compiler. 1994. Official lists of endangered and potentially endangered flora and fauna in Florida. Florida Game and Fresh Water Fish Commission. Tallahassee, FL.

Woolfenden, G.E., B. Pranty, J.W. Fitzpatrick, and B.S. Nelson. 1996. Western Wood-Pewee recorded in Highlands County, Florida. *Florida Field Naturalist* 24: 61–67.

AMERICAN BIRDING ASSOCIATION
PRINCIPLES OF BIRDING ETHICS

*Everyone who enjoys birds and birding must always respect wild-
life, its environment, and the rights of others. In any conflict of
interest between birds and birders, the welfare of the birds and
their environment comes first.*

CODE OF BIRDING ETHICS

1. Promote the welfare of birds and their environment.

1(a) Support the protection of important bird habitat.

1(b) To avoid stressing birds or exposing them to danger, exercise restraint and caution during observation, photography, sound recording, or filming.

Limit the use of recordings and other methods of attracting birds, and never
use such methods in heavily birded areas or for attracting any species that is
Threatened, Endangered, or of Special Concern, or is rare in your local area.

Keep well back from nests and nesting colonies, roosts, display areas, and important feeding sites. In such sensitive areas, if there is a need for extended
observation, photography, filming, or recording, try to use a blind or hide, and
take advantage of natural cover.

Use artificial light sparingly for filming or photography, especially for
close-ups.

1(c) Before advertising the presence of a rare bird, evaluate the potential for disturbance to the bird, its surroundings, and other people in the area, and proceed
only if access can be controlled, disturbance can be minimized, and permission has been obtained from private land-owners. The sites of rare nesting
birds should be divulged only to the proper conservation authorities.

1(d) Stay on roads, trails, and paths where they exist; otherwise keep habitat disturbance to a minimum.

Respect the law and the rights of others.

2(a) Do not enter private property without the owner's explicit permission.

2(b) Follow all laws, rules, and regulations governing use of roads and public areas,
both at home and abroad.

2(c) Practice common courtesy in contacts with other people. Your exemplary behavior will generate goodwill with birders and non-birders alike.

Ensure that feeders, nest structures, and other artificial bird environments are safe.

3(a) Keep dispensers, water, and food clean and free of decay or disease. It is important to feed birds continually during harsh weather.

3(b) Maintain and clean nest structures regularly.

3(c) If you are attracting birds to an area, ensure the birds are not exposed to predation from cats and other domestic animals, or dangers posed by artificial hazards.

Group birding, whether organized or impromptu, requires special care.

Each individual in the group, in addition to the obligations spelled out in Items #1 and #2, has responsibilities as a Group Member.

4(a) Respect the interests, rights, and skills of fellow birders, as well as those of people participating in other legitimate outdoor activities. Freely share your knowledge and experience, except where code 1(c) applies. Be especially helpful to beginning birders.

4(b) If you witness unethical birding behavior, assess the situation and intervene if you think it prudent. When interceding, inform the person(s) of the inappropriate action and attempt, within reason, to have it stopped. If the behavior continues, document it and notify appropriate individuals or organizations.

Group Leader Responsibilities (amateur and professional trips and tours).

4(c) Be an exemplary ethical role model for the group. Teach through word and example.

4(d) Keep groups to a size that limits impact on the environment and does not interfere with others using the same area.

4(e) Ensure everyone in the group knows of and practices this code.

4(f) Learn and inform the group of any special circumstances applicable to the areas being visited (e.g., no tape recorders allowed).

4(g) Acknowledge that professional tour companies bear a special responsibility to place the welfare of birds and the benefits of public knowledge ahead of the company's commercial interests. Ideally, leaders should keep track of tour sightings, document unusual occurrences, and submit records to appropriate organizations.

PLEASE FOLLOW THIS CODE— DISTRIBUTE IT AND TEACH IT TO OTHERS.

Additional copies of the Code of Birding Ethics can be obtained from:

ABA, PO Box 6599, Colorado Springs, CO 80934-6599
(800) 850-2473 or (719) 578-1614; fax: (800) 247-3329
or (719) 578-1480; e-mail: member@aba.org; or
online at www.americanbirding.org/abaethics.htm

This ABA Code of Birding Ethics may be reprinted, reproduced, and distributed without restriction. Please acknowledge the role of ABA in developing and promoting this code.

7/1/96

Join the American Birding Association

When you become a member of the American Birding Association, you join thousands of birders who are eager to improve their knowledge and skills to get the most out of their birding experiences.

- ✔ Network with friends and share the passion of birding.

- ✔ Learn more about birds and birding.

- ✔ Sharpen and augment your birding skills.

- ✔ Participate in workshops, conferences, and tours.

- ✔ Receive our full-color magazine, *Birding*, and our newsletter, *Winging It*.

- ✔ Use our directory and catalogs to expand your birding horizons.

You don't have to be an expert birder to be a member of the American Birding Association. You're qualified simply by having a desire to learn more about birds, their habitats, and how to protect them.

ABA membership offers you the opportunity to meet and learn from experts and to improve your skills through our internationally attended conferences and conventions, Institute for Field Ornithology workshops, specialized tours, and volunteer opportunities. It is great way to get to know others who share your interests.

ABA Membership
P.O. Box 6599, Colorado Springs, CO 80934
Phone: 800-850-2473 * Fax: 719-578-1480
www.americanbirding.org

Sign Up Today!

American Birding
A S S O C I A T I O N

Name _____

Address _____

_____

City _____ State _____ Zip _____

Country _____ Phone _____

Email _____

Each level entitles members to certain benefits.
Visit <www.americanbirding.org/memgen.htm> or call 800-850-2473 to find out more.

❏ Individual . . . . US $45

❏ Joint . . . . US $52

❏ Student[a]. . . . . US $25

❏ International / Canada Individual[b]. . . US $55

❏ International / Canada Joint[b]. . . . . . US $63

❏ International / Canada Student[ab] . . . US $35

[a] Please include your birth date, school name, and graduation date
[b] Canadian dues include GST, which is paid to the Canadian government
All membership dues include $30 for **Birding** magazine and
   $10 for **Winging It** newsletter

Sent this form to:

ABA Membership
PO Box 6599
Colorado Springs, CO
80934-6599

You may also join by phone fax, or web:
Phone 800-850-2473
Fax 719-578-1480
www.americanbirding.org/join.html

Membership: $ _____

Additional Contribution: $ _____ for: ❏ Unrestricted ❏ Conservation ❏ Education

Total: $ _____

U.S. dollars; check or money order payable to American Birding Association, or charge to:

❏ VISA   ❏ Mastercard   ❏ Discover

Card # _____ Exp Date _____

Signature _____

ABA BIRDFINDING GUIDE SERIES

A Birder's Guide to Alaska
George C. West

A Birder's Guide to Arkansas
Mel White

A Birder's Guide to the Bahamas
Anthony R. White

A Birder's Guide to Colorado
Harold R. Holt

A Birder's Guide to Eastern Massachusetts
Bird Observer

A Birder's Guide to Florida
Bill Pranty

A Birder's Guide to Metropolitan Areas of North America
Paul Lehman

A Birder's Guide to Michigan
Allen T. Chartier and Jerry Ziarno

A Birder's Guide to New Hampshire
Alan Delorey

A Birder's Guide to Planning North American Trips
Jerry A. Cooper

A Birder's Guide to the Rio Grande Valley
Mark W. Lockwood, William B. McKinney, James N. Paton, Barry R. Zimmer

A Birder's Guide to Southeastern Arizona
Richard Cachor Taylor

A Birder's Guide to Southern California
Brad Schram

A Birder's Guide to the Texas Coast
Harold R. Holt

A Birder's Guide to Virginia
David Johnston

A Birder's Guide to Washington
Hal Opperman

A Birder's Guide to Wyoming
Oliver K. Scott

NEW GUIDES IN PROGRESS
Louisiana — Oregon

OTHER RECENT ABA PUBLICATIONS

Birding on Borrowed Time
Phoebe Snetsinger

Attu: Birding on the Edge
Charles E. Osgood

ABA SALES — 800-634-7736
www.americanbirding.org/abasales

Index

Q

R

Tampa Electric Company Manatee Viewing Center 136
Tanager
  Blue-gray 324
  Scarlet 15, 90
  Summer 15, 62, 67, 72, 82, 88, 90, 106, 111, 119, 150, 155, 158-159, 161, 324
Tates Hell Swamp 47
Ten Thousand Islands National Wildlife Refuge 201, 204
Tern
  Arctic 173
  Black 17, 58, 98, 116, 211-212, 294
  Bridled 16, 245, 266, 294
  Caspian 293
  Common 58, 98, 123
  Elegant 131, 293
  Forster's 294
  Gull-billed 58, 72, 98, 114, 117-118, 174, 211-212, 243, 293
  Least 55, 59, 98, 107, 138, 201, 294
  Roseate 245, 261-262, 265-266, 294
  Royal 59, 98, 198, 293
  Sandwich 58-59, 128, 195, 198, 293
  Sooty 16, 90, 245, 262, 264, 266, 294
Theodore Roosevelt Preserve 100
Thomas P. Smith Water Reclamation Facility 68
Three Lakes Wildlife Management Area 153-154
Thrush
  Bicknell's 319
  Gray-cheeked 319
  Hermit 14, 320
  Swainson's 319
  Varied 320
  Wood 60, 62, 77, 88, 320
Tigertail Beach County Park 200
Timucuan Ecological and Historic Preserve 98
Titusville 174
Tolomato River 105
Torreya State Park 62
Tosohatchee State Reserve 148
Towhee
  Eastern 90, 93, 190, 326
  Green-tailed 326
  Spotted 326
Tram Road Sewage Treatment Facility 69
Tree Tops County Park 220
Trimble Park 148
Tropicbird
  Red-billed 275
  White-tailed 262, 275
Turkey Creek Sanctuary 180

Turkey, Wild 65, 87, 139, 146, 149, 152, 154-155, 157, 159, 241, 272
Turnstone, Ruddy 95
Turtle
  Atlantic Green 183
  Leatherback Sea 183
  Loggerhead Sea 183
Turtle Mound, Canaveral Natl. Seashore 172
Turtle-Dove
  European 246, 296
  Ringed 296

U

Upper Key Largo 247, 249-250
Upper Tampa Bay Park 122

V

Veery 319
Venus 162
Venus Flatwoods Preserve 165
Vero Beach 183
Viera Wetlands 179
Vilano 104-105
Vireo
  Black-whiskered 15, 109, 123, 196, 200-201, 229, 232, 234, 245, 249-250, 254, 258, 315
  Blue-headed 14, 315
  Thick-billed 187, 215, 219, 245, 249, 262, 314
  Yellow-green 131
  Yellow-throated 67, 88, 90, 109, 112-113, 119, 135, 148, 314

W

W.J. Janes Scenic Drive 204
Wakodahatchee Wetlands 217
Wakulla Beach 72
Wakulla Ranger District, Apalachicola National Forest 69
Wakulla Springs State Park 70
Walk-in-The-Water Tract, Lake Wales Ridge State Forest 157
Walsingham Park 126